MW00465834

Internet and Society

Routledge Research in Information Technology and Society

1. Reinventing Government in the Information Age
International Practice in IT-Enabled
Public Sector Reform
Edited by Richard Heeks

2. Information Technology in Government
Britain and America
Helen Margetts

3. Information Society Studies
Alistair S Duff

4. National Electronic Government
Building an Institutional Framework
for Joined Up Government – A
Comparative Study
Edited by Martin Eifert and Jan Ole
Püschel

5. Local Electronic Government
A Comparative Study
Edited by Helmut Drüke

6. National Governments and Control of the Internet
A Digital Challenge
Giampiero Giacomello

7. The Politics of Cyberconflict
Security, Ethnoreligious and
Sociopolitical Conflicts
Athina Karatzogianni

8. Internet and Society
Social Theory in the Information Age
Christian Fuchs

Internet and Society

Social Theory in the Information Age

Christian Fuchs

Routledge
Taylor & Francis Group
New York   London

First published 2008
by Routledge
270 Madison Ave, New York, NY 10016

Simultaneously published in the UK
by Routledge
2 Park Square, Milton Park, Abingdon, Oxfordshire OX14 4RN

Routledge is an imprint of the Taylor & Francis Group, an informa business

First issued in paperback 2010

© 2008 Taylor and Francis

Typeset in 10 point Sabon Roman by IBT Global.

Frontispiece design by Birgit Palma.

All rights reserved. No part of this book may be reprinted or reproduced or utilised in any form or by any electronic, mechanical, or other means, now known or hereafter invented, including photocopying and recording, or in any information storage or retrieval system, without permission in writing from the publishers.

Trademark Notice: Product or corporate names may be trademarks or registered trademarks, and are used only for identification and explanation without intent to infringe.

Library of Congress Cataloging in Publication Data
Fuchs, Christian, 1976-
Internet and society : social theory in the Internet age / Christian Fuchs.
p. cm. — (Routledge research in information technology and society ; 9)
Includes bibliographical references and index.
ISBN 978-0-415-96132-5 (hardback : alk. paper)
1. Internet—Social aspects.   2. Information technology—Social aspects.
3. Information society.   I. Title.

HM851.F83 2008
303.48'33--dc22   2007021600

ISBN13: 978-0-415-96132-5 (hbk)
ISBN13: 978-0-415-88992-6 (pbk)

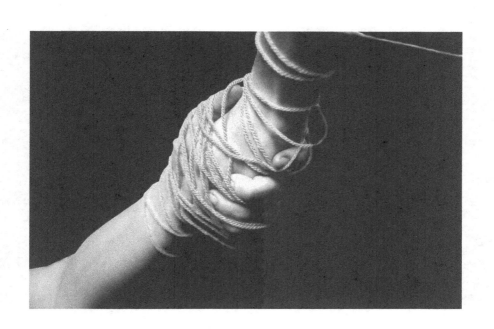

Contents

Preface   ix

1   **Introduction**   1

2   **Self-Organization and Cooperation**   11

   2.1 Characteristics of Self-Organizing Systems   11

   2.2 Self-Organization and Dialectical Philosophy   17

   2.3 Self-Organization as Ideology: Hayek's Theory of Competition 23

   *2.4 An Alternative: Self-Organization in Society as Human
Cooperation*   31

   2.5 Conclusion   34

3   **Society and Dynamic Social Theory**   35

   3.1 Anti-Luhmann: Niklas Luhmann's Revolution in Social Science? 35

   3.2 Humans and Society   40

   3.3 The Self-Organization of Social Systems   49

   3.4 Dialectics and Evolution   58

   3.5 Society as Dynamic System   62

   3.6 Modern Society as Dynamic System   71

   3.7 Conclusion   96

4   **The Rise of Transnational Informational Capitalism**   98

   4.1 Conceptualizing Contemporary Society   98

   4.2 The Rise of Transnational Informational/Network Capitalism 105

   *4.3 Conclusion: Cooperation and Competition in Transnational
Network Capitalism*   119

5   **Social Internet Dynamics**   121

   5.1 The Internet as a Dynamic Techno-Social System   121

5.2 *Web 1.0 as Dynamic Techno-Social System*   123

5.3 *The Rise of Web 2.0 and Web 3.0: Communication and Cooperation Online*   125

5.4 *Virtual Reality and Cyberspace*   136

5.5 *Conclusion*   138

6 **Competition and Cooperation in the Informational Ecology**   140

6.1 *ICTs and Transport*   140

6.2 *A Weightless Economy?*   142

6.3 *Virtual Products as a Foundation of a Sustainable Society?*   143

6.4 *Conclusion*   146

7 **Competition and Cooperation in the Internet Economy**   148

7.1 *The "Network Enterprise": Cooperation as Ideology*   148

7.2 *Informational Capitalism: Commodity or Gift Economy?*   157

7.3 *Class Competition in Informational Capitalism*   189

7.4 *Conclusion*   209

8 **Competition and Cooperation in Online Politics**   213

8.1 *Digital Exclusion: Digital Divides*   213

8.2 *Digital Inclusion: eParticipation as Grassroots Digital Democracy* 225

8.3 *The Absolute Violence of Competition in the Information Age: Information Warfare*   247

8.4 *Competition by Control: The Rise of Electronic Surveillance*   267

8.5 *Cooperating Social Movements Online: Cyberprotest*   277

8.6 *Conclusion*   294

9 **Competition and Cooperation in Cyberculture**   299

9.1 *Cyberculture Defined*   299

9.2 *Virtual Communities*   304

9.3 *Cyberculture: Socialization or Alienation?*   327

9.4 *Conclusion*   333

10 **Conclusion**   335

Notes   355
References   357
Index   381

Preface

Internet and society is an emerging research field. A number of strands are converging to feed this field. Among them are sociology of technology, new media studies, and social informatics. It does not come as a surprise that this field, as such, is in a premature state of affairs and has to search for its transdisciplinary foundation. Thus, social theory is challenged in the information age.

The present book is an attempt to fill the gap. What makes it distinct from other attempts are the following features:

First, it gropes for a unified approach by making use of a combination of two different theoretical backgrounds. On the one hand, there is a paradigm shift throughout science, including social science and humanities, initiated by the findings in thermodynamics regarding open, dynamical, nonlinear, complex, self-organizing systems. The concept of self-organization is considered being able to bridge the gap between system theory and action theory approaches in social theory. On the other hand, it is a fact that many theorists in information society research, in particular, the critics of the information society concept, are of Marxian origin. Christian Fuchs contends that some arguments of the Marxist tradition are still valid while some are not. He shows that by a proper merger of both lines of thought a grand social theory framework may emerge that is able to grasp capitalism in the age of the Internet.

Second, this theoretical framework is substantiated by a tremendous amount of empirical details found in the literature comprising every essential aspect of society from economy to politics to culture to technology to environment. The data regarding the impact the Internet has on each of these subsystems evidence the aggravation of system-specific manifestations of an underlying antagonism between cooperation and competition. The Internet may be interpreted as a technological catalyst of social struggles.

Third, in so doing, the data suggest the only reasonable and practicable conclusion for guiding action: a proactive attitude towards shaping the Internet for a global, sustainable information society that provides opportunities for all to participate and for survival, in the long run.

The book is worth reading for students, scholars, and practitioners interested in the bigger picture of the Internet society that affects us day by day.

Wolfgang Hofkirchner
Professor for Internet and Society
University of Salzburg
May 2007

1   Introduction

The Internet is ubiquitous in everyday life. On the Internet, we search for information, plan trips, read newspapers, articles, communicate with others by making use of e-mail, instant messaging, chat rooms, Internet phone, discussion boards, mailing lists, video conferencing; we listen to music and radio, watch videos, order or purchase by auction different goods, write our own blogs, and contribute to the blogs of others; we meet others, discuss with others, learn to know other people, fall in love, become friends, or develop intimate relations; we maintain contact with others; we protest, access government sites, learn, play games, create knowledge together with others in wikis, share ideas, images, videos; we download software and other digital data, and so forth. On the Internet, we also can feel being lost, disoriented, dissatisfied, scared, bored, stressed, alienated, lonesome, and so forth.

The Internet obviously is here to stay. How has this system transformed our lives and our society? What are the positive effects? What are the negative ones? Which opportunities and risks for the development of society and social systems are there? This book tries to contribute in helping people to find their own answers to such questions. Its main goal is to work out a theoretical understanding of the relationship of Internet and society. The problem that it addresses is the question of how society and the Internet need to be shaped by humans in order to avoid risks and maximize human happiness.

The study on Internet and society undertaken here takes place within a larger framework that has during the last years been labeled with categories like Internet research, ICTs and society, social informatics, informatics and society, new media research, information society theory, information society research/studies, Internet studies, Web research, etc.

Social informatics is a widely used term for this field of research. It was defined as "the interdisciplinary study of the design, uses, and consequences of ICTs that takes into account their interaction with institutional and cultural contexts" (Kling, Rosenbaum, and Sawyer 2005, 6). This definition implies that both the social design processes of ICTs and social ICT usage are important.

The terms *Internet* and *new media* are understood as technological concepts by many (although they are frequently described as techno-social systems by social scientists); hence my contention is that *Internet research* or *new media research* are not wisely chosen terms because they can convey the impression of a technological determinist understanding. I therefore consider the term *information and communication technologies & society research* (ICT&S) more suitable (Fuchs/Hofkirchner 2006).

ICT&S is also short for the Center for Advanced Studies and Research in Information and Communication Technologies & Society (ICT&S Center, http://www.icts.uni-salzburg.at) at the University of Salzburg. Its opening took place in March 2004; the idea for such a research center was created by Ursula Maier-Rabler, who is now the ICT&S Center's academic director. One of the center's units of competence is the eTheory unit, headed by Wolfgang Hofkirchner, who became professor at the center in October 2004. I joined the Center and the eTheory unit in October 2005 as assistant professor for Internet and society. It is the vivid atmosphere at the ICT&S Center—with all ups and downs attached to it—and at the University of Salzburg that has provided me with the intellectual climate for writing this book. Hence, I want to thank all the people at the ICT&S Center, my students, and my colleagues at the Department of Communication Science for giving me the opportunity for my own continuous learning and intellectual growth.

ICTs is a term that is used for technologies of cognition, communication, and cooperation that are computerized (i.e., work with digital logic) and networked. The term *Internet* frequently is used for a specific type of ICTs, the global network of computer networks that is based on the TCP/IP protocol and has developed from the ARPANET. Much of the analysis in this book is devoted to the Internet in this understanding; however, the category *Internet* is not only seen as one specific network but as the general phenomenon of the interconnection of networked knowledge-based technologies and networked social systems.

The research field of ICT&S deals with the interplay of new information and communication technologies (ICTs) and society. Two interconnected aspects of ICT&S research are:

- The social shaping/social design of ICTs.
- The impacts of ICT usage on society.

The task is the analysis of these relationships and the contribution to the design of society and ICTs so that a participatory knowledge society can emerge. ICT&S research deals with opportunities and risks of the knowledge society and the shaping of technology and social systems.

ICT&S research is a double process, consisting of (1) a process in which human actors design ICTs and in which it is analyzed how society shapes ICTs, and (2) of a process in which it is assessed how the usage of ICTs

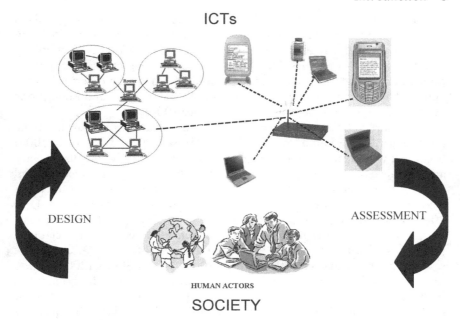

ICTs

DESIGN

ASSESSMENT

HUMAN ACTORS

SOCIETY

Figure 1.1 ICT&S Research.

transforms society (fig. 1.1). That ICTs are shown at another level than society here doesn't mean that they exist outside of it. Rather, ICTs are an immanent part of society.

Conceiving ICT&S as a double process of design and assessment implies that the relation of the two levels is inherently dynamic, they are mutually connected to each other, and they have constructive effects onto each other. Such dynamic thinking in philosophy can be found in the dialectical tradition. In dialectics, two separate entities become connected and form a higher-level unity that feeds back onto its parts. Dialectical development is a dynamic process of unity in diversity. In contemporary social science, dialectics has played a role, for example, in conceiving the relationship between social structures and human practices, as Anthony Giddens's structuration theory or Pierre Bourdieu's theory of habitus have exemplified.

Technological determinist accounts see technology as the driving force of society, as an independent factor outside of society that has linear effects on social systems. Social shaping approaches (such as social constructivism, actor network theory, neo-Marxist technology critique, cultural studies; for this distinction cf. Mackay 1995) consider technology as being invented, designed, changed, and used by humans and influenced by an overall societal context. The dialectical view advanced in this book, which conceives the relationship of ICTs and society as dynamic process, allows escaping the techno-deterministic view that only technology shapes society and the socioconstructivist view that only society shapes technology. The endless dynamic loop involved in this approach is based on the idea that humans in society shape (i.e., design and use) ICTs and that in this process technology conditions, that is, enables and constrains, human cognition, communication, and cooperation. Such a self-referential loop has been described as the approach of mutual shaping of society and ICTs (Lievrouw and Livingstone 2006; Herdin, Hofkirchner, and Maier-Rabler 2007).

What sort of science is ICT&S? Some argue that it is a transdiscipline (Hunsinger 2005; Lamb and Sawyer 2005; Sawyer and Tyworth 2006) because it would approach its object of study beyond and across disciplinary and interdisciplinary perspectives, there would be no single perspective, and researchers from different disciplines would cooperate in order to construct a common ground. Some say it is an interdisciplinary field of research (Duff 2000: 180). For others it is an emerging new discipline with its own journals, institutions, departments, studies, curricula, conferences, associations, projects, students, researchers, grants, a unified object of research, specific research methods, and so forth (Vehovar 2006). Wesley Shrum (2005) argues that Internet research is an indiscipline because it crosses the boundaries between traditional disciplines. No matter which position one takes here, it is obvious that ICT&S transgresses the traditional boundaries between the social and the engineering sciences. It is a boundary-deconstructing science.

Computerized network technologies change all areas of society; they pose challenges and opportunities in a networked globalizing world. Analyzing networks and networked social systems requires networking science. Transdisciplinarity means a higher-level system of research with a shared language, a unity in diversity of disciplines, approaches, methods, categories, theories, and so on. It emerges from the communication of scientists who have different backgrounds but share an interest in a common topic of research from different angles.

Some argue that Internet and society can be researched with traditional social science methods, whereas others argue that new methods are needed. My contention is that old methods are needed but that, due to the emergence of cyberspace, transformations of methods are also needed, as is shown by the emergence of methods of online social research (cf., e.g., Batinic, Reips, and Bosnjak 2002; Johns, Chen, and Hall 2004). The methods of ICT&S research are based on a dialectic of the new and the old: ICT&S needs all methods employed for designing and engineering ICTs, and it needs all methods employed for conceptualizing and analyzing society. Hence, a mix of methods from informatics and the social sciences forms a precondition for the existence of ICT&S. By their interplay, all of these methods can form a higher-level unity in diversity so that new cooperative methods emerge. Design produces applications; the latter's usage by humans changes society and social system. These changes need to be assessed, so that new design requirements emerge that again result in new applications, and so on. This dynamic process is at the heart of the methodological level of ICT&S.

ICT&S is not yet a fully developed field of research. There are many inter-acting parts that try to form a joint whole. The novelty of this field brings along excitement and openness as well as uncertainty about its future.

Kling, Rosenbaum, and Sawyer (2005, 6sq.) argue first that social infor-matics is empirically focused but then say that analytically it refers to studies that develop theories or to empirical studies that contribute to theorizing. If a theory is understood as a logically interconnected set of systematic hypoth-eses that describe worldly phenomena and the latter's foundation, structure, causes, effects, and dynamics; and empiricism as the observation and col-lection of data for constructing systematic and reflected knowledge, then one arrives at two levels of science. There is no theory that isn't grounded in empirical observations and no empirical research that doesn't make some theoretical assumptions. However, there can be a different stress of the two factors, and hence one can distinguish between theoretical research (pri-marily theoretically informed) and empirical research (primarily empirically informed). The work undertaken in this book is understood as a contribu-tion to a theory of Internet and society. Why is social theory important in this context? The emergence of the Internet has transformed society. In research this has resulted in a plurality of concepts such as Internet economy, digi-tal democracy, cyberculture, virtual community, cyberlove, eParticipation, eGovernment, eGovernance, online journalism, social software, Web 2.0, and so forth. There is no clear meaning of these terms; some of them remain very vague or contradictory. One of the goals of the work at hand is to con-tribute to the theoretical clarification of concepts that arise in the context of the relation of Internet and society. It is a theoretical approach grounded in a multitude of other theories and concepts that to a certain extent are dialectically synthesized so that a complex, multidimensional analysis that avoids deterministic understandings can emerge.

There are microlevel (individual), middle-range (organizational), and wide-range (society) theories and research designs in ICT&S research (Rice 2005). The approach undertaken in this work is predominantly located at the societal level; it is a wide-range theory of Internet and society that focuses on how society as a whole and its subsystems interact with Internet technologies.

Steve Sawyer and Michael Tyworth (2006) argue that social informatics is critical, but not in the sense of emancipation as advanced by critical theory, but more in the sense of an orientation that challenges accepted and taken-for-granted knowledge on ICT design, development, deployment, and use. Kling, Rosenbaum, and Sawyer (2005, 7) say that the critical orientation of social informatics is that it doesn't automatically and uncritically accept the goals and beliefs of the groups that commission, design, and implement ICTs. Critique for these authors means a critique of technological determin-ism. The work at hand understands itself not just as a social theory but also as a critical theory of Internet and society. The challenge of ideologies and accepted knowledge has always been one important aspect of the tradition of critical theory, although not the only one. One of the lines of thought that inform this book is the tradition of critical theory, as advanced by people like Herbert Marcuse, Theodor W. Adorno, Max Horkheimer, and Jürgen Habermas.

In summary, the main moments of critical theory that are also important for a critical theory of Internet and society are (cf. Horkheimer 1937; Marcuse 1937a):

- A dialectical critique of society doesn't focus on that which exists in society but on the possibilities of existence. It identifies moments and movements in society that negate dominant structures and open up possibilities for a Hegelian negation of the negation of existing structures.
- Critical theory is a lever of possible practice.
- It identifies differences of essence and appearance.
- It is concerned about the situation of human existence and is oriented on the improvement of human existence and happiness for all.
- It points out tendencies and real possibilities of development and human intervention, conditions, and perspectives of human practice.
- It transcends concrete reality and anticipates possible forms of being.
- It comments on the concrete forms of being.
- It develops categories that question the world that is and that which existing society has done to humans.
- The language of critical theory criticizes one-dimensional thought by creating a linguistic and theoretical universe that is complex and dialectical.
- Given categories and societal facticities are not considered as natural but as historical. Critical theory is a deconstruction of ideologies.
- It argues for humane conditions so that humans are reconciled with societal being that has been estranged from them.
- For critical theory the human being is more than an exploitable object.
- Critical theory argues that happiness, self-determination, and freedom can only be achieved by a transformation of the material conditions of existence.
- It stresses the importance and power of imagination for anticipating possible futures.
- Its goal is a reasonable society, an association of free people based on a sustainable utilization of technical means. It starts from the judgment that human life is livable or can and should be made livable and that in a given society there are specific possibilities for improving human life and specific ways and means for realizing these possibilities.
- Critical theory takes partisanship for oppressed humans.
- It strives for a condition without exploitation and oppression and for the emancipation of humans from enslaving relationships.

- It comprehends societal relationships as totalities.
- It points out the irrationality of the existing rationality and the rationality of irrationality in existing society.

In summary, this means that the approach worked out in this book is critical in the sense that it focuses on social problems in the context of Internet and society, it identifies opportunities and risks, sees them related to the larger social structure of contemporary society, and understands them as antagonistic forces.

Scott Lash (2002) has argued that critical theory in the information society must be immanent critique because there would be no outside space for transcendental critical reflection due to the immediacy of information (the speed and ephemerality of information would leave almost no time for reflection), the spatiotemporal extension caused by informatization and globalization processes, the vanishing of boundaries between human and nonhuman and culture as well as between exchange value and use value. Information critique would have to be an immanent critique without transcendentals. Critique of information would be in information itself, and it would be modest and also affirmative. The arguments in the book at hand are different: I argue that the information society has potentials for cooperation that provide a foundation for the full realization of the immanent essence of society—cooperation. Cooperation is seen as the very essence of society (an argument that can be found in the writings of young Marx, Marcuse, and Macpherson), it is an immanent feature of society and the human being as such, but this potential is estranged in modern society. This immanence is in contemporary society transcendental because the existence of society is different from its essence. The information society promises a new transcendental space—a cooperative society (or participatory democracy)— that is immanent in society as such (but not existent in alienated societies) and potentially advanced by information and information technology. But such a society isn't reached automatically because there is an antagonism between cooperation and competition immanent in capitalism and hence also in the capitalist information society that threatens the potentials for cooperation. Hence, for establishing an outside of and alternative to global informational capitalism, transcendental self-organizing political projects are needed that have alternative goals, practices, and structures of organization that, however, make use of existing structures (such as communication technologies) in order to transcend these very structures and create a new global space—a participatory democracy. The idea of this book is that information produces potentials that undermine competition but at the same time also produces new forms of domination and competition. The philosophical argument is based on the logic of essence and on the dialectic of immanence and transcendence. The line of argument assumes a formal identity of immanence and transcendence with society as the system of reference (cf. Fuchs and Zimmermann 2008). Transcendence is not something that is externally given to being but as immanent essence (and thus *wirklichkeit*) of that being. Transcendentals are societal forces that represent needs and goals that form the immanent essence of society but are repressed within the existing antagonistic totality and can't be realized within it. Hence, I don't agree with Lash that transcendental critique and dialectical critique (like the one of the Frankfurt school) are outdated. A dialectical framework of critique is needed for understanding the interconnected opportunities and risks of global informational capitalism. Facing Paul A. Taylor's (2006) critique that Lash's information critique is media determinist and risks becoming uncritical and conformist due to the lack of transcendentals, Lash (2006) now seems to argue for the dialectic of immanence and transcendence. One of my main points is that due to informatization the dialectics of thinkers like Hegel, Marx, and Marcuse gain a new topicality in transposed forms.

Another framework of the work at hand is self-organization theory. In the last decades, self-organization theory has emerged as a transdisciplinary theory that allows describing reality as permanently moving and producing novelty ("emergence"). The concept of self-organization grasps the dynamic, complex, evolving nature of systems in nature and society. The main motivation for taking up this notion is that contemporary society seems to be inherently complex, networked, and dynamic and that an explanation of its phenomena with this concept is manifest.

In the social sciences, the main representative of self-organization theory is Niklas Luhmann. I am impressed with the fact that Luhmann was one of those scientists who have shown that social theory is important today, but overall I am very critical of his theory because of its conceptual elimination of human actors from society. The understanding of self-organization advanced here is one that is oriented on human practice and puts humans and human interests into the very center of theory and society. Hence, a critique of Luhmann and the elaboration of a human-centered notion of social self-organization in the context of Internet and society runs throughout the book. The approach advanced is rather Habermasian than it is Luhmannian. Habermas argues that his critical theory of communicative action criticizes societies that don't make use of the learning capacities that they have and that surrender to an unguided increase of complexity, and it criticizes scientific approaches that can't deconstruct the paradoxes of societal rationalization because they consider complex societies only in abstract terms and neglect these societies' historical constitution (Habermas 1981, vol. 2, 549sq.). This means that Habermas understands his theory as a critique of the suppression of societal potentials and of ideologies that legitimize such developments.

However, other than Habermas, I think that it makes sense to employ a general notion of systems that are produced by human practice. For Habermas, systems are social relationships coordinated by the media money and power. He sees the systems concept related to instrumental reason and opposes it with the critical idea of a lifeworld of communicative discourse that has been colonized by systems in capitalist society. Habermas's theory lacks a universal concept that can explain the common ground of society and social relationships. If the concept of systems is defined on a very general level, one can describe society on a more general level that allows the distinction of different types of societies and systems (such as closed systems, coercive systems, capitalist systems, heteronomous systems, rigidly controlled systems, deterministic systems, purposive systems, heuristic systems, open systems, purposeful/purpose-seeking systems, lifeworld systems, participatory systems, etc.), the critique of coercive settings of society, and the advancement of liberating settings.

In systems thinking, there are some approaches that have been influenced by Habermas and critical theory. They have provided an alternative to the instrumental framework advanced by Luhmann. These are approaches such as critical systems thinking, critical systems heuristics, social systems design, and soft systems methodology. They have tried to integrate critical thinking and systems thinking. They can be considered as an incorporation of Habermasian ideas into systems theory. The understanding of systems advanced in the book at hand is close to the overall framework of critical systems theories that have tried to give the systems concept a humane twist.

The question how opportunities and risks emerge from the interrelation of Internet and society is reframed as an antagonism between cooperation and competition. The analysis of this antagonism in contemporary society runs as a thread throughout the book. Specific research questions that are treated are:

- What specific type of system is the Internet?
- In which society do we live?
- Which role do networks and knowledge play in contemporary society?
- Which role do cooperation and competition have in the information ecology?
- Which role do cooperation and competition have in the Internet economy?
- Which role do cooperation and competition have in online politics?
- Which role do cooperation and competition have in cyberculture?

In chapter 2, the notion of self-organization is introduced and related to dialectical thinking. These ideas are used throughout the book as theoretical framework that has ethical implications. In chapter 3, a general model of society is introduced, and the role of cooperation and competition in modern society is clarified. This model serves as the background for analyzing the Internet and society in the subsequent chapters. In chapter 4, the notion of the Internet is discussed. It is described as a techno-social system. After the two main categories (Internet, society) have been clarified in chapters 1–4, the relationship of Internet and society is discussed in chapters 5–9.

The arguments advance from the abstract to the concrete. In chapter 5, the question is discussed in which society we live and which key concept should be employed for analysis. The notions of transnational informational capitalism and transnational network capitalism are introduced. In chapters 6–9, it is subsequently shown how the antagonism between cooperation and competition shapes the relation of Internet and society in the ecological system (information ecology, chap. 6), the economic system (Internet economy, chap. 7), the political system (online politics, chap. 8), and the cultural system (cyberculture, chap. 9) of transnational informational capitalism. Phenomena relating to virtualization, dematerialization, resource and energy intensity of ICTs, information monopolies, open source, Internet gift economy, digital divides, digital democracy, information warfare, electronic surveillance, cyberprotest, and virtual community are subsequently discussed. In chapter 10, the main arguments of the book are brought together and an outlook is given.

There are certain phenomena of Internet and society such as eLearning, eHealth, digital art, Web art, online journalism, or cyberscience that can, due to limitations of space, not be analyzed in detail here but need to be addressed in separate publications in the future.

Figure 1.2 summarizes the dimensions of Internet and society that are treated in this book.

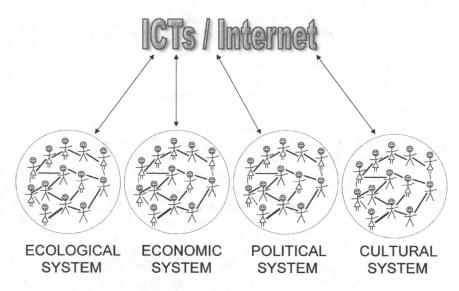

ECOLOGICAL   ECONOMIC   POLITICAL   CULTURAL
SYSTEM   SYSTEM   SYSTEM   SYSTEM

Figure 1.2 Dimensions of Internet and society.

2 Self-Organization and Cooperation

This chapter introduces the notion of self-organization as a foundational theory that will later be used for conceptualizing the relationship of Internet and society. First, principles of self-organizing systems are introduced (2.1), then the notion of self-organization is interpreted as a reformulation of dialectical philosophy (2.2), the usage of the self-organization concept in neoliberal theories is criticized (2.3), an alternative notion of self-organization as cooperative systemic agency is developed (2.4), and some conclusions are drawn (2.5).

2.1 CHARACTERISTICS OF SELF-ORGANIZING SYSTEMS

Self-organization is a process where a system reproduces itself with the help of its own logic and components, that is, the system produces itself based on an internal logic. Self-organizing systems are their own reason and cause; they produce themselves (*causa sui*). In a self-organizing system, new order emerges from the old system. This new order can't be reduced to single elements; it is due to the interactions of the system's elements. Hence, a system is more than the sum of its parts. The process of the appearance of order in a self-organizing system is termed *emergence*.

Some important characteristics of a self-organizing system that are mentioned in the literature and are summarized here are (cf. Arshinov and Fuchs 2003; Ebeling and Feistel 1994; Eigen and Schuster 1979; Fuchs 2003e; Haken 1978, 1983; Nicolis and Prigogine 1989; Prigogine 1980):

1. *Systemness:* Self-organization takes place in a system, that is, in a coherent whole that has parts, interactions, structural relationships, behavior, state, and a border that delimits it from its environment.
2. *Complexity:* Self-organizing systems are complex systems. The term *complexity* has three levels of meaning: (1) There is self-organization and emergence in complex systems (Edmonds 1999). (2) Complex systems are not organized centrally, but in a distributed manner; there are many connections between the system's parts (Kauffman 1993;

Edmonds 1999). (3) It is difficult to model complex systems and to predict their behavior even if one knows to a large extent the parts of such systems and the connections between the parts (Heylighen 1996, 1999; Edmonds 1999). The complexity of a system depends on the number of its elements and on its connections between the elements (the system's structure). According to this assumption, Kauffman (1993, 47) defines complexity as the "number of conflicting constraints" in a system; Heylighen (1996) says that complexity can be characterized by a lack of symmetry (symmetry breaking), which means that "no part or aspect of a complex entity can provide sufficient information to actually or statistically predict the properties of the others parts"; and Edmonds (1999) defines complexity as "that property of a language expression which makes it difficult to formulate its overall behavior, even when given almost complete information about its atomic components and their inter-relations". Aspects of complexity are things, people, number of elements, number of relations, nonlinearity, broken symmetry, nonholonic constraints, hierarchy, and emergence (Flood and Carson 1993).

3. *Control Parameters:* A set a parameters influences the state and behavior of the system.

4. *Critical Values:* If certain critical values of the control parameters are reached, structural change takes place; the system enters a phase of instability/criticality.

5. *Fluctuation and Intensification:* Small disturbances from inside the system intensify themselves and initiate the formation of order.

6. *Feedback Loops, Circular Causality:* There are feedback loops within a self-organizing system; circular causality involves a number of processes $p_1, p_2, \ldots, p_n$ ($n \geq 1$) and p_1 results in p_2, p_2 in p_3, $\ldots$, p_{n-1} in p_n and p_n in p_1.

7. *Nonlinearity:* In a critical phase of a self-organizing systems, causes and effects can't be mapped linearly; similar causes can have different effects and different causes similar effects; small changes of causes can have large effects whereas large changes can also only result in small effects (but nonetheless it can also be the case that small causes have small effects and large causes large effects).

8. *Bifurcation Points:* Once a fluctuation intensifies itself, the system enters a critical phase where its development is relatively open, certain possible paths of development emerge, and a choice concerning the future state of the system is required. This means a dialectic of necessity and chance. Bifurcation is phase transition from stability to instability.

9. *Selection:* In a critical phase, which can also be called point of bifurcation, a selection is made between one of several alternative paths of development

10. *Emergence of Order:* In a critical phase, new qualities of a self-organizing system emerge; this principle is also called order from chaos

or order through fluctuation. A self-organizing system is more than the sum of its parts. The qualities that result from temporal and spatial differentiation of a system are not reducible to the properties of the components of the system; interactions between the components result in new properties of the system that can't be fully predicted and can't be found as qualities of the components. Microscopic interactions result in new qualities on the macroscopic level of the system. Checkland (1981, 314) defines an emergent quality in similar terms "as a whole entity which derives from its component activities and their structure, but cannot be reduced to them". The emergence of order includes both (a) bottom-up emergence (a perturbation causes the system's parts to interact synergetically in such a way that at least one new quality on a higher level emerges) and (b) downward causation (once new qualities of a system have emerged, they, along with the other structural macroaspects of the system, influence, that is, enable and constrain, the behavior of the system's parts). This process can be described as top-down emergence if new qualities of certain parts (seen as wholes or systems themselves) show up.

11. *Information Production:* Information is a relationship between specific organizational units of matter. Reflection (*widerpiegelung*) means reaction to influences from the outside of a system in the form of innersystemic structural changes. There is a causal relationship between the result of reflection and the reflected. The reflected causes structural changes but doesn't mechanically determinate them. There is a certain, relative autonomy of the system. This autonomy can be described as a degree of freedom from perturbations. On the different organizational levels of matter we find different degrees of freedom. This degree increases along with complexity if we go up the hierarchy from physical-chemical to living and finally social systems. The causal relationship between the reflected and the result of reflection is based on a dialectic relationship of freedom and necessity. This means that information is a relationship of creative/active reflection between a system and its environment or interacting elements of a system, to be more precise between units of organized matter. Stimuli and fluctuations cause innersystemic structural change; the fluctuation is actively reflected within a system. Information is not a structure given in advance; it is produced within material relationships.

12. *Fault Tolerance:* Outside a critical phase, the structure of the system is relatively stable concerning local disturbances and a change of boundary conditions.

13. *Openness:* Self-organization can only take place if the system imports entropy that is transformed. As a result, energy is exported/dissipated.

14. *Symmetry Breaking:* The emerging structures have less symmetry than the foundational laws of the system.

15. *Inner Conditionality:* Self-organizing systems are influenced by their inner conditions and the boundary conditions from their environment.
16. *Relative Chance:* There is a dialectic of chance and necessity in self-organizing systems; certain aspects are determined, whereas others are relatively open and according to chance.
17. *Cohesion:* Cohesion means the closure of the causal relations among the dynamical parts of a dynamical particular that determine its resistance to external and internal fluctuations that might disrupt its integrity (Collier 2003, 2004). It is a "dividing glue" of dynamic entities (2004).
18. *Hierarchy:* The self-organization of complex systems produces a hierarchy in two distinctive senses: (1) The level of emergence is a hierarchically higher level, that is, it has additional, new emergent qualities that can't be found on the lower level that contains the components. The upper level is a sublation of the lower level. (2) Self-organization results in an evolutionary hierarchy of different system types. These types are hierarchically ordered in the sense that upper levels are more complex and have additional emergent qualities.
19. *Globalization and Localization:* Bottom-up emergence means the globalizing sublation of local entities, downward causation the localization of more global qualities (Fuchs 2003b).
20. *Unity in Plurality (Generality and Specificity):* On the one hand, a self-organizing system is characterized by a number of distinctive qualities that distinguish it from other self-organizing systems. On the other hand, each type of self-organizing system also shares general principles and qualities with all other types of self-organizing systems.

The concept of emergence is the central notion of self-organization concepts. Aspects of emergence are:

- *Synergism:* Emergence is due to the productive interaction between entities. Synergy is a very general concept that refers "to combined or 'cooperative' effects—literally, the effects produced by things that 'operate together' (parts, elements, or individuals)" (Corning 1998, 136). Synergy takes place and shapes systems on all organizational levels of matter. It is a fundamental quality of matter. Synergies between interacting entities are the cause of the evolution and persistence of emergent systems.
- *Novelty:* On a systemic level, different from the level of the synergetically interacting entities, new qualities show up. Emergent qualities are qualities that have not been previously observed and have not previously existed in a complex system ("a whole is more than the sum of its parts").
- *Irreducibility:* The new produced qualities are not reducible to or derivable from the level of the producing, interacting entities.

- *Unpredictability:* The form of the emergent result and the point of emergence can't be fully predicted.
- *Coherence/Correlation:* Complex systems with emergent qualities have some coherent behavior for a certain period of time (Goldstein 1999). This coherence spans and correlates the level of the producing entities into a unity on the level of emergence (ibid.).
- *Historicity:* Emergent qualities are not pregiven but the result of the dynamical development of complex systems.

Figure 2.1 summarizes the principles of self-organization: On the one hand, self-organization is a process in which, from the permanent complex interactions of agents structures are reproduced. If certain controlling forces reach thresholds, then a phase of instability and bifurcation emerges. One knows that in such a phase the overall system will be transformed, but one doesn't know the exact direction and form of change. New overall order of the system emerges; its structure is fundamentally changed. In dialectical philosophy, this process of the emergence of novelty is termed *aufhebung* (sublation), a German term that means preservation, elimination, and elevation. The unity of these three processes is characterized by the steplike process structure in the figure. In the bifurcation phase, there are several potential futures of the system (conditioned by the existing structures), but only one is

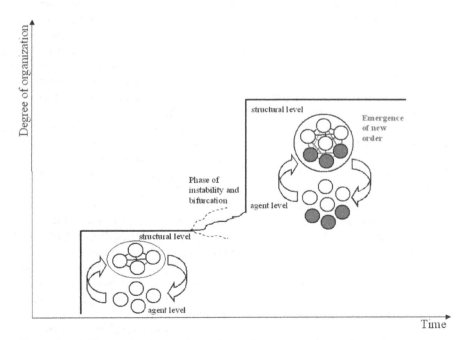

Figure 2.1 Self-organization as dynamic synchronous and asynchronous process.

realized. In the figure, the potential future development paths of the system are characterized by dotted lines, and the actual paths by a normal line.

I will now give an example for a self-organizing system on the Internet: MySpace is a social networking online platform that allows users to generate personal profiles on which they can upload pictures, text, videos, music, and keep their personal blogs. It networks users with a friendship system (users can add others to their friend list and post comments to their friends' guest books), discussion forums, interest groups, and a mail function. It was founded in 2003, and with more than 100 million registered users in 2006 it is one of the most accessed Web sites worldwide. MySpace is a system (P1); it is made up of human beings who make use of Internet technologies for interacting. It consists of various subsystems, that is, communities organized in the form of discussion boards and interest groups. Especially alternative music plays an important role here, but there are also communities focusing on film, comedy, philosophy, politics, and so on. The system is complex (P2); there are millions of actors and interactions; nobody can be fully aware of and can fully control these interaction flows. The system is dynamic; it is permanently reproduced by human actions and communications. MySpace is only a system as long as it is actively used by humans who act and interact in it in order to produce meaning and social relations. Self-organization (P10) here means that there is a dynamic emergence of new profile information (blog infos, links, videos, images, music, etc.) and new profiles produced by human action as well as the dynamic emergence of new social relations (accumulating friends in the friend lists), guest-book entries, e-mail messages and exchanges, discussion board discourses, entries and replies, blog interactions, and so on, produced by human communication. Self-organization of MySpace is a dynamic process in the sense that the system is transforming itself and growing permanently due to human cognition, communication, and cooperation. With the growth of the system, it also extends itself in space; users from different parts of the globe that are physically far away from each other emerge and form virtual communities that are localized in cyberspace (P19). MySpace is an interest-based community: People look for others who share their personal interests, or they maintain contacts with friends from whom they already know that they share their interests. Shared interest is a cohesive force of MySpace (P17). It is open for the emergence of new actors and relations (P13), although of course there are also nodes and links that cease to exist (e.g., if a user leaves the community). Information is produced (P11) as the MySpace structure changes dynamically due to human activity (adding digitized data) and communication (interacting with others). Existing structures (profiles, friendships, discourses) enable further activities, relations, and communications on MySpace from which new structures emerge. This is a recursive feedback process (P6) between MySpace actions (human cognition, communication, and cooperation) and MySpace structures (objectified digital information stored on servers and transmitted by the Internet). A decisive parameter of MySpace is its number of users, which has been rapidly growing since 2003. We can say that the number of users is a control parameter of the MySpace system (P3). If it reaches a certain critical value (P4), then an overall change can be expected. In 2005, MySpace came closer to 100 million registered profiles (which was finally reached in summer 2006), which was a critical value and generated economic interest in the platform. A fundamental change occurred (P5, P8, P10, P14): Rupert Murdoch's News Corp. purchased MySpace for half a billion US dollars. From different offers, the old owners of MySpace selected the one of News Corp. (P9). New ownership structures emerged in a phase of change (P5, P8, P10). This also changed the structure of MySpace: Its advertising strategy is enforced and MySpace is now used for promoting the content provided by Murdoch's Fox TV ("TV on Demand") in order to increase the TV station's competitiveness. It was determined that with the increasing popularity of MySpace, some changes would occur, but the exact form of change (change in ownership) wasn't predetermined but decided by economic agency and communication in a transformative phase (P7, P16). Due to the networked structure of MySpace, there is the potential for certain information to spread rapidly through the network, intensify collective social action, and result in what Howard Rheingold (2002) terms a *smart mob*. MySpace is a Web 2.0 application. Whereas Web 1.0 was a development phase of the Internet in which the latter was dominated by information production and reception, Web 2.0 is a phase that is dominated by human communication on the Net. Communication as a dominant function emerged with the rise of Web 2.0, but Web 1.0 and Web 2.0 have in common that they are both Internet technologies (P18, P20). Web 1.0 is an encapsulated part of Web 2.0. The development of the Internet forms an evolutionary hierarchy characterized by emergent properties.

2.2 SELF-ORGANIZATION AND DIALECTICAL PHILOSOPHY

Self-organization theory considers nature as dynamic and is hence opposed to the classical Newtonian worldview that characterizes nature and society as strictly determined, immutable, conservative, reducible to mechanics, and stabile. Hegel, Marx, and Engels were highly critical of the Newtonian worldview. They emphasized interconnection and processes instead of singularities and reduction. Hegel criticized atomistic philosophies (Hegel 1874, §§97, 98) by saying that they fix the One as One. The Absolute is formulated as Being-for-self, as One, and many ones. They wouldn't see that the One and the Many are dialectically connected. Marx criticized the reductionism of individualism in his critique of Max Stirner (Marx and Engels 1846, 101–438[1]) and put against this the notion of the individual as a social being that is estranged in capitalism and becomes a well-rounded individual in communism. Engels questioned the reductionism and individualism of "metaphysical thinkers" (Engels 1878, 20sq.; 1886a, 482). Due to the stress on dynamic development, self-organization theory can be considered as a reformulation of dialectical philosophy (Hodgson 2000, 65; Hofkirchner 1993, 1998; Prigogine and Stengers 1984; Steigerwald 2000; Woods and Grant 2002). "The idea of a history of nature as an integral part of materialism was asserted by Marx and, in greater detail, by Engels. Contemporary developments in physics, the discovery of the constructive role played by irreversibility, have thus raised within the natural sciences a question that has long been asked by materialists. For them, understanding nature meant understanding it as being capable of producing man and his societies" (Prigogine and Stengers 1984, 252). In Marxist thinking also, Ernst Bloch's concept of matter anticipated the modern theories of self-organization. Nature is for Bloch a producing subject; he says it is forming itself, forming out of itself (1963, 234). Bloch used the term *emergence* in stressing that all gestalt figures *emerge* from the dialectical process and from matter as developing, producing (*ausgebären*[2]) substance immanently as well as speculatively (Bloch 1975, 165).

The logic of self-organizing systems resembles the dialectical principles of the transition from quantity to quality, negation, and negation of the negation (Fuchs 2003e):

Georg Wilhelm Friedrich Hegel has outlined that the purpose of dialectics is "to study things in their own being and movement and thus to demonstrate the finitude of the partial categories of understanding" (Hegel 1874, note to §81). Self-organization refers to the forms of movement of matter and hence is connected to dialectical thinking. What is called control parameters, critical values, bifurcation points, phase transitions, nonlinearity, selection, fluctuation, and intensification in self-organization theory (principles 3, 4, 5, 7, 8, 9) corresponds to the dialectical principle of transition from quantity to quality. This is what Hegel has discussed as the Measure (Hegel 1874, §§107–111): The Measure is the qualitative quantum; the quantum is the existence of quantity. "The identity between quantity and quality, which is found in Measure, is at first only implicit, and not yet explicitly realised. In other words, these two categories, which unite in Measure, each claim an independent authority. On the one hand, the quantitative features of existence may be altered, without affecting its quality. On the other hand, this increase and diminution, immaterial though it be, has its limit, by exceeding which the quality suffers change. . . . But if the quantity present in measure exceeds a certain limit, the quality corresponding to it is also put in abeyance. This however is not a negation of quality altogether, but only of this definite quality, the place of which is at once occupied by another. This process of measure, which appears alternately as a mere change in quantity, and then as a sudden revulsion of quantity into quality, may be envisaged under the figure of a nodal (knotted) line" (ibid., §§108–109).

Hegel gives an example for the transition from quantity to quality: "Thus the temperature of water is, in the first place, a point of no consequence in respect of its liquidity: still with the increase of diminution of the temperature of the liquid water, there comes a point where this state of cohesion suffers a qualitative change, and the water is converted into steam or ice" (Hegel 1874, §108). In the language of self-organization theory, one can say that temperature is a control parameter. At zero degrees Celsius a critical threshold is reached; water changes its quality; ice emerges as a new quality. As other examples, Hegel mentions the reaching of a point where a single additional grain makes a heap of wheat; or the point where the bald-tail is produced, if we continue plucking out single hairs.

What is called emergence of order, production of information, or symmetry breaking in self-organization theory (principles 10, 11, 14) corresponds to Hegel's notions of sublation (*Aufhebung*) and negation of the negation. Something is only what it is in its relationship to another, but by the negation of the negation this something incorporates the other into itself. The dialectical movement involves two moments that negate each other, a somewhat and an other. As a result of the negation of the negation, "something becomes an other; this other is itself somewhat; therefore it likewise becomes an other, and so on ad infinitum" (Hegel 1874, §93). Being-for-self or the negation of the negation means that somewhat becomes an other, but this again is a new somewhat that is opposed to an other and as a synthesis results again in an other, and therefore it follows that something in its passage into other only joins with itself: it is *self-related* (§95). In becoming there are two moments (Hegel 1812, §§176–179): coming-to-be and ceasing-to-be: by sublation, that is, negation of the negation, being passes over into nothing, it ceases to be, but something new shows up, is coming to be. What is sublated (*aufgehoben*) on the one hand ceases to be and is put to an end, but on the other hand it is preserved and maintained (ibid., §185). In dialectics, a totality transforms itself; it is self-related. This corresponds to the notions of self-production and circular causality. The negation of the negation has positive results, that is, in a self-organizing system the negation of elements results in positive new qualities. Hegel speaks in this context of being determined (*bestimmtes sein*).

Friedrich Engels, in his *Dialectics of Nature* and his *Anti-Dühring*, developed a dynamic worldview in which motion is the mode of existence of matter (Engels 1878, 55). Examples that Engels (1878, 1886a) mentions for the transition from quantity to quality are the homologous series of carbon compounds, a certain current strength that is required to cause the platinum wire of an electric incandescent lamp to glow, the temperature of incandescence and fusion of metals, the freezing and boiling points of liquids, the critical point at which a gas can be liquefied by pressure and cooling, the change of form of motion and energy, or Hegel's example of the states of aggregation of water. As an example for dialectical development, Engels mentions the development process of a grain of barley: "Billions of such grains of barley are milled, boiled and brewed and then consumed. But if such a grain of barley meets with conditions which are normal for it, if it falls on suitable soil, then under the influence of heat and moisture it undergoes a specific change, it germinates; the grain as such ceases to exist, it is negated, and in its place appears the plant which has arisen from it, the negation of the grain. But what is the normal life-process of this plant? It grows, flowers, is fertilised and finally once more produces grains of barley, and as soon as these have ripened the stalk dies, is in its turn negated. As a result of this negation of the negation we have once again the original grain of barley, but not as a single unit, but ten-, twenty- or thirtyfold" (Engels 1878, 126). As similar examples, he mentions the development process of insects, geology as a series of negated negations, a series of successive chatterings of old and deposits of new rock formations, differential and integral calculus, the development of philosophy and society. Such development processes can also be described as self-organizing development: The control parameters that influence the development of the grain are time and natural conditions such as heat and moisture. During the development, new seeds show up. At a specific point of time, a critical point is reached and the grain ceases to exist. But at the same time, new grains emerge. Nodal lines or the transition from quantity to quality are today also studied in self-organization theory, especially in the theory of self-organized criticality (Bak 1996).

Dialectical processes and negation of the negation mean not just the emergence of other, new qualities; dialectic development also includes development process that results in *higher* qualities and other structural levels. Dialectical development is not just change or self-transformation and self-reproduction; it is also the emergence of higher levels of organization (Hörz 1976, 311sqq.). Hence, dialectical thinking assumes an immanent hierarchy in nature and evolutionary leaps. "The transition from one form of motion to another always remains a leap, a decisive change" (Engels 1878, 61). Self-organization theory is also dialectical in the respect that it frequently considers self-organization as emergent evolution. This means that there are hierarchical organizational levels of self-organization that differ in complexity. New qualities of organization emerge on upper levels. In self-organization theory, for example, Ervin Laszlo (1987) argues that evolution does not take place continuously, but in sudden, discontinuous leaps. After a phase of stability, a system would enter a phase of instability; fluctuations intensify and spread out. In this chaotic state, the development of the system is not determined; it is only determined that one of several possible alternatives will be realized. Laszlo says that evolution takes place in such a way that new organizational levels emerge. He identifies successive steps of evolution. Not all scientists who speak about self-organization include the development of higher qualities into their concepts. Hence, dialectical materialism can in this respect be considered as a broader evolutionary concept than self-organization.

The principle of relative chance, which is typical for self-organizing systems, has already been considered as dialectic of chance and necessity by Hegel, Marx, and Engels (Hegel 1874, §§144–149; Engels 1886a,

486–491). Engels has stressed that the dialectic of attraction and repulsion is an aspect of matter and its movement. Both elements are also described by self-organization theory: Chaos, noise, or instability are seen as disordered movement of the elements of a complex system. One can also say that the elements are repulsing each other. But this repulsion is one that turns into attraction, because the elements interact; there are processes of ordering and selection, that is, attraction takes place as the emergence of a coherent whole and new qualities.

Humberto Maturana and Francisco Varela (1992) applied self-organization theory to biology in order to find a consistent definition of life. They say that living systems are biologically self-organizing in the sense that they permanently produce themselves, their parts, and their unity. They term such self-producing systems *autopoietic* (*autos* = self, *poiein* = to make something). Engels pointed out the problem of defining life and intuitively anticipated autopoiesis theory. Of course, today we know a whole lot more about life than Engels did, especially since the discovery of the double helix. But what's important is that Engels anticipated the idea of autopoiesis. He says that life exists in the "constant self-renewal of the chemical constituents" it has (Engels 1878, 75); it is a "self-implementing process" (ibid. 76). Albumen would not only permanently decompose itself; it would also permanently produce itself from its components (Engels 1876a, 558f).

I am aware that, due to Marxist orthodoxy, dialectical materialism is today considered by many as a mechanic worldview that assumes that capitalism by natural laws collapses and that communism is an automatic result. Orthodox Marxism interpreted societal development as a natural process and neglected the role of agency. For me, speaking of self-organization means that novelty can emerge from the interactions of agents that are not determined but conditioned, that is, enabled and constrained, by existing structures. Self-organization in society is used as a category that stresses agency and the creativity of human cooperation. Linking these ideas to Marxian dialectical categories shall not revive a determinist conception of history but show the topicality of reading Marx's works as a theory of agency, cooperation, and self-determination. Traditional Marxism is not the same as Marxian ideas.

Antonio Negri argues that Hegelian dialectics is deterministic, a "schematism of reason and transcendentality" and a "reformist teleology" (Negri 2004, 84). The critique of dialectics by Negri holds true for vulgar dialectical thinking such as the one of Stalin and Mao, in which the development of society has been conceived as based on deterministic natural laws so that human practice could be considered as unimportant and the Soviet and Chinese systems could ideologically be legitimated as free societies because, according to dialectical materialism, socialism would, as a natural law, have to follow after capitalism. That these regimes were indeed highly repressive was ideologically concealed by a deterministic interpretation of Hegelian dialectics. Stalin (1938) misinterpreted Marx and argued that dialectics apply similarly to nature and society and cause a linear, successive development in both realms. Stalin overlooks that social dialectics differ from natural dialectics in the respect that human beings have a much greater degree of freedom of choice than nature does have; they can make a conscious difference that makes a difference in society. Stalin's interpretation of dialectics is structural, functionalistic, and deterministic. Based on the deterministic naturalization of society, he argues that "revolutions made by oppressed classes are a quite natural and inevitable phenomenon" and based on this mechanic determinism he says that "the U.S.S.R. has already done away with capitalism and has set up a socialist system" where "there are no longer exploiters and exploited". Stalin interprets the dialectical movement of society as a natural law in order to idealize the Soviet system that was indeed a system of terror, domination, exploitation, and repression. He argues that this system must be considered as a free society because it would be the system following capitalism, and according to historical laws and the natural development of society, a free society would follow capitalism. In Stalinism (and similarly in Maoism and some other isms), dialectics became an ideology. "[In Soviet ideology] the consciousness and action of the proletariat then are largely determined by the 'blind laws' of the capitalist process instead of having broken through this determinism. . . . the capitalist development, the transition to socialism, and the subsequent development of Soviet society through its various phases is presented as the unfolding of a system of objective forces that could not have unfolded otherwise. To be sure, strong and constant emphasis is placed on the guiding role of the Communist Party and its leaders . . . The subjective factor no longer appears as an integral element and stage of the objective dialectic" (Marcuse 1958, 147sqq.).

But it is a premature conclusion to oppose all dialectical thinking. The dialectic of society must be based on the dialectic of human subjectivity and societal objects in order to be truly dialectical and nondeterministic. Such a reading of dialectics can be found in the philosophical writings of Marx and was for the first time explicitly formulated against deterministic interpretations by Herbert Marcuse. Marcuse argues that capitalism is based on structural antagonisms that cause crises; the tendency of crises would be an aspect of objective dialectics: "Capitalist society is a union of contradictions. It gets freedom through exploitation, wealth through impoverishment, advances in production through restriction of consumption. The very structure of capitalism is a dialectical one: every form and institution of the economic process begets its determinate negation, and the crisis is the extreme form in which the contradictions are expressed" (Marcuse 1999, 311sq.). Marcuse wanted to avoid a deterministic understanding of dialectics; he wanted to accomplish a turn from structuralism towards human practice in Marxism. For doing so, he first turned to Heidegger's phenomenology, but Heidegger's fascist ideology and the publication of Marx's "Economic-Philosophic Manuscripts" in 1930 made him aware that there is a line of thought immanent in Marxian and Hegel's works that allows the accomplishment of a turn towards practice in Marxism. Capitalism would be dialectically negative by its very own antagonistic structure, but the negation of the negativity could only be achieved by human practice: "The negativity and its negation are two different phases of the same historical process, straddled by man's historical action. The 'new' state is the truth of the old, but that truth does not steadily and automatically grow out of the earlier state; it can be set free only by an autonomous act on the part of men, that will cancel the whole of the existing negative state" (Marcuse 1999, 315). "Not the slightest natural necessity or automatic inevitability guarantees the transition from capitalism to socialism. . . . The realization of freedom and reason requires the free rationality of those who achieve it. Marxian theory is, then, incompatible with fatalistic determinism" (Marcuse 1999, 318sq.).

Subjective practices are conditioned, that is, enabled and constrained, by objective antagonisms; vice versa, objective reality is a result of the subjective realization of certain objective potentials. For Marcuse, dialectics is dialectics of subject and object, freedom and necessity, a unity of subjective dialectics and objective dialectics. The rise and fall of the Soviet system has shown that there is no automatic historical development. Capitalism produces antagonistic potentials for cooperation that anticipate a cooperative society. If a cooperative society will emerge is decided in social struggles and by realized or unrealized potentials for social self-organization of oppressed groups in contemporary network capitalism. It is not predetermined. Subjective dialectics is dialectically connected to the objective dialectical structure of contemporary society. With the help of the concept of self-organization, I want to contribute to a subjective turn of dialectical thinking, that is, a dialectic of dialectics that overcomes the theoretical and practical gap between human subjects and social structures. A mechanic dialectic can be avoided by an emphasis on practice and subjectivity that argues that the objective dialectic sets conditions, that is, enables and constrains the subjective dialectic of human practice that can, based on conditioning structures, produce different historical alternatives of development. It is also important to stress that human dialectics differs from natural dialectics in the sense that humans are knowledgeable, creative, visionary, anticipatory, self-conscious, active social beings that, given certain societal conditions, can choose between different practices. In human practice we find much more (conditioned) degrees of freedom than in nature.

2.3 SELF-ORGANIZATION AS IDEOLOGY: HAYEK'S THEORY OF COMPETITION

Paradoxically, contemporary Marxism, much more than conservative thinking, stresses human agency (e.g., Hardt and Negri 2000, 2005). In certain forms of systems theory, self-organization has become a functionalist ideology that excludes the potentials for social change by human agency.

Niklas Luhmann (2000, 215sq.) argues that the welfare state tries to solve all problems of society, but that this would be impossible and cause problems in a functionally differentiated society. For Luhmann, all subsystems of society (politics, economy, family, legal system, education, mass media, religion, science) are functionally differentiated, that is, they have their own autonomous self-referential autopoiesis and binary functions. Hence, it would be impossible for one subsystem like polity to intervene into others. Luhmann (1994, 325, 336sq., 340, 346) says that in a functionally differentiated society there is neither a top nor a center that could represent society in society. Representatives of evolutionary economics frequently argue that self-organization means the theorem of the invisible hand of Adam Smith (Witt 1997). Kevin Kelly (1995, 1999) says that the market is a self-organizing vivi-system that has the capacity to regulate itself. Andrew Dunsire considers governance as an autopoietic system and says that, hence, social systems are "unregulable from any center if not altogether ungovernable" (Dunsire 1996, 301).

The idea that markets and capitalism are self-regulating and that political influences are harmful has, in the context of self-organization theory, been most widely discussed by Friedrich August von Hayek.

Hayek defines competition as "the action of endeavouring to gain what another endeavours to gain at the same time" (1949, 96). This implies that one achieves an advantage at the expense of others: An asymmetrical distribution of resources and power will probably be the result. Capitalism would be based on unconscious self-organization. Cooperation in the narrow sense that has to do with solidarity and altruism would be a fundamental human instinct. The communities of "primitive" people would have been based on these instincts and collectivism. Hayek says that this is why they remained very small and limited. The development of civilization would depend on the emergence of rules that are passed on to following generations not by instincts but by traditions and that would consist of prohibitions that forbade man to do what his instincts demanded. Rules of human conduct that would have enabled man to enlarge civilization would be several: property, honesty, contract, exchange, trade, competition, gain, privacy, the market system, and money. Man would have had to restrain some 'good' instincts in order to advance civilization.

Adam Smith argued that an individual who in economic action "intends only his own gain . . . is in this, as in many other cases, led by an invisible hand to promote an end which was no part of his intention. . . . By pursuing his own interest he frequently promotes that of the society more effectually than when he really intends to promote it" (Smith 1976, 477). For Hayek, society is guided by Smith's invisible hand, which would help maintaining order, although social relationships wouldn't be actively planned but unconsciously and spontaneously organized. "We are led—for example, by the pricing system in market exchange—to do things by circumstances of which we are largely unaware and which produce results that we do not intend"

(Hayek 1988, 14). People would blindly obey abstract rules that they don't understand and haven't made themselves. This would enable them to profit from the activities and knowledge of others they don't know and will never meet. Striving for profit of individual actors would benefit the masses. The market and other institutions would enable human beings to use widely dispersed information that no central planning agency could ever know, possess, or control as a whole (ibid., 15).

Cooperation wouldn't be better than competition because the first would mean a sort of central planning that couldn't make, like competition, full use of the knowledge dispersed over society. "Cooperation, like solidarity, presupposes a large measure of agreement on ends as well as on methods employed in their pursuit. It makes sense in a small group whose members share particular habits, knowledge and beliefs about possibilities. It makes hardly any sense when the problem is to adapt to unknown circumstances; yet it is this adaptation to the unknown on which the coordination of efforts in the extended order rests. Competition is a procedure of discovery, a procedure involved in all evolution, that led man unwittingly to respond to novel situations; and through further competitions, not through agreement, we gradually increase our efficiency" (ibid., 19).

Profitability would be a sort of signal that guides selection towards what makes man more fruitful (ibid., 46); market information would enable individuals to act egoistically in order to achieve profit. This would strengthen the public good. The market would transmit information about material objects (ibid., 94), "enabling men to use, and put to work, much more information and skill than they would have access to individually" (ibid., 97). It would transmit knowledge about prices, "of the basic fact of how the different commodities can be obtained and used" and about "alternative possibilities of action" (Hayek 1949, 51). There would be a division of knowledge: "knowledge of the circumstances of which we must make use never exists in concentrated or integrated form but solely as the dispersed bits of incomplete and frequently contradictory knowledge which all the separate individuals possess" (ibid., 77). The anonymous, unconscious, spontaneous market-mediated combination of fragments of knowledge would bring about a distribution of resources which could be understood as if it were made according to a single plan, although nobody planned it (ibid., 54). Prices would coordinate the separate actions of different people.

Order would mean a classification of and relation between elements. Hayek distinguishes two types of orders: spontaneous, self-forming orders, which he calls *kosmos*, and deliberately arranged and planned orders, which he calls *taxis*. All cultural (and natural) evolution would be a process of continuous adaptation to unforeseeable events and contingent circumstances. Social development would, due to the complexity of social relationships, be something that is largely determined by chance; it would be "unavoidably unpredictable" (Hayek 1988, 25). Cultural evolution would depend on variation, adaptation, and competition. "Not only does all evolution rest on competition; continuing competition is necessary to preserve existing achievements" (ibid., 26). Historically, those tribes who would have introduced trade and competition as an evolutionary variation would have had advantages over others; the latter would have adapted to these developments in order to survive. Other such evolutionary advantages would have been trade, private property, and money; they would have been necessary conditions for progress. The enlargement of society would have resulted from the invention and extension of trade and markets.

The spontaneous evolution of rules of conduct would assist the formation of self-organizing macrostructures. Hayek emphasizes a spontaneous nature of society. In the marketplace there would be permanent unintended consequences of actions; the distribution of resources would be affected by impersonal processes, in which individuals who act for their own ends would not and could not know what the results of their interactions would be.

The extended order couldn't be designed because complexity and knowledge would be created permanently by people making many decisions independently from each other according to their own purposes. The market would spontaneously coordinate the activities in such a way that order is created. Some actors would gain economic and competitive advantages, but these advantages would be communicated to others over the market. This would allow them to adapt to these changes and would advance evolution. Evolution would happen spontaneously, not in a humanly guided way. It would be a "self-ordering process of adaptation to the unknown" (Hayek 1988, 76). In the extended order, most ends of actions wouldn't be conscious or deliberate. Anonymous competitive market activities would result in "synergetic collaboration" (ibid., 80) that makes use of dispersed knowledge in order to generate order and enhance productivity. "The efforts of millions of individuals in different situations, with different possessions and desires, having access to different information about means, knowing little or nothing about one another's particular needs, and aiming at different scales of ends, are coordinated by means of exchange systems. As individuals reciprocally align with one another, an undersigned system of higher order of complexity comes into being, and a continuous flow of goods and services is created that, for a remarkably high number of the participating individuals, fulfills their guiding expectations and values" (Hayek 1988, 95). Activities of single individuals would benefit other individuals whom they don't know and will never meet.

The fatal conceit and a distinguishing characteristic of all socialist thought would be the idea that the ability to acquire skills would stem from reason. In reality, it would be the other way round: Reason would be the result of a cultural evolutionary selection process in society. Man could neither create nor design the extended order by reason. The fatal conceit would be the assumption "that man is able to shape the world around him according to his wishes" (Hayek 1988, 27). Without capitalism and competition, large parts of mankind would be doomed to poverty and death. The advancement of cultural evolution would have again and again been halted by intervening governments that would have disturbed spontaneous and voluntary actions. Government would only be necessary for providing abstract rules that secure private property, that is, the invasion of the individual's "free sphere" (63).

Decentralized mechanisms like markets would allow the fullest exploitation of dispersed knowledge; central planning or active design would imply a central actor overseeing all social knowledge. But such perfect knowledge would be impossible; hence, socialism would have to fail and capitalism would be superior. Concern for profit would make possible a more effective use of resources. Decentralized control over resources, control through private property, would lead to the generation and use of more information than is possible under central direction (86). Cooperation, solidarity, and altruism would be impossible in an extended order because there would be a high complexity of dispersed, uncontrollable knowledge and social relationships. Human beings could best achieve their ends by "relying on the self-ordering forces of nature"; hence, they should keep from deliberately trying to arrange elements. "For in fact we are able to bring about an ordering of the unknown only by causing it to order itself" (83). "Most defects and inefficiencies" of spontaneous orders would result from "attempting to interfere with or to prevent their mechanisms from operating, or to improve the details of their results" (84). Socialism would be a threat to the welfare of the human race. The socialist effort of designing social relationships would be a longing for the life of the "noble savage" that is led by instincts and would mean a return to a "primitive" society.

Based on a certain interpretation of the notion of self-organization, scholars argue that all subsystems of society are operationally closed and autonomous and that state intervention is harmful and has unpredictable outcomes. Hayek's theory has been highly influential; it has had tremendous consequences for contemporary policy design. His reductionistic misconception of society leads to the assumption that all deliberate intervention is harmful; hence, humans should not intervene into social structures. This hypothesis ignores the role of creative human agency in social development, and that the self-organization of society is not something that happens only blindly and unconsciously but depends on conscious, knowledgeable agents and creative social relationships that result in actions that have both planned and unintended consequences. Hayek's methodological individualism doesn't see the necessarily societal and material interdependence of individuals and doesn't grasp their process of development because it limits itself to advise them that they should proceed from themselves, it doesn't adequately reflect the real conflicts in the world, and it reduces sociality to individuality. "The methodological individualists are wrong in so far as they claim that social categories can be reduced to descriptions in terms of individual predicates" (Giddens 1984, 220). Hayek's approach sees only the unintended consequences of intervention in complex systems and labels these as harmful because the operation of the invisible hand is seen as inevitably beneficial.

Hayek's assumptions have been empirically falsified. State policies in the industrialized countries have during the last 20 years been increasingly based on a reduction of social intervention into the economy. Hayek's assumption that the economy is capable of ordering itself spontaneously without regulation has been put to test. The result has not been what Hayek and other believers in the beneficence of the invisible hand predicted. There has been an increase of general wealth, but along with it the increasing rise of poverty, unemployment, wage inequality, asymmetrical distribution of income and wealth, and a massive increase of insecure and precarious living conditions have shown that an elite benefits at the expense of the majority. These consequences of economic liberalization contrast with the general rise in median wealth and the redistribution of wealth, at least in developed countries, during the period of politically motivated social investment in the decades following the Second World War.

Theories like those of Hayek and Luhmann are ideologically biased; they try to scientifically legitimize a rigid capitalistic order and the global dominance of economic logic. The practical realization of Hayek's theory of spontaneous order formation and of Luhmann's theory of functional differentiation can be characterized as neoliberal ideology. Neoliberalism aims at creating a framework for the economy that makes it possible to raise profits by minimizing the costs of investment, reducing social security, preaching the capability of the market to regulate itself without human intervention, as well as self-help and self-responsibility of the individual for his or her problems. This results in deregulation, precarious job relationships, the dismantling of the welfare state, deterioration of labor and social policies, the lowering of taxes on capital, flexible labor times, the privatization of formerly public services and industries, the liberalization of international trade policies, the rise of new free trade associations, and so on. Under the regime of neoliberalism, the instrumental reason of the capitalist economy colonizes political and cultural systems and everyday life; it is a process of the colonization of lifeworlds.

Neoliberal ideologies claim that the economy is independent from society, that the market is the best means of organizing production and distribution efficiently, and that globalization requires the minimization of state spending, especially for social security. These developments are presented as inescapable, self-evident, and without alternative. The economy and politics are mutually dependent; each can realize its dynamics only with the help of the other. The state depends on taxes that it derives from the production process and is related to economic conflicts and struggles; the economy depends on regulatory frameworks that the state guarantees with its monopoly of violence. Assuming independence is an ideological move.

Neoliberalism results in precarious living and working conditions for a large, steadily increasing part of the world population. It has caused the rigid dominance of the economic system in society; economic logic permeates all social realms. This is a form of centralization, showing that 'spontaneous market-based order formation' does not lead to decentralization, as assumed by Hayek and Luhmann. The structural coupling between the economy and other subsystems of society is becoming more rigid in the direction in which the economy influences these subsystems.

It is not feasible that a system like society works the best way when, as Hayek claims, responsible, decision-oriented political action is missing. Such theses overlook that the human being is an active being that possesses the ability to change reality in well-rounded and responsible manners and in such a way that all can benefit. The global problems of society are not due to the fact that there is not enough "free market"; they are due to the antagonistic and conflicting character of modern society. The capitalist economy is a crisis-ridden, antagonistic system that in its development produces "market failures". The state as a regulatory instance tries to compensate for these failures in many respects; hence, conscious state intervention is a necessary condition for the existence of capitalism. All societies are in need of mechanisms that enable the cohesion of social relationships. A mode of regulation describes the institutional framework of social processes. These institutions have public, semipublic, and private character and are oriented on decision-based actions. Collective decisions are necessary elements of the development of all social systems; hence, politics is an aspect of all social systems and societies. The self-organization of a system such as the economy is in need of political regulation. Without political regulation, that is, decision-oriented human action, there can be no society and no economy. Hence, it is wrong to argue that economic systems can or should be self-sustained and that political intervention is harmful. Without political regulation, that is, purposeful, institutionalized human agency, there would be no social order at all. Regulation is a necessary condition for the existence and self-organization of all social systems. It is a false illusion that modern society functions better by minimizing regulation. Society is a complex system that can't be fully planned. But this doesn't mean that human beings can't act in certain ways in order to increase the possibility that certain developments will be realized and others won't. Human beings can't steer the development of society, but they can design the context of complex social systems.

Hayek is right in stressing that one important feature of the failures of "actually existing socialism" was that a central planning agency couldn't manage the complexity of society. Decentralized forms of self-organization and knowledge management seem indeed to be appropriate for establishing a socially and ecologically sustainable human order. But it is wrong to assume that cooperation means centralization and that competition means decentralization. Centralization can be defined as the control of resources and power by one or several specific subsystems of society. This implies an asymmetric distribution of resources and power, advantages of the centralizing subsystem at the expense of other subsystems. The countries of the Soviet Union were based on state-led centralization of society; the human beings were not able to immediately control their means of life assurance in a decentralized way. This doesn't imply that capitalism is a decentralized form of organization and that competition is an organization principle superior to cooperation. One can in fact learn from the failures of "actually existing socialism" that a just, fair, and humane society must have a fully participatory, decentralized, and cooperative character. Capitalism is an inherently centralistic order of human relationships. It is based on the asymmetric distribution of power and resources; it is a centralistic order where one class centrally controls the strategic economic resources and means of production. The concepts of competition and private property are not an expression of decentralization but of the immanent centralistic tendency of modern society. Competition does not mean, as Hayek claims, "decentralized planning by many separate persons" (Hayek 1949, 79) but asymmetric opportunities that favor certain interests and groups at the expense of others. The existence of economic classes is an expression of the centralistic character of modern society; monopolization as an economic phenomenon is an immanent feature of the logic of capital accumulation and market-based circulation.

For Hayek, cooperation and solidarity are an expression of a "primitive order"; complex social relationships would always be based on markets and competition. But modern society wouldn't exist without the historically increasing social character of production; the increasing division of labor has led from simple, individual production, where one producer produces one good all by himself, to complex, cooperative forms of production where one good is produced within complex social relationships that are highly spatially and temporally dispersed. The accumulation regime of post-Fordist capitalism is based on a highly cooperative character of production; the most successful corporations are frequently those engaging in participatory management, corporate networks of cooperation, decentralized methods of production, and computer-supported cooperative work. Production is increasingly based on communicative and cooperative labor and interaction. The highly cooperative character of the productive forces seems to falsify Hayek's assumption that cooperation is only part of an instinctive, primitive order. Cooperation is a mechanism for effectively making use of dispersed knowledge; no invisible hand is needed here, only synergies that result from cooperative social relationships and the enhancement of these relations by modern technologies. The fact that we are today witnessing a permanent aggravation of the global social problems is due to the fact that there is an antagonism between cooperation and competition that hinders social progress and the development of society. Cooperation is increased within an overall competitive social order; the increasingly cooperative character of the social forces collides with the individualization and tightening competitive character of social relationships. The social forces seem to put forward a new principle of decentralized, participative cooperation. Within the existing social order, the advantages of this principle don't seem to be achievable;

cooperative and competitive aspects of social existence collide and produce social problems.

A full development of cooperation and decentralization has neither been achieved by "actually existing socialism" nor by capitalism. Both have been based on the logic of accumulation and centralization. The fatal conceit of "socialism" as well as of capitalism has been the lack of participation, cooperation, and decentralization. Cooperation is the most effective means of managing dispersed knowledge because it favors large synergies between human actors that are due to different knowledge and capabilities that can be actively combined in such a way that emergent qualities result from the creative and productive combination of knowledge. Emergence requires active social relationships; anonymous market structures and competition don't put forward synergetical advantages; the indivisible hand is an unfounded misconception detached from social reality.

2.4 AN ALTERNATIVE: SELF-ORGANIZATION IN SOCIETY AS HUMAN COOPERATION

Self-organization is not only a neoliberal ideology; in everyday life it is also connected to ideas such as self-management, resistance, grassroots activity, participatory democracy, self-determination, opposition to heteronomy, alienation, and estrangement, the questioning of authorities, the abolishment of social hierarchies and classes, and so on. Such understandings are oriented on human agency, whereas the neoliberal meaning of the term *self-organization* is functionalistic and deprives humans of their capability and desires of active participation in and cooperative ownership of social systems. The task is to construct a theory of self-organization as creative and transformative human capacity.

Social self-organization in a broad sense covers the reproduction of society in very general terms that apply to all societies and all social systems, but it does not specify how exactly this self-organization of society takes places on a more concrete level. So ascending from the abstract to a more concrete level, one has to distinguish different forms of how society can reproduce itself and aspects of power, domination, and class will play an important role.

Self-organization in a broad sense can be understood as re-creation or self-reproduction of society. In a narrower, more political sense, social self-organization is based on cooperation, participation, self-determination, and grassroots democracy. Alternative theories of social self-organization have in common that they associate an ethical vision of a cooperative society with the notion of social self-organization (cf., e.g., Böcher 1996; Bühl 1991; Espejo 2000; Hofkirchner 2002; Hörz 1993; Schlemm 1999; Zeyer 1997). They are not so much interested in a functionalist interpretation of the concept that describes how society reproduces itself and how it *is*; they are interested in visions, utopias, and in how society *could be*. Social self-organization is interpreted in terms of cooperation, participation, grassroots democracy, respect, solidarity, responsibility, and tolerance. These theories argue that:

1. Democracy is an expression of self-organization, dictatorship an expression of heteronomy.
2. Humans are not just auxiliary persons of objective laws but can and should positively intervene into society; hence, they are designers of their future.
3. Self-organization of social system is oriented on making possible the effective and humanistic satisfaction of human needs.
4. The conditions of living should take on forms where all can recognize themselves, determine themselves, and realize themselves.
5. Self-organization puts forward the notions of responsibility and solidarity.
6. Self-organization in terms of self-determination means the possibility for a person, group, or society to give them their own laws and sense.
7. There should be active hope for a better society. It wouldn't be decisive if certain actions are successful, but it would be decisive that they can be successful.
8. Social self-organization is the principle of bottom-up social organization that stimulates the capacity to act.

Cooperation in a general sense is a cohesive force; the interactions of agents produce synergies that result in new, higher, emergent properties of a system. Self-organization is a process where a system reproduces itself with the help of its own logic and by the synergetic activities of its components, that is, the system produces itself based on an internal logic. Self-organizing systems are their own reason and cause; they produce themselves (*causa sui*). Hence, self-organization is not based on the assumption of an external creator of the universe but on the immanence of the universe; it is a scientific worldview that has atheistic consequences.

Cooperation is a topic that has been widely ignored in traditional sociology. Marx defined it as numerous laborers working together side by side, whether in one and the same process or in different but connected processes (Marx 1867, 344). He was right that cooperation means working together, but this is not only an economic but rather a universal social phenomenon that is not confined to a single branch of society. In society, cooperation acquires additional emergent qualities. It is more than the coaction of agents in natural systems; it is based on the active, knowledgeable, transformational societal capacities of human beings:

1. In cooperation the involved actors are mutually dependent.
2. All participating actors benefit from cooperation.

3. Cooperation is based on a shared symbolic system.
4. Cooperating actors have to a certain extent shared goals or at least a shared view of certain parts of reality.
5. By cooperating, actors can reach their goals more quickly and more efficiently than on an individual basis.
6. Cooperation is based on communication about goals and conventions in order to reach a common understanding.
7. In cooperation, the actors make concerted use of existing structures in order to produce new structures. Cooperation is based on sharing the existing and the newly produced structures.
8. Cooperation involves mutual learning and the common production of new reality.
9. Cooperation doesn't mean the absence of conflict; conflict on a nonescalating level can be productive. Controversy can be constructive and conflict creative.
10. In cooperative social relationships there is a high degree of networked, interconnected activity. The actors depend on each other. Mutual interconnectivity and mutual responsibility emerge.

Cooperation is a specific type of communication where actors achieve a shared understanding of social phenomena, make concerted use of resources so that new systemic qualities emerge, engage in mutual learning, all actors benefit, and feel at home and comfortable in the social system that they jointly construct. Cooperation is the highest principle of morality; it is the foundation of an intersubjective and objective dimension of ethics, a cooperative ethics. All human beings strive for happiness, social security, self-determination, self-realization, inclusion in social systems so that they can participate in decision processes, codesigning their social systems. Competition means that certain individuals and groups benefit at the expense of others, that is, there is an unequal access to structures of social systems. This is the dominant organizational structure of modern society; modern society hence is an excluding society. Cooperation includes people in social systems; it lets them participate in decisions and establishes a more just distribution of and access to resources. Hence, cooperation is a way of achieving and realizing basic human needs, competition a way of achieving and realizing basic human needs only for certain groups and excluding others. We argue that cooperation forms the Essence of human society and that competition estranges humans from their Essence. One can imagine a society that functions without competition; a society without competition is still a society. One can't imagine a society that functions without a certain degree of cooperation and social activity. A society without cooperation isn't a society; it is a state of permanent warfare, egoism, and mutual destruction that sooner or later destroys all human existence. If cooperation is the Essence of society, then a truly human society is a cooperative society. Cooperation as the principle of morality is grounded in society and social activity itself; it can be rationally explained within society without the need to refer to a highest transcendental absolute principle such as God that can't be justified within society. Cooperative ethics is a critique of lines of thought and arguments that want to advance exclusion and heteronomy in society; it is inherently critical; it subjects commonly accepted ideas, conventions, traditions, prejudices, and myths to critical questioning. It questions mainstream opinions and voices alternatives to them in order to avoid one-dimensional thinking and strengthen complex, dialectical, multidimensional thinking. The method of critique goes back to Socrates; in the twentieth century it has been advanced by approaches such as critical theory and discourse ethics.

All social systems are self-organizing in the broad sense of the permanent dynamic self-reproduction of structures and actions. But not all societies and social systems are cooperative. Indeed, modern society is largely structured by competition. Hence, cooperative self-organization is one form of systemic self-organization; it is a transformative human practice that aims at creating a higher form of society that corresponds to society's Essence, that is, a cooperative society.

2.5 CONCLUSION

In a self-organizing system, new order emerges from the old system. This new order can't be reduced to single elements; it is due to the interactions of the system's elements. Hence, a system is more than the sum of its parts. Concepts from self-organization theory such as control parameters, critical values, bifurcation points, phase transitions, nonlinearity, selection, fluctuation, and intensification in self-organization theory correspond to the dialectical principle of transition from quantity to quality. What is called emergence of order, production of information, or symmetry breaking in self-organization theory corresponds to Hegel's notions of sublation (*aufhebung*) and negation of the negation. In order to critically confront neoliberal understandings of self-organization that want to deprive humans of their agency in order to legitimate the domination of capitalist structures that colonize society, self-organization is understood as cooperative grassroots agency and human capacity that has the potential to fundamentally transform permanently self-reproducing dynamic social systems. If cooperation and self-organization are the Essence of society, then contemporary capitalist society is estranged from its Essence, but there is a potential (that is not automatically realized) that society could become fully itself by grassroots processes of social self-organization and cooperation. This would be the emergence of a cooperative society.

In order to develop a theoretical framework for understanding Internet and society, we need to conceptualize society as a self-organizing system, which shall be accomplished in the next chapter.

3   Society and Dynamic Social Theory

In this chapter, foundations of a dynamic theory of society will be worked out. This theory shall function as the background for the analysis of the relationship of Internet and society. First, Niklas Luhmann's concept of social systems and self-reference are discussed (3.1), then the relation of humans and society is considered (3.2), the notion of social self-organization is introduced (3.4), society is described as a dynamic system (3.5), the dynamics of modern society are analyzed (3.6), and some conclusions are drawn (3.7). The arguments advance from the more general level of analysis to the more concrete one.

3.1 ANTI-LUHMANN: NIKLAS LUHMANN'S REVOLUTION IN SOCIAL SCIENCE?

The idea of social self-organization is frequently associated with the works of Niklas Luhmann on social systems. He failed to adequately incorporate the conceptual apparatus supplied by the philosophical implications of self-organization theory that could help to overcome dual oppositions and dualistic conceptions in the social sciences. Luhmann (1995) conceives society in functional terms, applies Maturana's and Varela's autopoiesis concept sociologically, and sees society as a self-referential system with communications as its elements. He says that a system can only differentiate itself if it refers to itself and its elements. It generates a description of itself and a difference between system and environment. Self-observation means that a system/environment difference is introduced into the system. All social systems can observe themselves.

Luhmann argues that individuals are (re)produced biologically, not permanently by social systems. If one wants to consider a social system as autopoietic or self-referential, the permanent (re)production of the elements by the system is a necessary condition. Hence, Luhmann says that not individuals but communications are the elements of a social system. A communication results in a further communication; by the permanent (re)production of communications a social systems can maintain and reproduce itself.

"Social systems use communications as their particular mode of autopoietic reproduction. Their elements are communication which are recursively produced and reproduced by a network of communications and which cannot exist outside such a network" (Luhmann 1988, 174). For Luhmann, human beings are sensors in the environment of the system. He says that the "old European humanistic tradition" conceives humans within and not on the outside of social systems. Systems theory would have no use for the subject and the human being could not be the measure/standard of society. Luhmann stresses (communicative) processes instead of human beings. The "revolution" in social science that he wanted to bring about is one that conceptually excludes human actors from society.

Luhmann resolves the sociological problem of how social structures and human actors are related dualistically, which results in inconsistencies and theoretical lacks. He can't explain how one communication can exactly produce other communications without individuals being part of the system: "There is no significant attempt to show how societal communication . . . emerges from the interactions of the human beings who ultimately underpin it. Without human activity there would be no communication. . . . It is one thing to say analytically that communications generate communications, but operationally they require people to undertake specific actions and make specific choices. . . . One communication may stimulate another, but surely it does not *produce* or *generate* it" (Mingers 1995, 149sq.). An autopoietic conception of society must show consistently that and how society produces its elements itself. Beyerle (1994, 137sq.) criticizes that Luhmann does not show how communications are produced. Luhmann only mentions that communications *result* in further communications. He can explain that society is self-referential in the sense that one communication is linked to other ones, but he can't explain that it is self-producing or autopoietic.

Luhmann does not conceive society as a dialectic process of social structures and human actors as suggested by the philosophical implications of the new sciences of complexity (cf. chap. 2.2). He states that he is opposed to traditional Western science, but as typically for the dominating line of Western worldviews (see Jantsch 1975) he solves the tension between opposites one-sidedly, not in terms of a unity or synthesis of the opposites.

In Luhmann's theory, not humans but only social systems act; he describes systems in human terms and neglects human agency. The characterization and critique that Giddens (1984) gives of functionalism also holds for Luhmann's social systems theory: Functionalism tries to study social systems synchronically in a sort of timeless snapshot, but in reality a social system exists in and through its reproduction in time. Functionalism is unable to see human beings as reasoning, knowledgeable agents with practical consciousness and argues that society and institutions have needs and fulfill certain functions. This sometimes results in views of a subjectless history that is driven by forces outside the actors' existence that they are wholly unaware of. The reproduction of society is seen as something happening with mechanical inevitability through processes of which social actors are ignorant. Functionalism and structuralism both tend to express a naturalistic and objectivistic standpoint and emphasize the preeminence of the social whole over its individual, human parts.

For Luhmann, modern society is functionally differentiated: Its subsystems are operationally closed networks of communication; each has its own binary code that organizes the communications of the specific subsystem. For example, law: legal/illegal; economy: paid/unpaid; science: true/false; politics: holding/not holding office—government/opposition; education: good/bad marks; morals: good/bad; religion: immanence/transcendence; mass media: informed/uninformed; art: beautiful/ugly; health: healthy/sick, and so on. In this conception, subsystems form part of each other's environment; they can influence each other in certain ways, but each subsystem is autonomous. The social subsystems are structurally coupled, that is, one subsystem can influence or perturb but never determine the other. Society is centerless for Luhmann and consists of a multiplicity of autonomous subsystems. For Luhmann, each subsystem of modern society has to deal with one specific problem and has one specific function. Modern organizations are networked organizations; in a network society it is unlikely that the activity of systems is functionally separated because networks transcend systemic boundaries. Luhmann's theory can't grasp the importance of networks in contemporary society. In each social system there is more than one binary code, for example, a hospital doesn't only deal with health issues but also with technological, social, political, economical, juridical questions, and so on (Martens 1997, 304). One could at most speak of the dominance of one binary code in a specific subsystem.

As argued in chapter 2.3, conceiving society as functionally differentiated legitimates neoliberalism because it argues that systems or humans can't and shouldn't intervene into the economy because the latter is functionally differentiated. The function of Luhmann's social systems theory hence is the production and communication of ideology in society. The consequence of Luhmann's exclusion of humans and their interests from his theory is a blindness for social problems that created an affirmative uncritical theory that describes society as it is, not also as it could be. So Luhmann (1996a), for example, claims that the mass media can't manipulate humans because they, just like every system, would construct a legitimate reality. The function of the mass media for him is that they provide topics for communication and hence advance the autopoiesis of society. There is no analysis of simplification, scandalization, and emotionalization as media tactics, one-dimensional reporting, staged media events, the role of the Internet in the mass media, media monopolies, and so on. For Luhmann, there are only positive, no problematic aspects of the mass media—and of contemporary society at a whole.

The dramatic implications of Luhmann's theory become most apparent in his discussion of protest movements. He argues that social movements are alternatives without alternatives (Luhmann 1996b, 75sqq.), that they protest against the functional differentiation of society (76), operate within society against society (103, 204), have no alternatives to offer (104), fetishize opposition and alternative thinking (159), are made up by a notoriously mentally instable public (204), stage provocation as end in itself (206), possess no analytical depth and don't know why something is as it is (207), stage protest as pseudoevents (212), are a form of refractory communication against communication (214), constitute a disturbing aspect of modern society (Luhmann 1984, 545), and act as negators that weaken the affirmation of society (ibid., 549sq.). For Luhmann, protest movements are reactive, aimlessly, and dangerous. Each protest movement has values and certain political goals; hence, it wants to change society. Social movements are not reactive but active and proactive. Luhmann's characterization aims at discrediting protest; if the latter is not seen as a positive function of society, alternatives are considered as undesirable. A society that forestalls critique is a totalitarian society; a theory that considers critique and opposition as undesirable is an affirmative and totalitarian theory. The role of sociology in society is critique and reflection of society; a pure description of society as it is as the best form of society is uncritical and affirmative. For Luhmann, the function of protest movements is that they convert the negation of society in society into operations (ibid., 214). According to Hegel, a contradiction is not purely negative but a determinate negation, that is, a contradiction results in the negation of the negation; it is sublated and produces positive results. Protest movements are a negation of existing structures and values, but they strive for changing society, that is, for a negation of the negation and for sublation. They are movements because they move society and want to guarantee dynamic change.

Luhmann (2004) argues that a system forms its border by the system/ environment difference, that society is the all-enclosing social system of communications and that nature forms the environment of society. His approach is based on an ontology that considers systems as self-centered, endogenous, and closed; there are no causal relationships between systems, only irritations and disturbances. "The relationship of system and environment is constituted by the system's closing off its self-reproduction against the environment by internal circular structures and by being only exceptionally—only on other levels of reality—irritated, built up, and put into oscillation. We term this case resonance" (Luhmann 2004, 40; author's translation). For Luhmann, systems are not open, interconnected, in complex causal relationships, and in processes of exchange. Contact between a system and its environment is only considered as an exception from the rule and as a very weak disturbance for the normal systemic functioning. Based on such a dualistic concept of system and environment, Luhmann can neither explain how ecological problems are caused nor how they could be solved; he is only interested in how society communicates about ecological problems (ecological communication) and argues that ecological problems are only problems because society communicates them as problems (Luhmann 2004, 63), which suggests a radical constructivist perspective that doubts the existence of real problems. In such an approach, ecological problems are not real but only constructed.

Christoph Görg (2001) says that Luhmann has stressed in later works that nature and society are structurally coupled and that hence Luhmann has accepted causalities between the two systems. Structural coupling does not imply a stronger form of causality than Luhmann's concept of resonance because this notion that stems from Maturana and Varela means that the environment can't determine structural transformations of a system, but can only cause perturbations. This concept operates like Luhmann's theory in terms of closed, autonomous, differentiated systems.

Luhmann's main argument is that modern society is functionally differentiated, that is, it is organized in the form of autonomous subsystems where each fulfills a specific function that is based on a specific dual code and a specific program. Such systems are operationally closed. He tries to show that none of these subsystems (he mentions economy, legal system, science, polity, religion, education, and ethics) is responsible, appropriate, or competent for dealing with ecological problems or solving them because all of them would be concentrated on their own system-specific problems and operations that would leave no place for external problems. In case of the economy, Luhmann argues that this system is only interested in prices and hence deals only with ecological problems if they can be expressed in the language of prices. Luhmann simply ignores that the economy is the system where the metabolism between society and nature is organized and that the industrial form of economic production has resulted in global ecological problems. There simply seem to be no solutions for ecological problems for Luhmann, and he seems to be willing to accept such problems as irrevocable reality. Luhmann tells us that ecological problems are simply too complex to be solved by society and that problem solution by specific subsystems would be determined to fail because these systems would be functionally differentiated and would by attempting solutions try to act as centers of society, which would generate new problems. Luhmann's systemic fatalism is ignorant and ideologically distorted. The Green movement and the New Social Movements earn only scorn and derision in Luhmann's account of ecological problems; he argues that they protest against functional differentiation, are self-righteous, lack theory, have no real solutions, name only enemies, stir up and communicate fears. In the end, Luhmann argues that he doesn't want to explain how ecological communication could contribute to a solution of ecological problems and that there can be no privileged location in society that can formulate norms, rules, or guidelines for the solution of these problems (Luhmann 2004, 249). Luhmann's dualistic systemic approach can't explain how society and nature are related, how in modern society this relationship generates problems, and it doesn't contribute any insight to possible solutions. The function of Luhmann's theory for society is that it is completely useless. Luhmann's insight is that nothing can be done because society functions as it functions; he is blind to the insight that social and ecological problems are due to the antagonistic dysfunctions of modern society and that more far-reaching social changes are needed.

The Habermas/Luhmann debate has shown that there is a difference between critical thinking and functional thinking (Habermas and Luhmann 1971). Habermas's main criticism of Luhmann is that the latter considers society as instrumental and describes it as it is and not as it could be. Luhmann is only interested in describing society, whereas Habermas argues that ignoring social problems and aspects of how to improve society and how to advance human interests and human emancipation means to reduce sociology to the logic of instrumental and functional reason. Habermas says that Luhmann ignores the intersubjective and democratic dimensions of social relationships, that is, that consensus and participation can be achieved by communicative action in ideal speech situations that satisfy the four validity claims of truth, truthfulness, rightness, and comprehensibility. Habermas considers Luhmann's theory as technocratic and functional, that is, oriented on a logic that only wants to improve the functioning of the system and is blind for human interests. Luhmann argues that modern society is too complex for allowing discursive decision taking. For Luhmann, human beings are outside observers of social systems, not active participants. It is no wonder that based on such a dualist concept of society he is blind to social problems and human interests. For Habermas, the lifeworld consists of the private sphere and the public sphere; these two parts would in modern society be colonized by money and power, which results in cultural homogenization, a lack of public discourse, and a centralization of decision power (Habermas 1981, Vol. 2, 449–488). In the administered society (Adorno 1970) there would be a lack of self-determination and freedom of action (Habermas 1981, Vol. 1, 470). I would term the two colonizing processes commodification (Habermas prefers to speak of monetarization; cf. Habermas 1981, Vol. 2, 566) and bureaucratization. Habermas's colonization hypothesis builds on critical theory's insight that instrumental reason and the cultural industry produce a one-dimensional society, false needs, and false consciousness, and on Max Weber's critique of the centralization of power. Habermas's approach is close to critical thinking, Luhmann's close to instrumental thinking. Because I intend to construct a critical theory of Internet and society, Habermas is a more valuable influence than Luhmann.

3.2 HUMANS AND SOCIETY

Sociological theories can be categorized by the way they relate structures and actors. Individualistic and subjectivistic theories consider the human being as an atom of society and society as the pure agglomeration of individual existences. Structuralistic and functionalistic theories stress the influence and constraints of social structures on the individual and actions. Dualistic sociological theories conceive the relationship of actors and structures as independent, arguing that actors are psychological systems that don't belong to social systems. Finally, dialectical approaches try to avoid one-sided solutions of this foundational problem of sociology and conceive the relationship of actors and structures as a mutual one. Functionalistic and structuralistic positions are unable to see human beings as reasoning, knowledgeable agents with practical consciousness and argue that society and institutions as subjects have needs and fulfill certain functions. This sometimes results in views of a subjectless history that is driven by forces outside the actors' existence that they are wholly unaware of. The reproduction of society is seen as something happening with mechanical inevitability through processes of which social actors are ignorant. Functionalism and structuralism both express a naturalistic and objectivistic standpoint and emphasize the preeminence of the social whole over its individual, human parts. Mechanistic forms of stucturalism reduce history to a process without a subject and historical agents to the role of supports of the structure and unconscious bearers of objective structures.

In individualistic social theories, structural concepts and constraints are rather unimportant, and quite frequently sociality is reduced to individuality. There is a belief in fully autonomous consciousness without inertia. For example, methodological individualists such as von Mises, Schumpeter, and Hayek claim that social categories can be reduced to descriptions of the individual.

In Hegelian terms, individualism reduces society to individual Being-in-Itself or Abstract, Pure-Being, whereas structuralism and functionalism consider the role of the human being in society merely as Being-for-Another and Determinate-Being. Only dialectical approaches to society consider the importance of both aspects, unity as Being-in-and-for-Itself. Already Hegel criticized atomistic philosophies (Hegel 1874, §§97, 98) by saying that they fix the One as One, the Absolute is formulated as Being-for-Self, as One, and many Ones. It doesn't see that the One and the Many are dialectically connected: The One is Being-for-Itself and related to itself, but this relationship only exists in relationship to others (Being-for-Another) and hence it is one of the Many and repulses itself. But each of the Many is One, or even one of the Many; they are consequently one and the same. As those to which the One is related in its act of repulsion are ones, it is in them thrown into relation with itself and hence repulsion also means attraction.

Also, Marx criticized the reductionism of individualism in his critique of Max Stirner (Marx and Engels 1846, 101–438) and put against this the notion of the individual that is estranged in capitalism and that can only become a well-rounded individual in communism. Stirner says that the individual can only be free if he or she gets rid of dominating forces such as religion, state, and even society and humankind. He argued in favor of a "union of egoists" and stressed the superiority of the individual and the uniqueness of the ego. Social forces would be despotic; they would limit and subordinate the ego of the individual.

Marx interposes that (1) Individualism doesn't see the necessarily social and material interdependence of individuals and doesn't grasp their process of development because it limits itself to advise them that they should proceed from themselves. "Individuals have always and in all circumstances 'proceeded *from themselves*', but since they were not *unique* in the sense of not needing any connections with one another, and since their *needs*, consequently their nature, and the method of satisfying their needs, connected them with one another (relations between the sexes, exchange, division of labour), they *had to* enter into relations with one another" (Marx and Engels 1846, 423); (2) Individualism wouldn't adequately reflect the real conflicts in the world, and due to an idealistic inversion of the world it would replace political praxis by moralism. Stirner wants to do away with the "private individual" for the sake of the "general", selfless man, but consciousness is separated from the individual and its existence in the real, material world. Marx: "It depends not on *consciousness*, but on *being*; not on thought, but on life; it depends on the individual's empirical development and manifestation of life, which in turn depends on the conditions obtaining in the world. If the circumstances in which the individual lives allow him only the [one]-sided development of one quality at the expense of all the rest, [If] they give him the material and time to develop only that one quality, then this individual achieves only a one-sided, crippled development. No moral preaching avails here" (Marx and Engels 1846, 245sq.). Individualism has had its rise with the emergence of modern, that is, capitalist, society and is related to ideas that have been developed during the course of the Enlightenment such as a free will as well as rationally and responsible acting subjects. The Enlightenment formed an integral element of the process of establishing modern society. The concept of the modern individual is also one that has been made possible by questioning religious eschatologies of an unalterable and God-given fate of humankind. The rise of this modern notion of the individual has also been interrelated with the rise of the idea of "free" entrepreneurship in market society. Freedom has been conceived in this sense as an important quality and Essence of the modern individual. The idea of the modern individual can be seen as a logical consequence of the liberal-capitalist economy. According to this concept, morally responsible and autonomous personalities can develop on the basis of economical and political freedom that is guaranteed by modern society. It also stresses that society guarantees individuality by removing obstacles to individual freedom and to rational and reasonable actions. In the ideology of individualism, individuality is clearly identified with economic self-interest. Egoism and selfishness are often fetishized by assuming that they are natural characteristics of all individuals and that they emerge from rational and autonomous thinking. But it can also be argued that modern society is not reasonable because it does not guarantee happiness and satisfaction of all human beings. In fact, these categories are only achievable for a small privileged elite.

Nowadays individuals are not only seen as owners of a free will; it is also generally assumed that this free will can be applied in order to gain ownership of material resources and capital, which makes it possible to realize individual freedom. So freedom is seen as something that can be gained individually by striving towards individual control of material resources. This shows that the concept of the modern individual is connected with the idea of private property. The idea of the individual as an owner has dominated the philosophical tradition from Hobbes to Hegel and still dominates philosophical ideas about the Essence of mankind. But this concept has never been applied to all humans that are part of society because the majority of the world population still does not possess all these idealistically constructed aspects of freedom and autonomy; this majority is rather confronted with alienation and the disciplinary mechanisms of compulsions, coercion, and domination. Hence, the modern idea of the individual can be seen as an ideology that helps to legitimate modern society. The idea of already existing autonomous individuals may be a nice ideal but might be nothing more than imagination and self-deception.

An individual is a self-conscious and social being. He or she has the ability to consciously create new qualities, to reflect about its actions, and to select one action from several possible ones. He or she can consciously repeat past actions and actively plan future situations. Humans can reflect their own and other actions; they can draw conclusions from and apply them to future actions. Human beings are social beings; they enter social relationships, which are mutually dependent actions that make sense for the acting subjects. Individual being is only possible as social being; social being is only possible as a relationship of individual existences. Marx has pointed out the dialectic of individual and social being: "The individual *is the social being*. His manifestations of life—even if they may not appear in the direct form of communal manifestations of life carried out in association with others—are therefore an expression and confirmation of *social life*. Man's individual and species-life are not *different*, however much—and this is inevitable—the mode of existence of the individual is a more *particular* or more general mode of the life of the species, or the life of the species is a more *particular* or more general individual life" (Marx 1844b, 538sq.). Man is the subjective existence of society and he exists as a totality of human manifestation of life.

Marx says that social analysis has to begin with "individuals producing in a society" (Marx 1857, 615). These individuals are "dependent and . . . belong to a larger whole" (616). He considers man as a *zoon politikon* (political animal) that is not only a social animal but also an animal that can be individualized only within society. Man would be a social being; the concept of a "solitary individual outside society" would be preposterous.

For Marx, the individual is of great importance in his social analysis, not as an isolated atom but as a social being that is the constitutive part of qualitative moments of society and has a concrete and historical existence. "The first premise of all human history is, of course, the existence of living human individuals" (Marx and Engels 1846, 20). He considers the individual in its abstract being-for-self, its connectedness to others, and its estrangement in modern, capitalist society. The individual as a social, producing being ("individuals cooperating in definite kinds of labor") results in phenomena such as modes of life, increase of population (family), forms of intercourse (*verkehrsformen*), separation of town and country, forms of politics (nation-state), division of labor, forms of ownership (tribal ownership, ancient communal and state ownership, feudal or estate property [feudal landed property, corporative movable property, capital invested in manufacture, capital as pure private property]), production of ideas, notions, and consciousness. For Marx, a certain mode of production is combined with a certain mode of cooperation (Marx and Engels 1846, 30), and the history of humanity is closely connected to the history of the economy. Opposing the atomism of Max Stirner and Bruno Bauer, Marx writes that the "individuals certainly make one another, physically and mentally, but do not make themselves" (ibid., 37).

In the *German Ideology*, Marx speaks of social relationships as forms of intercourse. He later replaced this term by the one of relationships of production. He says that with the development of the productive forces, the form of intercourse becomes a fetter, and in place of it a new one is put which corresponds to the more developed productive forces and hence "to the advanced mode of the self-activity of individuals"—a form which in its turn becomes a fetter and is then replaced by another one, and so on. The history of the forms of intercourse would be the history of the productive forces and hence the history of the development of the forces of the individuals themselves (ibid., 72).

The behavior of animals is largely based on instinct, although learning exists to a certain limited extent. The range and complexity of learned behavior in human beings is by far greater than in any animal. In contrast to all animals, the behavior of humans is not genetically programmed and led by instincts. Humans rely much more on learned and socialized patterns of behavior. The plurality of human culture shows that the human genetic code does not contain specific instructions to behave in certain ways. You won't find this plurality concerning, for example, nests built by birds, dwellings built by apes, and so on.

Sociality does not only simply mean that some beings act together in order to achieve something. Already Max Weber (1978) pointed out in his fundamental definitions of sociological categories that in a social system we always find the production of meaning. He argued that all human action is directed by meanings. Actions have a specific meaning for the actors, which they use for making sense of the world. Social actors have motives; they can identify reasons for their actions and have planned intentions in concrete situations. They can choose between different alternative actions in a situation; they can consciously reflect the state of the world (and its change) and can identify their role and position in the world. Human beings can interpret social situations in different ways; by this, meaning (the definition of situations by actors) is produced. So making sense of the world involves intended actions, reflection, the identification of reasons for actions, intentions, freedom to choose between different alternative actions, identification of one's own role in the world, and (different) interpretations of the world. All sociality involves the production of sense, and this has to do with self-consciousness. Animals do not have self-consciousness, and they cannot make sense of the world. Hence, one would not describe birds building a nest, working bees, or chimpanzees playing together with the terms *societal* or *sociality*. Both concepts are solely related to the human realm.

Human beings begin to distinguish themselves from animals by starting to produce their means of subsistence by which they are indirectly producing their actual material life (Marx and Engels 1846, 21). Marx pointed out that man, like animals, lives from inorganic nature; he must remain in a continuing physical dialogue with nature in order to survive. Animals produce only their own immediate needs. "Animals produce one-sidedly, whereas man produces *universally*; they produce only when immediate physical need compels them to do so, while man produces even when he is free from physical need and truly produces only in freedom from such need; they produce only themselves, while man reproduces the whole of nature; their products belong immediately to their physical bodies, while man freely confronts his own product. . . . man also produces in accordance with the laws of beauty" (Marx 1844b, 517).

In the production of his life that includes the metabolism between society and nature and social reciprocity, man as the universal, objective species being produces an objective world, that is, a world of produced artifacts, and reproduces nature and his species according to his purposes. With the human being, history emerges: "The more that human beings become removed from animals in the narrower sense of the word, the more they make their own history consciously, the less becomes the influence of unforeseen effects and uncontrolled forces of this history, and the more accurately does the historical result correspond to the aim laid down in advance" (Engels 1886a, 323). "The animal merely *uses* external nature, and brings about changes in it simply by his presence; man by his changes makes it serve his ends, *masters* it. This is the final, essential distinction between man and other animals, and once again it is labor that brings about this distinction" (Engels 1886a, 452). Klaus Holzkamp (1985) speaks in this context of a reversal of ends and means; humans produce and preserve means independent from immediate ends.

As Friedrich Engels (1886a) has shown, the breakup of immediacy of behavior (which is a foundation of the emergence of society) started with the erect posture in walking that resulted in the specialization of the hand, which implies tools. Tools imply production as human activities that transform nature. A differentiation of certain bodily forms can result in other organic differentiations. The specialization of the hand resulted in labor and the utilization of nature. The emergence of labor and production resulted in a coevolution of society and consciousness. The genesis of man is due to a dialectic of labor and human capabilities (hand, language, increase of brain volume, consciousness, etc.), which resulted in developments such as hunting, stock farming, agriculture, metal processing, navigation, pottery, art, science, legislation, politics, and so on. Idealistic conceptions of the development of man, as, for example, the traditional philosophy of consciousness, argue that consciousness existed prior to human beings as beings in society. Symbolic interactionism (e.g., George Herbert Mead), on the other hand, has pointed out that the development of consciousness can only be explained by assuming social interactions and social actions mediated by the usage of symbols. Both explanations are reductionistic; they assume either consciousness or society as determining the historical process. The emergence of the individual as a social being can only be explained adequately by a dialectical coevolution of society (especially categories such as labor and production) and human abilities.

By interacting and entering social relationships, individuals frequently exchange and generate symbols. The generation of symbols that are basic representations of parts of the world is a social process and takes place within the framework of social relationships. Symbols gain meaning by cultural signification and influence individual lifestyles, ways of life, and thinking.

As pointed out by Marx (1844b, 516), man is also a species-being—not only in the sense that he reproduces the species biologically but also in the sense that he lives from inorganic nature and natural products: "Nature is man's inorganic body—that is to say, nature insofar as it is not the human body. Man lives from nature—i.e., nature is his body—and he must maintain a continuing dialogue with it if he is not to die". Unlike the animal, man has conscious life activity. The animal produces only its own immediate needs, whereas man (re)produces himself and the whole of nature universally, and this results in the practical human creation of an objective world. Modern society has estranged man from himself and nature; this results in the exploitative appropriation of both; life has become alienated life. Marx already described man as a self-reproducing being: This does not only mean the internal autopoietic self-reproduction of the organism, as suggested by Humberto Maturana and other theoreticians of autopoiesis; it also means an external, social as well as natural type of self-reproduction: Man reproduces himself by social activities and by exchanging matter and energy with his natural environment (= labor). Material production, social activities, and a relationship between man and nature are necessary for the self-reproduction of man and the reproduction of the whole of society and nature by human activities. The aspect of the conscious reproduction of the man-nature relationship is grasped by the concept of the species being.

Human beings exchange matter and energy with their natural environment. Labor is a social process that results in the production of use values and social resources that are useful for humans, satisfy human needs, and are produced in order to simplify existence and achieve defined goals. Labor is only possible as an active shaping of nature and the world; man appropriates nature in order to produce use values. In this sense man is an active natural being. The relationship between man and nature is mediated by technologies. Humans produce technologies in order to better organize the labor process. Technology can be defined as a purposeful unity of means, methods, abilities, processes, and knowledge that are necessary in order to achieve defined goals. Humans have the ability to consciously think about their environment, to set themselves self-defined goals, and to find different ways to achieve these goals. Technologies mediate attainment of human goals and the social labor process.

Humans make use of objects in the world, and they actively create new objects in the labor process. Hence, man is objective man. In this process, his living labor power is being objectified in use values that are a type of dead labor that stores information about the world and society. This objectivity of human existence also finds an expression in the fact that all human organs and senses are in their *orientation to the object*, the appropriation of the object, the appropriation of human reality (Marx 1844b, 539). So the objective world becomes the world of man's essential powers for man in society and "all *objects become* for him the *objectification* of himself, become objects which confirm and realise his individuality, become his objects: that is, man *himself* becomes the object" (Marx 1844b, 541). Man is a *corporeal*, living, real, sensuous, objective being that has real, sensuous objects as the object of his being, and he can only express his life in real, sensuous objects.

Man exists within and by the use of language (Krippendorff 2006) and the social production of symbols. Interacting by language is also one of the necessary conditions for man as a cultural being. Culture involves the whole ways of life, man's ways of thinking and acting, and the emergence of social norms and values. Socially accepted and established norms are guidelines that direct conduct in particular situations. Norms define acceptable and appropriate behavior in particular social situations. Domination refers to the disposition over the means of coercion required to influence others or processes and decisions. Domination always includes sanctions, repression, threats of violence, and an asymmetric distribution of power. Power can be regarded as the disposition over the means required to influence processes and decisions in one's own interest. In societies that are imprinted by domination, norms are usually enforced by positive and negative sanctions that may be formalized or not. Values are more general guidelines than norms. Socially established and accepted values are beliefs that something is good and desirable. They define what is considered as important and worth striving for. Human beings have the ability to create norms, values, habits, traditions, and different ways of life, and their behavior is influenced and imprinted by existing cultural modes. As typical expression of cultural activities, man creates cultural manifestations such as art, literature, music, science, ideologies, world outlooks, and so on.

Creativity is a basic skill of the individual. Creativity means the ability to create something new that seems desirable and helps to achieve defined goals. Man can create images of the future and actively strive to make these images become social reality. Man has ideals, visions, dreams, hopes, and expectations that are based on the ability of imagination, which helps him to go beyond existing society and to create alternatives for future actions. Based on creativity, man designs society (Banathy 1996): Design is a future-creating human activity that goes beyond facticity, creates visions of a desirable future, and looks for a solution to existing problems. Design creates new knowledge and findings. Man designs machines, tools, theories, social systems, physical entities, nature, organizations, and so on, within social processes.

Human beings have the ability to create their own history depending on the constraints and influences of existing social forces and relationships. Society is the result of human activity and is not a static being; it is dynamically becoming by the influence of the relationships humans enter and the relationships of these social relationships.

Due to its self-conscious, active, and creative being, the human being can strive towards freedom and autonomy. Freedom includes the absence of dominating and controlling forces and the possibility for individuals and groups to choose and design the conditions of their own life all by themselves. This means freedom in terms of self-determination, a maximum of participation, and man's control over himself. Freedom is not only an individual but also a collective category because the individual can only be free if a maximum of self-determination for all others can be achieved and because collective or social freedom can only be reached when an optimum of individual autonomy (the possibility to choose one's own way of life and interests that do not conflict with other lifestyles and interests) is enforced. There is no individual freedom without collective freedom and no collective freedom without individual autonomy. Collective and individual freedom are not automatically given but form something that man has the ability to envision and to struggle for. In chapter 2.4, the notion of cooperation was introduced. Man is not just a social being; his sociality to certain degrees takes on the form of cooperation, depending on the character of overall societal structures.

Summing up, it can be said that the individual is a social, self-conscious, creative, producing, reflective, cultural, symbol- and language-using, active natural, laboring, objective, corporeal, living, real, sensuous, visionary, imaginative, designing, cooperative being who makes his or her own history and can strive towards freedom and autonomy.

3.3 THE SELF-ORGANIZATION OF SOCIAL SYSTEMS

If the concept of self-organization is closely connected to dialectical thinking and to the conception of systems as dynamic entities in which new structures emerge from interacting agents, then applying self-organization to society implies that one should conceive social systems as a dialectic of social structures and social actions. What is needed hence is a dialectical solution of the foundational problem of sociology of how structures and practices are related. Traditionally it has been solved in a reductionistic manner: Action theory and symbolic interactionism (Max Weber, George Herbert Mead, Jürgen Habermas, etc.) have argued that society and social systems are constituted by social actions, whereas structuralism and functionalism (Emile Durkheim, Robert Merton, Talcott Parsons, Niklas Luhmann, etc.) have seen the basic social process as the structuring of social existence by existing social structures and systems that fulfill certain functions. Action theory underestimates the structural constraining of social actions whereas functionalist theories often do not leave enough space for a certain degree of freedom of actions and thinking. "If interpretative sociologies are founded, as it were, upon an imperialism of the subject, functionalism and structuralism propose an imperialism of the social object" (Giddens 1984, 2). In contemporary sociology, the main representatives of sociologies that try to bridge the gap between action theory and structural approaches are Anthony Giddens and Pierre Bourdieu. Hence, it is feasible to connect the concept of social self-organization to Giddens's and Bourdieuian sociology.

One of the central themes in Anthony Giddens's works has been the opposition to one-sided solutions of the problem how social structures and actions are related, which, for example, can be found in functionalism, structuralism as well as methodological individualism (see Giddens 1981, 15–20, 44, 53sq., 64–68, 171, 215; Giddens 1984, 1sqq., 6, 26, 207–221). Giddens wants to avoid "the twin pitfalls of objectivism and subjectivism in explaining social reproduction" (Giddens 1981, 64). A similar motive can be found in the works of Bourdieu, who wanted to "escape from the ritual either/or choice between objectivism and subjectivism in which the social sciences have so far allowed themselves to be trapped" (Bourdieu 1977, 4). To do so, objectivist knowledge would have to be embedded into practical experiences. This could be achieved by a dialectical methodology, by a "science of the dialectical relations between the objective structures to which the objectivist mode of knowledge gives access and the structured dispositions within which those structures are actualized and which tend to reproduce them" (Bourdieu 1977, 3).

For Giddens, social structures don't exist outside of actions; they are "rules and resources, or sets of transformation relations, organised as properties of social systems" (Giddens 1984, 25). Structuration theory holds that the rules and resources drawn upon in the production and reproduction of social action are at the same time the means of system reproduction (19). Human social activities are recursive because actors continually re-create them. In and through their activities, agents reproduce the conditions that make these activities possible (2). "According to the notion of the duality of structure, the structural properties of social systems are both medium and outcome of the practices they recursively organise" (25) and they both enable and constrain actions (26).

I suggest that integrating aspects of the theory of structuration into a theory of social self-organization can help to avoid the dualistic shortcomings and the neglect of the human subject that dominates conceptions of social self-organization. Conceptual affinities between Giddens's theory and the philosophical assumptions of self-organization theory are quite obvious (cf. also Küppers 1999; Mingers 1995, 1996, 1999): Giddens is describing society in terms of mutual and circular causality, and he is critical of reductionism. He has understood that conceptions that place a totality above its moments, reduce the totality to its moments, or conceive the relationship of a totality and its moments as a dualistic one, don't help in describing complex systems adequately. The concept of the duality of structure grasps the dialectical and complex nature of society and overcomes the structure/actor dichotomy that has long dominated the social sciences and that in systems theory has especially been sustained by Niklas Luhmann.

For arguing that social self-organization means the self-reproduction of a social system, one must specify what is being reproduced. Applying the idea of self-(re)production to society means that one must explain how society produces its elements permanently. By saying that the elements are communications and not individuals, as Luhmann does, one can't explain self-reproduction consistently because not communications but human actors produce communications. One major problem of applying autopoiesis to society is that one cannot consider the individuals as components of a social system if the latter is autopoietic. "If human beings are taken as the components of social systems, then it is clear that they are not produced by such systems but by other physical, biological processes" (Mingers 1995, 124). Applying autopoiesis nonetheless to society will result in subjectless theories such as the one of Luhmann that can't adequately explain how individuals (re)produce social structures and how their sociality is (re)produced by these structures. Another alternative would be to argue that society can reproduce itself by the biological reproduction of the individuals. There have been some conceptions that have tried to describe the reproduction and autopoiesis of certain social systems such as the family in biological as well as sociological terms: "The components within the family (the family boundary) are produced through the family interactions . . . Sons are transformed into fathers, fathers into grandfathers, mothers and fathers produce sons and daughters ... To become the 'head of the family' is an internal social production ... Men and women biologically produce children" (Zeleny and Hufford, 1992). Here, biological and social processes are confused and biological mechanisms are interpreted as fundamental sociological concepts; the *differentia specifica* of society is lost in such theories (even more by the fact that Zeleny continues his argumentation by saying that all autopoietic systems are social systems). Attempts to describe the reproduction of society and social systems should be located within the social domain. Society does not produce individuals biologically because this is mainly a biological, not a social process of reproduction.

Neither the assumption that society is a self-referential communication system nor the description of society in terms of biological reproduction provides us with an adequate idea of how the self-reproduction of society takes place. Society can consistently be explained as a self-reproducing system based on human practice if one argues that man is a social being and has central importance in the reproduction process. Society reproduces man as a social being and man produces society by socially coordinating human actions. Man is creator and created result of society; society and humans produce each other mutually. Such a conception of social self-organization acknowledges the importance of human actors in social systems and is closely related to Giddens's duality of structure. Saying that man is creator and created result of society corresponds to Giddens's formulation that in and through their activities agents reproduce the conditions that make these activities possible (Giddens 1984, 2).

Marx (1858/59, 8) argued that in "the social production of their existence, men inevitably enter into definite relations, which are independent of their will". For economic relationships this is surely true. But there are also other social relationships, ones where humans often can choose whether they want to enter them or not. For example, I cannot choose if I want to enter a labor relationship because I have to earn a living, but I can choose which political party I want to belong to and which concert I will attend (given the condition that I have enough money or that there is free entry). So one can say that concerning the totality of society, individuals enter social relationships that are partly independent and partly dependent on their will. By social actions, social structures are constituted and differentiated. The structure of society or a social system is made up by the total of regularized social behavior and relations that are continuously reproduced over certain timespans. By social interaction, new qualities and structures can emerge that cannot be reduced to the individual level. This is a process of bottom-up emergence that is called agency. Emergence in this context means the appearance of at least one new systemic quality that cannot be reduced to the elements of the system. So this quality is irreducible and it is also to a certain extent unpredictable, that is, time, form, and result of the process of emergence cannot be fully forecast by taking a look at the elements and their interactions. Social structures also influence individual actions and thinking. They constrain and enable actions. This is a process of top-down emergence where new individual and group properties can emerge. The whole cycle is the basic process of systemic social self-organization that can also be called re-creation because by permanent processes of agency and constraining/ enabling, a social system can maintain and reproduce itself (see fig. 3.1; the model was first introduced in Hofkirchner 1998 and subsequently elaborated in Fuchs 2003c, 2003d). It again and again creates its own unity and maintains itself. Social structures enable and constrain social actions as well as individuality and are a result of social actions (which are a correlation of mutual individuality that results in sociality).

Re-creation denotes that individuals that are parts of a social system permanently change their environment. This enables the social system to change, maintain, adapt, and reproduce itself. What is important is that the

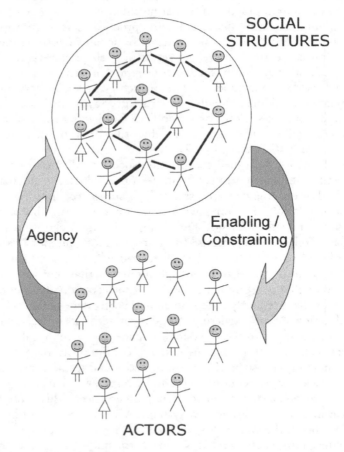

Figure 3.1 The self-organization/re-creation of social systems.

term *re-creation* also refers to the ability of humans to consciously shape and create social systems and structures, an ability that is based on self-consciousness and, in Giddens's terminology, the reflexive monitoring of action. As Erich Jantsch says, social systems are re-creative ones because they can create new reality (Jantsch 1979, 305), the sociocultural human being has the ability to create the conditions for his further evolution all by himself (343). Individuals can anticipate possible future states of the world, society as it could be or as one would like it to become; and they can act according to these anticipations. The understanding of design as a fundamental human capability takes into account man's ability to have visions and utopias and to actively shape society according to these anticipated (possible) states of the world. It is opposed to an understanding of design as a hierarchical process and as the expert-led generation of knowledge about the world and solutions to problems. As Ernst Bloch (1986) pointed out, desires, wishes, anxieties, hopes, fantasies, imaginations play an important role in society and hence one should also stress the subjective, creative dimension in the constitution of human and social experience. Bloch has shown that hopes and utopias are fundamental motives in all human actions and thinking. These are also important differences between animals and humans.

Terming the self-organization of society re-creation acknowledges the importance of the human being as a reasonable and knowledgeable actor in social theory. Giddens has stressed that the duality of structure has to do with re-creation: "Human social activities, like some self-reproducing items in nature, are recursive. That is to say, they are not brought into being by social actors but continually *recreated* by them via the very means whereby they express themselves as actors" (Giddens 1984, 2). Saying that society is a re-creative or self-organizing system corresponds to the notion of the duality of structure because the structural properties of social systems are both medium and outcome of the practices they recursively organize and both enable and constrain actions.

Giddens has frequently stated that functionalist thought argues that certain institutions, structures, or systems work or function in certain ways. These entities are often described in analogy to organisms and the descriptions often convey the impression that structural entities work as autonomous agents or even subjects. It's true that the reproduction of society only takes place within and through human social activities; hence, when I'm speaking of the *self*-organization of a social system, I don't mean that social systems or structures are autonomous actors or subjects of social change. Structures don't act; they only exist within and through social actions and the term *social self-organization* refers to the dialectical relationship of structures and actions that results in the overall reproduction of the system. The creativity and knowledgeability of actors is at the core of this process and secures the re-creation of social systems within and through self-conscious, creative activities of human actors. A social system and its structures don't exist outside of human activities; structures are medium and outcome of actions, and this recursive relationship is essential for the overall re-creation/self-reproduction of society. The term *self*-organization refers to the role of the self-conscious, creative, reflective and knowledgeable human being in the reproduction of social systems.

Durkheim's social facts have sometimes been interpreted as emergent properties of society because he says that social structures are different from individual consciousness and don't belong to the parts of society. Giddens is very critical of the notion of emergence because Durkheim's implicit usage of the term conveys the impression that structures exist outside of and external to actions (Giddens 1984, 169–174). Giddens furthermore says that Durkheim seems to argue that human actors are separated and come together ex nihilo to form a new entity. I have mentioned that emergence is an important notion in self-organization theory and that social structures and individual ideas and actions are properties of social systems that result from bottom-up- and top-down-emergence. Emergence in society refers to the fact that social reproduction takes place by the constitution of new social and individual properties that can't be reduced to prior existing properties. This doesn't mean that emergent properties exist outside of or external to social activities; in fact, emergent social properties in a structural sense are medium and outcome of social activities that can only exist due to the complex interactions of human beings and can't be reduced to single actions or actors. Social emergence is due to the productive synergies that occur in the relationships between individual human actors and the relationships between collective actors (organizations). In top-down processes, there is the emergence of new aspects of actions and consciousness that is made possible by the enabling and constraining synergetic effects of social structures. These newly emerging properties can't be reduced to single structural entities.

I have argued that Giddens's duality of structure as well as the notion of the re-creation of society suggests a *dialectical* relationship of structures and actors. One should clarify why exactly this is a dialectical relationship. In society, structures and actors are two opposing, contradictory moments: A structure is a Somewhat opposed to an Other, that is, actors; and an actor is also a Somewhat opposed to an Other, that is, structures. The Becoming of society is its permanent dialectical movement, the re-creation or self-reproduction of society. Being-for-Itself or negation of the negation in society means that something social becomes an other social, which is again a social Somewhat, and it likewise becomes an other social, and so on ad infinitum. Something social refers to aspects of a social system such as structures or actions. In the dialectical movement these two social moments in their passage become another social moment and therefore join with themselves; they are self-related. The permanent collapse and fusion of the relationship of structures and actors results in new, *emergent* properties or qualities of society that can't be reduced to the underlying moments. In the re-creation process of society, there is coming-to-be of new structural and individual properties and ceasing-to-be of certain old properties. "Becoming is an unstable unrest which settles into a stable result" (Hegel 1812, §180). Such stable results are the emergent properties of society that are constituted by the dialectical process termed duality of structure by Giddens. In respect to Hegel, the term *social self-organization* also gains meaning in the sense that by the dialectical process where structures are medium and outcome of social actions, a social somewhat is self-related or self-referential in the sense of joining with itself or producing itself. By dialectical movement, social categories opposing each other (structures and actions) produce new social categories. A social Something is opposed to a social Other and by sublation they both fuse into a unity with emergent social properties that again produces an opposition. So this unity is again a social Somewhat opposed to a social Other, and so on. By coming-to-be and ceasing-to-be of social entities, new social entities are produced in the dialectical social process.

For explaining the *Science of Logic* and dialectical movement, Herbert Marcuse refers to the relationship of structures and (individual) actors as an example of dialectics in the social realm. For Hegel, all being "must even transgress the bounds of its own particularity and put itself into universal relation with other things. The human being, to take an instance, finds his proper identity only in those relations that are in effect the negation of his isolated particularity—in his membership in a group or social class whose institutions, organization, and values determine his very individuality. The truth of the individual transcends his particularity and finds a totality of conflicting relations which his individuality fulfils itself" (Marcuse 1999, 124).

Saying that man is creator and created result of society, as well as Giddens's formulation that in and through their activities agents reproduce the conditions that make these activities possible, corresponds to Marx' formulation that "the social character is the general character of the whole movement: just as society itself produces man as man, so is society produced by him" (Marx 1844b, 537). Marx can be reread as having constructed a dialectical philosophy of practice that anticipated the idea of the dialectics of structures and agency. He argued that the individual is a particular mode of existence of society and that society is a more general individual life (ibid, 538sq.). "Man, much as he may therefore be a particular individual (and it is precisely his particularity which makes him an individual, and a real individual social being), is just as much the totality—the ideal totality—the subjective existence of imagined and experienced society for itself; just as he exists also in the real world both as awareness and real enjoyment of social existence, and as a totality of human manifestation of life" (ibid., 539).

The notion of social self-organization can also be connected to Pierre Bourdieu's theory in which a dialectic of structures and practices is achieved with the help of the concept of the *habitus*. Habitus can be understood as specific systems of dispositions (i.e., specific ways of thinking and acting) characteristic for specific social groups. The habitus is "a subjective but not individual system of internalized structures, schemes of perception, conception, and action common to all members of the same group or class constituting the precondition for all objectification and apperception" (Bourdieu 1977, 86). "The habitus is not only a structuring structure, which organizes practices and the perception of practices, but also a structured structure: the principle of division into logical classes which organizes the perception of the social world is itself the product of internalization of the division into social classes" (Bourdieu 1986a, 170).

These quotes don't mean that all members of a group or class act, think, and perceive the same way. The language Bourdieu uses is a rather sophisticated one, and this opens up numerous possible interpretations. If one takes a look at Bourdieu's work as a whole, one will see that quite commonly he didn't refer to the habitus as a structure that fully determines actions and thinking of group members. Bourdieu says that uncertainty is an aspect of all social situations (Bourdieu 1990a, 78), that actors always have strategies for avoiding the most probable outcomes (Bourdieu 1977, 9), and that the habitus means *invention* (Bourdieu 1977, 95; 1990b, 55). This inventive dimension of the habitus refers to knowledgeable, creative actors. The creative human being is not a pure object of social structures; he has relative freedom of action due to creativity and self-consciousness. In society, creativity and invention always have to do with relative chance and relative indeterminism. Social practices, interactions, and relationships are very complex. The complex group behavior of human beings is another reason why Bourdieu assumes a degree of uncertainty of human behavior (Bourdieu 1977, 9, 1990a, 8). What Bourdieu suggests is not mechanical determinism but that habitus *both* enables the creativity of actors and constrains ways of acting. Hence, he says that the habitus gives orientations and limits (Bourdieu 1977, 95); it neither results in unpredictable novelty nor in a simple mechanical reproduction of initial conditionings (Bourdieu 1977, 95). The habitus provides conditioned and conditional freedom (Bourdieu 1977, 95); that is, it is a condition for freedom, but it also conditions and limits full freedom of action. This is equal to saying that structures are medium and outcome of social actions (Giddens 1979, 1984). For Bourdieu, practices are relatively unpredictable but also limited in diversity (Bourdieu 1990b, 55). Due to the creative ability of human beings, the habitus also has to do with vagueness and indeterminancy (Bourdieu 1990a, 77). The habitus not only constrains practices; it is also a result of the creative relationships of human beings. Bourdieu wants to express this when he says the habitus is both *opus operatum* (result of practices) and *modus operandi* (mode of practices; Bourdieu 1977, 18, 72sqq.; 1990b, 52). Habitus can be seen as a matrix of patterns of cognition, perception, and action that produces in interplay with actual context conditions of the social field an actor is situated in, the praxis of this actor. It is a concept that is based on the dialectic of necessity and chance, social objects, and subjects.

On the dialectic of structures and practices, Bourdieu says that there is a "dialectical relationship between the objective structures and the cognitive and motivating structures which they produce and which tend to reproduce them, ... these objective structures are themselves products of historical practices and are constantly reproduced and transformed by historical practices whose productive principle is itself the product of the structures which it consequently tends to reproduce" (Bourdieu 1977, 83). This complex formulation means that society is being reproduced by the productive relationships of individuals (and the mapping of their cognitive and motivating structures onto emerging social structures), that is, their existence as beings who enter groups, and that the human being is at the same time a produced result of society. Actors who engage in social practices and relationships that reproduce society reproduce cognitive structures. Social structures are reproduced by the actors' production of cognitive structures of individuals that have social practices. In social systems there is a dialectic of the internalization of externality and the externalization of internality, a dialectic of incorporation and objectification (Bourdieu 1977, 72).

Bourdieu's emphasis is not only on the structuring of thinking and actions by social structures and the distribution of capital; he equally emphasizes the creative and inventive capacities of social actors. The habitus is indeed a dialectical category that mediates between objective structures and subjective, practical aspects of existence. Being defined as "systems of durable, transposable dispositions, structured structures predisposed to function as structuring structures, that is, as principles of the generation and structuring of practices and representations" (Bourdieu 1977, 72), there is an emphasis on dispositions, which mean on the one hand results of organizing actions (structures) and on the other hand also designate ways of being, habitual states (especially of bodies; Bourdieu 1977, 214, fn 1). This shows that the habitus on the one hand is a structural category and that it is on the other hand very closely related to the human being and his or her practices. The habitus can neither be simply ascribed to social structures nor to the actor; it is a category that dialectically mediates the relationship of society and actors.

The self-transformation of society, social systems, and human practices is achieved with the help of the habitus. The interaction of the two moments (structures and actors) takes place through the habitus, which both involves objectivity and subjectivity. It is important for Bourdieu that the mutual relationship of structures and actors is enabled through practices. It is this emphasis on practice and class struggles that shows that Bourdieu considers the mutual interactions of group members that result in the production of lifestyles as important constituting aspects of the dialectical process of society. In society, internalities become part of externalities and externalities part of internalities not through individual practice but through the practical relationships of an individual to the other members of his or her social group. In this context Bourdieu points out the practical character of knowledge and says that practical knowledge, based on the continuous decoding of the perceived indices of the welcome given to actions already accomplished, continuously carries out the checks and corrections intended to ensure the adjustment of practices and expressions to the reactions of expectations of the other agents (Bourdieu 1977, 10). Practical schemes would enable the agents to produce the practices necessary for social existence. With the examples of gift exchange and the question of honorability in challenges from the society of the Kabyles, Bourdieu shows that every exchange—not only the exchange of gifts but also the practical, interactive exchange present in all social situations—contains a challenge for riposte. There is a "dialectic of challenge and riposte" (Bourdieu 1977, 14) in the social world; "calls to order from the group" (ibid., 15) result in permanent social activity. It is this social activity that drives forward the dialectical process of society because it enables the dialectical relationship of structures and actors in which both moments are mutually connected by the internalization of externalities and the externalization of internalities. For Bourdieu, the individual is not an isolated atom and can only exist in relationship to others. He stresses that the individual is *practically* and in its struggles connected to others and that this connectedness is the decisive aspect of the social process.

Bourdieu's works show that the habitus mediates the two levels of social systems; it secures conditioned (constraining) and conditional (enabling creativity and invention) freedom; it enables the creative, inventive dimension of practice but also gives orientations and limits to invention. The habitus mediates the mutual relationship of social structures and actors/groups; it is the mediating structure that makes possible the constraining and enabling of (collective and individual) practices. It provides conditioned and conditional freedom (Bourdieu 1977, 95); that is, it is a condition for freedom, but it also conditions and limits full freedom of action. This is equal to saying in Giddens's terminology that structures are medium and outcome of social actions. Very much like Giddens, Bourdieu suggests a mutual relationship of structures and actions as the core feature of social systems. The habitus is a property "for which and through which there is a social world" (Bourdieu 1990b, 140). This formulation is similar to saying that habitus is medium and outcome of the social world.

3.4 DIALECTICS AND EVOLUTION

In this work there is a stress on dialectical thinking and the Marxian form of dialectic. But hasn't history proven that Marxism and dialectics got it all wrong? Aren't both mechanistic and deterministic conceptions of history? This is certainly true for some forms of Marxism, but as I want to show in this chapter not for the Marxian dialectic. Hence, what I want to accomplish is a rereading of Marx with a stress on human practice and its application to contemporary society and technology.

Anthony Giddens opposes evolutionary theories of society (see Giddens 1984, chap. 5[1]) because he says that almost all of them are based upon some notion of adaptation, in which societies adapt to the material conditions of the environment (Giddens 1981, 20–22) and where adaptation would be conceived in almost mechanical fashion (ibid., 82). Societies wouldn't 'adapt' because it would be their conscious, knowledgeable human members that influence social and historical change. Evolutionary theories would conceive change as endogenous change and 'unfolding' models. Giddens argues that historical materialism is a determinist conception of history because it would believe—as typical for evolutionary theories—in an automatically progressive development from Asiatic society, ancient society, feudalism, capitalism to (finally) communism. "Marx never abandoned the idea that a progressive evolutionary process can be traced out from the initial dissolution of tribal society to the developments which bring humankind to the threshold of socialism" (Giddens 1981, 76; cf. also 235sq., 240, and Giddens 1977, 188, 192–202). Evolutionary theories would be highly prone to merge progression with progress (Giddens 1984, 232).

Marx argued that economical changes in the forces of production are a medium of social change. Giddens says that class struggle and the dialectic of productive forces and relations of production are important in social transformations of capitalism but not in overall history because in other types of society political power would have been a more important influence than economic power. The ideology of modernity has since the Enlightenment been coined by a belief in linear progress and history as progress. Giddens is right in criticizing deterministic conceptions of history and social change; it is true that there are certain formulations by Marx and Engels that without careful consideration could make one believe that their conception of history is a deterministic one. For example, Marx says that "the Asiatic, ancient, feudal and modern bourgeois modes of production may be designated as epochs marking progress in the economic development of society"; that the "bourgeois mode of production is the last antagonistic form of the social process of production" (Marx 1858/59, 9); and that "capitalist production begets, with the inexorability of a law of Nature, its own negation" (Marx 1867, 791). Engels argued that "with the same certainty with which we can develop from given mathematical principles a new mathematical proposition, with the same certainty we can deduce from the existing economic relations and the principles of political economy the imminence of social revolution" (Engels 1845, 555) and that revolution and socialism would result with inevitable necessity from the existing conditions of society (Engels 1850, 242).

Nonetheless, I otherwise than Giddens think that Marx's and Engels's conception of history is not a deterministic one because they frequently stressed the role of revolutionary action in history. But if history depends on agency and the subject, it can't be a linear but only a discontinuous, broken process that is, though conditioned, relatively open and does not automatically result in progress. Marx, for example, stresses that "the greatest productive power is the revolutionary class itself" (Marx 1846/47, 181), that all social life is essentially practical and that the coincidence of the changing of circumstances and of human activity or self-changing can be conceived and rationally understood only as *revolutionary practice* (Marx 1845, 371sq.). Decisive is the "historical self-initiative ["self" is missing in the English translation although it can be found in the German original, CF]" (Marx and Engels 1848, 490) of the dominated and that history is "the history of class struggles" (ibid., 462). Engels stresses the role of the human being in history by saying that in contrast to animals, for which history is made and for which it occurs without their knowledge, "the more that human beings become removed from animals in the narrower sense of the word, the more they make their own history consciously, the less becomes the influence of unforeseen effects and uncontrolled forces of this history, and the more accurately does the historical result correspond to the aim laid down in advance" (Engels 1886a, 323). Marx and Engels in fact acknowledged the importance of conscious, creative human beings in the historical process as also another quotation from Engels shows: "Men make their own history, whatever its outcome may be, in that each person follows his own consciously desired end, and it is precisely the resultant of these many wills operating in different directions, and of their manifold effects upon the outer world, that constitutes history" (Engels 1886b, 297). Writings such as the *Economical and Philosophical Manuscripts, Holy Family, German Ideology, Poverty of Philosophy*, and *Theses About Feuerbach* show a lot of concern for the importance of the creative human being in social processes and social theory.

Although Marx conceived progress in the capital quantitatively as "progress in the productiveness of labour" (Marx 1867, 535), he and Engels knew that the development of the productive forces doesn't automatically result in humane, qualitative progress. Marx says that capitalism means "progress here, and retrogression there" (Marx 1894, 270), and Engels mentions that capitalism is "the period that has lasted until today in which every step forward is also relatively a step backward" (Engels 1886a, 68). In a letter from Engels to Marx, the first argues that against the enlightened prejudice that since the dark Middle Ages there has been a steady progress to the better, one should not only stress the antagonistic character of progress but also the retrogressions (Marx and Engels 1985, 128). History is not fully determined for Marx and Engels and not an automatically progressive process; it is conceived in relationship to social practice that can result but will not automatically result in qualitative progress. If all social life is essentially practical and human beings make their own history, the subject cannot be seen as a simple bearer of structures who carries out universal laws.

Certainly many Marxists have *interpreted* Marx in a determinist manner, but this doesn't mean that Marx's own conception of history is a deterministic one. Statements such as "Marx's evolutionism is a 'world-growth story'" (Giddens 1984, 243) do not adequately acknowledge the importance of human practice in Marx's writings. Giddens himself says that historical materialism's assumption that human beings make history corresponds to the theory of structuration, but the common Marxist use of the term would be a deterministic and economically reductionistic one (Giddens 1984, 243sq.). Giddens also suggests that history is neither pure accident nor fully determined. Marx himself suggested the dialectic of chance and necessity that shapes social change. Knowledgeable human beings make history, but the conditions and possibilities of these changes are *conditioned* by the existing social structures and the material world. This dialectic of freedom and necessity is an important fact about Marx's works that shouldn't be forgotten; capitalist development conditions and triggers situations in which history is relatively open and agency is very important for attaining a desirable result. "Men make their own history, but they do not make it as they please; they do not make it under self-selected circumstances, but under circumstances existing already, given and transmitted from the past" (Marx 1852, 115).

The term *evolution* doesn't necessarily, as Giddens assumes, imply a deterministic conception of progress and historical change. In recent years, there have been usages of the term in self-organization theory that acknowledge the importance of human creativity in social change. For example, Charles François (1997) defines evolution in a very general sense as the accumulative transformation of systems undergoing irreversible changes, and Bela H. Banathy (1996) coined the terms *evolutionary systems design* and *social systems design* in order to stress that the creativity of human beings allows them to intervene into social processes and enables them to give direction to evolution, although a complete steering of social systems is not possible due to their complex nature. Self-organization theory as a theory of evolutionary systems puts forward the idea that the development of complex systems is neither fully determined nor fully accidental. Complex systems are dynamic systems where nonequilibrium states and discontinuity are important aspects of development. Such systems are not in permanent stability as concepts such as adaptation or homeostasis suggest; they are permanently becoming and processlike. Change is taking place permanently in such systems. Self-organization theory tries to employ the term *evolution* in a nondeterministic manner and corresponds much more to Giddens's structuration theory as one might imagine at a first glance. The concept of self-organization can be interpreted as a form of nondeterministic dialectical societal development that is guided by human practices and social struggles and constrained by existing structures.

Ervin Laszlo (1987), one of those system theorists keen on employing the term *evolution* in a nondeterministic and non-Darwinian manner, argues that in the development of complex systems, the latter do not remain stabile; if certain parameters are crossed, instabilities emerge. These are phases of transition where the system shows high entropy and high degrees of indetermination, chance, and chaos. Evolution would not take place continuously but in sudden, discontinuous leaps. After a phase of stability a system would enter a phase of instability; fluctuations intensify and spread out. In this chaotic state, the development of the system is not determined; it is only determined that one of several possible alternatives will be realized. Such points in evolution are called bifurcation (Laszlo 1987). Social self-organization can, on the one hand, be understood as self-reproduction or re-creation; on the other hand, the way the concept is used by Ilya Prigogine, Laszlo, and others, it refers to the emergence of order from chaos when a system enters a phase of instability that results in bifurcation.

3.5 SOCIETY AS DYNAMIC SYSTEM

Society can be conceived as consisting of interconnected subsystems that are not independent and based on one specific function they fulfill but are open, communicatively interconnected, and networked. In each of these systems the basic process of self-organization that interconnects actors and structures takes place permanently. The subsystems of the model of society outlined here are the ecological system, the technological system, the economic system, the political system, and the cultural system. Why exactly these systems? In order to survive, humans in society have to appropriate and change nature (ecology) with the help of technologies so that they can produce resources that they distribute and consume (economy), which enables them to make collective decisions (polity), form values, and acquire skills (culture). The core of this model consists of three systems (economy, polity, culture). This distinction can also be found in other contemporary sociological theories: Giddens (1984: 28–34) distinguishes between economic institutions, political institutions, and symbolic orders/modes of discourse as the three types of institutions in society. Bourdieu (1986b) speaks of economic, political, and cultural capital as the three types of structures in society. Jürgen Habermas (1981) differs between the lifeworld, the economic system, and the political system.

Each of these systems is coined by human actors and social structures that are produced by the actors and condition the actors' practices.

Each subsystem is defined and permanently re-created by a reflexive loop that productively interconnects human actors and their practices with social structures. Figure 3.2 shows a general model of society as a dynamic, dialectical system that is made up of reflexive, self-referential subsystems. The dynamic loops that constitute these systems will be described subsequently.

Matter is the totality of objects that constitute reality and is itself constituted in space and time by an interconnected totality of bodies that react

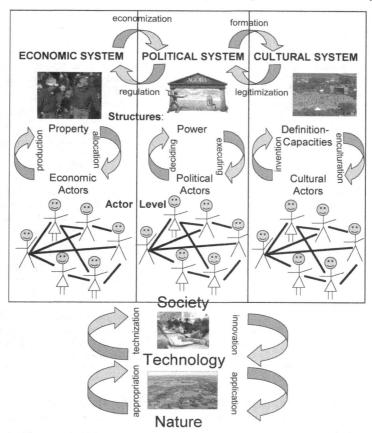

Figure 3.2 Society as dynamic, dialectical system.

on one another (motion), that is, they repulse and attract each other. Matter is the totality of objectively existing systems that are interconnected and accord to different physical laws. As organizational level of matter, society is part of nature, but it also possesses qualities that can't be found in biological and physical matter. Hence, it is a higher-level system that encompasses and encapsulates parts of biological and physical nature. Those parts of nature that are appropriated by man form a specific subsystem of society, the eco-system, that constitutes the biological and physical environment of human societal activity. Society and culture are a sublation of nature; nature and society are dialectically connected. When we speak about nature we always speak about systems that are observed and changed by human beings. Nature is part of society; for human beings there can be no observation of and encounter with nature from the outside of society. The relationship of nature and society/culture is neither exclusive nor inclusive in character, that

Table 3.1 An overview of structures in society.

Type of structure	Structure	Definition
Ecological structures	(Natural) resources	Physical matter that is extracted in labor processes from nature and that is changed by human activities.
Technological structures	Tools	Artifacts, means, methods, skills of action that are used by humans in order to try to achieve defined goals.
Economic structures	Property	Goods and resources that are produced, distributed, and used by humans for satisfying defined needs.
Political structures	Power	The capacity and means for influencing collective decisions according to one's own will.
Cultural structures	Definition-capacities	The capacity to define and acquire values, skills, and practices that shall give meaning to life and help re-create human minds and bodies.

is, nature and society are neither fully different nor fully identical. Society is the realm of human activity and interaction; it forms one specific, small part of nature. But for human beings this small part of the universe forms their overall context of activity. All human activity and observation take place within society; there is no position of humans external to society. Hence, nature as physical realm of activity of human labor, production, and communication is itself a part of society. In transforming and observing nature in economic, technological, cultural, and scientific processes, the human being integrates nature into society. Hence, there is no relationship between nature and human beings external to society; all metabolic and observational processes that establish a relationship between nature and human beings function within society. Nature has produced the human being and society, but the human being integrates (certain parts of) nature as a subsystem of society into its own sphere of activities. Hence, when we speak about "nature and society" we speak about society as the total realm of activity where we focus on social interactions between human beings and about the ecosphere as the interaction processes between humans and ecology and the interaction processes between natural systems that are observed by human beings. Society is a sublation of nature; in production humans consume natural forces. Hence, nature is a foundation of society and continues to exist in society. Humans transform nature in such a way that use values and social relationships emerge that have a specific social function that doesn't exist in nature as such.

The technosphere is the system of society where human beings design and apply technological tools and capabilities in order to satisfy their needs. This is a process in which they change society and nature with the help of technologies. New technologies emerge from social processes that reflect dominant interests, power structures, and worldviews—this is the process of *innovation*. Technologies are applied by humans in social systems in order to achieve certain goals—technology changes society; this is the process of *technization*. Innovation and technization are two dynamic processes that constitute the differentiation and reproduction of the technosphere. Technology can be defined as a purposeful unity of artefacts, means, methods, abilities, processes, and knowledge that are necessary in order to achieve defined goals.

The ecosphere is the subsystem of society where humans use tools in order to appropriate nature in order to produce goods that satisfy their needs. In this subsystem, physical and biological systems form a life-support system of society. The technosphere is the system that mediates between sociosphere and ecosphere; that is, technologies are means that are produced and applied by humans in order to transform and appropriate nature, to satisfy human needs, and to simplify human life. Humans, with the help of technologies, *appropriate* nature; the results are extracted natural resources that are used in the economy for producing use values. By applying tools in order to achieve defined goals, humans transform society, that is, social relationships, but also parts of nature, that is, the material foundation of society. Human interaction permanently changes the physical state of nature in technological *application* processes.

The self-organization of nature (the dissipative and autopoietic production and reproduction of dead and living material systems) and the self-organization cycle of the sociosphere are mutually connected in a productive cycle where natural self-organization serves as the material foundation that enables and constrains social self-organization and human production processes transform natural structures and incorporate these very structures into society as means of production (technologies, raw materials). "The economic process of reproduction, whatever may be its specific social character, always becomes intertwined in this sphere . . . with a natural process of reproduction" (Marx 1885, 359). Nature can exist and self-organize without society, but society can't exist without a natural base. The ecosphere, as the socially constructed part of nature, is shaped and transformed by society. The economy is that part of the sociosphere where the relationship between nature and the sociosphere is established: In the economic system, nature is appropriated in the form of resources that are applied and transformed by human labor in such a way that property forms that function as use values and satisfy human needs are produced and can be distributed, circulated, and consumed. Hence it makes sense to argue that the economy is more material and fundamental in character than polity and culture and that it forms, together with the ecosphere and the technosphere, the material foundation of society. In the relationship of nature and society, human actors (society) produce objective structures; they externalize and objectify their labor power in social processes that result in material objects (use values). Hence, the process of the production of use values is a process of objectification of the subjective. Nature, as objective material being, enters society in the form of raw materials, technologies, and use values that are consumed as the foundation of production that is appropriated by nature and incorporated into human labor practices and experiences. Hence, this process is a process of subjectification of the objective. The whole self-organization cycle that connects society and nature hence is based on the dialectic of the (inter)subjective (labor power, social relationships) and the objective (natural forces, technologies, raw materials, use values), the objectification of the subjective and the subjectification of the objective. The sociosphere can be considered as the subjective or intersubjective and the ecosphere as the objective aspect of the society-nature system.

The interconnection of nature and economy is achieved in labor processes. These are special productive activities exercised by humans with defined aims in social processes so that nature is appropriated and parts of it are used as resources for the production of property so that certain human needs can be satisfied. Labor is only possible as an active shaping of nature and the world. Humans make use of existing worldly objects in order to actively create new objects in labor processes. Hence, man is objective man, a being that objectifies its labor power in property structures that shall satisfy certain needs.

Nature enters the economy in the form of natural and technological means of production (natural forces, technological tools, raw materials, auxiliary materials). The economic system is based on the dialectical relationship of productive forces and relations of production. Relations of production form the structural level of the economy; the term grasps the ways of social mediation between humans that act as agents or as (opposed or cooperating) social groups in economic processes. The productive forces are a systemic totality of living labor force and factors that influence labor. Living labor of human actors and its factors form a relationship that changes historically and is dependent on a concrete formation of society (such as capitalism). The central aspect of the productive forces is laboring human actors. The influencing factors can be summed up as subjective ones (physical ability, qualification, knowledge, abilities, experience), objective ones (technology, science, amount and efficacy of the means of production, cooperation, means of production, forms of the division of labor, methods of organization), and natural ones. These forces can only be viewed in their relationship to living labor. The system of productive forces can't be reduced to these forces; the system is only possible in combination with human labor. It is more than the sum of its parts; it is an integrated whole that lies at the foundation of economic processes.

Generally speaking, one can say that human beings make use of (subjective, objective, natural) productive forces as foundation of production processes; they employ tools in order to enter a metabolism with nature that results in the change of the material state of nature. As a result, nature is appropriated, differentiated, and transformed into a social fact, that is, labor power produces economic goods and relations with the help of productive forces that enable and constrain human economic practices, that is, use values that satisfy human needs and routinized economic relations emerge (*production*). The production of economic resources takes places within specific social relationships/structures, that is, relations of production that have a specific historical form such as in capitalism the relationship between wage labor and capital that is a form of dependence and exploitation. Capital and labor are specific forms of organizing property relations; they are social forms of determining who produces and who owns property. Produced economic goods are distributed and consumed (allocation); thereby they enter the system of the productive forces and function as part of the foundational system of human labor. Hence, the whole process takes on the form of a productive cycle that interconnects productive forces (the system of laboring human actors) and relations of production (economic structures) in such a way that in the economic system of society we find the permanent emergence of economic property resources from human labor practices. Hence, the economic system is a dynamic system.

The political system deals with collective decisions concerning the way life conditions are set (including how economic resources are used and how they are distributed). Power is a political structure; it can be defined as the disposition over means required to influence collective processes and decisions in one's own interest. Domination is a specific form of power; it refers to the disposition over the means of coercion required to influence others, collective processes, and decisions. Power is a social force in the sense that it can be considered as a materialization of the relationships of political groups. In modern society, power structures are, for example, collective decisions (such as laws), political institutions (such as government, parliament, councils, ministries, bureaucracy, courts, public offices, and departments), political positions (member of government, chancellor, etc.). Such structures reflect existing power relationships and the existing distribution of power. Political actors are either individuals or groups that have certain interests that they want to achieve in the political process by political actions. They want to determine political decisions in their interest, enter relations with each other, form groups, and enter certain (more cooperative or more competitive) relations with other interest groups. On the actor level of the political system we find citizens and political groups with certain political practices. As a result, political relationships/structures are formed. These relations determine how power is constituted, distributed, allocated, and disposed. Political structures are both the foundation of political actors' practices and are differentiated and developed by political practices.

Political practices result in the emergence of new and the reproduction of already existing power structures. These structures enable and constrain the actions of the human beings in a society and result in new political activities that set themselves goals of changing or maintaining existing rules and dispositions of power. In the political system we find a mutual relationship of political practices and political structures: The active relationships between political groups (governmental parties, opposition parties, nonparliamentary opposition, and support groups) result in the emergence of new power structures (decisions, laws, rules, political institutions, allocation of offices, appointment of civil servants, etc.) (*deciding*). These forces enable and constrain the life and behavior of citizens as well as political actions of political groups (*executing*). Further political commitments, new goals, ideas, and so on, emerge at the actor level. The political system is a dynamic system that is based on the continual reproduction and emergence of power structures by political practices.

Culture is a social process that produces common meanings that signify certain social entities. This process is based on a mutual productive relationship between the subjective culture of human beings (ideas, norms, values, beliefs) and objective cultural structures (meaningful cultural artifacts with symbolic content, and collective norms, ideas, values, rules, traditions, worldviews, morals). Culture is about defining one's own life and that of the social systems and the society one lives in. It is about the question who controls these definition capacities and about ways of life that practically realize such definitions. Culture is not only "high culture"; it is lived in everyday life. It is, as Raymond Williams has pointed out, ordinary and a whole way of life: "We use the word culture in these two senses: to mean a whole way of life—the common meanings; to mean the arts and learning—the special processes of discovery and creative effort. . . . Culture is ordinary, in every society and in every mind" (Williams 2001, 11).

In cultural systems, human actors, based on their subjective ideas, norms, values, and beliefs, enter social relationships in which they produce and reproduce collective meaningful artifacts (such as pieces of music, books, films, artworks, etc.) and social-value structures (collective cultural values). This process is termed *invention* because it is based on human creativity. Cultural structures enable and constrain human thinking (*enculturation*), what we think, how we live and act, how we define ourselves (identity) and our role in society; which values we have is conditioned by existing collective values and definitions that we are confronted with in the social systems that we live in. We don't necessarily share dominant values, although many of us frequently do, but we have to form opinions concerning these values and decide in how far we let them shape our behavior and thinking and in how far we form differing individual values. Collective definitions condition further social practices that produce and reproduce further collective cultural structures, which again enable and constrain our individual values and ideas, and so on. Culture hence is a dynamic process in which individual values and collective values are interconnected so that meanings, identities, and lifestyles emerge. The totality of individual and collective values and the ways of life based on it forms the cultural system, which signifies a certain "structure of feelings" (Williams 1961, 48; 1977, 131sq.) of a period in societal development, that is, the historically distinct lived experiences of groups, organizations, and societies. A structure of feelings is not homogenous but is made up of different cultural definitions (that can based on the overall societal character and be more or less competitive or harmonized).

Raymond Williams has, as early as 1973, in his paper "Base and Superstructure"—one of the foundational texts of Cultural Materialism—coined the terms *emergent meaning* and *emergent culture*. "By 'emergent' I mean, first, that new meanings and values, new practices, new significances and experiences are continually being created" (Williams 2001,170sq.). Emergent meaning is the permanent discontinuity and novelty through which culture can reproduce and organize itself. Williams notes that dominant culture is alert "to anything that can be seen as emergent" (ibid., 171). Williams didn't connect this notion of cultural emergence to the sciences of complexity, which were just about to emerge full-scale in the 1970s, but he intuitively anticipated the idea that self-organization in the sense of the self-reproduction of a system requires the permanent constitution of new qualities of a system.

The economic, the political, and the cultural systems of society don't work as autonomous units but are open and interconnected. The complexities of the economic system and the lifeworld of the cultural system provide the necessity for the political system to take collective decisions of how the social systems of society shall be shaped. The economic system provides resources (such as money in contemporary society) to the political system as well as problem areas that require decision making to the political system (*economization*). In the political system, to a certain degree, rules are defined that are also binding for the economy and influence the behavior of economic actors (*regulation*). That certain collective decisions are taken influences the everyday life and behavior of the individuals that live in a society; they must position themselves towards these decision structures, form values and opinions on them, and decide to which extent they find it useful or disturbing to act according to these decisions (*formation*). The collective values defined in the cultural system (which can be competing values) influence the collective decisions taken in the political system; certain worldviews try to give legitimacy to certain decisions, whereas other worldviews contest certain decisions (*legitimization*).

All social systems have natural, technological, economic, political, and cultural aspects. Hence, when we act in a certain social system we are confronted with all five different structures simultaneously. So, for example, in a hospital the beds, facilities, and so on, are made of natural resources; there are medical technologies, economic calculations, rules how patients should be treated, aspects of health politics that are discussed, certain values of patients, nursing staff, practitioners, management, and so on. But one of these aspects is the dominant aspect and hence one can argue that each social system has a dominant perspective and structure and hence can be seen as forming a part of a specific subsystem of society. So, for example, when we take a walk in a remote forest we feel being part of the natural system of society; the Internet and the actors that use it form part of the technological subsystem of society; corporations oriented on capital accumulation are part of the economic system; protest movements and governments are members of the political systems; and when we go to a museum or a film we enter the cultural system.

Does it make sense to speak of base (nature, technology, economy) and superstructure (polity, culture) in society, or does this mean that one reduces all social existence to economic facts? The superstructure is not a mechanic reflection, that is, a linear mapping, of the base, that is, the relations and forces of production. It can't be deduced from or reduced to it. Orthodox Marxism for a long time didn't realize this. That the base is not the mechanic reflection of the superstructure has for a long time not been realized by idealism. All human activity is based on producing a natural and social environment; it is in this sense that the notion of the base is of fundamental importance. We have to eat and survive before we can and in order to enjoy leisure, entertainment, arts, and so on. The base is a precondition, a necessary, but not a sufficient condition for the superstructure. The superstructure is a complex, nonlinear creative reflection of the base, the base a complex, nonlinear creative reflection of the superstructure. This means that both levels are recursively linked and produce each other; economic practices and structures trigger political and cultural processes; cultural and political practices and structures trigger economic processes. The notion of creative reflection grasps the dialectic of chance and necessity/indetermination and determination that shapes the relationship of base and superstructure. There isn't a content of the superstructure that is "predicted, prefigured and controlled" by the base; the base "sets limits and exerts pressure" on the superstructure (Williams 2001, 165). If one rereads Marx and bears in mind that our material reality is our social reality, then materialism means that all our life is socially constructed and shaped by the dominant practices, relations, and structures of society. My social theory is a materialistic one, but not a form of mechanical materialism, rather a dynamic materialist social theory. Basic social and economic production processes constrain, but don't mechanically determine, superstructural practices and structures. They are a necessary but not a sufficient condition for polity and culture. The economy enables and constrains the political and cultural systems, which in return enable and constrain the economic system of society.

Given this basic general theoretical framework that describes dynamic processes in all types of society, one can next take a look at how modern society is a concrete expression of this model.

3.6 MODERN SOCIETY AS DYNAMIC SYSTEM

Modern society is characterized by an antagonism between self-determination and heteronomy, inclusion and exclusion, cooperation and competition. Heteronomy, exclusion, and competition are the dominant features that coin the overall character of contemporary society. Humans are not able to fully participate in the economic, political, and cultural system; they are confronted with property that they produce, but that is owned by others, with decisions that affect their lives, but are taken not by themselves, and with values and lifestyles that they have to share in order to be accepted, although they are defined by others.

Marx pointed out that with the division of labor a contradiction between the interest of the separate individual and the communal interest of all individuals who have intercourse with one another emerged. The structures of modern society are alien powers; they are not controlled by all but by certain classes. In modern society individuals and groups compete for the control and accumulation of structural resources, which separates society into classes who own, decide, and define and those who don't or do so to a limited extent. If cooperation and participation are the Essence of society as such, then modern society is not a fully developed society, its existence doesn't correspond to its Essence, and individuals and society are alienated from the immanent Essence of society. Modern society hence is an alienated society; individuals in this society are class individuals. In contrast to a society dominated by competition, a cooperative society is a society in which Essence and Existence correspond. Hegel defined such a correspondence philosophically as truth. Such a community is the "reintegration or return of man to himself, the transcendence of human self-estrangement", "the real *appropriation* of the *human* essence by and for man", "the complete return of man to himself as a *social* (i.e., human) being" (Marx 1844b, 536).

In modern society social structures are capital, that is, the aim of this society is the ever more accumulation of social structures in the hand of certain competing groups. Modern society is shaped by the competition for the accumulation of property, power, and definition capacities. These structures function as economic, political, and cultural capital, that is, structures that are accumulated, which implies competition, an asymmetrical distribution of capital, and an asymmetrical distribution of ownership, power, and hegemony. Hence, modern society is a capitalist society.

Modern society is also a class society. The logic of competition and accumulation has originated in the capitalist economy, but it has simultaneously colonized the political and cultural system; hence, it is not limited to the economy but has a more general meaning. It would be a mistake to conceptualize class only as an economic phenomenon because traditionally this has often meant to reduce political and cultural phenomena to the economy and to leave out of sight their relative autonomy. In order to avoid a reductionist concept, I find it tempting to define class with Bourdieu in a more general sense. He does not as in classical Marxism define class as depending on the position in the economic relations of production but as depending on the volume and composition of capital. The social position and power of an actor depends on the volume and composition of capital (i.e., the relative relationship of the three forms of capital—economic, political, and cultural capital) that he owns and that he can mobilize as well as the temporal changing of these two factors (Bourdieu 1986a, 114). The main classes of society are for Bourdieu a result of the distribution of the *whole* (i.e., economic and political and cultural) capital. This results in a social hierarchy with those at the top who are best provided with capital and those at the bottom who are most deprived. Within the classes that get a high, medium, or low share of the total volume of capital, there are again different distributions of capital, and this results in a hierarchy of class fractions. For example, within the fraction of those who have much capital, the fractions whose reproduction depends on economic capital (industrial and commercial employers at the higher level, craftsmen and shopkeepers at the intermediate level) are opposed to the fractions that are least endowed with economic capital and whose reproduction mainly depends on cultural capital (higher-education and secondary teachers at the higher level, primary teachers at the intermediate level; ibid., 115). Bourdieu says that orthodox Marxism can't explain new forms of social struggles that are, for example, linked to the contradictions resulting from the functioning of the educational system (Bourdieu 1993, 32). He points out that one should not only take economic capital into consideration.

If the subsystems of modern society take on competitive, asymmetric forms then it does not suffice to term these systems economy, polity, and culture; one rather needs to find terms that better capture the qualities of capitalism. Economic property in capitalism is private property controlled by economic classes and produced by subsumed classes. It takes on the form of commodities and money capital. In line with French regulation theory, I use the term *regime of accumulation* for signifying a specific historical model of the accumulation of money capital (Aglietta 1979; Lipietz 1987). The regime of accumulation describes the concrete forms of capital accumulation, production, distribution, and consumption in a specific mode of development. Its result is the accumulation of economic capital within the framework of antagonistic economic structures (money, commodities, markets, class relations). It includes aspects of production such as the productivity of labor, the degree of mechanization, the distribution between branches of production, norms of productivity, technologies of production, means of labor and organization, connections between different modes of production and organizational modes of decision, class relationships, the existing forms of the appropriation of nature and knowledge, as well as aspects of consumption such as conditions that shall secure demand, modes, patterns, and norms of consumption and channels of distribution.

In regulation theory, the political system is termed the *mode of regulation* (Boyer 1990; Lipietz 1986). The mode of regulation refers to the institutional framework that enables and constrains capital accumulation. Its result is the accumulation of political capital within the framework of antagonistic political forms (laws, the state) and political relationships. Regulation means agency that works as a sort of cohesive force on the economy.

For regulation theory, economy and polity are the two systems of capitalist society. However, it leaves out the cultural aspect of society that has been stressed in other Marxist theories (such as critical theory, Gramsci's theory of hegemony, and Althusserianism): ideology. Regulation theory overlooks the relative autonomy of culture and hence subsumes ideological and cultural aspects within the mode of regulation. To avoid these shortcomings, I suggest to add a third aspect: the disciplinary regime which is made up by mechanisms that shall secure the hegemonic consent of the oppressed to the dominating mode of societal development. It produces hegemony, ideologies, and dominating norms and values and results in the accumulation of cultural capital within the framework of cultural forms (dominating norms, knowledge, values, ideologies) and cultural relationships. Hegemony can be seen in accordance with Antonio Gramsci as "the 'spontaneous' consent of the masses who must 'live' those directives, modifying their own habits, their own will, their own convictions to conform with those directives and with the objectives which they propose to achieve" (Gramsci 1971, 266). Hegemony always has political and cultural aspects; it is formed in the framework of the complex relationships between politics and culture. In this process of enforcing consent between dominators and the dominated, political institutions such as law and the repressive state apparatus are important, but also cultural institutions, that is, institutions, which organize ways of life and socialization, are necessary. Cultural institutions involve, for example, the family, churches, religion, media, the educational system, schools, art, and science. Hegemony can only work in and with ideology. An ideology is a system of ideas and beliefs that dominates the consciousness of a human being or a social group (Althusser 1971). Ideology is a 'representation' of the imaginary relationship of individuals to their real conditions of existence, that is, they do not map reality but are social constructions that show how certain groups want to define reality in order to make others see reality the same way. Someone who favours a certain ideology takes part in certain practices (going to church, meetings, consumption of information and culture, etc.). These practices show that ideologies have a material existence and are not confined to the ideational realm. Ideology calls human beings as subjects; this is a process termed *interpellation* by Althusser. Ideology interpellates individuals as subjects and makes them become subjects (members of families, churches, associations, parties, etc.). An interpellation takes place in the name of an absolute subject (god, leader, state, boss, guru, etc.). The individual is interpellated as a free subject so that he or she voluntarily submits to the will of the absolute subject.

Capitalism develops in certain phases, that is, there are periods that are characterized by certain overall qualities that change due to the antagonistic structures of modern society. A concrete historical phase of capitalism is termed a mode of (capitalist) development; it is a coherent unity of a regime of accumulation, a mode of regulation, and a disciplinary regime.

Capital Accumulation and Competition in the Modern Economic System

As in all societal formations, in capitalism goods are produced that satisfy human needs. The specific ways this is done distinguish different societal formations. In capitalism the production process is based on the fact that economic actors produce goods which are sold on the market after their production in order to achieve a profit that allows reinvestment, more production, the selling of more commodities, hence again more profit, and so on. Marx called this process the accumulation of (money and commodity) capital. Capitalist production doesn't satisfy immediate needs (as was, e.g., the case in the production of the medieval craftsman), but each capitalist is in need of the so-called anonymous market for the socialization of products. That the single capitalist enterprise produces in an isolated way is not something biologically given but a social relationship. Marx says that private labor produces commodities. Another foundation of capitalism has been the detachment of the means of production from the workers. Marx is speaking of "double free wage-labor"; the workers don't own the means of production and the produced goods, and they are forced to sell their labor power (Marx 1867, 181–183). Wage labor and the industrial division of labor (which has been enabled by machine technologies; Marx mentions machine-systems, large industry, or the cooperation of many similar machines that are powered by a motor mechanism such as the steam engine; see Marx 1867, chap. 13) are necessary conditions for the full development of capital accumulation.

Capital accumulation is an autopoietic cycle that has been described by Marx as the expanded reproduction cycle of capital in his labor theory of value. The starting point is money capital that forms a social relationship. The capitalist buys with money (M) the commodities (C) labor power (L) and means of production (Mp). This means that here a relation between relations of production and the productive forces is established. The means of production are considered in their value form as constant capital (c) and can be subdivided into circulating constant capital (the value of the utilized raw materials, auxiliary materials, operating supply items, and semifinished products) and fixed constant capital (the value of the utilized machines, buildings, and equipment; Marx 1885, chap. 8). The value of the employed labor power is termed variable capital (v). Constant capital is transfused to the product, but it doesn't create new value. Only living labor increases value—labor produces more value than it needs for its own reproduction. In production, due to the effects of living labor onto the object of labor, surplus value (s) is produced. This means that in the economic system an autocreative process takes place: Living labor (i.e., human subjects) makes use of the objective, material part of the system in order to produce something new; a new good emerges. This good is more than the sum of the parts of the old system. A surplus that is due to living labor power is objectified in it. This creative process is itself a self-organization process within the overall economic autopoietic cycle; something new emerges. The value of a produced commodity is $C' = c + v + s$; this value is larger than the value of the invested capital ($C = c + v$). The difference of C' and C (ΔC) exists due to the production of surplus value and is itself surplus value. In the production process (the upward arrow in the economic cycle of fig. 3.2), living labor within class relations produces surplus value that is objectified in commodities. Surplus value is transformed into profit (surplus value is "realized") and value into money capital by selling the produced commodities on the market. By the sale and purchase of commodities, the latter are allocated to human consumers (the downward arrow in the economic cycle of fig. 3.2); consumption helps reproducing activities in society such as labor power. A further (re)production process is started by capital by the repurchase of labor power and means of production; labor again produces surplus value and commodities that are first sold so that profit is realized and then consumed so that new production processes are enabled, and so on. This is a dynamic process in which there is an overall self-reproduction and self-transformation of the economic system, that is, the accumulation of capital (see fig. 3.3).

This autopoietic process is based on exploitation, alienation, and estrangement. In capitalism, social structures are alienated social structures; they aren't controlled by their immediate producers but are structures of the dominating groups. They are imposed on the individuals as interest "alien" to them and are to a certain extent independent of them in the sense that they can't control them. This is not only true for the economy but for all realms of modern society. The self-reproducing (i.e., self-increasing, self-valorizing, self-expanding) cycle of capital just outlined exists in and through agency, that is, human labor: The actors enter social relationships and with the help of their labor power produce emergent properties (surplus value, commodities, profit). Human labor produces and reproduces surplus value and ever more money capital as structure that is accumulated in antagonistic class relations. Capital as structural moment is based on human action (labor) and can only reproduce itself autopoietically by reflexive actions that are enabled and constrained by the reproduced structures.

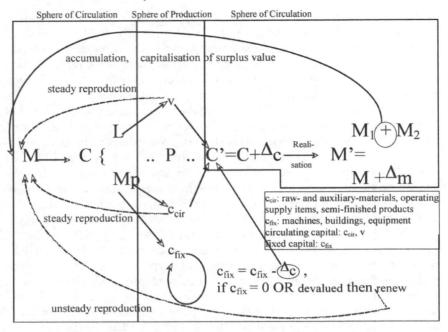

Figure 3.3 The economic self-reproduction of capital: The expanded reproduction cycle of capital.

Not necessarily can all produced commodities be sold; hence, not all surplus value is necessarily transformed into profit. But normally after the whole process there is more money capital than has been invested into production, and such "surplus value generating money" is termed *money capital* and is partly reinvested into new production (accumulation). Modern society is an antagonistic system; it can't reproduce itself permanently and steadily. So self-reproduction, that is, self-expansion and self-valorization, only occurs in a phase of stabile (economic, political, or cultural) accumulation. Due to the antagonistic character of this process, the system is from time to time driven into crisis: crisis means discontinuity and disruption of accumulation.

Capital Accumulation and Competition in the Modern Political System

In modern society, the state system is the organizational unit of political self-organization. It is based on organized procedures and institutions (representative democracy in many cases) that form the framework of the competition for the accumulation of power and political capital. Various groups compete for gaining power; an increase of power for some groups automatically means a decrease of power for other ones. The state is based on asymmetrical distributions of power, domination, the permanent constitution of codified rules (laws) in the process of legislation (*deciding*), the sanctioning and controlling execution of these rules, and the punishment of the disobedience and violation of these rules (jurisdiction, *executing*). Political parties/groups want to shape these processes according to their own will and hence compete for influence and the accumulation of power.

The basic process of the state is based on competitive relationships between political groups that result in a certain distribution of power and the permanent emergence of new features of this distribution (laws, regulations, cases, filling of public offices and civil services according to specific political interests, etc.). These new emergent qualities enable and constrain political practices, political engagement for stabilizing or changing a certain constellation of power. Political practices that constitute the modern state include running for political offices, elections, parliamentary debates, the working out of bills, the passing of laws, political discussions (also in everyday life), political media coverage (press, television, radio, Internet, etc.), protests (petitions, demonstrations, strikes, etc.). Existing laws, political institutions, and political events (the outcomes of the enactment of laws and the processes of establishing new laws) stimulate political organization; they result in new, emergent properties on the level of political groups, that is, in new ways of thinking and acting that try to stabilize or change the existing distribution of power. The development of the state is not a static but a dynamic process; it is based on the permanent political interactions of various political groups that result in the emergence of new political capital, that is, decision-oriented power structures that stimulate further political actions which try to stabilize or change the existing distributions of power. Competition and accumulation of power are fundamental aspects of the dynamics of the modern nation-state.

Elections are important mechanisms for stabilizing and changing existing distributions of power within the state. Political parties compete for votes that determine the distribution of power within the system of rule. Elections and economic markets have certain similarities. Both the economic and the political system of modern society are based on accumulation and competition. A central feature of modern representative democracy is the accumulation of power and votes; the central motive of politicians is the pursuit of power in order to realize their political ideas and programs. Politics in modern society is oriented on its exchange value: Political decisions and positions that are based on a certain amount of votes are exchanged for an increase or decrease of votes in the next elections. The political process that is based on elections can be described in the form V–D–V' or P–D–P': votes–decisions–more votes, power–decisions–more power. However, the accumulation of power is uncertain because an election is an evaluation of the work of politicians, and only if the voters are satisfied with a government will they increase the government's power. This means that in the formula $P' = P + dP$, dP can be negative or positive; there can be either an increase or a decrease of power for each party that runs in an election. Politicians hope that after the end of a legislative period their work will be evaluated positively and they will increase their power. Elections are based on the exchange of representation/decisions and votes; they are procedures for increasing and decreasing the power of political groups that are part of the system of rule. Parties also try to increase their (political and economic) power by increasing the number of memberships.

Elections take place every couple of years. This means that the distribution of power within the system of rule changes slowly; this subsystem of politics is reproduced in a process of slow, conservative change, whereas the whole state system permanently reproduces itself due to synergetic interactions between political groups that result in new qualities. Political power changes permanently in the sense that new political groups, laws, views, ideas, regulations, and so on, emerge, but the distribution of power between the elements (i.e., parties) of the system of rule only changes slowly. Chance and discontinuity is only introduced once every couple of years into the system. Representative democracy and its electoral system are based on a conservative form of change that results in certain dichotomies and asymmetrical distributions of political power. It functions based on dichotomies of government/opposition and parliament/people. This means the constitution of exclusiveness and the delegation of the competence of reaching decisions to certain political groups. In the representative political system, we are confronted with asymmetries and dichotomies in a double sense. First, the dichotomy of electorate/elected politicians. Second, the dichotomies or binary codes of government/opposition and majority/minority. The organization of the state functions in accordance with the principles of exclusion and competition; the political laws that are produced are exclusive social structures. Dynamic types of political self-organization, where decision power is redistributed and reproduced permanently, occur in organizations and systems that are based on the principles of direct democracy and self-government. In such systems there is a more symmetrical distribution of power, and all individuals concerned, by certain collective decisions, participate in the constitution of these decisions. In processes of discursive communication, they try to reach a consensus on certain decisions. In modern society, laws are constituted by a certain subsystem of politics (government, parliament). Such a type of political autopoiesis is inherently hierarchical, asymmetrical, and a type of top-down constitution of decisions.

The state system has certain functions that it fulfills in modern society:

1. Economic regulation

    The state and the economy are structurally coupled and mutually dependent; the economy is in need of certain laws that enable economic accumulation; the state depends on economic accumulation and the taxes derived from capital and wage labor. The economy can't cope with its own complexity; it can't organize itself all the conditions necessary for its self-organization. Hence, the state takes over certain of these tasks and integrates them into its own dynamics and helps to reduce the complexity of the economy. These activities of the state can include welfare, wage policy, labor legislation, subsidies, taxation, property rights, regulation of competition, antitrust laws, contract laws, research politics and subsidization, central bank policies, the organization and maintenance of infrastructures like transportation, energy supply, communication, education, and so on. These infrastructures *can* have and frequently do have a public character, but this must not be the case, as the privatization and deregulation of public infrastructure that has taken place in many countries in recent years shows.

2. Control of the means of violence

The state holds a centralized control/monopoly of the means of violence and is organized within a certain natural and social territory. The processes of the state take place within strictly defined boundaries. Means of violence are used in order to secure the organization of society; the state protects society from external and internal influences that threaten its self-reproduction. The nation-state is based on a certain territory; it has natural and social boundaries that are defended with the threat of using violence. The nation-state is a precondition of the organization of an economic system of accumulation because regulatory rules and the organization of the infrastructure of the economy are efficiently possible only within a bounded territory that is controlled by a system that monopolizes the means of violence. The development of the modern economy and the modern state system was a process of coevolution; hence, both are based on similar principles and depend on each other. Economic self-organization is based on wage labor; the effective organization of wage labor relationships is only possible within a bounded territory that is controlled by the nation-state. The modern nation-state is both based on the notion of the individual as citizen that has certain basic rights and the idea of the individual as private owner of property and labor power. The state's monopoly of violence consists of both internal defense (police, legal system, secret service) and external defense (military, secret service). The differentiation between internal and external aspects of defense of the system's boundary has resulted in the differentiation between the police and the standing army. Political colonialism means the enlargement of the border of the state by making use of violent means. Warfare is the central means of the state for defending and enlarging its bounded territory.

3. Legitimization

The existence of the means of violence in the hands of the state and their usage must be explained and justified. The legitimization of violence has become a permanent affair of politics. One can observe this phenomenon especially during times of warfare and its prearrangements.

4. Surveillance for the self-observation of society

   The nation-state is a power container, a metastorage of social information structures and a system that implements the self-observation of society. In order to maintain and reproduce itself and to foster the various autopoietic self-reproductions of its subsystems, society must observe itself. Surveillance, understood in the sense of information gathering about the activities of the citizens in order to organize and run administration and avoid and punish crime by coercive means, is a central feature of the nation-state's observation of society. These processes of observation are based on information generation and processing. "Surveillance as the mobilising of administrative power— through the storage and control of information—is the primary means of the concentration of authoritative resources involved in the formation of the nation-state" (Giddens 1985, 181).

5. Individualization

   In order to simplify the self-observation of modern society that is organized by the state, the modern state is based on individualization into individual citizens, labor forces, commodity owners, private owners, and voters. The individual is granted certain rights such as the rights to organize, express himself, vote, run for public office, assemble himself with others, make use of different sources of information, and to choose his own religion. These citizenship rights are necessary conditions for the economic and political self-organization of modern society.

6. Definition and control of membership in society

   The state as a modern organization is based on the definition of membership; it organizes the rights it grants to individuals along the differentiation between citizen/noncitizen. In order to maintain a border of the modern state system, it is necessary to define who is allowed to live, work, vote, and contribute to economic, political, and cultural processes. The nation-state is necessarily based on exclusion and a differentiation of membership status. The members of a territorially bounded society have different rights that are determined by their status and along the definition of citizen/noncitizen. The formation and maintenance of a bounded territory is based on the formation and violent maintenance of a difference between the system and its environment. This border between system and environment defines a differentiation between inside and outside of society.

7. Self-description of society

   In order to legitimize and maintain itself, the state system must describe itself. National identity is the result of the self-description of society. The state constructs a common identity of its members in order to create the unity that is necessary for maintaining the autopoietic processes that constitute a society that is organized within national boundaries. In describing itself, society refers to and fosters constructed symbols of unity such as language, traditions, origin, money, culture. The existing boundaries of a nation-state are a result of various conflicts, wars, and international treaties. Originally culturally, economically, and politically relatively autonomous groups of people have been artificially united within one nation-state. The existence of various minorities and regional traditions, idioms, symbols, practices, and habits is an expression of the artificial character of the nation. A united, centrally controlled territory is in need of an identity that legitimizes the common sharing of a part of space-time by a vast number of people. This organization and unification of space-time is a necessary condition for the economic and political autopoiesis of modern society. The nation is a symbolic, imaginary community that functions as the self-description of the state and is the result of the process of describing society that is organized by the state. The education system is an important institution in establishing and maintaining the ideological self-description of society. The self-reproduction of modern society is necessarily based on a definition of inclusion/exclusion concerning membership, national identity, and the family. The state organizes these three integrated and interrelated elements of modern society. The construction of artificial, imaginary identities concerning origin, ethnicity, and gender are central features of the ideological function of the state. The description of society generated by the state produces clear cut identities along the lines of origin, ethnicity, and gender and assigns certain roles to each identity and its opposite by fostering the difference between these roles. Each identity generated in the process of self-description comprehends itself in opposition to other identities that are frequently perceived as threats. The state's involvement in migration and territorial control has 'racial' implications; its involvement in organizing citizenship has ethnical implications; and its involvement in family policy has gender implications.

8. Population policy

The systems of modern society are in need of active human agents (labor forces and citizens). One role of the state is the facilitation of population growth by managing population policy. All social self-organization processes within society are in need of biological autopoiesis in the sense that the reproduction of the species is necessary for supplying active human beings that enter social relationships in order to maintain and reproduce social systems. Biological autopoiesis of the human being is in modern society coupled to the dynamics of the economy and politics; people have to enter and actively participate in these systems in order to survive and maintain their own biological and social autopoiesis. The family is the germ cell of economic and political processes in modern society; its autopoiesis produces human beings that sustain the social processes of modern society.

The modern state regulates the economy; it organizes and defends the autopoiesis of society within a bounded territory by making use of the monopoly of the means of coercion; it organizes the self-observation, self-containment, and self-description of modern society and is a meta-storage mechanism of social structures.

Dynamic processes in which political actors interact in such a way that political power structures are permanently differentiated constitute the political system, that is, new aspects emerge. Political structures (power structures, political institutions, political decisions) enable and constrain political practices that result in the differentiation of political structures; that again conditions further political practices, and so on. This mutual productive process of political actors and political structures is the dynamic political process of political self-organization.

Political processes in modern society are not only shaped by governments and parties, but also by extraparliamentary opposition and protest movements. Antonio Gramsci stressed that the state means "political society + civil society" (Gramsci 1971, 263). It consists of two major subsystems: the system of political rule and the system of civil society. The system of political rule is made up by the parties that are represented in parliament, official political institutions such as parliament, government, ministries, public offices, police, military, courts, and the secret service. This system forms the core of the process of constituting and enacting laws. Civil society is the system that is comprised by all nonparliamentary political groups. These groups either run for elections, but are not represented in parliament, or don't run for elections because they rely on nonparliamentary forms of political practice. Political groups that are part of civil society represent certain aims and interests and try to influence power relationships in such a way that their ideas and interests are represented. Their chief practice is the lobbying for certain political ideas (lobbying doesn't only include procedures of influencing powerful political actors that are based on personal and cultural relationships as well as on economic resources; also all forms of protest can be considered as a type of lobbying for certain ideas and material interests). The self-organization of the state system can only be accomplished by complex interactions between the system of political rule and civil society; it is not solely comprised by interactions within the first. The two subsystems are structurally coupled, that is, each perturbates the other but can't determine the practices and structures of the other to a full extent. Lobbying as the main practice of civil society is a perturbation for the ruling system; it will result in a change of existing structures, that is, a sort of response, but it is not determined how this change will look like, to which extent it will take place, and whether it will be a rather important, major change or a rather unimportant, minor change. In many nation-states, referenda that can be initiated by civil society are a sort of nonparliamentary political procedure. Lobbying also includes the membership in political parties of members of a group that belongs to civil society. Political events that take place within the system of rule (new laws, appointments, etc.) perturbate civil society in the sense that the organizations of civil society form opinions and views concerning these events. Political events stimulate political practices. It is not determined whether or not this will result in support or opposition. Certain political events can result in political mobilizations within civil society that support or protest against certain events in the system of rule. It is not determined in advance what will happen, how civil society will react to new emergent properties of government. It is determined that such emergence will result in further political practices within both subsystems of politics but not in which ones. The political system contains both aspects of chance and necessity. As an effect of the emerging new networked forms of politics that are due to the changes that have affected society during the last 30 years, the growth rate of the research literature on civil society and governance (a term employed for describing political practices that are organized within civil society and significantly diverge from governmental practices) has massively increased. There are various ideas about governance and civil society; most scientists involved with these issues agree that both notions have to do with voluntary political action in order to advance common purposes.

Social protest movements are collective actors and social systems; they are part of the civil society system. They form dynamic social systems that permanently produce and reproduce events and political topics that signify protest against existing social structures and the search for alternative goals and states of society. Protest movements are a reaction to social problems, an expression of fear and dissatisfaction with society as it is and a call for changes and for the solution of problems. The ecology movement is a reaction to the problem of ecological degradation; the women's movement is a reaction to gender-specific oppression; the antiracist movement is a reaction to the problem of racial discrimination; antifascism is a reaction to the problem of right-wing extremism and neofascism; the human-rights movement and the civil-rights movement are reactions to the problem of human-rights violations; the antiglobalization movement is a reaction to the global problems of poverty, lack of political participation, and to the negative consequences of neoliberal policies; indigenous movements and landless movements are reactions to the problem of land expropriation; the homosexual movement is a reaction to the problem of sexual discrimination; the antipsychiatric movement is a reaction to the discrimination of the mentally ill; the disability-rights movement is a reaction to the discrimination of the disabled; the open-source movement is a reaction to the problem of the valorization and privatization of knowledge and public goods; the peace movement is a reaction to the global problem of war; the student movement is a reaction to the problem of cutbacks in the educational sector; the unemployment movement is a reaction to the problem of unemployment; the youth movement and alternative (sub)cultures are reactions to the problem of the lack of perspectives for young people in late capitalism;

esotericism, sects, and spiritualism are reactions to the crisis of religion and belief systems caused by individualization processes; Third World initiatives are a reaction to the problem of poverty; fundamentalist movements are reactions to global cultural homogenization; neofascist movements are reactions to the failures of overcoming fascist traditions and thinking and to the problems of modernization, and so on.

Some authors have distinguished between (new) social movements and nongovernmental organizations (NGOs). The first would be self-organizing, political, unprofessional, temporary, discontinuous, decentralized, nonbureaucratic, critical, and conflict-oriented; the latter rather instrumental, apolitical, professionalized, continuous, formally organized, bureaucratic and centralized, reformist, and consensus-oriented (Demirovic 1997, 272). If one understands an organization as a temporally continuous, formally organized social system that is based on clearly defined membership rules, resources, and defined rules and has strategic goals and behavior, then spontaneous or informal social movements can't be understood as NGOs. If one understands also self-organized spontaneous informal social systems, in which the actors have strategic goals and behavior, as organizations, then one must distinguish between rather formal and rather informal NGOs and both form parts of social movements. This discussion is further complicated by the notion of social movement organizations (McCarthy and Zald 1977), which conceives civil society as an expression of instrumental reason. As the stress in the work at hand is on self-organization processes, which includes the term organization, I tend to interpret organizations in a broader meaning as social systems in which actors form social relations in order to act together strategically so that they can achieve certain goals and realize interests. Organizations are mainly economic and political social systems, characterized by strategic end-rational actions. Formal NGOs are based on formal rules, membership status, hierarchies, a division of labor, defined rules, continuity, and strategically mobilized resources. Informal NGOs are based on superficial rules, spontaneity, grassroots structures, decentralization, undefined rules, and discontinuity. A social movement is a network of NGOs; the latter can all have a rather formal or a rather informal character or there is a mix of formal and informal NGOs. Civil society, then, is a network of NGO networks, a network of social movements, or the totality of all social movements in society.

Social movements are political answers of civil society to ecological, economic, political, social, and cultural problems of modern society. The problems produced by the antagonistic structures of society are a condition for the emergence of protest that organizes itself within the civil society subsystem of the political system. Social problems and protest are couplings of societal subsystems with the political systems (or a self-coupling of the political system in the case where protest is an answer to political problems).

Each social movement is reactive in the sense that it reacts to strains and protests against the existence of certain social structures, but each is also proactive in the sense that it wants to transform society and holds certain values and goals that shall guide these transformation processes.

The emergence of a social movement presupposes social problems as a material base. Protest is a negation of existing structures that result in frictions and problems and a political struggle that aims at the transformation of certain aspects of society or of society as a whole. Protest is the essential activity of social movements; hence *protest movement* is a term that is similar to the one of *social movement* but stresses the central activities of such social systems. Neither the aggravation of problems nor the structural opening of new political opportunities or the increase of resources for protest movements results automatically in protest. "In some cases strains will persist for decades, only giving way to movement formation when a shift in opportunities or resources makes this possible. In other cases opportunities and resources may be in abundance, but there will be no movement until new strains emerge. In other cases still all the pieces may be in place save for a precipitating event which sets them alight, and so on" (Crossley 2002b, 188). The transition in the Soviet Union and the student movement of 1968 are examples of protests in situations of increasing political opportunities and resources, whereas the emergence of the labor movement and the anti-globalization movement can be considered as reactions to aggravating social stratification.

Only if social problems are perceived as problems and if this perception guides practices, protest emerges. Hence, "cognitive liberation" and rebellious consciousness are necessary (McAdam 1982). The difference between objective structures and subjective expectations is an important aspect of protest. "When the 'fit' between objective structures and subjective expectations is broken the opportunity for critical reflection and debate upon previously unquestioned assumptions is made possible" (Crossley 2002b, 185). As long as one-dimensional consciousness dominates a social system, protest can't emerge even if social problems get worse. That protest and social problems are nonlinearly related has been one of the central insights of Herbert Marcuse. In late capitalism ideologies such as racism, the performance principle, consumerism, esotericism, and competition are factors that limit and constrain the possibilities for social protest. Protest presupposes social problems, the perception of these problems as problems by human actors, the assessment that these problems are unbearable and a value-based indignation that activates and mobilizes practices. That a problem is perceived as a problem that should be solved doesn't automatically result in the emergence of protest but maybe in attempts to organize protest. Such attempts are only successful if possibilities and resources for protest can be found and mobilized.

Identities are meanings by which social groups define themselves. Social movements question dominant values and identities; they produce values and goals that contradict dominating structures and that shape their identity. These values and goals guide collective practices that aim at transforming the institutions, material structures, and values of society. Historically such practices have been demonstrations, boycotts, strikes, sit-ins, blockades, civil disobedience, refusals to obey orders, sabotage, desertion, demolition of property, kidnapping, terrorism, armed struggle, and so on. There are nonviolent and violent forms of protest. Protest is a collective search for and a production of alternative meanings and values. Each protest group has a certain identity, an adversary, and goals. These three aspects guide practices of protest. Jürgen Habermas has in this context stressed the importance of cultural aspects of NSMs (new social movements). "In the past decade or two, conflicts have developed in advanced Western societies that deviate in various ways from the Welfare State pattern of institutionalised conflict over distribution. They no longer flare up in domains of material reproduction; they are no longer channelled through parties and associations; and they can no longer be allayed through compensations. Rather, these new conflicts arise in domains of cultural reproduction, social integration, and socialisation; they are carried out in sub-institutional—or at least extraparliamentary—forms of protest; and the underlying deficits reflect a reification of communicatively structured domains of action that will not respond to the media of money and power. The issue is not primarily one of compensations that the welfare state can provide, but of defending and restoring endangered ways of life. In short, the new conflicts are not ignited by distribution problems but by questions having to do with the grammar of forms of life" (Habermas 1987, 392).

Protest movements are political phenomena and part of civil society, as oppositional and alternative movements (i.e., they formulate alternatives to the dominating conditions of society) they have an important role in modern society because by producing alternative topics and demands they guarantee the dynamic of the political system that is given by the confrontation of dominating structures by opposition. The political system is based on the dispute between different values and views. Conflict guarantees possibilities of change and dynamic. A political system without opposition is static and totalitarian; protest and critique are important aspects of democratic political systems. The role of protest movements in modern society is that they point out ways of social change and transformation.

Communication organizes collective practices of protest movements such as demonstrations, petitions, boycotts, civil disobedience, media and information work, publications, discussions, and so on. These collective practices of social movements (which form collective actors) produce and reproduce as part of the system of civil-society alternative and oppositional topics and values in the political public sphere. Hence, they have a communicative function in society; they communicate and describe antagonisms of society that have resulted in social problems as well as alternative social structures as possible solutions. They want to produce public attention for topics and problems that are ignored and not communicated by dominant actors and institutions; they are a form of alternative political communication. Social movements fulfill the role of being a noninstitutionalized civil-society mechanism of self-criticism of society. Based on actual political and societal events and the identity of a movement, protest practices and protest communication are enabled that result in the production and reproduction of protest structures, events, regularized interactions, protest topics, and protest values that enable the reproduction of identity and communication of the movement, and so on. Protest is not a singular event; it normally takes on the form of a continuous succession of protest events that stretches in time; it is organized in the form of campaigns. Protest movements are dynamic communication systems that permanently react to political and societal events with self-organized protest practices and protest communications that result in the emergence and differentiation (production and reproduction) of protest structures (events, oppositional topics, alternative values, regularized patterns of interaction and organization). The dynamic of social movements is based on the permanent emergence and mutual production of protest practices and protest structures. Protest practices are forms of nonparliamentary action and communication of social groups that are aimed at the transformation of society or a social system, question and criticize dominant relationships and structures, react to certain frictions of society, and suggest alternative solutions to phenomena that they consider as social problems. Protest structures are political events, topics, resources, regularized organizations, and values produced by protest practices that question the status quo of a social system or society, identify frictions and problems, and suggest alternative solutions to these identified problems. A protest group or movement exists as long as there are actors that communicate protest oriented on certain topics. Dynamic is an important aspect of protest; protest exists only as long as there is mobilization of actors, resources, meanings, knowledge, and public attention that enable practices and structures of protest. If the goals of the movement are reached or it is externally or internally smashed or its resources are exhausted, the movement immerges; it ceases to exist and stops communicating. The self-organization of a social movement is a vivid process; it is based on the permanent movement and differentiation of actors and structures that communicate public protest; a social movement is only a movement as long as it communicates protest and moves itself.

The totality of all protest groups of society forms the subsystem of social protest. The role of this self-organizing social system in society is that it communicates oppositional values and goals in the political public sphere. Protest system is just another expression for the system of civil society. The emergence of social movements is closely coupled to societal development and the emergence of societal problems. A critical phase of the system of social protest emerges if social antagonisms and problems are considered as unbearable, that is, a critical mass of people is dissatisfied with the structure of society; the number of opponents of certain structures has increased to such an extent so that dissatisfaction and a will for change can be experienced. Such a critical phase is not the necessary result of an aggravation of social antagonism (e.g., the intensification of poverty, unemployment, or environmental degradation) but the result of the perception and the consciousness of the aggravation of an antagonism. Herbert Marcuse's insight that manipulation, control, and technological rationality can forestall protest is still very important in this context. The antagonistic structure of society is a foundation, that is, a necessary condition of protest, but it is not a sufficient condition. Protest depends also on the possibilities and conditions of struggle and on the consciousness of these possibilities. Liberation must be socially possible and humans must have understood the reasons for the existence of social problems; they must have the desire for change; they must feel the need for social transformation and possess the consciousness of the possibilities of liberation. Liberation has both material and cognitive aspects that must coincide in order to result in concrete attempts of liberating practice. Only if such a coincidence is given, the system enters a critical phase and protest emerges. Date, time, form, and result of protest are not determined but emerge from protest practices and communications that produce synergetic results. Productive communication is an important feature of protest movements. In critical phases of protest, new social systems of protest emerge whose form, content, and effects are not determined but depend upon old structures, that is, old structures enable and constrain new structures. A new order of protest emerges, that is, the social system of protest is fundamentally transformed; a new protest movement or a new network of protest movements emerges.

Struggles of social movements are a necessary condition for social change, but the outcome of these struggles is not predetermined. It can be successful in terms of effecting social change to different degrees, ranging from hardly any changes to more fundamental changes in the institutional settings of society. The protest system as a whole is, like society, a dynamic evolving system that has its own laws of movement that are structurally coupled to the overall evolution of society. From time to time new issues, structures, identities, organizational forms, and methods of protest emerge in the system and transform the overall system. These transformations are due to societal changes that demand adaptation of the protest system to changing economic, political, cultural, technological, and ecological conditions. The emergence of new protest issues, methods, identities, structures, and organizational forms starts as singular innovation. If it is widely imitated, then it spreads within the protest system and transforms the system as a whole; novel qualities sublate the old structure of the total system. In terms of Hegelian dialectics, this means that novel qualities sublate the old structure of the total system, that is, the system is transformed, reaches a higher level, incorporates old qualities, and creates new qualities. That novelty emerges doesn't mean that old forms, methods, and structures of protest vanish but that new qualities are added that enable new collective practices and structures of protest. The evolution of the protest system has both external and internal aspects; it is caused to certain degrees by both changes in the societal environment of movements and processes of internal communication, cooperation, conflict, competition, adaptation, innovation, and negotiation.

Members of social groups communicate in the form of conflicts, alliances, splitting, networks, joint demonstrations, petitions, and so on. The same is true for communication between protest groups, that is, there is both intra- and intersystemic protest communication. The system of social protest is dynamic, that is, the groups organized in it communicate in ways that allow certain degrees of spontaneity of the system. Hence, social protest is frequently undetermined and unpredictable. The system of protest changes permanently; new alliances, networks, demonstrations, forms of protest, boycotts, alliances, petitions, declarations, and so on, emerge permanently; old alliances and networks disappear, and so on.

The emergence of order in complex systems is triggered by small singular events that result in small disorder that intensifies itself and cause phases of instability where novelty emerges. Social protest is conditioned by social structures and social antagonism but triggered by singular events. On December 1, 1955, Rosa Parks, a black lady in Montgomery, Alabama, refused to give her bus seat to a white man and was arrested. This event sparked off large protests and the emergence of the civil-rights movement. The social conditions of segregation were considered as being unbearable any longer at these times; a singular event that could not be predicted and that had nondetermined outcomes triggered social protest.

Social development can't be steered and forecast. Due to the rising complexity and globalization of society, we are confronted with an end of certainties—indeterminism, irreversibility, chance, and nonpredictability shape society today. Chance is an opportunity; liberation can't be centrally steered; it can only be self-organized in decentralized processes. In critical phases, protest can intensify itself. This reflects the idea of complexity thinking that small causes can spontaneously have large effects. Herbert Marcuse has described the intensification of protest as a domino effect (1966, 67; 1969a, 50; 1972, 42). A recent British empirical study of protest has shown that contagion effects are important aspects of protest, that is, that protests can temporarily raise the protest potential of the public as a whole (Sanders, Clark, and Stewart 2005).

The emergence and growth of social movements is a process of spontaneous self-organization that has its roots in the antagonistic structure of modern society, is triggered by certain political or societal events, and is based on antagonisms, the conscious perception of antagonisms as unbearable social problems, and the mobilization of resources that enable protest.

Civil society and protest movements both provide legitimization to modern society and are a space for the start of potential changes of society, which are not determined, but a possibility.

Capital Accumulation and Competition in the Modern Cultural System

Capitalism is an antagonistic social formation that is based on divisions into social groups that compete for economic (property: money, commodities), political (power: social relationships, origin), and cultural capital (definition capacities, qualification, education, knowledge; Bourdieu 1986a, 1986b). This stratified class structure produces social struggles that aim at accumulating capital in the hands of certain groups at the expense of other groups. These divisions are at the heart of the cultural evolution of modern society. Hence, cultural development has both internal (the antagonistic logic of the accumulation of cultural capital) and external (the antagonistic logic of the accumulation of economic and political capital) causes. The cultural antagonism is one between unity and plurality. Dominant groups try to ideologically impose their worldviews upon other groups in order to accumulate more capital and to enlarge their sphere of influence and their social system. They aim at creating a unity without plurality that is frequently challenged by the dominated groups, who themselves aim at a reversal of hegemony, that is, a radically negated new unity without plurality or separation (plurality without unity). The stratified structure of capitalism that is the result of the antagonistic logic of accumulation is opposed to a unity in plurality because it separates social groups and makes them have to compete against each other in the race for capital.

The capitalistic process of cultural self-organization is one of competition, accumulation, and separation.

The antagonisms of modern society are due to the logic of accumulation and result in class struggles. Capital structure and the practice of conflict are the driving forces of the development of modern society. By being confronted with tastes and schemes of perception of other classes and class fractions, specific lifestyles of a class or class fraction emerge (Bourdieu 1986a, 170sq.). A lifestyle can be seen as a system of classified and classifying practices and distinctive signs. People, families, and groups in modern society commonly strive for upclassing, and if it becomes necessary they struggle against downclassing. This dialectic results in class struggles; these are material (strikes, protests, refusal of work) and symbolic conflicts.

Symbolic struggles are fights over symbolic capital and tastes that shall establish distinction between classes in order to ideologically secure the domination of certain groups (Bourdieu 1986a). Symbolic capital is a "capital of honour and prestige" (Bourdieu 1977, 179). Symbolic struggles are cultural struggles in the sense that they make use of signification processes in order to produce signs that draw borders, erect a social hierarchy, and produce distinction. Cultural struggles are semiotic struggles in the sense that meaning is contested, that is, there are fights about who defines and controls values and knowledge in society. Modern culture is characterized by competition, that is, struggles for the accumulation of cultural capital.

Cultural signification processes are of large importance in capitalism because they constitute a symbolic dimension of class struggle that is not just imaginative but has real material results. Cultural forms like language, music, clothing, artworks, furniture, styling, food, drinks, toiletries, books, newspapers, magazines, sports, records, toys, body care, cosmetics, appearance, manners, and so on, are symbols that signify class differences in modern society and are used as forms of class distinction. Distinction is a principle that is at the heart of the antagonistic cultural development in modern society; it produces cultural classes and symbolic struggles.

Fundamental changes in worldviews can result from symbolic and material class struggle when they either shift the balance of power in such a way that new classes or class fractions gain dominance or when ruling classes employ new strategies of symbolic class struggle in order to secure their position by producing new cultural distinctions. Hence, fundamental cultural change can both be disintegrative or integrative; it can destabilize or stabilize the existing class structure. Cultural change that operates with the help of the logic of symbolic struggle, distinction, exclusion, competition, and so on, is heteronomous in character and typically for the capitalist social formation. This means that as long as the logic of distinction and capital accumulation is at the heart of society, social and cultural change will always aim at reproducing the class structure (although there might be deep changes in the social structure). Hence, the most fundamental cultural change would be one that eliminates the logic of distinction and symbolic accumulation. Symbolic accumulation doesn't mean that dominant classes accumulate meanings at the expense of dominated classes who lack meanings. All social classes permanently accumulate symbolic cultural capital, that is, tastes and lifestyles that make a difference and define others, that is used as a weapon in the struggle for the accumulation of economic, political, and cultural capital, that is, they permanently aim at transforming symbolic capital into material (economic, political, and cultural) capital. But specific groups have more power in defining which tastes and lifestyles are considered as dominant, important, and trend-setting in society; they control cultural definition capacities. Symbolic capital is accumulated by both dominant and dominated classes in a hegemonic field of active symbolic struggle that is articulated with the field of material struggle. The outcome of social struggles determines the social hegemony of certain meanings and social groups.

That cultural forms in modern society are signs that produce symbolic difference and symbolic class struggle means that culture has in this social formation an ideological character. Culture fulfills "a social function of legitimating social differences" (Bourdieu 1986a, 7). This is not to say that ideology is the mere reflection of economic relationships of production but that ideology is a cultural practice of signification linked to all areas of social production (economic, political, cultural) that produces difference, tastes, and distinction in order to reproduce the class structure of modern society. Hence, ideology doesn't have an economic, but a social function; it is a cohesive factor that secures the principles of accumulation, class division, competition, and exclusion. Structuralistic thinkers like Althusser (1971), Barthes (1972), and Wallerstein (1990) have shown that modern culture functions as ideology, but it should be added that ideology is a site of struggle between different meanings that try to win active consent (hegemony). Not only dominant but also oppositional codes function as ideologies in modern society; they both interpellate subjects and try to invoke certain preferred meanings. Ideology does not map reality but is a social construction that shows how certain groups want to define reality in order to make others see reality the same way. Someone who favors a certain ideology takes part in certain practices (going to church, meetings, consumption of information and culture, etc.). These practices show that ideologies have a material existence and are not confined to the ideational realm. Ideologies divert attention from social divisions and social stratification. But ideology is not something that is simply imposed upon dominated classes by the dominators; it is actively produced and reproduced by all individuals and social classes; it is a relatively autonomous principle that secures cultural accumulation and distinction. As a process of signification that has overall social importance, it secures accumulation in all subsystems of society.

Stuart Hall (1999) has pointed out that a certain degree of determinism in the form of hegemonic meaning, as well as a certain degree of indeterminism in the form of negotiated meaning and oppositional meaning, is present in the cultural reception process. Dominant meaning means that "there exists a pattern of 'preferred readings'; and these both have the institutional/ political/ideological order imprinted in them and have themselves become institutionalised" (Hall 1999, 513). Negotiated meaning is decoding that "contains a mixture of adaptive and oppositional elements" (ibid., 516); oppositional meaning means "to decode the message in a globally contrary way, . . . within some alternative framework of reference" (ibid., 517). The main achievement of Hall is that he has shown that there is no necessary correspondence between encoding and decoding. Different interpretations exist in parallel and even in opposition and antagonism to each other. It seems realistic to me to conceive the relationship of production/encoding and reception/decoding of texts dialectically by assuming that social relationships in modern society are whole ways of social struggle that are reflected in the symbolic realm as symbolic struggles and hence constitute a limited plurality of hegemonic/dominant, negotiated, and oppositional meanings that are assigned to social realities in such processes of material and symbolic struggle. The causality of this relationship is one of dialectical determinism or conditioned chance: The social reality of the modern world, that is, antagonistic social relationships, condition a number of possible conflicting meanings of cultural forms; there is a variety of possible meanings conditioned by class and power relationships; real meanings are determined in active social processes.

Antonio Gramsci's concept of hegemony helps in describing ideology not as a passive structural imposition on the masses but as an active production process. Gramsci stressed that superstructures cannot be reduced to the economic base and that culture involves the creation of (new) world outlooks and morals of life (Gramsci 1980). The concept of hegemony has been frequently stressed by cultural studies in order to show that culture is a site of class struggle where hegemony is actively produced, reproduced, and challenged. Hegemony, as a concept that doesn't reduce the masses to passive cultural dupes and bearers of structures, shows that culture is an ideology in the form of dominant codes, but it enables alternative readings, oppositional codes, and practices. Culture is an integrative process that consists of processes of bottom-up *invention* and top-down incorporation of collective meanings, rules, and values (*enculturation*). Gramsci's concept of hegemony helps to conceive the relationship of actors and structures in cultural theory dialectically. "The value of the Gramscian theory of hegemony is that of providing an integrating framework which both sets of issues [the structuralistic stress on imposed culture and the culturalistic stress on constructed and spontaneously oppositional culture] might be addressed and worked through in relation to each other" (Bennett 1986, 222).

Implications of Competition and Accumulation for the Ecosphere and the Technosphere

Since the fifteenth century, Enlightenment thinking, which forms the heart of the ideology of modernism, has considered nature mainly as a machine, passive, inert, and a thing that needs to be controlled and mastered by man. Society and nature have been considered as two separate realms. Nature and technology are in modern society coined by the logic of competition and accumulation. The enlightenment caused a movement from magic to science, ritual to technology, belief/religion to reason—from nature to society. This shift in ideology was accompanied by the shift from agricultural society to industrial society; man was separated from nature and land, and the working class as a propertyless industrial social group emerged.

Nature organized in the form of technologies increases productivity and hence cheapens commodities insofar as it replaces labor. The reason why capital is enthusiastic about the organization of nature in the production process in the form of technology is that it increases the productivity of labor and hence reduces the costs of variable capital (total amount of wages) and increases the speed of the production of surplus value. Marx stresses that technology is a means of relative surplus value production, that is, for producing more surplus value in less time by advancing productivity. This could result in elevated levels of unemployment. He both stresses the consequences of the capitalist usage of technology as well as the social framework for the usage of technology and its effects on society. Marx says that social problems are not caused by technology as such but that the capitalist use of technology contributes to such problems. He sees technological determinism as a means of bourgeois thinkers in order to persuade the workers that their opponent is not capital as a social relationship but technology as such. "The contradictions and antagonisms inseparable from the capitalist employment of machinery, do not exist, they say, since they do not arise out of machinery, as such, but out of its capitalist employment" (Marx 1867, 465).

Nature as capital in accumulation processes doesn't produce new value; its value is transfused to commodities by human labor that creates surplus value. It has been termed constant capital by Marx because it doesn't create new value in the production process. Raw and auxiliary materials get used up in single stages of production; all of their value instantly enters the commodity, whereas machines are employed for a longer time period in production; their value gradually enters commodities. Machines are fixed in the production process for a certain time; hence, Marx terms them, along with buildings and equipment, fixed constant capital. Raw materials are more fluid and dynamic; hence Marx terms them circulating constant capital.

Capital accumulation is based on constant and variable capital as inputs of production; hence, it consumes natural resources as raw materials (both in the form of principal substances of goods and accessory raw materials), and the longer it continues to be oriented primarily on surplus value and profit, nonrenewable resources will continue to diminish. The goods produced in these processes are partly returned to nature after consumption in the form of nonrecyclable waste. Waste and scarcity of natural resources cause costs for society, but capital normally doesn't pay for these results of capitalist production; hence, it can increase profit by omitting expenditures for ecological restoration and putting these burdens on society. Capital is keen on reducing the costs of labor, nature, transport, rent, health, education, and so on, in order to lower its investment costs, which in turn increases profit. Nature in the form of raw materials functions as cheap or free resources for the economy; a heightened rhythm of capital formation results in increased consumption of nature and production of waste. Capital expands itself by technological progress, that is, by increasing productivity, that is, a certain amount of employed labor is able to process a larger quantity of raw materials in a shorter time period than at earlier historical stages of production. Capital is blind for ecological degradation as long as it is allowed to maximize profit by externalizing ecological costs. As a result of economic accumulation processes, there is an increase of the mass of constant capital and a decrease of the mass of variable capital, that is, the organic composition of capital increases and natural resources are continuously appropriated at an increasing pace. Ecological degradation impairs both society and the economy; capital accumulation is short-sighted and oriented on profit. Hence, it externalizes the costs of ecological destruction to society and nature.

Modern industrialism is unsustainable in two ways: (1) Accumulation processes result in the depletion of nonrenewable natural resources; limits to extraction and accumulation are herewith created. (2) Economic production and consumption result in residues of goods that are shoved into nature by society in the form of waste. Hence, ecological degradation includes both depletion and pollution. One can describe ecological degradation as a double process of the depletion of nature (in the direction where nature is appropriated by society) and the pollution of nature by society (in the direction where society transforms nature).

Unsustainable ecological development is a process by which depletion and pollution of nature by society cause the breakdown of more and more material (living and nonliving) cycles of self-organization in nature and create threats to the survival of the whole ecosystem that forms the material foundation of society. Hence, the destruction of nature also threatens the survival of society and humankind.

Just as capitalism gives more value to profit than to human life, it also gives more value to profit than to nature. Capitalism destroys both the life of human beings—who are reduced to function as labor power that doesn't control its own products and has to a certain extent work for free in order to survive—and of nature that forms the material foundation of human life processes. Hence, there is a double impairment of the life of exploited persons and groups; they are confronted by precarious social conditions and have to bear the effects of the destruction of the ecosphere, whereas the economically well-off classes can buy both undamaged social and natural conditions and enjoy a good life. Capital externalizes costs to nature, that is, one method for saving investment costs in order to increase profit is to use nature as a free tap and sink.

In the line of thought of ecological Marxism, James O'Connor (1998) has argued that, besides a contradiction between productive forces and production relations that takes on the form of a contradiction between production and realization of value, there is a "second contradiction of capitalism" (O'Connor 1998, 158–177), "the contradiction between capitalist production relations (and productive forces) and the conditions of capitalist production, or 'capitalist relations and forces of social reproduction'" (O'Connor 1998, 160). I doubt that there is only one or that there are only two contradiction(s) of capitalism because due to the complexity of capitalism it is unlikely that crises are always caused by one and the same antagonism in all crises situations occurring during the history of capitalism. But O'Connor makes an important point by stressing that there is an antagonism between natural forces and the mode of production. I would add that this is not only a capitalistic antagonism but one that has shaped the entire formation of modern society that has been based on a mode of production that has been made up by a destructive form of industrialism. Both the economy of capitalism and the Soviet system have been shaped by this "ecological antagonism".

The capitalist economy aims at the accumulation of money capital; its criterion of efficiency is not the reduction of entropy production but production of surplus value. With the accumulation of capital the entropy of the natural environment generally increases because capitalist production functions like a machine that devours ever more resources in order to disgorge ever more money capital. It is economically efficient to produce in ecologically unsustainable ways; the natural global commons are increasingly used up and polluted by the processes of capital accumulation. The latter is only possible due to increasing inputs of energetic and natural resources. The economic expansiveness of the modern economy is at the root of ecological problems; capitalism treats nature as a tap and a sink.

Alternative energy forms and ecotechnologies don't seem to be real options for the capitalist system because they are much less economically profitable than fossil and nuclear energy. Besides the problem of the limitation of natural resources, it seems questionable that the capitalist production model that is based on mass production and mass consumption that enable capital accumulation could reduce the amount of waste generated by the superabundance of commodities without impairing economic profitability. Hence, capitalistic economic rationality seems to antagonistically contradict ecological sustainability. A true alternative only seems to be the introduction of new technological systems based on renewable resources and energy forms and a solar revolution that requires a fundamental institutional change and an alternative economic and political model.

Marx anticipated the idea of sustainable development (of nature and society): He argues that in a free society the globe must be improved by human beings and passed on to succeeding generations in such a condition. "From the standpoint of a higher economic form of society, private ownership of the globe by single individuals will appear quite as absurd as private ownership of one man by another. Even a whole society, a nation, or even all simultaneously existing societies taken together, are not the owners of the globe. They are only its possessors, its usufructuaries, and, like *boni patres familias*, they must hand it down to succeeding generations in an improved condition" (Marx 1894, 784). If one compares this passage to the most common definition of sustainable development by the Brundtland Commission—"Sustainable development is development that meets the needs of the present without compromising the ability of future generations to meet their own needs" (World Commission on Environment and Development 1987, 43)—one finds a striking concurrence.

3.7 CONCLUSION

In chapter 3, I have outlined the foundations of a social theory that tries to bridge the gap between structures and practices by introducing dialectical dynamics, in which practices produce and reproduce structures that enable and constrain further practices. Self-organization and cooperation are at the heart of society and its dynamics. But modern society are estranged from its

Essence; it is dominated by competition, accumulation, class formation, and the asymmetric distribution of structures that take on the form of economic, political, and cultural capital. Modern society is shaped by an antagonism between cooperation and competition. Competition dominates over cooperation; capitalist economy aims at accumulating money, capitalist polity at accumulating power, and capitalist culture at accumulating definition capacities that shall secure hegemony. The result is an alienated society that is not controlled by its producers in all realms but by dominant classes. An alternative would be a truly cooperative and self-organized society that realizes society's Essence. As has been indicated by the rather detailed discussion of self-organization processes of protest movements, the latter are not only a realm of legitimizing domination and securing hegemony but also the active hope for struggles that aim at more cooperation, self-organization, and participation in society.

Based on this theoretical model of society, the further task of this work is to show how the identified subsystems of modern society have been transformed by the rise of Internet technologies and which role the basic capitalist antagonism between cooperation and competition plays in the "Internet society". A first step will be accomplished in the next chapter by discussing which key concept could be used for describing contemporary society.

4 The Rise of Transnational Informational Capitalism

In this chapter it is discussed which category should be employed for describing the overall character of contemporary society. First various concepts that have been used in scientific literature for discussing aspects of the "information society" will be introduced (4.1). The order presentation of the different key concepts is chronological. Then the notion of transnational network capitalism or transnational informational capitalism is introduced (4.2). Finally some conclusions are drawn (4.3).

4.1 CONCEPTUALIZING CONTEMPORARY SOCIETY

Concepts such as knowledge/information economy, postindustrial society, postmodern society, information society, network society, informational capitalism, network capitalism, and so on, show that it is an important sociological question in which society we live and which role technologies and information play in contemporary society. Both aspects are central issues of information society theory.

Fritz Machlup (1962) has introduced the concept of the knowledge industry. He has distinguished five sectors of the knowledge sector: education, research and development, mass media, information technologies, and information services. Based on this categorization he calculated that in 1959, 29 percent of the gross national product (GNP) in the United States had been produced in knowledge industries.

Peter Drucker (1969) has argued that there is a transition from an economy based on material goods to one based on knowledge. Marc Porat (1977) distinguishes a primary (information goods and services that are directly used in the production, distribution, or processing of information) and a secondary sector (information services produced for internal consumption by government and noninformation firms) of the information economy. Porat uses the total value added by the primary and secondary information sector to the GNP as an indicator for the information economy. The Organisation for Economic Co-operation and Development (OECD) has employed Porat's definition for calculating the share of the information economy in the total economy (e.g., OECD 1981, 1986). Based on such indicators, the information society has been defined as a society in which more than half of the GNP is produced and more than half of the employees are active in the information economy (Deutsch 1983).

For Daniel Bell, the number of employees producing services and information is an indicator for the informational character of a society. "A postindustrial society is based on services.... What counts is not raw muscle power, or energy, but information.... A post-industrial society is one in which the majority of those employed are not involved in the production of tangible goods" (Bell 1976, 127, 348).

Alain Touraine already spoke in 1971 of the postindustrial society. "The passage to postindustrial society takes place when investment results in the production of symbolic goods that modify values, needs, representations, far more than in the production of material goods or even of 'services'. Industrial society had transformed the means of production: postindustrial society changes the ends of production, that is, culture.... The decisive point here is that in postindustrial society all of the economic system is the object of intervention of society upon itself. That is why we can call it the programmed society, because this phrase captures its capacity to create models of management, production, organization, distribution, and consumption, so that such a society appears, at all its functional levels, as the product of an action exercised by the society itself, and not as the outcome of natural laws or cultural specificities" (Touraine 1988, 104). In the programmed society also the area of cultural reproduction, including aspects such as information, consumption, health, research, education, would be industrialized. That modern society is increasing its capacity to act upon itself means for Touraine that society is reinvesting ever larger parts of production and so produces and transforms itself. This idea is an early formulation of the notion of capitalism as self-referential economy.

Radovan Richta (1977) argues that society has been transformed into a scientific civilization based on services, education, and creative activities. This transformation would be the result of a scientific-technological revolution based on technological progress and the increasing importance of computer technology. Science and technology would become immediate forces of production.

Jean-François Lyotard (1984, 5) has argued that "knowledge has become the principal force of production over the last few decades". Knowledge would be transformed into a commodity. Lyotard says that postindustrial society makes knowledge accessible to the layman because knowledge and information technologies would diffuse into society and break up grand narratives of centralized structures and groups. Lyotard denotes these changing circumstances as postmodern condition or postmodern society.

Similarly to Bell, Peter Otto and Philipp Sonntag (1985) say that an information society is a society where the majority of employees work in information jobs, that is, they have to deal more with information, signals, symbols, and images than with energy and matter.

Nico Stehr (1994, 2002a, 2002b) says that in the knowledge society a majority of jobs involves working with knowledge. "Contemporary society may be described as a knowledge society based on the extensive penetration of all its spheres of life and institutions by scientific and technological knowledge" (Stehr 2002b, 18). For Stehr, knowledge is a capacity for social action. Science would become an immediate productive force; knowledge would no longer be primarily embodied in machines, but already appropriated nature that represents knowledge would be rearranged according to certain designs and programs (ibid., 41–46). For Stehr, the economy of a knowledge society is largely driven not by material inputs but by symbolic or knowledge-based inputs (ibid., 67); there would be a large number of professions that involve working with knowledge and a declining number of jobs that demand low cognitive skills as well as in manufacturing (Stehr 2002a).

Also, Alvin Toffler argues that knowledge is the central resource in the economy of the information society: "In a Third Wave economy, the central resource—a single word broadly encompassing data, information, images, symbols, culture, ideology, and values—is actionable knowledge" (Dyson, Gilder, Keyworth, and Toffler 1994).

In recent years the concept of the network society has gained importance in information society theory. For Manuel Castells, network logic is, besides information, pervasiveness, flexibility, and convergence, a central feature of the information technology paradigm (2000a, 69 sqq.). "One of the key features of informational society is the networking logic of its basic structure, which explains the use of the concept of 'network society'" (Castells 2000a, 21). "As an historical trend, dominant functions and processes in the Information Age are increasingly organized around networks. Networks constitute the new social morphology of our societies, and the diffusion of networking logic substantially modifies the operation and outcomes in processes of production, experience, power, and culture" (Castells 2000a, 500). For Castells, the network society is the result of informationalism, a new technological paradigm. Jan Van Dijk (2006) defines the network society as a "social formation with an infrastructure of social and media networks enabling its prime mode of organization at all levels (individual, group/organizational and societal). Increasingly, these networks link all units or parts of this formation (individuals, groups and organizations)" (Van Dijk 2006, 20). For Van Dijk, networks have become the nervous system of society, whereas Castells links the concept of the network society to capitalist transformation, Van Dijk sees it as the logical result of the increasing widening and thickening of networks in nature and society. Darin Barney (2004) uses the term for characterizing societies that exhibit two fundamental characteristics: "The first is the presence in those societies of sophisticated—almost exclusively digital—technologies of networked communication and information management/distribution, technologies which form the basic infrastructure mediating an increasing array of social, political and economic practices. . . . The second, arguably more intriguing, characteristic of network societies is the reproduction and institutionalization throughout (and between) those societies of networks as the basic form of human organization and relationship across a wide range of social, political and economic configurations and associations" (Barney 2004, 25sq.).

On the one hand, the notion of the network society points towards important changes of capitalism: Capital accumulation (in the sense of the accumulation of economic, political, and cultural capital as put forward by Bourdieu) is globalizing and we witness the rise of a flexible regime of accumulation (Harvey 1989). On the other hand, the concept is an ideology that obscures domination because phenomena such as structural unemployment, rising poverty, social exclusion, the deregulation of the welfare state and of labor rights, the lowering of wages in order to maximize profits, and so on, can easily be legitimized in a society where networks are seen as natural organization patterns. Hence, the problems of contemporary "network society" can be presented as inevitable and as something to which people have to adapt and not as a situation which is open to fundamental criticism and that requires political intervention and change (Barney 2004, 180). Steven Shaviro in this context speaks of "soft fascism" (Shaviro 2003, 4). The term *network society* also obscures that, first of all, we live in a capitalist society that is restructuring and changing its organizational form. Networks are characteristic for all systems; hence, they are not only specific for contemporary Western society. The historically novel quality is that in more and more systems, such as the economy, polity, and the Internet, we find transnational actors that operate on a global scale; they are transnational/global networks. Hence, it is more appropriate to speak of transnational/global capitalism, transnational/global network capitalism, or transnational/global informational capitalism in order to stress the dialectic of continuity and discontinuity and the role of information and new information and communication technologies (TNCs) in society.

The major critique of concepts such as information society, knowledge society, network society, postmodern society, postindustrial society, and so on, that has mainly been voiced by neo-Marxist scholars is that they create the impression that we have entered a completely new type of society. "If there is just more information then it is hard to understand why anyone should suggest that we have before us something radically new" (Webster 2002a, 259). Neo-Marxists such as Frank Webster argue that these approaches stress discontinuity, as if contemporary society had nothing in common with society as it was 100 or 150 years ago. Such assumptions would have ideological character because they would fit with the view that we can do nothing about change and have to adapt to existing political realities (Webster 2002b, 267). These neo-Marxist critics argue that contemporary society first of all is still a capitalist society oriented on accumulating economic, political, and cultural capital. They also acknowledge that information-society theories stress some important new qualities of society (globalization and informatization) but that they fail to show that these are attributes of overall capitalist structures. There would be a dialectic of continuity and discontinuity; capitalist development would have entered a new phase of development.

For describing contemporary society based on a dialectic of the old and the new, continuity and discontinuity, neo-Marxist scholars have suggested several terms, such as:

Digital capitalism (Schiller 2000; cf. also Glotz 1999): "Networks are directly generalizing the social and cultural range of the capitalist economy as never before" (Schiller 2000, xiv)

Virtual capitalism: The "combination of marketing and the new information technology will enable certain firms to obtain higher profit margins and larger market shares, and will thereby promote greater concentration and centralization of capital" (Dawson and Foster 1998, 63sq.).

High-tech capitalism (Haug 2003) or informatic capitalism (Fitzpatrick 2002)—to focus on the computer as a guiding technology that has transformed the productive forces of capitalism and has enabled a globalized economy.

Informational capitalism: Other scholars prefer to speak of information capitalism (Morris-Suzuki 1997) or informational capitalism (Castells 2000a; Fuchs 2005a; Schmiede 2006a, 2006b). Manuel Castells sees informationalism as a new technological paradigm (he speaks of a mode of development) characterized by "information generation, processing, and transmission" that have become "the fundamental sources of productivity and power" (Castells 2000a, 21). The "most decisive historical factor accelerating, channelling and shaping the information technology paradigm, and inducing its associated social forms, was/is the process of capitalist restructuring undertaken since the 1980s, so that the new techno-economic system can be adequately characterized as informational capitalism" (Castells 2000a, 18). Castells has added to theories of the information society the idea that in contemporary society dominant functions and processes are increasingly organized around networks that constitute the new social morphology of society (Castells 2000a, 500). Nicholas Garnham (2004) is critical of Castells and argues that the latter's account is technologically determinist because Castells points out that his approach is based on a dialectic of technology and society in which technology embodies society and society uses technology (Castells 2000a, 5sqq.). But Castells also makes clear that the rise of a new "mode of development" is shaped by capitalist production, that is, by society, which implies that technology isn't the only driving force of society.

Jan Van Dijk (1999) argues that in Castells's approach, networks are considered as actors, and content of society, actors, and struggling movements would be rather neglected, policy implications would be avoided, and a technological determinist approach advanced. I agree with Van Dijk that networks are relational categories that connect human actors, but as argued in the preceding paragraph I don't share the view that Castells's approach is a form of technodeterminsim.

The Empire: Antonio Negri and Michael Hardt argue that contemporary society is an Empire that is characterized by a singular global logic of capitalist domination that is based on immaterial labor. With the concept of immaterial labor, Negri and Hardt introduce ideas of information society discourse into their Marxist account of contemporary capitalism. Immaterial labor would be labor "that creates immaterial products, such as knowledge, information, communication, a relationship, or an emotional response" (Hardt and Negri 2005, 108; cf. also 2000, 280–303), or services, cultural products, knowledge (Hardt and Negri 2000, 290). There would be two forms: intellectual labor that produces ideas, symbols, codes, texts, linguistic figures, images, and so on; and affective labor that produces and manipulates affects such as a feeling of ease, well-being, satisfaction, excitement, passion, joy, sadness, and so on (ibid.).

In *Multitude* Hardt and Negri (2005) speak of three forms of immaterial labor: communication, symbolic analysis, and the manipulation of affects. "Immaterial" labor is a problematic term because it implies that there is a material and a non-material—i.e., spiritual—part of the world. This either means that spirit is the substance of the world or that there are two independent substances—matter and spirit—in the world. Hence the concept is either a form of a monistic philosophical idealism or a form of a dualistic philosophical framework. In any case, it is a non-materialistic concept. A dynamic materialistic philosophical approach on society argues that the whole universe is organizing itself by the dynamic movement and active self-development of matter, it is monistic, but at the same time dynamic. The dynamic interaction of material systems produces higher forms of systemic organization and systemic levels of organization that have emergent qualities. Hence the human mind is just another form of the organization of matter, although one with specific emergent qualities. Hence there is no "immaterial labor"—human cognition and communication and its products are material because they are based on the brain's materiality and bodily mediations. "Immaterial labor" is like all labor material because it is activity that changes the state of real world systems. The difference to manual labor is that it doesn't primarily change the physical conditions of things, but the emotional and communicative aspects of human relations. A better term than immaterial labor is informational labor—cognitive, communicative, and cooperative labor (in contrast to manual labor).

Overall, neo-Marxist accounts of the information society have in common that they stress that knowledge, information technologies, and computer networks have played a role in the restructuration and globalization of capitalism and the emergence of a flexible regime of accumulation (Harvey 1989). They warn that new technologies are embedded into societal antagonisms that cause structural unemployment, rising poverty, social exclusion, the deregulation of the welfare state and of labor rights, the lowering of wages, warfare, and so on.

I prefer neo-Marxist terms to radical discontinuous terms like information society or postmodern society, but some of them convey the impression that technology (digital, virtual, high-technology) determines society, that is, that the relations of production are a linear result of the productive forces. Change in contemporary society affects forces and relations, structures and actions. Hence, I prefer to speak of knowledge capitalism, informational capitalism, or network capitalism in order to stress that knowledge work and information technologies shape capital production and accumulation in contemporary society.

Other than Marxist approaches that focus on the objective structural technological changes of capitalism, Carlo Vercellone (2007) sees the transformation of capitalism as a subjective turn and hence speaks of "cognitive capitalism," a formation that is characterized by "the hegemony of knowledges, by a diffuse intellectuality, and by the driving role of the production of knowledges by means of knowledges connected to the increasingly immaterial and cognitive character of labour" (Vercellone 2007, 16). There would be a "preponderance of the knowledges of living labour over knowledges incorporated in fixed capital and in corporate organization" (Vercellone 2007, 32). The emerging antagonism between the living knowledge of labor and the dead knowledge of fixed constant capital would cause a crisis of the law of value and an antagonism between capital's attempt to enforce the law of value artificially (e.g. by intellectual property rights) and the socialization of knowledge by its incorporation in the brains of the collective workers of the general intellect.

The rise of knowledge in production is neither only a subjective, nor only an objective transformation, but based on a subject-object-dialectic: The search of capital for new strategies and forms of capital accumulation transforms labour in such a way that cognitive, communicative, and cooperative labor forms a significant amount of overall labor time (a development enforced by the rise of the ideology of self-discipline of 'participatory management'), but at the same time this labor is heavily mediated by information technologies and produces to a certain extent tangible informational goods (as well as intangible informational services). The notion of informational capitalism grasps this subject–object–dialectic, it conceptualizes contemporary capitalism based on the rise of cognitive, communicative, and cooperative labor that is interconnected with the rise of technologies of and goods that objectify human cognition, communication, and cooperation. Informational capitalism is based on the dialectical interconnection of subjective knowledge and knowledge objectified in information technologies. That the role of technology doesn't vanish as claimed by Vercellone can e.g., by seen by the fact that among the worldwide largest corporations (measured by a composite index of sales, market value, assets, and profits, e.g., the Forbes Global 2000 list from 2007) there are not only financial, banking, insurance institutions, and oil corporations, but increasingly also information technology-producers like AT&T, Verizon Communications, IBM, Telefónica, Hewlett-Packard, Deutsche Telekom, Nippon, or Microsoft.

4.2 THE RISE OF TRANSNATIONAL INFORMATIONAL/NETWORK CAPITALISM

I consider the approach of the *Political Economy of Communication and the Media* as more suitable for analyzing contemporary society than theories of discontinuous development. Such an approach is characterized by addressing the nature of the relationship of media and communication systems to the broader structure of society; it looks at how capitalist structures, ownership, support mechanisms, and government policies influence media systems; the issues of social class and the concentration of ownership are considered as important (McChesney 1998). Relevant questions of the political economy of the media are, for example, "Who owns the media?" (Gomery 1989/1997); and "What economic functions do they serve?" (Smythe 1977/1997, 438). Political economy decenters the media; it avoids communication essentialism by situating media and communication in dominant structures of production and power (Mosco 1996). Generally speaking, the political economy of the media aims at "understanding the relations between the institutions of political economy and the processes of communication" (Melody 1993, 80). Most political economists will agree that in the analysis of media the "recognition that the mass media are first and foremost industrial and commercial organizations which produce and distribute commodities" (Murdock and Golding 1974/1997, 35sq.) is important and that the media should be analyzed as "economic entities with both a direct economic role as creators of surplus value through commodity production and exchange and an indirect role, through advertising, in the creation of surplus value within other sectors of commodity production" (Garnham 1990/1997, 61). Although not all political economists agree on the importance of the ideological dimension of the mass media (cf., e.g., Garnham 1990/1997), one can nonetheless say that in the political economy of the media the analysis of how mass media "disseminate ideas about economic and political structures" (ibid., 4) has been of relevance. One idea that needs to be added to these approaches is a Bourdieuian and Habermasian influence that the economic logic of capitalism has colonized other subsystems of society, which has resulted in a generalization of accumulation, capital, and political economy and the structuring of society as totality by instrumental reason and technological rationality. Robin Mansell (2004) has stressed that only a tiny part of research on new media is on aspects of political economy and power and that the political economy of new media perspective should be strengthened. I understand this book as a contribution to research on the political economy of new media, with a specific emphasis on a generalized concept of political economy that analyzes processes of accumulation and competition in society in general and how they relate to the Internet.

In order to explain the increasing importance of transnational networks, we have to take a closer look at the restructuration of capitalism during the last decades. The mode of development that dominated Western societies from the time after the Second World War until the mid-1970s was Fordist capitalism. Its mode of regulation can be characterized by qualities such as:

- State intervention into the economy
- Bureaucratization
- The welfare state
- State-planned monetary, fiscal, industry, research, growth, employment policies
- Acknowledgment of labor unions as political forces
- Corporatism
- "Security State"
- The system of Bretton Woods

The accumulation regime of Fordism—a system of standardized mass production and mass consumption—was based on Taylorism, characterized by qualities such as:

- Division of the production process
- Strict command and control
- Separation of manual and mental labor
- Optimization of the production process
- Standardization of tools, components, and goods
- Hierarchic and central organizational control by the management
- Centrally organized organizations
- Strict regulation of the working day

In the early 1970s, the Fordist mode of development of capitalism entered crisis (for a detailed discussion of the subsequent arguments on the crisis of Fordism, see Fuchs 2002). One of the reasons was that the hierarchical Taylorist model of organizing work reached its limits and promoted refusal of work and class struggle because the work force couldn't stand the permanent and extraordinary psychological and physical burdens. Other reasons were the technological and organizational limits the centralist Taylorist methods had reached. As a result, the growth rate of productivity decreased and wages (variable capital) and constant capital (costs of means of production) relatively increased. The centralized and hierarchic forms of economic organization increasingly proved to be inflexible and rigid. The costs of wage labor had increased relatively fast during the 1960s due to the power of the organized interest of the working class. The growth of productivity was relatively slow during the 1960s, the growth of wages relatively fast. These two factors negatively influenced profit rates. The upward pressure on variable capital caused by labor organization and the downward pressure on constant capital by the limits of Taylorism resulted in falling profit rates. The economic hegemony of the United States was questioned during the 1960s by the fast economic development of European countries and Japan. This competition, along with expenditures of the United States for financing the Vietnam war, resulted in a large budget deficit and in deficits of the balance of trade. The role of the US dollar as "world money" was increasingly questioned and finally the system of Bretton Woods broke down in the early 1970s. Stagflation appeared as a new economic phenomenon. The Keynesian policy of deficit spending was based on the assumption that the crises of capitalism could be overcome, but once the crisis of Fordism began and the profits fell, the state also entered crisis because it heavily depends on taxes that stem from the production process (taxation of wages and profits). The increasing international character of production came into conflict with the nationally organized policies of regulation. The antiwar movement, the students' protests, and the emergence of new social movements questioned the Fordist way of life. Taken together, all these tendencies produced an overall economic, political, and ideological crisis of world society. Fordism reached its end during the first half decade of the 1970s.

After the second world economic crisis in the mid 1970s, there was a transition from the Fordist to the post-Fordist mode of capitalist development. In order to increase profits, new strategies of accumulation and domination emerged; the main idea is to increase profits by putting pressure on nation states to lower wages and by decentralizing and globalizing the production process in order to reduce wage costs and investment and reproduction costs of capital so that variable and constant capital decrease, which can result in rising profits.

The regime of accumulation of post-Fordist capitalism has been termed flexible accumulation regime (Harvey 1989) or flexible specialization (Piore and Sabel 1984). Some aspects of the post-Fordist accumulation regime are:

- Customer-oriented production
- Teamwork
- Decentralization
- Flat hierarchies in corporations
- Simultaneous engineering
- Just-in-time-production and outsourcing
- Kanban system: only those parts that are needed are supplied
- Autonomation
- Networked units of production
- The rise of transnational corporations
- The triadization of world trade and capital investment

The role of the state has changed in post-Fordist society. When a social system enters crisis, it is determined that a new order will emerge, but it is not predetermined how that order will look. The outcome depends on social practices and struggles; it is influenced by the prior existing social structures in the sense that they condition a field of possibilities. The capitalist nation-state has been transformed from a Keynesian intervention state into a neoliberal competitive state. We have been witnessing the rise of a neoliberal mode of regulation characterized by some important qualities:

- The withdrawal of the state from all areas of social life.
- Destruction of the welfare state and of collective responsibility.
- The preaching of self-help, self-responsibility of the individual for his/her problems, and of the capability of the market to regulate itself without human intervention.
- Growth, productivity, and competition are presented as the only goals of human action.
- Old ultraliberal ideas are presented as modern and progressive.
- Homogenization of the money and finance markets under the dominance of a few nations.
- A new social Darwinist ideology that puts across the message that only the strong and remarkable survive in society and on the market is advanced.
- Establishment and institutionalization of a permanent insecurity of wages and living conditions ("flexploitation") and of an individualization of work contracts.
- State assistance and subsidies for large corporations.
- Neoliberal ideologies claim that the economy is independent from society, that the market is the best means of organizing production and distribution efficiently and equitably, and that globalization requires the minimization of state spending, especially for social security.
- Such developments are presented as something inescapable, self-evident, and being without alternatives.
- The neoliberal state creates the legal framework for flexible wages and flexible working times.
- Collective bargaining systems are increasingly superseded by systems at a sectoral, regional, or company level.
- The state tries to facilitate capital investment and technological progress by subsidies, R&D programs, funds, and institutional support.
- The transition to the information society has produced new areas of regulation such as data protection, data security, intellectual property rights, e-commerce, and cybercrime.
- The state increasingly tries to activate entrepreneurial thinking of the individual by creating new forms of self-dependence and self-employment, reducing unemployment benefits and welfare, tightening

eligibility criteria, installing sanctions and coercive activation programs ("workfare", "welfare to work").

- Pensions are increasingly cut and the retirement age lifted; private pension funds are encouraged.
- Universities are considered as enterprises and cooperation between universities and corporations is encouraged.
- Regulation is increasingly important on and shifted to the supranational, regional, and local level; networks/links between cities, regions, and federal states are established (also on a cross-border basis).
- Certain state functions are shifted to civil society (neocorporatism). Public enterprises and services are increasingly privatized and commercialized. Welfare is shifted from the private to the corporate level.
- TNCs have become important political actors and the state has transformed itself into a competitive nation-state (Cerny 1997; Hirsch 1995, 2002; Jessop 2002).

A central mechanism of Postfordist, neoliberal, informational capitalism is what David Harvey terms "accumulation by dispossession" through privatization and commodification of public assets, financialization, the creation, management, and manipulation of crises by institutions such as the IMF, and state redistribution from lower to upper classes through cutbacks in state expenditures and revisions of the tax code (Harvey 2005, 159–165; Harvey 2003, 137–182). Capitalism is a permanent accumulation by dispossession because the surplus value produced by labor is dispossessed by capital through economic property rights and economic coercion in order to generate profit. What is happening under neoliberalism is the dispossession of the commons in order to generate new spaces of accumulation and an intensified dispossession of income and wealth in order to raise profits. The effects are on the one hand the extension and intensification of economic colonization—the commodification of everything—and what I term the extension and intensification of alienation—the almost entire loss of control over economic property, political decision making, and value-definition by lower classes in all realms of life. The extension and intensification of alienation is brought about by a centralization of ownership, power, and cultural-definition capacities.

Toni Negri and Michael Hardt argue in their book *Empire* that in post-Fordism "sovereignty has taken a new form, composed of a series of national and supranational organisms united under a single logic of rule" (Hardt and Negri 2000, xii). They call this global system Empire and say that it is decentered, deterritorializing, encompasses the spatial totality, rules over the entire "civilized" world, and has no territorial boundaries that limit its reign. It is a "dynamic and flexible systemic structure that is articulated horizontally" (ibid., 13).

The increasing importance of computer networks and global network organizations is an instrumental result of capitalist development. Computer technology and the Internet weren't invented in economic but in military contexts and in respect to the Second World War (computer) and the cold war (Internet). But the societal diffusion of these technologies is due to the role they have played primarily for the economic restructuration of capitalism. Hence, it was the economic subsumption of computer technology and computer networks that caused their diffusion and the reorganization of capitalism. Computer networks are the technological foundation that has allowed the emergence of global network capitalism, that is, regimes of accumulation, regulation, and discipline that are helping to increasingly base the accumulation of economic, political, and cultural capital on transnational network organizations that make use of cyberspace and other new technologies for global coordination and communication.

The economic diffusion of information and communication technologies (ICTs) is related to the crisis of global Fordism. As a reaction to the relative fall of profit rates, computerization and automation have been put forward in order to save labor costs and to increase the rates of profit. ICTs are medium and result of the economic globalization of capitalism. On the one hand, they make the generation of temporal and spatial distance possible; hence, local processes are influenced by global ones and vice versa. ICTs make global communication and world trade easier. They push ahead globalization, decentralization, and flexibilization of production, are a medium of the territorial restructuring of capitalism. The generation of networks of production that are typical for transnational corporations has been advanced by ICTs; the latter are also a result of the economic movements of restructuring that are typical for capital. So ICTs are not only medium of globalization processes; they are also their results.

ICTs make outsourcing, rationalization, and decentralization of production, teamwork, the flexibilization of jobs, and the flattening of organizational hierarchies much easier. They have contributed to the shift of the employment sector from a focus of industrial jobs to service jobs. In most advanced countries the service sector today makes up two-thirds of total employment. The post-Fordist economy is a flexible regime of accumulation that is enabled by ICTs and is based on the outsourcing, decentralization, and "flexibilization" of production; lean management, just-in-time production, the flattening of internal hierarchies in corporations, small organizational units in corporations, delegation of decision making from upper hierarchical levels to lower ones, decentralization of organizational structures, teamwork, strategic alliances, innovation networks, semiautonomous working groups, network organizations, tertiarization and informatization of the economy, triadization of international trade and of capital export, participatory management, a new phase of economic globalization, diversified quality production, automation and rationalization mediated by computerized information and communication technologies (ICTs). Speculative ("fictive") capital that is detached from material production and constitutes fast, self-increasing, unstable ("bubble economy") global flows of capital, is gaining importance. It is due to the fact that ICTs dissolve temporal and spatial distances that corporations can flexibly manage production and make use of global interconnected flows of capital, technology, labor, and information. Network organization is a characteristic of the post-Fordist global economy: networks of firms, networks of suppliers and distributors, financial networks, strategic alliances, joint ventures, financial markets that are based on fast global flows of increasingly "immaterial" speculative capital that are transmitted and manipulated digitally by making use of network technology.

Globalization can generally be defined as the stretching of social relationships, that is, communication networks, in space-time, a globalizing social system enlarges its border in space-time; as a result, social relationships can be maintained across larger temporal and spatial distances (Fuchs 2003b). The spatial scale of society reaches from the individual as starting point to local immediate relationships, such as family, friendships, or colleagues, to local intermediary structural relationships, such as local city council, transmediary (national) structural relationships like institutions of the state or national markets, to international structural relationships like international agreements or the European Union, and finally global or transnational structural relationships of worldwide reach like the Internet, the world market or human rights (at least by idea). In modern society these processes of globalization are based on a logic of accumulation of natural resources, tools, money capital, power, and hegemony. The main problem that modern society tries to solve is how to accumulate ever more capital. Whenever an existing regime/mode of accumulation reaches its inherent limits and enters crisis, new strategies and areas of accumulation are needed in order to revert to ordered processes of accumulation. Hence, globalization is in modern society inherently driven by the logic of capital accumulation that results in the appropriation and production of new spaces and systems of accumulation. The antagonism between structures and actors characteristic for modern society (social structures are alienated from their producers, that is, they are controlled by certain groups that exclude others from control) results in a clash of estrangement and self-determination that is characteristic for all subsystems of modern society. The basic conflict is that many people can't cope with the increased complexity of the world because their lives are increasingly shaped by global alienated structures that are out of their reach and that they can't participate in.

Global network capitalism is based on a transnational organizational model; organizations cross national boundaries. The novel aspect is that organizations and social networks are increasingly globally distributed, that actors and substructures are located globally and change dynamically (new nodes can be continuously added and removed), and that the flows of capital, power, money, commodities, people, and information are processed globally at high speed. Global network capitalism is a nomadic dynamic system in the sense that it and its parts permanently reorganize by changing their boundaries and including or excluding various systems by either establishing links, unions, and alliances or getting rid of or ignoring those actors that don't serve or contribute to the overall aim of capital accumulation.

Human society is organized in space and time; it is organized within a natural environment (physical and biological space) that is socially constructed by human agents in social processes that produce meaning (social space). Networked computer usage has resulted in a real-time globalization of social relationships (Fuchs 2003b). Knowledge flows today transcend national borders; they result in the globalization, intensification, time-space-distanciation of social relationships (Giddens 1990), and establish a more intensive and extensive interconnection of humans (Robertson 1992). They cause a sort of supraterritoriality (Scholte 1999), time-space compression (Harvey 1989), action at a distance (Held, McGrew, Goldblatt, and Perraton 1999), and accelerating interdependence. Knowledge is today quite substantially detached from territorial space, it cannot be situated at a fixed and limited territorial location; it operates largely without regard to territorial distance—it transcends territorial space.

New knowledge-based technologies like the computer facilitate the delocalization and disembedding of communication in the sense of the generation of spatial and temporal distance. One of the main characteristics of knowledge-based technologies is that they increase the speed of delivery of data massively and hence are a medium of the time-space distanciation of communication. They contribute to the disembedding and delocalization of social systems and relationships and hence reshape society. But they also further the reeembedding and localization of disembedded social relationships, for example, the globally available information on the Internet is embedded into local cultural contexts of action by users. Globalization and localization are intrinsically coupled; Roland Robertson (1992) has suggested the term *glocalization* for this phenomenon.

The twentieth century has seen an unprecedented increase in intensity, extensity, and velocity of global communication that is closely related to the rise of radio, television, satellite transmission, the microelectronic revolution, and digital fibre-optic cable networks/digital data processing. The transatlantic cable of 1866 reduced the time of transmission of information between London and New York by over a week; the telephone increased the velocity of messages by a few minutes; the Internet reduced it not much at all in comparison to the telephone (Keohane and Nye 2000, 80). This doesn't imply that technological globalization is a myth but that one should also stress qualitative aspects such as new qualities of communication such as many-to-many communication, interactivity, hyperlinking, digital compression, multimedia, conversion, simulated virtual realities, the decontextualization and derealization of communication, implications of computer-mediated communication for the formation of identities, online cooperation, and so forth.

The common theme underlying Giddens's concept of disembedding (Giddens 1990), Castells's concepts of timeless time and the space of flows (Castells 1989, 2000a, 2000b, 2001, 2004), and Harvey's (1989) concept of time-space compression is that modern technologies such as the computer accelerate and flexiblize social relationships. The history of modern society is a history of globalization and of the technological acceleration of transportation (of data, capital, commodities, people) that makes the world a smaller place in the sense that it increasingly mediates social relationships more efficiently so that it appears like distances are disappearing. Technological progress has resulted in an increasing separation of the movements of information from those of its carriers; the movement of information gathered speed on a pace much faster than the travel of bodies (Bauman 1998, 14). Especially, transportation and communication technologies (railway, telegraph, broadcasting, automobile, TV, aviation, digital computer-based communication technology, and most recently digital network technology) have increased the speed of global flows of capital, commodities, power, communication, and information. The Earth has been increasingly transformed into a global communication network that affects all realms of society. Castells has stressed that in the "network society" a new type of space, the space of flows, emerges that replaces the space of places and is based on timeless time and placeless space. He considers global network capitalism not as existing out of space—an assumption that would have to result in the demise of the space concept—but giving rise to a transformation of space. One should add that this transformation means the emergence and an increasingly dominant function of transnational/global social spaces in economy, polity, and culture. The emerging global space is the spatial form of organization of global network capitalism; it consists of global technological systems and transnational (economic, political, cultural) organizations and institutions that enable global flows of capital, power, and ideology that create and permanently re-create a new transnational regime of domination.

Some scholars argue that networks are inherently nonhierarchic and inclusive (e.g., Deleuze and Guattari 1976; Goguen and Varela 1979), whereas others say that networks are not automatically politically progressive and participatory but can be segmented, centralized, and hierarchic (Castells 2000a, 2004; Van Dijk 2006; Hardt and Negri 2005). In network research a network is generally defined in very broad terms as a system of interlinked nodes that don't imply full connectivity and a symmetric flow of resources (Barabási 2003). Hence, in a network there can be hubs and centers that are of strategic importance because they have much more direct links from and to other nodes than other nodes; they store and centralize resources and hence also control the flow of resources throughout the network. A network is not necessarily a map (as argued by Deleuze and Guattari in regard to their concept of the rhizome) but can also be a tracing. A network can have different degrees of centrality and hierarchy; there can either be a rather polycentric, pluralistic, and decentralized structure, or there can be central actors that dominate the system. The degree of decentralization refers to the distribution or control of resources such as knowledge, activists, money, decision power, infrastructure, technologies, and cultural definition power. Geert Lovink (2005) argues that networking is "notworking" in the sense that it is not automatically progressive but is today indeed connected to problems and institutionalization mechanisms that result in new hierarchies and forms of control such as precarious labor conditions of many knowledge workers. Networks wouldn't dissolve power but transform it. Networks don't automatically annihilate domination and hierarchy; they flexibilize and mobilize hierarchy and domination. Lovink uses the term *organized networks* in order to point out that networks "are infected by power" (Lovink 2005, 18) and have "internal power relations" (ibid., 19). I understand the term as characterizing, on the one hand, the fact that networks are used in contemporary society as mechanisms of domination and, on the other hand, the need of a certain institutionalization of alternative networks because in order to progressively transform contemporary society a networked protest movement is in need of money, continuous funding, and power; it must go beyond voluntarism, loose relationships, and informality and hence must build more durable structures and strategies so that it can act as a real counterpower. This discussion reminds me of Herbert Marcuse's critique of the anarchism and informality of the New Left and the students' movement in the 1970s. Marcuse argued that the movement is in need of powerful, permanent institutions such as media, political, and educational organizations in order to really challenge domination. Marcuse has coined in this context the term *organized spontaneity* (Marcuse 2004, 109sq.; cf. Fuchs 2005a, 46, 84–87, 89–93). Self-organizing systems need triggers that initiate the dynamic emergence of order; there are ordered patterns as well as intervention. For alternative networks, this implies that self-organization can't be left to pure chance but needs to be organized and institutionalized to a certain extent. An appropriate political strategy is not, as John Holloway (2002) has argued, to "change the world without taking power" but to organize self-organization so that processes of self-empowerment can take place (cf. Fuchs 2005a, 84–87).

Networks and knowledge are closely connected. Networks form the morphology of dynamic systems; they characterize the elements and relations in a system (Fuchs 2007b). Knowledge characterizes the dynamic change of networks, how the nodes in the network interact and form new structures. Knowledge here is used interchangeably with the term (social) *information*, although in other literature sometimes knowledge is used in the sense of human capacities or practical information and information in the sense of information technology. In information science research (e.g., in the foundations of information science [FIS] community) the term *information* is generally used in a very general transdisciplinary sense, and knowledge as the manifestation of information in society (cf. Fuchs and Hofkirchner 2005). As networks and knowledge are closely related, the term *transnational network capitalism* is used interchangeably with the term *transnational information* (or knowledge) *capitalism.*

In order to show how knowledge is related to economic accumulation, I first want to summarize some of its basic characteristics:

- Knowledge is a manifestation of information in the human-social realm. Knowledge doesn't exist in nature as such; it is a human and cultural product.
- Cognition, communication, and cooperation are three aspects of knowledge (Hofkirchner 2002; Fuchs and Hofkirchner 2005).
- Knowledge exists both in the human brain and in social structures and artifacts. It has subjective and objective aspects that are mutually connected. Subjective and objective knowledge is constituted in social practices of active, knowledgeable human beings; knowledge is related to human practice. Hence, the main question of the sociology of knowledge is, according to Karl Mannheim: "What categories, what systematic conceptions are used by the different groups at a given stage in accounting for one and the same fact uncovered in the course of practical operations? And what are the tensions which arise in the attempt to fit these new facts into those categories and systematic conceptions?" (Mannheim 1952, 195, 147).
- Objective knowledge is stored in structures and enables time-space distanciation of social relationships. It reduces the complexity of social systems; foundations of human existence don't have to be reproduced permanently due to its storage function. Such storage mechanisms of social knowledge include rules, resources, technologies, property, decision power, norms, values, traditions, myths, worldviews, codes, routines, guidelines, databases, organizations, and institutions. Objective knowledge is a supraindividual structural entity (Willke 2001; Argyris and Schön 1996; Etzioni 1971; Sveiby 1997), but is based on human agency; it is medium and outcome of social actions; it constrains and enables human practices. Giddens (1981, 35, 39, 94sq., 144, 157–181; 1984, 180–185, 1985, 13sq., 172–197) argues in this context that there are storage capacities in society (such as human memory, tradition, myths, writing, notation, cities, lists, timetables, money, money capital, nations-states, communication and transportation technologies in general, and especially the rapid-transit transportation and electronic communication technologies [including electromagnetic telegraph, telephone, and computer-mediated communication]) that allow the storage of information on allocative and authorative resources across time-space distances.
- Individually acquired knowledge can be put to use efficiently by entering a social coordination and cooperation process. Synergetical advantages that could not be achieved on an individual basis can be gained by such a coordination of knowledge. Emergent knowledge and qualities

show up and are due to the synergies produced by the cooperating efforts of knowledgeable actors. Intelligent organizations are based on the effective use and management of emergent knowledge.

- Knowledge must be permanently enhanced and updated.
- Knowing is intrinsically coupled to not knowing: Heinz Von Foerster (1993; cf. also 1999, 62; 2002, 306) has stressed that there can be no absolute knowledge; there is much that we can't and don't know. The unknowable would consist of undeterminables and undecidables. If epistemology is a theory of knowledge or of understanding understanding, then one would also need a theory of the unknowable. Von Foerster calls such a theory *lethology*. This term is derived from Greek mythology in which one assumed that one must cross the river Lethe in order to reach the Elysium and that during this journey one would loose memory. In the knowledge-based society, scientific and technological knowledge produces risks and hence phenomena that we don't know and can't fully predict. Willke (2002) speaks in this context of a crisis of knowledge.
- Knowledge has relevance for a system and is constituted within and as part of human experiences (Willke 2001).
- Knowledge is a social, common, public good that has a historical character. Knowledge production is a social process. In order to produce new knowledge, one must refer to prior knowledge produced by others. Frequently knowledge production has a highly networked and cooperative character.
- Knowledge is a self-expanding resource but can be artificially transformed into a scarce resource (e.g., by intellectual property rights).
- Knowledge production is in many cases a cooperative and networked process.
- Public knowledge gains importance when it is distributed freely in high numbers; proprietary knowledge looses importance when the same happens to it.
- Knowledge is a nonsubstantial (*nichtstofflich*) process and good that is generally not used up by its manifold usage.
- Knowledge expands during its usage.
- Knowledge can be compressed.
- Knowledge can replace other economic resources.
- In fast networks, knowledge can be transported at the speed of light.
- Purchasers of knowledge only buy copies of the original data.
- The costs of reproducing knowledge are generally very low and are further diminished by technological innovations and progress.
- In contrast to capital, knowledge appreciates with use; its marginal utility increases with use.
- The depreciation of knowledge is purely moral; in contrast to most physical products, it isn't used up by usage, nonusage, or the effects of natural forces.

- Knowledge is dynamic and dialectic. Karl Mannheim's sociology of knowledge has stressed the historical character of knowledge. For Mannheim (1952), knowledge doesn't exist metaphysically outside or above history but is constituted in social processes. New knowledge would incorporate old knowledge; a higher level of knowledge would eliminate but also preserve the old system. New knowledge sublates old knowledge (Mannheim 1952, 170). "The attainment of new knowledge consists in incorporating new facts into the old framework of definitions and categories, and ascertaining their place therein" (Mannheim 1952, 148). Norbert Elias has stressed that knowledge is a process and has the "character of a structured flux" (Elias 1971, 364).
- Knowledge is a collective cultural heritage of humanity; parts of this heritage are used as the foundation for the production of new knowledge that enters the historical assets of society in order to be used as foundation for the production of further knowledge. Knowledge is a dynamic, self-perpetuating process; it is self-producing and self-organizing.
- Knowledge can't be measured. It emerges as a collective good from the cooperation of many networked individuals and groups that partly don't know each other (cf. Gorz 2000, 177; 2004).
- By digitization, knowledge stored on different media, such as records, videos, film, paper, or images, can be combined in a multimedium.

There are subjective concepts of knowledge (knowledge as cognition), objective ones (knowledge as transferable thing), dualistic ones (knowledge existing in two separated domains, an objective and a subjective one), and dialectical ones (Fuchs and Hofkirchner 2002). In dialectical approaches, knowledge is conceived as a dynamic process in which, based on subjective cognitive processes, social relations emerge (communication), in which new systems and qualities can be formed (cooperation). Knowledge in this concept is a threefold dialectical process of cognition, communication, and cooperation (Fuchs and Hofkirchner 2005). Knowledge is seen as a dynamic, relational social process; the triad can also be seen as one of the individual, social relations, and social systems. This corresponds to the three steps of development in Hegelian dialectics (being-in-itself/identity, being-for-another, being-in-and-for-itself) and to Peirce's triad of firstness, secondness, and thirdness. Such a dynamic understanding of knowledge has been grounded by the works of Klaus Fuchs-Kittowski (2002), who argues that information is a triad of form (syntax), content (semantics), and effects (pragmatics), and a process of transfiguring outside influences complexly into inner syntax structures (in-forming), interpretation, and evaluation. For me also Klaus Krippendorff's (1993; 2004) notion of information as distinctions drawn within a present domain that lead to distinctions that matter in another domain is a dynamic understanding.

All human labor is based on a dialectical interconnection of mind and body. Hence, it is both mental labor and manual labor. But nonetheless a distinction between mental labor and manual labor can be made: the first is mainly based on cognition, reflection, logical operations, and so on, the second on the human production of physical energy. All societies are based on human activity that produces subjective and objective knowledge. But nonetheless we don't characterize all types of societies as "knowledge-based societies" (KBS) or "knowledge societies". In the current phase of development of capitalism, all areas of society are to a certain extent shaped by knowledge, that is, by mental labor, cognition, communication, and cooperation. In knowledge capitalism, mental labor, social labor, that is, the production of social relationships by communicative and cooperative labor, affective labor, and the production and use of information technologies are of crucial importance. There is hegemony of mental over physical labor; knowledge has become a decisive factor of production and in the form of knowledge products a profitable commodity. Computers and Internet, as new systems of production, information, communication, and cooperation, shape all parts of society and accelerate the time-space distanciation of social and political relationships as well as of capitalist production and circulation (globalization). Although the current development phase of society can be distinguished from the industrial society, the knowledge society doesn't bring an end to industrial production, but its transformation. The knowledge society is not a postcapitalist societal development phase, but capitalism enters an informational mode of development. Knowledge in the sense of subjective (cognition), intersubjective (communication, cooperation), and objective knowledge (knowledge goods) has, just like physical labor, capital, and power, become a defining characteristic and mechanism of modern society. This manifests itself, for example, in a boom of service and knowledge industries, an increasing importance of innovation, universities, expertise, research, Internet and computer technologies, knowledge work, and knowledge products.

Just as letters, books, television, radio, telephone, fax, telegraph, and so on, the computer is a knowledge-based technology or medium. It is not just a medium of cognition and communication but also a system for production and cooperation. A particular feature of the computer is that it enables the convergence of traditional media in a single digital medium: knowledge representation in the computer can combine written text, spoken words, audio, video, and animations in one medium. This can be achieved by the digitization of the represented knowledge. The computer enables many-to-many communication; it is an interactive medium that allows new forms of cooperation and relationships across spatiotemporal distances. In respect to interactivity, the computer differs from traditional media. Traditional machines, as well as the computer, are an objectification of human knowledge; their technological structure is based on human knowledge produced by science. Manual labor and raw materials are the input of traditional machines such as the assembly line; their output, the product of a transformation process, consists of goods that are an objectification of manual labor. The input of a computer is mental labor that is transformed by binary operations; its output consists of knowledge products that are an objectification of mental labor.

4.3 CONCLUSION: COOPERATION AND COMPETITION IN TRANSNATIONAL NETWORK CAPITALISM

Networks shape systems in nature and society; they are structures of communication that are organized by producing and re-creating spaces as settings and contexts of interaction. Social space is the locale of human communication; it involves a setting of human bodies and artifacts, changing distances between humans and objects, certain borders, and communication technologies that allow the stretching of system boundaries in time-space. The history of communication technologies is a history of the stretching of social systems and their communication networks in time-space.

The need to find new strategies for executing corporate and political domination has resulted in a restructuration of capitalism that is characterized by the emergence of transnational, networked spaces in the economic, political, and cultural system and has been mediated by cyberspace as a tool of global coordination and communication. Economic, political, and cultural space have been restructured; they have become more fluid and dynamic, have enlarged their borders to a transnational scale, and handle the inclusion and exclusion of nodes in flexible ways. These networks are complex due to the high number of nodes (individuals, enterprises, teams, political actors, etc.) that can be involved and the high speed at which a high number of resources is produced and transported within them. But global network capitalism is based on structural inequalities; it is made up of segmented spaces in which central hubs (transnational corporations, certain political actors, regions, countries, Western lifestyles, and worldviews) centralize the production, control, and flows of economic, political, and cultural capital (property, power, definition capacities). This segmentation is an expression of the overall competitive character of contemporary society.

Competitive networks of corporate power, political domination, and cultural homogenization are the reality of the "network society". But spaces not only have actual realities; they also have potential realities, that is, each space is also a space of its own possible future state; it is a state of possibilities (a state space with current and possible future trajectories) that is enabled and constrained by the existing network structures. Global network capitalism has created novel methods and qualities of domination and competition, but at the same time it has advanced new opportunities for cooperation and participation that question domination and point towards alternative futures. It is an antagonistic space that by producing new networks of domination also produces potential networks of liberation that undermine the centralization of wealth and power that has thus far been achieved by networking. The networking, globalization, and informatization of capitalism is shaped by the modern antagonism between competition and cooperation; global network capitalism has both potentials for new forms of cooperation and competition that today exist simultaneously and stand in antagonism. Today, competition dominates cooperation. Global network capitalism is characterized by an economic antagonism between proprietary and open space, a political antagonism between dominated and participatory space, and a cultural antagonism between one-dimensional and wise space (cf. Fuchs 2003b). Network logic in contemporary capitalism has effects that advance both cooperative, inclusive potentials and the overall competitive and exclusive character of society. The central conflicts and struggles of modern society (on property, power, and skills) have been transformed in the Information Age; transnational networks and knowledge have become strategic resources in these struggles. Network commons challenges network capitalism, networked control is challenged by networked participation, and networked manipulation is challenged by networked wisdom.

The dialectical antagonism between cooperation and competition lies at the heart of informational capitalism. In the subsequent chapters, this antagonism will be characterized and analyzed concerning the relationship of the Internet and the different subsystems of contemporary society that have been identified in chapter 3. For doing so, we first need to find an understanding of the Internet, which shall be accomplished in the next chapter.

5 Social Internet Dynamics

For discussing what the Internet is, how it can be conceived as a dynamic system, and which role cooperation plays in it, first its dynamic character is discussed (5.1), then the early World Wide Web (Web 1.0) is analyzed as a self-organizing system (5.2), Web 2.0 and social software (5.3) and their aspects of cooperation are characterized (5.3), notions of cyberspace and virtual reality are introduced (5.4), and some conclusions are drawn (5.5).

5.1 THE INTERNET AS A DYNAMIC TECHNO-SOCIAL SYSTEM

It is well known that the Internet originated from the ARPANet, a decentralized military computer-based communication network that was set up in the 1960s by the US government and was expected to survive a nuclear attack. Important Internet-based applications have been, for example, Telnet, FTP, Gopher, LISTSERV, Archie, Finger, IRC, Talk, Usenet, MUD, Email, X.500, WHOIS, WAIS, Veronica, Ping, Netserv, Netfind, Knowbot, Hytelnet. Probably the best-known and most influential Internet-based technology is the World Wide Web (WWW), which was created by Tim Berners-Lee at CERN in 1990. This concept allows a user-friendly browsing in a shared information space by making use of a Web browser like Mosaic, Internet Explorer, Netscape, Lynx, Viola, Opera, Mozilla, or Safari. The user friendliness of the WWW is one of the factors that contributed to the boom of the Internet. The Internet is generally considered as a global technological system of networked computer networks, a network of computer networks that works based on the TCP/IP protocol. Standard definitions, such as the one of the Federal Networking Council or the RFC 2026 of the Internet Engineering Taskforce (IETF), have advanced such a techno-deterministic understanding that forgets that knowledgeable human activities make the Internet work; the technological structure can't be separated from its human use and the permanent creation and communication of meaningful information through the Internet. A purely technical understanding conceives the Internet as static system because computer technologies are strictly mechanic systems;

in computational logic the outputs are predetermined; there is no freedom, chance, irreducibility, unpredictability, and indeterminacy.

The Internet is a global techno-social system that is based on a global, decentralized technological structure consisting of networked computer networks that store objectified human knowledge. Human actors permanently re-create this global knowledge storage mechanism by producing new informational content, communicating, and consuming existing informational content in the system. The technological infrastructure enables and constrains human cognition, communication, and cooperation. The self-organization of the Internet is based on a self-referential loop of self-organization (see fig. 5.1): In a top-down process the existing technological structure that stores objective human knowledge enables human activity, that is, there is the subjectification of objective knowledge in human brains when one consumes knowledge that is represented in the Internet or communicates or cooperates with other human beings via the Internet. In this sense the technological structure mediates human activities and results in emergent aspects of thinking and action. In a bottom-up-process, human beings act, communicate, or cooperate in such a way that the knowledge stored by the technological structure changes, is actualized, and extended. Here objective knowledge emerges from the cooperation of human actors; the actors coordinate their communication in such a way that parts of their

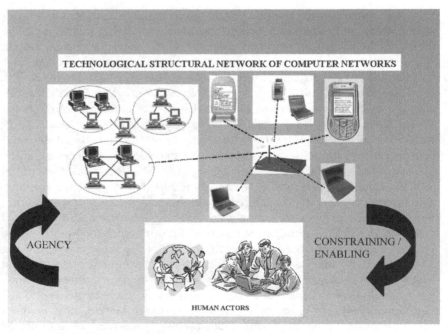

Figure 5.1 The Internet as dynamic techno-social system.

subjective knowledge are synergetically shared and coordinated in such a way that new embedded and objectified knowledge emerges that is stored in the technological structure. This double process of bottom-up emergence of objective knowledge and top-down emergence of subjective knowledge constitutes the basic productive loop that is characteristic for the self-organization of the Internet system.

The Internet consists of both a technological infrastructure and communicating human actors. The technical structure is medium and outcome of human agency; it enables and constrains human activity and thinking and is the result of productive social communication and cooperation processes. The technological structure/part of the Internet enables and constrains human communication and is itself produced and permanently reproduced by the human communicative part of the Internet. The Internet consists of a technological and a social subsystem that both have a networked character. Together these two parts form a techno-social system; the technological structure is a structural mass medium that produces and reproduces networked communicative and cooperative actions and is itself produced and reproduced by such practices. The Internet is not a mass medium; only its technological part functions as a reflexive medium of cognition, communication, and cooperation.

5.2 WEB 1.0 AS DYNAMIC TECHNO-SOCIAL SYSTEM

The first phase of the development of the World Wide Web (WWW, Web 1.0) was dominated by hyperlinked textual structures. In which sense is Web 1.0 a dynamic self-organizing system? Emergence in the WWW means emergence of new Web sites. The structure of the Web changes dynamically, pages disappear, reappear in alternative forms, are mirrored on other servers, new pages appear, and so on. The detailed structure of the Web can't be known, predicted, and controlled to a full extent; its complexity steadily increases with its growth. The number of Web sites and links in the WWW is a measure of this complexity. When a new Web site is introduced, it is embedded into the existing Web and extends the latter. In order for a Web page to be "visible" on the net, links must be created that lead from and to this Web page. Hence, each Web page is based on other Web sites, search engines, link lists, and so on, but it can't be reduced to them (except in the case when one page is an exact mirror of another) because it has its own specific content and structure. Hence, one can say that in the self-organization of the WWW, new Web pages emerge out of other Web pages. The Web "is continuously expanding, moving, and transforming itself. The World Wide Web is a flux" (Lévy 2001, 140). The emergence and self-organization of the WWW is not a purely technological process; it is in need of active, knowledgeable human actors who create the structure of the WWW, links, new Web sites, and so on, and browse the Web. Without human beings, the Web is a dead mechanical entity that is not self-organizing. One can only speak of the self-organization of the WWW when one considers it not as a techno-logical system but a techno-social system in which human beings make use of a technological medium in order to act, communicate, and cooperate. The Web grows and self-organizes only through human activity. The metaphor of the Internet as a carpet that is woven and permanently rewoven by millions of people that are distributed all over the world describes cyberspace's dynamic nature. It is a carpet of networked, shared meaningful information that permanently re-creates itself and permanently reemerges.

Web sites are written in a specific language, the Hypertext Markup Language (HTML). Users make use of tools like Dreamweaver, FrontPage, Homesite, and so on, in order to produce HTML code. A hypertext is a network of informational nodes that contain informational pieces (texts, images, sounds, videos, animations) and are interlinked. Hypertext has a distributed nature; it can consist of texts, images, sounds, videos, animations, and so on (hence, one also speaks of hypermedia) that are not necessarily stored on one computer, but all over the WWW, and of links to distributed Web pages. Links from all over the WWW lead to a hypertext; it can be produced jointly and at a distance by making use of cooperative work systems; it can be used and maybe extended or changed by people who are globally distributed. The hypertext is essentially dynamic, fluid, transitory; it has no fixed place. A specific hypertext forms a node in the Web that develops dynamically in such a way that links from and to this hypertext frequently appear and disappear.

Creating links is the essential operation of networking in Web 1.0. It is a self-referential medium in the sense that when a new link is created the system refers to itself by actualizing its content. Each Web page refers to a number of other Web pages that again refer to other Web pages, and so on. Self-referentiality is the essential nature of the hypertext; by creating links a hypertext is connected to a hypertext; the hypertext system of the WWW is referring to itself. This self-referentiality is based on human activities, that is, on the creation of new hypertexts that are embedded into the existing system. The interlinked structure of the WWW defines possible paths that are discovered by active human beings that browse the Web and create their own personal path. "A hypertext is a matrix of potential texts, only some of which will be realized through interaction with a user" (Lévy 1998, 52). A hypertext system reproduces itself by the permanent self-reference of the category text.

Designing a Web page is an essentially human creative activity, not only a technological one. Not only the production of new Web sites is a central feature of the self-reproduction of the Internet; also, its permanent usage as well as computer-mediated human communication and cooperation is important and productive. Certain subsystems of the Internet, such as specific chats, bulletin-board systems, newsgroups, mailing lists, and so on, can maintain and reproduce themselves only due to the fact that human actors make use of the technological structure as a medium of their symbolic exchange. As long as they communicate, the Internet is alive and organizes itself. The order of the system emerges due to communicative synergies. As soon as they stop using it, the specific self-organizing subsystem of the Internet breaks down. It might still be available technologically, but without meaningful communicated information it is not self-organizing. There is also the possibility that the self-organization of such a subsystem ends because it is technologically disconnected from the Internet. The Internet and the WWW consist of many different self-organizing spaces that are organized around special interests. Many of these subsystems are interlinked; they are not fully communicatively autonomous.

Due to its globally distributed, decentralized technical structure, small causes can have large effects in the Internet and can amplify themselves through the Net. Probably the best examples are computer viruses that spread over the Internet. These small pieces of code can do hardly any damage in a nonnetworked, local computer environment, but it can cause a lot of damage at distant places when it enters the Internet. The same is true for communication. Communicating specific information over the Internet can, under certain circumstances, cause social transformation in many distant places. The Internet enables action- and communication-at-a-distance. An example (Lubbers 1997): When in 1995 Steven Fishman published data and a declaration in lieu of oath on the Dutch server Xs4all.nl that documented the dubious tactics of Scientology, the sect threatened to prosecute Fishman and the Internet service provider (ISP). It aimed at censoring how former members felt about the practices of Scientology. After Scientology effected a search warrant of Xs4all's headquarters, a global campaign was started by making use of the Internet. People all over the world joined the coalition and mirrored the incriminated data. Hence Scientology was unable to sue all of these individuals and ISPs and finally had to abandon the lawsuit against Xs4all. This example shows that small events or pieces of data (like a single Web page about Scientology) can spread over the Internet and cause large effects like a protest campaign that transforms society.

5.3 THE RISE OF WEB 2.0 AND WEB 3.0: COMMUNICATION AND COOPERATION ONLINE

The era of web 1.0 was one of text-based websites, although there were of course also communicative features, the Internet was dominated by the phenomenon that everyone could easily publish his information online and embed it into the global web. Web 1.0 was predominantly a system of cognition. Since the millennium, the character of the web has been successively changing. With the rise of new heavily frequented platforms such as MySpace, YouTube, Facebook, Wikipedia, Friendster, etc., communication and cooperation have become more important features of the web. According to the three aspects of information a web dominated by cognition is termed web 1.0, a web dominated by communication web 2.0, and a web dominated by cooperation web 3.0[1]. My impression is that around 2005, web 2.0 fully emerged and that the web has entered a new phase of development. Web 3.0 does not yet exist, but it shines forth in online cooperation systems such as Wikipedia, wikis, Writely, or Google Docs & Spreadsheets. All software is social in the sense that it is a product of social processes, it is produced by humans in social relations, objectifies knowledge produced in society, and is applied and used in social systems. All software applications are hence social in the sense of Durkheim's social facts, they are fixed and objectified social structures, present even if a user sits in front of a screen alone and browses information on the World Wide Web because according to Durkheim they have an existence of their own independent of individual manifestations. Web pages and other web 1.0 technologies are Durkheimian social facts: "A social fact is every way of acting, fixed or not, capable of exercising on the individual an external constraint; or again, every way of acting which is general throughout a given society, while at the same time existing in its own right independent of its individual manifestations" (Durkheim 1982, 59).

For Max Weber not all action is social, but only in so far as it is oriented on and takes account of the behavior of others. "The term 'social relationship' will be used to denote the behavior of a plurality of actors insofar as, in its meaningful content, the action of each takes account of that of the others and is oriented in these terms" (Weber 1978, 26). "Not every kind of action, even of overt action, is 'social' in the sense of the present discussion. Overt action is not social if it is oriented solely to the behavior of inanimate objects. For example, religious behavior is not social if it is simply a matter of contemplation or of solitary prayer. (. . .) Not every type of contact of human beings has a social character; this is rather confined to cases where the actor's behavior is meaningfully oriented to that of others" (Weber 1978, 22sq).

Browsing the web hence for Weber is a non-social action, but communicating (e.g.,, in a chat room, by instant messaging, or by voice-over-ip) or cooperating (e.g.,, by collectively writing a wiki) with others on the Internet is social action in the Weberian sense. Web 2.0 and 3.0 signify an expansion of the meaning of sociality in the Internet from a Durkheimian and non-Weberian towards a Durkheimian and Weberian understanding. Hence the term social software is both Durkheimian and Weberian in contrast to forms of Web 1.0 software that are Durkheimian and non-Weberian.

Web 3.0 technologies like wikis are not only communicative, but also cooperative. Web 3.0 reflects an understanding of the social as cooperation that can be traced back in its most pure form to the works of Marx. For Marx and Engels cooperation is the essence of the social: "By social we understand the cooperation of several individuals, no matter under what conditions, in what manner and to what end. It follows from this that a certain mode of production, or industrial stage, is always combined with a certain mode of cooperation, or social stage, and this mode of cooperation is itself a 'productive force' " (Marx and Engels 1846, 30).

Capitalists would exploit the collective labor of many workers in the form of the appropriation of surplus value and cooperation hence would turn into alienated labor. This antagonism between the cooperative character of production and private appropriation that is advanced by the capitalist development of the productive forces would be a factor that constitutes crises of capitalism and points towards and anticipates a cooperative society. The true species-being would only be possible if man "really brings out all his *species*-powers—something which in turn is only possible through the cooperative action of all of mankind" (Marx 1844, 574). For Marx a cooperative society is the realization of the cooperative Essence of humans and society. Marx speaks of such transformed conditions as "the cooperative society based on common ownership of the means of production" (Marx 1875, 19) in which "the springs of cooperative wealth flow more abundantly" (Marx 1875, 21).

The basic idea underlying Marx's notion of cooperation is that many human beings work together in order to produce goods that satisfy human needs and that hence also ownership of the means of production should be cooperative. The idea of goods as emergent qualities of human cooperation is reflected in definitions of social software and the new web that focus on the qualities of collaboration and collective intelligence (e.g., O'Reilly 2005, Kolbitsch and Maurer 2006, Tapscott and Williams 2006).

Social networking platforms (e.g., MySpace) are focused on online communication and have the potential to foster virtual communities. Community is on the one hand a feature of durable online communication, on the other hand certain online communities (but not all of them as there are also competitive stratification mechanisms present today) or parts of it are characterized by virtual togetherness, friendship, love, altruism—they gain an aspect of affective cooperation. Social networking hence is always an aspect of web 2.0 and hence based on a Weberian understanding of the social—in the case of an affective cooperative virtual community also an understanding of the social as a community in the sense of Tönnies (focused on feelings of togetherness, cf. section 9.2 for a detailed discussion of the notions of community and virtual community) is present. Web 2.0 then turns into web 3.0.

Web 1.0 is based on an understanding of the social as Durkheimian social facts, Web 2.0 adds the Weberian idea of communication, Web 3.0 the Marxian idea of collective cooperative production and Tönnies' idea of communities.

- Web 1.0 is a tool for thought.
- Web 2.0 is a medium for human communication.
- Web 3.0 technologies are networked digital technologies that support human cooperation.

What is termed "social software", "web 2.0" or "web 3.0" reflects a shift from Durkheimian sociality towards Weberian, Marxian, and Tönnian notions of the social in the world of computing and society.

Peter Kollock and Marc Smith (1999) distinguish 6 forms of online communication tools: e-mail/discussion lists (asynchronous, centralized control, push media), usenet/BBBs (asynchronous, pull media), text chat (synchronous, centralized control), MUDs (synchronous text-based visual realities), WWW Web sites (multimedia interfaces for hosting synchronous and asynchronous online information and communication), and graphical worlds (synchronous online conversations enhanced by multimedia). But meanwhile the range of tools has become more complex, so, for example, blogs and wikis must be added. Saveri, Rheingold and Vian (2005) identify eight clusters of technologies of cooperation, but they don't provide theoretical criteria that ground the typology and the differences of these technologies. Furthermore, no distinction between cooperating machines (in the case of self-organizing mesh networks and community computing grids) and cooperating humans (in the case of the other five technologies) is made.

Information is a threefold process of cognition, communication, and cooperation (Hofkirchner 2002; Fuchs and Hofkirchner 2005): A single individual (cognitive level) connects itself by using certain mediating systems to another individual and a feedback is established (communication). From communication processes a system of shared or jointly produced resources can emerge (cooperation). Networked computer technology enables cognition, communication, and cooperation processes that are spatially disembedded and either temporally synchronized or not. The level of information (cognition, communication, cooperation) and the type of temporality characterize networked computer technologies. Synchronous temporality means that users are active at the same time ("in real time"), asynchronous temporality that the users' actions are temporally disembedded. In both cases, technology enables a spatial disembedding of users. Another aspect of network technologies is the type of relationship that they enable: one-to-one relationships (o2o), one-to-many relationships (o2m), or many-to-many relationships (m2m). O2o technologies allow one user to reach one other, o2m-technologies allow one to reach many others, and m2m-technologies allow many users to reach many others. The following table provides a typology of Internet technologies characteristic for each of the three aspects of information.

In addition to cognition, communication and cooperation are also becoming more important aspects of the Internet. That has been stressed recently by the concepts of social software and Web 2.0 that focus on the transition from information consumption and publishing to applications that support more communication, cooperation, and participation on the Internet (O'Reilly 2005). Tim O'Reilly (2005) has stressed that the transition from Web 1.0 to Web 2.0 means a change from the Web as a publishing platform to a tool supporting communication. Communication applications

Table 5.1 A Typology of Internet Technologies

	Synchronous	*Asynchronous*
Cognition (Internet 1.0)	Peer-to-peer networks for filesharing (o2o, m2o, o2m)	Web sites (o2m), online journals (o2m, m2m), alternative online publishing (e.g., Indymedia, Alternet, o2m, m2m), online archives (o2m, m2m), e-portfolio (o2m), Internet radio/podcasting (02m) social bookmarking (o2m, m2m) social citation (o2m, m2m) electronic calendar (o2m) real simple syndication (RSS, o2m)
Communication (Internet 2.0)	Chat (o2o, o2m, m2m), instant messaging (o2o, o2m), Voiceover IP (o2o, o2m, m2m), video conferencing systems (o2o, o2m, m2m)	E-mail (o2o, o2m), mailing-lists (m2m), bulletin-board systems (usenet, m2m), Web-based discussion boards (m2m), blogs (o2m, m2m), video blogs (v-blogs)/photo blogs (o2m, m2m), group blogs (m2m), social network services (e.g., online dating and friendship services like MySpace, o2o), social guides (o2m, m2m), mobile telecommunication (e.g., SMS and cellular phones; o2o, o2m), online rating, evaluation, and recommendation systems (e.g., Tripadvisor, eBay and Amazon Market Place user ratings, listing of similar items at Amazon, o2m, m2m)
Cooperation (Internet 3.0)	Multiuser Dungeons (MUDs) (o2o, o2m, m2m), MUDs Object-Oriented (MOOs) (o2o, o2m, m2m), graphical worlds (o2o, o2m, m2m), MMORPG (Massive Multiplayer Online Roleplaying Games, o2o, o2m, m2m) Synchronous groupware (collaborative real-time editing shared whiteboards, shared application programs, m2m)	Wikis (m2m), shared workspace systems (e.g., BSCW) (m2m), asynchronous groupware (m2m), knowledge communities (e.g., Wikipedia)

have been supported by the Internet since its beginning, but at least since the rise of the World Wide Web it has been dominated by information provision applications. With the rising importance of social software, the character of the WWW changes; many-to-many communication and cooperative knowledge production seem to become new dominant qualities of the Web. Social software (like discussion boards, mailing lists, wikis, blogs) has become a central foundation of Internet activities. "Social software is a set of tools that enable group-forming networks to emerge quickly. It includes numerous media, utilities, and applications that empower individual efforts, link individuals together into larger aggregates, interconnect groups, provide metadata about network dynamics, flows, and traffic, allowing social networks to form, clump, become visible, and be measured, tracked, and interconnected" (Saveri, Rheingold, and Vian 2005, 22).

Maria Bakardjieva (2005) distinguishes between a rationalistic model of Internet communication and committed online communities. In the first model, users focus on finding information for instrumental reasons; in the second model, the central value is sociability, and an important characteristic is interpersonal commitment. The first would be a consumption model of the Internet, the other a community model. "The qualitative distinction between the two models lies in the absence or presence of users' involvement with one another" (Bakardjieva 2005, 180). I think that these two social models can be mapped to the two versions of the Web: Web 1.0 was more oriented on infosumers; Web 2.0 (and Web 3.0) is more oriented on community or what Bakardjieva calls virtual togetherness.

A blog is a Web site on which users can post messages that are chronologically stored and other users can comment on these entries. It is a sort of online diary that has public character and hence breaks down the border between private and public. The main difference between mailing lists/newsgroups and a blog is that a blog is always Web-based and archived in reverse chronological order (newest entries first). A wiki is a dynamic Website on which all pages can be edited by all users with the help of special editing tools in which users make use of a wiki markup language.

In the self-organization of Web 1.0, what permanently emerges are new Web sites and links. The users permanently browse Web sites and links and hence give meaning to the provided data (see section 5.2). In newsgroups and mailing lists, self-organization means the dynamic emergence of new postings and replies. In blogs, self-organization is achieved by the emergence of new postings by one author in the case of an individual blog and by many authors in the case of group blogs, by the browsing of entries, and by the production of comments to postings by many users. In a wiki, self-organization is achieved by permanent changes to content pages by many different authors, and new pages of text emerge dynamically. The entity that is permanently produced and reproduced is the overall hypertext structure in the WWW, postings in the case of newsgroups, mailing lists, blogs, and content pages in the case of wikis. The World Wide Web and wikis are page-centered, but a single wiki page is much more dynamic than most Web pages and allows many/all users to permanently make changes, whereas ownership of a Web page is individualized. If one could compare technologies metaphorically to political systems, then a Web page would be close to the capitalist idea of individual property in the means of production and wikis close to the communist idea of public property in the means of production. Mailing lists, newsgroups, and blogs are post-centered; individual contributions in the form of single messages and comments that have one author are the units of reproduction of the overall system.

Table 5.2 shows some differences between Web pages, newsgroups, mailing lists, blogs, and wikis: A push medium is a communication system in which the user is automatically provided with new information; a pull medium is a communication system in which the user must take some activity (e.g., opening a Web site or a discussion board) in order to receive information. There are three aspects of knowledge (cf. Fuchs and Hofkirchner 2005): cognition (information), communication, and cooperation. Higher-level forms of knowledge have lower-level forms of knowledge as a necessary precondition and show emergent qualities. Web pages are mainly tools for publishing and reading information, mailing lists, newsgroups, and blogs support, besides cognition, also communication; wikis are, besides tools of cognition and communication, also systems of human cooperation for shared knowledge production. The information flow can be one-to-one (o2o), one-to-many (o2m), and many-to-many (m2m). The content data can be stored on a server where it is archived or not stored, but only distributed to subscribers (who store the data locally on their hard drives). Each application type has its own mode of editing information that allows a different number of users (from one to many or all) to change content.

Some important aspects of social software—Web 2.0 and Web 3.0—are:

- Many-to-many communication: Social software enables many users to reach many recipients; each receiver can be a sender of information, each consumer a producer. The dialectical figure of the prosumer emerges.
- Cooperation: Wikis enable users to collaboratively produce digital knowledge without being physically copresent. Users read existing texts or create new ones (cognition), they discuss how texts could be changed, appended, and enhanced (communication), and they together produce new content (cooperation).
- Open source/content: The wiki software is open source; wiki pages are open content—everyone (in a user group) can access and edit them. People write wikis not for earning money but because they want to share knowledge. The motivation for producing wikis is in many cases social and universal, not instrumental and economic. Large wikis like the Wikipedia attract interest by being freely available on the Internet, that is, one doesn't have to pay for accessing and editing it. Hence,

Table 5.2 Differences of Web Sites, Newsgroups, Mailing Lists, Blogs, and Wikis

	Web site	Newsgroup	Mailing list	Blog	Wiki
Push/pull medium	Pull	Pull	Push	Pull	Pull
CnCmCp	Cognition	Cognition, communication	Cognition, communication	Cognition, communication	Cognition, communication, cooperation
Information flow	o2m	m2m	m2m	o2m, m2m	m2m
Information storage	On server	On server	Not automatically, only if a Web archive is available	On server	On server
Editing	Web site can only be changed by one user or group of users	Each user is able to add new postings and to add comments to other postings in a thread	Each user is able to make new postings to the list and to answer to other postings	In individual blogs, one user is able to post messages and others are able to post replies and comments to original postings. In group blogs, many or all users are able to post messages and to reply to messages	All pages can be changed by all users
Unit of production and reproduction	Hypertext	Posting	Posting	Posting	Wikipage

the knowledge of Wikipedia and other open content projects isn't a commodity from which economic actors derive profit; it transcends the instrumental logic of accumulation, profit, competition, and commodification and is based on an ethos of cooperation, public goods, and shared knowledge that constitutes a new logic, the one of a gift economy. However, that wikis and open content projects are noncommodified should not be taken for granted; one can imagine that such systems are suddenly colonized by capitalist logic, that is, that their knowledge is sold in order to accumulate money capital. Noncommodified open-content projects are what Jürgen Habermas has described as life world-spheres of communicative action that enable rational cooperation but are threatened by the influence of the steering media money (commodification, big business) and power (bureaucratization, big power). This would mean that all active users have produced surplus value for absolutely no wage. Such a strategy would be an extremely sophisticated and perfidious way of exploiting knowledge labor. But such an ideology would probably also put an end to such projects because, for many users, the nonproprietary character and free availability of open-content knowledge is a driving factor for their commitment.

- Real participation versus participation as ideology: Stephen Coleman (2005) argues that blogs could help establish a new politics of listening in which everyone has a voice. They could become "sophisticated listening posts of modern democracy" and sources "of nourishment for a kind of democracy in which everyone's account counts" (Coleman 2005, 274). A centralized control of public opinion by totalitarian regimes or market forces (as in the case of private media monopolies) can be undermined by Internet platforms that pose opportunities for alternative information and communication. Web 2.0, due to its ability of supporting many-to-many-communication, has a potential for acting as a tool that helps establish a more participatory democracy in which decisions are discussed and taken by those affected by them. It can also strengthen the voices of civil society and hence help create alternative public spheres that are critical of dominant societal structures and communicate protest. Hence, Web 2.0 can act as a tool supporting cyberprotest. Chris Atton (2004, 26) speaks in this context of an alternative Internet that creates a counterpublic sphere and is "opposed to hierarchical, elite-centred notions of journalism as a business". But for all of these positive developments to take place, what is first of all needed are institutional changes. Web 2.0 is not automatically progressive; it can be used for advancing democracy just as it can for advancing fundamentalism, right-wing extremism, and terrorism. The impact of Web 2.0 on the political system depends on the societal embeddedness of technology. Blogs can also be appropriated by politicians, parties, and the representative political system for giving voice to the people without listening and giving people a say in political decisions so that they can communicate political ideas and have the illusionary impression that they can make a difference, but in reality can't influence policies. In such a case, blogging becomes an ideology and an expression of repressive tolerance (Marcuse 1969b). Social software can support grassroots digital democracy just as it can support representative and plebiscitary forms of digital democracy. It is an ethical and political choice which of these models one considers as more desirable and democratic. Blogs that are not used for citizen-citizen communication, but mainly for the communication of politicians with citizens within the existing representative institutions and without establishing more participatory institutions, are not a form of participatory digital democracy but of representative digital democracy. In the US Presidential preelections of 2004, Howard Dean was very successful in mobilizing supporters and funds by making use of blogs (Kline and Burstein 2005), and the blog of the Bush campaign was successful but didn't invite comments from readers (ibid.). This shows that Web 2.0 can be incorporated into big politics (as well as big business) that can result in a destruction of its participatory potentials. In such cases, Web 2.0 is colonized in the Habermasian sense of the word by power and money. Web 2.0 can have empowering effects if it is used as a tool for communication and cooperation in civil society. David Kline and Dan Burstein (2005, xiv) argue that blogging can contribute "to restoring the lost voice of the ordinary citizen in our culture" and that it can broaden "the range of voices and issues for political debate" (9). There is certainly a potential of Web 2.0 to support the rise of alternative public spheres, but this is not technologically determined; there is no technological fix to the lack of institutions that guarantee political participation; besides technological tools, most importantly institutional reforms are needed. There is no automatism in the effects of blogging; it will not, as Kline and Burstein claim, "inevitably lead to a strengthening of the civic mindedness of the citizenry" (Kline and Burstein 2005, 11). The effects of technology are not determined as techno-deterministic positions argue; they depend on the social embeddedness and construction of technology.

- Self-organized structures: Open-content projects that are based on Web 2.0 or 3.0 software are in many cases not controlled by an elite group that takes decisions, but self-managed networks of activists.
- Citizen journalism vs. corporate journalism: In journalism, blogs can be an opportunity for marginalized voices to be heard and listened to because blogging doesn't require as much money capital as establishing a newspaper does. All citizens can, in principle, become journalists by political blogging. Dan Gillmor in this context considers blogs as online grassroots journalism. He argues that they "can be acts of civic engagement" (Gillmor 2006, 139) and establish a "read/write Web"

(24). For Chris Atton, blogs are a less reticulated and less social move-ment-minded version of alternative online media that applies "similar principles of native reporting, media critique, discussion, and dialogue amongst its writers and readers" (Atton 2004, 55). However, that everyone is in principle able to post political ideas in a blog doesn't mean that he or she will be heard and listened to because blogging today takes place in a hierarchical and stratified society in which pub-lic attention can be bought and is controlled by media corporations and political elites. Hence, a blog run by established actors might be more listened to than one by marginalized actors. Widespread blog-ging alone doesn't solve the problem that there is a lack of political participation; institutional reforms of society are needed besides tech-nological change that can support, but not substitute, such reforms. Social software like blogs could challenge and weaken the domina-tion and monopolization of political information and communication by large media corporations that commodify and industrialize cul-ture, but it is not determined that it has positive effects on the public sphere.

- Collective intelligence: A wiki is more than the knowledge of single individuals and more than the agglomeration of knowledge of many single individuals. Due to cooperation, knowledge emerges that is more than the sum of the knowledge of the contributors and as a new qual-ity has a shared perspective to which the contributors all agree. Pierre Lévy (1997) has termed the new quality of such emergent knowledge systems *collective intelligence.*

Some people argue that blogging is an inherently self-centered activity without political relevance. This might indeed be the case for individual blogging that supports the dominant idea of distinctive lifestyles as strategy for accumulating symbolic capital, but there is a more radical potential in group blogs and the political usage of blogs. There are many examples for the influence of political blogs, such as their role in the debate on the French plebiscite on the European constitution in 2005 and the protests against the deregulation of dismissal protections for young French people in 2006, in the Iraq war (war blogs), in communicating political opposition in Iran, or in the US Presidential elections in 2005. Richard Kahn and Douglas Kellner (2004) argue that the political developments after 9/11 have produced a social movement that makes use of the Internet for political activism. These activities would transform the Internet itself and result in phenomena such as political blogs that form a "vital new space of politics and culture" (Kahn and Kellner 2004, 94).

The blogosphere is the "world of blogs as a collective group" (Kuhns and Crew 2006, 7), "an alternative universe created by the aggregation of hundreds of thousands of blogs". It is a network of blog systems; blogs are interrelated by permalinks and can be indexed, searched, and assessed with the help of metablog systems such as Technorati, Feedster, Bloglines, Blog-pulse, Pubsub, or Blogdex.

Web 2.0 and Web 3.0 are more dynamic than Web 1.0. They can support grassroots journalism and activism and participatory democracy. But these phenomena are not automatic implications of technologies; they need to be self-organized in social relations that change the overall competitive character of society.

5.4 VIRTUAL REALITY AND CYBERSPACE

William Gibson introduced the term *cyberspace* in his science-fiction novel *Neuromancer* (Gibson 1984, 51). "Cyberspace, a consensual hallucination experienced daily by billions of legitimate operators, in every nation, by children being taught mathematical concepts. . . . A graphic representation of data abstracted from the banks of every computer in the human system, unthinkable complexity. Lines of light ranged in the non-space of the mind, clusters and constellations of data. Like city lights, receding. . . ." Gibson here pointed out some important aspects of the cyberspace: It is a complex system (interlinking information and hence creating a Web of knowledge); it transcends national boundaries; it is based on a networking of computers; it is virtual in the sense of creating an artificial reality; it seems to be a nonspace because it transcends boundaries, but at the same time it seems to constitute a new space that here is compared to a city.

The term *cyber* in cyberspace derives from "cybernetics". Cybernetics emerged in the twentieth century as the study of the communication and control of regulatory feedback both in living beings and machines and in combinations of the two (Wiener 1948). During the last three decades, the focus of cybernetics shifted from controlling and steering systems to the analysis of how systems self-organize. The notion of self-organizing systems is the central idea of second-order cybernetics as introduced by Heinz von Foerster (second-order cybernetics as "cybernetics of cybernetics"; cf. Von Foerster 1995). The connection of cybernetics and space points out that cyberspace is a technological space produced by human beings (social space). The stress of "cybernetics" also makes it feasible to analyze the Internet and the social relations connected to it as a self-organizing system.

Cyberspace obviously changes space and time: When we communicate per e-mail, we do not need to be in the same place with our communication partners, and the process works asynchronously. In a chat, we need temporal copresence but no spatial copresence. The traditional sociological concept of space has been associated with borders and fixity. The fact that new information and communication technologies transcend borders has caused a crisis of the space concept in sociology (Löw 2001; Funken and Löw 2003). On the other hand, spatial descriptions such as "global village" (McLuhan 1962), "cyberspace" (Gibson 1984), "digital city" (Iglhaut,

Medosch, and Rötzer 1996), "space of flows" (Castells 2000a), or "virtual community" (Rheingold 2000) indicate a desire of scientists and stakeholders to describe cyberspace as a new type of space. Cyberspace is a type of social space where communication is technologically mediated and that is organized on a global time-space scale. Its subsystems are specific virtual communities, that is, topic- and interest-oriented social systems that make use of specific Internet applications (such as newsgroups, chats, mailing lists, ICQ, peer-to-peer technologies, etc.) in order to establish communication that is globally stretched in time-space (see chapter 9.2 for a detailed discussion of the notion of virtual community). A virtual community is not a space that is constituted by shared values, identities, or traditions. What connects people in a virtual community is a shared interest in certain issues and communication oriented on these topics. Cyberspace doesn't mark the end of space but the acceleration of communication and the extension of some social systems to a global scale.

Another term used for signifying the Internet is *virtual reality*. Virtual Reality (VR) means a space where information is not stored in the human brain but in computer networks that enable human communication and activity at a distance. VR is an extension of human reality in the sense that is based on human beings, their actions and interactions; it is a socially created space that has a technological substratum and is inhabited by human beings. VR is not the opposite of reality and it doesn't abandon reality. The experiences and practices we have through VR are real; hence Castells (2000a) speaks of "real virtuality". The culture of real virtuality would be "virtual because it is constructed primarily through electronically based, virtual processes of communication. It is real (and not imaginary) because it is our fundamental reality, the material basis on which we live our existence, construct our systems or representation, practice our work, link up with other people, retrieve information, form our opinions, act in politics, and nurture our dreams. This virtuality is our reality" (Castells 2001, 203). VR means a technological multiplication of reality, a simulation that constructs a new level of imagination and reality (Poster 1995a, 1995b). VR is characterized by three *I*'s: immersion, interactivity, information intensity (Heim 1998). *Immersion* means that virtual reality creates new human experiences; *interaction* means that the state of an application changes according to changes of the human body that are fed as an input into the technical system; *information intensity* means that a virtual world can offer special qualities like telepresence that show a certain degree of intelligent behavior.

When we browse the WWW, we are immersed in an artificial space that we navigate by clicking links and entering commands with the help of interaction devices such as the mouse and the keyboard. Certain human senses are observed by the system in order to gather input and change the state of the system; the output that the system produces appeals at least to our eyes and ears; the computer digitally combines data that can appeal to several of our senses; and it digitally converts input of multiple senses into data that is used for changing the system's state. Hence, the computer is a multimedium. Digitization allows the convergence of text, sound, images, videos, animations, and so on. Human-computer interaction (HCI) involves a potentially endless feedback loop between the human user and the computer in which the activity of a human being's sense organs changes the system's output and the output changes sensual human experiences. This process is the basic loop involved in interactivity. The WWW is not a fully immersive medium because our senses are not fully concentrated on interaction with the technology: You can see, hear, feel, smell, and taste stimuli that are not produced by the WWW while you are browsing. The Internet is a partly immersive system.

Full immersion can be achieved in a virtual-reality system that makes use of 3D graphics, a data glove or data suit, and a head-mounted display. A fully immersive virtual reality system isolates the human senses totally from the outside environment; they are fully concentrated on interaction with the technology; the only sensual input into the body during the time of virtual experience is produced by the technology. The system exactly measures the user's position and movements and hence allows the user's control of artificial agents that move in a world that is presented to the user via the head-mounted display. The only thing he or she sees is the virtual world; it is not possible to observe the outside environment as it is when you surf the WWW. Frequently, the virtual worlds are not purely artificial but a simplified representation of reality. Examples are the virtual operating room and the virtual cockpit of a warplane. The simulation of 3D spaces on a 2D monitor can provide midlevel immersion. This is, for example, the case in 3D arcade games like Duke Nukem or Silent Hill, VRML (Virtual Reality Modelling Language) spaces like cybertown.com, and role-playing games like Second Life.

Pierre Lévy (1998, 2001) argues that the virtual is not the opposite of the real; philosophically it would mean that which exists potentially rather than actually, a field of forces and problems that is resolved through actualization. Hence, one can consider VR systems as objective systems that contain a mass of human knowledge that can be potentially actualized as subjective human knowledge. When one reads a piece of information in the WWW, objective knowledge is transformed into subjective knowledge; potential subjective reality is actualized into actual subjective reality.

5.5 CONCLUSION

The Internet is not simply a technological network of computer networks but a dynamic techno-social system in which new qualities emerge dynamically. The rise of Web 2.0 and 3.0 software has brought about new potentials of cooperation. These are technologies of communication and cooperation, but the potentials are not automatically realized due to the overall competitive character of contemporary society.

Some characteristics of the Internet are:

- **Interactivity:** Users can change the state of Internet applications by entering commands via interfaces and by using input devices.
- **Multimedia:** Based on digitalization of data, the Internet combines text, sound, images, animation, and video in one medium that integrates all senses.
- **Hypertextuality:** The World Wide Web, as one part of the Internet, is based on a network of interlinked texts; each node represents a digital content that can contain links to other nodes that can be followed by the user with the help of a browser software that displays Web pages.
- **Globalized communication:** The Internet advances the spatiotemporal disembedding of social relationships and communication.
- **Many-to-many communication:** Due to the decentralized structure of the Internet, each receiver/consumer of information is a potential sender/producer of information.
- **Cooperative production:** In comparison to traditional mass media such as telegraph, telephone, radio, television, books, or newspapers, the Internet is not just a communication medium but also a system that enables cooperative working processes. With the help of the Internet, human beings can form social systems, share information, and jointly produce digital content without spatiotemporal copresence (examples are open source projects, open theory, and wikis).
- **Decontextualization:** In the Internet the context of digital information (authorship, time and place of production, the physical location of the server that stores the digital content, etc.) gets lost; Web information frequently is an emergent whole that is made up of many decontextualized pieces of information.
- **Derealization:** The Internet blurs the boundaries between reality and fiction; it creates a virtual reality where fictive and real information become intermixed.

Based on the thus far elaborated theoretical foundations, we can now discuss how the Internet changes society and is shaped by society. For doing so, we will subsequently discuss the antagonism between competition and cooperation in the ecological (chap. 6), the economic (chap. 7), the political (chap. 8), and the cultural system (chap. 9) of informational capitalism.

6 Competition and Cooperation in the Informational Ecology

In chapter 3, I pointed out that in modern society there is an antagonism between natural forces and the mode of production that is due to the fact that the competitive interest in capital accumulation dominates over the cooperative Essence of society. With the rise of the Internet the question is posed how the man-nature relationship changes. The discourse on this question predominantly assumes that information and communication technologies (ICTs) bring about a shift towards ecological sustainability. This view shall be deconstructed because of its techno-deterministic character. In this chapter I try to show how the competitive character of capitalism plays a role in the informational ecology and limits positive potentials. This question will be discussed relating to the areas of transport (6.1), resource intensity (6.2), and virtual products (6.3).

"Our contention is that, as ICT becomes more sophisticated and more embedded in our organizational structures and everyday life, we are in a better position than ever before to make sustainable development work" (Alakeson et al. 2003, 5). Counter to this quotation, I don't think that ICTs automatically advance ecological sustainability but that they pose both new opportunities and risks for the ecosphere.

6.1 ICTS AND TRANSPORT

The question is whether private and business Internet communication automatically reduces the need for traveling. This can be the case if people consciously choose to avoid unnecessary traveling and transport by plane and car; but Internet communication also makes it easier to connect people globally and to initiate and maintain social relationships, and hence it can also raise the desire or need to meet people face to face more frequently.

Some scientists argue that due to the fact that telework allows knowledge workers to overcome spatiotemporal distances and to work from home, the need for transport and hence environmental pollution would be reduced. The same argument can be employed for teleconferencing, saying that by substituting personal meetings by teleconferences, traveling can be reduced. But teleworkers normally don't work full time at home because they need to stay connected personally and face to face with their social work environment; the number of teleworkers is generally relatively low (in Europe the share of teleworkers in the total labor force ranges from less than 2 percent to more than 10 percent; cf. Schallaböck et al. 2003, 9). Traveling to work produces only a relatively small share of total carbon dioxide emissions. Working from home doesn't automatically imply less transport because online work can produce new contacts that might generate the need for meeting people personally. Working at home can have negative environmental effects, for example, people can't go shopping on the way home from work but might take an extra trip by car from home to shops and supermarkets. A German study has shown that the total distance traveled per employed person has been constantly rising (Schallaböck et al. 2003). Hence, telework doesn't yet seem to have positive effects on work-related transport.

Companies often paint an optimistic picture of the effects of teleworking on the ecosystem, but studies show that although teleworkers frequently reduce their commuting distances, "the overall distance travelled for commuting is growing, though not very fast. That the last 3 years represent the highest figures, does not support the thesis which suggests that transport savings have been made because of telework" (Schallaböck et al. 2003, 26). A study by the Wuppertal Institute for Austria, Germany, Japan, the Netherlands, and the US concludes that business trips are still increasing in number and that home-based telework hasn't reduced the number of commuting trips and the commuting distances traveled (ibid.). The European reality seems to be that telework and teleconferencing are simply too unimportant for having positive effects on transport savings and that there are rebound effects from online communication on the increase of traveling. About 5 percent of the labor force in Europe can be considered as teleworkers. Roughly 10 percent of the working days of the complete European labor force can be considered as home-based telework (ibid., 52). The result of another study is that "homeworkers are spending more time traveling than conventional workers" (Marletta et al. 2004). A German study has shown that the distance traveled by teleworkers per week (360 km) is three times as large as the one traveled by conventional workers (120 km, Schallaböck et al. 2003).

Telework and teleconferences certainly pose an opportunity for reducing traveling, but this opportunity has thus far not been adequately realized. What is needed is a conscious commitment of business and individuals to reduce the amount of travels by car and plane. ICTs alone don't solve the problem. The reality of work and life today is that in a flexible economy and society individuals have to be flexible because they *compete* for jobs and capital and have to travel long-distances in order to maintain work-related and private social relationships.

6.2 A WEIGHTLESS ECONOMY?

Some scientists argue that the shift from the "industrial society" to the "information society" means that the economy becomes less resource intensive and that hence there is a "dematerialization" of production that creates a "weightless economy" (Coyle 1997; Kelly 1999; Leadbeater 2000; Quah 1999) that advances ecological sustainability. "On the one hand, there are (in the service sector) the traditional occupations that statisticians call 'community, social and personal services': haircuts, cleaning, babysitting, teaching, nursing, government administration and so on. On the other there are 'high value added' services such as currency trading, creating financial derivatives, software development, gene research or making programmes for satellite television. Most of these are high-technology, depending for their existence on modern computer power and telecommunications. They are also dematerialized, or weightless" (Coyle 1997, 2). The argument of such scholars is that knowledge-based industries and services are less resource intensive than industrial production; that ICTs can reduce negative environmental impacts of traditional industries by allowing more efficient ways of production and distribution; that certain products and services could be dematerialized/virtualized, which would reduce their environmental impact; that such goods are traded and transported over the Internet, which would reduce the amount of physical transport; and that ICTs can increase the efficiency of transportation.

A study by the Wuppertal Institute concludes that the ICT sector's resource productivity is higher than the one of the total economy, that is, that it is cleaner per unit value added generated, but that the ICT sector's contribution to total value added is relatively low (5–8%) (Kuhndt 2003). The "old economy" is still important.

In Germany the energy intensity and the CO_2 emission of the ICT sector is lower than in the traditional economy. In 1999 the production of information goods with a total value of 34 million Euros resulted in the emission of one ton CO_2, whereas in the total economy goods with a value of 2 only million euros resulted in the same emissions (Kuhndt 2003, 23).

In Germany, the ICT sector made up only 7.9 percent of the total value added in 2000 (ibid., 19). A study by the World Resource Institute concludes that, although the ICT sector has a better resource and emission efficiency than the overall economy, "part of the explanation for the continued increase in overall waste quantities lies in the fact that traditional industries, despite their declining relative economic importance are not necessarily declining in terms of their physical operations. . . . Fossil fuel combustion is the dominant activity of modern industrial economies and is the single largest contributor to material outflows to the air and on land. Most of these flows are hazardous to human health or the environment" (WRI 2000, 19, 41).

The reality of dematerialization seems to be that fully virtualized products and the ICT sector constitute only a small portion of the economy, that the total resource use of the economy is constantly rising, and that hence thus far there has not been a massive "greening" of production and consumption induced by knowledge products and ICTs. It is not true that "economic value is dematerializing" (Coyle 1997, 1).

Postindustrial capitalism as a dematerialized ecologically sustainable economy is a "dangerous myth" (Foster 2002, 24). Touraine has argued in this context that the information society is a "hyperindustrial society" (Touraine 1988). It is not a new society that is characterized by intangible goods but a new phase of development of capitalism that is both continuity and discontinuity of industrial capitalism and has emergent qualities such as the central importance of cognitive, communicative, and cooperative labor.

The knowledge economy is not an economy of invisible and intangible goods. There indeed are many physical information commodities that are transported and sold. Huws (2001) argues that in capitalism there is a major tendency to transform services into physical products (commodification; cf. Fleissner 2005) because, with the help of the latter, capital accumulation would be easier to achieve than with the first due to higher potentials for technological rationalization and outsourced/globalized production. Profit interests in this context seem to contradict ecological sustainability.

6.3 VIRTUAL PRODUCTS AS A FOUNDATION OF A SUSTAINABLE SOCIETY?

Another argument is that certain products and services can be entirely virtualized and transported in digital form over the Internet and that hence material and energy savings can be made. For example, the Wuppertal Institute (Türk 2003) found out in an analysis that downloading a CD over the Internet is 2.5 times as resource efficient as buying it in a music store. This way savings concerning energy and matter in production and transport surely can be made. But many users have the habit of not only storing files on their computers; they rather choose to burn music files on CDs because they prefer to play music on their CD players. Hence there are again material and energy impacts.

MP3 players that are portable and can be connected to a hi-fi system surely pose a good alternative that to a certain extent allows resource savings, but the example shows that virtualization doesn't automatically result in ecological sustainability. The same is true for books, journals, and newspapers. If they are distributed in digital form, online resource savings in production and distribution can be made. Also, new flexible production technologies that are based on just-in-time-production (e.g., books on demand) allow resource savings. But almost no one wants to read a book or a whole newspaper online because it is not very comfortable to read on screen. Therefore, many people print out articles or whole books, which results in a high consumption of paper, toner, and ink. There are certain alternatives such as e-paper that can be reused. Companies thus far have not widely supported reusable or ecofriendly equipment (such as e-paper, the "green PC", or refillable ink cartridges for printers) because reusable computer equipment is not only less resource intensive but also in the long term probably less profitable.

The antagonism between capitalism and ecology has thus far also had negative influences on companies' support for ecologically sustainable ICT equipment. The use of recyclable and reusable equipment could indeed reduce the environmental impact of ICTs, but for doing so the logic of capital accumulation needs to be subordinated under ecological and social awareness. The relationship of ICTs and sustainability is not only a question of ethical consumerism but also one of corporate social and ecological responsibility. In capitalism, not those technologies that most benefit society and ecology are promoted but those that enable capital accumulation. Hence it is, for example, not solar or wind energy or the reusable computer that is promoted but nuclear energy, fossil fuels, the automobile, and nonrenewable computer equipment. "In recession times, decision-makers try to survive. Questions beyond the survival of their companies do not interest them at all; most common recipe: replace people by machines and save money, i.e.: jobs are played against profits and (ecological) reforms" (Mettler 1997, 7). As long as a company is profitable, it might be open-minded for ecological and social goals, but capitalism is based on *competition* and economic crisis is an inherent feature of the system; hence, in the end, in many cases the logic of profit will outstrip social and ecological awareness.

Moore's law says that the speed of computers doubles every 18 months. Thus far this law has proven true. It results in a fast moral depreciation of computers, and people frequently buy new computers in order to participate in technological progress. For ecological sustainability we don't necessarily have to slow down technological progress, but the ways hardware is manufactured and diffused surely have to change because the short life span of computers is detrimental to reaching ecological goals. Advances in chip technology today (under capitalist conditions) result in an increasing reduction of the life span of computers. The average lifetime of a business PC is two to three years, the one of a mobile phone eighteen months in Europe (European Information Technology Observatory (EITO) 2002, 256).

What is needed are reusable, recyclable, and upgradeable computer hardware and periphery. One should also add that ICTs are industrial products; their production and disposal generates waste and emissions. The knowledge society is not an immaterial society but a new phase in the material reality of capitalism. It requires a large material infrastructure made up by computers, periphery, servers, routers, switches, network cables, and so on. The hardware industry makes profit by selling computers and periphery. If computers were used for a longer time or if it were increasingly possible to renew only certain parts in order to come up to date with technological progress and not have to buy a whole new computer, environmental improvements could indeed be made. But this would require some steps away from the logic of profitability towards the logic of ecological sustainability. Hence, it would mean to accept lower profits in order to protect the environment. Such moves are possible, but they contradict the dominant economic logic. If corporate social responsibility shall not only be an ideology, corporations must be ready to go beyond and to question to a certain extent capitalist logic.

Computers and the Internet run by consuming energy. The Wuppertal Institute found that in 2000 the Internet accounted for 5 percent of Germany's total energy use (Langrock, Hermann, and Takeuchi 2001). It is not only based on a material infrastructure but also consumes energy that constitutes another material aspect of the information society.

A study by the Fraunhofer Institut für Systemtechnik und Innovationsforschung in cooperation with the Centre for Energy Policy and Economics (2005) has found that ICTs in business and households account for about 8 percent of total energy use in Germany. It is estimated that until 2010, ICT energy use will rise from 38 TWh (terawatt hours, 2001) to 55.4 TWh (ibid., 275). Especially television sets, hi-fi systems, computers, servers, mobile phone infrastructure networks, mobile phones, and fixed phone lines are considered as being very energy intensive (ibid.). There are technological possibilities to reduce the energy consumption of television sets and monitors (by using LCD monitors and television sets and selling such machines at reasonable prices) as well as computers (by including components that automatically detach computers from energy supply if they are not used for a certain time: switched mode power supply).

But the interests of the energy industry might be detrimental to establishing "green ICTs" because high amounts of energy use mean high profits. What is needed are political pressure and unified laws that define minimum standards of energy efficiency of ICTs and require producers to include energy consumption labels on ICTs. This might have negative consequences on profitability, but if sustainability shall be achieved the domination of society by economic logic must be challenged.

The miniaturization of ICTs doesn't automatically result in less environmental impacts because ICT production itself produces wastes and toxic emissions. ICT equipment such as personal computers or mobile phones contains toxic substances such as lithium or cadmium batteries. Environmental performance assessments of computer technologies show that the latter doesn't heavily reduce material outputs; the production of one PC requires sixteen to nineteen tons of material resources and more than 5,000 kWh of energy; the emission of the production of one piece includes 60 kg of waste, 1,850 kg of carbon dioxide, 2 kg of sulfur dioxide, and 1 kg of nitrogen oxide (Grote 1994; cf. also European Information Technology Observatory (EITO) 2002, 25). The EU produces 6 million tons of waste of electrical and electronic equipment a year (European Information Technology Observatory (EITO) 2002, 256).

The predominant competitive logic, that is, the interest in accumulating capital, seems to be detrimental to resource- and energy-saving technologies because it is a profitable business to sell hardware and energy.

6.4 CONCLUSION

ICTs neither automatically produce positive or negative ecological effects; there is no techno-deterministic relation to nature. It all depends on how ICTs are designed and into which societal context they are embedded. There seem to be certain potentials for resource and energy savings in ICTs, but under competitive capitalist conditions these potentials have not been realized and it seems like the colonization of society by the *competitive* logic of profitability is not compatible with a sustainable ecology.

A sustainable information society is a society that makes use of ICTs and knowledge for fostering a good life for all human beings of current and future generations by strengthening biological diversity, technological usability, economic wealth for all, political participation of all, and cultural wisdom. Achieving a sustainable information society costs; it demands a conscious reduction of profits by not predominantly investing in the future of capital but the future of humans, society, and nature. Environmental problems are social problems, not technological problems; they are neither caused by science and technology as such nor can they be solved by science or technology as such. Science and technology have, due to their unsustainable social design, contributed to environmental degradation; they have been turned into destructive forces by social forces. Heavy promotion of computer usage is not an appropriate means and automatism for achieving ecological sustainability; the latter requires alternative models of economic production. If humankind is interested in a sustainable society, the destructive character of the economy must be sublated; new models of economic production and social relationships are needed.

The information ecology—that is, the ecology that is influenced by ICTs—is characterized by an antagonism between sustainable potentials and unsustainable realities This is an antagonism between the sustainable and the unsustainable information ecology that is today shaped by the overall competitive character of contemporary society. Figure 6.1 shows some qualities of this antagonism.

ICT Opportunities
(Logic of Co-operation)

ICT Risks
(Logic of Competition)

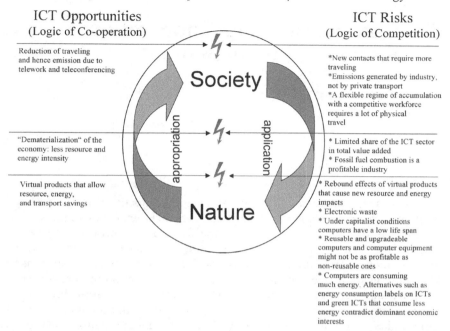

Reduction of traveling
and hence emission due to
telework and teleconferencing

*New contacts that require more
traveling
*Emissions generated by industry,
not by private transport
*A flexible regime of accumulation
with a competitive workforce
requires a lot of physical
travel

"Dematerialization" of the
economy: less resource and
energy intensity

* Limited share of the ICT sector
in total value added
* Fossil fuel combustion is a
profitable industry

Virtual products that allow
resource, energy,
and transport savings

* Rebound effects of virtual products
that cause new resource and energy
impacts
* Electronic waste
* Under capitalist conditions
computers have a low life span
* Reusable and upgradeable
computers and computer equipment
might not be as profitable as
non-reusable ones
* Computers are consuming
much energy. Alternatives such as
energy consumption labels on ICTs
and green ICTs that consume less
energy contradict dominant economic
interests

Figure 6.1 The antagonism of sustainable and unsustainable information ecology.

7 Competition and Cooperation in the Internet Economy

In this chapter, processes of cooperation and competition in the Internet economy are analyzed. Before doing so, it is first shown how capital is organized in informational capitalism in the form of decentralized "network enterprises" that use cooperation as ideology in order to advance competitive capital accumulation (7.1). In section 7.2 the concrete manifestations of the antagonism between competition and cooperation in the Internet economy are analyzed. It is shown that this antagonism takes on the form of an antagonism between the informational gift economy and the informational commodity economy. Sections 7.1 and 7.2 focus on the organizational form of capital. But it is also necessary to discuss aspects of labor; hence, section 7.3 focuses more on knowledge labor in the Internet economy and advances the notion that knowledge labor is both a class and a nonclass.

7.1 THE "NETWORK ENTERPRISE": COOPERATION AS IDEOLOGY

The rise of organizational networks and computer networks in the economy has transformed firms into what Manuel Castells (2001, 67; 2000a, 180, 185, 187) has termed the "network enterprise". Firms are increasingly based on flat hierarchies, decentralized organizational structures, global outsourcing, flexible production mechanisms, and participatory management. These changes affect corporations at two levels: at the innerfirm and at the interfirm level.

Corporations and Teamwork

On the internal level of corporations, teamwork and semiautonomous working groups are gaining increasing importance. Relatively autonomous groups of workers are formed that must perform certain tasks until certain deadlines; how they organize the work internally and which means and methods they use are left to themselves. Autonomy can refer to the following areas: the type of commodities, the amount of produced goods, labor time, place of labor, production methods, the division of work and responsibilities within the group, questions of internal management and leadership, selection of group members, internal and external communication. The rise of teamwork is accompanied by the use of computer networks for internal and external communication and work coordination and by strategies of "participatory management" that want to create cooperative relationships between owners, management, and employees, favor the flattening of hierarchies (which means in most cases a decreasing importance of middle management), and propagate work as fun, the blurring of the boundaries between leisure and labor, and the company as a place to feel at home. This reflects the shift from a disciplinary society (Foucault 1979), in which domination operates through hierarchical control, enclosure, and surveillance, to a society of control (Deleuze 1995) in which domination operates through self-control, identification, and inclusion. Disciplines are methods that secure the submission to external forces by surveillance and punishment (Foucault 1979). They are inherent in modern institutions such as schools, prisons, families, universities, hospitals, corporations, and so on, because these milieus try to enclose the individual. Disciplines were also incorporated into the Fordist apparatuses of mass production, especially into assembly lines. These aspects still exist today to a certain extent, but there is a shift towards the society of control: Employees who feel at home at work, have fun at work, and can to a certain degree influence internal decisions will work more and better, that is, they will create more surplus value in less time. Hence, we witness not the rise of a new economic system but of a new ideology and a new type of integrative domination. Participation and cooperation are understood in a very limited sense in such ideologies because they leave the asymmetrical, exclusive, nonparticipatory, noncooperative distribution of economic property untouched. The shift from hierarchical expert management towards participatory management reflects an ideological shift in modern society that no longer involves a dominance of hierarchical control but a strategy of integration that is expected to result in a rise of profits.

For Deleuze, controls are internalized disciplines, forms of self-discipline that are presented as liberating and operate in a subtle manner. He compares the individual in disciplinary society to a mole and the individual in the society of control to a serpent.

Controls are internalized disciplines, forms of self-discipline that present themselves as liberating and operate in a more subtle manner: "Enclosures are molds, distinct castings, but controls are a modulation, like a self-deforming cast that will continuously change from one moment to the other, or like a sieve whose mesh will transmute from point to point. . . . The old monetary mole is the animal of the space of enclosure, but the serpent is that of the societies of control. We have passed from one animal to the other, from the mole to the serpent, in the system under which we live, but also in our manner of living and in our relations with others. The disciplinary man was a discontinuous producer of energy, but the man of control is undulatory, in orbit, in a continuous network. . . . The coils of a serpent are even more complex than the burrows of a molehill" (Deleuze 1995). The mole as a symbol of disciplinary society is faceless and dumb and monotonously digs his burrows; the snake is flexible and pluralistic. Luc Boltanski and Ève Chiapello (2006) argue that the rise of participatory management means the emergence of a new spirit of capitalism that subsumes values of the political revolt of 1968 and the subsequently emerging New Left such as autonomy, spontaneity, mobility, creativity, networking, visions, openness, plurality, informality, authenticity, emancipation, and so on, under capital. The topics of the movement would now be put into the service of those forces that it wanted to destroy.

The individual in Fordist capitalism was expected to carry out monotonous labor; management expects individuals in post-Fordist capitalism to be flexible, innovative, motivated, dynamic, modern, young, and agile, and it wants them to identify with the corporation and to have fun at work. Strategies of participatory management aim at the ideological integration of laborers into corporations. This is a new quality of the disciplinary regime that aims at a rise of profits by an increase in productivity and cost reductions achieved by the workers' permanent self-discipline. Bonus systems, teamwork, share options, corporate identity, attractive design of the workplace, construction of a community between management and workers ("we" identity), advancement of spirit of enterprise within the workforce, and so on, are part of this strategy that constitutes new qualities of the disciplinary regime of capitalist society. Studies found that the reality of the network firm is decentralization of production and management combined with centralization of capital and control (Van Dijk 2006, 75). Rudi Schmiede (2006b, 458sq.) argues that decentralization concerns only the organizational structure of corporations but is accompanied by a centralization of capital, financial control, and economic power.

In organization and management theory, "participation" is understood in a rather narrow sense of the term that excludes overall societal and political issues. Full participation would have to include an inclusive control and ownership of products and the means of production and on the political level overall grassroots democracy in the sense that people affected by decisions take these decisions collectively and all by themselves. "Participatory" management is a method of rationalizing and optimizing the production process in such a way that profit can be achieved effectively. The division of labor inherent in capitalism that requires a class relationship between those owning the means of production and the results of the production process and those depending on the entrance into labor relationships is maintained in informational capitalism. Despite all the changes we are witnessing today, the antagonism between the owners of property and the owners of labor remains an unchanged central characteristic of society. "There is still a division between those who own the valuable resources on which the information economy is dependent and those who merely own their ability to labour in such an economy. . . . In the information economy even if knowledge creators are themselves individuals, the ownership of the bulk of valuable knowledge resources remains with capital" (May 2000). Participatory methods of management help to ideologically forestall social change towards a real participatory society and uphold what has in critical theory been termed false consciousnesses

Khandwalla (1977) characterizes elements of participatory organizations: Superiors have trust and confidence in subordinates; subordinates feel free to discuss any job-related matters with their bosses; reward systems, participatory set goals, improvement programs, evaluation of progress; great deal of upward, downward, and horizontal communication; extensive, friendly interaction between superior and subordinates; great deal of cooperative teamwork; decision making is done throughout the organization and is integrated through interlinked groups; awareness of organizational problems throughout the organization; subordinates are fully involved in decisions related to their work; consensus-oriented team decision making at the level of top management; decision making is designed to motivate the implementation of decisions; team goals are established by group discussions; participation in control functions; use of human relations in effecting organizational changes and securing better cooperation from employees; use of techniques such as sensitivity training and managerial grid for organizational development. This is a narrow understanding of economic participation that serves economic interests; a participatory and cooperative ownership of the means of production and the products is avoided as a characteristic here. True economic participation would imply a stronger cooperative character of ownership.

Khandwalla suggests that "another aspect of the participative mode's ideology is the notion that cooperation is better than competition, and warm, friendly relations among organizational members are more desirable than mutual hostility and suspicion. This is best achieved by power equalization, in sharp contrast to the power struggles characteristic of the coercive mode" (Khandwalla 1977, 418). Cooperation indeed is better than competition in order to achieve economic democracy, but this requires full economic cooperation, not a selective and opportunistic type of cooperation that bases only those aspects of an organization and of society on cooperation that help ideological integration and don't conflict with profit-oriented production.

The increasing importance of knowledge work in corporations and the resulting interest in yielding economic profit from knowledge have resulted in the emergence of new scientific areas such as research on knowledge management (KM) and organizational learning (OL). Mark W. McElroy (2000) points out that first-generation KM was a rather hierarchic and technology-centric approach oriented on capturing, codifying, distributing, and delivering information, whereas second-generation KM would be more oriented on organizational knowledge creation and learning. In this new generation, the three formerly separated approaches of knowledge management, organizational learning, and complexity/systems thinking would converge. KM and OL approaches frequently use notions such as self-organization, participation, and cooperation in order to stress that knowledge can be created and used most efficiently and democratically if organizations flatten hierarchies and allow certain degrees of autonomy and self-managed decision making by workers. McElroy points out that complexity thinking and self-organization theory (such as the complex adaptive systems approach) are particularly suited in this context because they provide models and a theory of how dynamically changing organizations create knowledge.

In KM, Ikujiro Nonaka and Hirotaka Takeuchi (Nonaka 1994; Nonaka and Takeuchi 1995) have created the SECI model of organizational knowledge creation that shows how tacit knowledge and explicit knowledge can be created and mutually converted by processes of socialization, externalization, combination, and internalization (SECI). They link their concept to ideas from complexity thinking such as self-organization, synergetics, or order from noise in order to suggest forms of knowledge management. For example, Nonaka argues that one "way to implement the management of organizational knowledge creation is to create a 'field' or 'self-organizing team' in which individual members collaborate to create a new team" (Nonaka 1994, 22). Creative chaos (evoking tension and a sense of crisis by proposing challenging goals), redundancy (promoting trust by sharing extra information), and requisite variety (giving access to necessary information by information channels) are besides self-organized teams introduced as important methods of KM.

In the field of OL, Peter Senge (1990) has introduced systems thinking as the fifth discipline that helps to see the world as made up of interconnected systems. Systems thinking would be the theory and practice for bringing together the four other disciplines of personal mastery, mental models, shared vision, and team learning so that learning organizations can emerge. A learning organization would be "an organization that is continually expanding its capacity to create its future" (Senge 1990, 14). Such learning would be generative and not adaptive. Senge stresses teamwork and dialogue; by dialogue and discussion a commonality of direction, an alignment, could emerge. The emerging commonality would be a shared vision and shared understanding. Senge presents team learning as a self-organizing system in the terms of Hermann Haken's Synergetics (without explicitly naming Haken or Synergetics, cf. Senge 1990, 234sq.).

That management theory now employs concepts such as self-organization, participation, and cooperation that are typical for grassroots thinking is characteristic of an ideology that employs new terms and models for organizing the old model of capital accumulation in corporations more effectively. The advanced ideas and their practical reality remain only partial because they hardly touch the question of the ownership of the means of production and remain on the microorganizational level of decision making within teams. The full consequences of thinking in terms of self-organization—which implies the full sublation of heteronomy and alienated structures—are not realized. New management methods try to install a regime that works with unconscious controls that make workers produce more surplus value more quickly by engaging in self-exploitation because they feel a sense of fun, duty, commitment, and community in the corporation. It is speculative and probably not yet decidable if the uptake of grassroots vocabulary by management theory and practice will result in an intellectual and political climate that is more open for ideas of a self-managed society.

The role of computer networks in innerorganizational restructuration is that they act as a medium for information storage and exchange, coordination, communication, and cooperation within and between teams/organizational units so that if desired operation over spatiotemporal distanciation is enabled. The ability of computer networks to enable organizational information, communication, and cooperation at a distance has resulted in the introduction of concepts such as the virtual corporation (Davidow and Malone 1992), the virtual organization (Mowshowitz 2002), and the virtual team (Lipnack and Stamps 2000). The concept of virtual corporation focuses on the interorganizational use of computer networks, the notion of virtual teams on intraorganizational use: "The virtual corporation is a temporary network of independent companies, suppliers, customers, even erstwhile rivals—linked by information technology to share skills, costs and access to one another's markets. It will have neither central office nor organization chart. It will have no hierarchy, no vertical integration" (Byrne, Brandt, and Port 1993, 36). "A virtual team is a group of people who work interdependently with a shared purpose across space, time, and organization boundaries using technology" (Lipnack and Stamps 2000, 18).

I see two problems with such concepts:

1. If it is not stressed that the virtual and the real are intertwined, the impression can be created that virtual organizations and teams are only those social systems that exist fully online and where there is no face-to-face contact of human actors. As economic activity requires the formation and continuous reproduction of empathy which can more easily be created offline than online, it is unlikely that the majority of corporations that make heavy use of computer networks will be based on pure online relationships. Hence, such a narrow concept of the virtual and of virtual teams/organizations hardly makes sense because it applies only to a small share of cases.

2. To characterize contemporary economic organizations as virtual distracts from the fact that they are first of all still capitalist in nature and hence oriented on profit generation.

Transnational Corporations: Cooperation for Competition and Profit

Corporations are increasingly organized on a transnational level by breaking the production process down into small units that are organized by subfirms or subcontracted corporations that can be located and distributed throughout the globe depending on where the best conditions of economic investment (such as low wages, low corporate taxes, political stability, neoliberal policies, weak unions, etc.) are given. Computer networks allow the global coordination of activities of transnational corporations from remote places; they make corporate control relatively independent of fixed times and places.

Economic globalization is today shaped by the rise of transnational corporations (TNCs). Restructuring (decentralization, flexiblization, outsourcing, lean management, flattening of hierarchies, just-in-time-production, etc.) is aimed at increasing profits by cutting costs. The model for transnational capitalism is the Japanese lean-production system of Toyota; hence, one also speaks of Toyotism. The goals of the existing forms of automation and computerization are the decrease of labor costs in order to increase profits. Transnational corporations are an important aspect of the post-Fordist economy. Their number has increased from 7,000 in 1970 to an estimated 53,600 in 1998 (French 2000). Transnationalism is different from the export strategy and multinationalism. In a corporation that employs an export strategy, a foreign branch of the corporation distributes the corporation's commodities in a specific country and is controlled by the center of the corporation that resides in one country. Multinational corporations are based on the idea that all establishments should be relatively autonomous and should try to autonomously control certain local, regional and national markets. Transnational corporations break the production process down into small units and make use of outsourcing and subcontracting in order to produce each unit in parts of the world where the conditions of production are attractive. Transnational corporations have a globally distributed and networked character; they produce and diffuse different and diversified products and services all over the world on local, regional, national, and international markets. TNCs account for around two-thirds of world trade and a quarter of world output (Held, McGrew, Goldblatt, and Perraton 1999, 236, 272).

Global trade and global capital investment are increasingly centralizing within the triad of North America, Europe, and Southeast Asia (especially Japan). Third World countries (especially African ones) are frequently not exploited by Western corporations and countries, but economically excluded. Other important economic trends are the increasing importance of information commodities, mental labor, the service sector, information industries, the liberalization of markets, the privatization of public services, production and delivery on demand, e-commerce, more and more nonstandard forms of labor such as precarious and semi-independent freelance workers, homeworkers, part-time workers, temporary workers, self-employees who constitute a new class of working poor (increasing unemployment due to technological productivity gains), central control of markets (such as in the culture, computer, and software industries), and global financial markets with flows of fictive capital that are detached from real capital accumulation and create financial speculation bubbles.

ICTs simplify the outsourcing, rationalization, and decentralization of production, teamwork, the flexiblization of jobs, and the flattening of organizational hierarchies. They are medium and result of the economic globalization of capitalism. They make the generation of temporal and spatial distance possible; hence, local processes are influenced by global ones and vice versa. It is due to the fact that ICTs dissolve temporal and spatial distances that corporations can flexibly manage production and make use of global interconnected flows of capital, technology, labor, and information. ICTs make global communication and world trade easier. They push ahead globalization, decentralization, and flexiblization of production; they are a medium of the territorial restructuring of capitalism. The generation and maintenance of networks of production that are typical for transnational corporations has been made much easier by ICTs. The diffusion of the Internet in society was not just a technological innovation but was also driven by the economic interest of capital to create new spheres of accumulation. Hence, the rise of ICTs is also result of the economic movements of post-Fordist restructuring that are typical for capital. So ICTs are not only medium of globalization processes; they are also a result of them.

Economic globalization means globe-spanning social relationships of commodity and finance markets and corporations. Large corporations increasingly outsource production to foreign small and medium-sized enterprises (SMEs). On the intercorporate level, corporations are involved in transnational production and innovation networks between firms in order to lower investment costs and increase profits. Strategic alliances and joint ventures concern especially joint research and development (R&D); there is a sharp rise in such alliances. Hence, Dunning (1997) speaks of "alliance capitalism". Strategic alliances are a cooperative effort to develop competitive advantages. Neil M. Coe et al. have in this context coined the term *global production* (Coe et al. 2004, 471). In another paper, Coe and Bunnell (2003) have worked out a similar concept of transnational innovation networks.

A systemic form of centralization characterizes the global economy of network capitalism. "If the global economy is to be understood as a set of interlocking networks of economic activity, then we must be prepared to ask who is excluded from such networks, and why" (Dicken et al. 2001, 95). The networks that are created on micro- and macrolevels of the economic system have resulted in an asymmetric distribution and centralization of resources and property. An increasing class of (working and nonworking) poor faces a small elite of rich managers, owners, and new economy employees. The Third World is excluded from the global geography of economic space; its position is only marginal and its social problems are aggravated due to the closure of global society. A small elite of transnational corporations that determine consumption, political decisions, and living conditions of the world population dominates the economy. Many people feel the effects of this rigid economically dominated type of globalization and feel estranged because decisions that affect their lives are made by anonymous powers that they don't know and whose actors they will never meet and are physically detached from local contexts. This economic dominionism could well result in the long persistence of a global informational empire. If capitalism is indeed organized as a global network economy, then one has to stress that the spatial geography of this economy is devised in such a way that there is a class of central hubs (corporations, countries, cities, city zones, regions, occupational groups, classes, individuals) that controls the flows of property, money, and goods in the network and hence creates an asymmetrical, divided, exclusive economic space where the majority of people is marginalized and kept outside of the network and a divided geography is created. Zygmunt Bauman (1998) argues in this context that contemporary globalization has resulted in a polarization between the globalized rich and the localized poor. The globals would be cosmopolitan, extraterritorial elites who traverse space easily and in a self-determined way. They would live in time; space wouldn't matter for them, since spanning every distance would be instantaneous. The locals would be fixed in space and locality (the "locally tied"); they would live in space that ties down time and keeps it beyond their control.

The economy of global network capitalism is based on a network logic that affects the internal structures (the horizontal corporation, semiautonomous work groups) and the external relationships/the environment of corporations (interfirm networking, corporate strategic alliances, global business alliances). But this doesn't result, as Castells (2000a) argues, in a "network economy" or as Van Dijk (2006) says in a "flow economy" because networks and flows of resources are characteristic for all types of economies. A more accurate signifier is the term *global capitalist network economy*.

In order to maximize profits by reducing constant and variable capital costs, firms take on global networked forms by outsourcing production to areas where labor costs and rights are minimal and by entering strategic alliances with other corporations. The result is global cooperation of relatively autonomous globally distributed firm units and cooperation between separate corporations in order to maximize profit and achieve competitive advantages. Hence, this form of cooperation advances the overall competitive and centralized character of capitalist society. Cooperation and competition are antagonistically intertwined; cooperation is used for advancing competition and profit generation (at the expense of certain actors).

7.2 INFORMATIONAL CAPITALISM: COMMODITY OR GIFT ECONOMY?

In April 2000, Microsoft was found guilty by a US court, in first instance, to offend the trust right and to try to secure itself a monopoly in the operating-system and the Web-browser market by distributing Windows in combination with Internet Explorer. The decision was that the enterprise should be separated into two parts. It was reverted in 2001 by an appeal court. The encryption of the source code of software makes possible a control by license rights. Users can't adapt the software further to their own needs; this possibility is reserved for the software company. Since the middle of the 1980s, the operating system Linux and corresponding application programs have been distributed as free software, that is, the source code is accessible and the programs can be developed further by users. Hence, it will be difficult or even impossible to obtain profit with such software. Special licenses (copy left) for free software, for example, the GNU (GNU is not Linux) general public license and the open source license, were developed. The open-source principle was expanded to other knowledge forms; the result are cooperative, global, networked knowledge production projects like the encyclopedia Wikipedia or open theory projects, creative commons licenses, that is, standard license agreements with which authors can grant rights for usage and differentiation of their works (texts, books, music pieces, etc.). The consumer becomes thereby the producer (prosumer), the reader the writer. Open source promises the participatory grassroots production of knowledge.

In July 2000, a guideline for the introduction of software patents was rejected by the European Parliament. It was argued that such patents could result in monopolies, quality loss, increasing prices of software, and the end of free software. ATTAC (Association Pour Une Taxation Des Transactions Financières Pour L'Aide Aux Citoyens) Germany and Campact organized an online demonstration against the introduction of software patents. Patents protect the economic use of new ideas and guarantee to the patentee a monopoly for use. People who infringe patent laws or refuse to pay royalty fees for the use of an idea can be prosecuted. An example: Adobe holds a patent for special dialogue menus since 1995 in the United States and since 2001 in Europe. The software enterprise Macromedia had to pay 2.8 billion euro to Adobe because it violated this patent. Certain types of software applications, algorithms, and input dialogues are standardized and widespread; they are used globally and hence can be considered as common knowledge of informatics. All object-oriented software engineering tools allow the usage of very similar input dialogues. If such an element is patented and I use it in my software application, I can be sued due to the violation of patent rights.

The TRIPS agreement (Agreement on Trade Related Aspects of Intellectual Property Rights) regulates that the World Trade Organization's member states must issue laws that secure intellectual property and that the penalties must be severe enough in order to avoid violations. It specifies, among other things, that there must be a copyright on computer programs, films, and live performances. By such means the unauthorized copying, diffusion, and transfer of digital contents shall be avoided.

Since the beginning of the millennium, file-sharing Internet applications, which work with the peer-to-peer technology (P2P) and allow the direct exchange of data between computers, have become ever more popular. They permit the free distribution of digital knowledge (music, pictures, video, films, software, etc.). Altogether the total amount of users of file-sharing systems exceeds 100 million. The music and film industry sees file sharing as an economic threat and hence files legal suits against operators of such services. Due to a complaint of the Recording Industry Association of America (RIAA) against Napster, the latter organization had to go offline in July 2000. In September 2002, after a complaint of the RIAA, the file-sharing system Audiogalaxy was transformed into a proprietary service. In March 2002, a Dutch appeal court ruled that the provider of Kazaa is not responsible for copyright infringements by its users. The verdict from November 2001 against Kazaa, that it must prevent copyright infringements, was reverted. During past years there has been a boom of file-sharing systems such as KaZaA Lite, LimeWire, Morpheus, Edonkey, WinMX, iMesh, Bearshare, Blubster, SoulSeek, BitTorrent, Overnet, Toadnode, and Grokster. The knowledge industry now also sues users of P2P networks in order to create precedents and deterring examples. In the year 2004, the Virgin Megastore, Vienna's largest retailer of music, went bankrupt. The management indicated that apart from heavy competition, file-sharing systems also would have led to strong losses in turnover.

In December 1999, the European Patent Office granted a patent to the University of Edinburgh for the extraction of embryonic stem cells from animals and humans. This patent on genetic information also included the right for breeding stem cells. After protests and objections, the patent was limited in July 2002. In 1990, the Human Genome Project started trying to decode the genetic information stored in the human genome. From 1981–1995, approximately 1,200 patents were granted on human DNA sections.

In the Internet there are databases in which lyrics of popular songs are stored and can be browsed. The Berlin-based law firm Wollmann und Partner sent over 200 warnings in the name of music publishers to over 40 operators of such Web pages in April 2005. The operators were requested to sign omission explanations and to pay 1,600 euro in lawyer fees per song. The operators concerned were to a large extent pupils and young people who were plunged into debt. The databases were freely accessible and not commercially oriented; the operators understand the publication of lyrics as advertisement for and support of artists.

These examples are characteristic for the Internet economy and show that the latter shows aspects of both a commodity and a gift economy. In the twenty-first century, knowledge is a hard-fought resource. The new property and class struggles are conflicts on the collective or private ownership of resources.

The dialectical antagonistic character of social and technical networks as motor of competition and cooperation in informational capitalism reflects Marx's idea that the productive forces of capitalism are at the same time means of exploitation and domination and produce potentials that go beyond actuality, point towards a radically transformed society, and anticipate a fully cooperative design of the means of production. The productive forces of contemporary capitalism are organized around informational networks. It is due to three specific characteristics of such structures that they come in contradiction with the capitalist relations of production and are a germ form (*keimform*) of a society that is based on fully cooperative and socialized means of production:

- Information as a strategic economic resource is globally produced and diffused by networks. It is a good that is hard to control in single places or by single owners.
- Information is intangible. It can easily be copied, which results in multiple ownerships and hence undermines individual private property.
- The Essence of networks is that they strive for establishing connections. Networks are in Essence a negation of individual ownership and the atomism of capitalism.

It certainly is right that in network capitalism surplus extraction reaches all aspects of society, both production and consumption. But this is not its central characteristic (as argued by Shaviro 2003, 249) because this leaves out the antagonistic dialectical movement in which informational networks both extend and undermine capital accumulation.

Informational networks aggravate the capitalist contradiction between the collective production and the individual appropriation of goods. "The contradiction between the general social power into which capital develops, on the one hand, and the private power of the individual capitalists over these social conditions of production, on the other, becomes ever more irreconcilable, and yet contains the solution of the problem, because it implies at the same time the transformation of the conditions of production into general, common, social, conditions" (Marx 1894, 274).

In one of the most well-known, but also most misunderstood, passages of Karl Marx's works he says that the "material conditions for the existence" of "new superior relations of production" mature "within the framework of the old society" and that the "productive forces developing within bourgeois society create also the material conditions for a solution of this antagonism" (Marx 1857/58, 9).[1] The informational networks that form the major productive forces of informational capitalism have turned into fetters of the relations of production. The misinterpretation of Marx is that he argued that the development of the productive forces automatically results in revolution and a free society. But Marx always spoke of material conditions of a new society. If productive forces are tied up by existing relations, there is in no way assured that they can be freed; they can remain enchained and will remain enchained as long as individuals let enchain themselves. Networks are a material condition of a free association, but the cooperative networking of the relations of production is not an automatic result of networked productive forces, a network society—in the sense of a distinctive sublation of network capitalism that constitutes itself as "associations of free and equal producers" (Marx 1869, 62) and an "association, in which the free development of each is the condition for the free development of all" (and vice versa!, Marx and Engels 1848, 482) and that is self-organizing according to the principle "From each according to his ability, to each according to his needs" (Marx 1875, 21)—is something that people must struggle for and that they can achieve under the given conditions but that could very well also never emerge if the dominant regime will be successful in continuing its reign. Networks anticipate a society in which "the antithesis between mental and physical labor has vanished", "the productive forces have also increased with the all-around-development of the individual", and "the springs of cooperative wealth flow more abundantly" (Marx 1875, 21). Networks are forms of development as well as fetters of capitalism; paraphrasing Marx one can say that informational capitalism is a point where the means of production have become "incompatible with their capitalist integument" (Marx 1867, 791).

Manuel Castells (2006, 20) argues that Marx's insight of the antagonism of the productive forces and the relations of production is important in the network society as rentier capitalism of the Microsoft type blocks in contrast to other models (such as open source) the expansion of innovation. This antagonism would be "the only lasting contribution from the classical Marxist theory" (Castells 2006, 20). This antagonism is the most important insight of Marx and it subsumes many important Marxian ideas such as the crisis-ridden nature of capitalism, social relations as class relations and potentially resulting class struggles, potentials of cooperation, the simultaneously productive and destructive role of technology in capitalism, and the material foundations of an alternative society. Hence, the antagonism is not the only lasting contribution of Marxian thinking but an indication for the importance of many Marxian categories for the analysis and practical critique of contemporary society.

For Slavoj Žižek (2001), the advancement of the antagonism between the productive forces and the relations of production shows the topicality of Leninism because Lenin would have seen elements of capitalism such as central banks as anticipations of communism. I agree with Žižek that the Internet has an explosive potential for capitalism and that elements of the new develop within the old. But the idea of Lenin was that capitalism creates monopolies that anticipate the state ownership of private property. The Internet economy, on the one hand, has monopolistic tendencies, which are, on the other hand, permanently questioned by the free sharing and cooperative production of digital knowledge with the help of a global decentralized network. The Internet doesn't anticipate a state-oriented centralized ownership of the digital means of production but grassroots cooperation and decentralized free access. This is not a Leninist form of socialism but a form of grassroots socialism. The comparison of the WWW to central banks by Žižek is inappropriate; not Lenin but Marx was "developing the theory of a role of World Wide Web" (Žižek 2001).

The antagonistic economic character of network capitalism has two colliding sides, the cooperative one of the informational gift economy and the competitive one of the informational commodity economy. The two sides and their antagonism will be analyzed in the next two subsections.

Cooperation in the Internet Economy: Open Source and the Informational Gift Economy

Knowledge is in global network capitalism a strategic economic resource; property struggles in the information society take on the form of conflicts on the public or proprietary character of knowledge. Its production is inherently social, cooperative, and historical. Knowledge is in many cases produced by individuals in a joint effort. New knowledge incorporates earlier forms of knowledge; it is coined by the whole history of knowledge. Hence, it is a public good and it is difficult to argue that there is an individual authorship that grounds individual property rights and copyrights. Global economic networks and cyberspace today function as channels of production and diffusion of knowledge commodities; the accumulation of profit by selling knowledge is legally guaranteed by intellectual property rights. Richard Stallman (2005) argues that the practice of persecuting the unauthorized redistribution of knowledge by robot guards, harsh punishments, information ads, legal responsibility of Internet service providers, and propaganda reminds him of Soviet totalitarianism in which the unauthorized copying and redistribution known as *samizdat* was prohibited.

In cyberspace, an alternative production model has been developed that sees economic goods not as property that should be individually possessed but as common goods to which all people should have access and from which all should benefit. This model stresses open knowledge, open access, and cooperative production forms; it can, for example, be found in virtual communities like the open-source community that produces the Linux operating system, which is freely accessible and to which, due to the free access to the source code of its software applications, people can easily contribute. The open access principle has resulted in global open-source production models where people cooperatively and voluntarily produce digital knowledge that undermines the proprietary character of knowledge (if knowledge is free and of good quality, why should one choose other knowledge that is expensive?). The open-source principle has also been applied to other areas, such as online encyclopedias (Wikipedia) and online journalism (Indymedia).

Open-source software or free software is software that provides four kinds of freedom for the user (Free Software Foundation 1996):

- The freedom to run the program, for any purpose.
- The freedom to study how the program works and adapt it to specific needs. Access to the source code is a precondition for this.
- The freedom to redistribute copies so that someone can help his neighbor.
- The freedom to improve the program and release these improvements to the public, so that the whole community benefits. Again, access to the source code is a precondition for this.

Open-source software has been realized mainly within projects such as the Linux operating system. Special licenses (termed *copy-left*) such as the GNU public license have been developed for assuring that free software has an open access to its source code. Free software hardly yields economic profit; it is freely available on the Internet and constitutes an alternative model of production that questions proprietary production models. Eric S. Raymond (1998b) argues that proprietary software is like a quiet, reverent, hierarchic cathedral, whereas the Linux community resembles "a great babbling bazaar of differing agendas and approaches". I agree that the Linux community represents a grassroots model, but I wouldn't compare this to a bazaar because bazaars are markets and the market mechanism and competition form principles of the commodity economy, whereas gifts and cooperation are principles of the gift economy. In a gift economy, property is freely given away, there is no accumulation, no money or other medium of exchange, and no exchange value. The idea can in philosophy be traced back to nineteenth century social anarchist thinkers like Peter Kropotkin (1902), who argued that a free economy should be organized as free association of humans who engage in free agreements, cooperation, and voluntary mutual aid. In the twentieth century, anthropologists like Marcel Mauss used the term for describing economic phenomena in traditional societies like the Kuala ring and for distinguishing gifts from commodity economies (Cheal 1988; Hyde 1983; Mauss 1954; Titmuss 1970). There is no agreement in the anthropological literature whether in traditional societies gifts can be free or are always based on the obligation for reciprocal exchange. With the rise of free software and the free sharing of digital information on the Internet, the notion of the free gift economy has been revived (e.g., Barbrook 1998; Veale 2003).

Lawrence Lessig employs the term *free culture* for the idea that technology "could enable a whole generation to create ... and then, through the infrastructure of the Internet, share that creativity with others" (Lessig 2002, 9). For Lessig, as for Richard Stallman, freedom in this context doesn't mean that digital knowledge should be provided at no costs but that users should be allowed to reuse and change knowledge. Marx considered freedom as a gift economy, a realm of freedom that is characterized by well-rounded individuality, pluralistic activities, abundance, the abolition of hard work and wage labor due to technological productivity, the disappearance of the performance principle and exchange, the free production and distribution of goods ("from each according to his ability, to each according to his needs"), and free time for idle and higher activity. The concept of freedom that Marx and Engels put forward questions freedom as the freedom of private property in means of production and understands it as freedom from scarcity and domination and as a community of associated individuals that provides wealth, self-ownership, self-realization of human faculties, and self-determination for all. Based on such a concept of freedom, a free culture doesn't only mean that digital knowledge can be freely used but that it also isn't exchanged for money as a commodity but provided for free. The exchange economy is sublated by the gift economy. A free culture is based on a broad concept of freedom; it is a noncapitalist culture.

Garrett Hardin (1968) argues that the commons are facing a tragedy: If they are freely available to all, the problem could arise that public resources are depleted. A feedlot available to all would be attractive for herdsmen because they could let their cattle graze for free. But if many would do so the feedlot would become bald and no one would any longer be able to benefit. Freedom in a commons would bring ruin to all. The problem with this example is that in it there is privately owned cattle and hence the interest of herdsmen to accumulate as much individual profit as possible by grazing cattle. If also cattle were treated as a common good, the herdsmen would try to find solutions from which all can benefit. Knowledge isn't used up by consumption (like grass on a meadow); it is a durable good. It isn't destroyed but enhanced by productive usage and it isn't a scare good; hence, it can't be argued that it shouldn't be treated as common free good because it faces the tragedy of the commons.

Digitization allows the easy copying of knowledge such as texts, music, images, software, and videos. The Internet enables the fast and free global distribution of knowledge with the help of technologies such as peer-to-peer-networks (Napster, Audiogalaxy, KaZaA, KaZaA Lite, LimeWire, Morpheus, Edonkey, WinMX, iMesh, Bearshare, Blubster, SoulSeek, BitTorrent, Overnet, Toadnode, Grokster, etc.). The informational content can be stored on different physical carriers; the possession of digital information by one person doesn't imply the nonpossession of it by others. Information is an intangible good; its characteristics have implications for ownership that are different from those implied by tangible goods. In the case of physical property, there can only be one possessor; in the case of information, the good can be shared without not being able to use it. If someone takes my house from me, I am deprived of it and can no longer live in it. But if someone takes an idea from me, I can still use it; I am not deprived of it. Hence, the Recording Industry Association of America (RIAA) sues operators of such network applications, but whenever one operator has been forced to quit its services, others have emerged. This shows that information and informational networks like the Internet are hard to control and that one should consider whether it is just and fair to monopolize and commodify information and to destroy its public character. All sorts of networked open-source activities show the power of cooperation and the possibility of enhancing cooperation by making use of digital networks.

In the Internet, each consumer of information is also a potential producer and vice versa; with the Internet, we see the emergence of the prosumer. Also, each receiver is a potential sender and vice versa; and each reader a potential writer and vice versa. The traditional relationship of the author and the reader is broken up. The Internet is closely connected to concepts like open source, open content, open theory, etc. It fosters the networked, cooperative production of information; you can download existing code, data, images, and so on, reuse and improve them. The open-source standards of the Internet software have in fact been one of the factors that have fostered its rapid growth. "The openness of the Internet's architecture was the source of its main strength: its self-evolving development, as users became producers of the technology, and shapers of the whole network" (Castells 2001, 27). Open-source software is one of the key features of the Internet's evolution.

Open-source communities and peer-to-peer networks are global networked spaces of production that advance principles of open access, free distribution, cooperative production, and common ownership of goods. Networking not only produces new models of capital accumulation but also alternative production models that undermine corporate power and suggest social spaces in which goods are jointly produced and freely distributed.

Proprietary models that aim at accumulating capital with the help of the Internet form another reality of the Internet economy. This realm that is connected to the formation of informational monopolies will be discussed in the next section.

Competition in the Internet Economy: Informational Monopolies

In society, information can only be produced jointly in cooperative processes, not individually. Hence, Marx argued that knowledge "depends partly on the cooperation of the living, and partly on the utilisation of the labours of those who have gone before" (Marx 1894, 114). Whenever new information emerges, it incorporates the whole societal history of information, that is, information has a historical character. Hence, it seems to be self-evident that information should be a public good, freely available to all. But in global informational capitalism, information has become an important productive force that favors new forms of capital accumulation. Information is today not treated as a public good, rather as a commodity. There is an antagonism between information as a public good and as a commodity. This antagonism stems from the fundamental capitalistic antagonism between products as use values and as exchanges values. Exchange value dominates use value; not the usefulness of a product is its main aspect but its commodification and valorization.

Traditional mass-media institutions (especially TV and cinema) make use of network technologies for reaching global audiences and providing globally available stations and programs. There is a fierce competition between a few global players in the mass-media market for global audiences and ratings. CNN and Hollywood are the main symbols of the globalization of mass-media markets. The digitalization of TV and radio broadcasting puts forward new forms of entertainment such as pay-per-view and video-on-demand. This can, on the one hand, enhance leisure time and education; on the other hand, it can, especially under the influence of monopolization and competition, standardize programs (unpretentious programs sell) and undercut the provision of cheap information and entertainment sources.

Contemporary cultural globalization means homogenization in the sense that culture has increasingly and worldwide a commercial character and is dominated by a few cultural TNCs. However, this process of homogenization makes use of difference and plurality; for example, CNN makes use of local reporters and knowledge; the cultural industry appeals to feelings of difference by consuming certain individualized products. Individualization and difference (micromarketing) have indeed become marketing strategies for homogenizing markets. "Media globalization may have a homogenizing effect, yet this homogenizing effect is more limited than previously anticipated, and it often occurs with a particularising effect" (Wang 1997, 317). This form of homogenization doesn't automatically mean the formation of global "false consciousness"; there are indeed different readings and interpretations of cultural products that have to a certain extent an unexpected character and can also be oppositional in character (Fiske 1996). But besides oppositional readings/codes, there are also what Stuart Hall (1999) calls hegemonic codes that employ dominant values and patterns and have a dominant character and hybrid forms of codes.

Political coverage in the mass media frequently makes use of principles such as emotionalization, concentration on selective facts, limitation to the methodical, demonstrative harmlessness and inoffensiveness, classificatory thinking, decontextualization, emergent meaning, and recoding. This results in misrepresentations and manipulation of reality. Monopolization is an important aspect of the mass media. Media corporations engage in both horizontal and vertical integration; they try to monopolize existing areas of specialization but also to settle down and expand their influence in other areas of mass media. They aim at both selling content (film, music, videos, books, TV programs, etc.) and acting as providers and distributors (media megastores, TV channels, cinemas, etc.). Production and distribution of media contents is converging. The system of the mass media is technologically multidimensional (multimedia), but institutionally there is an increasing lack of plurality; it is controlled by a few large global players that engage in such different areas as software, Internet, film, broadcasting, music, and so on, at the same time. The mass media are dominated by a few large transnational corporations (AOL Time Warner, Disney, Viacom, Bertelsmann, News Corporation (Murdoch), AT&T, Sony, Seagram, Polygram, NBC, Phillips, TCI, etc.; McChesney 2003). The largest one is Time Warner Inc., which was a result of the fusion of Time and Warner in 1989 and of Time Warner and Turner Broadcasting in 1996. In 2000, AOL, the largest Internet provider, merged with Time Warner, the largest media and entertainment corporation, in order to create AOL Time Warner. The danger of the vertical integration of an Internet infrastructure provider (AOL) and a media content provider (Time Warner) is that capitalist logic implies that the corporation will try to limit the content that is provided with the help of AOL's infrastructure to Time Warner products and hence will preferentially offer these commodities in order to accumulate ever more capital. Diversity is limited, consumption controlled by one huge corporation. The system of the mass media has a capitalistic character and to a certain extent pursues economic goals. The contemporary transformations of the global economy also apply for these media TNCs: transnational corporation structure, market concentration, privatization, and so on.

Whereas in premodern and agricultural societies the main actors of cultural globalization were world religions and empires, with the rise of modern society the rationalistic Enlightenment ideology that heavily focuses on economic interests became the main medium of cultural globalization. Today we witness the intensification and acceleration of modernization; the mass media and cultural TNCs have become the main aspects of cultural globalization. The symbolic cultural contents that people are confronted with today (books, films, broadcasts, food, magazines, digital content, etc.) have an increasingly segmented global character in the sense that they reach consumers across the globe but mainly stem from Western countries (especially the United States). Concentration in the cultural industry moves along a horizontal and a vertical axis. Horizontal integration means that cultural TNCs focus on mergers with corporations that offer the same services, whereas in vertical integration they try to acquire both large channels of production and distribution in order to control the consumption process. Hence, there is a convergence in ownership of content production and distribution networks.

For ranking the largest companies in the knowledge industries, I have referred to the *Forbes* list of the 2,000 largest corporations for 2007 and have filtered out those companies that operate in knowledge-based industries. Corporations are ranked by capital assets (table 7.1). As knowledge-based industries, I consider here classical mass media (TV, radio, press, publishing, audio/music), telecommunication services (hardware, operators, services), and computer industries (semiconductors, hardware, software). The concept of knowledge-based industries/services is here used as a collective term for what Manfred Knoche (1999) has termed *media capital* (capital invested in

Table 7.1 The 20 Largest Corporations in Knowledge Industries

Rank	Name	Country	Category	Assets ($ Billion; 2007)
1	AT&T	USA	Telecommunications Services	270,63
2	Vodafone	UK	Telecommunications Services	220,17
3	Verizon Communications	USA	Telecommunications Services	196,76
4	Deutsche Telekom	Germany	Telecommunications Services	159,90
5	Nippon	Japan	Telecommunications Services	152,65
6	Telefónica	Spain	Telecommunications Services	132,30
7	Time Warner	USA	Media	131,67
8	France Telekom	France	Telecommunications Services	125,01
9	Comcast	USA	Media	110,41
10	Telecom Italia	Italy	Telecommunications Services	110,19
11	Siemens	Germany	Conglomerates	109,12
12	IBM	USA	Software & Services	103,23
13	Sprint Nextel	USA	Telecommunications Services	97,16
14	Sony	Japan	Technology Hardware & Equipment	88,75
15	Hitachi	Japan	Technology Hardware & Equipment	82,51
16	Hewlett-Packard	USA	Technology Hardware & Equipment	81,31
17	Samsung Electronics	South Korea	Semiconductors	72,90
18	Microsoft	USA	Software & Services	66,37
19	Matsushita Electric Industrial	Japan	Technology Hardware & Equipment	66,06
20	Tyco International	Bermuda	Conglomerates	63,68

Source: Forbes 2000, 2007 Listing of World's Largest Corporations, March 29th 2007.

content production in traditional mass media), media-related capital (capital invested in the production of media technologies), and media infrastructure capital (capital invested in infrastructure for the storage and transportation of data and in communication services). It should be noted that knowledge-based industries are capitalist in nature; hence, a more appropriate term might be knowledge-based capital. Table 7.2. shows the largest companies in ICT industries (hardware, software, Internet).

The total GDP of all 53 African states was 1000,913 billions US$ in 2007 (data according to World Economic Outlook Online Database, April 2007, retrieved on June 25th 2007). The total assets of the top six knowledge corporations (AT&T, Vodafone, Verizon, Deutsche Telekom, Nippon, Telefónica) were 1132,41 billion US$ in 2007 and hence are larger than the total African GDP. This shows the huge economic power of knowledge corporations. Knowledge that is produced, transmitted, and communicated with the help of technologies influences human thinking and decisions. Hence, the existing agglomeration of economic capital by knowledge corporations gives them a tremendous power for influencing human thinking and decisions. They control definitions of reality and are able to create one-dimensional views of reality that neglect negation and critique of dominant views that represent dominant interests.

According to onestat.com (August 14, 2006), Microsoft Windows had a market share of 96.9 percent in the area of operating systems (Apple: 2.47%; Linux: 0.36%) in 2006. With capital assets of 66,37 billion US$ in 2007 Microsoft is the 18th largest knowledge-creating company and the largest (pure) software corporation in the world. In July 2006, Google accounted for 43.7 percent of searches done by Internet users in the United States (Source: searchengingewatch.com, September 13, 2006). Google had capital assets of US$10.27 billion in 2006; it was ranked number 106 in the list of the largest knowledge-creating corporations, was, according to these data, the eighth largest software company in 2006 (Microsoft was the leading software company in 2006, followed by First Data, Electronic Data Systems, Softbank, Computer Sciences, Yahoo, SAP, and Google), and was in 2006 ranked by *Forbes* magazine as the fastest-growing technology company in terms of the growth of annual earnings (30%) and five-year sales (497%; forbes.com, September 13, 2006). In 2007 Google's capital assets increased to 18,47 billion US$ and it became the fifth largest software corporation in the world (cf. table 7.2).

What's the problem with monopolies in the computer and software industries?

- Ideology: Corporations that produce or organize digital content (like the Microsoft Encarta or Google's page-rank algorithm) have the power to define what people consider as correct and valuable views of reality and as truth. So there are, for example, many Web pages that are not found by Google (the so-called Hidden Web) and hence are excluded

Table 7.2 The 20 Largest Corporations in the Computer Industries

Rank	Name	Country	Category	Assets ($ Billion; 2007)
1	IBM	USA	Software & Services	103,23
2	Hewlett-Packard	USA	Technology Hardware & Equipment	81,31
3	Samsung Electronics	South Korea	Semiconductors	72,90
4	Microsoft	USA	Software & Services	66,37
5	Intel	USA	Seminconductors	48,37
6	Cisco Systems	USA	Technology Hardware & Equipment	46,25
7	First Data	USA	Software & Services	34,46
8	Fujitsu	Japan	Technology Hardware & Equipment	31,86
9	NEC	Japan	Technology Hardware & Equipment	30,83
10	Oracle	USA	Software & Services	28,93
11	Dell	USA	Technology Hardware & Equipment	23,15
12	Alcatel-Lucent	France	Technology Hardware & Equipment	22,87
13	Apple	USA	Technology Hardware & Equipment	19,46
14	EMC	USA	Technology Hardware & Equipment	18,57
15	Google	USA	Software & Services	18,47
16	Taiwan Semiconductor	Taiwan	Seminconductors	18,02
17	Electronic Data Sys	USA	Software & Services	17,95
18	Symantec	USA	Software & Services	17,90
19	Softbank	Japan	Software & Services	15,18
20	Nortel Networks	Canada	Technology Hardware & Equipment	14,48

Source: Forbes 2000, 2007 Listing of Largest Corporations, March 29th 2007 (excluded were companies that don't derive their products from predominantly selling computerized ICTs and ICT equipment, but sell such goods among others[6]).

from searches. Monopolies hence have an ideological function; they can potentially lead to the simplification of complex realities. Visibility on the Internet is a commodity; a high rank in search results can be purchased. Awareness of information generates economic profit.

- Labor standards: Monopoly corporations can set low labor standards (especially concerning wages) in their industry sector.
- Political power: In capitalism, money is entangled with political power; hence, monopolies enable huge political influence of small groups of people.
- Control of prices: They have the economic power to control prices of information goods.
- Control of technological standards: They have the power to define and control technological standards. Lawrence Lessig (2002) argues that monopolies like the one held by Microsoft in the area of operating systems, intellectual-property rights on technology, and software patents destroy the original idea of the Internet, which is based on an existing common architecture—code, that is, protocols and software that make protocols run—everyone can create applications and content. Monopolists like Microsoft or AOL would aim at monopolizing technological systems and limit the potential diversity of code, content, and applications. Monopolization would threaten the existence of free software code and free content.
- Dependency of customers: Controlling the power to define technological standards also means that the need of customers to buy ever more software and versions (that only run on certain systems such as Windows or Apple) in order to remain up to date can be generated. Hence, a potential result is an increasing dependency on commodities produced by one corporation and increasing monopoly profits.
- Economic centralization: They deprive others of economic opportunities.
- Quality: A monopolist might care less about quality because there are no alternatives to choose from for consumers.
- Surveillance and censorship: If content and applications are monopolized, that is, most users have to rely on certain products of single companies, operations of surveillance (i.e., monitoring, statistically evaluating, and recording what users are doing online, which content they create, consume, and how and what they communicate) and censorship can be carried out more easily and more completely than in the case of several competing companies. For example, Google gained a license for operating in China, given the condition that it censors certain political search results and blocks links to certain servers. The economic interest of reaching more than 100 million Chinese Internet users obviously was the driving force for Google's censorship. More and more users upload private pictures and videos to the Internet with the help of platforms such as MySpace, Flickr, or YouTube. If software

for biometric face recognition were combined with a search database such as Google, it would be potentially possible to identify the names and other data of individuals who are shown on digital pictures or in videos. If such a service were introduced either for state authorities or private users, privacy rights would be violated.

In order to characterize the formation of monopolies in the information-producing sector of the economy, Peter Drahos and John Braithwaite (2002, 2sq.) use the term *information feudalism*, by which they mean the "transfer of knowledge assets from the intellectual commons into private hands. These hands belong to media conglomerates and integrated life sciences corporations rather than individual scientists and authors". Private monopolistic power would be the effect; Drahos and Braithwaite speak of "infogopolies" secured by patents and intellectual-property rights. I consider information feudalism as a misleading term: Feudalism was a societal formation in which the class of the aristocrats owned the means of production (land), which were rented to peasants. The peasants were bond slaves of the lords and had to pay rent (in the form of labor, products, or money). This means that part of the working day they worked for earning a living; the other part they worked for free for the lord; they had to transfer the results of their labor. One could find money and markets, but no money capital, that is, money that is accumulated by being invested in the production of ever more commodities that are sold on markets and that is accumulated at increasing pace by a technologically mediated process of rising productivity. Feudalism was an agricultural society, whereas capitalism is based on modern industry, "double-free" wage labor, and the globalization of production and markets. The feudal peasant is tied to the land and owns his own tools, whereas wage labor has to sell its capacities on the labor market and doesn't own the produced goods as well as the utilized tools. The term *information feudalism* is incorrect because a central structural feature of contemporary society is that it is capitalist. Hence, it is more appropriate to speak of, for example, informational capitalism that has a tendency for trying to form monopolies.

Competition and cooperation in the Internet economy are not two separate models. In the next section it will be discussed how cooperation is used for advancing the competitive logic of capital accumulation. The gift and the commodity economy interlock antagonistically.

The Gift Commodity Internet Economy: Strategies of Accumulation in Informational Capitalism

In this section I want to show different strategies that are used for accumulating capital with the help of the Internet. It will also be pointed out that the relationship of information commodities and information gifts in the Internet economy is truly dialectical, which means that there is not a simple opposition of the two but an entanglement of gifts within the commodity form. On the one hand, gifts today hence are subsumed under capital and yield profit; on the other hand, they point towards the future and anticipate a fully developed gift economy.

First I want to discuss how capital accumulation takes place with the help of information commodities and information technologies. Kenney (1997) argues that one must distinguish between physical- and knowledge-based production of value. The driving force of the economy would be the production of knowledge today. Hence, knowledge that is part of a commodity would be the determining factor of value production. Value would today mainly be produced by mental creations of knowledge workers. Kenney misunderstands that mental and material production cannot simply be treated separately. Today, mental labor quite often manifests itself in physical commodities (such as compact discs, videos, computer games, etc.). Marx argued in many passages that such a material foundation of the accumulation of capital and the production of surplus value is a necessary stipulation of capitalism.

James Curry (1997) says that knowledge is not a thing but a social process, a general abstraction outside the nexus of capital, a general pool that is nonproprietary and available for everyone. When it is subsumed under capital, knowledge would become information. Applying Hegel's categories of universality, particularity and individuality, Curry argues that knowledge is a universal determination, information something particular that is related to ideas and meaning, and data something individual related to syntactic aspects. All material products of human activity would contain knowledge and as commodities information. The use value of information products would be their information content. All commodities would have a knowledge composition consisting of the technical knowledge embodied in both the design and production of a commodity and an ideational content which is a symbolic aspect created through marketing and advertising. With the rise of informational capitalism, the information content of commodities would have increased. The value of an information commodity would be relatively autonomous from its material form (paper, film, magnetic media, etc.) and there would be no value without circulation; the value form would have to be consumed in order to have meaning in capitalism. "The vast majority of the value of a particular knowledge-content commodity comes from the content, i.e., Spielberg's or Lucas' idea" (Curry 1997).

If this means that the surplus value contained in an information commodity is mainly an ideational content that is derived from an innovating idea, one must be careful with such assumptions because this would mean that an idea by Spielberg or Lucas is the source of surplus value and that hence there must be a tendency of exploitation decreasing or vanishing. In fact, there is an idea for a book, a piece of software, and so on, but there are also a number of workers realizing that idea, which results in the actual information commodity that has a material reality. They are employed and exploited by a corporation. The actual value of a single piece of an information commodity is relatively low due to the qualities of information that favor capitalist interests. Information is only produced once but copied millions of times very cheaply. The average value of one piece can be calculated by counting the number of necessary working hours and the number of produced pieces in a certain period and figuring out the average number of working hours needed for the production of one piece. This will be a very low number compared to traditional industrial production. In my view, information products don't have a high value due to their symbolic value; they have very low value but are sold at prices much higher than their value. And for justifying this it is argued that it has a high symbolic value. The surplus value contained in an information commodity is related to the time spent by employees in material and ideational production. Value isn't something subjective that is related to ideas (this would mean that the more important an idea, the more value the commodity that represents this idea), as sometimes suggested by postmodern theory (e.g., Baudrillard); value is something objective, a relationship in the material world that emanates from human beings' practical existence in the real world. It is true that frequently more time is spent developing marketing strategies and the knowledge contained in an information commodity than is spent in doing the actual reproduction process (software is a very good example for this), but at a whole information commodities don't have more but much less value than traditional commodities. Nonetheless, they are a major source of profit due to the difference between value and price that is justified by the ideological construct of the importance of subjective ideas and symbolic importance. So it is important to say that the ideational content doesn't have subjective value but objective value in the sense of hours spent in production by employees who are dependent on the wages paid by capitalists. Surplus value can only be created by variable capital; it exists prior to circulation and consumption and is only transformed into profit by its selling on the market. A commodity that doesn't sell still does have value but doesn't result in profit.

The work of Kenney and Curry (1999) is an important contribution that suggests that the advent of the computer and data communication networks has accelerated knowledge creation, but with this has come a more rapid obsolescence in the things that objectify this knowledge. "Production equipment loses market value quickly and simultaneously as factories become more automated there is more capital at risk. Profits must be made before the equipment is superseded by a dramatically superior machine. This gives real meaning to the term "speed-based" competition. The introduction of electronics makes machines more productive, but simultaneously, because it helps accelerate technological change, the machine's productive life decreases making it a wasting asset. In many fields, the factory comes under increased pressure to operate constantly, because physical depreciation no longer bears any relationship to obsolescence". Nonetheless, the authors argue in a rather idealistic manner that there is a dematerialization of the economy and commodities, that software is entirely a creation of the mind, and that the Internet represents an extremely powerful dematerialization.

Such formulations don't take into account the material nature of informational capitalism and of value production in the information age.

Modern society is not only based on the domination of human labor by capital; also, technology and science as means for increasing productivity and the speed of commodity production are subsumed under capital. Technology is a means that enables labor to produce ever more value in ever less time. As a result, there is an antagonism of producer and means of production: "Within the capitalist system all methods for raising the social productiveness of labour are brought about at the cost of the individual labourer; all means for the development of production transform themselves into means of domination over, and exploitation of, the producers; they mutilate the labourer into a fragment of a man, degrade him to the level of an appendage of a machine, destroy every remnant of charm in his work and turn it into a hated toil; they estrange from him the intellectual potentialities of the labour-process in the same proportion as science is incorporated in it as an independent power" (Marx 1867, 674). In a similar passage, Marx says: "Every kind of capitalist production, in so far as it is not only a labour-process, but also a process of creating surplus-value, has this in common, that it is not the workman that employs the instruments of labour, but the instruments of labour that employ the workman. But it is only in the factory system that this inversion for the first time acquires technical and palpable reality. By means of its conversion into an automaton, the instrument of labour confronts the labourer, during the labour-process, in the shape of capital, of dead labour, that dominates, and pumps dry, living labour-power" (Marx 1867, 446).

Substituting living labor by technology is an economic interest of contemporary society; it is necessary for reducing the costs of investment and reproduction of capital and for shortening its turnover time so that an increase of profit can be achieved. The continuous overthrow and revolution of technology by science are conditions of existence and reproduction of capital. Hence, during capitalist development the importance of the technological means of production (fixed constant capital [cfix])—and hence of knowledge labor—increases and the one of living labor (variable capital [v]) decreases. Marx argues that the organic composition of capital (the relation c:v) grows continuously: "The accumulation of capital, though originally appearing as its quantitative extension only, is effected, as we have seen, under a progressive qualitative change in its composition, under a constant increase of its constant, at the expense of its variable constituent" (Marx 1867, 657). To put it more simply: Technology substitutes labor. The mass of constant and variable capital increases continuously in the accumulation process, but in the long run constant capital grows faster than variable capital. Variable capital decreases relatively to constant one.

By the increase of constant capital (the value of the means of production), the relative mass of total labor oriented on the reproduction of capital and the mass of labor occupied with the reproduction of the means of production that includes machinery (technologies for communication and transport, buildings) rises (Marx 1861–63, 190). Production becomes ever more dependent on knowledge, the "General Intellect" (Marx 1857/58, 602), the "universal labour of the human spirit" (Marx 1894, 114), "the power of knowledge, objectified" that becomes "a direct force of production" (Marx 1857/58, 602). The rise of knowledge in production is based on the inner tendency of capitalism for a rising organic composition of capital that at a certain nodal point results in a turn from quantity to quality, that is, a qualitatively new phase of capitalist development. We don't live in a knowledge or information society; rather, the dynamics and dialectic of continuity and discontinuity of modern production have resulted in a new capitalist mode of development: informational capitalism/knowledge capitalism.

Obtaining profit from commodified knowledge is tied to the existence of intellectual property rights that artificially transform knowledge into a scare resource by creating an artificial monopoly for the diffusion of certain knowledge forms and contents. The idea of aesthetics that art has form and content (Adorno 1970) can be generalized for knowledge. For the monopolization of knowledge forms and types, patents are used; for the monopolization of knowledge contents, copyrights. In the categories of the Marxian labor theory of value, the value of a product is the objectified labor time needed for producing the good. In this context Marx formulated the law of value: "We see then that that which determines the magnitude of the value of any article is the amount of labour socially necessary, or the labour time socially necessary for its production. . . . In general, the greater the productiveness of labour, the less is the labour time required for the production of an article, the less is the amount of labour crystallised in that article, and the less is its value; and vice versa, the less the productiveness of labour, the greater is the labour time required for the production of an article, and the greater is its value. The value of a commodity, therefore, varies directly as the quantity, and inversely as the productiveness, of the labour incorporated in it" (Marx 1867, 54sq.).

The value of a commodity is made up of the value of the necessary raw materials (constant capital), the value of the necessary labor (variable capital), and the newly generated value (surplus value): $V = c + v + s$. Knowledge has little value, that is, not much labor is necessary for producing a copy of knowledge. If knowledge is produced once, it can be copied and transported with the help of media such as CDs, DVDs, and the Internet almost at no cost. The copying of a music CD costs less than 1 euro, but copies are sold at 15–20 euros. Capital is so interested in commodifying knowledge because the latter has a low value, it doesn't depreciate by consumption, and can be reproduced cheaply. The sale of knowledge at prices far above its economic value is the central value-theoretic mechanism in the process of accumulating capital with knowledge products.

Let's consider an example that shows that capital can make use of the specific characteristics of information in order to yield large profits with information commodities. Imagine the production of a mass software with a certain turnaround time; the production time of the necessary knowledge is best assigned to the first turnover period of capital. We assume that all copies are sold, that already after the first turnaround a profit is achieved, and that there is no interest and rent to be paid. Let the market price of one piece of software be 1,190 euros. We have to distinguish the constant and variable capital in the production of knowledge (c_1 and v_1) from the capital involved in the physical reproduction process (c_2 and v_2). Let's also assume that at the first turnover 100,000 pieces of commodity are produced, that c_1 = 10 10^6 €, v_1 = 50 10^6 €, c_2 = 5 10^6 €, v_2 = 2 10^6 €.

Hence, the total investment costs are 67.10^6 €. We assume a rate of surplus value of 100%. The mass of constant capital is c = c_1 + c_2 = 15 10^6, the mass of variable capital v = v_1 + v_2 = 52.10^6. Due to a rate of surplus value of 100%, the mass of surplus value produced is s = 52 10^6 €. All copies are sold, hence the revenues are 1190*100 000 = 119.10^6 euros. Subtracting the investment costs from this sum results in a profit of 52.10^6 euros for the first year. The average value of a single copy is v = c_d + v_d + s_d, where c_d, v_d, and s_d describe the average proportions for one commodity of the total constant and variable capital as well as of the total surplus value produced. Hence the average commodity value is

$$v = \frac{15 \times 10^6}{10^5} + \frac{52 \times 10^6}{10^5} + \frac{52 \times 10^6}{10^5} = 1190 .$$

In this example, the value of the commodity equals its market price. Let's take a look at the second turnover of capital: We assume that the conditions of production, the costs and the total amount of produced commodities remain the same. How does profit develop? The investment costs for knowledge production don't have to be spent by the capitalists this time due to the specific characteristics of information (c_1 = 0, v_1 = 0). Hence the average commodity value is reduced to

$$v = \frac{5 \times 10^6}{10^5} + \frac{2 \times 10^6}{10^5} + \frac{2 \times 10^6}{10^5} = 90 .$$

This means that the average value of a single piece of software has massively decreased without a change in the conditions of production! This is due to the fact that knowledge only has to be produced once; it only has what Marx called a "moral" devaluation but doesn't loose value by deterioration, use, or nonuse; it can be reproduced easily and very cheaply, and so on. The software is still sold at 1,190 euros; hence, the profit increases from 52.10^6 euros to 112.10^6 euros. This amounts to an increase of average profit from 520 euros to 1,120 euros per commodity and an increase of the profit rate from 0.78 to 16 (profit rate = profit / (c+v))! This shows that the value of a piece of software is much lower than its market price and that the specific characteristics of knowledge are the mechanism that enables capital accumulation in the software industry.

A typology of the Internet economy will now be presented. The typology is based on some categories: First, a distinction between hardware industry (including hardware such as computer and periphery as well as infrastructure such as networks and hardware configurations for, e.g., mail accounts and Web pages), software industry, and content industry is made. The second category describes what is provided by the organizations: a traditional physical good (such as books, cars, furniture, etc.), digital products (software, digitized music/films/images, etc.), or services, that is, not physical objects but social relationships (i.e., that which is provided is primarily oriented on human action that helps users or customers to achieve certain goals and not on things that help users achieve goals). Another category describes which technological dimension the organization makes predominant use of in order to achieve their goals (computer hardware, network infrastructure, software, digital content). This category doesn't focus on what the organization provides or sells but on the means that it makes use of to do so. The next category describes aspects of circulation: It is shown if the goods and services are diffused online or offline (i.e., if they are digital or not/take place on digital networks or not). Another category describes if the organization is oriented on achieving money profit or not. The last category grasps if the goods or services provided have costs (commodity, exchange value) or not (gift, use value). Note that there are organizations that focus on generating profit but provide gifts. So, for example, Google provides its service of searching for information on the World Wide Web for free for users but is mainly oriented on achieving money profit by selling online advertisement space to customers. Concerning payment, there are the following possibilities: One pays once for a good or service; one pays for each usage or for the amount consumed; there is a regular subscription fee; one doesn't pay for usage, but advertisers pay for the marketing of their products and services on the platform, or the product or service is provided for free (i.e., with no costs).

Table 7.3 doesn't assert the claim to be a complete overview of accumulation strategies in the Internet economy, but it tries to show how some important models work. Capital is dynamic; it only exists as long as it can be increased. Capital that is fixed in certain products and industries is under constant threat of crisis: If markets become saturated, the purchasing power of potential customers drops, or competing corporations can offer better, similar products at cheaper prices because they have a higher productivity; then a firm enters crisis, that is, its profit rate begins to drop. In order to avoid such situations, capitalist corporations permanently seek to innovate new products, new technologies, and to reach new markets, that is, capital is expansive. Manfred Knoche (1999) argues that capital moves to different areas of the economy if it expects to achieve higher profit rates there. There would be capital strategies that search for markets in the area of new

Table 7.3 Economic Strategies in the Internet Economy

Model	Product	Technologies Used	Distribution Method	Orientation	Method for Achieving Goals
IBM Model	Physical	Hardware and Infrastructure (Computers, periphery like printers and input devices)	Offline	Profit	Products sold on market
GoDaddy Model	Physical, Digital	HW Infrastructure (Domain, Webspace, Mail Account, Internet Account)	Offline, Online	Profit	Products sold on market, payment once, regularly, or per amount/duration of use
Yahoo Model (Mail) Geocities Model (Webspace)	Physical, Digital	HW Infrastructure (Webspace, Mail Account)	Online	Profit	Gift economy and advertisements
Wireless Community Model	Physical, Digital	HW Infrastructure	Offline	Non-Profit	Gift economy
Community Network Model	Physical, Digital	HW Infrastructure (Webspace, Mail Account, Internet Account)	Offline, Online	Non-Profit	Gift economy or donations
Microsoft Model	Digital	Software	Online and Offline	Profit	Products sold on market
Norton Antivirus Model	Digital	Software	Online and Offline	Profit	Subscription
Mozilla Model	Digital	Software	Online	Profit	Gift economy and advertisements
Linux Model	Digital	Software	Online and Offline	Non-Profit	Gift economy
EDS Model	IT Services	HW, Infrastructure, SW	Offline	Profit	Products sold on market

Model	Platform type	Object	Mode	Orientation	Revenue model
ITunes Model	Digital information platform	Content sold in an online shop	Online (transfer of files)	Profit	Products sold on market
Wall Street Journal Model	Digital information platform	Content (text, images, videos, music), Web platform	Online	Profit	Subscription for access
Google Model	Digital information platform	Content (text, images, videos, music), metainformation, Web platform	Online	Profit	Gift economy and advertisements
Indymedia Model, Soulseek Model	Digital information platform	Content (text, images, videos, music), Web platform	Online	Nonprofit	Gift economy
Microsoft Outlook Model	Digital communication platform	Social relationships, online tool	Online	Profit	Products sold on market
The Well Model	Digital communication platform	Social relationships, online platform	Online	Profit	Subscription for access
MySpace Model	Digital communication platform	Social relationships, online platform	Online	Profit	Gift economy and advertisements
mIRC Model	Digital communication platform	Social relationships, online platform	Online	Nonprofit	Gift economy
IBM Lotus Model	Digital cooperation platform	Digital content production, online platform	Online	Profit	Products sold on market
Socialtext Model	Digital cooperation platform	Digital content production, online platform	Online	Profit	Subscription for access
Writely Model	Digital cooperation platform	Digital content production, online platform	Online	Profit	Gift economy and advertisements
Wikipedia Model	Digital cooperation platform	Digital content production, online platform	Online	Nonprofit	Gift economy

media and strategies that try to establish new market segments in established media sectors. The expansive nature of capital pointed out by Knoche explains why media capital is invested in Internet business; the new technology promises new opportunities for the accumulation of capital, which results in the investment of capital of established media corporations and the formation and capital investment of new corporations. Internet capital tries to make profit with the help of different accumulation strategies. Finding new accumulation strategies and differentiating existing ones seems to be a condition of survival of capital in the Internet economy. Capital strategies related to the Internet concern the use of the Internet for the marketing of already existing products and for the commercial distribution of newly generated digital content. Hence, the Internet economy is intertwined with already existing capital and markets, but it is also an economic space for the formation of new capital and markets.

The rise of the Internet economy has taken place in a societal situation that is characterized by the diffusion of economic logic into all spheres of society, which can be characterized as neoliberal capitalism. The privatization of formerly state-owned media sectors, such as telecommunications, television, and radio, is a symptom of this area. Capital is looking for new spheres and strategies of accumulation in order to avoid crisis. Manfred Knoche (2001) points out that there is not just an economization but a capitalization of media industries that is part of the capitalization of lifeworlds and society at large. Capitalization doesn't only affect the traditional mass media such as print, radio, television, recording, and film, but also the Internet, which, first of all, is a sphere for the advertisement of commodities, for capital formation and accumulation, and for the reduction of transaction and communication costs of corporations.

I have termed the different economic strategies according to trendsetting organizations. Don Tapscott argues that the digital economy—which he defines as "new economy based on the networking of human intelligence" (Tapscott 1996, xiii)—is made up of e-business communities—"networks of suppliers, distributors, commerce providers, and customers that execute substantial business communications and transactions via the Internet and other electronic media" (Tapscott 1999, xiii). The business models presented here are based on economic networking, but to speak of communities obscures the fact that they are first of all oriented on capital accumulation, which is a competitive process.

It should be noted that these are not only profit-oriented organizations. Indeed, most accumulation strategies are accompanied by a nonproprietary version that contradicts the proprietary model and in which products and services are offered for free (without payment). The Internet economy is an antagonistic and contested space in which commodification and decommodification processes are present and contradict each other (Fleissner 2005). Decommodification technologies threaten to undercut the commodification of the Internet and hence the profit of "new economy" corporations.

There is a commodified Internet economy and a noncommodified Internet economy. Only those aspects of the Internet economy that are nonprofit gifts, that just have use value and no exchange value, hence are provided without costs for the users and without selling advertisement space, can be considered as decommodified or noncommodified. Examples are file-sharing platforms, Wikipedia, Linux, and Indymedia. Commodified Internet spaces are always profit oriented, but the goods they provide are not necessarily exchange value and market oriented; in some cases (such as Google, Yahoo, MySpace, YouTube, Netscape), free goods or platforms are provided as gifts in order to drive up the number of users so that high advertisement rates can be charged in order to achieve profit. In other cases, digital or nondigital goods are sold with the help of the Internet (e.g., Amazon), or exchange of goods is mediated and charged for (online marketplaces such as eBay or the Amazon Marketplace). In any of these cases the primary orientation of such spaces is instrumental reason, that is, the material interest of achieving money profit, that is, a surplus to the invested capital.

Generally speaking, one can distinguish between direct (payment once, regular payment, payment according to duration or amount of consumption) and indirect (advertisement, subsidies) forms of revenue in the Internet economy (Zerdick 1999, 25). In the models identified here, we generally distinguish between advertisement, payment once, regular payment (subscription), and pay per use (duration, amount of transfered data). Besides e-commerce for physical and digital products, advertisement on the Internet is also of particular importance. Besides legal advertising, where users agree that by using certain platforms information on their online behavior is collected and sold to advertising agencies that confront them with personalized advertisement, there are also illegal forms of data mining and advertisement, for example, organizations that collect or sell e-mail addresses in order to enable companies to send unsolicited commercial spam mail to users.

First there are hardware and hardware infrastructure models: *The IBM model* is based on the production and circulation of hardware technologies such as computers, laptops, printers, scanners, monitors, digital cameras, mp3 players, network infrastructure, etc. Computers and computer networks are the material foundation for going online. In the *GoDaddy model* technologies that are needed for accessing and operating the Internet on workstations are sold by companies. This includes the provision of Internet access (Internet access providers), of domain names and web space for websites, e-mail accounts, etc. Payment is either done once, regularly, or per duration/amount of usage. In the *Yahoo (mail)* and *Geocities (webspace) models* such services are offered as gifts to users, profit is made by selling advertisement space to customers, the ads are delivered to the users of the free e-mail programs and web sites. Internet access, web space, e-mail accounts, etc. can be considered as being both physical and digital, they require physical features (such as modems, network cables, servers, etc.), but also digital applications for administering accounts.

Proprietary hardware and hardware infrastructure models are questioned by community models: In the *wireless community model* (e.g., SFLan in San Francisco, Seattle Wireless, Funkfeuer in Vienna, the ICT&S WLAN at Max-Reinhard-Platz in Salzburg, etc.) in which wireless Internet access is offered for free. Closely related to this model is the idea of public access: Internet access and computers are offered for free in public spaces.

Providers of completely non-profit and non-commercial hardware infrastructure are rare, but can nontheless be found. For example, Piranho offers unlimited web space without advertisements for free and the Open Webmail Project is a non-commercial open source initiative for developing a web-based freemail program. Many community networks offer to their members free or cheap Internet access, web pages, and e-mail accounts on a non-profit basis. Some of them expect or charge modest annual donations and provide certain groups with free access (e.g. in the LA Free Net access for students and classrooms is free, the Seattle Community Network provides free services, but expects donations on a pay-what-you-can basis). Hence in this context one can speak of the *community network model*.

In the *Microsoft model*, operating and application software is marketed and sold online and offline (i.e., on the Internet and in traditional software stores). Customers have to purchase licenses and digital applications that are installed on computers in order to be allowed to legally run certain software packages. Other software models include the subscription model, as in the case of *Norton Antivirus*, and the proprietary gift model financed by advertisement, as in the case of *Mozilla*. Mozilla makes profit with its Firefox browser by adding search engines for Google, Yahoo, and so on, to the user interface. Also, the creation of Web solutions (applications, content) belongs to the realm of software models. Such solutions are either sold as package that the customers pay for once or for a regular fee that includes a regular update of software and content.

The *Linux model*, in which the source code of software is freely available, contradicts the proprietary software models. In this model, the software can be further developed by anybody as long as the source is kept free. In most cases, such applications are distributed for free. In the *EDS model* (electronic data systems) certain IT services are offered to customers: the integration of hardware and software in a certain environment; the setting up of servers, networks, and workstations; the repair of hardware and operating systems, and so on. Other Internet services include companies such as DoubleClick, which supports its customers in placing advertisement on the Internet, for example, in the form of banner ads, and online social and market research companies such as Nielsen/Netratings. IT services are offered for free in cases where one knows competent people (friends, colleagues, etc.) that are willing to provide their expertise and help for free due to specific social bonds. Completely nonprofit and noncommercial Internet services are rare but can still be found. For example, Piranho offers unlimited Web space without advertisements for free and the Open Webmail Project is a noncommercial open-source initiative for developing a Web-based free-mail program. In the Amazon model, online shopping software is used for marketing physical products online and organizing the purchase and payment process. The products (mainly books and CDs) are distributed offline. Online shops that sell physical products form a separate category: They sell physical products by making use of Internet software (online shop) for marketing and purchase.

Hardware and software form the foundation for the execution of human action online. Human action is informational, that is, it is a process of cognition, communication, and cooperation (Hofkirchner 2002; Fuchs and Hofkirchner 2005): Humans form ideas based on content they are confronted with (cognition); they socially relate to each other so that ideas are exchanged and behavior is modified (communication); and they act together in order to produce new qualities and structures of social systems (cooperation). Each process is a sublation of the prior one; the three moments are encapsulated. On the content level of the Internet economy, organizations provide applications that support cognition, communication, and cooperation processes. For each of these three types of applications there are four different models: In the first one, users purchase certain products; in the second, users pay a regular subscription fee; in the third, they have free access and profit is made by advertisement; in the fourth, there is free access and no advertisement. This results in a total of twelve different models of the Internet economy on the content level that will now be further described.

The cognition level is focused on the download and browsing of digital content: The *iTunes model* is a form of online shopping in which the sold commodities are digital, hence are distributed over the Internet. In both the Amazon and the iTunes model the customers pay for each purchased commodity once and separately. Related to these models are also online marketplaces such as eBay and the Amazon Market Place, where fees are charged for the establishment and mediation of exchange relationships between two parties. Comparable to Amazon are online travel agencies like STA Travel Online, with the difference that they sell intangible services and not physical goods. Financial online corporations also sell services online; they offer online banking (e.g., ING DiBa) or online money transfer (PayPal). Online banking, travel agencies, and money transfer can be subsumed under IT services.

In the *Wall Street Journal model*, customers pay a regular subscription fee for accessing digital content (text, images, videos, music, animations, etc.) online. It is a proprietary digital information platform operating on central servers. Probably the most popular and profitable subscription content is of sexual nature (e.g., *Playboy* Online). In some cases, such as Slashdot, there is not a regular but a metered subscription, that is, you pay a certain amount per viewed page. In the *Google Model*, digital content and metainformation are provided for free; selling advertisement space generates profit. This model is also popular with online newspapers and journals that provide free issues online. Most of them charge users a subscription fee for accessing the digital archive. There are exceptions, such as *Time* magazine, which provides a free online archive for all of its issues since 1923 and finances its services by advertisements. Also, file-sharing programs are digital information platforms. Some of them, like Kazaa and eDonkey, make profit by selling advertisements and using spyware. The *Indymedia model* and the *Soulseek model* are noncommercial digital information platforms for the free distribution of content (software, music, videos, text, images, etc.). Here, noncommercial file-sharing systems such as Soulseek, BitTorrent, Kazaa Lite, and LimeWire are important.

On the communication level of the Internet economy, one first finds proprietary online communication software that is sold by companies (*Microsoft Outlook model*). In the *Well model*, access to online communication and online communities is offered for a certain period to users if they pay a subscription fee. Here also, cyberdating platforms such as Parship and video sex chats such as Cams.com are important. The *MySpace model* has become of particular importance during the last years: The establishment of social relationships online is offered for free with the help of online communication platforms; revenue is generated by advertisement placement and the delivery of personalized ads to the users. Nonprofit, noncommercial alternatives to MySpace, Facebook, Friendster and other social networking software are hardly existent; one example of such an ongoing project is Manusya. The *mIRC model* is characterized by nonprofit, noncommercial online communication platforms; users can download the software for free and there are no advertisements. JBother is a noncommercial Internet messaging program; Miranda Internet Messenger is a free Internet messaging software that supports six IM networks. Also, online games are a form of digital communication platforms. There are noncommercial, nonprofit online games such as Aardwolf (noncommercial MUD) or Daimonin (opensource massiveley multiplayer online role-playing game, MMORPG). And there are profit-oriented online games such as EverQuest, World of Warcraft, Second Life (commercial MMORPG) that require the payment of subscription fees. Voice-over IP is another communication-oriented type of online application: Skype offers Internet telephony from computer to computer for free and charges for calls to fixed or mobile lines and for sending SMS (Skype Out, Skype SMS). Skype Out is an example of an application that is based on the principle of pay per use or pay per amount/duration. Speak Freely is an example of a noncommercial open-source voice-over IP application.

Besides a cognition and a communication level, there is also a cooperation level of the Internet economy: Online cooperation means that humans use cyberspace in order to jointly produce digital content without being spatially copresent. Cooperation technologies help to overcome spatiotemporal distances. Proprietary cooperation software tools that are sold by corporations are. for example, *IBM Lotus* Notes, Microsoft Exchange, and Novell

GroupWise. In the *SocialText model*, the availability of collaboration software and server space is sold for a limited period to subscribers. SocialText is commercial wiki software. *Google's Writely* application can be downloaded for free; it allows online cooperation and is financed by advertisement. Free wiki software constitutes the gift model of online cooperation. It can be accessed for free and is free of commercials. The most well-known example is Wikipedia; that's why this type has been termed the Wikipedia model.

In the early phase of the World Wide Web, platforms that provide content were important business models. Many new stock companies in the areas of Internet content and Internet services had emerged since the mid-1990s. They were set up with the help of venture capital and their stock quotations vastly increased. There was a difference between the real value in terms of profits and the fictional stock market value of the companies. The high stock values were due to the hope of the investors that the interest in the Internet products and services would increase so fast that after a certain time high profits and hence dividends could be achieved. In spring 2000, the NASDAQ index started falling, which was triggered by the results of the trial against Microsoft, which declared the company a monopoly and by saturated consumption due to the Y2K frenzy. The result was a blast of the finance bubble. The stocks of many ICT companies crashed; they went bankrupt and had to lay off their employees. This concerned, for example, companies like WorldCom, XO Communications, Global Crossing, NTL, Metromedia Fiber, and Adelphia. Large corporations like Amazon and eBay survived, but it took some years until the crisis of the new economy was overcome and new fields of investment of the Internet economy emerged. By the years 2005 and 2006, the Internet had shifted from a primary focus on information to a focus on communication and cooperation. Internet 2.0, social software, and Web 2.0 emerged, which constitute a new phase in Internet development characterized by new business strategies. The crisis and the new boom weren't a result of technological development but of the behavior of investors and venture capitalists, that is, of strategic capitalist decisions where to invest and withdraw money.

Commercial Web 2.0 applications are typically of no charge for users; they generate profit by achieving as many users as possible by offering free services and selling advertisement space to third parties and additional services to users. The more users, the more profit, that is, the more services are offered for free, the more profit can be generated. Although the principle of the gift points towards a postcapitalist society, gifts are today subsumed under capitalism and used for generating profit in the Internet economy. The Internet gift economy has a double character; it supports and at the same time undermines informational capitalism. Applications such as file-sharing software question the logic of commodities, whereas platforms such as Google and MySpace are characteristic for a capitalist gift economy. Internet 2.0 is characterized by this antagonism between information commodities and information gifts. Mark Coté and Jennifer Pybus (2007) have applied the concept of immaterial labor to Web 2.0 activities in social networking platforms like MySpace. They speak of immaterial labor 2.0, which would be a "more accelerated, intensified, and indeed inscrutable variant" (Coté/ Pybus 2007, 89) of immaterial labor. Immaterial labor 2.0 would reflect a subjective turn of labor and be a specific form of the immaterial labor Hardt, Negri and Lazzarato speak about because it would be about "the active and ongoing construction of virtual subjectivities" (Coté/Pybus 2007, 90) and the production of surplus value by activities focuses on affects online and user-generated content. The labor that characterizes Web 2.0 systems is labor that is oriented on the production of affects, fantasy (cognitive labor) and social relations (communicative, cooperative labor)—it is like all labour material because it is activity that changes the state of real world systems. The difference to manual labor is that it doesn't primarily change the physical conditions of things, but the emotional and communicative aspects of human relations. It is also material in the sense that in its current forms it is in the last instance to a certain extent oriented on the economy, subsumed under capital, and oriented on producing economic profit. A better term than immaterial labor 2.0 hence is cognitive, communicative, and cooperative labor—informational labor (in contrast to manual labor). Richard Barbrook (1998) argues in this context that the hi-tech gift economy (that he sees as really existing anarcho-communism) and digital capitalism are not just in conflict with each other but also coexist in symbiosis so that anarcho-communism on the Net is now sponsored by corporate capital. What is missing in this account is the Marxian idea that productive forces mature within capitalist relations of production and hence are also subsumed under and exploited by capital but nonetheless point towards alternative forms of existence that can be realized by human agency.

Google makes use of freedom for advancing unfreedom, of free access for achieving profit. The more users freely access Google for searching online information, the higher the moral value of the corporation and the higher the advertisement prices can be raised. Free access and commodification are not mutually exclusive but are antagonistically intertwined in capitalism. Although the first concept points towards higher forms of existence that transcend capitalism, it is trapped in capitalist structures and within these contributes to the perfection of profit generation. I will now discuss some further examples of the capitalist gift economy.

YouTube is a Web platform that allows users to upload and share videos without being charged for uploading or downloading. YouTube was founded in 2005 by three former employees of PayPal. Its operation is based on a capital of $11.5 billion provided by the venture capitalist firm Sequoia Capital. YouTube makes money by putting commercial adds on its site that accompany the videos. It has made a deal with Warner Brothers that the latter company provides copyrighted material on YouTube and in return receives parts of the advertising revenue generated by that content. Among the first content provided by Warner on YouTube were music videos by

Paris Hilton. Other than Warner, Universal Music has considered YouTube a threat to copyrighted material and has requested YouTube to respect property rights. Other ideas for a YouTube business model are "participatory" video ads, advertisement videos that can be rated and commented by users; or the introduction of preroll ads, which are short advertisement videos played before a selected video starts. But YouTube is careful with introducing too much advertisement because there is the danger that users leave the platform or produce another one if they feel pestered by too much advertisement, which would drive down the market value and hence the advertising prices of YouTube. In October 2006, YouTube was bought by Google for $1.6 billion. Google operates Google Video, a platform that is very similar to YouTube; the merger with YouTube hence can be interpreted as a practical expression of the interest of gaining monopoly profits.

MySpace is a Web platform that allows users to generate personal profiles on which they can upload pictures, text, videos, music, and keep their personal blogs. It networks users with a friendship system (users can add others to their friend list and post comments to their friends' guest books), discussion forums, interest groups, chat rooms, and a mail function. Rupert Murdoch's News Corp. owns MySpace, which it purchased in 2005 for half a billon dollars. These services are provided for free to the users. MySpace, like YouTube, is making profit by selling advertisement space. Google has paid $900 million in 2006 for placing search and keyword services on MySpace. Fox, the TV station owned by News Corp., has started to offer videos of episodes of some of its TV series. This is called TV on demand. Hence, MySpace is used for promoting the content provided by Fox in order to increase the TV station's competitiveness. A specific player must be installed by the user in order to watch the Fox content on MySpace so that downloading the videos is not possible (which could actually result in a distribution of the content on the Internet, which would question Fox's copyright). MySpace shows how media corporations are vertically integrated and try to make use of all media available for accumulating capital. The Internet is used by News Corp. as large advertisement space with which it can reach many users who are offered the opportunity to upload content and connect to others for free and are confronted at the same time with the advertising messages of News Corp. and other companies to which advertisement space is sold. In 2006, Universal Music threatened to sue MySpace for copyright infringement. This shows that social networking platforms such as MySpace and YouTube at the same time advance and threaten capitalist interests.

Flickr is a Web platform for the sharing of images. It was launched in 2004 and bought by Yahoo in 2005 for a two-digit million dollar amount. Users can generate their own profiles on Flickr and write comments for the pictures of others. Flickr sells advertising space, makes money by offering photo printing and unlimited premium accounts (for $24,95 a year in 2006) to users. The upload limit for a free account was 20 MB per month in 2006, for a premium account 2 GB.

Facebook is a Web platform that allows the networking of students with the help of photos, blog messages (Facebook notes), personal profiles, friend groups, e-mails, guest-book entries (The Wall), and interest groups. Facebook is based on networks of users that one can join (e.g., colleges, high schools, companies in the United States and the United Kingdom, and country networks). The concept of Facebook is very similar to the one of MySpace; a difference is that one can only join a college or work network with an e-mail address within the organization, which shall allow more privacy and restricts communication. Not each user can see the profile of all others. MySpace allows users to post videos and pictures in the guest book of others; Facebook limits such entries to text. Facebook doesn't support videos, whereas MySpace does. Like MySpace, Facebook generates revenue from selling advertisement space.

Currently, social networking portals don't sell the content that the users upload. But in principle they could commodify the content if certain license agreements (which most users don't read before they agree) were introduced. In 2006, the British socialist folksinger Billy Bragg protested against the MySpace license by withdrawing his songs from the platform. The license said that MySpace can reuse and resell all content. As a reaction, MySpace issued new terms that read that "MySpace.com does not claim any ownership rights in the text, files, images, photos, video, sounds, musical works, works of authorship, or any other materials (collectively, "content") that you post to the MySpace services". In the terms of use, MySpace reserves the right to charge the users for the service. This is currently not the case. If subscription fees were introduced, the question is if it could be profitable or if most of the users would simply leave MySpace and look for another free social-networking service. The privacy policy of MySpace says that it doesn't transfer personal information to third parties in general, only if a user agrees to such a transfer in a promotion, sweepstake, or contest on MySpace. Advertisement partners of MySpace are allowed to set cookies that transfer information on where the users are located and which advertisements they click so that targeted advertisement is possible.

The terms of use of YouTube allow the company to resell the videos posted by users. The privacy notice of YouTube says that it allows other companies to receive the IP addresses of users and to read cookies in order to deliver personalized advertisement to the users. It would not provide personally identifiable information (e-mail address, name, address, etc.) to such third parties, but users would be selected by specific criteria (age, gender, interests, and geographic area) in order to be delivered with specific advertisement.

The terms of use for Flickr are now those of Yahoo. Users are required to create a Yahoo ID. The Yahoo terms of use say that concerning photos, graphics, audio, and video, "Yahoo is allowed to use, distribute, reproduce, modify, adapt, publicly perform and publicly display such Content on the Service". This means that Yahoo can't sell photos that users upload to Flickr to other companies, but it can use the photos for advertising or add advertising messages to them on its own site. Concerning other content (e.g., text), Yahoo retains the right to "incorporate such Content into other works in any format or medium not known or later developed". The Flickr privacy policy says that Yahoo allows other companies to show personalized advertisements to users with the help of cookies and information transferal to the third parties.

Facebook has the right to use and sell the photos and content of its users. Its terms of use say that the users grant "to the Company an irrevocable, perpetual, non-exclusive, transferable, fully paid, worldwide license (with the right to sublicense) to use, copy, perform, display, reformat, translate, excerpt (in whole or in part) and distribute such information and content and to prepare derivative works of, or incorporate into other works, such information and content, and to grant and authorize sublicenses of the foregoing". The Facebook privacy policy allows the company to sell profile information (without disclosing personal information) to other companies in order to enable personalized advertisement on Facebook.

In the preceding subsections, I have tried to show how capital accumulation works in the capitalist information economy. What has thus far been rather left out is the question how labor is organized in informational capitalism. This question will be treated in the next section.

7.3 CLASS COMPETITION IN INFORMATIONAL CAPITALISM

Class is an expression of competition: There are some groups in society that have opposed interests; some exploit others in order to gain competitive advantages.

Ulrich Beck (1992) argues that contemporary society is a risk society, in which risks and dangers such as radioactivity, harmful and noxious substances in the air, water, and food are not class specific, but affect all humans. "Even the rich and powerful are not safe from them" (Beck 1992, 201). Risks would have an equalizing effect. "In this sense risk-societies are not class societies, nor can their conflicts be comprehended as class conflicts" (205). There would be a transition from class to risk-society (207). Beck announces the end of class, but he overlooks that the logic that has produced global risks that threaten the further survival of humankind as a whole is the modern logic of instrumental reason that treats humans and nature as mere exploitable resources for production. Instrumental reason is the very logic that modern class societies are built upon. Hence, there is no end of class, but class societies today are high-risk class societies. The unequal distribution of wealth here still plays a role because those who are well off can afford to purchase risk-avoiding strategies (e.g., moving to another country or continent after a nuclear event). So, for example, Michael

Perelman (1998, 33) argues that the information society is a society with a hardening class system because "more and more wealth and income flows to the upper classes, leading to a scandalous distribution of income".

In another work, Beck (1983) argues that class locations have become detraditionalized by processes of individualization that have been caused by increased mobility, the rise of the welfare state, improved educational opportunities, more competitive social relationships, urbanization, and the expansion of wage-labor relationships. The effect would be the destruction of unified experiences and lifeworlds of classes and the rise of individualized forms of existence, in which people have to manage their lives all by themselves and hence also have to individually cope with risks that have become more likely to occur. He argues that individualization processes and class formation are reciprocally proportionally related. For Beck, risk is a subjective category oriented on common lifeworld experiences and class solidarity. But that there is less class consciousness and class solidarity today than some decades ago doesn't mean that classes don't exist, because another logical possibility is that classes still exist objectively but that they have been transformed and perceive themselves less as classes. Individualization is not the opposite of class formation, but an expression of class separation as an objective class formation process in the age of neoliberal capitalism. It is a typical move of neo-Weberians to conceive class in subjective terms linked to attitudes. Also, Anthony Giddens (1980) argues that a class has a common awareness and acceptance of similar attitudes and beliefs linked to a common style of life. I find more convincing the position of representatives of critical theory such as Herbert Marcuse, who argued that in contemporary capitalism we find classes without class consciousness because of manipulation, ideology, the scientific-technological revolution, and increasing relative wealth. Under these circumstances the working class for Marcuse is "revolutionary class 'in-itself' but not 'for-itself', objectively but not subjectively" (Marcuse 1969a, 54).

The approach taken in this work is oriented on Marxist thinking and hence stresses the concept of exploitation in objective class formation. The two main approaches on class in the social sciences are the Marxian and the Weberian concepts of class.

How did Marx and Engels conceive class? "By bourgeoisie is meant the class of modern capitalists, owners of the means of social production and employers of wage labour. By proletariat, the class of modern wage labourers who, having no means of production of their own, are reduced to selling their labour power in order to live" (Marx and Engels 1848, 462, fn*). In this footnote to the *Communist Manifesto* written by Engels in 1885, the proletariat is considered as the class of industrial wage labor. This definition might not be suitable for grounding a more expanded notion of the working class in the information age because it excludes nonwage labor. The traditional concept of the working class implies "productive or useful activity, which would leave all who were not working class unproductive and useless" (Williams 1983, 64). Using such a concept hence means to argue that reproductive workers, the unemployed, knowledge workers, and so on, are useless and unproductive, which under extreme political conditions can also imply that they are considered as parasites that need to be annihilated.

But fortunately a more appropriate definition of class has been given by Marx: He argued that members of the exploited class are "free from, unencumbered by, any means of production of their own", which would mean the "separation of the laborers from all property in the means by which they can realize their labour" in a "process which takes away from the labourer the possession of his means of production; a process that transforms, on the one hand, the social means of subsistence and of production into capital, on the other, the immediate producers into wage-labourers" (Marx 1867, 742). Here Marx argues that the exploited class can't control its conditions and means of production and that capital is exploitative. The exploited class is "double-free labour", free from serfdom so that it can offer its labour power on the market and hence "has no other commodity for sale, is short of everything necessary for the realisation of his labour-power" (Marx 1867, 183). For wage labor and self-employed labor, this condition is true in the sense that capital appropriates the produced goods, owns them, sells them on the market, and owns the resulting profit. Self-employed labor (which owns certain means of production by itself, doesn't hire labor, but sells its own labor to capital) also produces goods and value that is appropriated by capital. Self-employed labor, just like wage labor, is "double-free"; both "live only as long as they find work, and who find work only so long as their labour increases capital" (Marx and Engels 1848, 468). These two classes, as well as the nonwage labor classes and the irregular labor class, work under conditions under which capital takes away from them the fruits that they have produced, either (material or immaterial) goods if they are employed directly by capital or in any case the common goods that are produced by society, under indirect command of capital, appropriated by capital, and transformed into profit. Marx in his analysis had to limit the class concept to wage labor under the conditions of nineteenth-century industrialism, but his idea of the capitalist class separating, exploiting, and taking away factors of production and goods in order to achieve profit is still valid for an expanded model of classes that is appropriate for informational capitalism. Exploitation is a central notion to the Marxian concept of class. This category is closely related to the one of surplus value in Marxian theory. In informational capitalism, the exploitation of nonwage and irregular labor as a necessary condition for the production of surplus value has become of high importance; exploitation, class, and surplus value have a more general societal character.

Marx highlights exploitation as the fundamental aspect of class in another passage where he says that "the end and aim of capitalist production" is "to exploit labour-power to the greatest possible extent" (Marx 1867, 350). From exploitation, antagonistic class relations would arise: "The control exercised by the capitalist is not only a special function, due to the nature of the social labour-process, and peculiar to that process, but it is, at the same time, a function of the exploitation of a social labour-process, and is consequently rooted in the unavoidable antagonism between the exploiter and the living and labouring raw material he exploits" (Marx 1867, 350). The living and laboring raw material that is exploited by capital is of a more general nature today; it is the whole socially productive multitude that includes, besides regular wage labor, also self-employed labor, nonwage labor, and irregular labor.

The stress on exploitation distinguishes the Marxian class concept from the Weberian concept in which a class is understood as a group of people who have in common certain life chances in the market; these chances would have to do with the possession of goods and opportunities for income and would be represented under the conditions of the commodity or labor market (Weber 1978, 926). A class for Weber is made up of "all persons in the same class situation", that is, those who share "a typical probability of 1. Procuring goods, 2. Gaining a position in life and 3. Finding inner satisfaction" (Weber 1978, 302). Weber tends to see the kind of services offered and the type of goods produced as important characteristics of class. Exploitation and the different conditions generated by it are not considered as important factors of class. The most well-known neo-Weberian class model is the one of John H. Goldthorpe (2000), who distinguishes a total of eleven classes. The criteria for drawing distinctions in this model are the type of employment relationship (labor contract or service relationship) that allows different extents of monitoring difficulty and the asset specificity concerning skills. Goldthorpe's class model, on the one hand, distinguishes different occupations (farmers, self-employed, small employers, nonmanual employees, service employees, manual workers) and, on the other hand, different skills (upper skills, semiskills, unskilled). Who appropriates and controls capital and profit is no explicit criterion; hence, it is not surprising that capitalists are missing in the scheme. Goldthorpe's neo-Weberian model might be appropriate for distinguishing different types of occupation, but it fails to grasp exploitation, contradictions, and struggles as important moments of class. In this model, there is a service class and a manual class; hence, a sharp distinction is drawn based not on the position in the relations of production and towards the means of production but based on the type of output one produces. Another neo-Weberian model is the one of Anthony Giddens (1980), who distinguishes classes according to which type of market capacity they control: the upper class (property in the means of production), the middle class (educational or technical qualifications), and the working class (manual labor power). Just like Weber, who differentiates in his model of four social classes, besides the petty bourgeoisie and classes privileged through property and education, between the working class and the propertyless intelligentsia and specialists, Giddens identifies manual labor and white-collar labor as two different classes. Here we can see the typical characteristic of Weberian approaches to distinguish classes by the types of occupation and products or services that they produce. But the question is if today the class position of, for example, an unskilled blue-collar assembly-line worker in a car factory is so different from the one of, for example, an unskilled white-collar call-center agent—both have to sell their labor power, have rather low wages, hardly any authority, and low skills.

Based on a Marxist-inspired notion of class, I want to discuss if knowledge labor forms a class or not. Seven approaches on knowledge and class in the information society can be identified

1. Internet users as a new class (e.g., Terranova 2000).
2. Knowledge labor as a new class (e.g., Berardi 2003; Castells 2000a; Huws 2003; Wark 2004).
3. Knowledge labor as revolutionary class (e.g., Hardt and Negri 2000, 2005).
4. Precarious knowledge labor as new class (e.g., Dyer-Witheford 1999, 2006; Gorz 1980; Peery 1997).
5. Knowledge labor as unproductive subsumed labor class (e.g., Resnick and Wolff 1987).
6. Knowledge labor and knowledge capital as one new class (e.g., Florida 2002; Kroker and Weinstein 1994).
7. Knowledge labor as petty bourgeoisie (Poulantzas 1973/1982; Wayne 2003).

These approaches are very diverse and range from considering knowledge labor as a revolutionary class to seeing it as part of the bourgeoisie. Given this plurality, I want to position myself in this debate. My own approach is based on a theoretical assumption that might seem paradox at a first sight: knowledge labor is both a nonclass and a class.

Knowledge Labor as Nonclass

What does class in the information society mean? So what then are knowledge workers? Are they a new class? In a first approximation to answers to these questions, we will assume that this is not the case because knowledge work is quite heterogeneous. Think, for example, of a manager who exerts command and control in a company, which are primarily informational and communicative activities, and compare this job to the one of a call-center agent who is low paid, low skilled, and has hardly any authority. Or compare the call-center agent to a software engineer who receives a high wage, is highly skilled, and has a medium level of authority in the team he works in. Although all of these workers produce knowledge, they have different levels of wages, skills, and authority. Economic class is a category that describes groups that have comparable amounts of economic (property, income), political (authority, power), and cultural capital (skills) in economic production processes. Related to this category is the formation of different classes and the phenomena of economic exploitation, organizational exploitation, and skills exploitation.

Given such circumstances, knowledge labor is not a class category but a category that can be applied at the vertical dimension of the economy, at the level of describing which types of goods or services are produced in different sectors of the economy. In all economic branches in which one finds classes, classes and class fractions are made up of workers (capitalists) that stem from different economic sectors. Class is a category that spans over several economic sectors.

Here is an overview of a four sector model of the economy:

1. Primary sector: Here natural products are produced in agriculture and mining.
2. Secondary sector: Here industrial/physical products are manufactured in branches such as utilities, construction, metal, wood, machinery, electrical equipment, vehicles, furniture, food, drinks, tobacco, textiles, or chemicals.
3. Tertiary sector: In this sector we find labor that produces services that don't belong to agriculture, manufacturing industries, or knowledge services/manufacturing. These are activities in the areas of trade, transportation, warehousing, real estate, rental, leasing, finance, insurance, accommodation, food, and waste management. One can say that these are services for distributing, managing, and taking care of manufactured products and money
4. Quaternary sector: Here knowledge goods and services are produced by knowledge labor. Knowledge labor is labor which produces information, communication, social relationships, affects, and information and communication technologies. This involves the manufacturing of information and communication technologies (computers, computer equipment, paper, printing), information and communication goods and services (music industry, motion-picture industry, software industry, publishing industry, broadcasting, telecommunications), scientific services, technological services, legal services (legal affairs are primarily communicational and informational activities), management and administration (these are primarily cognitive and communicative tasks of command and control, including governmental administration, except military and government enterprises), educational services (these are activities that help individuals in developing skills and producing knowledge), arts and entertainment (both art and entertainment are forms of cultural knowledge), and health and social care. I have hesitated to include health care in the knowledge sector because it is about regenerating body and mind, and the body is traditionally considered as external to knowledge. But I have come to the conclusion that health and social care are primarily about aid that experts

provide for individuals not primarily due to instrumental economic reasons but due to more altruistic motives. Aid, altruism, and coopera-tion are an expression of emotional care and lie at the very heart of society and social action. Hence, I consider health and social care as knowledge work.

In comparison to the distinction of traditional transformative labor, tra-ditional services, and postindustrial services provided by Erik Olin Wright (1997, 138), I haven't included finance and insurance in the postindustrial sector because I think that handling money hasn't so much to do with knowl-edge because money is a very traditional medium of circulation. Other than Wright, I consider entertainment as part of the knowledge sector because it is oriented on recreating the mind.

The next two tables show the distribution of wage labor in the four sec-tors of the US economy in 2005. Due to statistical reasons that don't allow an exact sector matching, the statistics here are limited to employees and don't include the self-employed. The economic structure has been modeled for the following calculations according to the definitions of the four eco-nomic sectors given above.

The analysis shows that in 2005, 44.21 percent of US wage labor was employed in the knowledge sector, 40.19 percent in the traditional service sector, 14.15 percent in the secondary sector, and 1.44 percent in the pri-mary sector. There was a total of approximately 141,217,000 part- and full-time workers, of which 89.8 percent were full-time workers and 10.2 percent part-time workers. It is interesting to see that the share of part-time workers in the tertiary and quaternary sector is significantly higher than in the primary and secondary sector. Hence, knowledge work and traditional service work seem to be predestined for irregular employment relations.

Knowledge Labor as Class

In order to develop my own model of class, I first have to outline some foundations of class theories that I consider important. The most important neo-Marxist concept of economic class, on which the theoretical model out-lined here is based, is the one of Erik Olin Wright (1997, 10; 2005, 23), who defines three aspects of exploitation and hence class formation:

1. Inverse interdependent welfare: The material welfare of one group of people causally depends on the material deprivations of another.
2. Exclusion: The exploited are asymmetrically excluded from access to certain productive resources (frequently by force and with property rights).
3. Appropriation: The fruits of labor of the exploited are appropriated by those who control the productive resources.

Table 7.3 Distribution of Labor in Different Sectors of the US Economy

		Full and part time (in 1000) 2005	Full time (in 1000) 2005	Part time (in 1000) 2005
Agriculture, forestry, fishing, and hunting	Primary	1,473	1,279	194
Mining	Primary	564	557	7
Total Primary		**2,037**	**1,836**	**201**
Utilities	Secondary	554	545	9
Construction	Secondary	7,567	7,315	252
Manufacturing, durable goods				
Wood products	Secondary	579	564	15
Nonmetallic mineral products	Secondary	508	496	12
Primary metals	Secondary	465	459	6
Fabricated metal products	Secondary	1,525	1,504	21
Machinery	Secondary	1,166	1,148	18
Electrical equipment, appliances, and components	Secondary	436	429	7
Motor vehicles, bodies and trailers, and parts	Secondary	1,100	1,093	7
Other transportation equipment	Secondary	673	669	4
Furniture and related products	Secondary	569	556	13
Miscellaneous manufacturing	Secondary	670	651	19
Manufacturing, nondurable goods				
Food and beverage and tobacco products	Secondary	1,687	1,627	60
Textile mills and textile product mills	Secondary	389	376	13
Apparel and leather and allied products	Secondary	312	301	11
Petroleum and coal products	Secondary	111	109	2
Chemical products	Secondary	876	862	14

Table 7.3 *(continued)*

		Full and part time (in 1000) 2005	Full time (in 1000) 2005	Part time (in 1000) 2005
Plastics and rubber products	Secondary	802	791	11
Total Secondary		**19,989**	**19,495**	**494**
Wholesale trade	Tertiary	5,850	5,652	198
Retail trade	Tertiary	15,763	13,723	2,040
Transportation and warehousing				
Air transportation	Tertiary	500	475	25
Rail transportation	Tertiary	198	188	10
Water transportation	Tertiary	60	57	3
Truck transportation	Tertiary	1,420	1,350	70
Transit and ground passenger transportation	Tertiary	417	397	20
Pipeline transportation	Tertiary	38	36	2
Other transportation and support activities	Tertiary	1,159	1,102	57
Warehousing and storage	Tertiary	586	557	29
Real estate and rental and leasing				
Real estate	Tertiary	1,535	1,410	125
Rental and leasing services and lessors of intangible assets	Tertiary	673	601	72
Finance and insurance				
Federal Reserve banks, credit intermediation, and related activities	Tertiary	2,899	2,783	116
Securities, commodity contracts, and investments	Tertiary	822	789	33
Insurance carriers and related activities	Tertiary	2,291	2,203	88
Funds, trusts, and other financial vehicles	Tertiary	89	86	3

Table 7.3 (continued)

		Full and part time (in 1000) 2005	Full time (in 1000) 2005	Part time (in 1000) 2005
Accommodation and food services				
Accommodation	Tertiary	1,837	1,684	153
Food services and drinking places	Tertiary	9,190	7,274	1,916
Other services, except government	Tertiary	6,901	5,839	1,062
Administrative and waste management services				
Waste management and remediation services	Tertiary	339	325	14
Government, federal, general government				
Military	Tertiary	2,250	1,550	700
Government enterprises	Tertiary	883	726	157
Government, state and local, general government				
Government enterprises	Tertiary	1,060	1,033	27
Total Tertiary		**56,760**	**49,840**	**6,920**
Manufacturing, durable goods				
Computer and electronic products	Quaternary	1,311	1,296	15
Manufacturing, nondurable goods				
Paper products	Quaternary	484	469	15
Printing and related support activities	Quaternary	664	644	20
Information				
Publishing industries (includes software)	Quaternary	939	849	90
Motion picture and sound recording industries	Quaternary	382	323	59
Broadcasting and telecommunications	Quaternary	1,323	1,292	31
Information and data processing services	Quaternary	436	401	35

Table 7.3 *(continued)*

		Full and part time *(in 1000)* 2005	Full time *(in 1000)* 2005	Part time *(in 1000)* 2005
Professional, scientific, and technical services				
Legal services	Quaternary	1,331	1,255	76
Computer systems design and related services	Quaternary	1,201	1,132	69
Miscellaneous professional, scientific, and technical services	Quaternary	4,964	4,680	284
Management of companies and enterprises	Quaternary	1,748	1,724	24
Administrative and waste management services				
Administrative and support services	Quaternary	7,800	7,140	660
Educational services	Quaternary	2,911	2,582	329
Health care and social assistance				
Ambulatory health care services	Quaternary	5,245	4,722	523
Hospitals	Quaternary	4,331	4,040	291
Nursing and residential care facilities	Quaternary	2,850	2,566	284
Social assistance	Quaternary	2,595	2,238	357
Arts, entertainment, and recreation				
Performing arts, spectator sports, museums, and related activities	Quaternary	500	418	82
Amusements, gambling, and recreation industries	Quaternary	1,481	1,237	244
Government, federal, general government				
Civilian	Quaternary	1,958	1,815	143
Government, state and local, general government				
Education	Quaternary	9,915	7,906	2,009
Other	Quaternary	8,062	6,964	1,098
Total Quaternary		62,431	55,693	6,738

Source: Bureau of Economic Analysis Statistics (http://www.bea.gov).

Table 7.4. Overall distribution of labor in the four sectors of the US economy

	Full- and Part Time	Full Time	Part Time
Primary	1.44%	1.45%	1.40%
Secondary	14.15%	15.37%	3.44%
Tertiary	40.19%	39.29%	48.21%
Quaternary	44.21%	43.90%	4694%

If only the first and the second criteria are given, Wright speaks of non-exploitative economic oppression. For Wright, groups such as the unemployed, retirees, the permanently disabled, students, people on welfare, and houseworkers form underclasses that are not exploited but excluded and hence economically oppressed by capital (Wright 1997, 26–28). This idea doesn't take into account that the "economically oppressed" are growing in number and hence can't be seen as a side effect of economic exploitation. Wright limits his concept of economic class to wage labor and capital (as well as contradictory class positions).

In informational capitalism the brain has become an important productive force. Many precarious labor forces—which are characteristic for service jobs and knowledge labor—work as freelancers, one-man companies; hence, formally they are self-employed and they own and control their means of production (brain, computer, etc.), but they are forced to permanently sell their own labor power per contracts to capitalist corporations that outsource or subcontract labor power. This class of self-employed workers, which owns its own means of production, doesn't hire others but sells its own labor power, has been characterized by Wright and Pierre Bourdieu as the petty bourgeoisie. I don't think that such a term is suitable because it implies that this class is more part of the capitalist class than of the proletariat. I don't think that this is the case because many in this class struggle to survive and have very low earnings. Hence, I would more precisely describe this class as self-employed labor class. This class is a characteristic expression of capital's move under neoliberal conditions to outsource labor (which means not having to take care of labor rights, ancillary wage costs, technology, etc.) in order to reduce variable and constant capital costs. Knowledge labor requires little physical capital and hence is predestined for new forms of employment and exploitation (Wright 1997, 130, 135). Self-employed labor in informational capitalism is frequently precarious labor; it is not a fixed but a dynamic category as many of these individuals shift from self-employment to temporary labor, unpaid labor, and back again, and so on.

Wright argues that under contemporary conditions a more complex economic class model is appropriate, and hence, besides the relation to the means of production, he adds authority (or political capital in Bourdieuian terms) and skills/knowledge (or cultural capital in Bourdieuian terms) as defining characteristics of class position. Based on this distinction, he arrives at a class model that is based on twelve different class locations. There are similarities between the class models of Wright and Bourdieu. One can see Wright's class concept as an expanded Marxist model of economic class that takes into consideration the two structural aspects of political/social capital and cultural capital that have been stressed by Bourdieu as important aspects of class formation besides economic capital. For Wright, skills exploitation means that higher-skilled workers "receive incomes above the costs of producing those skills" (Wright 1989, 12); they have some extra remuneration due to their position. "For a skill to be the basis of exploitation, therefore, it has to be in some sense scarce relative to its demand, and there must be a mechanism through which individual owners of scarce skills are able to translate that scarcity into higher incomes" (Wright 1989, 21). The same would be true for organizational assets/authority, which would allow managers to "extort wages out of proportion to the costs of producing managerial labor power" (Wright 1989, 201). Wright here speaks of organizational exploitation.

Philippe Van Parijs sees jobs as scarce assets in advanced capitalism; hence, he argues that there is an "unequal distribution of job assets among the employed" (Van Parijs 1989, 235) and an exploitation of the unemployed by wage labor. He speaks of a "job exploiter" as "someone who would be worse off if job assets were equally distributed" and sees a job exploited as someone who would be better off under these conditions (Van Parijs 1989, 233). It is a courageous move of Van Parijs to leave behind the orthodoxy of considering the unemployed as an unorganized and hence, for class struggle, unimportant group (as expressed by the Marxian term *lumpenproletariat*) and to define it as part of the exploited multitude that is itself antagonistically constituted by exploiting and exploited classes and class fractions. Based on these concepts, Van Parijs has developed the concept of asset-based inequality and external endowments for arguing that humans have a right for a universal guaranteed basic income (Van Parijs 1995).

The argument has thus far been that knowledge labor isn't a class but forms an economic sector. This argument will now shift and it will be shown that knowledge can be considered as the foundation of a broad exploitation process in informational capitalism. If one defines economic exploitation as the existence of an exploiting class that deprives at least one exploited class of resources, excludes them from ownership, and appropriates resources produced by the exploited, one stays within a Marxist framework of class but needs not necessarily exclude the "underclasses" from this concepts if one considers knowledge labor as central to contemporary society. Knowledge labor is labor which produces information, communication, social relationships, affects, and information and communication technologies. It is a direct and indirect aspect of the accumulation of capital in informational capitalism: There are direct knowledge workers (either employed as wage labor in firms or as outsourced, self-employed labor) who produce knowledge goods and services that are sold as commodities on the market (e.g., software, data, statistics, expertise, consultancy, advertisements, media content, films, music, etc.) and indirect knowledge workers (unpaid or paid) that produce and reproduce the social conditions of the existence of capital and wage labor, such as education, social relationships, affects, communication, sex, housework, common knowledge in everyday life, natural resources, nurture, care, and so on. These are forms of unpaid labor that are necessary for the existence of society; they are performed not exclusively but to a certain extent by those who don't have regular wage labor—houseworkers, the unemployed, retirees, students, precarious and informal workers, underpaid workers in temporal or part-time jobs, and migrants. This unpaid labor is reproductive in the sense that it reproduces and enables the existence of capital and wage labor that consumes the goods and services of unpaid reproductive workers for free; hence; both capital and wage labor exploit reproductive workers—which is just another term for indirect knowledge workers. Capital can't be accumulated without a common societal infrastructure in the areas of education, spare time, health and social care, natural resources, culture, art, sexuality, friendships, science, media, morals, sports, housework, and so on, that it takes for granted and doesn't pay for (in the form of shares of its profit). Wage labor is reproduced, that is, it consumes the reproductive and public goods and services in order to restore its labor power; it exploits reproductive workers in order to be able to be exploited by capital. Hence, we can define the multitude as the class of those who produce material or knowledge goods and services directly or indirectly for capital and are deprived and dispossessed of resources by capital. Such exploited resources are consumed by capital for free. Here the arguments of Tiziana Terranova (2000) and Michael Hardt and Antonio Negri (2000, 2005) are important: In informational capitalism, knowledge has become a productive force, but knowledge is not only produced in corporations in the form of knowledge goods but also in everyday life by; for example, parents who educate their children; citizens who engage in everyday politics; consumers of media, who produce social meaning and hence are prosumers; users of MySpace, YouTube, Facebook, and so on, who produce informational content that is appropriated by capital; radio listeners and television viewers who call in live on air in order to discuss with studio guests and convey their ideas that are instantly commodified in the real-time economy, and so on. Hence, the production process of knowledge is a social, common process, but knowledge is appropriated by capital; and by this appropriation the producers of knowledge become, just like traditional industrial labor, an exploited class that can, with reference to Negri and Hardt (2005), be termed the multitude. The multitude is an expanded notion of class that goes beyond manual wage labor and takes into account that labor has become more common.

The multitude as the class of all those who are in some sense exploited consists of the following class fractions:

1. Traditional industrial workers, who produce physical goods in wage relationships. Capital appropriates the physical goods of these workers and the surplus value contained in them.

2. Knowledge workers, who produce knowledge goods and services in wage relationships or self-employed labor relations. Capital appropriates the knowledge goods and services of these workers and the surplus value contained in them. One must note that public servants in areas such as health, education, transport, social care, housing, energy, and so on, are not under direct command of capital, but most of them are waged knowledge workers who produce parts of the commons that are a necessary condition for the existence of society and capital. The latter exploits these public goods in an indirect way.

3. Houseworkers: These workers—who are still predominantly female—produce knowledge in the broad sense of communication, affects, sexuality, domestic goods and services that are not sold as commodities but consumed by capitalists and wage laborers for free in order to reproduce manpower.

4. The unemployed: This class is deprived of job assets by capital and wage labor. It is the result of the tendency of the organic composition of capital to rise, which is due to technological progress. The unemployed are, just like houseworkers, involved in unpaid reproductive knowledge labor that is a necessary condition of the existence of capital. Furthermore, the unemployed are frequently forced to take on very low-paid precarious or illegal jobs and hence are also subjected to extreme economic appropriation. Increasingly, unemployed persons are forced by the state to perform extremely low-paid, compulsory, overexploited work.

5. Migrants and workers in developing countries: Migrants are frequently subjected to extreme economic exploitation in racist relations of production as illegal, overexploited workers. They are exploited by capital and this exploitation is ideologically supported by a certain share of wage laborers who hope to increase their wages and to reach better positions if migrants can be forced to do unpaid or extremely low-paid unskilled work. Developing countries are either completely excluded from exploitation or they are considered as a sphere of cheap, unskilled wage labor that is overexploited by capital by paying extremely low wages and ignoring labor rights and standards.

6. Retirees: Retirees are exploited to the extent that they act as unpaid reproductive workers in spheres such as the family, social care, home care, and education.

7. Students: Students are exploited in the sense that they produce and reproduce intellectual knowledge and skills that are appropriated by

capital for free as part of the commons. Students are furthermore frequently overexploited as precarious workers, a phenomenon for which terms such as *precariat, generation internship*, or *praktikariat* (from the German term *Praktikum*, which means internship combined with the term *precariat*) can be employed.

8. Precarious and informal workers: Part-time workers, temporary workers, the fractionally employed, contract labor, bogus self-employment, and so on, are work relations that are temporary, insecure, and low paid. Hence, these workers are overexploited by capital in the sense that such jobs would cost capital much more if they were done by regularly employed wage labor (the same is true for racist labor relations and compulsory work done by unemployed persons). Also, the core workforce with full-time contracts benefits in material terms from the subordination of the periphery workforce.

9. Self-employed persons who don't employ others themselves are forced to sell their own labor power by contracts; they control their means of production but produce surplus for others who control capital and use the appropriated labor for achieving profit.

I have used the term *overexploitation* here several times. By overexploitation, capital can gain extra surplus value, *extra surplus value* is a term employed by Marx for describing relations of production in which goods are produced so that the "individual value of these articles is now below their social value" (Marx 1867, 336). By employing illegal migrants, unemployed compulsory or illegal workers, students, precarious and informal workers, capital can produce goods at a value that is lower than the average social value because it pays less wages than in a regular employment relationship; hence, the commodities produced contain less variable capital but are nonetheless sold at regular prices so that an extra profit can be obtained. The total value of a commodity is $V = c + v + s$ (constant capital + variable capital + surplus value). By overexploitation, variable capital and the total value of the commodity are lowered, the commodity can be sold at regular market prices, and extra profit can be achieved.

Very influential for developing expanded conceptions of class have been the contributions of Marxist feminism that have questioned the mechanical treatment of patriarchy as superstructural phenomenon (Ehrenreich 1997/1976, 68). The most important insight of Marxist feminism is that reproductive labor is necessary for the reproduction of manpower and the existence of capital. Reproductive workers don't receive a wage; they either work for free or receive a small share of family income. Capital isn't able to pay for all labor that is necessary for its accumulation—hence, there is the phenomenon of unpaid labor that is indirectly consumed by capital. Double free wage labor—that is, "free" of ownership of capital and "free" to offer its labor power on the market—is free in a threefold sense because it is also free of the reproductive labor that is accomplished by reproductive workers (who are predominantly female). For accumulating, capital is in need of colonies such as housework, nature, and developing countries.

Rosa Luxemburg (1913) argued that the process of primitive accumulation is not finished but that capital generates milieus and spheres of unpaid labor that are exploited by violent means: "capital feeds on the ruins of such organisations, and, although this non-capitalist milieu is indispensable for accumulation, the latter proceeds, at the cost of this medium nevertheless, by eating it up" (Luxemburg 1913, 363).[3] This idea was used for explaining the existence of colonies of imperialism by Luxemburg and was applied by Marxist feminism in order to argue that unpaid reproductive labor can be considered as an inner colony and milieu of primitive accumulation of capitalism (Bennholdt-Thomsen, Mies, and Werlhof 1992; Mies 1996; Werlhof 1991).

In post-Fordist capitalism, the inner colonies of capitalism are expanded so that profits rise by generating milieus of low-paid and unpaid labor. This phenomenon has been termed *housewifization* (Bennholdt-Thomsen, Mies, and Werlhof 1992; Mies 1996); more and more people live and work under precarious conditions that have traditionally been characteristic for patriarchal relations. People working under such conditions are, like housewives, a source of uncontrolled and unlimited exploitation. The economic logic underlying housewifization is oriented on the reduction of variable capital. Identifying inner colonies of capitalism as classes means to argue, like Hardt and Negri (2005), that class relationships have become generalized and that the production of value and hence exploitation are not limited to wage labor but reach society as a whole. Hence, beside wage labor, also houseworkers, the unemployed, migrants and developing countries, retirees working in reproduction, students, precarious and informal workers should be considered as exploited classes that form part of the multitude that is antagonistic in character and traversed by inner lines of exploitation, oppression, and domination that segment the multitude and create inner classes and class fractions. Nonetheless, the multitude is objectively united by the fact that it consists of all those individuals and groups that are exploited by capital, live and produce directly and indirectly for capital that expropriates and appropriates resources (commodities, labor power, the commons, knowledge, nature, public infrastructures and services) that are produced and reproduced by the multitude in common.

Based on influences by Negri/Hardt, Marxist feminism, and Philippe Van Parijs, it is possible to expand Wright's class model so that the growing number of those who produce the commons and are exploited outside of regular wage relationships are included as exploited classes (cf. fig. 7.1). The model presented here is based on Erik Olin Wright's class model but adds some aspects relevant for considering the production and exploitation of the commons. Note that an individual can be positioned in more than one class location at one time. Class positions are not fixed but dynamic, that is, in informational capitalism people have a fluid and transit class status. So,

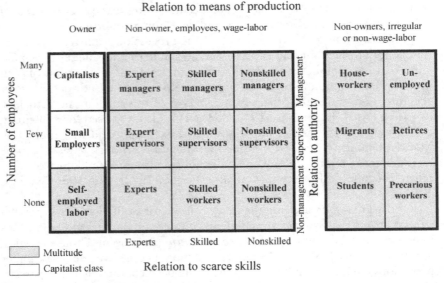

Figure 7.1 An expanded class model.

for example, female workers are frequently at the same time houseworkers; many students are also precarious workers; many precarious workers form a type of self-employed labor, and so on. That class positions are antagonistic also means that there is no clear-cut separation between the multitude and the capitalist class, so, for example, managers can be considered to have a contradictory class position: they work for a wage but at the same time execute command over workers in the name of capital.

Knowledge is a social and historical product; new knowledge emerges from the historical heritage of knowledge in society and is in many cases produced cooperatively. Hence, Marx argued that knowledge "depends partly on the cooperation of the living, and partly on the utilisation of the labors of those who have gone before" (Marx 1894, 114). Nature, knowledge, and societal infrastructures are due to their collective or natural form of production common property; they are not produced and controlled by single individuals. Knowledge and infrastructures can only exist due to the collective activities of many; nature produces itself and is transformed into resources by metabolic processes organized by many. Knowledge, nature, and infrastructures are collective goods that cost nothing for capital, but they are a necessary condition for capital accumulation, enter production processes, and capital profits from them. Capital consumes the commons for free; it exploits the results of societal and natural production processes such as education, science, health, reproductive labor, and so on. The Essence of the commons is its social character; in capitalism the commons are individually appropriated as proprietary goods by capital. In categories of the

Hegelian logic, one can argue that Essence and Existence of knowledge and the commons are nonidentical; exploitation alienates the Existence of the commons from their Essence and their Truth, Reason, and Reality.

Philippe Van Parijs (1995) argues that the right for a universal basic income guarantee can be derived from the share of collective resources that each person is entitled to. He speaks of external endowments as wealth that is available without human activity and that must not be earned and is available due to, for example, the appropriation of nature, inheritance, or privileged economic positions (Howard 2002).

Van Parijs (1995) argues that there is an unequal access to external assets; in order to attenuate this inequality a universal basic income guarantee should be available to all. Knowledge can be considered as an external asset in Van Parijs's understanding. Knowledge and skills are produced in processes of education and in everyday life; they form an input to production that is consumed for free by capital in the form of technology and the skills of workers. Knowledge is not produced once but continuously, and it is reproduced permanently by parents, teachers, children, pupils, scientists, students, schools, universities, the cultural system, and so on (Gorz 2004, 2000). For capital, it is a gratis resource that it subsumes and exploits.

Nature is consumed by all humans in forms such as water, air, meadows, food, and so on, in order to survive. Corporations as a general rule consume much more natural resources and produce more environmental impact in the form of the waste generated by production than private individuals and households. They consume a relatively high share of the collective resource nature and make use of it in order to produce economic profit.

All humans benefit from knowledge in society that was produced in the past (inherited, historical knowledge) in the form of organizations that allow the development of skills (educational knowledge), cultural goods (music, theater performances, literature, books, films, artworks, philosophy, etc.) that contribute to mental reproduction (entertainment knowledge), and in the form of traditional practices as aspect of education and socialization (practical knowledge). These three forms of knowledge are handed down to future generations and enriched by present generations during the course of the development of society; all humans contribute and benefit. Another form of knowledge is technological knowledge, that is, knowledge that is objectified in machines and practices that function as means for reaching identified goals so that labor processes are accelerated and the amount of externalized labor power can be reduced. Not all humans and groups benefit to the same extent from these four types of knowledge. Corporations especially consume an overaverage share: Educational, entertainment, and practical knowledge are aspects of the reproduction of manpower. These processes are performed to a large extent outside of firms and labor time by individuals and society. Technological progress helps corporations in increasing productivity, that is, the ability of capital to produce ever more profit in ever less time. Technological knowledge doesn't enter the production process indirectly as the other three forms of knowledge; it is directly employed by capital in the production process. Technological knowledge is produced by society, but it is individually appropriated by capital as a means of production. One argument that some scholars employ is that corporations pay for technological progress in the form of machines, software, hardware, and so on, that they buy as fixed capital. But the value produced by labor with the help of technology is much larger than the value of technology as such, and each individual technology is based on the whole history of technology and engineering that enters the product for free. Another argument is that technological knowledge and progress are created in technology-producing industries and in the research departments of corporations. This argument is deficient because a certain part of knowledge is produced in public research institutions and universities and each technological innovation is based on the whole state of the art of science for which one doesn't have to pay but is consumed by research departments and technology-producing corporations for free as an external resource.

The result of this discussion is that corporations consume the commons of society that consist of nature, educational knowledge, entertainment knowledge, practical knowledge, technological knowledge, and public infrastructures (labor in the areas of health, education, medical services, social services, culture, media, politics, etc.) for free. Hence, one important form of exploitation in the knowledge society is the exploitation of the commons by capital, which is also exploitation of the multitude and of society as a whole. But aren't capitalists and small employers also part of the multitude in the sense that they contribute to the production and reproduction of the commons in everyday life? There is no doubt that all humans contribute certain shares of unpaid labor to the production and reproduction of nature, knowledge, and public services, and so on. But the capitalist class is the only class in society that exploits and expropriates the commons; it is the only class that derives economic profit and accumulates capital with the help of the appropriation of the commons. All humans produce, reproduce, and consume the commons, but only the capitalist class exploits the commons economically. Hence, this class shouldn't be considered as forming a part of the multitude.

Hardt and Negri argue that due to the networked and cooperative form of immaterial labour and the latter's dominance over industrial labor labor time would become immeasurable and the Marxian law of value (that says that the value of a commodity is the total labor time needed for producing it) inapplicable. "Each of us produces in collaboration with innumerable others. [. . .] labour power has become increasingly collective and social; [. . .] labour cannot be individualized and measured." (Hardt and Negri 2005, 144, 403). Hardt and Negri interpret a passage from Marx's (1857/58, 601) *Fragment on Machines* in the *Grundrisse*—where he says that with the rise of the General Intellect (=knowledge) labor time will cease to become the measure of wealth and the production based on exchange will break down—in such a way that they argue that this is the case today. But a closer expection shows that Marx argues that in a Communist society (that is a realm of freedom from necessary labor) this is the case. Labor time can still be measured today: 1. One can measure the aggregate labor time in a company that is spent by all its employees in total per year for physical and informational labor (including contracted work). 2. There is one important aspect that Hardt and Negri touch upon: There is much labor in society that is done for free, but necessary for the existence of capital and there is labor that is common, i.e. it can't be attributed to the production of certain companies, commodities, or even industries—but is consumed or needed by many (or all) capitalists simultaneously in order to accumulate profit. It is free common labor that doesn't produce surplus value directly, but in an indirect way. The amount of this labor time can be measured by counting how many hours of unpaid work that benefit capital indirectly are done per year. This labor can be characterized as indirect common surplus labor. It includes unpaid or public work that produces educational knowledge, entertainment knowledge, practical knowledge, technical knowledge, scientific progress, affects, communication, social relations, etc. It includes labor in areas such as private households, public education, public health, public science and research, social care, etc. The exploitation of the commons can in principle be measured.

7.4 CONCLUSION

Capital accumulation with the help of knowledge commodities is in knowledge capitalism based on the specific characteristics of information: It is generally not used up by its manifold usage; it expands during its usage; it can be compressed; it can replace other economic resources; it can be transported at the speed of light over the global information networks; and the costs of reproducing information are generally very low and are further diminished by technological innovations and progress. Hence, knowledge as commodity can be produced and diffused very cheaply; the mechanism for gaining profit from information commodities is that such goods are sold at prices that are much higher than the commodity values.

The Internet economy is characterized by an antagonism between cooperation and competition, between the informational gift economy and the informational commodity economy. This antagonism has two specific expressions:

1. The level of corporations:
   The logic of networking has transformed corporations, which are increasingly organized on the transnational level and decentralize and flexiblize their internal structures. This is a new strategy, which allows accumulation by integration, identification, and a new spirit

of corporate 'participation' and 'cooperation'. The new strategies of accumulation are connected to the rise of new scientific models and concepts such as virtual teams, virtual organizations, virtual corporations, knowledge management, or organizational learning, which create the impressions that post-Fordist corporations are democratic institutions, but in fact they have a very limited notion of participation. Corporations use cooperation as an ideology in order to advance the logic of competition, that is, the accumulation of money capital, by reducing the constant and variable capital costs.

2. The level of the economy as totality:

Informational networks are at the core of the productive forces of informational capitalism. Due to the characteristics of information and networks (global diffusion, intangibility, connectivity), the classical Marxian antagonism of the productive forces and the relations of production take on a new form: Information in the Internet economy is, on the one hand, a commodity that is controlled with the help of intellectual property rights; on the other hand, the informational productive forces point towards the alternative economic model of a gift economy because information is an open, societal good. Hence, the informational productive forces collide with the capitalist relations of information production, which results in class struggles in which the open or proprietary character of information is contested

At a first glance the model of information gifts and the model of information commodities seem to be two very different models. Information gifts form a part of the Internet economy in which goods are distributed for free and are openly accessible. Information commodities constitute a subsystem of the Internet economy in which goods are sold and controlled with the help of intellectual property rights. Competition in the proprietary Internet economy results in a tendency for the formation of informational monopolies.

At a second glance, one sees that the gift model and the commodity model are antagonistically entangled: Especially newer strategies of profit generation (social networking platforms, social software, Google, etc.) in the Internet economy make use of information as a gift in order to achieve a high number of users and to build monopolies in certain fields so that they can charge high advertisement rates. This shows that, although the gift model transcends the commodity model, it is also subsumed under capital.

Knowledge forms part of the commons of society; it is a social product produced and consumed by all. The commons of society that are produced and consumed by all consist of nature, educational knowledge, entertainment knowledge, practical knowledge, technological knowledge, and public infrastructures (institutions in the areas of health, education, medical services, social services, culture, media, politics, etc.). All humans cooperate, produce, reproduce, and consume the commons, but only the capitalist class exploits the commons economically. Hence, this class shouldn't be considered as forming a part of the multitude. The multitude is an expanded Marxist class category that is used for describing the common labor class that produces the commons in cooperation and is exploited by capital that appropriates the commons for free and subsumes them under capital in order to gain profit. In the expanded notion of the multitude, besides regular manual and mental wage labor, also groups such as houseworkers and reproductive workers, the unemployed, migrants, developing countries, retirees, students, precarious and informal workers are included as class fractions that live and produce under the rule of capital and are expropriated by capital. One political implication of the exploitation of the commons and the multitude by capital is that one can argue that everyone should have the right to receive a guaranteed basic income that guarantees a living and is financed by taxation of capital. The argument underlying these political implications is that nobody is unproductive, rather all are productive workers producing and reproducing the commons of society that are appropriated by capital, which in return has to give something back to society in the form of taxes that are used for compensating society and its members for the theft of the commons by installing the common form of a guaranteed basic income. The commons that are cooperatively produced by the multitude are exploited by capital for its competitive and particular goals of profit generation.

The antagonism between the informational gift economy and the informational commodity economy (information as free good and as commodity) is summarized in the following figure. The commons are part of the material

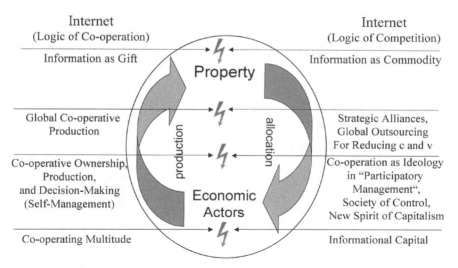

Figure 7.2 The antagonism of the informational gift economy and the informational commodity economy in the Internet economy

foundation of exploitation in informational capitalism. These exploitation processes generate (potential) struggles that have undetermined results: The future could either be a society totally controlled by political-economic monopolies, which could very well result in a new totalitarianism or fascism, or a cooperative society in which the common production processes of the multitude become the determining societal force so that self-determination, cooperative ownership, and participatory democracy can flourish.

8 Competition and Cooperation in Online Politics

The political system of society deals with collective decisions that refer to the way life conditions are set. Power is the disposition over means required to influence processes and decisions in one's own interest. Domination refers to the disposition over means of coercion that are employed for influencing others, processes, and decisions. It is a way of establishing asymmetric power relations by force and violence. In modern society, domination is institutionalized for securing the accumulation of power; it is shaped by the logic of competition. Cooperation is an alternative, democratic, grassroots way of constructing power relations. The modern antagonism between cooperation and competition in politics takes on the form of an antagonism between eDomination and eParticipation when politics goes online. The potentials for domination and participation take on networked, Internetted forms. Digital divides are an expression of the logic of competition because they give benefits to those who participate in the Internet and deprive others of those benefits; it is a phenomenon of exclusion (section 8.1). On the other hand, there seem to be new potentials of grassroots digital democracy that can advance more inclusion and cooperation, but in digital democracy the two phenomena of cooperation and competition also intertwine (8.2). eDomination takes on its most violent form in information warfare (8.3) and its most controlling form in electronic surveillance (8.4). eDomination is challenged by protest movements that make use of the Internet in order to struggle for more inclusion and participation—this is the phenomenon of self-organized cyberprotest from below (8.5).

8.1 DIGITAL EXCLUSION: DIGITAL DIVIDES

Manuel Castells defines the digital divide as "inequality of access to the Internet" (Castells 2001, 248). Access to the Internet is moreover "a requisite for overcoming inequality in a society which dominant functions and social groups are increasingly organized around the Internet" (Castells 2001, 248). Jan van Dijk defines the digital divide as "the gap between those who do and do not have access to computers and the Internet" (Van Dijk 2006, 178).

Pippa Norris sees it as "any and every disparity within the online community" (Norris 2001, 4), Ernest J. Wilson III as "an inequality in access, distribution, and use of information and communication technologies between two or more populations" (Wilson 2006, 300).

Which types of the digital divide can be identified? Jan Van Dijk and Kenneth Hacker (2003) argue that there are four forms of barriers to access:

- The lack of "mental access" refers to a lack of elementary digital experience.
- The lack of "material access" means a lack of possession of computers and network connections.
- The lack of "skills access" is a lack of digital skills.
- The lack of "usage access" signifies the lack of meaningful usage opportunities.

Van Dijk has demonstrated that in terms of physical access to computers and the Internet, the digital divide is closing in developed countries, whereas in developing societies it is still growing. In terms of skills access and usage access, the digital divide is both widening and deepening. He argues that information skills (the skills needed to search, select, and process information in computer and network sources) and strategic skills (the capacities to use these sources as the means for specific goals and for the general goal of improving one's position in society) as aspects of the skills access are "extremely unevenly divided among the populations of both developing and developed societies" (Van Dijk 2006, 181). Concerning usage access, Van Dijk has found that people with high levels of education and income tend to use database, spreadsheet, bookkeeping, and presentation applications significantly more than people with low levels of education and income, who favor simple consultations, games, and other entertainment (Van Dijk 2006, 182sq.). It is naive to believe that mental and material access is enough so that problems of skills access and usage access will diminish (Van Dijk and Hacker 2003). But faith in bridging the digital gap in this way is widespread in science.

Pippa Norris (2001) describes the digital divide as a multidimensional phenomenon; she distinguishes between the global digital divide, the social divide, and the democratic divide:

For Norris, the social divide includes the income gap, which makes a difference between those who can afford computer and Internet access and those who can't. Castells furthermore identifies an education gap, an ethnical divide, an age gap, a family/single gap, and an ability/disability gap (Castells 2001). For Wilson (2006), there are eight aspects of the digital divide: physical access (access to ICT devices), financial access (cost of ICT services relative to annual income), cognitive access (ICT skills), design access (usability), content access (availability of relevant applications and information online), production access (capacity to produce one's own content),

Table 8.1 Pippa Norris's dimensions of the digital divide (Norris, 2001: 4)

Types of Digital Divide	Signified by
Global divide	Divergence of Internet access between industrialized and developed societies
Social divide	Gap between information rich and poor in each nation
Democratic divide	Difference between those who do, and do not, use the opportunities of digital resources to engage, mobilize, and participate in public life

institutional access (availability of institutions that enable access), and political access (access to the governing institutions where the rules of the game are written). Wilson relates these eight aspects to six demographic dimensions of the digital divide: gender, geography, income, education, occupation, and ethnicity.

As outlined in chapter 3, the core of society consists of three subsystems: the economic system, in which use values and property that satisfy human needs are produced; the political system, in which power is distributed in a certain way and collective decisions are taken; and the cultural system, in which skills, meaning, and competencies are acquired, produced, and enacted in ways of life. This distinction can, for example, be found in the works of Anthony Giddens, who says that symbolic orders and forms of discourse are concerned with the constitution of rules (culture), that political institutions deal with authoritative resources (polity), and that economic institutions are concerned with allocative resources (economy; cf. Fuchs 2003d); as well as in the works of Pierre Bourdieu, who distinguishes economic, political, and cultural capital as the three structural features of society (cf. Fuchs 2003c). Hence, besides general social forms of the digital divide, there is also an economic divide, a political divide, and a cultural divide.

Technologies enable and constrain human practices. Their main dimensions are the material access to them (in modern society mainly with the help of money as technologies are sold as commodities), the capability to use them, the capability to use them in such ways that oneself and others can benefit, and embedding institutions. The digital divide refers to unequal patterns of material access to, usage capabilities of, and benefits from computer-based information and communication technologies that are caused by certain stratification processes that produce classes of winners and losers of the information society, and of participation in institutions governing ICTs and society. Material access refers to the availability of hardware, software, applications, networks, and the usability of ICT devices and applications. Usage and skills access refer to the capabilities needed for operating ICT hardware and applications, for producing meaningful online content, and for engaging in online communication and cooperation. Benefit access refers to ICT usage that benefits the individual and advances a good society for all. Institutional access refers to the participation of citizens in institutions that govern the Internet and ICTs, and to the empowerment of citizens by ICTs to participate in political information, communication, and decision processes. Stratification patterns are, on the one hand, social hierarchies such as age, family status, ability, gender, ethnicity, origin, language, and geography (urban/rural). These categories have resulted in different types of the social divide. On the other hand, unequal patterns of material access, usage capabilities, benefits, and participation concerning ICTs are also due to the asymmetric distribution of economic (money, property), political (power, social relationships), and cultural capital (skills). Hence, there is also an economic divide, a political divide, and a cultural divide. In modern society, structures take on the form of capital that is accumulated and unevenly distributed so that different social classes and class fractions with a different (high, medium, low) total amount of economic, political, and cultural capital are created (cf. Fuchs 2003c). The reason why there are gaps in access, usage/skills, benefit, and participation concerning ICTs is the multidimensional class structure of modern society that creates structural inequalities. People with high income, far-reaching and influential social relationships, good education, and high skills are much more likely to have access to ICTs, to be capable of using ICTs, to benefit from this usage, and to be supported in political participation by ICTs than people who are endowed with only a little amount of economic, political, or cultural capital. Table 8.2 summarizes aspects and dimensions of the digital divide.

Jeffrey James (2003, 45) defines the global digital divide as "the strikingly differential extent to which rich and poor countries are enjoying the benefits of information technology" and as "the unequal distribution of computers, Internet connections, fax machines and so on between countries" (James 2003, 23). What Pippa Norris and Jeffrey James call the global digital divide is mainly an aspect of the economic divide because it concerns the difference in access to and usage of ICTs between rich countries and poor countries. Poor countries are those endowed with little economic capital, people there are much less likely to be able to access ICTs, to know how to use them, to benefit from usage, and to participate in embedding institutions. Developing countries are not only economically excluded but also deprived of political power and cultural skills needed for active participation in the information society.

In 2006, although Africa made up 14.1 percent of the world population, only 3 percent of all Internet users lived there (Source: Internet World Statistics: http://www.internetworldstats.com/stats1.htm, data accessed on November 1, 2006). In 2006, of fifty-seven African countries only three had access rates higher than the worldwide Internet usage rate of 16.7% (Reunion, Saint Helena, Seychelles), and only six of fifty-seven African countries had access rates higher than 10 percent (Fuchs and Horak 2007a). Twenty of the

Table 8.2 Aspects and Dimensions of the Digital Divide

	Economic Capital	Political Capital	Cultural Capital	Age	Family Status	Gender	Ability	Ethnicity	Origin	Language	Geography
Material access											
Usage and skills access											
Benefit access											
Institutional access											

fifty-seven African countries in 2006 had access rates lower than 1 percent (ibid.). This shows that the digital divide is a very pressing problem—most African countries are excluded from informational capitalism. If the information society should really be a global village (Marshall McLuhan), a digital agora, or virtual community (Howard Rheingold), Internet access and usage for developing countries would have to be assured because communities and democracy are inclusive and participatory rather than exclusive and segmented. Cyberspace in its current form as a techno-social system that only gains meaning through human activities and communication is a segmented space that reflects the inequalities of society. Concerning Africa, one hence can also speak of a digital apartheid that has real-world causes, such as the unequal global distribution of resources. Digital apartheid means that certain groups and regions of the world are systematically excluded from cyberspace and the benefits that it can create.

Neoliberal stakeholders frequently argue that foreign direct investment and total privatization and deregulation of the telecommunications sector in developing countries will increase infrastructure, wealth, and income and hence bridge the digital divide. There are several reasons why it is unlikely that such policies will promote universal access for all in developing countries:

- Privately led companies are first of all profit oriented, which means that they will provide cheap access only as long as they are not faced by crisis, which is an integral feature of capitalism and competitive markets. Hence, there is an antagonism between cheap (or even free) access and the capitalist crisis economy.
- Increasing quality and speed of services require continuous investments; the fixed capital costs will increase, which requires increases in tariffs so that profitability is assured. Hence, the poor and low-income classes might not be able to afford access. This is especially a problem in countries with high income inequality such as Nigeria.
- Private firms might see the poor and low-income classes as financially weak and might want to focus on financially strong customers and hence exclude the first from their services.
- Private investment and privatization might attract foreign capital and hence make available an Internet infrastructure. But it is not automatically the case that wages rise and the mass of people has access to the Internet because it is not assured by markets that profit remains within the country, that high wages are paid, and that income inequality is avoided.

Specific case studies undertaken by the author and a colleague concerning three African countries with heavily privatized and deregulated telecommunications markets (Ghana, Nigeria, South Africa) have shown examples of how neoliberal policies failed and haven't bridged the digital divides (Fuchs and Horak 2007a, 2007b). Within these countries, due to investments Internet infrastructure and services are available, but only a tiny elite (and in some cases Western corporations) have benefited; the mass of people can't afford Internet access.

I agree with Jan van Dijk that "most likely, the digital divide within developing countries and between them and the developed world will continue to rise" (Van Dijk 2005, 185). But this is only the case if the current unequal economic and social development of global society continues, which clearly is not a foregone conclusion. Now six potential strategies for dealing with the global digital divide will be discussed.

Wolfgang Hofkirchner (2002) has introduced a typology of worldviews that is based on the potential relationships between two categories: Reductionism establishes identity by eliminating the difference for the benefit of the smaller, less differentiated part; projectionism establishes identity by eliminating the difference for the benefit of the larger, more differentiated side; dualism eliminates identity by establishing a difference of the two sides, it is a disjunctive approach; finally, dialectical thinking integrates the two sides so that the two sides have different and identical aspects; they yield a unity in diversity. Applying this typology to the realm of identifying potential solutions for the digital divide means to consider technology as one category and society as the other. Technology in this case is the less differentiated side; it forms a part or subsystem of society.

Strategy 1: Technological reductionism 1 (innovationism): Wait and see; market and technological development will cheapen access. Some say that, historically, new technologies such as electricity, the car, the telephone, or television have at first always been expensive and reserved to a small elite before they have diffused into society and have become accessible for the broad masses. Concerning the Internet, the same would be the case, and hence one should just wait because after a certain time the digital divide would decline due to declining costs of technology and the effects of Moore's law[1] (e.g., Compaine 2001; Norris 2001). This argument is not suitable for the topic of the global digital divide because the wealth gap between Western and Third World countries is continuously increasing and developing countries

Table 8.3 A Typology of Potential Solutions to the Digital Divide

Worldview	Technology	Society
Reductionism	Technological reductionism: innovationism, leapfrogging, technophilia	
Projectionism		Market fundamentalism
Dualism	Technophobia	Technophobia
Dialectics	Dialectical integrationism	

are systematically excluded from wealth and technological progress. Hence, to wait and see won't solve the problem. Also, older technologies such as electricity, the telephone, or TV are not widespread in developing countries; there is a general global technological divide.

This strategy can be seen as a form of technological reductionism because it is believed that the digital divide can be solved due to the characteristic feature of computer technology that it develops rapidly.

Strategy 2: Technological reductionism 2 (leapfrogging): By entering into markets and competition, Third World countries will be able to leapfrog directly into information societies. Will ICTs help developing countries in leapfrogging certain stages of technological development and the industrial development stage so that they will catch up with Western societies and become information societies? Technological leapfrogging means "the implementation of a new and up-to-date technology in an application area in which at least the previous version of that technology has not been deployed" (Davison et al. 2000, 2). "In developed economies, newer versions of technology are often used to upgrade older versions, but in developing economies where still older versions of technology are often prevalent (if they exist at all), the opportunities for leapfrogging over the successive generations of technology to the most recent version are that much greater" (Davison et al. 2000, 2). Leapfrogging might indeed be possible (e.g., establishing wireless communication in developing countries without requiring the earlier stage of a well-developed wire-line infrastructure), but the important question is not if leapfrogging is possible but if it will benefit all people or only a tiny class. Market liberalization doesn't automatically result in the affordability of ICTs for all human beings; hence, the author doubts that liberalization enables leapfrogging as, for example, argued by Pippa Norris (2001, 42): "Given a high-speed backbone, and market liberalization of telecommunication services, African nations may also be able to 'leapfrog' stages of industrialization through new technology by investing in fully digitized telecommunications networks rather than outdated analog-based systems".

This strategy is also technologically reductionist because it argues that computer technologies are so flexible that they allow the instant introduction of the newest standards and that the availability of these standards automatically transforms developing countries into information societies.

Strategy 3: Technological reductionism 3 (technophilia): Technologies for the Third World. Jeffrey James (2003) argues that one possibility for solving the global divide is to transport old computers from rich to poor countries. The lifetime of a Western business computer is only 2–3 years; this is due to rapid technological progress and the nonupgradeability of most hardware, which causes people to buy new computers every 2 or 3 years, as well as heavy profits of the hardware and software industry. The danger in exporting old computers to developing countries is that the latter will become dumps for electronic waste just like many Western corporations and countries consider them as dumps for atomic waste. Besides that, we see no reason why developing countries should not have the same right as Western countries to benefit to a full extent from technological progress just as other countries do. Nicholas Negroponte and the One Laptop Per Child (OLPC) association have introduced the $100 laptop as a strategy for advancing computer technology in developing countries. The problem is that this is a technology that is inferior to Western standards (very slow processor, no hard disk and drives, etc.) and hence can be produced and sold rather cheaply. If the $100 laptop is widely diffused in the Third World, Western actors selling these computers will derive profits, and a global divide in technological progress and standards will emerge that separates advanced Western technology users from users of less-advanced technologies in the Third World. What is needed are not new business strategies but solutions to the material and social causes of the global digital divide as well as free advanced hardware, infrastructure, and software that are based on open standards and copy-left licenses. That Microsoft and Intel are critical of the $100 laptop doesn't mean that it is automatically a good idea; this is rather a manifestation of the competition for profit and customers in developing countries. Open-source technologies have a potential to transcend market logic. What is needed is an advanced $0 laptop with free software for people in developing countries as well as criticism of the capitalist logic that has caused the divide between developing and developed countries and solutions to the social, economic, political, and cultural inequalities that underpin the global digital divide.

Open-source software has been realized mainly within projects such as the Linux operating system. Special licenses (termed copy-left) such as the GNU-public license have been developed for assuring that free software has an open access to its source code. Free software hardly yields economic profit; it is freely available on the Internet and constitutes an alternative model of production that questions proprietary production models. The main reason why free software is a good opportunity for developing countries is not that it is cheap (James 2003) but rather that by using free software developing countries don't depend on Western corporations such as Microsoft which aim not primarily at solving the digital divide but at accumulating capital in developing regions by creating dependencies on Western technological standards such as Windows. Examples for a large-scale adoption of open-source software can be found, for example, in Mexico, China, Zimbabwe, Ethiopia, and Mozambique (Grassmuck 2004, 323–328).

The technophile strategy is a specific form of technological reductionism; it is very optimistic concerning the introduction of new and alternative computer technologies and argues that such technologies should be given to the Third World for free or at low cost.

Strategy 4: Economic projectionism (market fundamentalism): Attracting foreign capital will increase wealth for all and access in developing countries. Some stakeholders and scientists argue that liberalizing telecommunications markets in developing countries will attract Western corporations to invest in the ICT sector in these regions and that this will result in economic growth that benefits all and lowers Internet and phone prices due to competition (e.g., Murelli 2002). It is naive to assume that capitalists aim primarily at solving the digital divide. Western investment is only due to the search for new opportunities of expanding capital accumulation. The reality is as that the economic growth caused by Western investments in ICT markets benefits Western corporations and a small local elite but does not at all assure access for all to ICTs and benefits from ICTs for all (Fuchs and Horak 2007a, 2007b).

ICT applications in the areas of e-commerce, e-travelling, e-government, e-transport, e-health, e-education, e-learning, and so on, are mainly developed in Western countries and benefit under current conditions mainly Western corporations if they are exported to developing countries because these corporations can extract profit by establishing dependencies on Western-defined standards. The Third World is not only largely excluded from wealth but also from technological progress. In 1999 there was $56 billion in Western foreign aid for the Third World, and the latter paid $136 billion debt service to Western countries (Fuchs 2002, 370). Hence, in total there was a value transfer from developing countries to developed countries. Although Africans makes up 14.1 percent of world population, Africa accounts for only 3 percent of the number of global Internet users.

The World Summit on the Information Society (WSIS) sees a sustainable information society as a society in which ICTs promote participation and poverty eradication. For achieving a sustainable information society in developing countries, the WSIS Plan of Action (WSIS 2003) argues, on the one hand, that debt cancellation is needed and on the other hand that more private national and international markets for ICTs should be provided by developing countries. What is missing is the insight that markets don't automatically eliminate poverty because they don't determine how wealth is distributed. Hence, public institutions and regulatory practices are needed that ensure that all can enjoy benefits from ICTs and economic production. WSIS sees capital only as a positive factor in achieving sustainable development. It assesses ICT markets as very positive means for advancing social sustainability, neglects aspects of political regulation of the economy and income distribution, and gives priority to economic logic.

The market-oriented strategy is a form of projectionism; it argues that the solution to the digital divide can be achieved within only one subsystem of society, the economy. Market-driven and profit-oriented development is considered as best practice.

Strategy 5: Dualistic technophobia: The Third World doesn't need technology. Some analysts argue that there is no need for technology in the Third World because there would be more basic problems such as poverty, health issues, and illiteracy. For example, Ted Turner, the founder of CNN, has argued: "We talk about the digital divide. We talk about it all the time at Time-Warner too. We want to get computers in everyone's hands. But half the people in the world don't have electricity. Over a billion don't have access to clean drinking water. Forget the digital divide, they need food, water, clothing, shelter and a chance for an education".[2]

Information and communication are, just like social security, a fundamental human right. This right is explicitly mentioned in article 19 of the Universal Declaration of Human Rights: "Everyone has the right to freedom of opinion and expression; this right includes freedom to hold opinions without interference and to seek, receive and impart information and ideas through any media and regardless of frontiers". In information societies, opinions are increasingly expressed and articulated with the help of the Internet and other new media. Hence, material, usage, and skills access to new technologies is a contemporary expression of a fundamental human right. It is unjust that Western citizens enjoy more human rights and economic, social, cultural, and technological resources than citizens in developing countries.

The technophobe strategy is dualistic, it considers technology as completely unimportant, as a mechanism that can under no societal circumstances do any good. Technology and society are completely separated and technology is considered as unimportant.

Strategy 6: Dialectical integrationism: An integrated strategy combining the global redistribution of wealth, educational and health programs, digital literacy programs; public and free access to computers and technologies, open source technologies, and computers for the Third World. All five strategies discussed so far are reductionistic and one-dimensional; they don't see the interconnectedness of technology access, social factors, uneven development, human rights, and global capitalism. In order to tackle the global digital divide, a fundamental redistribution of resources is needed as a precondition. Modern society is so rich and productive that it could easily afford a modest income, social security, literacy, and free access to computers and the Internet for all humans. If this is a real possibility, then the best and most desirable option is to realize it. But this requires a redesign of global society because the digital divide is not first of all a technological problem; it is an economic, social, and political issue. The digital divide is not only a divide in the access to and benefits from technology but also an expression of a more general divide in wealth and power. In order to close the global divide, first of all measures such as a fundamental global redistribution of wealth, a full cancellation of all debts of development countries, a multiplication of development aid, the provision of free public-health and educational programs, and a basic income guarantee for all absolutely poor individuals (that could be financed, e.g., by a Tobin tax) could be realized. Based on such a material foundation, further measures, such as the support of publicly provided free access to computers and Internet for all, the public provision of digital literacy programs, local hardware production that aims at free or cheap local products, and the large-scale adoption and production of free software technologies (that are adapted to local needs) by developing countries, seem to be feasible. Western actors or countries could also provide computers and equipment for free to the Third World, but these technologies should be technologically advanced, noncommercial, nonproprietary, free of cost, and open source in order to avoid the deepening of existing or emergence of new dependencies. Access to technologies should be universal, guaranteed by the public, free of cost, and based on open source. That it should be universal means that it should be guaranteed to all people. This can best be achieved if provided not by private organizations but by public ones (such as communities) because the latter are not based on profit interests that might undermine universality but on the common interest in common goods. The best guarantee for avoiding the emergence of capitalist interests in technology that might undermine universal access and the dependency of developing countries on Western capital, technologies, and interests is the provision and development of technologies that are free of cost ("free access for all") and open source (accessible source code in order to advance cooperative engineering, high quality, and free access). Open source technologies can advance the emergence of local and regional communities for cooperative technology development that act independently from Western interests and the logic of profitability.

One innovative measure is to establish public funds for free access telecommunication services. In Brazil the Partido dos Trabalhadores (PT) government has established a fund for universal telecommunications services (FUST) financed in part by a 1 percent tax on the gross revenues of telecommunications service providers. It provides ICT resources for schools, health facilities, and rural communities. Such funds can be financed, as the Brazilian example shows, by taxing capital and/or by development aid. An integrative strategy of fundamental redistribution mechanisms, free public access, educational and health programs, a gift economy, open source and open access technologies seems most promising to us. One-dimensional strategies ignore the interconnectedness of technological and societal issues. For overcoming the digital divide, more fundamental strategies that aim at changing society and departing from the dominance of capitalist logic are needed.

The strategy of dialectical integrationism unites societal and political measures in the areas of poverty reduction, development aid, debt service, health, or education, with the introduction of alternative technologies that can support local societal development and are in line with local knowledge and needs. This strategy is not one-sided and much more complex and realistic than the other five.

Digital exclusion is challenged by digital inclusion. Besides the digital divides, there are also movements and ideas of establishing a participatory society in which all decide all, all own all, and so on, that could be supported by ICTs. This phenomenon of eParticipation will be discussed next.

8.2 DIGITAL INCLUSION: ePARTICIPATION AS GRASSROOTS DIGITAL DEMOCRACY

For discussing the phenomena of digital democracy and eParticipation, three traditions of democracy and democracy theory are first identified. Then the three lines of thought are mapped to approaches on digital democracy: Representative digital democracy, plebiscitary digital democracy, and grassroots digital democracy are discussed.

In objective concepts of power, power is located in coercive institutions that realize the particular will of a group by commanding and sanctioning other groups and individuals. In subjective approaches it is a productive, transformative human capacity that is immanent in the human body and social relationships. My own understanding is a dialectical synthesis of the two notions: power is a dialectical process in which human actors enter social relationships that are to certain degrees competitive and cooperative in order to reach decisions so that decision-oriented structures emerge and are reproduced that enable and constrain further decision-oriented social practices. Power is conceived as a self-referential autopoietic process.

Based on the three different concepts of power, three corresponding models of democracy will be discussed:

- Representative democracy (corresponding to the objective concept of power)
- Direct democracy (corresponding to the subjective concept of power)
- Grassroots democracy (corresponding to the dialectical concept of power)

Democracy and Participation

Etymologically, the term *democracy* stems from the Greek "demokratia," which is made up of the two words *demos* (people) and *kratos* (rule). Democracy hence literally means rule/sovereignty/power by the people.

In the concept of representative democracy, democracy is conceived as a parliamentary system that consists of elected parliamentarians who each represent a certain share of voters and who, based on majority votes, pass bills. In parliamentary democracies, such as Great Britain, government is formed by a majority of representatives and is based on parliamentary majority votes. In presidential democracies, such as the United States, government is elected separately and can under normal circumstances not be overturned by parliament. In competitive democracies (e.g., the United States, the United Kingdom, and France) conflicts are solved by majority votes. In concordance democracies (e.g., Belgium, Netherlands, Austria, and Switzerland) one tries to achieve consensus or compromises by negotiation mechanisms. In majority democracies, the majority party forms government and there is a majority voting system. In consensus democracies, a parliamentary majority forms government so that coalitions might be required and there is proportional representation.

In the concept of direct democracy, democracy is conceived as immediate decision making by the people. In this tradition, it is considered desirable that as many decisions as possible should be discussed and taken by the citizens. Many modern democracies contain direct democratic elements in the form of referenda and petitions for referenda. Mechanisms of direct democracy are especially important in Switzerland, Italy, France, Ireland, Denmark, Australia, and New Zealand. In Switzerland, there are four instruments of direct democracy. In a facultative referendum, a plebiscite concerning already existing laws is held if at least 50,000 citizens sign a referendum. If a public initiative attains 100,000 signatures, parliament must discuss certain proposed amendments of the Swiss constitution. Parliament can work out an alternative proposal and the citizens and cantons select one of the alternatives in a plebiscite. There are also facultative referenda concerning international treaties or the entry of Switzerland into international organizations as well as obligatory referenda where the citizens can vote on the retention or abolition of constitutional amendments or emergency laws one year after they have been passed.

A plebiscitary system is a political system in which ruling parties or charismatic leaders decide on which issues referenda should be taken and how the questions for such plebiscites are formulated; citizens then vote directly on these issues. The main criticism of this concept is that it is prone to manipulation and that a plebiscitary system can easily turn into totalitarianism. Max Weber favored a plebiscitary system based on charismatic leadership. Carl Schmitt considered, twelve years after the death of Weber, a dictatorship based on plebiscitary legitimation as the best form of government (Schmitt 1932) and conceived plebiscitary leadership as the foundation of the political model of the National Socialists known as the *Volksgemeinschaft*.

Classical thinkers of representative democracy, such as Montesquieu, John Stuart Mill, and John Locke, stressed democratic institutions, that is, power structures such as parliaments, governments, and constitutions. Their concept of democracy is based on an objective concept of power in which power structures represent citizens. For classical thinkers of direct democracy, such as Jean-Jacques Rosseau, who argued that the moment a people allows itself to be represented it is no longer free, democracy is a more subjective process, that is, it is based on the permanent decision making by citizens.

It is more desirable, just, and democratic that those affected by decisions are directly involved in decision making than the formation of decision-making elites by the election of representatives or the plebiscitary separation of decision preparation and decision taking that results in autocracy. In this context, the notions of participation and participatory democracy arise.

Participation means that humans are enabled by technologies, resources, organizations, and skills to design and manage their social systems all by themselves and to develop collective visions of a better future so that the design of social systems can make use of their collective intelligence. Decisions in a social system should be prepared, taken, and enacted by all individuals and groups affected by the operations of the system in bottom-up grassroots processes. Participatory systems are self-organized and self-managed systems.

Why is participation important?

- Participation is a human right.
- Participatory systems are more democratic and effective than heteronomous systems.
- Participation contributes to the contentedness and happiness of human beings.
- Participation is a precondition for consensus.
- Participation creates respect for one another.
- Participation can ensure that people take part in social systems more effectively and at a deeper level of commitment.
- Participation allows synergies to arise from cooperation and joint knowledge production.

A participatory social system is a system in which power is distributed in a rather symmetrical way, that is, humans are enabled to control and acquire resources such as property, technologies, social relationships, knowledge, and skills that help them in entering communication and cooperation processes in which decisions on questions that are of collective concern are taken. Providing people with resources and capacities that enable responsible and critical activity in decision-making processes is a process of empowerment; participation is a process of empowering humans.

A coercive or dominative system is a system that is a hierarchic oligopoly, autocratic, gives little regard to the desires and purposes of people in the system, and where the members are there only to serve the purposes of the system that are set by a limited number of people. Such a system is an exclusive, estranged, heteronomous, and alienated system. A participatory system, in contrast, is a system in which people are invited to make unique contributions, to participate in decision making, and to use their individual and collective creativity and intelligence. Such systems are inclusive and self-determined.

Representatives of participatory democracy stress that participation is not confined to the state system but also affects the economy, culture, and the lifeworld. It is not limited to decision making; rather, it also includes processes such as producing and owning (economic), setting goals, forming knowledge, values, images and visions, communication, and self-realization (cultural). Hence, in participatory systems there is not only cooperative decision making, but also an asymmetric distribution of the means of production and of skills are avoided; economic resources and human capacities (knowledge, skills) are considered as means of empowerment. In participatory systems, owning, producing, deciding, living, and learning are cooperative and inclusive processes. Citizenship is attached to ownership of property, human capacities, and decision power. Bela A. Banathy, the founder of participatory social systems design, argues in this context that democracy is a dynamic process: "Participative democracy comes to life when we individually and collectively develop a design culture that empowers us to create, govern, and constantly reinvent our systems" (Banathy 1996, 37). Participation would be the Essence of true democracy: "The notion of 'empowering' people to make decisions that affect their lives and their systems is a core idea of true democracy. Much of this power today is delegated to others" (ibid., 344). For Banathy, the notion of participatory systems design implies a self-governing, self-creating society.

In the concept of participatory democracy, political life is not separated from everyday life. Politics is not conceived as an exclusive sphere dominated by a political elite but as an inclusive sphere of political communication and cooperation constituted by affected, knowledgeable, active citizens. Besides what Antonio Gramsci (1971) has called the political society, there is also the political sphere of civil society, the sphere of voluntary political action in nongovernment organizations that aims at advancing common purposes. Participatory democracy empowers civil society; it is based on communication and cooperation processes within civil society. A dialectical concept of participation conceives democracy as a permanent emergence of power structures from participatory communication in civil society: Affected citizens enter political communication processes that are organized as public forms of discourse and deliberation wherein different problems, standpoints, and possible solutions are discussed controversially; in deliberation and cooperation processes, they try to achieve agreements (in the ideal case in the form of informed consensus or alternatively by majority votes or by chance). These agreements become power structures (i.e., institutionalized, collectively binding decisions that have a certain temporal continuation) by being enacted by public authorities. As such, they enable and constrain further political ideas, practices, communication, and cooperation in civil society from which further power structures emerge, and so on. Hence, participatory democracy is a dynamic process in which civil society communication and public administration act mutually upon each other and guarantee the overall reproduction of the political system.

The importance of civil society has been shown by the increasing relevance of nongovernment organizations and protest movements in society. They can be understood as calls for a more participatory society wherein those affected by decisions are involved in decision-making processes. The fascination that these movements exert on many people is partly due to the fact that they make grassroots democracy vivid, noticeable, and sensible within a world of heteronomy and alienation.

Political communication and cooperation processes in civil society result in the emergence of a public sphere for political discourse and discursive, deliberative will formation. For Jürgen Habermas (1968, 1981), the private sphere and the public sphere are part of the lifeworld. The public sphere differs from the private sphere insofar as it is a freely accessible space of communication that is not limited to family and friends in which public opinions (understood as criticism of a ruling class by a public body of citizens) are formed (Habermas 1968, 11sqq.; 1981, 471sqq.). For Habermas, the public sphere is a space for the solution of problems by communicative action. This would be possible by nondominative discourse, that is, communication that adheres to the validity claims of truth (according to facts), truthfulness (correspondence of statements and intentions), normative rightness (adherence of general norms of communication), and comprehensibility. Habermas's approach is important because it has shown that communication is an important aspect of participation. In participatory systems, communicative action is the process that allows civil society to form a discursive public sphere in which there is reasoned, knowledgeable discussion. Public criticism and arguments on different political opinions that can be stated and heard at length are voiced and subject to public scrutiny. From these critical communication processes, collectively binding power structures emerge. The public sphere is not a single system but a whole that is made up of spheres of political communication that emerge in everyday life wherever people engage in political arguments and controversies that are open for others to join. Nancy Fraser (1982) has pointed out that the bourgeois public sphere has excluded women, workers, and ethnic minorities and that hence counterpublics have developed that, on the one hand, "function as spaces of withdrawal and regroupment; on the other hand, they also function as bases and training groups for agitational activities directed toward wider publics" (Fraser 1982, 124). Counterpublics are alternative public spheres in class-segmented societies (class employed in the multidimensional Bourdieuian sense of the term) that allow dominated groups to voice their opinions in public. In the bourgeois public sphere, access and openness for all are not guaranteed; both are ideals of true public spheres.

The idea of participatory democracy can best be described as the concept of self-organized democracy. Self-organization is a process of order formation that comes from within a system. In the case of political order formation, self-organization means that affected citizens are enabled to take decisions all by themselves in bottom-up grassroots processes; self-organized democracy is a process of self-determination and self-management that maximizes the involvement of affected humans in political discourse and decision taking and avoids the formation of political elites that constitute heteronomous political systems that are alienated from direct involvement of citizens.

The notion of self-organized democracy is close to other concepts of participatory democracy such as Crawford Brough Macpherson's concept of democracy as the maximization of developmental power, Benjamin Barber's strong democracy, Murray Bookchin's libertarian municipalism, David Held's democratic autonomy, and Cornelius Castoriadis's autonomous self-institution.

Macpherson (1973) understands power in opposition to the definition of power as domination as the possibility to use and develop essential nondestructive human faculties such as "the capacity for rational understanding, for moral judgement and action, for aesthetic creation or contemplation, for the emotional activities of friendship and love, and, sometimes, for religious experience" (= developmental power; Macpherson 1973, 4). Complete democracy would maximize the developmental power of all. Macpherson advances an understanding of power as potential that in philosophy can, for example, be found in the writings of Spinoza (cf. Fuchs and Zimmermann 2008). Capitalism would be based on extractive power, that is, the transfer of the faculties of the nonowning class and the goods that they create into the hands of the owning class. Hence, there would be inherent limits of modern society to complete democracy. The right to unlimited appropriation would undermine freedom, security, and justice for others. There would be an antagonism between the freedom to unlimited appropriation of the faculties of others and the (undermined) right to the development of human faculties. Macpherson grounds his concept of democracy in the Marxian picture of man as creative being who has become alienated in modern society and can realize its human Essence only under transformed power relations. He understands complete democracy as a society that guarantees political freedom and extends democracy from the political to the economic and the cultural realm as participation in ownership of resources and means of production for all and the right to good life for all. The realization of well-rounded individuality for all would require the access to economic resources, political freedom, as well as material and immaterial life-sustaining goods that enable the development of human faculties. Under such conditions, property would not only mean property in material resources but also include the participation in power that controls productive resources and the right to a society that guarantees a complete and fully developed human life for all. Macpherson was a neo-Marxist political scientist who grounded the idea of participatory democracy and extended the notion of democracy from the political to the economic and cultural realms with the help of the Marxian idea of human Essence that can be found in early writings such as the *Economic-Philosophical Manuscripts*. Macpherson's concept of complete democracy is more radical than the notions of participation advanced by thinkers like Barber or Dahl, who argue that there are certain necessary limits to participation. Macpherson's analysis is visionary and transcends dominant reason; nonetheless, he remains realistic and hence can be considered as the most important influence on the development of the eParticipation concept in the book at hand.

Barber has defined a strong democracy as a system "where citizens are engaged at the local and national levels in a variety of political activities and regard discourse, debate and deliberation as essential conditions for reaching common ground and arbitrating differences between people in a large multi-cultural society. In strong democracy, citizens actually participate in governing themselves, if not in all matters, all of the time, at least in some matters at least some of the time" (Barber 1998).

Murray Bookchin has conceived a grassroots democracy at municipal level that is confederated in the form of a commune of communes and that is based on a self-managed, municipalized economy. "With regard to its origin in classical Athens, democracy as I use it is the idea of the direct management of the polis by its citizenry in popular assemblies. . . . Democracy generically defined, then, is the direct management of society in face-to-face assemblies—in which policy is formulated by the resident citizenry and administration is executed by mandated and delegated councils" (Bookchin 1994).

David Held's concept of democratic autonomy is based on the idea of a participatory society understood as "a society which fosters a sense of political efficacy, nurtures a concern for collective problems and contributes to the formation of a knowledgeable citizenry capable of taking a sustained interest in the governing process" (Held 1996, 271). Autonomy, for Held, means that people should be able to participate in a process of debate and deliberation, open to all on a free and equal basis, about matters of pressing public concern (ibid., 302) and that they are enabled to do so by representative state institutions and a bill of rights that guarantees political rights, social rights such as child care, education, and health, as well as economic rights realized among other things in the form of a guaranteed basic income for all (ibid., 318sq.).

Cornelius Castoriadis argues that society is in need of institutions that decide what is to be done and not to be done, that is, institutions set limits. He conceives democracy as a permanent bottom-up process that he terms autonomy or self-institution. "Democracy is the regime of self-limitation [autolimitation], in other words, the regime of autonomy, or of self-institution [autoinstitution]. Democracy is a regime that self-institutes itself explicitly in an ongoing [permanent] manner" (Castoriadis 2005, 202sq.). The affinity of the concept of self-organized democracy to these notions is straightforward in the sense that they all conceive power formation as a grassroots process from below, although one can object to Barber and Bookchin that in the age of the Internet participatory democracy is not necessarily confined to local and national scopes and to face-to-face assemblies but can acquire a global dimension.

Social information or knowledge can be conceived as a threefold dynamic process of cognition, communication, and cooperation (Fuchs and Hofkirchner 2005): Individuals perceive the world and form ideas in cognitive processes that are recursively linked to social communication processes in which symbolic interaction is achieved and that are recursively linked to synergetic cooperation processes from which new system qualities emerge. In the case of political information processes, humans form political opinions by engaging with political information sources (discussions and mass media) that are the cognitive foundation for political discourses and controversies (communication) from which political decisions and their administrative implementations emerge. Collective binding decisions, as results of political cooperation in processes of downward causation, feed back on political communication; they enable and constrain discourses that, furthermore, enable and constrain the cognitive formation of political opinions that again act as the foundation of discourses from which new decisions emerge, and so on. Hence, the dynamic process of power generation and reproduction can, on the informational level, be conceived as an interconnected process of political cognition, communication, and cooperation (see fig. 8.1). All three aspects can have a more centralized or decentralized character. In contemporary society, opinion formation and political discourse are mainly confined to the mass-media system in which there are a few senders and many recipients and to everyday political discussions; decision taking is organized in the form of elections and representative institutions. Hence, the contemporary political information structure is rather centralized.

A self-organized (participatory) democracy implies a decentralization of all three levels:

- Cognition: Mechanisms of opinion formation that allow a plurality of information sources and in which every recipient can also be a sender that is heard and taken seriously by others.
- Communication: Mechanisms of rational public discourse that are open and accessible for all citizens and enable humans to acquire the resources and capacities they need for active, knowledgeable, informed participation.
- And finally, on the cooperative level, institutions of decision taking and enactment that are directly controlled by and responsible to all citizens.

The role of civil society in contemporary society has a communicative and a cooperative dimension as nongovernment protest groups engage both in

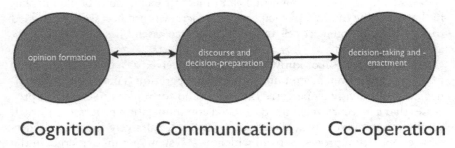

Cognition   Communication   Co-operation

Figure 8.1 The political information process.

the formation of alternative discourses (information campaigning, alternative media, etc.) and influencing decisions (by various methods of protest and lobbying). The three aspects of political information identified here correspond to the ones that Roza Tsagarousianou (1999) has considered as important for digital democracy: obtaining information, engaging in deliberation, participating in decision making.

Based on the discussion of models of democracy in this section, I will identify three understandings of digital democracy in the next section:

- Representative digital democracy (corresponding to the representative model of democracy)
- Plebiscitary digital democracy (corresponding to the model of direct democracy)
- eParticipation: Grassroots digital democracy (corresponding to the model of participatory democracy)

eParticipation and 3 Concepts of Digital Democracy

There are different concepts of digital democracy that are related to different concepts of democracy. Jan Van Dijk (2000) argues that telepolls, telerefernda, and televoting are mainly favored by plebiscitary and libertarian versions of digital democracy, tools for online communication between citizens and governments by legalist and competitive versions, and political mailing lists and discussion boards by participatory, pluralist, and libertarian versions.

I will now discuss different definitions of digital democracy and relate them to three important concepts of democracy: (1) Representative democracy; (2) Direct, plebiscitary democracy; (3) Participatory democracy.

Many definitions of digital democracy and related concepts are very vague, broad, and neutral; they describe all forms of politics that make use of new ICTs for political activities. They don't acknowledge that such diverse activities as contacting a parliamentarian by e-mail, voting online, or discussing in an online forum are related to different democratic concepts and traditions.

Hacker and Van Dijk define digital democracy in very general terms; their concept implies that online politics are necessarily activities of physically separated people and ignores the more blended character of contemporary online politics as it is practiced, for example, by social movements. "We define digital democracy as a collection of attempts to practice democracy without the limits of time, space and other physical conditions, using ICT or CMC instead, as an addition, not a replacement for traditional 'analogue' political practices" (Hacker and Van Dijk 2000, 1; cf. also Van Dijk 2006).

Another vague definition says that digital democracy "can be defined as encompassing all the uses of information and communication technology (ICT) which might affect and change the functioning of a democracy—and more especially the fundamental operations of expressing opinions, debating, voting, making decisions" (Catinat and Vedel 2000, 185).

Martin Hagen (1997) has identified three different concepts of digital democracy: The idea of teledemocracy stresses direct democracy in the form of electronic voting; the notion of cyberdemocracy focuses on direct democracy in the form of virtual communities, online discussions, and online activism that challenge centralized state power; in the concept of electronic democratization, representative democracy should be enhanced by direct feedback links between voters and representatives (electronic town meetings) and political online information systems that allow more and freer access to crucial government information. Hagen's (1997) concept of electronic democracy is so general that it encompasses all three forms; he defines it as the usage of computer networks "to carry out crucial functions of the democratic process—such as information and communication, interest articulation and aggregation and decision-making (both deliberation and voting)"—it lacks a normative preference for a certain concept.

Besides such general neutral definitions, there are also ones that are closer to specific concepts of democracy.

Representative Digital Democracy

Representative concepts of digital democracy mainly stress top-down digital communication of governments and citizens and intragovernment digital communication. Technologies that are favored include political guest books, newsletters, chats and online conferences with politicians on special occasions, e-mails to politicians, online administration tools (such as online tax declarations, downloading and submitting forms online, etc.), citizen information systems, online election campaigning, online policy proposals, online consultation, citizens' juries, citizens' panels, or the electronic town hall.

Here are some definitions of digital democracy that focus on representative ideas. "The Internet provides a forum for consultation. . . . For a specific form of consultation, the public can easily access the documentation put forward by government. The medium allows one to learn by browsing or searching" (Richard 1999, 74). Pippa Norris argues that the extensive debate about the role of digital technologies for strong and direct democracy "can be regarded as a distracting irrelevance, a buzzing mosquito" (Norris 2001, 104) because many countries would first of all need well-functioning representative institutions (governments, parliaments). In her understanding of digital democracy, she hence focuses on "the potential function of Internet in strengthening the institutions of representative governance and civic societies worldwide" and "how far governments and civic society learn to use the opportunities provided by the new channels of information and communication to promote and strengthen the core representative institutions connecting citizens and state" (Norris 2001, 104). This is a narrow understanding of digital democracy; it cancels off the desire of human beings for grassroots democracy. Political problems today not only stem from a lack of democratic institutions in the world but also from a feeling of alienation that many people have about governing institutions that they feel don't represent their interests well, and that implies a need for more grassroots participation. A focus on "the ability of the Internet to provide information, promoting the transparency, openness and accountability of governing agencies" ignores the importance of political communication, political protest, and nongovernment organizations for digital democracy. An empirical study of 3,000 government department Web sites conducted by Norris in 1999 concludes that "the opportunities for 'bottom up' interactivity in communicating with official departments are far fewer than the opportunities to read 'top down' information" (Norris 2001, 130). It comes as no surprise that governments prefer centralized top-down information technologies to decentralized grassroots communication technologies because established political actors in contemporary representative political systems aim at accumulating and stabilizing power relationships. Interactive technologies like public online discussion boards or wikis allow oppositional voices to criticize governments and parties, which might shed negative light on the latter and might be detrimental to the interest of accumulating votes. Vilém Flusser (1996a, 1996b) described such centralized information distribution mechanisms as conservative, protofascist, and totalitarian modes of communication; the focus on one-to-many information technologies discloses a very restricted and dangerous view of democracy by many governments.

Representative digital democracy is a competitive view of politics in which there is an exclusion between government and the people and government and opposition.

Plebiscitary Digital Democracy

Plebiscitary concepts of digital democracy mainly stress bottom-up digital communication of citizens and governments. Technologies that are favored are, for example, online surveys, online polls, online voting, and online referenda.

Electronic democracy is considered by Hacker as being close to plebiscitary democracy, electronic democratization as a way to improve the institutions of representative democracy. "The term electronic democracy signifies a system of participation in which direct electronic expression and voting are viewed as replacements for democracy by representation. By contrast, electronic democratization is defined here as the enhancement of a democracy, already initiated, with new communication technologies in ways that increase the political power of those who usually have minimal roles in key political processes" (Hacker 1996).

William H. Dutton (1999, 179) argues that "ICTs like interactive cable TV and the Internet could enable citizens to vote and be polled on matters of public interest from their homes", which might clash with traditional paradigms of representative democracy. For Richard Moore, electronic democracy means "the use of electronic networking to bring about a more direct form of democracy, to short-circuit the representative process and look more to net-supported plebiscites and 'official' online debates in deciding issues of government policy" (R. K. Moore 1999, 55). Theodore Becker and Christa Slaton see televoting from the home as a central feature of teledemocracy that they define as "a new democratic political communications system that includes televoting, deliberative polling, electronic town meetings and the Internet, one that is facilitated globally via the Internet" (Becker and Slaton 1997, 24). Alvin Toffler (1980, 429) argues that "spectacular advances in communications technology open, for the first time, a mind-boggling array of possibilities for direct citizen participation in political decision-making" (Toffler 1980, 429).

Christopher Arterton (1987, 14) defines teledemocracy as "the use of communications technology to facilitate the transmission of political information and opinion between citizens and their public leaders". This definition is close to both a representative and a plebiscitary understanding of democracy. In his study he focuses on plebiscitary mechanisms of televoting and communication between governments and well-informed citizens achieved by new technologies. Citizen-citizen communication and civil society communication are excluded from this understanding of teledemocracy; it focuses on political elites and how they can connect to citizens by the means of communication technology.

Representatives of plebiscitary digital democracy consider televoting, telepolling, and telereferenda as empowering citizens and weakening centralized bureaucratic power. They reduce democracy to direct decisions in the form of voting and ignore that democracy is first of all a process of communicative action and deliberation. The conceptual focus on voting instead of on deliberation and communication is underestimating the danger of the potential usage of televoting for installing push-button and point-and-click decision systems that give legitimacy to authoritarian leadership that manipulates public opinion. Such leadership is an expression of elite formation, competition, and exclusion.

eParticipation: Grassroots Digital Democracy

I don't want to give a definition of digital democracy that contributes to the dominant conceptual chaotic plurality without unity. It might be best to coin a new term for grassroots digital democracy and to use the term *digital democracy* as a very general notion describing different methods, tools, practices, and concepts of using ICTs in democratic politics. The term *eParticipation* is employed for describing methods, tools, practices, and concepts of employing ICTs in politics that are close to the tradition of participatory, self-organized democracy. eParticipation is a term that describes that computer-based information and communication technologies (ICTs) can be used for empowering cognition, communication, and cooperation processes of humans so that they can jointly construct participatory social systems. In eParticipation processes, ICTs empower humans, groups, and society, that is, they provide individuals with capacities and resources for changing organizations and society according to their will, they provide groups and organizations with capacities and resources for changing society and better including individuals, and they provide society with capacities to better include groups and individuals.

The grassroots concept of digital democracy (eParticipation) mainly stresses citizen-citizen digital communication and communication processes of and in nongovernmental civil society protest groups and movements. Whereas plebiscitary and representative models of digital democracy stress the relationship of governments and citizens, the concept of grassroots digital democracy stresses the communication of civil society and citizens and has the vision that from these communication processes an alternative participatory society that is self-managed and self-organized could emerge. Technologies and tools that are favored for online politics include online-discussion boards (Web-based, non-Web-based), mailing lists, wikis, political blogs, political chats, cyberprotest tools, online petitions, and online protest campaigns.

Ann Macintosh (2004) argues that e-voting and e-participation are the two aspects of electronic democracy. She sees three dimensions of participation: e-enabling information access, e-engaging citizens in policy consulting, and e-empowering, which "is concerned with supporting active participation and facilitating bottom-up ideas to influence the political agenda" (Macintosh 2004, 3). For me, e-enabling and e-engaging are more aspects of representative digital democracy than of eParticipation. The stress in the concept of eParticipation should be not just on the idea that citizens should be able to influence political decisions, but on the idea that all those served and governed should be those serving and governing. eParticipation is not one complementary aspect of representation and e-voting, but an alternative to representative and plebiscitary digital democracy.

The concept of eParticipation is close to the models of bottom-up-digital democracy of Manuel Castells, Benjamin Barber, and Howard Rheingold.

Manuel Castells (2004) argues that digital democracy will be exclusive and one-way as long as it is controlled by parties and governments; he is optimistic concerning the use of ICTs by nongovernment organizations and citizens and speaks of an "empowerment for grassroots groups using the Internet as an instrument of information, communication, and organization"; he argues that "the Internet can contribute to enhance the autonomy of citizens to organize and mobilize around issues that are not properly processes in the institutional system" and that a "new kind of civil society" and the "electronic grassrooting of democracy" could emerge (Castells 2004, 417).

Another grassroots understanding is provided by Benjamin Barber: "The Net offers a useful alternative to elite-mass communication in that it permits ordinary citizens to communicate directly round the world without the mediation of elites—whether they are editors filtering information or broadcasters shaping information or facilitators moderating conversation. By challenging hierarchical discourse, the new media encourage direct democracy and so, as I suggested fifteen years ago, can be instruments of strong democracy" (Barber 1998).

Howard Rheingold (2000) has argued that many-to-many communication in virtual communities has a potential for enhancing democratic deliberation if the interests of "big power" and "big money" (xix) can be kept out and learning people form an informed population. Commercial media would have co-opted and narrowed political discourse; open virtual communities in which "every citizen can broadcast to every other citizen" could "revitalize citizen-based democracy" (xxix). The effects of computer-mediated communication on society could either be a panopticon or an "electronic agora", the latter understood as "the vision of a citizen-designed, citizen-controlled worldwide communication network" (xxx), a "worldwide citizen-to-citizen conversation" (133). Rheingold's focus is on online discourse and the challenging of information monopolies by many-to-many communication, not on online voting and plebiscites. He is aware that media-manipulated plebiscites as political tools go back to Joseph Goebbels and that they can easily advance authoritarian politics (306sq.). In a chapter added to the revised 2000 edition of "The Virtual Community" (originally published in 1993), Rheingold answers his critics by stressing that there is no techno-deterministic development of society, that the future of the Internet depends on social forces, and that just like in "real life" one finds both the establishment of strong and weak relationships and isolation in virtual life. "No tool can make democracy happen without the actions of millions of people—but those millions of people won't succeed without the right tools" (382). I read Rheingold's book as an indication for virtual communities being techno-social potentials for participatory democracy that can only be realized in a society that avoids the colonization of communication and public spheres by commodification and bureaucratization. Rheingold describes that he experienced himself that the turning of virtual communities into commodities threatens open access and communication when the online community The WELL (The Whole Earth 'Lectronic Link) was commercialized and when he founded Electric Minds with venture-capital financing (chap. 11).

The term *electronic agora* is also employed by Gerhard Vowe and Martin Emmer (2001), but their account lacks an explicit definition. I understand an electronic or digital agora as a participatory social structure that is based on permanent political discussion of citizens, aims at finding political agreements, has no primary focus on voting but on decision making by communicative action, and makes use of new ICTs for supporting communication processes.

Concerning citizen-citizen communication, online discussion boards are particularly important for eParticipation because they have potentials to advance rational discourse and nondominative dialogue from which a critical public sphere supported by ICTs might emerge. But research has shown that these potentials have not yet been realized (Wilhelm 1999; Jankowski and Selm 2000; for the description of countertendencies, see Winkler 2002). What is needed are not just new tools and frameworks for democracy but also media literacy and political education. What is mostly needed for enabling citizens to engage critically, actively, and constructively in political discourse is the advancement of critical political education—a modern form of the ancient Greek *paideia*. The capacity for advancing political discourse arises from the Internet's decentralized structure that enables many-to-many communication. The Internet is in need of a decentralized social structure (that has not yet been established) in order to advance dialogic political communication that satisfies the four Habermasian claims of validity.

In the concept of eParticipation there is also a stress on the political usage of ICTs in civil society. Since recently the term *cyberprotest* has been employed for describing the usage of ICTs by protest groups and movements for providing alternative online media, networking themselves, communicating and coordinating protest online, and organizing protest not only with the help of but also within cyberspace itself (see section 8.5).

The main criticism of grassroots models is that they can only work at a local level and that modern societies are too complex and large for grassroots democracy. Due to the assumed complexity of society, representation and elite formation would be unavoidable in politics. Political efficiency is considered as the most important value by such arguments. The (yet to be realized) vision of a participatory information society gives contemporary answers to such arguments. In the information society, economic productivity has gained a level that could enable human beings to minimize compulsory labor time and to maximize freely chosen activities and free time so that huge free spaces for political activity could emerge. Furthermore, new ICTs enable local, regional, and global many-to-many communication that could allow humans to form interest groups and to rationally discuss problems. Rational discourse can be easier achieved in smaller communities, for example, at the municipal level. What about communities of thousands or millions of individuals? Here models of confederation might be practicable, that is, federal councils that involve delegates from all organizational units that are organized on lower levels. A major issue is if the delegates can decide all by themselves or if they are only seen as communicators. Some council models argue that delegates should be elected and that their base should have the possibility to withdraw their decision, which will result in the end of the delegates' function. An alternative is a horizontal model in which delegates only organize and simplify the communicative flows between different organizational units or interest groups. If a federal decision shall be reached, delegates of all units and groups that are affected meet and discuss the problem. But they can't reach a decision before they consult their social bases. New arguments might emerge; the ideas and views of some groups and units might be altered by extensive communicative flows. And it could be possible that members of different groups and units who are not delegates meet in order to discuss the problem. One possibility for exchanging views, besides face-to-face assemblies, is electronic discussion (supported by tools such as Web-based discussion boards, newsgroups, mailing lists) and social software (wikis, blogs, etc.). Decision mechanisms for federated councils are consensus, majority votes taken by all affected citizens or by their delegates, weighted majority votes, or chance decisions. Communities might deselect their delegates at any time and a frequent rotation (decided democratically or by chance) can guarantee a dynamic democratic process. The concept of decentralized communes and federated communes of communes that reach from the local to the regional to the global level seems feasible in the age of the Internet, which allows decentralized, global many-to-many communication. Networking individuals, interest groups, communities, organizations, and municipalities on the local, the regional, and the global level is a foundation of a participatory society because networks allow the sharing of ideas and resources. In a network society, achieving more democratic participation of all in decision processes has become a real possibility.

In the Internet each receiver is a possible transmitter, a prosumer. It is technologically based on a decentralized network that forms a polydirectional medium of interaction where many-to-many communication can take place. In comparison to traditional media, which were based on one-to-many communication, this is a new quality that has a fundamental political potential that is not automatically realized. Traditional media such as television, radio, or printed media have a one-dimensional character; they only work in one direction from the sender to the receiver without possibilities for mutual interaction. The interactivity of the Internet can extenuate the elitist character of traditional media; there is a shift from one-to-many to many-to-many and all-to-all communication. The technological networking of the world puts forward a new principle: all-embracing, participative, networked cooperation and grassroots direct democracy in all realms of society. It is up to human beings to change society in such a way that it can make full use of and realize the opportunities the Internet poses.

Vilém Flusser (1996a, 1996b) has distinguished between dialogic and discursive forms of communication. Dialogue would mean exchanging and sharing information in order to produce new information jointly and cooperatively; discourse would mean the distribution of existing information. Discourses would be conservative and totalitarian because they would try to conserve and distribute existing information. The traditional media would operate in the form of amphitheater discourses where there is one sending center functioning as a channel that transmits information to the mass of passive receivers. Another form of communication would be network discourses that could mainly be found in daily life as gossip and spreading rumors. The existing communication structure would be dominated by a combination and synchronization of the amphitheater discourses of the mass media and gossiping network dialogue. The amphitheater discourses would program unambitious, manipulating information in the form of techno-images (symbolic patterns that signify linear texts that signify pictures that signify parts of the world, images that signify concepts/texts) that would be realized by the gossiping network dialogues in the lifeworld. The character of network dialogue would be shaped and dominated by discourses.

In the times of the new media, there would not only be a potential for a new totalitarianism but also one for a new level of human communication (Flusser, 1996b, 50) that means real human communication (ibid., 157). Television could easily be transformed into a dialogic medium that functions like a telephone (ibid., 203) and enables a democratic cosmic village (ibid., 204). Adding feedback structures to existing mass media wouldn't be a technological problem (ibid., 226); doing so could open up new possibilities for a cosmic creative dialogue (ibid., 228). Computer-based technologies could help transform society into a new dialogic polis (ibid., 286–299). Telematics (telecommunication + informatics) would have a democratic potential for helping to realize a fully dialogic society, a "telematic society" (Flusser 1996a) that is not based on intercourse between techno-images and human beings but on intercourse between human beings that is mediated by techno-images that enable democratic dialogue (ibid.). The idea of using media as forms of dialogic many-to-many communication for strengthening democracy was in critical theories of society first formulated in Bert Brecht's (1932) radio theory and later further developed e.g. by Walter Benjamin (1934) who described the author as producer and by Hans Magnus Enzensberger (1970) with the concept of emancipatory media usage.

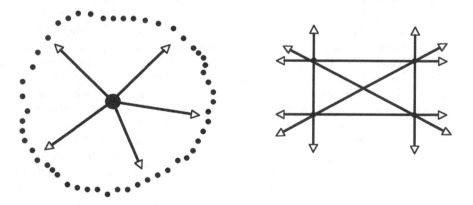

Figure 8.2 Amphitheater discourse and network dialogue as two forms of communication (drawing based on Flusser 1996b, 27, 32).

Flusser died in 1991; he didn't live long enough to see and describe the emergence of the Internet as a mass phenomenon. But he has clearly seen that computer-based networks pose both new opportunities and risks. The Internet forms on its technological level a system of networked dialogue, but on the social level society doesn't make adequate use of this potential because it is dominated by discourses in all realms of social life. Realizing the democratic potential of the Internet would mean that a technological system of network dialogue is coupled to a social system of network dialogue. A democratic form of network dialogue would replace the old system of amphitheater discourse that still dominates society in all of its realms. The form of network dialogue that Flusser describes as simplistic gossip and the spreading of "false consciousness" in the lifeworld would be transformed into a form of network dialogue that is participatory, cooperative, inclusive, and directly democratic. Human beings would be enabled to shape their lives and decisions all by themselves; self-determination, permanent dialogical decisions, and consensus democracy would be central aspects of the dialogical society. Social network dialogues would no longer be dominated by discourses but would be fully dialogic and supported in their democratic character by a technological infrastructure that is organized itself as network dialogue.

For Flusser, discourse means conservative stabilization and distribution of information; it forms a tracing where there is a lack of openness, modification, and connectedness. Moving from discourse to dialogue, from the tracing to map, from the segmented Internet to the rhizomatic Internet, from the segmented society to the rhizomatic society, means to realize the inclusive, cooperative, participatory, direct democratic potential that is immanent in the new media and to move from the conservative distribution model of information to the progressive model of the participatory constitution of information. The Internet has a rhizomatic potential; the human being can realize and build the rhizome but doesn't automatically do so.

Benjamin Barber (1997, 1998, 2002) argues that ICTs speed up life whereas for strong democracy slowing down is needed, that their binary dualism might foster a reductive and simple participatory democracy, that they advance advertising, manipulation, and propaganda by the power of imagery it provides for corporative interests, that they compartmentalize knowledge and hence lack an integrative common ground of knowledge, and that they have a privatizing nature that lacks the empathy needed for community building. For Barber, ICTs imply speed, simplicity, solitude, pictorialness, and segmentation, qualities that impair the possibilities for a strong democracy; as well as lateralness and immediacy (due to being a point to point medium) that might advance strong democracy. Similarly to Barber, Murray Bookchin (1987) argues that electronic media can't produce interdependence because they lack body language, personal intimacy, and face-to-face modes of expression. That ICTs can advance isolation is only one side of the story. Empirical studies show that cyberspace in its current form both advances individualism (e.g., Nie et al. 2002) and new forms of community (e.g., Howard et al. 2002; Katz and Rice 2002). It is both a tool for the reinforcement and shrinking of sociability (see chap. 9.3 of this book for a more detailed discussion). The phenomenon of cyberlove, that is, people that learn to know each other in chat rooms or online dating forums and fall in love after having met each other face to face or not, shows the power of the Internet to mediate the establishment of social relationships and social bonds. Social capital can indeed be created online; if this is possible in personal relationships, then it might also be possible in political relationships if society provides individuals with much more time, resources, and capacities to develop more interest in politics and political activity. Under more participatory societal conditions, the Internet could potentially mediate the emergence of global, regional, and local public spheres. Probably such spheres can be most dynamic and alive if they have a blended character, that is, contain a mixture of online and face-to-face relationships. An inclusive cyberspace enables the emergence of global public spheres or what John Keane (2000) terms "macro-public spheres" that link citizens worldwide and enable millions or billions of people to interact politically. This is due to the fact that the Internet transcends spatial and temporal borders; it is a system that enables the spatiotemporal distanciation of communication and cooperation. Due to the existence of global problems such as ecological degradation, poverty, wars, exploitation, unemployment, precarious working conditions, and so on, global public spheres of concerned citizens that share equal values and experiences, although they live far apart, have already emerged. Protest movements, such as the movement for democratic globalization, make use of the Internet for communicating and coordinating protest and for staging protest online. The public spheres that have emerged from these global political communications are blended ones, partly taking place online and partly in face-to-face meetings, assemblies, and protests. The majority of virtual communities are not purely taking place in cyberspace; they are places for maintaining friendships and creating and maintaining relationships over spatiotemporal distances. Many people who build trusting relationships online also meet offline, and many who have trusting relationships communicate online in order to stay more easily in touch. Continuous relationships today are frequently a combination of online (mediated by communication technologies) and offline communication. Especially for social groups (such as political ones), maintaining permanent relationships is supported by new communication technologies that enable people to stay in touch, exchange opinions, create further contacts, and to plan meetings and activities. In many cases, these activities wouldn't be possible without technological support because finding time and space for meeting frequently in order to discuss and plan activities is often rather difficult for groups that are larger than two people. Computer-mediated communication enables groups to cooperate without meeting permanently face to face, and it enables the building of relationships with people whom one would never meet offline. Global political activists feel a sense of belonging together and commonality, although many of them have learned to know each other on the Web. Alternative public spheres on the Internet are marginal, but they nonetheless exist; hence, it is wrong to argue that the net lacks "common places to gather and common turf on which grieve or celebrate" (Barber 1998). Virtual communities form around shared interests. People in contemporary society have frequently much more to say to individuals on the Net whom they have never met and with whom they share interests than to most people in their neighborhood with whom they hardly share cultural and political interests. Neighborhood and proximity today don't automatically mean open communities, but in many cases "narrow-mindedness and bigotry" that lack alternative outlooks and experiences (Rheingold 2000, 361). Depending on the type of relationships one establishes, virtual communities can both advance open-minded and narrow-minded thinking; like neighborhoods, they are spaces for contact with the difference that in cyberspace you have much more potential options of whom you want to meet and whom not; and hence it potentially enables users to learn from people who have different experiences and live under different societal circumstances.

Jürgen Habermas has argued that the Internet has, besides broadening the media sphere and making it more egalitarian, also resulted in a fragmentation, a "deformalization of the public sphere" (Habermas 2006b), "the fragmentation of large but politically focused mass audiences into a huge number of isolated issue publics" (Habermas 2006a, 423). "The price we pay for the growth in egalitarianism offered by the Internet is the decentralized access to unedited stories. In this medium, contributions by intellectuals lose their power to create a focus" (Habermas 2006b). Today there is a general marginal representation of intellectual thinking in mass media and cyberspace that is not due to the effects of the Internet on the public but due to (in Habermas's theoretical categories) the colonizing effects of monetarization/capitalization and bureaucratization on lifeworld communication processes in the private and the public sphere (including Internet communication and mass-media communication). The deformalization of the public sphere is due to the structure of capitalist society.

If ICTs can advance participatory democracy is not just a question of the availability of participatory technologies such as wikis and Web-based discussion boards; it crucially depends on the availability of resources such as technologies, money, time, and skills to humans. One first prerequisite for advancing digital democracy is the closing of digital divides (see section 8.1). A public sphere is by definition open and universal, that is, accessible for the whole community. If the Internet shall become a public sphere, all digital divides have to be closed and free access for all needs to be achieved. Market forces can't establish the closure of digital divides because they make access dependent on money; and hence in stratified societies those having more money will always have better access to technologies. An alternative is to advance free public access points (such as WLAN [wireless local area network] and free access terminals in public spaces) and open-source software. Nicholas Garnham (1990, 120) has argued in this context that public information and communication services are superior to market-driven ones because they can provide "all citizens, whatever their wealth or geographic location, equal access". Counter to such arguments the authors of the *Magna Carta for the Knowledge Age* (Dyson, Gilder, Keyworth, and Toffler 1994) from a conservative and neoliberal point of view have argued that new technologies promote the end of bureaucratic organization, that private ownership of technologies means dynamic competition, empowerment, and freedom in the sense of private ownership as ownership by the people. For achieving a third-wave society, intellectual property rights and a massive deregulation of telecommunications and computing industries would be needed. This view neglects the fact that private ownership doesn't guarantee diversity of opinions but in many cases has resulted in economic monopolies that threaten to manipulate and control public opinion. Private monopolies are as threatening as state censorship of information and communication; governments much more than markets and corporations have the ability to guarantee free access to ICTs for all because they don't have to market, sell, and derive profit from technologies. Langdon Winner (1997) characterizes the cyberlibertarian ideology as technological determinism (the Internet would automatically result in a better democracy, an "electronic neighbourhood"), radical individualism, and oriented on deregulated free-market capitalism—as being close to right-wing political thought.

Limited concepts such as the "digital nation" (Katz 1997) run counter to the idea of a universal public sphere that closes digital divides. Jon Katz argues that the citizens of the digital nation are young, educated, affluent, and disproportionately white. What should be a warning sounds, in Katz's words, very proud when he proclaims that this privileged minority forms a social class. A universal digital public sphere is a much more democratic vision than a digital nation, which implies borders, closure, and exclusion. It is wrong that "the ascending young citizens of the Digital Nation can, if they wish, construct a more civil society, a new politics based on rationalism, shared information, the pursuit of truth, and new kinds of community" because a civil society requires the participation of as many humans as possible. The notion of the "digital nation" was also employed by Anthony G. Wilhelm (2004) for describing "a more productive and inclusive" (Wilhelm 2004, 4) information society. An inclusive digital nation is an oxymoron because nations are always closed and have a limited, selective membership. One aspect of Internet communication is that it has the potential to transcend spatiotemporal boundaries, which means that it doesn't confine communication to a limited territory such as a nation.

Material and social security are other preconditions for the emergence of active, knowledgeable citizens. Only those who don't have to struggle each day for survival will find the time and energy to engage in politics. Hence, it is of importance to eliminate poverty and scarcity by taking measures such as the elimination of debt burdens on Third World countries and providing a guaranteed basic income for all humans worldwide. A rapid increasing number of people has to live under precarious living and working conditions, is affected by poverty and unemployment. This is due to the antagonism between profit-oriented production and the increasing supersession of human labor power by technology caused by rising levels of productivity. If the focus of the economy were less on profit and more on human interests, the high levels of productivity could easily guarantee the elimination of toil, the minimization of necessary labor time, the guarantee of wealth for all, and the maximization of free time. A postscarcity society where humans maximize their freely chosen activities is a precondition for participatory democracy. Macpherson (1973) argues in this context (with similar arguments and concepts like Herbert Marcuse 1964b) that contemporary societies have reached a level of technological productivity that allows the end of scarcity, necessary labor, and drudgery and the realization of a complete democracy—this is the democratic notion of human Essence or what he terms the maximization of developmental power. This would also mean the end of the idea of the Essence of man as a market-oriented being.

Knowledgeable citizens are in need of education that provides them with possibilities for developing critical faculties and intellectual capacities for engaging in public discourse, knowledge production, critical assessment, complex thinking, and a reflective outlook on society, its problems, and possible solutions. Education needs to be open, participatory, and public in order to enable humans to become well-rounded individuals who are interested in society and willing to engage in constructively changing society. In ancient Greece, the civic education needed for becoming a responsible, active citizen was termed *paideia*. The information society still largely lacks the paideia necessary for establishing digital agoras of the information age. Robin Mansell, in this context, argues that people are not just in need of new technologies and skills for operating these media but also need cognitive capacities and the ability to discriminate between alternative choices. Her focus is on media literacy that empowers people "to improve their own lives", to "express their own opinions about what they value" (Mansell 2001, 5), to "achieve what they value in their lives" (self-actualization, 9), to "strengthen their own freedom to decide between alternative ways of living" (10) and between social alternatives (16), "to contribute to deliberative democratic processes" (14). Mansell stresses that not only the availability of technologies is important but also how they are used and which quality the information that is provided has for the life and choices of humans; she hence sees a necessity for "public investment in information intermediaries that develop and make available the toolkits and other resources that would enable citizens themselves to acquire capabilities to become critical, informed participants in democratic processes" (20).

In early cyberspace theory, optimists like Marshall McLuhan argued that cyberspace will strengthen political participation and will result in a global village, pessimists like Neil Postman argued that new media will result in a totalitarian technopoly, whereas others, like Vilém Flusser, said that new media have various potentials that can result in a democratic telematic society or an undemocratic technopoly. In the contemporary discourse on e-democracy, similar arguments can be found. It is dominated by one-sided views. For example, Nicholas Negroponte (1996) has argued that digital technology is a global common language that has harmonizing and empowering effects and draws people into greater world harmony by its very nature. I think that neither techno-optimism nor techno-pessimism is appropriate but a dialectical view that sees cyberspace as a contradictory space that is embedded into societal antagonisms and hence is shaped by various conflicting tendencies of development. There are both opportunities and risks to eParticipation. In the table below, such dialectical tendencies of eParticipation are identified. It shows 10 antagonisms of eParticipation. The important aspect here is that none of these tendencies asserts itself automatically or by immanent qualities of technology; which ones will prevail and shape our future is determined by human practices in social struggles. The tendencies are ordered along the three aspects of information (cognition, communication, cooperation); the opportunities represent the logic of cooperation, the risks the logic of competition.

Next we will shift back from the logic of cooperation and eParticipation to the logic of competition and eDomination: The phenomenon of information warfare will be discussed.

8.3 THE ABSOLUTE VIOLENCE OF COMPETITION IN THE INFORMATION AGE: INFORMATION WARFARE

In order to work out a notion of information warfare, first the concept of war is discussed, then the relationship of war-technology-globalization is analyzed, and a theoretical notion of information warfare is introduced.

What Is War?

Carl von Clausewitz (1997, 5) defined war as an "act of violence to compel our opponent to fulfill our will". For him, war is the utmost use of violent force as a political instrument for achieving political goals against the will of those who are seen as enemies. Hence, he describes war as called forth by a political motive (Clausewitz 1997, 21) and as "a mere continuation of policy by other means" (Clausewitz 1997, 22). Hostile feelings, the tendency to destroy the adversary, the aim to disarm the enemy, uncertain outcomes due to the imperfect knowledge of circumstances, attack and defense, polarity, courage, and self-reliance would be important aspects of war. For Clausewitz, violence is physical force.

Johan Galtung defines violence as "the cause of the difference between the potential and the actual, between what could have been and what is"

Table 8.4 Opportunities and Risks of Online Politics

ICT- and Knowledge-Related Opportunities and Risks	Political Cognition	Political Communication	Political Cooperation
Opportunity	*Many-to-many online communication vs. One-to-many online communication:* Open and freely accessible ICTs can foster a media structure in which every recipient of information is also an information producer, a prosumer. This can foster a plural public.	*Online discussion vs. online isolation:* CMC can facilitate open, lively, public political discussions.	*Cyberprotest vs. chaotic political online communication:* The decentralized structure of ICTs advances many-to-many communication that might be used by active, knowledgeable citizens to foster grassroots politics that give voice to their interests, challenge the representative system, and aim at realizing the vision of a self-organized grassroots democracy. The idea of a grassroots digital democracy constituted by nongovernmental protest movements is connected to the emergence of alternative media, counterpublics, and counterpower that question and criticize the asymmetrical distribution of power caused by capitalization and bureaucratization. Social movements can use the Internet for coordinating and communicating protest or for protesting online.

Risk	*One-to-many online communication vs. many-to-many online communication:* Commercialized ICTs can advance a monopolistic structure of the mass media in which there are only a few or one sender(s) and many recipients that are prone to manipulation and one-sided information. Monopoly in the area of the media is a form of censorship because it will only give power to selected voices that represent corporate interests. The plurality of consumer choices advanced by e-commerce and the multiplication of available channels of communication doesn't imply more diversity, quality, and critical content of communication. People looking for information online might feel overwhelmed, lost, and disoriented if they are confronted with a complex plurality of information sources and articles on a certain topic. Hence, techniques of knowledge management for sorting out the most important information and gaining a quick overview are required.	*Online isolation vs. online discussion:* ICTs can foster the isolation and individualization of life.	*Chaotic political online communication vs. cyberprotest:* Self-organized grassroots communication that makes use of ICTs might undermine the creative role of educators and mediators in learning processes who can support and help people in organizing themselves. The outcome might be a chaotic plurality of opinions voiced in self-organized communities that are not able to find common grounds and to make decisions.

Table 8.4 (Continued)

ICT- and Knowledge-Related Opportunities and Risks	Political Cognition	Political Communication	Political Cooperation
Opportunity	*Vivid alternative online media vs. repressive online plurality:* ICTs can foster a public sphere where everyone can produce information and voice his or her opinions that are heard by others if the structure of the mass media is democratic and pluralistic and people have time and competences for engaging with the views of others. Alternative online media are particularly important in this context.	*Undermining censorship vs. surveillance on the Internet:* ICTs can be used for bypassing censorship and limitations of the freedom of speech and press.	*Online public spheres vs. plebiscitary online voting:* ICTs can advance the emergence of public spheres that work online and face-to-face, where rational discourse takes place and humans try to achieve consensus concerning problems that affect them.
Risk	*Repressive online plurality vs. vivid alternative online media:* ICTs can foster the voicing of a plurality of opinions and views, but based on an undemocratic and rather monopolistic media structure people aren't interested in a plurality of information sources because they are conditioned by advertising and propaganda to listen mainly to the voices of the big players in business. Not only the existence of information but also the attention to information is important in the information age.	*Surveillance vs. undermining censorship on the Internet:* ICTs can easily be used for the systematic massive surveillance of human cognition and communication by governments.	*Plebiscitary online voting vs. online public spheres:* ICTs can advance a plebiscitary system in which leaders decide which questions are raised for votes, politics is a big entertainment business, and manipulated voters engage in an online push-button-decision system that legitimates totalitarianism.

Opportunity	*Multimedia politics vs. low-quality political online information:* Political information can be presented in appealing ways by making use of the Internet's possibilities for employing multimedia and hyperlinking.	*Open source technologies and information vs. information commodities:* Free and open access to ICTs, open-source software, and the sharing of information can foster human involvement and activity in cyberspace.	*Cyberprogress vs. cyberhate:* Cyberspace is a global medium that can advance the decentralized communication and coordination of progressive political protest movements that aim at building a self-organized, participatory society.
Risk	*Low-quality political online information vs. multimedia politics:* The concern with the usability, attractiveness, look, and feel of Web sites might negatively impair the time needed for guaranteeing a high quality and level of critique of the content of information. The technical means offered by the Internet might privilege form over content of information.	*Information commodities vs. open source technologies and information:* Intellectual property rights and commercialization of cyberspace advance various forms of the digital divide.	*Cyberhate vs. cyberprogress:* Cyberspace can also advance the communication and coordination of fundamentalist or terrorist groups that want to build societies that either limit basic freedoms or are totalitarian in character. Examples are Islamic fundamentalists like Al Qaeda, Christian fundamentalists like the Christian Coalition or the Family Research Council, neofascists like the NSDAP/AO, militant sects like Aum Shinrikyo, etc.
Opportunity	*Overcoming social distance online vs. no truthfulness and rightness of online communication:* CMC can foster political debate by overcoming social distance caused by prejudices deriving from race, appearance, look, habitus, gesture, language, clothing, etc.		

Table 8.4 (Continued)

ICT- and Knowledge-Related Opportunities and Risks	Political Cognition	Political Communication	Political Cooperation
Risk		*No truthfulness and rightness of online communication vs. overcoming social distance online:* The validity claims of truthfulness and normative rightness are much harder to achieve in online discussions than in face-to-face meetings because they are often anonymous, lack gestures, facial expressions, body language, and bodily signs, and are frequently much more heated and nonnormative than traditional communication. Misunderstandings can arise more easily in online communication. Hence, it might frequently be harder to build solidarity and social cohesion online. Virtual communities are easy to leave, which might also make it harder to build trust but also allows individuals to gain a plurality of experiences and to experiment with different identities in various communities.	

(Galtung 1975, 111). This means that violence is a mechanism that hinders individuals and groups from acting as they would like to act or could potentially act. For Galtung, violence is given in the case of direct force, structures that incorporate violence, and cultural values that legitimate violence. In the case of war, violence means that direct and indirect means that aim at destroying the opponent and his infrastructure are employed in order to assure that certain potential actions of the enemy are made impossible.

Based on Galtung's definition of violence, one can argue that the political systems of modern societies are institutionalized forms of violence because the aim of these systems is the control of collective decision power by certain groups against the will of others. In the case of representative democracy, these groups represent the majority of the population; in the case of dictatorship, an elite monopolizes this capacity. In any case, there is a group of people that is excluded and that has to accept the dominant will in order to avoid being exposed to the violence of the juridical and law-enforcement system. Regular political activities include power struggles in the form of elections, strikes, protest, and so on. War is an irregular situation in a political system in which groups try to achieve political goals against the will of groups that are considered as enemies and who are either participants in the same or another political system with the help of violent means that are employed systematically in order to destroy, intimidate, or disarm the enemy so that the latter has to surrender. War, in any case, is an armed violent conflict for controlling political capital; other objects of war can be economic capital (such as territory) and cultural capital (such as values and ideology). War is absolute competition; competing ideas and behavior shall be eliminated by killing or intimidating its human actors.

For Clausewitz, war is limited to certain spaces of territory at certain times and stretches over a particular timespan. It would be spatially limited and temporally extended: "Now it is possible to bring all the moveable military forces of a country into operations, but not all fortresses, rivers, mountains, people, etc., in short not the whole country, unless it is so small that it may be completely embraced by the first act of war". A "complete concentration of all available means in a moment of time, is contradictory to the nature of war" (Clausewitz 1997, 11).

War either aims at the expansion of economic resources (goods, territory), power, or status or at the defense of such structures. Hence, it as a violent strategy of accumulating economic, political, and cultural capital or defending a certain share of these forms of capital.

War, Technology, and Spatiotemporal Distanciation

War in modern society has been predominantly war either within nations or war between certain nation-states. Hence, it has frequently a supranational character, except in the case of civil war. In the twentieth century, war has reached a global dimension by two world wars and the threat of global

nuclear extinction. David Held et al. (1999) see the increasing military globalization as a feature of the military system in the twentieth century. The
network of worldwide military ties and relations would be expanding and
military technologies would bring the centers of military power into closer
proximity and potential conflict so that a single geostrategic space would
have emerged (Held et al. 1999, 88sq.). Twentieth-century military affairs
have been different from earlier periods due to two world wars that involved
most of the globe in one overall conflict at the same time and the global
threat of nuclear extinction of humankind posed by the cold war. The contemporary situation is characterized by the permanent threat of networked
warfare (netwar) in which it is uncertain at which time and where the global
attacks could be carried out by the opposing sides. Other indicators of military globalization are the global arms race, the global distribution of high-
technology weapons and the production capacity of such weapons, global
outsourcing, strategic alliances, and joint ventures in the arms-producing
industry, the emergence of global and regional military bodies such as the
NATO, the UN, the Collective Security Treaty Organization (CSTO), the
Organization for Security and Cooperation in Europe (OSCE), or the Western European Union (WEU), and international laws regulating warfare such
as The Hague Conventions or the Geneva Convention (Held et al. 1999,
87–148).

A specific characteristic of contemporary warfare is its privatization and
its dynamic character. Nation-states don't control the monopoly of violence
in warfare; there are various private organizations, terrorist cells, and guerrilla groups involved in warfare. Today one can find private military firms,
such as Executive Outcomes, that sell warfare and killing as commodities
that can be purchased on the market. Various illegal groups also control,
besides relatively simple means like explosives, chemical and biological
weapons—as the gas attack of the Aum Shinrikyo on the Tokyo metro in
1995 has shown. Warfare has gained a global dynamic in the sense that one
doesn't know and can't foresee at which point in time and at which point on
the globe warfare and attacks will be carried out next. War has to a certain
extent gained a networked character; military groups tend to be organized
as decentralized cells that are connected to other units by receiving flows of
money, weapons, information, and ideas as inputs, but they don't operate
by central command but as autonomous units that decide by themselves
how to carry out an attack, where and when to strike, and which means are
employed.

Space and time of attack are highly uncertain in contemporary warfare;
the opponents have to reckon with attacks anywhere and anytime. There
can be long phases where no attacks occur and then intensive phases of
attacks. In contemporary warfare, there is no clear temporal beginning and
end (Arquilla and Ronfeldt 1996, 13). Local wars are still wars waged for
the control of a certain limited territory but different from the two world
wars. Contemporary wars are not limited to certain parts of territories at

certain times, and they don't expand or shrink in space depending on the success of offense and defense; but autonomous cells can be found all over the territory right from the beginning and they are ready to strike not by confronting their enemies directly and with warnings but by surprise. The whole territory or the whole globe is the front of war. Warfare has gained a more uncertain and arbitrary character. Especially in premodern warfare, the situation was different; one strategy of warfare was to concentrate troops spatially and temporally on the battlefield in order to defeat the enemy. Modern and "postmodern" warfare is characterized by a time-space distanciation of killing processes and violence in warfare.

The events of 9/11 have made clear that high-technology society is vulnerable; even with the most advanced technologies it can never fully control the population and potential enemies. Technologies themselves, such as airplanes, can relatively easily be turned into destructive weapons. Al Qaeda makes use of civilian means for attacking civilian targets in order to express and symbolize political goals. It creates fear by showing that the omnipresent control that high technology promises is a chimera and that suicide bombings, the lack of fear of death of terrorists, and the use of civilian means/technologies (such as airplanes and skyscrapers) for terror pose an uncontrollable threat that deconstructs the dreams of technological control and instrumental reason and shows that modern technological civilization has, by gaining imperial dimensions, created an overall state of fear.

The evolution of killing technologies has had a distancing effect on warfare. Whereas in premodern wars without firearms direct contact with the enemies was necessary for killings, the development of gunpowder, cannons, firearms, explosives, machine guns, tanks, warplanes, the atom bomb, chemical and biological weapons, long-distance missiles, and computer-controlled missiles has created a spatiotemporal distance between the attacker and the attacked. The attack is launched in other places at prior times; the attackers don't directly witness how people are killed and damage is created. Günther Anders (1980) has argued that a difference between producing and products and fantasy and product, which he terms *Promethean gap*, is created by the complexity of modern technologies. As a result, man would become blind for the apocalypse that he creates. So. for example, the crew of the Enola Gay that dropped the nuclear bomb "Little Boy" on Hiroshima on August 6, 1945, must have experienced this act mainly as dealing with a complex technology and not as the killing of 100,000 people. They might have been much more hesitating if each of them had had to kill one Japanese by hand. With the rise of virtual cockpits of warplanes that make war feel like a computer game, the Promethean gap and apocalypse blindness reach a new dimension; now killing seems not only to be an unreal technological act but a game simulated on screens by symbols and animated images. But the effects of warfare are real, and the combatants lose the inhibitions to kill in virtual warfare. Devisualizing the enemy, the dead, and misery causes a disinhibition of killing. Just as in the presence of a division of labor in killings, nobody feels responsible.

Making use of civilian technologies in networked wars ranges from the employment of mass media's interest in sensations for transporting symbolic messages and producing fear to the usage of letter post for mailing letters and other bombs to victims and the usage of computer networks for coordinating and planning attacks and carrying out online attacks in order to destroy or manipulate the enemy's information infrastructure.

That computers change weapons and warfare doesn't mean that older forms of warfare no longer exist. The employment of rather primitive means, such as machetes and knives, for slaughtering civilians in conflicts and genocides such as in Rwanda (1994) shows that high technology is a new quality, but not the only existing quality, of contemporary warfare. Different forms of warfare not only coexist, but they are also entangled as, for example, the war in the former Yugoslavia (1991–1999) has shown.

Information War

For Martin Libicki (2000), information warfare is a general concept for describing that information, information technologies, and information systems are increasingly important for warfare. Cyberwarfare, for Libicki, is one of seven types of information warfare. It would consists of three subtypes: Information terrorism would target individuals by attacking data stored about them in databases. In semantic attacks, computer systems would simulate to operate correctly but be damaged in the background. Similar-warfare battles would be simulated on the computer in order to approximate conflict (Libicki 2000, 102–104). Other strategies that he mentions and that involve computer technologies are hacker warfare, in which the aim is to destroy the enemy's computer systems; Gibson warfare, in which one finds battles of virtual characters; intelligence-based warfare, in which artificial-intelligence systems are used for gathering data on the enemy; electronic warfare, in which the information flows of the enemy are decrypted or manipulated; economic information warfare and command and control-warfare, in which information infrastructures (including computer systems) are destroyed. Psychological warfare is the type of information warfare that Libicki mentions that is least based on computers. In contrast to Arquilla and Ronfeldt, for Libicki cyberwarfare is always connected to computer systems, but it is not clear how exactly cyberwarfare can be distinguished from the other forms of information warfare and why exactly he chooses the three subtypes and not other ones. Also for Sandor Vegh (2003), cyberwar has to do with computers; he defines it as a sustained conflict of *hacktivism* at the state level connected to an ongoing conventional armed conflict. Vegh misses that cyberwar might also involve nonstate actors.

Arquilla and Ronfeldt (1997, 30) speak of information war as cyberwar: "Cyberwar refers to conducting, and preparing to conduct, military operations according to information-related principles". For Eric H. Arnett (1992), the war in Iraq in 1991 was the first cyber- or hyperwar. By these terms he understands a war in which autonomous weapons and robots do much of the killing and destroying without direct instructions from human operators.

These examples show that terms such as *cyberwar, information war*, and *hyperwar* are employed with different meanings by various authors.

In the information age, the mass media not only report on war but are themselves part of the battlefield. Counter to Clausewitz's definition of war, which limits the term to the exertion of physical violence for political means, today psychological warfare, that is, trying to intimidate the enemy and trying to create fear in the enemy population, has become of great importance in warfare. The mass media are a means of psychological warfare. In this type of warfare, communicating to the enemy that he has to be afraid of the effects the military powers of his opponents could cause forms a central element. Terror communicates fear to the enemy and strength to those people whom the terrorists represent because the act of terror symbolizes that there are opportunities for resistance against the omnipotent opponent.

Information warfare means that information has become a strategic factor in warfare that supports the physical destruction of enemies. Information warfare is here conceived as a relatively general and broad notion; it includes psychological, communicative, and networking operations.

Information warfare can be grounded in a theoretical notion of knowledge that considers the latter as a threefold dynamic process of cognition, communication, and cooperation: Systems are based on internal structures, interact with other systems, and form new higher-level systems by building relationships (Fuchs and Hofkirchner 2005). This allows seeing information warfare as a general umbrella concept of war in the information age (see table 8.5).

The attacks of September 11, 2001, show that, besides destruction, contemporary warfare has also gained massive symbolic dimensions. The Twin Towers were symbols of the American empire and they were strategically selected; the terrorists and their supporters wanted to show their radical opposition to the system that the towers represented.

Al Qaeda makes use of modern technologies for communication. Bin Laden allegedly uses satellite phone terminals to coordinate activities. CD-ROM disks are used to store and communicate information, and e-mail, bulletin boards, encryption technologies, and the World Wide Web are used (Zanini and Edwards 2001). ICTs enable global communication and coordination of netwar.

Some stakeholders argue that information war can become a bloodless war that avoids civilian or human casualties so that a humane face of war emerges (e.g., M. Moore 2006). Information and computer technologies don't exist independently of humans; they are inherently tied to the construction and usage in social systems. Hence, destroying or manipulating

Table 8.5 Aspects of Information Warfare

Level of Information	Description
Cognitive information war	The intimidation of the enemy and the production of fear by targeting the psyche of the enemy's military forces and population, observers, and public spheres with the help of information politics and mass media. This level also involves the gathering of data on the enemy, its infrastructures, and the battlefield that are processed by military forces as well as the targeting of persons by gaining control of, manipulating, or destroying their personal data or data that they depend on.
Communicative information war	The destruction and manipulation of the information infrastructures, flows, contents, meanings, and effects of enemy communication. Also involved here are "intelligent" soldiers and weapons that, with the help of computer systems, are provided with communicated real-time data so that an effective targeting of enemies and their infrastructures is enabled; as well as the employment of cryptography and radar systems for encrypting messages in order to achieve secure communication and for decrypting or manipulating enemy messages.
Cooperative information war (netwar)	In a narrow sense, war is never cooperative because it is destructive and doesn't produce mutual benefits but rather winners and losers, death, and sorrow. In a more general sense, war is cooperative when social networks are built that support a more efficient destruction of the enemy. In this regard, all military alliances (such as the Coalition of the Willing of 49 countries in the war on Iraq in 2003) as well as decentralized networks of coordinated autonomous military cells can be considered as forms of networked war (cooperative information war).

information and computer technologies doesn't automatically put an end to the enemy's capacity for action so that it is also likely that as long as war exists not only infrastructures of human activity will be damaged but also humans will be targeted and killed.

In the next three sections, the three levels of information war will be discussed.

Cognitive Information War: Media Manipulation

For Hakim Bey (1995), information war or hyperreal war means the fight "for the acquisition of territory indigenous to the Information Age, i.e. the human mind itself". We think that information doesn't only involve the mind, that is, cognition, but also communication and social relationships. Hence, we don't restrict the term *information war* to psychological warfare, as Bey does, but see cognitive information war as one type of information war.

US officials and media have been keen on not showing pictures or videos of dead soldiers in recent years because this could create an alternative image of war to the one of the sanitized high-tech war presented by most mainstream media. Media are involved in propaganda warfare themselves and have a hard time avoiding being used as channels for the manipulation and influence of public opinion during times of warfare. Pictures that show the violent side of war can influence public opinion in such a way that voices that oppose warfare increase. When the number of American casualties increased massively during the war against Vietnam and especially since the Tet offensive in 1968, pictures of the violent outcomes of warfare were quite present in US media. Many say that this contributed to the enlargement of the antiwar movement and put pressure on US politics. The most famous image from Vietnam that was published in the media was the one of the little girl Kim Phuc, who was shown running screaming, her clothes seared from her body and her body burnt by an American Napalm bomb that was dropped on the village Trang Bang in June 1972. The photographer Nick Ut won a Pulitzer Prize for this picture, which, as is said by many, became a symbol for the strengthened antiwar movement.

In 1991, the coverage of the attacks on Iraq was dominated by pictures broadcast by CNN that mainly showed Baghdad by night illuminated by flashes and radar images, as well as military analyses. Almost no dead bodies were shown; the media created the image that this was a clean, surgical war without civilian casualties. For many observers, the pictures seemed realistic because they were broadcast live; they took what they saw for representing the reality of war. But the decisive question in war correspondence is not what is shown but what is not shown, and it is strange when there are no reports on casualties and the horrors of warfare. This war was the first hyperreal war; the images broadcast consisted mainly of simulated, fictitious, virtual reality detached from the real world of war. Media coverage changed the public perception of war; war became a media event that entertains people and that one can watch live on TV 24 hours a day (Best and Kellner 2001).

The situation was a little bit different in the 2003 Iraq war: The Internet as a new medium for alternative coverage had emerged; there were Web sites and blogs where citizens, independent journalists, and alternative agencies reported directly from Iraq. This can help in establishing a plurality of sources from which observers can choose and which they can compare in order to create their own opinions. This time also, many European countries, along with large media institutions, opposed the war and hence provided alternative sources of information. Six hundred reporters were "embedded" with British and US troops and reported directly from the front. All of these journalists had to sign an agreement that defined "ground rules" (see Katovsky and Carlson 2003, 401–417) and set strict limits for coverage.

The coverage directly from the front has further transformed media coverage of warfare into a spectacle that excites and thrills the viewers; pictures of dead soldiers, that is, the horrifying effects of war were not shown. One can question whether it makes sense to embed journalists and whether this results in a more balanced coverage. These journalists face all the dangers that the fighting soldiers are confronted with, and hence their reports might be distorted and might reflect their subjective fears and angers more than in traditional coverage. Can "embedded" journalists report independently and impartially on warfare they are involved in personally? Can they adequately maintain distance from their objects of coverage? Which stories are shown on TV; which ones are missing? Do 24-hour-live coverage and reports directly from the front democratize and pluralize media coverage, or do they create yet a new dimension of hyperreality, media spectacles, and simulated, false, one-dimensional realities? The reality of death and destruction might get lost amid the high-tech imagery delivered by the mass media. Was the embedding experiment really "a demonstration of democratic values and freedom of speech in action" (Katovsky and Carlson 2003, XIX), or rather an integrative strategy of manipulation?

Due to Vietnam experiences, US governments in the subsequent decades tried to keep the mass media out of war zones and invaded countries. This was, for example, the case in Grenada and Panama. Since the 1990s and starting with the Iraqi war in 1991, a different strategy has been employed, one that focuses on integration instead of repression. This shift is an expression of a larger ideological shift in society from "disciplinary society" to the "society of controls" (see chap. 7.1 in this book). Embedded journalism is an integrative strategy of media self-censorship, an expression of mechanisms of the Deleuzian society of control (this interpretation was first advanced in Fuchs 2005b). The repressive political strategy tried to discipline the mass media; the integrative strategy in addition tries to provide a certain degree of flexibility (such as embedding journalists) and freedom of movement that is kept within clearly defined limits. It tries to produce identity between the mass media and political strategies. This strategy is one of ideological integration. The ground rules were a discipline, but in many cases there was no need to apply them due to the ideological identity established by the practice of embedding, which dissolves distance. This ideological shift can not only be observed in the mass media but also in the area of production, where strategies of participative management aim at the ideological integration of the workforce into corporations. Bonus systems, teamwork, share options, corporate identity, attractive design of the workplace, construction of a community between management and workers ("we" identity), advancement of spirit of enterprise within the workforce, and so on, are part of this strategy, which constitutes new qualities of the disciplinary regime.

In 2003, there was no longer a CNN monopoly on war coverage. Murdoch's FOX TV heavily competed with CNN; there were alternative press institutions that mainly made use of the Internet in order to provide alternative sources of war information. The competition for topical news and ratings among large channels, such as Fox, CNN, ABC, CBS, and MSNBC, didn't automatically result in a more democratic and pluralistic type of coverage. Driven by the run for ratings, such competition can easily result in a media competition for who can present the war in the most sensationalistic and spectacular way. The result won't be the representation of alternative views but mass one-dimensional coverage. The problem that alternative media are facing is that they are hardly recognized and hardly known and that the war-waging parties try to control and influence information and war coverage.

Communicative Information War

The concept of the cyborg was first introduced by Manfred Clynes and Nathan Kline (1960), who defined it as a self-regulating man-machine system. The concept was popularized by Donna Haraway (1985, 7), who sees the cyborg as "a cybernetic organism, a hybrid of machine and organism, a creature of social reality as well as a creature of fiction". For Haraway, the cyborg means both the (technophile) hope for a postgender world and the emergence of new forms of domination such as cyberwar. Haraway (1985, 8) says that modern war is a "cyborg orgy". That the boundary between man and machines is crossed in contemporary warfare means that computers play an important role in war-related information gathering, manipulation, communication, networking, and destruction. This is best expressed by the emergence of the military concept of C4I (Command, Control, Communications, Computers, and Intelligence; cf. National Research Council 1999). Cyborg warfare is the communicative dimension of information war: Communication and computer systems allow the encryption, decryption, surveillance, and manipulation of communicative flows and soldiers to communicate on the battlefield and to be provided with real-time data; intelligent weapon systems interact with the environment and with systems that surveil the location of targets in order to find, pursue, and destroy enemy targets. Surveillance is an important aspect of communicative information war.

Chris Hables Gray (2002, 56) speaks of cyborg soldiers as integrated human-machine-weapons systems that make use of computers. As examples, he mentions smart weapons and information displayed on windshields, visors, or into the eyes of weapon operators. For Gray, as for Best and Kellner (2001, 78), cyberwar means that computer technologies and networks become important aspects of warfare. Such a usage of the term differs from Arquilla and Ronfeldt (1997), who, as already mentioned, conceive cyberwar very generally as information-related warfare. Cybernetics was originally defined by Norbert Wiener (1948) as the study of communication and control in animals and machines (Greek: *kybernetes* = steersman). Based on such a definition, cyberwar should indeed be conceived in more general terms. But one central aspect of cybernetics is the development of computer systems, and with the rise of the Internet the term *cyberspace* was created. Such an understanding is closer to the other definition of cyberwar. Cyberwar is a vague term (Brush 2003); I hence prefer to speak of either information war or computer-related warfare. Computer-related warfare plays a role at all three levels of information war.

What's the reality of communicative information war? Here are some examples. The United States Army pushes multiplayer recruitment online games such as "America's Army" (cf. Bayer 2006). Military research in countries such as the the United States, Israel, and France works on the development of unmanned combat air vehicles (UCAVs) that work with precision-guided weapons. Unarmed UAVs that monitor and collect data on enemy targets are in use in many armies. The Indoor Simulated Marksmanship Trainer is an example for a computer-training system used in the United States Army: Soldiers fire with laser rifles at targets on a screen. In the 2003 war on Iraq, the United States used GPS (global positioning system) for navigating UAVs and several thousand smart bombs (D. Webb 2006). With the increasing importance of recognizing and monitoring enemy targets with the help of location technologies, C4I has been renamed to C4ISR (Command, Control, Communications, Computer, Intelligence, Surveillance and Reconnaissance; cf. National Research Council 2004). Airborne warning and control system (AWACS) airplanes can radar-detect targets and transmit the coordinates to bombers. The B-2 Stealth Bomber, which can drop GPS-guided bombs, was first used by the United States Army in the Kosovo war in 1999 and subsequently in Afghanistan in 2002 and in Iraq in 2003. Target coordinates collected by GPS satellites or UAVs were transmitted to aircraft in real time by e-mail and there was a real-time display of forces on computer screens (Larkin 2006, 123). Joint direct attack munitions (JDAMs) are smart bombs equipped with a guidance computer that permanently receives positioning data from GPS systems. The AGM-154 joint standoff weapon (JSOW) is another GPS-guided smart bomb. Both type of weapons were dropped by B-2, B-1, B-52, and F-117A bombers on Iraq in 2003 (*Time* magazine, March 21, 2003, 39; *Time* magazine, April 21, 2003, 33; *Newsweek*, March 31, 2003, 24sq.). Tomahawk cruise missiles that are guided by data that they receive from GPS were launched from ships and submarines (*Time* magazine, March 21, 2003, 38). A hacker warfare between China and the United States involving hacks of government Web sites and servers erupted in cyberspace after the US forces accidentally bombed the Chinese embassy in Belgrade during the Kosovo war on March 7, 1999. The attack was carried out by a misguided JDAM bomb, which shows that such weapons are, besides technological errors (e.g., if the GPS signal connection to the satellite fails and the bomb hits a wrong target because the position couldn't be dynamically actualized), still prone to human error (e.g., if there is a wrong input of initial target coordinates) and that a bloodless cyberwar is hence unlikely. After a US spy plane collided with a Chinese fighter jet and had to make a forced landing on Chinese territory in April 2001, a war between Chinese and American hackers who defaced Web sites erupted. The M1 Abrams battle tank employed in the Iraq war 2003 is equipped with a computerized fire-control system that, with the help of sensors, collects data, calculates target solutions for the gunners, and can automatically fire at the target (*Time* magazine, March 21, 2003, 42). Joint expeditionary digital information systems, which link ground troops via satellite so that they can, for example, call in missile strikes, are being developed by the US military (Rheingold 2002, 162sq.).

The reality of information war today consists of media manipulation, smart weapons, virtual reality training, encrypted communication, and hacking. The targets of war are still material and human; war hasn't become a pure simulation, as is sometimes claimed in postmodern theories. War is mediated by information technology so that there is not much direct human contact, and attacks at a distance are enabled; humans control and operate war technologies, but they gain more distance to the enemies that they kill with the help of information war. There are no purely virtual battlefields with virtual soldiers.

Cooperative Information War: Netwar

Netwar can be defined as warfare—that is, politically motivated acts of violence that aim at defeating or destroying certain groups that are considered as enemies so that a political will that is alien to the defeated is forced upon them—that is organized in the form of a decentralized network in which there are relatively autonomous units that organize attacks independently, control their own resources and people, and are connected via flows of information and money to other units with which they share overall values and goals. The organizational form is decentralized, which doesn't mean that there is necessarily no central figure on which values are oriented (such as Osama bin Laden in the case of Al Qaeda). Values and doctrines are common and can even be centralized; tactics and organization are decentralized.

John Arquilla and David Ronfeldt (1996, 5) define netwar as "an emerging conflict (and crime) at societal level, involving measures short of war, in which the protagonists use—indeed, depend on using—network forms of organization, doctrine, strategy, and communication. These protagonists generally consist of dispersed, often small groups who agree to communicate, coordinate, and act in internetted manner, often without a precise central leadership or headquarter. Decisionmaking may be deliberately decentralized and dispersed". Netwar actors would consist of a web of dispersed, interconnected nodes (individuals, groups, organizations) and there would be a flat structure (no central command, little hierarchy, much consultation, local initiative, dense communication). As examples, they mention Hamas, the EZLN (Ejército Zapatista de Liberación Nacional [Zapatista Army of National Liberation]) in Mexico, the Christian Identity Movement, the Asian

Triads, Chicago's Gangsta Disciples, and the Chechen separatists. These net-worked groups would be different from hierarchical groups such as Leninist cadres, the PLO (Palestine Liberation Organization), or the Ku Klux Klan.

The problem with the definition given by Arquilla and Ronfeldt is that it includes most nonstate actors; besides military groups, also transnational criminal organizations and NGOs. If war is political, as pointed out by Clausewitz, and hence forms a part of the political system, then criminal networks don't form a part of war, as they are in most cases economically oriented and not politically and hence are a distinct aspect of the economic system. That the two authors conceive "NGO activists" that "challenge a government or another set of activists over a hot public issue" (Arquilla and Ronfeldt 1996, 72) as forming a specific type of netwar (social netwar) seems problematic to me because many academics that study social movements agree that legal extraparliamentary political opposition forms an important aspect of a vivid democracy and for the practical existence of freedom of speech. By describing NGO activities as a form of warfare, a strict separa-tion between democratic politics and NGOs is erected, as the latter are put into the same line with terrorists and war-waging parties. War is never a democratic endeavor; to see NGOs as war-waging parties means to con-sider them as undemocratic as such. Arquilla and Ronfeldt don't see social movements as such as negative; they even argue that transnational NGOs could help constitute a global civil society and form an integral part of the emergence of noopolitik in which soft power and cooperation substitutes hard military power (Arquilla and Ronfeldt 1999). But when they speak of an "ambivalent dynamic of netwar" in which NGOs form the "forces of the bright side" and terrorists, criminals, and ethnonationalists the "dark side of netwar" (Arquilla and Ronfeldt 2001, 314), it again becomes clear that they see social movements and NGOs as "waging social netwar" (Arquilla and Ronfeldt 2001, 347). War is always a state of emergency and oriented on the physical destruction of the enemy. As many of the contemporary social-movement organizations struggle for a global democracy with peace-ful means, it is totally inappropriate to employ the image of war here. Social struggle is not automatically warfare; it does imply conflict and trying to change the distribution of political power and society as a whole, but this doesn't imply physical destruction of the lives and infrastructures of politi-cal opponents.

Arquilla and Ronfeldt (2000, 8) term the military strategy of netwars *swarming*, by which they mean "the systematic pulsing of force and/or fire by dispersed, internetted units, so as to strike the adversary from all directions simultaneously". Probably the most infamous example of swarming are the coordinated suicide attacks on the World Trade Center and the Pentagon car-ried out by four coordinated autonomous Islamic fundamentalist cells.

In the twentieth century, strategies of netwar could be found numerous times. Some examples are the Yugoslavian partisans in the Second World War, guerrillas in the Chinese Civil War (1927–1949), the Castro troops in the Cuban revolution (1953–1959), the Vietcong in the Vietnam War (1964–1975), guerrillas in anticolonial wars such as in Algeria (1954–1962), Angola (1959–1974), Guinea Bissau (1963–1974), and Mozambique (1964–1975).

Netwar or guerrilla warfare is a tactic or strategy of waging war. Partisan forms of netwar mainly see the opponent's army and military infrastructure as the target of their attacks and they operate from within their own territory, whereas terrorists see the opponent's whole society as the target of their attacks and operate from within their enemy's territory.

Che Guevara (2005) has described guerrilla warfare as a clandestine network of relatively autonomous groups. Each group would consist of at least a head and persons in charge of supplies, transport, information, finances, urban actions, and contacts with sympathizers. There would be a general command but freedom of implementation. The interesting point here is that Guevara described guerrilla warfare as networked. Carlos Marighella (1975) has conceived urban guerrillas as networks of autonomous firing groups.

The most infamous form of netwar is terrorism as it could be found in the twentieth century, for example, in groups such as Al Qaeda, Brigate Rosse, Hamas, Hezbollah, Euskadi Ta Askatasuna (ETA), Irish Republican Army (IRA), Ku Klux Klan, Ulster Freedom Fighters, Liberation Tigers of Tamil Eelam, Red Army Faction, and so on. These groups have different ideologies and motives, but they are united by their strategies of warfare: They operate clandestine within the territory of their enemies, are organized as autonomous cells within a larger network, are involved in asymmetric wars where the enemies have more manpower and military potential, don't face their enemies on the battlefield, but in situations where they strike the enemy unprepared and by surprise; they try to stay invisible for their opponents; they don't accept international conventions such as the Geneva Conventions, The Hague Conventions, and the United Nations Charter that define legitimate and illegitimate violence in warfare; and it is unlikely that they directly negotiate with their enemies. Terrorists can't and don't want to defeat their enemies and achieve their goals by military superiority but by creating large-scale fear by arbitrary attacks that could hit anybody. Cases such as illegal kidnappings of Arabs and their imprisonment as "unlawful combatants" in the Guantánamo Bay detainment camp and the torturing of Iraqi prisoners by American and British soldiers show that the violation of international conventions such as the Geneva Convention on the Treatment of Prisoners of War and the prohibition of torture by the Universal Declaration of Human Rights blurs the boundaries between elements of terrorism and nation-states that wage war. If the central element of terrorism is the attempt to create fear in the enemy by violence, then such tactics must also be considered as containing elements of terror. Noam Chomsky (2001) argues that the United States in the past has supported terrorism, for example, in Nicaragua, or the car-bomb attack on the Hezbollah leader in Beirut in 1985 in which many civilians were killed or the 1998 bombing of the Al-Shifa pharmaceutical factory in Khartoum (Sudan), which could have resulted in a shortage of medicine in Sudan that would have caused many deaths. Such attacks would have increased hate in the Arab world. No matter which causality one sees here at work concerning the causes, from a system theoretic point of view it is clear that there is a vicious cycle in which terrorism and US military intervention mutually reinforce each other, which results in a highly dangerous situation.

There isn't one generally accepted definition of terrorism, and the definitions of the term given by political bodies reflect political interests. A widely cited and accepted academic definition, to which 80 percent of academic respondents in a study agreed, is the one given by Alex Schmid: "Terrorism is an anxiety-inspiring method of repeated violent action, employed by (semi-) clandestine individual, group or state actors, for idiosyncratic, criminal or political reasons, whereby—in contrast to assassination—the direct targets of violence are not the main targets. The immediate human victims of violence are generally chosen randomly (targets of opportunity) or selectively (representative or symbolic targets) from a target population, and serve as message generators. Threat- and violence-based communication processes between terrorist (organization), (imperilled) victims, and main targets are used to manipulate the main target (audience(s)), turning it into a target of terror, a target of demands, or a target of attention, depending on whether intimidation, coercion, or propaganda is primarily sought" (Schmid 1993, 8). Here, elements such as the production of fear, violence, randomness, clandestine organization, symbolic targets, and communicating threats to the population are stressed. I don't agree that terrorism can have criminal reasons because, if it is considered as a specific form of war, then, according to the definition by Clausewitz, it is politically motivated.

What distinguishes Al Qaeda from other forms of netwar is that it doesn't want to defend a specific territory against invasion (e.g., the case with ETA, IRA, Hamas, etc.), but it questions the Western system of values and opposes it by a radical Islamic value system. As in the cold war, we here find a confrontation of two different societal systems, but in this case one of them is not represented by nation-states but by a certain religiously oriented community that is transnational in character. Fundamentalist forms of terrorism don't distinguish between civilians, combatants, and rulers, whereas other forms of terrorism are specifically oriented on strategic attacks against powerful actors. In any case, terrorism's primary target is, in many cases, not armed military forces.

Netwar frequently makes use of technological networks for communication. So, for example, the US military uses the SIPRNET (Secret Internet Protocol Router Network) for transmitting classified information and the NIPRNET (Nonclassified Internet Protocol Router Network) for transmitting unclassified information.

Another aspect of eDomination is the gathering of data on individuals and groups for controlling and coercing them. This phenomenon of electronic surveillance is discussed in the next section.

8.4 COMPETITION BY CONTROL: THE RISE OF ELECTRONIC SURVEILLANCE

In order to get an impression of how Internet technologies play a role in contemporary surveillance, first electronic surveillance is defined, then the theoretical influence of Foucault and Orwell is discussed, and it is shown how electronic surveillance has changed since 9/11.

Electronic Surveillance Defined

For Kevin Robins and Frank Webster (1999), new ICTs are an extension of Bentham's panopticon because they "monitor the activities, tastes and preferences of those who are networked. . . . Power expresses itself as surveillance and Panopticism, now on the scale of society as a whole" (Robins and Webster 1999, 118, 122).

For Kevin Haggerty (2006), the employment of the category of Bentham's panopticon, introduced by Foucault into surveillance studies, is not suitable for analyzing surveillance in the information society because surveillance would no longer serve the single coherent purpose of control as with, for example, Weblogs and Webcams more and more people are viewers at home, work or leisure (cf. also Bogard 2006, who argues, with Deleuze and Guattari, that surveillance today is not only repressive capture, but also a line of flight from oppression; and Koskela 2006). For characterizing the plural character of surveillance, Haggerty and Ericson (2000) have coined the concept of the surveillance assemblage. Haggerty (2006) argues that surveillance would now also be conducted by private actors. Revealing personal information such as pictures, videos, or intimate thoughts on Webcam broadcasts, Weblogs, video blogs, social networking platforms such as MySpace, YouTube, Google Video, or Facebook, and so on, are self-determined decisions of individuals who aim at making social connections with people who share similar interests and whom they wouldn't be able to know without this global medium. For most of them, being monitored by others and monitoring others is pleasurable in mental or even sexual respects and experienced as life enhancing. Electronic surveillance by nation-states and corporations aims at controlling the behavior of individuals and groups, that is, they should be forced to behave or not behave in certain ways because they know that their appearance, movements, location, or ideas are or could be watched by electronic systems. In the case of political electronic surveillance, individuals are threatened by the potential exercise of organized violence (of the law) if they behave in certain ways that are undesired but watched by political actors (such as secret services or the police). In the case of economic electronic surveillance, individuals are threatened by the violence of the market, which wants to force them to buy or produce certain commodities and helps reproducing capitalist relations by gathering and using information on their economic behavior with the help of electronic systems. In such forms of surveillance, violence and heteronomy are the ultimo ratio, whereas in private forms of displaying oneself on the Internet violence in most cases does not play an important role. In private surveillance, the individuals being watched agree to it in many cases; in economic and political surveillance they don't and in most cases don't even know that they are under surveillance. Hence, I would distinguish between electronic monitoring as a general notion of providing and gathering information with the help of electronic systems and electronic surveillance as the gathering of information on individuals or groups in order to control their behavior by threatening the exercise of institutionalized violence or exercising economic violence. I agree with Ogura (2006) that a common characteristic of surveillance is the management of population based on capitalism and/or the nation-state. Haggerty (2006) argues that there are also forms of surveillance of nonhuman entities such as bacteria, space, nature, and so on, but that the metaphor of the panopticon is always directed at humans. These are forms of monitoring and only forms of surveillance if the gathered information is used for coercing humans. The problem with the approach of Haggerty is that he conceives surveillance as a very general phenomenon so that repressive aspects directed against humans can't be accentuated. The distinction between political surveillance and economic surveillance corresponds to Lyon's distinction between categorical suspicion and categorical seduction. Ball and Webster (2003, 8) have added (a) categorical care and (b) categorical exposure as two other forms of surveillance by (a) health/welfare services and (b) the media. I suggest seeing these two types as subcategories of (a) political and (b) economic surveillance.

Electronic Surveillance: Foucault and Orwell

There are two dominant readings of Foucault's (1979) work on the panopticon. One argues that contemporary surveillance is a deepening of the panoptic principles; the other says that surveillance today is not only state-centered, but more plural, and hence nonpanoptic. Foucault describes Bentham's panopticon as a prison architecture where prison cells are organized in a circle so that each inmate can be watched from a central observation point so that a visibility of the individuals is established. He "is seen, but he does not see; he is the object of information, never a subject in communication" (Foucault 1979, 208). Surveillance is a power that is "capable of making all visible, as long as it . . . [can] itself remain invisible" (Foucault 1979, 222). Foucault describes how surveillance has become a fundamental mechanism of modern society that is pervasive in all institutions so that less direct violence is needed and people discipline themselves because they are aware of surveillance and afraid of potential sanctions or are disciplined by punishment. Electronic and digital surveillance have helped producing a general state of surveillance in which people's behavior, ideas, movements, look, and so on, can be permanently watched and assessed at a distance without their awareness. It is true that Foucault didn't relate panopticism to computer technology and is pretty much focused on the state control of the mechanisms of discipline. But the prevailing truth of Foucault's work, which still holds in the information society, is that surveillance has become pervasive today, a process that has been supported by computer technologies, and that it is a rather invisible technology of power and control. In cyberspace and everyday life, we leave traces that are digitally recorded and can be assessed and combined; state and corporations are especially interested in gaining such data. In many cases, we don't know who sees and assesses these traces or we are not even aware that we leave such traces. The principle of being seen without seeing has become generalized with electronic surveillance. Nonetheless, it is true that in various monitoring processes in everyday life (reading blogs, using Webcams, etc.) we are seeing subjects that make use of technologies to observe others. But in most of these cases there is no violence involved and there are more symmetric relationships; hence, there is no state of surveillance, but of monitoring. Foucault's analysis is still topical in the information society.

Also important in this context is the discussion of George Orwell's *1984*. "The telescreen received and transmitted simultaneously. Any sound that Winston made, above the level of a very low whisper, would be picked up by it, moreover, so long as he remained within the field of vision which the metal plaque commanded, he could be seen as well as heard. There was of course no way of knowing whether you were being watched at any given moment. . . . You had to live—did live, from habit that became instinct—in the assumption that every sound you made was overheard, and, except in darkness, every movement scrutinized" (Orwell 1990: 4sq.).

David Lyon (1994, 78) argues that Orwell's dystopia can't grasp the increasing importance of nonviolent and consumerist methods of surveillance that are not in need of state violence. Orwell's novel is still topical in the sense that electronic surveillance is a pervasive mechanism of being seen without being aware of it and without knowing who sees you when: Today's telescreens are not monitors that individuals are confronted with passively, but rather Internetted telescreen systems, in which digital traces are left that can potentially be assessed by others without the users' knowledge.

Lyon (2003, 5; cf. also 2001, 2, 16) defines surveillance as "routine ways in which focused attention is paid to personal details by organizations that want to influence, manage, or control certain persons or population groups". Although Lyon doesn't speak of surveillance as a form of violence, coercion is an immanent aspect of his notion of surveillance. Surveillance means the collection of data on individuals or groups that are used to control and discipline behavior by the threat of being targeted by violence. Surveillance operates with uncertainty, invisibility, and psychological threats. Foucault (1979) has stressed that discipline and potential punishment are important aspects of surveillance in the sense that the latter aims at the control and subjugation of bodily movement. One can add that besides behavior, mental activity and communication also shall be controlled by surveillance.

Surveillance is an expression of instrumental reason and competition because it is based on the idea that others are watched and data on their behavior, ideas, look, and so on, are gathered so that they can be controlled and disciplined and choose certain actions and avoid others that are considered as undesirable. Competitive interests and behaviors are involved; the controlling group, class, or individuals try to force the surveilled to avoid certain actions by conveying to the latter that information on them is available that could be used for actions that could have negative influences on their lives. Surveillance operates with threats and fear; it is a form of psychological and structural violence that can turn into physical violence.

For Giddens, surveillance means the accumulation of information defined as symbolic materials that can be stored by an agency or collectivity as well as the supervision of the activities of subordinates by their superiors within any collectivity (Giddens 1981, 169). The modern nation-state would from its beginning have been an information society because it would collect and store information on citizens (births, marriages, deaths, demographic and fiscal statistics, 'moral statistics' relating to suicide, divorce, delinquency, etc.) in order to organize administration. "Surveillance as the mobilising of administrative power—through the storage and control of information—is the primary means of the concentration of authoratative resources involved in the formation of the nation-state" (Giddens 1985: 181).

Other than Foucault, Giddens doesn't see surveillance as something entirely negative and dangerous and argues that these phenomena also enable modern organization and simplify human existence. Giddens and others don't use surveillance as a critical but a relatively neutral notion. The violent and coercive aspects of surveillance can't be criticized adequately within such frameworks. To limit the notion of information society to surveillance is a narrow perspective that ignores the specific role of knowledge and information technologies in contemporary capitalism.

Although watching reality TV series such as *Big Brother, Survivor, MTV Real World, The Osbournes, Candid Camera, Trigger Happy TV, Scare Tactics,* and so on, reading Weblogs, watching people on their personal Webcams or sexcams (Koskela, 2004, speaks of sexcams as "empowering exhibitionism" that creates new subjectivities), using location-based services on mobile phones, ambient intelligence, and so on, is fun for many people and enhances their lifeworlds, a significant point about these phenomena is that they have an ideological function and help to normalize surveillance in everyday life. If surveillance is considered as a ubiquitous phenomenon, people might be less inclined to critically question coercive surveillance by states or corporations. Hence, real-life surveillance is two edged, poses both opportunities and great risks.

If in everyday life, for example, a husband spies on his wife, installs programs to find out her e-mail passwords, reads her mail because he doesn't trust her, and finally threatens her because he finds out information that she wanted to keep as a secret, then this is also a form of surveillance because information gathering, coercion, and violence are involved. Hence, surveillance is not strictly limited to the political and the economic system but also occurs in interpersonal relationships in everyday life. But political actors, such as states, and economic actors, such as corporations, possess the most power in society, which allows them to organize large-scale surveillance because surveillance capacity depends on the availability of allocative and authoratative resources. All surveillance is political action no matter if it is undertaken by political actors, economic actors, or private individuals because it aims at influencing the decision capacity of others to select certain actions with the help of information-gathering mechanisms that are means of exerting and accumulating power. The distinction between economic, political, and everyday surveillance hence is based on the type of surveilling actors involved, but surveillance always takes place as an action within the political system of society.

Gary T. Marx (2004, 275; cf. also Marx 2002) speaks of new surveillance that he defines as "scrutiny through the use of technical means to extract or create personal or group data, whether from individuals or contexts". Contemporary surveillance is linked to information technology, but the repressive aspects of surveillance are not included in the definition.

Privacy and Electronic Surveillance after 9/11

Many of us leave digital traces in computer databases by having health records, financial and tax data, residence, income, nationality, educational performance, criminal records, and so on, stored in databases; withdrawing money from ATMs with cash cards, paying by using a credit card, using smart cards in our roles as patients, citizens, customers, and so on; applying for benefits, sending short messages and calling people with our mobile phones, surfing the Internet, shopping online, sending personal and business-related e-mails, leaving messages in discussion boards, consuming music and videos online, being watched by CCTV (closed circuit television) cameras in shops and public places and some of us by Webcams at home, talking to friends and strangers in chat rooms, by instant messaging, or on social networking platforms, and so on. The major threat is not that there are digital databases as such but that computer networks allow the combination and assessment of different databases so that, in principle, it becomes possible for those who have access to enough data to construct integrated profiles and to know where we are at which times, what we do, what we like, how we act, how we think, and so on—or at least to make assumptions on our behavior.

David Lyon (1994, 2001) has argued that the intensification of surveillance by computer technologies has resulted in a surveillance society. Surveillance is not the only main feature of contemporary society; there are a whole lot of others, such as capital, knowledge, networks, flows, globalization, neoliberalism, etc. Hence, the notion grasps just one feature, which is nonetheless a quite important and dangerous one.

Potential privacy intrusion is one problem of electronic surveillance. Why is privacy so important for human beings? Each individual is a complex personality characterized by a lot of different qualities and behaviors. In modern society, revealing too much information about oneself can in certain situations result in personal disadvantages or dangers because there are power differentials and different interest groups in society that might view certain aspects of the personality or life of an individual as immoral or unacceptable, which might cause hostile reactions. Hence, privacy means to be able to control the intensity of social relationships all by oneself, informational self-determination and autonomy, the right to decide by oneself if one wants to disclose certain personal information, to whom, when, to which extent, and so on. "To claim privacy is to claim the right to limit access or control access to my personal or private domain" (Introna 2000, 190). "We seek protection from strangers who may have goals antithetical to our own" (Moor 2000, 205). Privacy is most directly linked to the human right to freedom of opinion and expression. Privacy is, on the one hand, a typically modern value and ideology, an expression of the notion of humans as individual citizens and private property owners. On the other hand, in class societies it has the positive function of trying to safeguard individuals from interference of alien interests into the small part of their life that remains relatively self-determined. Privacy is undermined by the state interest in surveillance of citizens' activities, an interest that is nourished by the state's fear of activities that undermine the legitimacy of the economic and political system. The outcome is a culture of distrust and control.

Privacy intrusion is not the only problem of electronic surveillance. As electronic surveillance is based on the assumption that certain characteristics make individuals suspicious, social exclusion of certain groups is advanced (e.g., in the current predominant post-9/11 culture of suspicion and fear, Arabs are now all considered as potential terrorists, which has racist implications because people here are considered dangerous due to their ethnicity, origin, or nationality). David Lyon (2003) speaks in this context of surveillance as a mechanism of social sorting.

Whereas in industrial capitalism surveillance was more oriented on direct social contacts and the monitoring of activities (e.g., of factory workers) by overseers and punishment in the case of misbehavior, electronic surveillance is more anonymous, indirect, invisible, and technologically mediated. People know that they could be watched but are often not certain about it. This uncertainty can result in self-discipline and anticipatory compliance. For Gary Marx (2004), self-surveillance of individuals is an important aspect of the surveillance society.

In the economy, surveillance is about guaranteeing that workers continue to produce surplus value and about producing needs to consume commodities.

From the early modern phase until the end of the Fordist accumulation regime, economic surveillance was visible and workers were physically controlled by hierarchic power structures. In post-Fordist capitalism, surveillance is also based on technologies that document and assess behavior and communication and on the ideologies of participatory management, identification, and teamwork. Such mechanisms increasingly produce forms of self-control, self-discipline, and anticipatory obedience because individuals who are uncertain about being watched or not, and compete with other employees, might be more likely to internalize the instrumental performance ethic and to have existential fears of losing their jobs than Fordist workers who knew exactly when they were watched and when they could try to slow down or stop work.

In the area of consumption, corporations are keen on knowing our consumption preferences in order to target us with personalized advertisements online. They do so either legally, when you agree in an electronic contract to an analysis of your consumption preferences and to receive advertisements, for example, by e-mail or when you browse a Web platform, or illegally, by sending spam mail or invisible spyware that watches and transmits passwords and online behavior.

In the surveillance society, the state is suspicious of individuals; everyone is suspected of being a potential criminal; the principle that you are not guilty before proven guilty seems to be reverted; one seems to be automatically suspected of being guilty as long as one can't prove that one doesn't have criminal or terrorist intents. This phenomenon has become increasingly pressing since September 11, 2001.

After September 11, 2001, electronic surveillance has been intensified (cf. Ball and Webster 2003; Lyon 2003; M. Webb 2007). Here are some examples:

- In Newham, London, England, CCTV cameras are linked to the Mandrake facial recognition software (M. Gray, 2003, speaks of the rise of a facial recognition society in which thoughts that normally remain hidden to others are made visible with the help of new technologies). The United Kingdom has been at the forefront in the installation of CCTV (Gras 2004; Webster 2004).
- Biometrical iris scanners or facial recognition software for identity matching have been installed in numerous airports such as Frankfurt, Gatwick, Heathrow, Amsterdam Schiphol, Sydney, Melbourne, Boston Logan, and Manchester.
- In Europe, the United States, and Canada, biometric passports with digital photos and RFID (radio frequency identification) computer chips that store personal data have been introduced. In Canada, such passports have no chip. Biometric passports shall make passports fraud resistant and enable identity authentication.
- Immediately after 9/11, many Internet service providers agreed to install Carnivore computers, a data surveillance system operated by the FBI.

- Based on the Alien Registration Act, fingerprints of several tens of thousands of Arab immigrants were taken after 9/11 in the United States.
- Section 201 of the United States Patriot Act, which was passed in October 2001, allowed the interception of wire, oral, and electronic communications relating to terrorism if approved by a federal judge.
- Section 210 widened the scope of subpoenas for records of electronic communications to include, for example, identifying numbers such as temporary IP addresses.
- Section 217 allowed the interception of communications of a person who trespasses (access without authorization) a financial or US government computer.
- Section 503 allowed the United States to collect DNA samples from offenders of terrorism and violent crime.
- Section 505 of the Patriot Act, which allowed the FBI to obtain data on any user from Internet service providers, was declared unconstitutional in 2004.
- Section 814 set the punishment for attempting to damage protected computers to up to ten years in prison and the punishment for unauthorized access and subsequent damage to up to five years in prison.
- In late 2005 and in 2006, there were press reports and concerns that the NSA performed warrantless eavesdropping on citizens' phone calls and Internet traffic (cf., e.g., "Bush Lets US Spy on Callers Without Courts", *The New York Times*, December 16, 2005).
- The US-VISIT program requires travelers entering the United States from certain countries to have their fingerprints digitally scanned and to be digitally photographed.
- In 2002, the Bush administration planed to implement the Terrorism Information and Prevention System in which data on suspicious citizens gathered by workers who had access to private homes (such as mailmen) would have been stored in databases.
- Total Information Awareness (TIA) was a project started after 9/11 by the US Information Awareness Office that aimed at identifying potential terrorists by methods of collecting information and combing and assessing data from different already existing databases. Following heavy public criticism and civil-rights concerns, Congress suspended the program in spring 2003.
- In 2004, an agreement between the United States and the European Union was signed that required European airlines to transmit passenger-name records (PNRs) on transnational flights to the United States, in advance of flights, to US authorities. PNRs include 34 data sets such as full name, passport details, date and place of birth, contact details, address, phone number, e-mail address, flight data, and form of payment. In 2006, the European Court of Justice annulled the agreement, and a new temporary agreement was reached in fall 2006. The

main difference between the old agreement and the new is that data are passed from airlines to the US Department of Homeland Security (DHS) based on requests (data push), whereas in former times the latter had continuous access to the databases of the first (pull). The requests are not limited in number; rather transfer is defined as required by the DHS.

- In spring 2006, the European Union adopted the Date Retention Directive, which requires all member states to pass bills that require communication providers to store connection data (identity of source and receiver of a communication, date, time, length, provider, location data of mobile phones during calls, etc.) of all phone and Internet communications for a period of between six months and two years.
- The Computer Assisted Passenger Prescreening System (CAPPS) has been introduced in US aviation. It compares PNRs with data of the FBI and other agencies in order to calculate a terrorism risk score so that extra screening of certain people and their luggage becomes possible.
- The Echelon system is a UK-US spy network that can intercept radio and satellite communication, phone calls, e-mails, and Internet data (cf. Lyon 2003, 96sq.; Wright 2005). Not much is known about this system and its functions; hence, one can only speculate on its increasing importance after 9/11.

Contemporary systems of electronic surveillance don't have to store data in one central database; electronic networks allow the combination of data from different databases in real time. The result are large-scale surveillance mechanisms that operate with decentralized data storage but operate as one overall surveilling force that observes the activities of citizens like a central big brother. Electronic surveillance after 9/11 has been massively intensified in extensity and intensity, which in turn has further deepened the culture of fear and suspicion. A new quality is that you are automatically considered a terrorist if you match certain criteria that are calculated and assessed by computers as long as counterevidence is not found. Besides high transparency and ubiquitous surveillance, ideology more and more normalizes the state of permanent intensive surveillance so that people don't find surveillance problematic but as a routine aspect of their daily lives.

The societal context of the intensification of surveillance is neoliberal capitalism. Increased social insecurity, risks of social descent, a lack of institutions that provide real help in such situations, and the knowledge that one might be left all alone in such situations produce large-scale fear in society. But due to an ideological twist, individuals are not only afraid of social insecurity but are continuously told that becoming a victim of crime is the largest threat, which can cause an increasing willingness of citizens to support surveillance and law-and-order politics. Fear of the personal consequences of neoliberalism are manipulated and hence projected into the fear of crime. Surveillance, policing, and law-and-order policies are not only superficial methods of crime prevention that ignore social causes; they also form an ideology and method of control that aim at preventing and controlling intensified class struggles (in all its manifold manifestations) that could potentially result from neoliberalism. Another function of contemporary surveillance is the exclusion of victims of capitalism (such as the homeless or drug addicts) from public spaces so that "clean spaces" of consumption are created. Terrorism is the very product of modern society and of the deprivation of self-determination, economic, political, and cultural resources in certain regions of the globe. Intensified surveillance doesn't remove the social causes and hence the probability of terrorism because the latter is rather decentralized and hard to control. Fear of terrorism is used as an excuse for intensifying surveillance and hence population control.

Pete Fussey (2005) argues that in the implementation of CCTV, local public consultations, local governments, and private-public partnerships have played an important role and that hence the neo-Marxist assumption that CCTV is an extension of state power is not correct. But local governments and civil society are part of the state. That local autonomy and New Public Management (NPM) play a more important role means that the form of organization of state power has changed. If decisions to implement CCTV and supply more police are taken at the local level and supported by central government ideologically and financially, as in the case of the United Kingdom, then this still means an extension and intensification of state control and state power. The localization of power is an expression of the individualistic idea that large-scale problems of society can be solved individually and at a local level. The globalization of social insecurity is approached by the ideology of local crime prevention. Purely local explanations and approaches don't suffice for understanding and tackling the causes of contemporary social problems. It is not true that neo-Marxist approaches can't explain community consent on surveillance (Fussey 2005) that are due to fear of crime. There is a strong emphasis on ideology in many lines of thought of Marxism (such as Gramsci, Althusser, critical theory). Fear of crime is an ideology emanating from contemporary capitalism that manipulates people at the local level to demand an intensification of surveillance.

A future trend might be the emergence of an Internet of things, that is, chips are included in things in our environment and interact with mobile devices so that certain services are automated. For such phenomena, terms like ubiquitous computing, pervasive computing, and ambient intelligence (AmI) have been coined. "Long-term the PC and workstation will wither because computing access will be everywhere: in the walls, on wrists, and in 'scrap computers' (like scrap paper) lying about to be grabbed as needed. This is called 'ubiquitous computing', or 'ubicomp'. . . . Ubiquitous computing has as its goal the enhancing computer use by making many computers available throughout the physical environment, but making them effectively invisible to the user" (Weiser 1993, 71). So, for example, in an intelligent home, sensors might recognize when you enter the house and could automatically turn on specific music, depending on your communicated mood. In an intelligent city, one could input the place where one wants to go and a mobile device could interact with public databases (timetables and real-time data of public transport, etc.) in order to calculate the shortest way that is communicated to you and shown to you on maps. On the one hand, AmI has the power to make everyday life easier because routines can be automated. On the other hand, an intelligent computerized environment that interacts with mobile devices that people carry produces a vast network of large data flows that by storing, assessment, and combination of data allows the monitoring and reconstruction of location, behavior, and movements of people. Location has from the very beginning been considered as a central feature of ubiquitous computing: "ubiquitous computers must know where they are" (Weiser 1991, 95). Hence, AmI can become a powerful and dangerous mechanism of electronic surveillance that threatens privacy and permanently controls people. Rheingold (2002, 185) argues that there are threats to liberty: "Pervasive computing is converging with ubiquitous surveillance, providing the totalitarian snoop power depicted in Orwell's 1984". A technology assessment study of AmI scenarios in the areas of home, work, health, shopping, mobility, leisure, and entertainment from more than 70 AmI R&D projects found that all scenarios postulate benefits, but hardly refer "to the threats associated with AmI at the same time" (Friedewald et al. 2007, 24).

In sections 8.3. and 8.4, the focus was on eDomination. We will now shift back to the logic of cooperation and eParticipation. For eParticipation and participation in general, protest movements are of particular importance because they struggle for more inclusion and cooperation in society. When protest movements enter cyberspace, the phenomenon of cyberprotest, which will be discussed next, emerges.

8.5 COOPERATING SOCIAL MOVEMENTS ONLINE: CYBERPROTEST

In order to get an idea of what cyberprotest is, the phenomenon is first considered as a dynamic process; then, three levels of cyberprotest are introduced (cognition, communication, and cooperation). Cyberprotest is related to the Deleuzian category of the rhizome, and the role of the movement for democratic globalization is discussed as an example of networked protest.

The Self-Organization of Cyberprotest

The character of the Internet as a system of the cooperative production of knowledge, the global sharing of knowledge, real-time- and many-to-many communication allow the emergence and permanent reproduction of social systems of global protest that have collective values, practices, goals, and identities. By Internet communication, protestors produce shared meanings that constitute collective identities and practices. The logic of the Internet and of new global protest movements is characterized by decentralization, networking, dynamics, and globality. Both systems are based on global self-organization processes. Hence, the Internet is suited as a medium of coordination, communication, and cooperation in global protest. Cyberprotest means the structural coupling of the Internet system and the protest system of society; the two systems interlock; their self-organization processes produce each other mutually and affect each other. Structural knowledge emerges on the technological level of the Internet by processes of communication and cooperation of protestors. This structural knowledge enables the dynamic emergence of protest structures and practices on the actor level, that is, the system of protest. We are witnessing the emergence of transnational protest movements; this process is not virtually caused but virtually mediated.

The structural coupling of cyberspace and progressive global processes into global and decentralized cyberprotest-from-below anticipates a new political mass movement that could take on the form of a transnational, cooperative, decentralized Fifth International, a "cyber-spatial international" (Escobar 2003) and the form of a virtual community "in which computer communications would provide the connecting threads for new forms of distributed collectivity capable of coordinating socioeconomic cooperation from the bottom up" (Dyer- Witheford 1997, 232).

Cyberprotest is a global structural coupling and mutual production of self-organization processes of the Internet and self-organization processes of the protest system of society. In cyberprotest, the self-organization of the Internet system and the self-organization of the protest system produce each other mutually in a self-organization process; hence, cyberprotest is a self-organization of self-organization processes, a form of second-order self-organization. Manfred Eigen has characterized such processes, in which self-organization processes produce each other mutually in cyclical causality, as hypercycles (Eigen and Schuster 1979). Cyberprotest is a global hypercycle of the techno-social Internet system and the protest system.

It is important to note that neither technological networks produce protest networks nor the other way round; both assumptions are one-dimensional and (techno- or socio-) deterministic. The network form of protest is not a result of the Internet; rather; protest movements welcome network technologies because they help them in advancing networked forms of protest. The other way round, the Internet and networked technologies are also not the result of global networked protests, but the latter transform networked technologies; and the adoption of Internet by such movements has caused the emergence of new technological qualities such as electronic mass media, war blogs, various types of online protest and online campaigning, and so on. Both global protest networks and electronic networks are an expression of an overall societal shift from the logic of fixed places to the logic of fluids, flows, and networks. This logic signifies overall changes of production and consumption patterns of economic resources, power, knowledge, and technologies that have been aiming at new post-Fordist strategies of accumulation of economic, political, and cultural capital. Global protest networks make use of networked technologies in order to advance their networked form of organization, and they produce novel aspects of network technologies such as the various forms of cyberprotest and cyberactivism. Hence, neither network technologies produce network protests nor the other way round, but both processes take place at the same time; network technologies are adopted, advanced, and changed by the use in global protests, and these technologies enable and constrain the protest practices of global protest movements. Social systems and technologies are dialectically related; they produce each other mutually in dynamic processes. Harry Cleaver (1999) describes this dynamic nature of cyberprotest with the help of the metaphor of a flowing ocean.

The Internet mediates the circulation of struggles of global protest movements, that is, the production of meanings and practices of protest is virtually distributed and can spread and intensify with the help of cyberspace. The circulation of struggles can be defined as "the fabrication and utilization of material connections and communications that destroy isolation and permit people to struggle in complementary ways—both against the constraints which limit them and for the alternatives they construct, separately and together" (Cleaver 1993). Cyberprotest is a virtual circulation of struggles of global protest movements. "New information technologies therefore appear not just as instruments for the circulation of commodities, but simultaneously as channels for the circulation of struggles. . . . Cyberspace is important as a political arena, not, as some postmodern theorists suggest, because it is a sphere where virtual conflicts replace struggles 'on the ground', but because it is a medium within which terrestrial struggles can be made visible to and linked with one another" (Dyer-Witheford 1999, 121sq.). This concept reflects the insight of self-organization theory that in complex systems local events can spontaneously spread; through cyberspace, protest and knowledge about protests can quickly be spread over large distances; protest can intensify itself (snowball effect, butterfly effect). Protest movements are frequently spontaneous, unpredictable, and uncontrollable. "Movement actions trigger chains of events which cannot always be foreseen or controlled and they sometimes provoke backlashes and other unintended responses" (Crossley 2002b, 9). Due to the possibility of the fast and efficient transmission and amplification of protest and protest knowledge through cyberspace, Internet is a medium of global political solidarity. Examples are the EZLN solidarity movement (cf. http://www.ezln.org, http://www.fzln.org.mx, http://www.laneta.apc.org/laneta/, http://www.ciepac.org) and the McLibel Internet campaign (http://www.mcspotlight.org).

The Ejército Zapatista de Liberación Nacional (EZLN) and its supporters have been early adopters of cyberspace and innovators of cyberprotest. They have been characterized as the first informational guerrilla (Castells

2004; cf. also Cleaver 1994, 1995) and as a germ form of the "antiglobal-ization" movement. It has made use of Web sites, mailing lists, discussion boards, electronic voting, and so on, in order to globally amplify its strug-gle, reach a global public, and produce a global support network (Cleaver 1999). Potential functions and characteristics of different forms of cyber-protest are consciousness raising, the mobilization of activists for protests, the organization of offline protest, the support of offline protests by online activities (such as e-mail-campaigns as virtual parts of political campaigns), forms of online protest, electronic civil disobedience/virtual forms of protest/ hacktivism (Vegh 2003). For protest movements, the Internet is a medium of communication that is used for preparing and coordinating protests, a discussion medium for exchanging views, strategies, and goals, an informa-tion and dissemination medium for the dispersion of alternative knowledge (e.g., Indymedia; cf. Kidd 2003), a medium of mobilization for so-called consciousness-raising groups, and a medium of cooperation for virtual pro-tests. Cyberprotest makes use of the three dimensions of knowledge and vir-tual knowledge: cognition, communication, and cooperation; hence, there are cognitive, communicative, and cooperative forms of cyberprotest.

The openness of the Internet simplifies the access to protest movements (but of course only for those who are connected) and the sharing of their values and identities; a characteristic of cyberprotest is an "instant ethos" (Gurak and Logie 2003, 31). An example that points up instant ethos is the online protest against software patents initiated by ATTAC Germany.[3] In July 2005, activists were asked to send small pictures of themselves that were combined online to a mosaic that formed the writing "NO ePATENTS" (fig. 8.3). This was a protest against the introduction of software patents by a directive of the European Union. The mosaic was printed on a banner that was hoisted in front of the European Parliament on July 6, 2005, the day when the directive should have been passed. Activists were able to input individual slogans that were displayed when one scrolled over their picture in the digital mosaic. The activists argued that software patents endanger cheap and free software, make software more expensive, decrease security and stability, block innovation, and cut jobs. In this campaign, many remote activists who didn't know each other joined by sending pictures and input-ting protest slogans. It was a decentralized, spatiotemporal, disembedded type of protest where one could join with a few mouse clicks.

There are three aspects of knowledge as a process: cognition, communi-cation, and cooperation (Fuchs and Hofkirchner 2005). Cyberprotest orga-nizes itself on all three levels as cognitive, communicative, and cooperative cyberprotest.

Cognitive Cyberprotest: Alternative Online Media

Protest movements need public visibility; they are unimportant if they are not perceived and get no attention. The Internet is a global space that is used

Figure 8.3 Online protest against software patents (source: screenshot from http://www.stopptsoftwarepatente.de).

by protest movements in order to be perceived by the global political public and to produce a counterpublic, an alternative public sphere. Cyberspace is mainly a sphere of commerce, sex, and entertainment; it is economically dominated and a stratified sphere that reflects social inequalities and class relationships; hence, it is an exclusive space to which the access is limited and impaired by stratifying categories such as income, education, gender, age, origin, race, and language (digital divide). It is at the same time a class-structured space and a space for the organization of an alternative political public sphere; it both puts forward new risks and opportunities. Lee Salter (2003) argues in this context, from a Habermasian perspective, that the steering media money and power constrain the public sphere of communication, discourse, and dialogue and that cyberprotest can strengthen the public sphere, communicative action, and the lifeworld. "In strengthening the lifeworld, the Internet can be seen as a foundational medium for civil society and the informal public sphere. In particular, the Internet, with its global reach, could be said to be of value to social movements. The Internet enables social-movement groups and organizations to communicate, to generate information, and to distribute this information cheaply and effectively, allowing response and feedback" (Salter 2003, 128). Cyberprotest can contribute to the constitution of an alternative public sphere, but it is also a segmented space. W. Lance Bennett (2003) argues that global activist networks are polycentric orders; they have many centers or hubs that are less likely than in old movements to be defined around prominent leaders. Cyberprotest poses both an opportunity for advancing the grassroots character of protest as well as a risk of setting up new centers of protest communication.

Alternative online media as protest-information systems form one dimension of cyberprotest. These are online platforms like Indymedia or Alternet, which have an open character, are produced in cooperative grassroots processes, provide alternative and oppositional political information, and function according to the principle "Don't hate the media, become the media". Alternative media use channels of distribution that are independent of the structures of large corporations; they are frequently characterized by self-managed grassroots structures; they are mostly noncommercial, articulate viewpoints that are dissonant from those of the dominant mass media, give visibility to unheard and marginalized voices and topics, and involve a great deal of audience participation and the subversion of the distinction between producer and consumer, author and writer (the emergence of the prosumer). The challenge and opportunity for alternative media is to negate and provide alternatives to the one-dimensional logic of thinking, writing, presentation, and speech that dominates the established mass media, that is, to put forward forms of reporting that reflect the complexity of the world and initiate critical, complex thinking. "The opportunity—and the challenge—for open publishing is to find new ways of writing which bring audiences closer to solutions to the problems under discussion. Stories that address complexity rather than reducing it to a good guys/bad guys schema. Stories that stimulate discussion and debate rather than constructing conflicts" (Meikle 2002, 100). Alternative media are "independently owned and managed; second, they articulate viewpoints which are in some sense dissonant from those of the wider media; and third, they foster horizontal linkages between their audiences, in contrast to the top-down, vertical flows of established print and broadcast media" (ibid., 60). The most well-known alternative online medium is the Indymedia network.

The main problem with alternative media is that frequently they don't own enough money in order to reach a large public. In contrast to traditional mass media, the Internet is a cheap, fast, and global publishing medium. But it is a segmented space that reflects the antagonisms of global informational capitalism. It is not decisive that there are alternative media in cyberspace; decisive is the question if they reach a large public. Hence, their central problem is to attain attention and to reach a wide public. The World Wide Web is characterized by the phenomena of information overflow and being lost in cyberspace; hence, alternative media must try to develop strategies that produce visibility in cyberspace. Just as in real society, it is also true for virtual spaces that visibility can be bought. Herbert Marcuse's (1972) suggestion that alternative media should become more capital-intensive should also be considered by alternative online media. One hypothesis in this context is that the Internet helps make existing protest movements more flexible, global, and open, but there are limitations concerning the mobilization of new activists and the production of counterpublic spheres that stem from the fact that the Internet is imprinted by capitalist structures and the mainly noncommercial character of alternative cybermedia. Alternative cybermedia like Indymedia are characterized by an open character; they are global do-it-yourself media from below; everyone can engage as critical journalist insofar as he actively uses the medium; cyberspace is a global counterpublic sphere that is limited in its reach to humans with alternative consciousness; virtual consciousness-raising processes are limited by the constraining effects of stratified virtual space and the domination of society by one-dimensional consciousness.

Communicative Cyberprotest: Online Protest Communication

Cyberprotest also takes place as communicative coordination of social protest (as in the case of "antiglobalization" protests that are mainly coordinated and prepared with the help of mailing lists, e-mail, online discussion boards, newsgroups, etc.). Communicative cyberprotest means that social movements make use of networked telecommunication infrastructures in order to communicate and coordinate protest.

Many people use the Internet and computers in order to copy, transmit, and freely distribute digital knowledge (software, music, videos, films, etc.). They are all hacktivists and part of the multitude's (Hardt and Negri 2005) struggle for the open and common character of knowledge and services, although many don't know that they are part of this movement. This struggle has various fronts, such as the struggles against the privatization of public goods, the struggles against the capitalist appropriation of traditional knowledge and genetic information, the struggles for free access to the Internet and new technologies and for the open-source character of digital knowledge, the struggles for global democracy and a critical public, and so on. The Internet is used in these struggles as a medium that helps producing and distributing alternative and critical knowledge, freely sharing knowledge and technology, producing technology cooperatively, and changing and destroying hegemonic knowledge by cyberattacks.

Analyses of Internet usage by new protest movements have shown that elements of interaction and real-time communication (mailing lists, forums, chats, wikis, etc.) have thus far not been used very much, protest Web sites are often intensively linked to each other, and that the focus of antiglobalization Web sites is mainly information concerning the effects of neoliberal globalization, protest calendars, and protest tutorials (Van Aelst and Walgrave 2004; Rosenkrands 2004).

The Association for Progressive Communication (APC) is an international network of civil-society organizations that supports individuals and groups that struggle for freedom, human rights, development, and environmental protection in the strategic usage of information and communication technologies. The APC has formulated a charter of Internet rights that should guarantee the human rights of free communication, free speech, free association, free organization, and protest. Further demands concerning the Internet are usability, access for marginalized groups, gender equality, affordability, the transparency of public information, free speech, the free exchange of information, no censorship of debates, political online debates, the right for the free organization of protests, the right for participation in online protests, the diversity of contents, the support of the usage of free software and open-source software, data protection, the right for encrypted communication, and freedom from surveillance. APC has developed the software ActionApps, which should help NGOs in a simple, distributed, and cooperative administration of Web sites and the sharing of knowledge. The APC has played a major role in the EZLN solidarity movement because it has spread the messages of the Zapatistas.

Cooperative Cyberprotest: Online Protest and Electronic Civil Disobedience

Cyberprotest also takes place fully immersed in virtual space itself as virtual protest. In cooperative cyberprotest, protest takes place online to a full extent; human actors cooperate in cyberspace in order to attack the information infrastructure of or criticize their opponents. Because of the Internet's being an important infrastructure and organizational medium of domination, electronic activists try to paralyze Web sites of their adversaries. Web sites like petitionsite.com are portals that offer ordered links to online petitions. Virtual petitions, ping attacks/denial of service attacks (with the help of software applications like FloodNet[4]) aiming at the blockage of servers, the hacking, defacing, and hijacking of Web sites, the spamming of e-mail addresses (e-mail bombs), and IRC jamming are virtual protest repertoires. One important characteristic of online protests is that these are forms of collective protest that, unlike demonstrations, strikes, sit-ins, the occupation of buildings, and so on, don't require spatiotemporal copresence of actors. The actors are "smart mobs", "people who are able to act in concert even if they don't know each other" (Rheingold 2002, xii). Cyberspace enables communication and cooperation that transcends spatiotemporal limits; it disembeds communication and makes action at a distance and time-space distanciation of social relationships possible. Hence, cyberprotest events or campaigns are spatially distributed events or series of events. Some of them are, to a certain extent, temporally disembedded (such as online petitions; there are certain time limits on when one must sign such a petition, but it must not be signed simultaneously at one certain point of time); some must take place at the same time but are spatially distributed (such as the flooding of Websites or servers with ping requests in order to block communication channels of political adversaries). Cyberprotest is to a certain extent a spatiotemporal distanced and disembedded form of social protest; it is globally distributed and networked.

Figure 8.4 shows an example of ecological cyberprotest: On the Web site of Friends of the Earth UK, it is possible to sign online petitions (in this case one that calls on President Bush to sign the Kyoto Protocol) that are automatically sent to the relevant stakeholders by e-mail. The Greenpeace Cybercentre is the online community of Greenpeace; on this Web site cyberactivists can sign online petitions, send e-cards, and discuss Greenpeace-related topics in online discussion boards. In the petition section it is possible to generate petition letters that are sent by e-mail.

The Electronic Disturbance Theatre (EDT) wants to support the struggles of the Mexican Zapatistas by "electronic civil disobedience". Other examples for virtual protest groups are the Electrohippies, Netstrike, the Critical Arts Ensemble, and Cult of the Dead Cow. Sandor Vegh (2003, 82sq.) distinguishes cyberattacks/hacktivism, cybercampaigns, and cyberwar. Hacktivism would be a single politically motivated virtual action of nonstate actors in order to gather public attention for a political topic and to express disapproval. Cybercampaigns would be coordinated cyberattacks as part of social conflicts, and cyberwar hacktivism at the level of nation-states an aspect of armed conflicts. Tim Jordan and Paul A. Taylor (2004) define a hacker as a person who illicitly breaks into other people's computer systems. Hacktivism would be politically motivated hacking. They distinguish between mass action hacktivism (MAH) and digital correct hacktivism (DCH). MAH would transfer traditional forms of protest (boycotts,

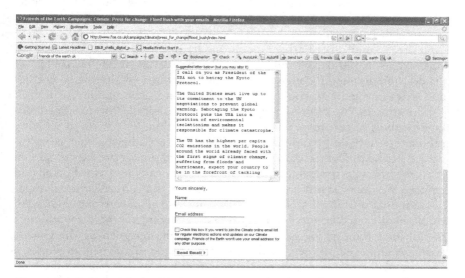

Figure 8.4 Friends of the Earth: environmental cyberprotest (source: screenshot from http://www.foe.co.uk).

demonstrations, sit-ins, strikes, civil disobedience) into virtual space. DCH would see information freedom as a human right; groups like Cult of the Dead Cow, which one can consider as forms of DCH, oppose the disturbance of communication channels (denial of service attacks etc.) by groups like the Electronic Disturbance Theater. They are against illegal actions and electronic militancy. MAH makes use of technology in order to reach non-technological goals. DCH considers electronic space as a political space that should be freely accessible. An example of another group that can be characterized as DCH is the Electronic Frontier Foundation: The fight for free access to the Internet, digital knowledge, and technology (which also involves the struggles of the open-source movement, the file-sharing movement, etc.) is part of a universal movement that struggles for the reappropriation of the common character of knowledge, technology, public goods, and nature. The common character of goods and services is increasingly destroyed by software patents, genetic patents, agreements such as GATS (General Agreement on Trade and Services), and TRIPS (Trade-Related Aspects of Intellectual Property Rights), and so on. As a result, a movement emerges that is reclaiming the commons (Klein 2004).

The term *tactical media* describes flexible usages of mass media in protests. It doesn't necessarily limit itself to cyberprotest; cyberprotest forms such as cyberattacks are one type of tactical media. The tactical-media strategy makes use of whatever media are necessary and accessible in order to stage protest events and campaigns (Garcia and Lovink 1997). ®™ark is an organization that funds acts of sabotage that criticize corporate power. It aims at the "intelligent sabotage of mass-produced items" (®™ark 1997); it satirically criticizes corporate and bureaucratic power. ®™ark, for example, set up a Web site that pretended to be a vote auction in order to criticize democratic deficits; it ridiculed the WTO's free-trade policies on a faked WTO Web site; it funded the Barbie Liberation Organization, which switched the voice boxes in 300 Barbie and GI Joe dolls in order to stress the problem of gender stereotyping in children's toys; and it sponsored altering song titles and lyrics in ways that would highlight the music's crass nature.

The strategy of culture jamming means to ironically reverse and sabotage symbols of corporate and political domination. It's a form of semiotic sabotage, symbolic juxtaposition, and information altering that is politically motivated (Dery 1993). Culture jamming can be related to all sort of mass media; cyberspace (e.g., in the form of politically motivated faked and defaced Web sites) is just one of them. Adbusters is a culture-jamming organization that operates a Web site, a magazine, and an advertising agency. An example of virtual culture jamming is "Google bombs"; these are attempts to influence the ranking of a given site in results returned by the Google search engine. Due to the way that Google's page-rank algorithm works, a Web site will be ranked higher if the sites that link to that page all use consistent anchor text. The first Google bomb mentioned in the popular press may have occurred accidentally in 1999, when users discovered that the query "more evil than Satan" returned Microsoft's home page. A search for "miserable failure" for some time brought up the official George W. Bush biography as number one result on Google, Yahoo, MSN, and Ask Jeeves. Also, the keyword *failure* produced Bush's biography as number one search result on Google.

Some years ago, Nike, in a campaign of micromarketing, offered customers to submit a word or phrase that they would stitch onto a pair of shoes. As an action of culture jamming, Jonah Peretti submitted the word *sweatshop* in order to criticize the labor conditions at Nike's production sites in the Third World. Nike refused to print such a slogan onto a pair of its sneakers. Peretti published the resulting e-mail exchange in the World Wide Web,[5] and the story reached the mass media and damaged the image of Nike because it was now frequently associated with sweatshops. "Nike rejected my request, marking the beginning of a correspondence between me and the company. . . . None of Nike's messages addressed the company's legendary labor abuses, and their avoidance of the issue created an impression even worse than an admission of guilt. . . . The e-mail began to spread widely thanks to a collection of strangers, scattered around the world, who took up my battle with Nike. Nike's adversary was an amorphous group of disgruntled consumers connected by a decentralized network of e-mail addresses. Although the press has presented my battle with Nike as a David versus Goliath parable, the real story is the battle between a company like Nike, with access to the mass media, and a network of citizens on the Internet who have only micromedia at their disposal. . . . I never expected my conversation with Nike to be so widely distributed; the e-mail began to proliferate without my participation" (Peretti 2001). This protest managed to produce an alternative, critical coding of a brand name by making use of e-mail, Internet, and the mass media. Cyberspace can play an important role in culture jamming and the production of critical subversions of symbols of domination. This example not only shows the connection of cyberspace and culture jamming but also that cyberprotest can make use of the characteristic of a self-organizing system that (virtual) communication can quickly intensify itself (in the Internet) and can create global contagion effects of protest. The example demonstrates that in complex, self-organizing systems small causes can have large effects and that cyberprotest forms such a system.

The emergence of a transnational, networked form of domination that makes use of new communication technologies, and has been termed *Empire* by Hardt and Negri (2005), has resulted in new forms of networked protest that challenge the Empire. Protestors make use of network technology; they use the logic the global system puts forward in order to battle against this system. This is a counterlogic that wants to appropriate, transform, and reverse the dominant logic in order to sublate and question this very logic. By doing so, activists have developed concepts like Digital Zapatismo (Dominguez undated), Hacktivismo (Cult of the Dead Cow undated),

Hacktivism (Electrohippies Collective 2003), Electronic Civil Disobedience (Critical Arts Ensemble 1996), Netstrike, and the Temporary Autonomous Zone (Bey 1991).

Cyberprotest and Rhizomes

Harry Cleaver (1999) has applied the concept of rhizomes by Gilles Deleuze und Félix Guattari (1976) in order to characterize cyberprotest as a transnational rhizome. In which respect is cyber protest truly rhizomatic? In order to give such an analysis we have to take into account the six qualities of a rhizome (Deleuze and Guattari 1976):

The principle of connection: Any point of a rhizome can be connected to any other thing, and must be. Elements that are connected are "diverse modes of coding (biological, political, economic, etc.)", "organizations of power, and circumstances relative to the arts, sciences, and social struggles" (ibid.).

The principle of heterogeneity: The elements of a rhizome can be connected according to different types of codes. A rhizome is not hierarchically and centrally organized like a tree structure but has an antihierarchical and decentralized form.

The principle of multiplicity: There are no points or positions in a rhizome, only lines. Multiplicities are defined by the outside according to which they change in nature and connect with other multiplicities. "Multiplicities are defined by the outside: by the abstract line, the line of flight or deterritorialization according to which they change in nature and connect with other multiplicities" (ibid.). Lines of flight are important aspects of rhizomes, they break open segmentary lines. Rhizomes tend to deterritorialize segmenting lines, that is, a rhizome constitutes lines of flight down which it constantly flees.

The principle of asignifying rupture: A rhizome may be broken or shattered at a given spot but will start up again on one of its old lines or on new lines.

The principles of cartography and decalcomania: A rhizome is a map and not a tracing. A map is not an image from which reality can be traced; it is a changing flux that is permanently reconstructed. A map is oriented towards experimentation; in contact with the real, it fosters connections, removes blockages, advances maximum opening, is open, connectable, detachable, reversible, susceptible to constant modification, and it has multiple entryways. A rhizome negates the reduction to simple parts. One can try to copy a map, but there will be no identical reproduction. The information flow in a map is nonhierarchical.

What do these principles mean for protest movements?

The principle of connection: A protest movement can only form a rhizome if its structures of decision and communication are inclusive and each actor is connected to the other actors. In order to take inclusive communicative decisions, the Internet is a suitable medium.

The principle of heterogeneity: The elements of a rhizome can be connected in different ways, that is, communication can take on different forms. The two most important ways are face-to-face meetings and computer-mediated communication (CMC). CMC is the main form of coordination of global protest. That a rhizome is antihierarchical and decentralized means for protest movements that a direct democratic grass-roots organizational form is important. Heterogeneous coding implies that the goals, values, and interpretation schemes of the groups and individuals in a movement are diverse and should be coordinated in the form of a unity in plurality. Access problems can be the result of the segmentation of the Internet (digital divides); hence, there is the danger of newly emerging hier-archies in the form of communication centers that develop within a global movement. This problem can be solved by a solidaristic pool of money and resources. The principle of mutual aid is important for democratic protest movements.

The principle of multiplicity: The line of flight is a cohesive force of pro-test movements; it organizes itself against a common enemy and with the help of common practices. That a rhizome is a multiplicity does not only mean the existence of lines of flight but also that plurality is important.

The principle of asignifying rupture: Global protest movements mostly have an open character: They are dynamic; new actors enter; old ones dis-appear; practices are newly defined, and so on. That a rhizome sprawls is an expression of its dynamic character. Internet and protest movements are dynamic systems; hence their combination in the form of global cyberpro-test is obvious.

The principles of cartography and decalcomania: Protest movements are rhizomatic only if they are not hierarchically organized but rather have a decentralized structure. There must be no central authority; decisions should be taken in a networked grassroots form. Communication should be global, flat, and dynamic. Hardt and Negri (2005) have argued that fun-damentalistic protest movements like Al Qaeda are globally networked sys-tems but that their inner structure is based on central leadership and their external goal is a hierarchical and repressive society. Hence, a protest move-ment is only rhizomatic if it is a grassroots organization and has progressive goals, such as the emergence of a global democracy. Transnational protest movements are not automatically rhizomatic, only in the case where they are open, dynamic, participatory, pluralistic, and hold humanistic politi-cal goals. Al Qaeda is not rhizomatic, whereas the movement for global democracy forms a transnational rhizome. A rhizome is at the same time multiplicity, heterogeneity, and connection; this means that the ideal orga-nizational structure of a global protest movement is the form of unity in plurality.

Networking Protest for Cooperation:
The Movement for Democratic Globalization

In the political realm, global grassroots networks that want to establish a more just and participatory society challenge global networks that centralize political power and hence advance the logic of competition. Participatory movements that want to create a global democratic public sphere question the establishment of new hierarchies with the help of networks and try to transform society into a cooperative society. The new forms of global networked domination have produced networked struggles that challenge the established system, express disagreement, and stand for alternative identities and models of society. "It takes a network to fight a network" (Hardt and Negri 2005, 58). The interactions in new social movements (such as the anticorporate movement) often have a cooperative grassroots character that is different from the traditional centralistic style of organization in parties, bureaucracies, and labor unions. Not all protest movements are organized in a decentralized and direct democratic manner, but many of them are indeed characterized by a flat organizational structure. The fascination that these movements exert on many people is partly due to the fact that they make grassroots democracy vivid, noticeable, and sensible within a world of heteronomy and alienation.

A social movement is not a singular group but a network of protest groups that are communicatively linked. Protest negates certain existing social structures and stands up for the negation of the negation (sublation) of certain social antagonisms that cause social problems. Protest groups such as ATTAC or Amnesty International are forms of critical protest, whereas, for example, Al Qaeda, neofascists, and antiabortionists are nonprogressive and noncritical protest groups. Protest as a social form is not automatically progressive and critical; what is decisive is the content of protest. Critical protest is oriented towards the future; it identifies possibilities within existing society that help to improve the situation of mankind and to reach a higher and progressive level of societal organization. Conservative protest movements are not oriented towards the future but towards the past or that which actually exists, that is, they don't want to substitute structures of domination by cooperative and participatory structures but rather want to conserve, transform, or rebuild domination.

The antiglobalization movement—which might better be termed movement for democratic globalization—is a new social movement that has emerged at the turn of the millennium and questions neoliberal globalization (cf. Fuchs 2007a). It can be considered as a reaction to the frictions and stratifications that have been caused by neoliberal globalization. There are both right-wing and left-wing antiglobalization activists. Extreme right-wing groups, such as the British National Party, the Nationaldemokratische Partei (NPD) in Germany, Front National in France, and the Austrian Freedom Party (FPÖ), see globalization as a threat to national economies and national identity and argue that the economy should be nationally controlled and immigration should be strictly restricted in order to guarantee national identity. Right-wing antiglobalism tends to argue that globalization is an ideology that is advanced by Zionism, Marxism, and liberalism. Globalization is presented as a worldwide conspiracy against national identity, Western culture, and/or the white man. Such arguments frequently have racist and anti-Semitic implications. For right-wing antiglobalism, neoliberal globalization is not the result of the structural logic of capitalism but the result of a conspirative political plan of powerful elites. They don't argue in favor of an alternative globalization but suggest nationalism and particularism as cure for the problems caused by the dominant form of globalization.

Far more important in number of activists and public attention than right-wing antiglobalism has been left-wing antiglobalism. It has called public attention by protests such as at the gathering of the WTO in Seattle in November 1999, at the gatherings of the IMF and the World Bank in Washington in April 2000 and in Prague in September 2000, at the G8 gathering in Genoa in July 2001, and by annually organizing the World Social Forum in Porto Alegre as a counterevent to the meetings of the World Economic Forum.

Nick Crossley has argued that global anticorporate struggles due to "the sheer diversity of groups, networks and ideologies involved" (Crossley 2002a, 674) don't form a social movement but a protest field in which numerous protestors, opponents, and mediating agencies are articulated in complex ways. In some definitions of social movements, collective identities, values, and goals are key definitional aspects. However, as anticorporate struggles are networks of actors, issues, and practices, one can also expect less homogeneity concerning the value structure of the protestors. What they share is a common adversary, reactivity to contemporary societal problems, and oppositional practices. Due to its power in mobilizing actors, I think it is a mistake to conceive anticorporate struggles not as a social movement because this diminishes its importance in analytical terms. In other papers, Crossley seems to agree and conceives anticorporate protests as an even newer social movement that wants to reclaim "'everyday life' (the lifeworld) from 'big business' (the system)" (Crossley 2003, 297). Another question is if right-wing antiglobalism should be considered as forming part of the movement or excluded in order to avoid definitional problems.

Left-wing antiglobalism can be considered, in the terminology of Jürgen Habermas, as a reaction to the increasing colonization of the lifeworld by capital and power. The *term anti-globalization movement* is mistakable because the movement is not purely defensive and reactive but a proactive movement for global democracy and global justice. Hence, it can better be characterized by terms such as movement for an alternative globalization or movement for democratic globalization. The insurgency of the Mexican Ejército Zapatista de Liberación Nacional (EZLN) against impoverishment, neoliberalism, NAFTA, land expropriation, and for freedom, dignity, justice, human rights, and democracy has resulted in the emergence of a global solidarity movement that makes use of the Internet. The EZLN has been characterized as the germ cell of the antiglobalization movement.

The emergence of a decentralized, global Empire has been challenged by a decentralized global protest movement that calls for global participation and global cooperation and suggests that the degree of democracy, justice, and sustainability of globalization should be increased. The organization principle of the movement is the one of global networked self-organization. For many of the activists, the protests anticipate the form of a future society as a global integrative and participatory democracy. The movement is a yearning for a society in which authorities don't determine the behavior of humans, but humans determine and organize themselves. It opposes globalization from above with self-organized forms of globalization from below.

The movement is a transnational protest movement that is global in character and has a decentralized, networked form of organization that mediates the production of common values, identities, goals, and practices that transcend spatial and temporal boundaries. It communicates mainly with the help of the Internet, which is used in order to organize worldwide protests and online protests, discuss strategies, reflect political events and past protests, and to build identities. Internet-based protest forms, mailing lists, Web forums, chat rooms, and alternative online media projects such as Indymedia are characteristic for this movement, which has a high degree of openness, accessibility, and globality.

The "antiglobalization" movement is pluralistic and to a certain extent contradictory. Groups that are involved include traditional and autonomous labor unions, art groups, landless peasants' groups, indigenous groups, socialists, communists, anarchists, autonomous groups, Trotskyists, parts of the ecology movement and the feminist movement, Third World initiatives, civil-rights groups, students, religious groups, human-rights groups, groups from the unemployment movement, traditional left-wing parties, critical intellectuals, and so on, from all over the world. It is a network of groups from different social movements, a global network of networks, a movement of social movements, a universal protest movement, a coalition of coalitions that aims at reclaiming the common character of goods and services that are increasingly privatized by agreements such as GATS (General Agreement on Trade and Services) and TRIPS (Trade-Related Aspects of Intellectual Property Rights).

Toni Negri and Michael Hardt (Hardt and Negri 2000, 2005; Negri 2002) have used the term *multitude* in order to describe the antiglobalization movement as a whole of singularities that act in common (Hardt and Negri 2005, 106), a decentred authority (ibid., 85), a polyphonic dialogue (ibid., 211), a constituent cooperative power of a global democracy from below (ibid., 237), an open-source society (ibid., 340), and a direct democratic government by all for all (ibid., 100). The multitude is "an open and expansive network in which all differences can be expressed freely and equally, a network that provides the means of encounters so that we can work and live in common" (ibid., xiii sq.).

Due to its structure and diversity, the movement is rather undogmatic and decentralized; it can't be controlled and dominated. The unity of this plurality emerges by the common mobilization against the neoliberal intensification of the global problems. The different issues and concerns of the involved groups are connected by the fact that they are all focused on problems that have been caused by the logic of capitalistic globalization. The movement is a network of groups from different social movements, a global network of networks, a movement of social movements, a universal protest movement, a coalition of coalitions that aims at reclaiming the common character of goods and services. The goals and practices of the movement are not homogeneous; there is, for example, a large difference between reformist and revolutionary activists and between nonviolent and militant methods of protest. Another difference concerns those parts that argue in favor of the strengthening of the regulation of capitalism at a national level and those parts that want to put a global democracy in place of national sovereignty.

As a collective actor that is composed of many interconnected, nonidentical parts, the movement can as a whole be considered as striving for global democracy, global justice and the global realization of human rights. It tries to draw public attention to the lack of democracy of international organizations and puts pressure to support democratization on dominant institutions. It is a global nonparliamentary opposition that acts and thinks globally. The movement is spontaneous, decentralized, networked, self-organizing, and is based on grassroots democracy. Its organizational form is an expression of the changing organizational features of society that is increasingly transformed into a flexible, decentralized, transnational, networked system of domination.

There are different forms of the globalization of social movements. International movements operate from one country but want to gather worldwide attention for their political goals; multinational movements have relatively autonomous operating suborganizations in nation-states and are held together by overall topics or campaign issues; transnational movements are globally distributed networks that share values, identities, and goals, communicate and organize protests across spatiotemporal distances. Transnational protest can take on the form of activists from all over the world mobilizing for one event or of simultaneous protest events aimed at a similar goal but taking place at different locations. The WTO protests in Seattle in 1999 were, for example, accompanied by simultaneous protests in more than 80 other cities around the world.

Protest labor is highly communicative and cooperative; protest networks produce knowledge and common values. Protest knowledge is knowledge about social problems and their possible solutions; it is oriented on the solution of social problems; it is critical knowledge if it is oriented on sustainable, humane, and participatory solutions. Existing knowledge is the foundation for further common knowledge and common practices of protest groups; their cooperation is based on knowledge and produces knowledge; protest knowledge permanently sublates itself due to the synergetic effects of cooperation. Critical protest labor is reflective and questions one-dimensional logic and instrumental reason. It is organized in the form of networks and is a form of collective intelligence or mass intelligence.

The vision of this movement is a self-organized society in which decisions are not alienated from those who are affected by them but are taken in inclusive bottom-up processes by affected citizens. They see ICTs as tools that support and empower political grassroots activism and participation. Protest movements use ICTs for communicating criticism and for voicing alternative opinions; their oppositional practices pluralize political opinions and guarantee a certain dynamic of democracy. A society without opposition is totalitarian; social movements and cyberprotest confront political elites and particular interests with the need for dynamising democracy and giving voice to marginalized and oppositional opinions. Cyberprotest and the movement for democratic globalization—which is a movement of movements in the sense that it networks the protest topics of all earlier new social movements—could strengthen the role of civil society. Civil society is both a realm of hegemony that legitimizes domination and a space of opposition and critique. The vision that emerges from these movements and their usage of the Internet is the one of a cooperative, self-organized society. If this is a realistic vision is another question, but what these movements do at least is that they make it possible to think of social change and voice ideas of cooperation as alternatives to competition. They contribute to breaking the continuum of repression that suppresses the voicing of alternative ideas that go beyond a competitive society.

8.6 CONCLUSION

The political system of modern society is based on competitive logic that drives actors towards competing for the accumulation of power, the capacity for influencing collective decisions in society. The underlying antagonism is one between competition and cooperation that takes on the form of an antagonism between domination and participation. Domination refers to the disposition over means of coercion that are employed for influencing others, processes, and decisions. It is a way of establishing asymmetric power relations by force and violence. Participation includes actors into systems; it enables them to influence collective decisions. A participatory society is one in which all decisions are taken by all who are concerned by them in communicative consensus-oriented actions. In participatory systems, power is distributed in a rather symmetrical way, that is, humans are enabled to control and acquire resources such as property, technologies, social relationships, knowledge, and skills that help them in entering communication and cooperation processes in which decisions on questions that are of collective concern are taken. eDomination and eParticipation are antagonistic phenomena that emerge when the political system shapes the Internet and is being influenced by the Internet (mutual shaping of polity and technology).

eDomination means the use of knowledge and networked computer technologies for trying to coerce others to act in certain ways in which they would potentially not act under other circumstances and for accumulating political capital (power). It is a competitive process. Phenomena of eDomination that were discussed are digital divides, information warfare, and electronic surveillance. The notion of the digital divide signifies that the Internet, under given societal conditions, is an exclusive social space not accessible to and available for all. It is a segmented space; this segmentation is due to structural inequalities in modern society that are caused by its competitive class character (class in the Bourdieuian sense). There is asymmetrical access to the physical infrastructure, digital skills, usage capacities, usage benefits, and the institutional context of new technologies. These asymmetries are visible along stratifying lines such as the distribution of economic, political, and cultural capital, age, family status, gender, ability, ethnicity, origin, language, and geography. Digital divides are an effect of the stratified class structure of informational capitalism that is based on a competitive logic that drives actors towards the interest of accumulating ever more economic, political, and cultural capital and from which asymmetries and inequalities emerge. Digital divides are political phenomena because political information, communication, and decision making are increasingly influenced by new technologies. Those who lack motivational, physical, usage, skills, benefit, and institutional access to these technologies automatically have a disadvantaged political position and can't use the Internet for empowering themselves.

Two other phenomena of eDomination are information warfare and electronic surveillance. War and surveillance are expressions of violent competitive politics. War aims at the destruction and intimidation of opponents that have competing interests so that the losers are forced to stop acting in ways that seem unacceptable to the winners. Surveillance means that powerful actors observe the behavior, movement, ideas, location, or appearance of others in order to force the latter to stop or avoid acting in ways that are considered as undesirable. In the information age, information war and electronic surveillance have become important forms of violent political competition. Surveillance and war have become to a certain degree based on information technologies, knowledge, and network structures. Tactics for eliminating and controlling competing actors that make use of info-technological dimensions are coined by the logic of violence and competition. Cooperation is only present here insofar as it allows more efficient methods of killing and control. The information society hence is not automatically a democratic and humane societal formation, but it is, in its contemporary form, predominantly characterized by instrumental reason, competition, alienation, and accumulation. Electronic surveillance and information warfare are at the heart of the violent, eliminatory, and hence barbaric nature of informational capitalism.

Information warfare means intimidation of the enemy and the production of fear by targeting the psyche of the enemy's military forces and population, observers, and public spheres with the help of information politics and the mass media and the gathering and manipulation of enemy data (cognitive and psychological level), the destruction and manipulation of the information infrastructures, flows, contents, meanings, and effects of enemy communication, encryption and decryption of military communication, battlefield communication, and intelligent weapons (communicative level), and the networking of war in military alliances and decentralized networks of coordinated autonomous military cells (netwar level). Information warfare aims at destroying the influence of enemies; it is based on a competitive separation into friends and enemies.

Electronic surveillance aims at controlling the behavior of individuals and groups, that is, they should be forced to behave or not behave in certain ways because they know that their appearance, movements, location, or ideas are or could be watched by electronic systems. In electronic surveillance, data on individuals are gathered with the help of digital systems. These data are known to powerful actors who have the authoritative and allocative resources needed to control these gathered, person-centered data that can be used for coercive means.

eDomination is challenged by eParticipation, which forms an antagonistic counterpart. eParticipation is a self-organizing grassroots political process; actors network in order to influence collective decisions and make use of Internet technologies that shall help them coordinate their activities.

eParticipation is a term that describes that computer-based information and communication technologies (ICTs) can be used for empowering cognition, communication, and cooperation processes of humans so that they can jointly construct participatory social systems. It is a form of grassroots digital democracy that is different from representative digital democracy (eGovernment: political parties and governments use new technologies in order to better inform citizens, communicate with them, and make administration more transparent, open, and efficient) and plebiscitary digital democracy (online decision taking based on electronic voting). In eParticipation processes, ICTs empower humans, groups, and society, that is, they provide individuals with capacities and resources for changing organizations and society according to their will; they provide groups and organizations with capacities and resources for changing society and better including individuals; and they provide society with capacities to better include groups and individuals. eParticipation is about active political communication and cooperation on the citizen-citizen level and the nongovernmental, nonparliamentary civil-society level.

In the concept of eParticipation there is also a stress on the political usage of ICTs in civil society. Since recently the term *cyberprotest* has been employed for describing the usage of ICTs by protest groups and movements for providing alternative online media, networking themselves, communicating and coordinating protest online, and organizing protest not only with the help of but also within cyberspace itself. In cyberprotest, protest movements make use of the Internet for coordinating, communicating, and networking protest, which can also take on global forms. In cognitive cyberprotest, one finds alternative online media; in communicative cyberprotest, online protest communication; and in cooperative cyberprotest, fully online protest and electronic civil disobedience.

Civil society has a double character: On the one hand, it legitimates domination and neoliberalism by being functionalized as an indicator of a vivid democracy, although in reality there might be serious limits to democracy, and by taking over social services formerly provided by the state. Hence it supports the colonization of society by instrumental economic reason. On the other hand, it is also a space of self-organization and critique that can anticipate an alternative mode of society based on cooperation, inclusion, and participation and act as a practical movement towards a cooperative society.

At the turn of the millennium, the movement for democratic globalization emerged. It networks different groups, worldviews, and activists all over the world (the globalization of social movements) and it networks the topics of the new social movements that emerged in the 1970s such as civil rights, human rights, gender-related rights, sustainable ecological development, peace, labor rights, economic justice, antifascism, antiracism, participation, and so on. It is a global network of protest movements, a network of networks, a universal protest movement, a movement of protest movements, a meta- and transprotest movement, and a coalition of coalitions that aims at reclaiming the common character of structures in informational capitalism. In chapter 7, it was argued that the multitude is the class of exploited actors in informational capitalism; it produces the commons of society (such as knowledge, content, social relationships, reproductive labor, nature, technology, social services, health, etc.) that are expropriated and exploited by capital. Contemporary society is coined by global class struggle from above, that is, the colonization of ever more realms of society by the instrumental economic logic of competition and accumulation. Many people today have the feeling that they can't participate in decisions and are not master of the conditions of the societies they live in. They live in an alienated society, devoid of real participation. The movement for democratic globalization is a protest of people who don't want to accept this colonization and have a vision of a more cooperative and participatory society. They challenge the logic of competition, exclusion, and accumulation with visions of cooperation, inclusion, and participation. They struggle for a more just and participatory society. If such a struggle is realistic and can be successful shall not

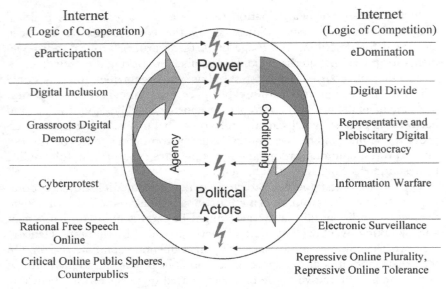

Figure 8.5 The antagonism between eParticipation and eDomination in online politics.

be judged and is unclear. The important point about these movements is that they voice critique of competitive relationships and try to make it possible to think and discuss alternatives to competitive, exclusive, dominative societies. They have revoked the ideas of social change and cooperation from the predominant continuum of repression.

The next figure summarizes the qualities of the antagonism between eParticipation and eDomination.

In the next chapter, we will move from the area of politics to the one of culture in cyberspace (cyberculture).

9 Competition and Cooperation in Cyberculture

Culture, as the system of production and reproduction of meaning, values, definition of life, and lifestyles, is dialectically related to the Internet. Modern culture is (as outlined in chap. 3) characterized by an antagonism between cooperative and competitive modes of value and lifestyle definition; the latter is dominant and results in asymmetric accumulation processes of cultural capital. To see how this antagonism is related to the Internet, first the notion of cyberculture will be explained (9.1). Then an understanding of the subsystems of cyberculture—virtual communities—is developed (9.2). Within this section also, the antagonism between cooperative and competitive virtual communities is introduced and examples are given. This antagonism is then further discussed as the antagonism between socialization and isolation/individualization in VCs (9.3).

9.1 CYBERCULTURE DEFINED

Arturo Escobar (1994) stresses that self-organization theory can establish studies of cyberculture that are critical of modernity because it stresses autonomy and self-organizing experiences. "Perhaps the language of complexity signals that it is possible for technoscience(s) to contribute to the design of forms of living that avoid the most deadening mechanisms for structuring life and the world introduced by the project of modernity. It is not a question of bringing about a technosocial utopia—decentralized, self-managed, empowering—but one of thinking imaginatively whether technoscience cannot be partially reoriented to serve different cultural and political projects" (Escobar 1994, 223).

My own approach on cyberculture is based on the concept of social self-organization because I think that it grasps important characteristics of the information society such as communication, complexity, dynamic emergence, and networking and allows culture to considered as a dynamic process in which structures and actions are interconnected. The self-organization concept has a political connotation that implies the ethical imperative of sublating alienation and exploitation and advancing participation in society.

Cyberculture is a dialectical system in which cultural action and cultural structures go online: It involves the permanent mutual production of practices and structures that produce and re-create mind (ideas, values, affects, meaning, taste) and body with the help of networked computer technology that allows to transcend spatial borders and takes place synchronously or asynchronously. Cyberculture develops dynamically; it is a self-organizing system in which cultural practices and structures permanently produce and reproduce each other in self-referential loops. Such a dialectical notion of cyberculture avoids the one-sidedness of subjective and objective approaches.

Cyberculture isn't the same as cybersociety. The concept of culture is less broad than the one of society; otherwise there would be no use for one of the two notions. For me, the information society consists of a number of interconnected, but nonetheless differentiated, subsystems like economy, polity, and culture that have relative autonomy.

Cyberculture can be differentiated from the virtual economy and digital democracy; it doesn't primarily focus on markets, commodities, or the accumulation of money and power but is more connected to online practices and structures in everyday lifeworlds. These lifeworlds have a different focus from the economy and polity but are nonetheless not fully autonomous but influenced and sometimes even colonized by money and power.

Conceiving cyberculture as a dialectical system implies that it is not homogenous but in modern society structured by antagonisms and struggles. The main antagonism of cyberculture is the one between cooperative cyberculture (socialization) and competitive cyberculture (alienation, isolation, fragmentation). The first culture is based on values, ideas, and structures of sharing and building relationships, the second on values, ideas, and structures that erect borders, construct classes, and separate people. Cooperative cyberculture is based on the idea of unity in diversity (Hofkirchner 2004)—a dialectical interconnection of the One and the Many—competitive cyberculture on the ideas of unity without diversity and diversity without unity—a separation of the One and the Many.

The antagonism between cooperative and competitive cyberculture is reflected within the dominant values of two groups of Internet users: the open-source community and the corporate cyberclass. Eric S. Raymond (1998b) characterizes the open-source community as an open, decentralized bazaar that challenges the centralized, cathedrallike software development methods of corporations. He considers code sharing, codevelopment, acknowledging others ideas, cooperative customs, self-organized production, and voluntarism as important values of the open-source community. Raymond (1998a) argues that from combining the level of zealotry (great, middle, moderate zealotry) with the level of anticommercial orientation (very and moderate anticommercialism, commercialism) nine different attitudes found in the open-source community can be identified. If digital products distributed as open source can be used and modified by anyone given the condition that he or she allows others to use and modify the artifact, it is not so easy to transform such goods into commodities because, as long as there are high-quality free alternatives, many people might choose not to pay for a proprietary version. Nonetheless, open-source licenses, such as the General Public License (GPL) or the Open Source License, don't forbid that open source software is sold; hence, there are certain possibilities for commodifying open-source goods and, contrary to the Free Software Foundation, the Open Source Initiative wants to advance open-source business models. Nonetheless, in the case of what Raymond considers anticommercial values, open source is considered as the expression of a gift economy that negates exchange economies. "It is quite clear that the society of open-source hackers is in fact a gift-culture. . . . Software is freely shared. This abundance creates a situation in which the only available measure of competitive success is reputation among one's peers" (Raymond 1998a). Such a gift culture negates dominant capitalist values like profit, accumulation, and competition. The values of the corporate cyberclass can be summarized as what Langdon Winner (1997) has termed cyberlibertarianism: The class would embrace technological determinism and be characterized by radical individualism, the idea of individual rights without responsibilities, attacks upon altruism, social welfare, and government intervention, the concept of free-market capitalism as formulated by Hayek, Friedman, and others, and the belief in digital democracy. Such values are typical for new-economy enthusiasts and businessmen. They are antistatist because they fear that profit accumulation is hindered by taxes imposed by political regulation on capital. Their vision is a commodified information society in which all goods and services are commodities that people have to pay for so that large corporations that privately own digital products and applications (with the help of licenses and intellectual property rights) can extract profit. Cyberlibertarianism is an expression of neoliberal thinking. "The combined emphasis upon radical individualism, enthusiasm for free market economy, disdain for the role of government, and enthusiasm for the power of business firms places the cyberlibertarian perspective strongly within the context of right wing political thought" (Winner 1997, 16). Cyberlibertarianism's main value is profit; it wants to accumulate capital by e-commerce, virtual enterprise, and the Internet economy. Such values, which are characteristic for institutions like *Wired* magazine, the Progress & Freedom Foundation, and individuals like John Perry Barlow, Stewart Brand, Esther Dyson, George Gilder, Kevin Kelly, George Keyworth, Nicolas Negroponte, or Alvin Toffler, are challenged by anticommercial open-source values. There is a contradiction between open, cooperative and proprietary, and competitive digital goods.

Steven Levy (1984, chap. 2) has pointed out some values that have guided the hackers' ethics:

- Access to computers should be unlimited and total.

- All information should be free.
- Mistrust authority, promote decentralization.
- Hackers should be judged by their hacking, not bogus criteria such as degrees, age, race, or position.
- You can create art on a computer.
- Computers can change your life for the better.

Open-source values seem to be close to the hacker values of free information and free access to computers, whereas the values of corporate cyberculture seem to interpret the hacker value of mistrusting authority as rejecting political regulation of markets that limits the authority and centralizing power of capital.

The basic antagonism that characterizes contemporary cyberculture is reproduced in specific forms within the subsystems of late-modern culture. Depending on how ICTs are socially designed and applied, they can have positive and/or negative effects on society. Within cyberculture, they can advance participatory online media and the plurality of political information and communication or one-dimensional online media in the mass-media subsystem; in the scientific subsystem, they can foster a higher publication rate and speed in science (scientific online journals and reviews) or have, due to the increasing publication speed, negative effects on quality standards provided by the peer-review system; in the subsystem of art they can put forward new forms of art (cyberart, electronic art) that involve audience participation or have negative influences on the authenticity of artworks; in education, they can support more cooperative or more individualized and competitive forms of learning; in the moral subsystem, they can foster cultural understanding or fundamentalism; in the health system, they can have positive (mature, aware patients; participatory relationship of doctors and patients; self-organizing communities of patients) and/or negative effects (self-diagnosing, hypochondriac patients) on health and medical awareness; in sports, they can advance and socialize or individualize and limit physical activity and games; and in the system of social relationships, they can be helpful in advancing friendships and love or the sowing of hate (as in the case of right-wing extremists using the World Wide Web). In all cases today, ICTs and information don't either have solely positive nor solely negative effects but both positive and negative ones at the same time. There are enabling and constraining tendencies of ICTs and information in culture and society at large.

People participate in cyberculture when they are confronted with cultural information online, or communicate or cooperate with others online on cultural topics such as scientific insights, art, health, sex, or love. The social systems within which these information and interaction processes take place can be termed *virtual communities*; these are systems of social activities that allow cultural processes that are mediated by networked computer technologies.

Table 9.1. Antagonism of the Subsystems of Cyberculture

Dimension of Cyberculture	Goal	Antagonism, Opportunities and Risks
Culture	Unity in diversity	Cooperative cyberculture vs. competitive cyberculture
Mass media	Wisdom, critical faculty	Wise, critical online journalism vs. one-dimensional, manipulative online journalism (false consciousness)
Science	Truth	Speed vs. quality of cyberscience
Art	Beauty, imagination	Aura gain and participatory art vs. aura and authenticity loss of works of art in cyberspace
Education	Skillfulness, well-roundedness	Cooperative, participatory vs. individualized, competitive e-learning
Morals/religion	The good	Open vs. fundamentalist cyberethics
Medicine	Health	Mature, aware, participating, self-organizing patients using e-health vs. self-diagnosing, hypochondriac patients using e-health
Sports	Fitness	Advancement/socialization vs. limitation/individualization of physical activity and games
Social relationships	Love	Cyberlove vs. cyberhate

Why are there eight subsystems of cyberculture? These are all systems that are in Essence not oriented on labor (economy) or power (polity) but on ideas, values, affects, and the body. These systems are not separated from the economic and the political system, which form a necessary foundation for culture; they are all interconnected and influence each other, but nonetheless each system has one dominant focus or orientation that exists besides all other factors. So, for example, in a museum that belongs to the art system, which forms a subsystem of the cultural system, the dominant orientation is beauty and imagination, although in modern society selling art, art as commodity, art politics, and so on, are also characteristic systemic features of art. By Essence, art is the system of beauty, although in modern society it actuality is estranged from its Essence and art is colonized by commodity logic.

Cyberculture is a lifeworld of online meaning and value production and reproduction that is organized in the form of virtual communities. A virtual community is a subsystem of the cyberculture system of society.

9.2 VIRTUAL COMMUNITIES

In order to discuss cooperation and competition in virtual communities, first the notion of community is introduced; then a dialectical model of virtual communities is discussed and the antagonism is explained; as an example of a cooperative online community, Wikipedia is explained; the role of identity in virtual communities is clarified; and we take a look at what happens when virtual communities become mobile.

What Is a Community?

Max Weber (1978), based on his basic categories of behavior, action, meaning, interpretation, rationality, social action, and social relationship, distinguishes four types of social action:

1. Traditional action, conditioned by accustomed habituation.
2. Affectual action, conditioned by affection and states of emotion.
3. Value-rational action, motivated by the conscious belief in values.
4. End-rational action, based on means for rationally calculated ends.

Weber distinguishes between society as social relationships based on value- or end-rational social action and community as social relationships based on traditional or affectual social action. "A social relationship, on the other hand, will be called 'communal' if the orientation of social action—whether in the individual case, on the average, or in the pure type—is based on subjective sentiment of the parties, whether affectual or traditional, that they belong together. Communal relationships may rest on various types of affectual, emotional, or traditional bases. Examples are a religious brotherhood, an erotic relationship, a relation of personal loyalty, a national community, a military corps" (Weber 1978, 54).

For Ferdinand von Tönnies, community (*gemeinschaft*) is the organization of life in traditional, agricultural formations, and society the organization of life in modern, capitalist formations. He argues that "the very existence of gemeinschaft rests in the consciousness of belonging together and the affirmation of the condition of mutual dependence" (Tönnies 1988, 69), whereas gesellschaft is for him a concept in which "reference is only to the objective fact of a unity based on common traits and activities and other external phenomena" (Tönnies 1988, 67). The following table shows the main differences between gemeinschaft and gesellschaft in Tönnies's conception.

For both Tönnies and Weber, community has to do with a feeling of togetherness and traditions. Whereas Tönnies makes a sharp distinction between community as premodern and society as modern, Weber doesn't see such a strict dichotomy. Both wanted to strengthen community, Tönnies by socialist corporatives, Weber by charismatic leadership.

Table 9.2 Community and Society in the Theory of Ferdinand von Tönnies

Community	Society
Harmonious consensus of wills	Rational will
Folkways, religion	Convention, agreement, public opinion
Mores	Law
Organic	Authoritative
Family	State, law
Village	Town, city
Kinship, inherited status	Class
Agriculture	Industry, commerce
Morality	Coercion, teaching
Essential will	Arbitrary will
Togetherness	Instrumentality

Communities are not automatically harmonious; the concept has in the past been used as a term for repressive systems, such as the Nazis' *volksgemeinschaft*, which is united by the belief in leadership and the superiority of "Aryans" to other groups that are considered as enemies that should be eradicated. Absolute authority and race defined community for the Nazis; they had a holistic understanding of the concept, which was blind for individual rights and power from below. Such oppressive usages of the term show that it doesn't make sense and is even dangerous to idealize communities.

In late-modern society, collective identities and institutions such as parties, families, unions, churches, associations, neighborhoods, village or town communities, and so on, which in the past have functioned as means of socialization, identification, and struggle, are continuously eroding. This tendency has been characterized as individualization (Beck 1983) or flexibilization (Sennett 1998). Manuel Castells argues that the individualization of the relationship between capital and labour, between workers and the work process, in the network enterprise, and the crisis of patriarchalism and the subsequent disintegration of the traditional nuclear family have resulted in networked individualism, "me-centred" social networks (Castells 2001, 128sq.). The Internet wouldn't cause but would support the diffusion of networked individualism. Jan van Dijk (2006) sees network individualism as the phenomenon that individuals spend "more time alone accompanied by technology (transport and communication means) and that they will spend more time being online. However, being online might be fully social"

(Van Dijk 2006, 168). In modern society, humans are considered individual citizens, labor forces, and property owners. Hence, individualization is an inherent characteristic of modernism. During the first modes of development of capitalism, economic production required huge amounts of labor forces that had a limited variety of activities and were located in central places. The resulting ways of life in production, politics, and culture were homologous for both the labor class and the corporate class. The individuals, due to comparable and relatively homogenous conditions of life, had homologous interests that were expressed in collective modes of organization and lifestyle. Fordist mass production and mass consumption were based on the standardization of production and culture. The emerging organizations were predominantly centrally and hierarchically organized and were coined by rigid command and control structures. The collective identities that many people shared were rather centrally defined and didn't allow a great deal of participation. This situation has changed; identity has shifted from collective communities to individualization and the flexible association in various networks that might be perceived as communities or not.

This has multiple causes:

- Global network capitalism: As a result of the crisis of Fordism during the mid-1970s, a flexible post-Fordist regime of accumulation emerged that decomposes centralized structures and is based on a tendency for globally dispersed, decentralized structures of production that require fast-changing flows of capital, power, money, commodities, people, and information that are processed at high speed on the local, national, and global level in order to produce profit. The emergence of the logic of global networks for restructuring capitalism displaces the individual because local and national organizations enter crisis and can no longer solve problems and hence give meaning to individuals in a situation where decisions are increasingly complex and taken at the supranational level that can't be controlled and understood by individuals who are fixed in local places.

- Knowledge society: Capitalist development demands a rise in productivity and hence the increase of the technical and organic composition of capital, that is, in order to accumulate and to increase profits technological progress is necessary, constant capital (technologies) continuously substitutes variable capital (human labor power) in processes of rationalization and automation. Capitalist development hence results in the permanent dynamic overthrow and recomposition of labor; there is a continuous decrease of exhaustive manual and industrial labor and an increase of intellectual, mental, communicative, social, and service labor. Knowledge-based capitalism and the decrease of industrial labor are the results of capitalist development and the evolution of capitalist technology. Knowledge work demands more agility, continuous change, and permanent learning; it is less homogenous than industrial labor, which has resulted in less homogenous ways of work and life that allow less points and situations of common identification.

- Neoliberal deregulation: The deregulation of labor times, contracts, and legislation, the decrease of the total wage sum by the rise of precarious working conditions (flexploitation) and low-wage jobs, the dismantling of social security, and cuts of state expenditures for education, health, and science are characteristic for the dominant post-Fordist model of politics. Society is considered as not being responsible for the welfare of the individuals, but the individual is considered as being solely responsible for his own welfare, fate, and future. This atomization separates individuals who have to see their colleagues, friends, neighbors, classmates, fellow citizens, and so on, primarily as competitors in existential struggles for survival. Networks of social security that allowed some form of shared central identity disappear; a system of competitive individuals who have to struggle under conditions that only allow high rise or absolute fall emerges. Competition under neoliberal conditions undercuts the possibility for more unified identities.

- Difference as commodified desire and ideology: Post-Fordist commodities are no longer standardized but are specialized and flexible. Commodities are now not mass products because they all look, sound, taste, smell, and feel the same but because there is such a huge mass of products that look, sound, taste, smell, and feel different. Consumption ideologies advanced by public relations and the mass media don't approach humans as mass or crowd but as individuals that are special and have specific needs and desires that commodity consumption promises to fulfill. Micromarketing and flexible specialization create, re-create, and commodify the desires of humans to be different, not to share common identities with others, and to develop individual identities. Difference sells and is a new ideology of capitalism.

The centrally and hierarchically defined identities characteristic for Fordist and pre-Fordist capitalism have not been superseded by new shared identities that are open, dynamically reconstructed, defined from the bottom, and allow a great deal of plurality and individual expression but by atomized individual identities that demand the competitive struggle for survival. The common aspect of individuals today is that they all have to see each other as competitors for survival, jobs, friends, payment, commodities, power, and differing lifestyles. The conditions for the understanding of the category of community have changed. Communities can no longer be conceived as homogenous values and ways of life of groups that allow identification, solidarity, and togetherness. Culture as the realm of production and reproduction of ideas, values, bodies, and meaning is no longer the realm of solitary communities but is fully affected by the logic of competition.

The decomposition of centralized collective identities is both an opportunity for the liberation of lifestyles and a risk of increasing poverty, unemployment, isolation, and precariousness. Under the current conditions, it allows great opportunities for few and high risks for most.

Anthony Giddens (1991) argues that individuals have a plurality of choices for action in high modernity because society is posttraditional, there are multiple milieus of action, numerous expert systems that individuals trust and distrust, globalizing effects of mass media, and because there is a transformation of intimacy. Giddens is certainly right in arguing that overall there are more alternatives of action today than in former times because society becomes more global and new activities, technologies, innovations, and knowledge are required permanently by the flexible regime of accumulation. But opportunities and risks are unequally distributed because the material and intellectual resources that underlie action are not accessible for and owned by all. Hence, there is a small class of people that is well equipped with resources and has great opportunities and a class of individuals that is increasing in size and is deprived of resources and opportunities and hence is facing sharp existential risks. There is a gap between risks and opportunities; the "risk society" is a class-structured society, and institutional security that minimizes risks is vanishing.

The reason why people are interested in virtual communities might be that they feel that society and the social systems they live and work in don't provide them with opportunities that guarantee participation and self-fulfilling activities. Many individuals feel alienated and search for new communities that function according to principles that transcend the dominant logic of competition and capitalism that today causes feelings of alienation. Andrew Calcutt (1999) argues in this context that there is a dialectic of virtual community and alienation. I don't agree with Calcutt that the only tie of cybercommunitarians is their alienation from the rest of the world and that the primary experience that they wish to share is that of the suffering victim (Calcutt 1999, 25–27). I rather think that alienation is a more general condition and feeling that many people have in late-modern society that causes a search for alternatives that is not purely passive but involves the active construction of new social relationships with the help of new media.

A Dialectical Notion of Virtual Community

In (inter)subjective concepts, virtual community is conceived as continuous communicative online practices that produce meanings and don't require homogenous interests and a consensus on values and interpretations. A VC wouldn't have a stable social meaning; "ongoing challenges are an intrinsic part of social life in most on-line communities" (Baym 1998, 62). Steve Jones argues that people who portray VC as impersonal and substituting real-world interaction often have an "idyllic (and often romantic) view of face-to-face interaction. . . . Face-to-face interaction does not necessarily break down boundaries, and to adopt it as an ideal will likewise not necessarily facilitate communication, community building, or understanding among people" (Jones 1995, 28sq.). VC wouldn't be idyllic but "an arena in which passions are formed, tyranny is exercised, love and death are braved, legacies are born, factions are splintered, and alliances dissolved" (Fernback 1999, 217).

Objective understandings of VC argue that the central feature is absolute, highest qualities such as shared values, shared identity and understanding, solidarity, unity, and togetherness. In contrast to subjective approaches, in such concepts not all online interaction systems are communities, rather only those in which intimacy, common values, unity, and togetherness are present. The stress here is not on communicative practices as in subjective approaches but on values, that is, on moral structures. "Not all virtual social gatherings are communities. Without the personal investment, intimacy, and commitment that characterizes our ideal sense of community, some on-line discussion groups and chat rooms are nothing more than a means of communication among people with common interests" (Fernback 1999, 216). Howard Rheingold stresses the importance of feelings in VCs: "Virtual communities are social aggregations that emerge from the Net when enough people carry on those public discussions long enough, with sufficient human feeling, to form webs of personal relationship in cyberspace" (Rheingold 2000, xx). For Rheingold, VC is not the same as computer-mediated communication (CMC) but continuous CMC that results in feelings of affiliation. Community would be established by the stability of nicknames, quick wit, and the use of words to construct an imagined shared context (Rheingold 2000: 181sq.). Maria Bakardijeva (2003) defines VCs as forms of virtual togetherness; Allucquère Rosanne Stone (1991) stresses the importance of common beliefs and practices that unite people in VCs.

Representatives of subjective concepts argue that people like Howard Rheingold, who sees virtual communities as online places where shared identities and feelings of togetherness and belonging develop, idealize online communication and hold on to an ideal of community that was characteristic for past epochs and was captured by traditionalists like Ferdinand von Tönnies almost a century ago. Representatives of objective concepts say that the intersubjective understanding of virtual community is too broad, sees all repeated online communication as community, doesn't allow qualitative differentiation, and has lost the ability of normative judgment.

But the different concepts of virtual community need not be seen as mutually exclusive. Subjective ones stress the importance of online communication; objective ones see the importance of moral structures and material artifacts that allow exchange and the potential for the emergence of togetherness, belonging, and shared understanding. An integrative approach captures all these moments as important for virtual communities by considering the latter as dynamic techno-social systems of communication and meaning production. The term *virtual community* seems to indicate that such systems have both a technological and a social subsystem. A dialectical approach connects these two aspects and describes the dynamic and processual character of the interconnected techno-social systems of online communication.

Raymond Williams (1983, 75sq.) has pointed out that the term *community* has been in use in the English language since the fourteenth century and stems from the French "communeté," the Latin "communitatem" (community of relations or feelings), and the Latin "communis" (common). In communities, participants have something in common. The extent and type of commonality can vary in virtual communities. Depending on the type and degree of commonality, I will now identify three levels of virtual communities (see fig. 9.1).

Level 1 of virtual communities: A common technological infrastructure of computer-mediated communication. In all virtual communities, users share a common technological infrastructure. All repeated online communication forms a virtual community in the sense of sharing common standards of hardware and software that are needed for establishing interaction. Networked digital technologies and corresponding applications form the material foundation of virtual communities. Information technology is a first factor that influences different types of virtual communities.

Level 2 of virtual communities: Computer-mediated communication. On the second level of virtual community, networked computer technologies are used for communication; the social level of the virtual community is

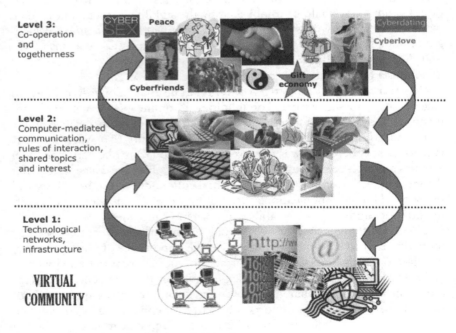

Figure 9.1 The three levels of virtual community.

established. Online communication is based on certain technologies and forms a community if it is continuously repeated. Hence, the common aspect here is continuous usage and a continuous interest in communicating online with others. At this level, continuous online communication is required but not consensus or common values. Also, specific guiding structures and rules of interaction (netiquette, chatiquette) emerge at this level of analysis.

Contemporary virtual communities are technologically mediated systems in which different interpretations of the world (meanings) of individuals meet. What the users share are not only certain technological standards but also an interest in using certain applications for certain overall goals. Users of online dating systems all share an interest in learning to know and love others. Users of Wikipedia all share the interest in producing open encyclopedia knowledge. Community on this level of analysis acquires the meaning of not only shared technology but also shared general interests and topics of communication.

Level 3 of virtual communities: Cooperation and appreciation. Modern society is characterized by an antagonism of cooperation and competition. Competition dominates social interaction and, in post-Fordist capitalism, colonizes cultural spheres of life that have, during Fordism, been more influenced by cooperation (such as friendships, everyday life, family, science, education, health, belief). One hence can't expect that under such conditions virtual communities are harmonious, solitary, consensus-oriented spaces that display a great deal of togetherness as expected by Tönnies and other early representatives of communitarian thinking. Virtual communities are social spaces that are shaped by the antagonisms of late-modern society and hence are characterized by both competitive and cooperative relationships. Competition (for prices and market shares of commodities) is obvious in economic virtual communities and is also rather easy to find in contemporary political virtual communities in the form of competition for better political arguments. Virtual communities are spatially disembedded and technologically mediated social spaces of continuous communication, fields where meanings—interpretations of the world—meet. These relationships take on the form of both cooperation and struggle for meaning. Virtual communities in late-modern society are social spaces for the production of symbolic distinction and status differences. Communication in such communities is often oriented on constructing identities in opposition to the identity of other users in order to produce unique online personae that act differently from others and communicate distinguishable meanings. Virtual communities today hence are social spaces for accumulating symbolic capital (in the sense of Bourdieu), a capital of status, rank, and reputation that produces differences that gives single users a feeling of superiority and communicates to others the impression that they are inferior. In such communities, cultural capital is accumulated by those who gain ever more capacity to define which identities, values, lifestyles, and so on, matter online and which ones are considered as inferior. Virtual communities are social spaces of semiotic struggles for the accumulation of differences that construct online identities. An example for a study that focuses on the asymmetrical accumulation of symbolic and cultural capital is the one of Catherine Dwyer (2007). She presents results of 19 qualitative semistructured interviews with users of social networking platforms and instant messaging and found that "in some respects, impression management seems to be the main point of social networking site".

But the competition of different worldviews and meanings for distinction and appreciated status is only one aspect; another one is the cooperative sharing of meaning and the joint production of new meaning online. Users communicate interpretations of the world (whether fictitious or grounded in their own life) in virtual communities; in doing so, they meet a lot of other personae communicating other meanings that signify interests, ideas, tastes, experiences, feelings, body look, and so on. The quality of anonymity enables users to potentially construct meanings (virtual meanings) that don't correspond to the meanings that represent their bodily, social, and cognitive identities ("real-life" meanings). Participants in virtual communities not only look for difference and status; they also look for friends, new acquaintances, shared interests in culture and politics, advice, opportunities for discussion, and so on. The construction of differences to other users might be used for impressing others. Besides competition, there is also a great deal of shared meanings and joint meaning production in virtual communities. This happens in conversations in which users discover interest in certain characteristics of other online personae (ideas, look, manner of online behavior, shared experiences, humor, shared hobbies or love for certain bands, movies, TV series, celebrities, political ideologies, destinations, etc.). It is probable that users engage in continued conversation with online persons with whom they share certain communicated meanings.

At this level, virtual community acquires a new dimension beyond common technologies and common general interests; a certain degree of togetherness, that is, an overlap of meanings, is discovered and creates attraction and continued conversations. The trajectory of such a conversation, that is, a common history of online persons, is undetermined and unpredictable. One might end the online contact once one discovers that the other doesn't fulfill certain expectations; one might transfer conversation to face-to-face meetings and either become friends (or even lovers) or never meet again afterwards; one might continue conversation at the virtual level for a long time, and so on. Everything's possible in the virtual world, just as in the "real" world, with the difference that online conversation requires more imagination as it is frequently less rich in contextual information and hence more prone to misunderstandings. Whenever online persons discover common interests and attraction, they start producing, to a certain extent, joint meanings that they agree on. Here, community acquires its original sociological sense as defined by Tönnies, Weber, and others; a virtual (i.e., technologically mediated) structure of feelings is produced that is characterized by a feeling of togetherness and belonging, shared meanings and beliefs, coconstructed new meanings, common values, intimacy, emotional commitment, bonds, emotional ties, consented values, and interpretations.

Not all virtual communities and not all users reach the third level; community in many cases remains a technologically mediated space of repeated communication. Raymond Williams (1983, 75) has pointed out that, etymologically, community, on the one hand, indicates actual social groups (in the sense of common people, state, people of a district) and, on the other hand, a particular quality of relationship (community of interests, community of goods, common identity and characteristics). All virtual communities and all online relations are communities in the broader first sense; not all of them are communities in the second understanding of the term. Levels number one and two of virtual communities are an expression of the first meaning of community; the third level is an expression of the second meaning of community.

It is important to stress that virtual communities are not idyllic and harmonious; they are an online arena of cooperation and struggle. Characteristics of late-modern society, such as the intense colonization of the lifeworld and the whole society by economic logic, are reproduced in cyberspace; hence, virtual communities are, besides being spaces of cooperation, also colonized by competition. Cyberspace is a contested terrain. On the one hand, it is coined by the forces of commercialization and commodification; on the other hand, it also is a space for a great deal of voluntary, altruistic cooperation as in the case of open-source and open-content communities, Wikipedia, online friendships, online love, and so on. Today, cyberspace is like society dominated by competition, a process that, following the theory of Jürgen Habermas, can be termed *colonization of virtual communities*. Howard Rheingold speaks in this context with a reference to Marx of the "notion of community as commodity" (Rheingold 2000, 341) and of the "commodification of community" (Rheingold 2000, 389). Colonization takes place, on the one hand, in the form of competition for status and prestige in VCs and, on the other hand, in the form of commodification of VCs, that is, the closure of VCs and the imposition of financial access barriers that make VCs nonpublic (i.e., freely accessible for all) spaces. But there is a real potential for change (of both society and cyberspace) towards a future space dominated by highly cooperative communities that engage in the joint production of meaning and digital resources. Virtual communities, then, will not only be spaces where humans share technological standards and broad interests that structure online communication but also social spaces of cooperation and participation from which strong ties and common identities emerge that are open, democratic, joyful, and allow plurality. But for achieving this condition, the predominantly competitive character of society will have to change towards much more cooperative conditions.

Some important qualities of virtual communities are:

- Anonymity: Communication is potentially anonymous communication.
- Identity building: Anonymity enables the construction of identities online. These identities are based on and connected to offline life; they are a continuously changing product of online activity and they feed back onto the offline world.
- Flexible membership: There is a nonbinding membership (retreat from communication is rather easily possible).
- General interest and topics: There is a shared interest or context that structures communication (technology, applications, topics, rules).
- Communication: There is continued interaction, that is, a certain temporal continuity of online communication.
- Rules: There are formal or informal conventions of online behavior, style, and language.
- Space-time: Communication is spatially disembedded and temporally synchronous or asynchronous.
- Meaning: Meaning is communicated and shared in VCs; new meaning is jointly produced and emerges from social practices and engagement with others in VCs.
- Voluntary: Interaction in virtual communities is voluntary.
- Global: Virtual communities have a global dimension.
- No contextual queues: In text-based VCs, verbal and nonverbal forms of expression (body language, gestures, facial expression, voice pitch) can't be communicated. VCs hence are more prone to misunderstandings than face-to-face communication and require more articulation work for communicating extra knowledge that conveys feelings and the context of communication (e.g., in the form of emoticons). Communicating emotions explicitly (to "emote") in text form is a strategy for overcoming contextual limitations of CMC. Text-based CMC can result both in a neglect of the body and an increased attention to the body (Döring 2003, 287).
- Expressive communication: Due to the potential anonymity and a lack of nonverbal expression in text-based VCs, the Habermasian claims to validity of truthfulness (correspondence of intention and statements) and normative rightness (clarification of and agreement on the normative context of communication) are often harder to achieve online than offline. Online communication hence is easier than offline communication, it shifts into a more expressive and affective mode, and it is more prone to violating normative rules of communication (e.g., in flame wars). In order to avoid such problems, moral rules develop in cyberspace and in VCs (netiquette, chatiquette).
- Speed: Relationships can become intense more quickly online than offline in a positive and a negative sense because anonymity and the lack of visual cues encourage projection (Turkle 1997, 206sq.). People

feel more courageous online than offline because they can more easily end a conversation, they feel that there are potentially less consequences for action in a symbolic than in a physical space, and they have more time for thinking before answering and arguing. The lack of physical presence and visual context queues and the invisibility of the communication partners might lower inhibitions. There are lower inhibition thresholds online than offline, and one arrives at private topics more quickly (Döring 2003, 457). Online communication in some respect seems to accelerate social contact and social relationships, which also means that online contacts are not only quickly created but can also be quickly abandoned. Anonymity allows masking handicaps and accentuating certain individual characteristics, which might lower inhibition (Döring 2003, 460). VCs are generally easier to join and to leave, which will result in more dynamic and continuous membership evolution (McLaughlin, Osborne, and Smith 1995).

- Sociality: Communication in VCs is a social activity, but it is in most cases carried out physically alone in front of a screen. Max Weber argued that "action is social, in so far, by virtue of the subjective meaning attached to it by the acting individual (or individuals), it takes account of the behaviour of others and is thereby orientated in its course" (Weber 1947, 88). Online communication of one individual is oriented on the messages typed/communicated by others; hence, it is always a social activity. That the individuals are not physically copresent and sit alone in front of a screen doesn't mean that online communication isn't social.

- Reflection: In a VC, other than in an offline community where people meet face-to-face, one can postpone reactions and take more time for reflection before giving answers to questions.

VCs are not necessarily global, Douglas Schuler (1996) has coined the term *community networks* for computer-mediated communication that encourages communication and participation in local communities. Examples are the Free-Nets in the United States and the Seattle Community Network.

Wikipedia as an Example of Cooperation in a Self-Organizing Virtual Community

Wikipedia is an open-content encyclopedia that can be read and edited by everyone having access to the Internet; it is based on the wiki technology. It is written collaboratively by volunteers; there are no access barriers. It was started in 2001 by Larry Sanger and Jim Wales and was planned as a more open alternative to Nupedia, a peer-reviewed online encyclopedia. Wikipedia is freely available, easily accessible, simple, can be edited by everyone, is noncommercial, has open content, fosters participation and communication of users, is based on the idea of the free sharing and joint production of knowledge, and allows up-to-date information. It is social software that advances interaction and cooperation of users. Ward Cunningham introduced the wiki concept in 1995 (cf. Cunningham and Leuf 2001); it is an easy way for the collaborative online production of knowledge. The term *wiki* is Hawaiian and means "quick". In January 2006, Wikipedia had more than 2,550,000 articles, including more than 902,000 in the English-language version and more than 757,000 registered users. There are over 200 language versions of Wikipedia: English is the largest one; German is the second largest one (in terms of number of articles). Referring to Wikipedia in press articles has become quite widespread. By adding articles to a watch list, Wikipedians can monitor how an article changes so that they can make new contributions if they feel that problems arise or the article should evolve in another way. Wikipedians can create a personal identity through their user page on which they can provide biographical information and links to articles they have worked on. Also, a discussion page, the "talk page", is associated with each user page. Users can contribute to articles anonymously; if they register they are able to create a user page and a watch list. Talk pages are also used to publicly express recognition of good articles and contributions. Featured articles are displayed for one day on the Wikipedia start page; these are articles that are considered as representing the best work done on Wikipedia. Works can be nominated as featured articles and are discussed by community members. Finally, votes are taken on featuring certain articles. Each Wikipedia article has a version history. Different versions can be compared, and it just takes one click to restore an older version. Hence, vandalizing can easily be undone. Wikipedia is an open-content project, which means that its content can be reused, improved, manipulated, and distributed if the new source is again an open-content document. This idea stems from the open-source software movement that has gained a broader meaning. Wikipedia is licensed under the GNU Free Documentation License provided by the Free Software Foundation.

As Wikipedia is a relatively new evolving networked collaboration space, Wikipedia research is also a newly emerging field (cf. e.g. Benkler 2002; Bryant, Forte, and Bruckman 2005; Cedergren 2003; Ciffolillo 2003; Emigh and Herring 2005; Kolbitsch and Maurer 2005; Lih 2004; Ma 2005; McKiernan 2005; Stadler and Hirsh 2002; Voss 2005; Winkler 2003). Susan L. Bryant, Andrea Forte, and Amy Bruckman (2005) interviewed 9 Wikipedia users. They found out that novices are concerned with correcting individual articles, whereas long-term users are more concerned with offering knowledge to the global public and strengthening the Wikipedia community. Lih (2004) compared Wikipedia articles before and after they had been cited in the mass media and found that press citation increased the quality of Wikipedia articles. Quality was defined in this study as the number of edits and the number of unique contributors for each node. William Emigh and Susan C. Herring (2005) measured the formality of Wikipedia articles and found that the articles mostly use formal language, avoid informal and colloquial features, and are "stylistically homogenous, typically describe only a single, core sense of an item, and are often presented in a standard format that includes labelled section headings and a table of contents". They conclude that the style of Wikipedia is statistically indistinguishable from print encyclopedias. Andrea Ciffolilli (2003) characterizes Wikipedia as a purpose-built virtual community that aims at creating a public good. Lih (2004) sees it as an example of participatory journalism, Stalder and Hirsh (2002) as open-source intelligence. Magnus Cedergren (2003) argues that Wikipedia users find it stimulating to work together with others, want to learn new knowledge, like the possibility for feedback, have an intrinsic motivation, are altruistic, see Wikipedia as a possibility for publicity, and want to provide benefits for the end user. The number of Wikipedia articles has been growing exponentially because more content leads to more traffic, which leads to more edits, which generate more content (Ma 2005; Voss 2005). Voss (2005) conducted a statistical analysis of Wikipedia and found that the number of distinct authors per Wikipedia article follows a power-law distribution and that the link-network of Wikipedia is scale-free on ingoing links, outgoing links, and broken links.

The main criticism of Wikipedia is that it is not peer-reviewed and hence lacks quality assurance and can easily be vandalized and attacked. Kolbitsch and Maurer (2005) argue that vandalism and edit wars are negative aspects of Wikipedia and that it is a problem that mechanisms to approve the expertise of authors or to verify the authenticity of descriptions do not exist. Due to the dynamic nature of Wikipedia, its articles wouldn't be useful as references or for quotation. The general counterargument by Wikipedians to such criticism is that watch lists and engaged users allow the immediate correction of acts of vandalism and that cooperation is a good principle for achieving good quality. In December 2005, the mass media reported that a Wikipedia article on John Siegenthaler Sr., a founding editor of *USA Today*, included erroneous information that linked him to the Kennedy Assassinations (*The New York Times*, December 4, 2005). The fake poster, Brian Chase, admitted that he planted the reference as a joke. Due to this story, some stakeholders questioned the reliability of the information on Wikipedia. In the same month, an article in the prominent journal *Nature*, which compared the quality of selected Wikipedia articles to articles on the same topic in the *Encyclopaedia Britannica*, concluded: "Wikipedia comes close to *Britannica* in terms of the accuracy of its science entries" (Giles 2005). This discussion shows that the quality of Wikipedia is a contested issue.

The research on Wikipedia conducted thus far has mainly concentrated on the formulation of hypotheses, the documentation of Wikipedia's history, statistical analyses of Wikipedia, and small-scale interviews. A more theoretical explanation of Wikipedia is missing. Hence, I want to briefly outline how Wikipedia can be conceived as a dynamic, self-organizing system in which structures and human communicative actions are of importance.

Marco Kalz (2005) argues that a framework theory for Wikipedia research is missing and suggests that Giddens's structuration theory could act as such a metatheory and that a combination of self-organization theory and structuration theory could be helpful in concrete Wikipedia research. My own social theory is based on a combination of dialectical structuration theories (Giddens, Bourdieu) and self-organization theory (Fuchs 2003c, 2003d). The central task for a framework theory is to first show how (and which) structures and communicative practices are interconnected and mutually produce each other in Wikipedia. The advantage of such a theoretical approach is that it allows a description of wikis as a dynamic, permanently changing communication system that grasps the characteristics of the Internet and online communication.

Which role do technological, economic, political, and cultural structures play in Wikipedia? The technological foundations of Wikipedia are the servers that store its information and the wiki software. A certain amount of money for financing the technological infrastructure and a few employees are required. Funding is mainly achieved by donations. Wikipedia doesn't accumulate economic capital; it is not financed by selling commodities or advertisements. Its content is freely accessible, it is not sold, and hence it negates the idea of economic money capital. Wikipedians work for free; they are not paid. Wikipedia could be turned into a commodity, which means that all the labor that has been done for free could be transformed into surplus labor. If access to Wikipedia were suddenly sold as a commodity, a tremendous amount of surplus value would have been produced without requiring any wages. It is unlikely that this will happen, but if it were the case, this would be a perfidious and sophisticated strategy for exploiting knowledge work. But most probably such a move would also put an end to the commitment of many users who value the open, altruistic, and cooperative character of Wikipedia. Wikipedia is a cultural resource; it is a knowledge system that is constituted by the dynamic interrelation of ideas of individuals that communicate and cooperate in order to produce articles. Wikipedia articles emerge from the knowledge of cooperating individuals; articles are emergent knowledge because they comprise many ideas and facts that the group of producers finds important and wants to publish.

What Bourdieu has termed political or social capital is referring to social relationships. Social relationships are established in Wikipedia in communication processes on how articles should be structured that take place in the discussion boards that accompany articles, the personal talk pages of users, and Wikipedia mailing lists. Reputation as a symbolic structure also plays a role in Wikipedia because users who are very active and help others are respected. There is a list of the most active users, which has a certain symbolic value. Value in Wikipedia is mainly symbolic and cultural, not material and economic; what is accumulated is not money capital but knowledge and, to a certain extent, reputation. Reputation is not gained by individual performance because production in Wikipedia is social; it is gained by cooperating with others and helping others. User groups are another symbolic aspect (aspects of rank and roles) of Wikipedia. They include banned users, bots, anonymous users, registered users, ambassadors, mediators, administrators (who can remove vandalism from page histories, block IP addresses from editing, and edit secure pages such as the main page), arbitrators (who mediate conflicts and can ban individuals), developers (who write MediaWiki software), stewards (who can set, give, and remove arbitrary user access [sysop, bureaucrat, steward, and bot]) levels, bureaucrats (who have the technical ability to give other users adminship), and Jim Wales (who has authority in policy decisions and acts as a "benevolent dictator"). Becoming an administrator or arbitrator is not difficult; being active in Wikipedia will create trust and people who want to do organizational work are welcome by the users.

Moral rules are cultural and political aspects of Wikipedia (Wikiquette) that structure communication and cooperation. Such rules are, for example, the neutral point-of-view policy (articles should be written without bias, representing all views fairly; debates should be described fairly without advocating any side) that users who act inappropriately are banned, that one should assume good faith, be polite, treat others as one wants to be treated by them, be prepared to apologize and forgive, give appreciation and praise when due, register (i.e., establish an identity and not remain anonymous) before contributing, argue facts instead of personalities, work towards agreement, avoid reverts and deletions if possible, answer questions, and so on (http://en.wikipedia.org/wiki/Wikipedia:Wikiquette). Anonymous contributions are considered as rather suspect. The Wikiquette defines norms of good behaviour; Wikipedia is based on the spirit of cooperation.

The technological structures of Wikipedia form the first level of virtual community, which enables social interactions and the emergence of knowledge and rules that take place at the second level. Many users see Wikipedia as community and argue that there is an overarching societal goal—"offering knowledge to the world at large"—that is publicly available (Bryant, Forte, and Bruckman 2005). Here, the third level of community, which involves values, feelings of togetherness, and common goals, is reached.

Technological (servers, wiki software), economic (donations, open-source goods), social (existing social relationships), cultural (knowledge, values), and symbolic (reputation and roles) structures are the foundation for human activities in Wikipedia; they enable and constrain cognition, communication, and cooperation. In cognition processes, users read Wikipedia articles; in communication processes, they debate with others in talk pages, discussion pages, and mailing lists on various issues concerning Wikipedia and on how articles should be structured. Other important communication mechanisms in Wikipedia are watch lists, which allow users to monitor changes to certain entries so that they can undo vandalism of articles to which they have contributed or engage in discussions if changes are made that they don't welcome. From human activities (writing a completely new entry, discussing with others, editing existing entries), new qualities of Wikipedia emerge; that is, new knowledge is added to Wikipedia, its structures are reproduced, changed, and enhanced. This is a permanent, dynamic self-organization process in which Wikipedia structures and Wikipedians' actions mutually produce each other in self-referential, circular, reflexive processes. The self-organization of Wikipedia is based on the permanent emergence of new knowledge and the browsing of existing knowledge. Wikipedia is grounded in human social action that produces and reproduces knowledge structures and rules and resources that enable the existence of the overall system.

In VCs, actors form identities and self-definitions of themselves as individuals and groups in cyberspace. This phenomenon will be discussed next.

Identity in Virtual Community

For Anthony Giddens (1991), self-identity means "the self as reflexively understood by the person in terms of her or his biography" (Giddens 1991, 53). It wouldn't be static but "something that has to be routinely created and sustained in the reflexive activities of the individual" (Giddens 1991, 52). Self-identity means the descriptions that an individual makes of his or her role in the world, of how he or she is different from others, and of what he or she has in common with others. It is influenced by and continuously produced and reproduced by social practices of humans in society. The various relationships that humans enter and the experiences they make in these relationships shape how an individual understands and describes himself or herself. Self-identity forms a foundation of communication processes in social relationships by which it is enabled and constrained. Especially phases of transition, loss, and the emergence of new roles in the life of an individual are also phases of instability of self-identity that can result in changes of self-description. In such phases, people enter or leave social groups that have certain collective identities and have to reposition their personal identities. They might enter new groups where they are confronted with new collective identities that enable and constrain their personal identities and that are influenced by actions and communications based on their personal identities. Individuals, to a certain extent, identify with the identity of social groups in which they act or of which they are part. Individual identity is a positioning of a human being towards all group identities with which she or he is confronted. Group identities emerge from continuous communication processes, which individuals enter with their personal identities, and they enable and constrain personal identities that again influence group identities, and so on. Hence, identity is a self-referential process that permanently connects an individual and a collective level.

Social life and society for many people have an impersonal character in contemporary society; they feel that they don't have control of their lives and of decisions that affect them. Globalization, commodification, and bureaucratization can result in feelings of alienation (= not being in control of the conditions of ones own life). In a global world, in which lifestyles and values are differentiating, intimacy is increasingly not found locally but with people who are spatially distanced and reached by the means of communication technologies. There is a globalization of intimacy, the need to organize personal relationships over spatial and temporal distances.

Allucquère Rosanne Stone (1991) speaks of computer cross-dressing. "Gendered modes of communication themselves have remained relatively stable (also online), but who uses which of the two socially recognized modes has become more plastic". Sherry Turkle describes "virtual cross-dressing and creating character descriptions that deconstruct gender" (Turkle 1997, 215). Online identity switching in most cases means that individuals claim that they have a certain social identity (gender, ethnicity, origin, age, sexual orientation, place of residence, etc.) that is not ascribed to them in the offline world.

"We can be multiple people simultaneously, with no one of these selves necessarily more valid than any other. These varied identities can have varied degrees of relation to the embodied 'self'" (Baym 2006, 41). In virtual communities, people are able to switch between different roles and characters and to create an unlimited number of new characters. Sherry Turkle (1997) argues that the Internet allows us to consider "identity as multiplicity. On it, people are able to build a self by cycling through many selves" (Turkle 1997, 178). She describes online identities as "multiple yet coherent" (Turkle 1997, 259). "We are encouraged to think of ourselves as fluid, emergent, decentralized, multiplicitous, flexible, and ever in process. . . . the culture of simulation may help us achieve a vision of a multiple but integrated identity whose flexibility, resilience, and capacity for joy comes from having access to our many selves" (Turkle 1997, 263sq., 268). Mark Poster speaks in this context of the "fluidity of identity" (Poster 1995, 90), a "decentered subject" (89), and postmodern virtuality, "communication practices that constitute subjects as unstable, multiple, and diffuse" (Poster 1995a, 87). For Poster (2001, 6, 16), the classical idea of the subject is based on the idea that the self is separated from material objects, which enables the exercise of reason. The postmodern subject wouldn't operate from the outside but from within a machine apparatus as a point in a circuit. For Kevin Robins (1995), online identities are dispersed, fluid, polymorphous, mobile, exploratory. "In this accommodating reality, the self is reconstituted as a fluid and polymorphous entity. Identities can be selected or discarded almost at will, as in a game or a fiction" (Robins 1995, 138).

In traditional concepts, identity is established in early years of life and remains relatively stable. In postmodern approaches, it is considered as pluralistic, dynamic, floating; each person would have multiple identities. Erik Erikson defined identity as "the immediate perception of one's selfsameness and continuity in time; and the simultaneous perception of the fact that others recognize one's sameness and continuity" (Erikson 1959, 22). Identity would develop itself in the form of phases and consolidate itself ever more in the course of time. Postmodern scholars such as Judith Butler (1990) see the assumption of fixed identities as ideology and an expression of domination; they argue that all groups and individuals construct their own identities, stress difference and multiple identities, and say that identities are free-floating, not connected to an Essence, and performances (which means that one can be anything and anyone that one wants to be and communicates to be). Kenneth Gergen (2003) argues that new communication technologies (especially mobile phones) undo the "bounded and centered self" and that "identity becomes fluid, shifting in a chameleon-like way from one social context to another" because "film, books, magazines, radio, television, and the Internet all foster communication links outside one's immediate social surrounds. They enable one to participate in alterior systems of belief and value, in dialogues with novel and creative outcomes, and in projects that generate new interdependencies. New affective bonds are created outside one's immediate social surrounds".

Applying these ideas to virtual identity means that traditional approaches see virtual identity as a linear mapping of the social identity of an individual, whereas postmodern approaches stress that cyberspaces allow multiple identities. In the first case, the relationship of social identity and virtual identity is conceived deterministically and with a stress on necessity; in the second case, it is conceived arbitrarily and with a stress on chance.

A dialectic approach sees virtual reality neither as being absorbed by nor as being separate from social reality. Virtual reality is part of our social reality; cyberspace is a system that mediates and influences our cognition, communication, and cooperation in everyday life. Hence, Manuel Castells stresses that virtual reality is not artificial but real and speaks of "real virtuality", "a system in which reality itself (that is, people's material/symbolic existence) is fully immersed in a virtual image setting, in the world of make believe, in which symbols are not just metaphors, but comprise the actual experience" (Castells 2000a, 381). The culture of real virtuality would be "real (and not imaginary) because it is our fundamental reality, the material basis on which we live our existence, construct our systems or representation, practice our work, link up with other people, retrieve information, form our opinions, act in politics, and nurture our dreams" (Castells 2001, 203). If virtuality is real, then also online identities are not purely artificial but form an aspect of social reality. The anonymity of cyberspace enables an endless space of possible identities that humans can construct in online communication. But not each individual makes use of these endless possibilities, because his or her identity is enabled and constrained by social structures, class relationships (in the broad Bourdieuian sense of the term), and by his or her endowment with economic, social, and cultural capital. Social experiences and the individual history of an individual influence and shape his or her online behavior. But this doesn't mean that social structures determine online identity in a linear way; they rather open up a space of possibilities in which each possible online identity is more or less likely to be constructed in virtual communities. In any case, online personae are connected to the social life of the individual who feels a desire to act and communicate in certain ways online. Online characters are an expression of real-world experiences, desires, fantasies, and ideas; they are connected to the offline world. If one knows the endowment of an individual with the different types of capital, one can't deduce his or her online identities, because there is a nonlinear, but not arbitrary, connection of the offline and the online world. Online identities have characteristics that give us a hint of which topics and ideas are important for an individual. But there is a continuum of how these topics and ideas are enacted online that ranges from a reversal of ideas, values, and behaviors, the enactment of behaviors that a person tries to develop with the help of CMC, to the affirmation and exaggeration of ideas, characteristics, and behavior of the offline individual. Studies show that the difference of online and offline identities is in many cases not as large as some scholars suspected in early Internet research (cf. Döring 2003, 351, 380, 398sq.). On the one hand, differences and discrimination concerning racial, sexual, gender, class, and bodily identities can have a lower importance online due to the anonymity of online communication; but on the other hand, users might feel more disinhibited online and might hence engage in identity-based discrimination more openly and directly. Lynn Schofield Clark (1998) interviewed 61 teens and 26 of their family members. She found that online teenage communication wasn't so different from the offline world concerning gender roles and homosexuality. "Indeed, there is evidence of much more that is socially reproduced into the chat rooms from the environment of 'real life' " (Schofield Clark 1998, 169).

I suspect that most people's online personae share many characteristics of their offline identities because they want to make contacts online that also work in the offline world, which might not be possible if others discover that the offline behavior is very different from the online behavior of persons whom they like and have learned to know in cyberspace. The World Wide Web allows an accentuation of certain personal characteristics that individuals consider important and realize by making use of hyperlinking, pictures, videos, animations, and social software that supports interaction online. One can expect that on platforms like myspace.com, which allow the self-presentation of individuals, most users aim at presenting and accentuating aspects of their self that can help them in creating contacts with others. Personal blogs can be considered as publicly available online diaries that allow accentuated presentations of individual selves (Döring 2003, 367). Nicola Döring (2003, 341sqq.) distinguishes between virtual self-presentation as the representation of an individual online by an application program (e.g., nickname, system-generated information) and virtual identity as the subjective and intersubjective representation of an individual online.

Due to post-Fordist flexiblization, the increasing importance of mobile phones, and convergence phenomena, mobility has emerged as a new trend in virtual communities. This phenomenon will be discussed next.

Mobile Virtual Communities

Wireless Internet connections and mobile phones connecting to the Internet can enable users to communicate with others independently of temporal and spatial constraints. In early virtual communities, participation was limited to being present at one place where an Internet connection was available. Virtual communities transcend space in the sense that the participants are not physically copresent, but frequently many users sit in the same places (living rooms, offices, etc.) in order to connect to these communities. In mobile virtual communities, the users are not tied to single places, but with the help of mobile devices they connect to the Internet and to other users at any time and from any place that they choose. I think that it is unlikely that mobile virtual communities that function based on many-to-many text communication (such as in chat rooms) are likely to be based on mobile phones because reading much text on a small display and typing much text on a small keyboard is exhausting, tiring, and not very user friendly. The effect would have to be that mobile devices increase in size so that users have larger displays and keyboards. Many users probably find it uncomfortable to carry large mobiles. People tend to read short messages on mobiles but not floating text or long articles. Therefore, I think that the stronger trend in the future will be that wireless Internet connection points will spread and that people will connect with their laptops in order to check and write e-mails, participate in virtual communities like chat rooms, read articles on the Web, search on Google, find new friends on MySpace, etc. Another possibility would be that devices become wearable and that the screen is simulated on glasses and that text inputs are recognized by typing on a virtual keyboard or by speech recognition. The future will show if the more important trend will be connected lightweight laptops or connected wearable devices. Small mobile devices seem to be more suitable for short messaging, e-mailing, and mobile blogging (Moblog, MoVlog) than for floating text services (so, e.g., since 2006 MySpace users who have a Helio mobile can check their accounts and post images to their blogs via the mobile).

What could be potential effects of the rise of mobile virtual communities? Some people would probably spend more time online in such communities with people that share their interests. This could intensify such relationships and build multiple social connections and friendships, also in the offline world. People could probably engage more with those persons whom they know online, which would increase the likelihood that they also want to meet these persons offline and could stay connected in real time to those whom they know offline. Individuals could switch dynamically anytime between different social networks from one and the same place. Another effect could be that people are present in certain places but don't recognize the people that surround them and hence are not willing to establish spontaneous face-to-face contacts because they prefer to interact in virtual spaces with people whom they already know or find more likely to share their interests. But mobile devices could also advance spontaneous face-to-face contact in the offline world. Think, for example, of an online platform where you can specify your interests and input which people you are looking for. If these interests are stored on your mobile along with a partner-matching algorithm, you could be notified by your device (e.g., via Bluetooth) if someone sharing your interests and matching your profile is close to you. This way, spontaneous contacts with people you have never met before could be established. In Japan, a device named Lovegetty has been developed for spontaneous dating. Howard Rheingold mentions Lovegetty as an example of smart mobs (Rheingold 2002, xvii, 164sq.), which "consist of people who are able to act in concert even if they don't know each other. The people who make up smart mobs cooperate in ways never before possible because they carry devices that possess both communication and computing capabilities. Their mobile devices connect them with other information devices in the environment as well as with other people's telephones" (Rheingold 2002, xii). The phenomenon of spontaneous meeting mediated by mobile devices has been termed *wireless dating* or *bluedating*. Applications include, for example, Nokia Sensor (Bluetooth based, connects you to other sensor users), Jambo (can be installed on a laptop and shows you which users are around that use the same application and are in certain specified social networks such as MySpace, Friendster, Facebook, Flickr, Del.icio.us, LiveJournal, etc., as well as their profiles), or Sixsense (uses wi-fi and Bluetooth to search for other Sixsense users, shows you their profiles, and allows you to interact with them). Helio is a mobile device that allows users to check and update their MySpace profiles. Enpresence allows users to specify their profile (interests, description, image) online, to download the application on their mobile, and to be connected to other users by Bluetooth. An advantage of wireless dating might be that the technological mediation makes it easier for people to catch up because the very first contact is not established by talking but by electronic signaling so that the unease that some people feel in establishing contact with strangers might diminish because using the mobile service is already something that the two people have in common and that they can talk about. So, for example, a Japanese user of Lovegetty reports: "When I'm shopping alone, I'm lonely of course. In such cases, it's fun to meet people, talk to new people, and make new friends. . . . It's very different from being picked up. When you're picked up out of the blue, there is always an element of suspicion, but when you're brought together through the Lovege, you're more at ease because you already have something in common. You already have something to talk about. I've never met anyone that was weird or scary" (*Wired News*, June 11, 1998).

Mobile meeting services can foster spontaneous social relationships, but they can also support surveillance and criminal acts (such as pedophiles looking for specific boys or girls); hence, privacy protection should be of high importance with such services. Location-sensing wireless communication (by GPS, Bluetooth, wi-fi, etc.) enables "people to act together in new ways and in situations where collective action was not possible before", but it also "makes possible a universal surveillance economy" (Rheingold 2002, xviii).

Mobile communication not just means that you use your mobile phone for talking to others; it means that computerized devices enable you to communicate in diverse ways (by transmitting speech, text, pictures, videos, images, emotions) with selected others at any time independently of where you are. Mobile devices enable a mobile Internet, that is, the access of information, communication, and cooperation anytime and anywhere. One can be in different spaces at one time and flexibly switch between different spaces, activities, and roles (work, business, friendships, traveling, entertainment, networking, sexuality, etc.). Traditionally separated roles and spaces become interconnected. Castells et al. (2007, 174, 250) argue that mobile communication allows "inserting communication into all the moments when other practices cannot be conducted, such as the 'in-between' time during transportation, in a waiting line, or simply during free time. . . . So the system of mobile communication enables the blurring, mixing, and recomposing of a variety of social practices in a variety of time/space contexts". Mobile communication, furthermore, allows the spontaneous coordination and realization of appointments and face-to-face interactions. Castells et al. (2007, 249) speak in this context of instant communities of practice.

The trend towards mobile instant communities of practice that are focused on peer groups of friends has also been verified empirically for social networking platforms. boyd (2006a) found in a case study of Friendster that the most common reasons for adding someone to friends lists were that these people were actual friends, acquaintances, family members, or colleagues. Social networking platforms like MySpace would be "full-time always-on intimate communities" (boyd 2006b).

Donath and boyd (2004) hypothesize that social networking platforms are technologies that are more suited for forming and maintaining weak ties than strong ties. Ellison, Steinfield, and Lampe (2006) conducted empirical research on the quality of social connections in the social networking platform Facebook. They conducted a quantitative empirical online survey with a random sample of 800 Michigan State University undergraduate students of which 286 completed the survey. The major result of the study was that "participants overwhelmingly used Facebook to keep in touch with old friends and to maintain or intensify relationships characterized by some form of offline connection such as dormitory proximity or a shared class". There was a stress on "connecting with offline contacts as opposed to meeting new people". This result is different from many studies of traditional virtual communities (especially chat rooms) in which people mainly look for building new social connections and friendships (cf., e.g., Parks and Floyd 1996). Facebook users use the platform for maintaining strong social ties and forming weak social ties. "Our findings suggest that the social affordances of tools such as Facebook may in fact facilitate maintenance of strong bonds as well as the creation of weak ones. . . . (The users) are using the online channel less to meet new people than to intensify and solidify relationships started online" (Ellison, Steinfield, and Lampe 2006). Facebook is specific in that it serves a geographically bound community (university campuses) by admitting individuals to one of its virtual communities only if they have organization-specific e-mail addresses. Hence, the results obtained by Ellison, Steinfield, and Lampe can't be generalized for other platforms such as MySpace. Facebook is specifically oriented on existing local communities.

In cyberculture, the antagonism between cooperation and competition is most clearly expressed in the question if it produces socialized (i.e., communicating and cooperating) or alienated (i.e., atomized and competing) individuals. This question shall be discussed next.

9.3 CYBERCULTURE: SOCIALIZATION OR ALIENATION?

I will first discuss and summarize some important findings of studies on the effects of communication in virtual communities. Then a synthesis of the results is worked out.

Socialized Cyberculture

Katz and Rice (2002) conclude from five successive quantitative surveys (1994, 1995, 1996, 1997, 2000) that "users tend to communicate with others through other media (especially telephone) more than do non-users, meet more with their friends, and interact more with others in general, although in a more widely dispersed physical environment . . . Clearly long-term Internet usage is associated with more, not less, frequent sociability" (Katz and Rice 2002, 135, 132).

Philip N. Howard (2004, 17), from a study based on more than 5,000 surveys, concludes that "overall, people who join society online believe that they know more people as a result". Howard, Rainie, and Jones (2002) conclude from a survey of over 12,000 American adults conducted in 2000 (Pew Internet Project) that "those who have ever gone online are 24 percent more likely than those who have never gone online to say they can turn to many people for support. . . . Moreover . . . people who have ever gone online are 46 percent more likely to have called a friend or relative just to talk on the previous day. This contradicts the assertion by some that the Internet detracts from other forms of socialization" (Howard, Rainie, and Jones 2002, 68).

John P. Robinson et al. (2002) conducted a time diary study with 948 respondents in 1998/99. They found that "Internet users did not spend notably less time in social contact, and they were slightly more active in family or home communication and home phone calls" (Robinson et al. 2002, 257).

Quan-Haase and Wellman (2002) analyzed data of 20,075 North Americans who participated in the National Geographic "Survey 2000" in 1998. They conclude that Internet users don't feel isolated but that "the more people use the Internet, the more positive their sense of online community", and that "those who are more active offline are more active online—and vice versa" (Quan-Haase and Wellman 2002, 318, 320).

In 1998, Hampton and Wellman (2002) studied wired and nonwired residents in Netville, a wired suburb in Toronto. They found that "wired residents have maintained higher levels of contact as a result of CMC and have been able to maintain contact at pre-move levels with network members living more than 50 km away. By contrast, non-wired Netville residents experienced a drop in contact with social ties at all distances in comparison to a year before their move" (Hampton and Wellman 2002, 365sq.).

Parks and Floyd (1996) conducted a survey of 176 Usenet users. "When we asked if our respondents had formed any new acquaintances, friendships, or other personal relationships as a result of participating in newsgroups, nearly two thirds (60.7%) reported that they had indeed formed a personal relationship with someone they had 'met' for the first time via an internet newsgroup". The authors argue that cyberspace "is simply another place to meet. Just like people who meet in other locales, those who meet in cyberspace frequently move their relationships into settings beyond the one in which they met originally".

Zhao (2006), based on the data from the General Social Survey (GSSS) 2000 ($N = 2,817$), found that those "using the Internet for interpersonal contact (e.g., email and chat) are likely to have more social connections than those who use it for solitary activities (e.g., web surfing), and there is indication, albeit not statistically significant, that solitary web users are likely to have fewer social ties than nonusers".

Alienated Cyberculture

Robert Kraut et al. (1998), in a longitudinal study of 231 participants' (coming from 73 households in Pittsburgh) first one or two years of Internet use, found that greater use of the Internet was associated with statistically significant declines in social involvement as measured by communication within the family and the size of people's local social networks, with increases in loneliness and depression, and decline in the size of the social circle. In a follow-up study, Kraut et al. (2002) collected data from 208 participants of the original study (done in 1995) in 1998 and found that after three years of internet usage "most of the negative outcomes initially associated with use of the Internet dissipated, except for its association with increased stress"

(Kraut et al. 2002, 67). The explanation that the authors provide for the dwindling effects is that from 1995 to 1998 the number of Americans with Internet access quadrupled and hence many more of the participants' close family and friends were likely to have obtained access. A new longitudinal study of the Internet use of 406 participants completing at least 2 of 3 surveys was undertaken in 1998/1999, which showed that "more use of the Internet was associated with positive outcomes over a broad range of dependent variables measuring social involvement and psychological well-being: local and distant social circles, face-to-face communication, community involvement, trust in people, positive affect, and unsurprisingly, computer skills. On the other hand, heavier Internet use was again associated with increases in stress. In addition, it was associated with declines in local knowledge and declines in the desire to live in the local area, suggesting lowered commitment to the local area" (Kraut et al. 2002, 67). Extraverts benefited more from Internet use than introverts.

Nie, Hillygus, and Erbring (2002) conducted a time-diary study of approximately 6,000 Americans in 2000. One of their findings is that "for each minute spent on the Internet during the last 24 hours there is a reduction of approximately one-third of a minute spent with family members" (Nie, Hillygus, and Erbring 2002, 224). They conclude that "time spent on the Internet reduces time spent in face-to-face relationships, and concomitantly increases time spent alone" (225, 227). My overall impression of this study is that a dichotomy of being alone online and social being offline (in face-to-face relationships) is constructed, as if online communication were not social itself.

Kimberly S. Young (1998) characterized individuals who in a study answered at least 5 out of 8 questions with "yes" as Internet addicts. The case study identified 396 dependent and 100 nondependent Internet users. She found that 58 percent of the dependents felt impairment in their academic life, 53 percent in their social relations, 52 percent felt financial impairment, and 51 percent felt impaired in their occupation. In another study, Young found that increased levels of depression are associated with those who become addicted to the Internet (Young and Rodgers 1998). Young (1998) concluded that the more interactive an Internet application, the higher the risk for the development of addictive use. This is a techno-deterministic understanding. Addiction is seen as being technologically caused; communication technology is analyzed as having simple, one-dimensional effects; the social context of technology is ignored.

Janet Morahan-Martin and Phyllis Schumacher (2000) conducted a survey of 277 undergraduate Internet users. Pathological Internet use was measured with the help of 13 yes/no questions focusing on aspects such as if others say about the respondents that they spend too much time online, if the respondents can't concentrate on offline life, go online when they feel down or isolated, cut short sleep to spend more time online, and have negative effects in life such as deteriorating performance and missing social engagements, classes, or work. "No symptoms (no) were reported by 74 (27.2%) students while 177 (64.7%) reported one to three symptoms (limited symptoms) and 22 (8.1%) reported four or more symptoms and were considered pathological internet users" (Morahan-Martin and Schumacher 2000, 19). They found that "pathological users were more likely to use the Internet for meeting new people, emotional support, talking to others sharing the same interests, and playing highly socially interactive games such as MUDs. Additionally, pathological users gained social confidence online" (Morahan-Martin and Schumacher 2000, 26). They would be friendlier and more open online and would find it easier to make friends online. Pathological users were significantly lonelier than others. From my point of view, Internet addiction is a misnomer because it conveys the image that technology as such is a means of addiction; hence, intensive usage would have to make everyone addicted, which is not the case. "Internet addicts" are not addicted to the Internet but to communication with others and to establishing social ties over the Internet. Hence, this addiction seems to be a very social activity.

Alienated cyberculture not only expresses itself in how people behave as individuals but also in how they behave towards others. One such phenomenon is cyberstalking/cyberharassment/cyberbullying, which can be defined as instilling fear and emotional distress in individuals, threatening them, or causing damage to them in social processes that are mediated by cyberspace (cf. Bocij 2004, 2003). Cyberspace gives a new quality to stalking because it allows stalkers a way of remaining relatively anonymous and for gathering and seeding information on their victims in a global fast system of information and communication. Studies have found that cyberstalking in most cases is combined with offline stalking (Alexy et al., 2005). Cyberspace might give a new quality to stalking, but it is not its cause; hence, there are no technological solutions to cyberstalking (such as censorship and surveillance of the Internet). Cyberstalking has its causes in the alienation of social relations in the contemporary competitive society; hence, first of all, feelings and societal conditions of alienation need to be tackled. However, superficial protective measures that can be taken nonetheless are improvements of privacy mechanisms on social networking platforms.

What to Make of the Results of Cyberculture Studies?

I think that it is a wrong understanding to argue that "the Internet" results in addiction, loneliness, community, and so on, because technology is embedded into social systems and doesn't have linear effects on society. Steven G. Jones (1995) argues that computer-mediated communication (CMC) doesn't have clear-cut effects on social relations; it would be likely "that social relations emerging from CMC are between the two poles of production (of new reality) and reproduction (of existing reality)" (Jones 1995, 14). How technology shapes society depends on the conditions users face in society and their personal histories and experiences within society. Technology enables a space of possible forms of cognition and interaction; there is a nonlinear and complex relationship between technological possibilities and social systems. Certain applications or patterns of usage can result in very different effects and behaviors depending on how the social systems that embed technology are shaped. Hence, what we can say and what the abovementioned studies show is that cyberspace is both a tool for the reinforcement and shrinking of sociability; it has an antagonistic character in the sense that, depending on the users' psychological and social context and capacities of online communication, it can enforce or diminish social relationships and feelings of alienation and isolation.

Sherry Turkle (1997) has demonstrated the nonlinear and contradictory effects of the Internet in a study of MUD players who experienced a lack of social contact and had serious psychological problems that were caused in childhood and adolescence. One user acted out his problems in cyberspace, whereas the other worked them through. The first couldn't improve his situation; the second could (Turkle 1997, 200). One user had deficits in early relationships that didn't allow him to identify with other players on the MUD who had qualities he wished to emulate, whereas another one had, besides his problems, a solid relationship with his mother that allowed him to constructively identify with others and the personae one creates online (Turkle 1997, 204sq.).

When we speak of virtual social relationships, we mean interaction processes in which the human beings are not physically copresent in one place and their communication is spatially disembedded. Virtual relationships can mean making new contacts online or maintaining offline relationships online. Frequently, offline relationships also turn into online relationships due to the globalization of life in late-modern society. And online relationships turn into offline relationships when people feel a desire to engage in face-to-face communication. The borders between offline and online social relationships are flexible; in a mediated society, most relationships are hybrid in character, take place both face-to-face and mediated by communication technologies.

One phenomenon that shows that the Internet has a potential for mediating the establishment of new social relationships is cyberlove. Aaron Ben-Ze'ev (2004, 4) defines *cyberlove* as "a romantic relationship consisting mainly of computer-mediated communication. Despite the fact that the partner is physically remote and is to a certain extent anonymous, in one important aspect this relationship is similar to an offline romantic relationship—the emotion of love is experienced as fully and as intensely as in an offline relationship". Nicola Döring (2002, 333) defines online love as a relationship that involves passion (shared arousal when articulating sexual fantasies), intimacy (support in times of personal problems), and commitment (regular contact) and is carried out via the asynchronous or synchronous exchange of digital text, tone, or image messages. It should be added to both definitions that in many cases cyberlove is not purely online but either involves regular offline contact and online contact during times of physical separation (e.g., in long-distance relationships) or is sooner or later supplemented by other forms of interaction (such as telephone or offline meetings).

Ben-Ze'ev argues that "cyberlove is characterized by detached attachment (detattachment)—physical distance with emotional closeness" (Ben-Ze'ev 2004, 56). In online love, at least the first contact is made online or communication in existing relationships is carried out online in order to bridge spatial distance. Ben-Ze'ev (2004, 129) also mentions, besides online relationships intended to find offline sexual or romantic partners, superficial cyberflirting, cybersex, and profound online-only romantic relationships as forms of online intimate activities. However, in most cases cyberlove doesn't take place fully online because people have desires for physical closeness and sexual intercourse. Hence, many cyberaffairs turn into offline love once the two online partners have met and fallen in love in the offline world. Cyberaffairs are likely to come to an end after an offline meeting, either because the partners are disappointed after a first real-life meeting or feel so attracted that they prefer offline sex/romance to online sex/romance.

Cyberlove requires imagination: Users imagine the look, charisma, gestures, and facial expressions of their partners. The high degree of imagination and the focus on mental aspects of an individual can result in idealizations and projections. There can be disappointments in offline meetings if chatters hide some of their central characteristics that their chat partners might not like in online interactions. The main risk of cyberlove is that there might be a certain discrepancy between how one imagines a person online and how one perceives her or him offline. But many people are willing to take that risk because they enjoy the great amount of choices and options that cyberspace provides for meeting people online. If one assumes that love involves, in most cases, attraction towards internal and external characteristics, then cyberlove moves from the inside out and offline love from the outside in.

Robert Sternberg distinguishes three aspects of love: intimacy ("feelings of closeness, connectedness, and bondedness"; Sternberg 1997, 315), passion ("drives that lead to romance, physical attraction, sexual consummation, and related phenomena"; ibid.), and commitment (continuity, commitment to maintain love, and decision to love a certain other; ibid.). Ben-Ze'ev (2004, 188sqq.) argues that intimacy and passion are higher in cyberlove than in offline love, whereas commitment is lower. Döring (2002) argues that especially intimacy is very pronounced in cyberromance because accelerated self-disclosure and the high frequency of contact create trust.

Online relationships develop in many cases more quickly than offline relationships; people more quickly get involved in personal and intimate communication because anonymity reduces the risk of harmful consequences, makes people more courageous, and enables them to end communication at any point of time.

9.4 CONCLUSION

Cyberculture develops dynamically; it is a self-organizing system in which cultural practices and structures permanently produce and reproduce each other in self-referential loops. In the cyberculture system, identities, lifestyles, communities, meanings, and values are permanently defined and redefined, produced, and reproduced online.

The main antagonism of cyberculture is the one between cooperative cyberculture (socialization) and competitive cyberculture (alienation, isolation, fragmentation). The first culture is based on values, ideas, and structures of sharing and building relationships, the second on values, ideas, and structures that erect borders, construct classes, and separate people. Cooperative cyberculture is based on the idea of unity in diversity—a dialectical interconnection of the One and the Many—competitive cyberculture on the ideas of unity without diversity and diversity without unity—a separation of the One and the Many.

Under given societal conditions, cyberspace is both a tool for the reinforcement and shrinking of sociability; it has an antagonistic character in the sense that, depending on the users' psychological and social context and capacities of online communication, it can enforce or diminish social relationships and feelings of isolation. Online socializing is an aspect of cooperation because it connects, networks, and brings individuals together; online alienation is an aspect of competition because it separates and atomizes humans.

The subsystems of cyberculture are virtual communities (VCs). A VC is a dynamic system that is based on computer networks and application programs (level 1) that enable continuous computer-mediated communication that is regularized and structured by general rules of interaction, shared interest, and general topics of interaction (level 2). From continuous computer-mediated communication cooperation, feelings of togetherness and belonging, shared identity, and common values can emerge (level 3). This level is not reached in all virtual communities; many are structured by competition and the accumulation of reputation and difference. Wikipedia is an example of a VC that has a spirit of cooperation and sharing.

In competitive virtual communities, actors try to accumulate symbolic and cultural capital at the expense of others, that is, they are about a competitive logic that values certain ideas, lifestyles, and identities positively and others negatively; strict distinctions are drawn between individuals and groups based on their tastes, look, ideas, and so on. Competitive differential identities emerge. In cooperative virtual communities, individuals connect to each other, share an open culture, and create a unity in diversity.

Commodified virtual communities are colonized by economic logic; their overall goal is the accumulation of capital, whereas real virtual communities are free and open for all and hence can reach a broader public. The next figure gives an overview of some qualities of the antagonism between socialized/cooperative and alienated/competitive cyberculture.

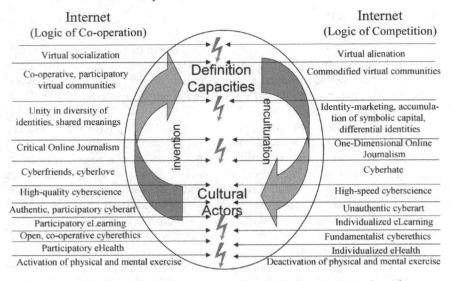

Figure 9.2 The antagonism between socialization and alienation in cyberculture.

10 Conclusion

The task of this chapter is to tie together the arguments presented in the single chapters of this book.

The theoretical framework chosen for this book is critical thinking and the notion of self-organizing systems. A self-organizing system is a system that dynamically produces and reproduces order from within and, based on its inner logic, it is autocreative and a *causa sui*, that is, it is its own cause and produces itself. Such systems are dialectical systems in the sense that its dynamics can be described in Hegelian terms: Concepts from self-organization theory such as control parameters, critical values, bifurcation points, phase transitions, nonlinearity, selection, fluctuation and intensification in self-organization theory correspond to the dialectical principle of transition from quantity to quality. What is called emergence of order, production of information or symmetry breaking in self-organization theory corresponds to Hegel's notions of sublation (*Aufhebung*) and negation of the negation.

Self-organization is based on the dynamic interactions of agents in complex systems; hence, synergetic bottom-up emergence from below, that is, from the microlevel at which agents interact to the macrolevel where new order emerges, is the central dynamic force at play. If this logic is applied to society, then this means that human communication and cooperation form the Essence of society and social systems. No social system is able to exist without at least a certain degree of cooperation, that is, positive social relations in which actors share meanings, cocreate structures, and mutually benefit. Cooperation, altruism, and solidarity are important parts of our everyday experience; these are the forces that make us feel at home in certain social systems. However, one can imagine social systems that are able to exist without competition, that is, negative social relations in which actors derive benefits at the expense of others. Hence, cooperation seems to be a more fundamental and important characteristic of society and social systems; philosophically speaking, it is the Essence of society. In Hegelian philosophy, truth means the correspondence of Essence and Existence of a phenomenon. If cooperation is the Essence of society, then a cooperative society is a fully developed, a true, and a real society.

Throughout the chapters of this book, it has been stressed that self-organization is a practical force, a human creative social action that produces structures in grassroots bottom-up processes. Such an understanding is an alternative to the predominant concept of self-reference and social autopoiesis in social theory as advanced, for example, by Niklas Luhmann and Friedrich August von Hayek. Luhmann argues that society is a functional self-referential system, that is, communication structures produce and reproduce themselves permanently so that one overall function of each subsystem oriented on a specific binary code is fulfilled. Luhmann excludes human actors from social systems; as a consequence, his social theory isn't oriented on social problems, critical thinking, and doesn't take into account how these problems could be solved and how society could be. My own approach can be read as a dialectical social theory oriented on human practice and the creative capacity of humans to self-organize cooperative social systems in bottom-up processes.

It was suggested that the foundational problem of sociology of how structures and actions are related can be solved dialectically in a dynamic social theory. A model of dialectical dynamics in social systems was introduced, in which practices produce and reproduce structures that enable and constrain further practices. This is a double process of agency and conditioning. Agency produces and reproduces social structures that enable and constrain human thinking, behavior, and social actions. This dialectical loop was connected to the theories of Anthony Giddens and Pierre Bourdieu. Giddens argues that structures are reflexive; they enable and constrain actions and are medium and outcome of social action. For Bourdieu, the habitus is a structuring and structured structure that mediates between human practices and the social structure of society.

I have tried to show that Marx's theory of society is not a mechanic-determinist interpretation of history, although one can find some determinist passages in his and Engels's writings. I have argued that it is fruitful to reread Marx as a philosopher of practice, a line of thought that can especially be found in his philosophical writings such as the *Economic and Philosophical Manuscripts* and the *German Ideology*. The dialectical relation of structures and actors was anticipated by Marx's position that society produces man and man produces society. Based on this conception, which puts human activity and struggle into the center of the analysis of society, Marx develops a vision of a self-organized and cooperative society that sublates human estrangement and in which man and society correspond to their Essence and become themselves. In this praxis-oriented understanding of Marx, society and its history are produced by man himself in self-organization processes: "History does nothing, it 'possesses no immense wealth', it 'wages no battles'. It is man, real, living man who does all that, who possesses and fights; 'history' is not, as it were, a person apart, using man as a means to achieve its own aims; history is nothing but the activity of man pursuing his aims" (Marx and Engels 1844, 98).

Based on the dialectic of actors and structures, society can be modeled as consisting of interconnected, networked subsystems that produce and reproduce themselves dynamically. The ecological system, the technological system, the economic system, the political system, and the cultural system have been identified as the subsystems of society in general. These systems are open and interconnected; each social system has structural aspects of all of these systems, but in each one overall structure is dominant.

Modern society is an alienated society in the sense that humans can only to a limited extent live in cooperative, participatory, inclusive social systems; they are confronted with situations of life in which they can't own what they produce, can't decide how they have to act, and can't determine what is considered as normal and acceptable way of life. They are confronted with an instrumental logic of competition that shapes modern society. The latter is based on an antagonism between structures and actors, competition and cooperation. Competition means, in this context, that actors have to strive for accumulating ever more economic, political, and cultural capital, which produces an asymmetrical distribution of structures and classes in society. In modern society, structures become capital, that is, they don't exist just in order to satisfy human needs but for achieving ever more profit by accumulating these different forms of capital. Structures become subsumed under the instrumental logic of competition and accumulation.

Only a dominant minority can control social structures, whereas others are excluded from or only minimally included into ownership, decision making, and definition setting. The central line of argument here is that modern society, due to the instrumental reason of competition, is estranged from society's cooperative and participatory Essence. This argument is based on Hegel's philosophy, in which truth is conceived as the correspondence of Essence and Existence. This logic of Essence was taken up in Marx's philosophical writings and in Herbert Marcuse's critical theory in order to construct critical theories of society. In modern society, competition, exclusion, and exploitation dominate over cooperation, inclusion, and participation. It is dominated by competition, accumulation, class formation, and the asymmetric distribution of structures that take on the form of economic, political, and cultural capital. The capitalist economy aims at accumulating money, capitalist polity at accumulating power, and capitalist culture at accumulating definition capacities that shall secure hegemony. The next table summarizes the central processes and structures for the subsystems of society in general and in modern society.

The further task of this book was to discuss how this basic antagonism of modern society is reproduced and transformed when networked forms of technology and organization emerge as important structuring patterns of society, that is, in the context of Internet and society.

Attributions of contemporary society, such as postindustrial society, information society, knowledge society, network society, virtual society, Internet society, and so on, are discontinuous conceptions that see differences

Table 10.1 The Central Structures and Processes in Society in General and Modern Society in Particular

Subsystem of Society	Structure	Central Process	Structures in Modern Society	Dominant Process (Logic of Competition)
Ecological system	(Natural) resources	Physical matter is extracted in labor processes from nature (appropriation) and is changed by human activities (application).	Ecological capital	Nature is considered as a resource that is continuously appropriated, depleted, and polluted in order to produce commodities. Nature is considered as a free external resource of economic production.
Technological system	Tools	Artifacts, means, methods, skills of action that are used by humans in order to try to achieve defined goals (technization); they are changed and emerge in innovation processes.	Technological capital	Technology is continuously used and innovated as a means for increasing the productivity of the production of commodities; it is a means for relative surplus production, control, and domination. As tool of communication, it is used for exercising and communicating ideology.
Economic system	Property	Goods and resources are produced, allocated, and used by humans for satisfying defined needs.	Economic capital	Labor power, with the help of technologies and resources, produces surplus value objectified in commodities that are sold on markets by competing private owners in order to accumulate money capital; needs are satisfied mainly by purchase and exchange that allow consumption.

Political system	Power	Collective decisions are taken based on a distribution of influencing capacities, and they are executed in order to enable and constrain complex societal processes.	Political capital	Political groups compete for the accumulation of power, which is institutionalized in dominative systems that regulate and control the overall conditions of life in society.
Cultural system	Definition capacities	Values, skills, and practices that shall give meaning to life and help re-create human minds and bodies are defined (invention), acquired, and lived (enculturation).	Cultural capital	Actors and groups compete in lifeworld processes for the accumulation of the capacity to define dominant values, meanings, lifestyles that are positively assessed in society and bring advantages to those who live by them. This is an accumulation of differences in meanings, tastes, symbols, values, norms, and lifestyles. Culture works as ideology, as worldviews that aim to bring about agreement of those who don't benefit.

and rather exclude the continuity of modern society and its competitive structures. In order to avoid an affirmative ideological functionalization of such concepts and to give them a critical twist, the notion of transnational network capitalism/transnational informational capitalism was introduced. Computer networks are the technological foundation that has allowed the emergence of global network capitalism, that is, regimes of accumulation, regulation, and discipline that are helping to increasingly base the accumulation of economic, political, and cultural capital on transnational network organizations that make use of cyberspace and other new technologies for global coordination and communication. The need to find new strategies for executing corporate and political domination has resulted in a restructuration of capitalism, which is characterized by the emergence of transnational, networked spaces in the economic, political, and cultural system and has been mediated by cyberspace as a tool of global coordination and communication. The transition from the Fordist to the post-Fordist mode of capitalist development has resulted in new strategies of accumulation that allow the reduction of variable and constant capital costs in order to increase profit. The informatization and globalization of society and its subsystems can be understood as such strategies. Economic, political, and cultural space have been restructured; they have become more fluid and dynamic, have enlarged their borders to a transnational scale, and handle the inclusion and exclusion of nodes in flexible ways. These networks are complex due to the high number of nodes (individuals, enterprises, teams, political actors, etc.) that can be involved and the high speed at which a high number of resources is produced and transported within them. Global network capitalism is based on structural inequalities; it is made up of segmented spaces in which central hubs (transnational corporations, certain political actors, regions and countries, Western lifestyles and worldviews) centralize the production, control, and flows of economic, political, and cultural capital (property, power, skills). This segmentation is an expression of the overall competitive character of contemporary society.

The relationship of Internet and society is characterized by antagonisms that are an expression of the modern antagonism between cooperation and competition. That this relationship is antagonistic means that it is nonlinear; technology doesn't determine society and doesn't have single effects. The relation is complex and dynamic; new technological applications can have several effects that exist simultaneously. In modern society, these effects are antagonistic. Which effects shape the overall character of social systems and society is determined by human practices and social relations; technology is embedded into social systems; humans produce and design technologies; they give them a certain shape. Simultaneously, the potentials of their ideas and behavior are conditioned by technological structures. In order to avoid a techno-deterministic understanding of the Internet that either sees only one-dimensional effects or only opportunities (techno-optimism) or risks emerging (techno-pessimism) in society from technology, the Internet wasn't conceived as a global technological network of computer networks but as a techno-social system that consists of a technological and a social system that mutually shape each other so that human knowledge is technologically stored and transmitted with the help of a global technological network of computer networks that conditions human meaning production, cognition, communication, and cooperation so that further knowledge emerges that is technologically stored and transmitted, so that further practices are conditioned, and so on. The Internet is conceived as a dynamic dialectical system in which technological structures and social structures/human practices produce each other. In contemporary society, this system advances both opportunities and risks.

Network logic in contemporary capitalism has effects that advance both cooperative, inclusive potentials and the overall competitive and exclusive character of society. The central conflicts and struggles of modern society have been transformed in the information age; transnational networks and knowledge have become strategic resources in these struggles. The capitalistic antagonism between cooperation and competition lies at the heart of global informational capitalism. The accumulation of money, power, and definition capacities is advanced with the help of network organizations and technological networks, but at the same time the global, decentralized, networked character of the Internet undermines the possibilities for the control of resources by specific dominant classes. The antagonism between cooperation and competition manifests itself in five specific antagonisms characteristic for informational capitalism (this idea was first introduced in Fuchs and Hofkirchner 2003; Hofkirchner and Fuchs 2003). In figure 10.1, these antagonisms are shown; the cooperative side is deliberatively

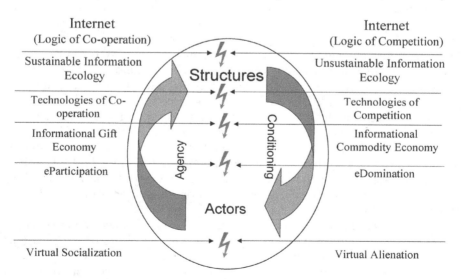

Figure 10.1 The antagonisms of informational capitalism.

printed on the left-hand side and the competitive side on the right-hand side because cooperation is considered as a bottom-up self-organization process and competition as a top-down domination process.

In the ecological system of society, the logic of Internet cooperation has produced opportunities for a more sustainable ecology such as potentials in reducing emissions due to telework and teleconferencing, in reducing the resource and energy intensity of the economy by virtual products and dematerialization. However, in a capitalist society shaped by instrumental competitive logic, there are limits to these opportunities and new risks emerge: A flexile economy requires individuals to travel frequently; new contacts emerge on the Internet that might require more business traveling; there is a limited share of the "cleaner" ICT sector in the total value added; fossil-fuel combustion is a profitable industry; there are rebound effects of virtual products that cause new resource and energy impacts; the production of computers results in a lot of emissions and waste; under capitalist conditions computers have a short lifespan (because this is a way to maximize profit) and electronic waste is an effect; reusable and upgradable computer equipment might not be as profitable as nonreusable ones; and computers consume much energy, which under current conditions benefits the fossil-fuel industry. The overall impression that emerges is that the logic of profit and accumulation severely limits the potential positive effects of ICTs on the ecology and produces new risks, pollution, and depletion of nature. Under the dominance of competitive logic, the informational ecology is unsustainable.

Networks enable connectivity and global diffusion of information, which is an intangible resource. Due to these characteristics, we find a reproduction and aggravation of the antagonism of the productive forces and the relations of production in the Internet economy. On the one hand, information is sold as a commodity with the help of intellectual property rights on the Internet; new spheres of capital accumulation emerge. On the other hand, information can be copied easily and cheaply, and it can be diffused at high speed all over the world in almost no time. From these characteristic of information, the phenomenon of its free sharing, which undercuts profitability of the Internet commodity economy, emerges. The commodity economy and the gift economy collide; social struggles and conflicts are a result of it. The productive forces have been transformed into networked global structures so that new spheres and more efficient methods of capital accumulation emerge. But at the same time, networking and globalization undercut the commodity character of the economy; they advance new forms of cooperation that question the logic of competition.

Capital accumulation, with the help of knowledge commodities, is in knowledge capitalism based on the specific characteristics of information: It is generally not used up by its manifold usage; it expands during usage; it can be compressed, can replace other economic resources, can be transported at the speed of light over global information networks; the costs of reproducing information are generally very low and are further diminished by technological innovations and progress. Hence, knowledge as commodity can be produced and diffused very cheaply; the mechanism for gaining profit from information commodities is that such goods are sold at prices that are much higher than the commodity values. The model of the cooperative gift economy and the competitive commodity economy are not altogether different; cooperation and gifts are subsumed under capital: Corporations in the Internet economy make use of gifts, free access, and free distribution in order to achieve a high number of users, which allows them to charge high advertisement rates and drive up profits. Especially Web 2.0 platforms make use of this model.

At the level of corporations, networking has transformed many corporations into transnational, decentralized, outsourced, distributed firms that make use of new technologies in order to coordinate production and allocation. Cooperating teams, production units, and corporations (strategic alliances) form a new strategy of cooperation for accumulating capital and gaining competitive advantages. Corporations functionalize cooperation as an ideology in order to advance the logic of competition, that is, the accumulation of capital by reducing the constant and variable capital costs. Corporations talk much about cooperation and participation; however, their understanding of these notions is very limited and instrumental and serves overall class interests.

In the realm of class formation, knowledge plays a crucial role in informational capitalism: Exploitation has become a universal condition of society; the commons of society (knowledge, communication, social relationships, education, skills, social services, medical services, health services, entertainment, reproductive labor, technology, nature, public infrastructures) form an immediate force of production; they are produced by all but appropriated only by capital in order to achieve profit. Capital consumes the commons for free in order to accumulate; it exploits not just wage labor but society at a whole, which includes groups such as houseworkers, the unemployed, migrants, people in developing countries, retirees, students, and precarious and informal workers. All humans cooperate, produce, reproduce, and consume the commons, but only the capitalist class exploits the commons. The exploited groups form one overall class-in-itself, the multitude.

In the political system, the antagonism between cooperation and competition is reproduced as antagonism between eParticipation and eDomination.

eDomination means the use of knowledge and networked computer technologies to try to coerce others to act in certain ways, in which they would potentially not act under other circumstances, and for accumulating political capital (power). It is a competitive process. Phenomena of eDomination are, for example, digital divides, information warfare, and electronic surveillance. Digital divide means that the Internet, under given societal conditions, is an exclusive social space not accessible to and available for all. It is a segmented space; this segmentation is due to structural inequalities in modern society that are caused by its competitive class character (class in the Bourdieuian sense). There is asymmetrical access to the physical infrastructure, digital skills, usage capacities, usage benefits, and the institutional context of new technologies. These asymmetries are visible along stratifying lines such as the distribution of economic, political, and cultural capital, age, family status, gender, ability, ethnicity, origin, language, and geography. Information warfare means that information has become a strategic factor in warfare, which supports the physical destruction of enemies. Information warfare has been conceived as a relatively general and broad notion; it includes psychological, communicative, and networking operations. Information warfare means intimidation of the enemy and the production of fear by targeting the psyche of the enemy's military forces and population, observers, and public spheres with the help of information politics and the mass media and the gathering and manipulation of enemy data (cognitive and psychological level), the destruction and manipulation of the information infrastructures, flows, contents, meanings, and effects of enemy communication, encryption and decryption of military communication, battlefield communication, and intelligent weapons (communicative level), and the networking of war in military alliances and decentralized networks of coordinated autonomous military cells (netwar level). Information warfare aims at destroying the influence of enemies; it is based on a competitive separation into friends and enemies. Electronic surveillance aims at controlling the behavior of individuals and groups, that is, they should be forced to behave or not behave in certain ways because they know that their appearance, movements, location, or ideas are or could be watched by electronic systems. In electronic surveillance, data on individuals are gathered with the help of digital systems. These data are known to powerful actors who have the authoritative and allocative resources needed to control these gathered, person-centered data that can be used for coercive means. After 9/11, both information warfare and electronic surveillance have been enlarged in extensity, speed, and intensity, and they have reached a new quality because there are forces that aim to convince people that war and surveillance are necessary for security and that civil rights could be limited in order to protect society.

The competitive logic of eDomination is challenged by cooperative phenomena of eParticipation. Participation is an integrative notion of cooperation; in participatory systems, people are included in ownership, decision making, and norm and value definition. eParticipation is a term that describes that computer-based information and communication technologies (ICTs) can be used for empowering cognition, communication, and cooperation processes of humans so that they can jointly construct participatory social systems. Opposed to the rather competitive logic of representative digital democracy and plebiscitary digital democracy is grassroots digital democracy, in which all those who are concerned with certain problems or phenomena participate in the decision-making process and try to find consensus by rational communicative action that is supported, but not substituted by, ICTs. In the concept of eParticipation, there is also a stress on the political usage of ICTs in civil society. The term *cyberprotest* has been employed for describing the usage of ICTs by protest groups and movements for providing alternative online media, networking themselves, communicating and coordinating protest online, and organizing protest not only with the help of but also within cyberspace itself. In cyberprotest, protest movements make use of the Internet for coordinating, communicating, and networking protest, which can also take on global forms. Civil society has a double character; it legitimizes domination but can also be or become a sphere of critique and of initiating potential social change.

The main antagonism of cyberculture is the one between cooperative cyberculture (socialization) and competitive cyberculture (alienation, isolation, fragmentation). The first culture is based on values, ideas, and structures of sharing and building relationships, the second on values, ideas, and structures that erect borders, construct classes, and separate people. Cooperative cyberculture is based on the idea of unity in diversity—a dialectical interconnection of the One and the Many—competitive cyberculture on the ideas of unity without diversity and diversity without unity—a separation of the One and the Many. Under given societal conditions, cyberspace is both a tool for the reinforcement and the shrinking of sociability; it has an antagonistic character in the sense that, depending on the users' psychological and social context and capacities of online communication, it can enforce or diminish social relationships and feelings of alienation.

Aspects of cooperative cyberculture are, for example, cooperative virtual communities like Wikipedia, critical online journalism, cyberfriends and cyberlove, high-quality cyberscience, authentic participatory cyberart, participatory eLearning, participatory eHealth. These phenomena of cooperation are challenged by predominant competitive forces such as commodified virtual communities, one-dimensional online journalism, cyberhate, fast low-quality cyberscience, unauthentic cyberart, individualized eLearning, or individualized eHealth.

One insight of the theoretical approach elaborated in this book is that the Internet is not a technological system that determines social systems; it doesn't have linear one-dimensional effects on society. In contemporary society, the Internet has produced both risks and opportunities that contradict each other. Neither techno-optimism nor techno-pessimism is appropriate because both have deterministic understandings of technology and society. Rather, feasible seems a position of techno-realism that assesses the actually existing effects, critically judges risks, and tries to help shape society in ways that advance opportunities and minimize the risks of new technologies.

On the one hand, ICTs are embedded into social systems and overall society; they are shaped by social forces and relations. On the other hand, ICTs condition, that is, enable and constrain, human social action. This relationship can be described as an endless dynamical evolving loop.

Another insight is that the antagonisms that structure modern society are reproduced on the Internet; existing trends are amplified into two directions, a cooperative and a competitive one. New media as such don't have clear-cut effects; they are antagonistically structured and embedded into the antagonisms of capitalist society. The antagonism between cooperation and competition that shapes modern society, limits self-determination and participation, also shapes the techno-social Internet system. Under the current societal conditions, which are characterized by the colonization of society by the instrumental logic of accumulation, the risks and competitive forces dominate over realized opportunities, cooperation, and participation on the Internet. The Internet is a class-structured, segmented, stratified social space.

The analysis could end here, but the question remains: Where can we go from here? It might seem odd to some that I talk about ethics in this context because the problems that we are confronted with concerning the Internet, such as electronic waste, digital divides, information war, electronic surveillance, the commodification of community, cyberhate (e.g., neo-Nazis on the Internet), are very material, social, real, and violent in character. Hence, what seems to be needed to solve these problems is material change and not *bonos mores* and spiritual reflection. For many people, ethics is purely ideological, ideational, and a form of philosophical idealism. However, I want to give an alternative understanding of ethics that sees it as a form of material practice for social change.

Marx and Engels considered morals as ideologies that try to legitimate religious, economic, and political domination and oppression and serve class interests by postulating the authority of an absolute subject. Marx considered religion and morals as opium of the people and right (the defense of morals in the form of laws by the state) as a mechanism for protecting private property. Marxists like Antonio Gramsci, Theodor W. Adorno, Max Horkheimer, and Louis Althusser have further elaborated this aspect of Marxism as critique of ideology. Marx and Engels argue that morals are an expression of coercive societies and that morality will vanish with the disappearance of class antagonisms because there will be no fundamental conflicts of interests that have to be legitimated ideologically. Moral theories would be a consequence of the economic conditions of society and morality class morality. They argue that their approach is not a moralistic but a scientific one because they would identify tendencies of the development of the productive forces that produce the potential for a higher form of existence. The alternative to preaching morality here seems to be the identification of deterministic laws of history. Steven Lukes (1985) has pointed out that the writings of Marx and Engels on moral questions are a paradox because, besides the stress on historical laws instead of morals, one can find a lot of moral expressions that condemn capitalism as oppressive, exploitative, alienating, estranging, heteronomous, and present the vision of a better world ("the realm of freedom") that is characterized by well-rounded individuality, pluralistic activities, abundance, the abolition of hard work and wage labor due to technological productivity, the disappearance of the performance principle and exchange, the free production and distribution of goods ("from each according to his ability, to each according to his needs"), and free time for idle and higher activity. The concept of freedom that Marx and Engels put forward questions freedom as the freedom of private property in means of production and understands it as freedom from scarcity and domination and as a community of associated individuals that provides wealth, self-ownership, self-realization of human faculties, and self-determination for all. They considered the bourgeois concept of freedom as narrow and as reducing freedom to free trade, free market, free buying, free wage labor, that is, to the sphere of money that radically constrains the practical alternatives of action. Bourgeois freedom would make the producers free from their product and would hence be a form of unfreedom. In this context, the notion of alienation arises and signifies compulsory wage labor, dispossession, and the crippling of human faculties.

Especially Lenin, Trotsky, and Stalin took up Marx's and Engels's concept of morality as class morality and of social development as lawful, predetermined process. Determinist readings of Marx argue that a better society doesn't come about because it is ethically justified but because it is causally produced. Paradoxically, this ended up in a new morality that became an ideology that legitimated an oppressive regime (Marcuse 1958; Fuchs 2005a, 140–150). Stalinism recoded bourgeois values, such as family, performance, hard work, in order to arrive at an alternative morality that argued that, under a socialist rule, old values serve higher principles. The result was a moral that resembled the Protestant ethic of capitalism but was characterized as socialist ethics. Soviet ethics were based on the idea that privations and dictatorship were needed in order to establish a free society and to develop the productive forces. The idea of freedom became an ideology and a transcendental absolute idea that legitimated a coercive system that was not all too different from capitalist principles of domination. The idea that history is a lawful process and that hence socialism follows capitalism became an ideology that allowed Stalin to persecute all critics because he argued that the Soviet system in any form is a socialist society because it is a social formation following capitalism and that any criticism of the system is counterrevolutionary and means critique of socialism and suggests a return to capitalism.

The alternative to a determinist interpretation of Marx and Engels is to acknowledge a certain importance of morality in Marxism and to understand it as a philosophy of praxis that aims at the sublation of domination and exploitation in the practice of human emancipation and self-organization. For Hegel, the Essence of things means that they have fundamental characteristics and qualities as such that frequently are different from their Appearance. Truth for Hegel is the correspondence of Essence and Existence of things; only true Existence would be Real and Reasonable. In Marxism, especially Herbert Marcuse has taken up Hegel's notion of Essence and has stressed that Essence is connected to possibilities and that a true society is one that realizes the possibilities that are enabled by its structural aspects such as technological forces, economic productivity, political power relations, worldviews, and so on (Marcuse 1937b, 1964a; Fuchs 2005c, 20–37). Essence in society is connected to what humans could be (Marcuse 1937b). Ernst Bloch (1986) in this context uses the category of "not-yet" to signify real (not abstract) potentials that could be, but have not yet been, realized. For Marcuse, ethics are connected with questions of that which can and should be because it can reduce pain, misery, and injustice (Marcuse 1964a, 106) and show how one can use existing resources and capacities in ways that satisfy human needs in the best possible way and minimize hard labor (ibid., 112). A false condition of society or a social system would mean that its actuality and its potentiality differ. Marcuse stresses, by especially referring to early works of Marx such as the *Economic and Philosophical Manuscripts* and the *German Ideology*, that in capitalism oppressed humans are alienated because they are dispossessed and that alienation means that humans and society are estranged from their Essence. The sublation of the alienation of labor and man by establishing a realm of freedom would mean the realization of the human and social Essence. One can read the works of Marx as a deconstruction of ideology, the identification of potentials that strengthen the realization of human freedom, and the suggestion that humans should act in ways that realize potentials that increase the cooperative character of society. Here both chance and necessity are important: Existing structures, that is, social relations and forces of production in economy, polity, and culture, determine certain potentials of societal development (necessity); the human being in its social practices realizes potentials by creating actuality (chance). Freedom hence is freedom to create novelty that is conditioned (enabled and constrained) by societal reality. Marx's works can be interpreted as an ethics of liberation and cooperation insofar as they suggest that humans should act in ways that bring society closer to the latter's cooperative Essence. Such a form of ethics doesn't have highest transcendental principles (such as God) that are ungrounded, unexplainable, and transcendental. The principle of cooperation as Essence of society emerges from the inner self of society and humans; it is an immanent principle of society that defines the latter's potentials.

Marx's stress on socialization and social relations shows that he saw cooperation as an essential societal phenomenon and considered the realm of freedom as the realization of the cooperative Essence of society. This is what Marx means, for example, when he speaks of "the return of man from religion, family, state, etc., to his human, i.e., social, existence" (Marx 1844b, 537), the "complete return of man to himself as a social (i.e., human) being" (ibid., 536), "the positive transcendence of private property as human self-estrangement, and therefore as the real appropriation of the human Essence by and for man" (ibid., 536). For Marx, cooperation is an objective principle that results in a categorical imperative that, in contrast to Kant, stresses the need for an integrative democracy: Marx argues that critique ends with the insight that "man is the highest essence for man—hence, with the categoric imperative to overthrow all relations in which man is a debased, enslaved, abandoned, despicable essence" (Marx 1844a, 385). Critique of domination and ideology is the consequence of this categorical imperative. Such an interpretation of Marx and Engels stresses that morals don't fade if injustice vanishes but that there is a potential for the emergence of an alternative cooperative ethics/morality, a "really human morality" (Engels 1878, 132).

Cooperation is a specific type of communication and social relation in which actors achieve a shared understanding of social phenomena, make concerted use of resources so that new systemic qualities emerge, engage in mutual learning, all actors benefit, and feel at home and comfortable in the social system that they jointly construct. Cooperation is the foundation of an objective dimension of ethics, a cooperative ethics: All human beings strive for happiness, social security, self-determination, self-realization, inclusion in social systems so that they can participate in decision processes, codesigning their social systems. Competition means that certain individuals and groups benefit at the expense of others, that is, there is an unequal access to structures of social systems. This is the dominant organizational structure of modern society; modern society hence is an excluding society. Cooperation includes people in social systems; it lets them participate in decisions and establishes a more just distribution of and access to resources. Hence, cooperation is a way of achieving and realizing basic human needs; competition is a way of achieving and realizing basic human needs only for certain groups and excluding others. Throughout this book it was argued that cooperation forms the Essence of human society and that competition estranges humans from their Essence. One can imagine a society that functions without competition; a society without competition is still a society. One can't imagine a society that functions without a certain degree of cooperation and social activity. A society without cooperation isn't a society; it is a state of permanent warfare, egoism, and mutual destruction that sooner or later destroys all human existence. If cooperation is the Essence of society, then a truly human society is a cooperative society. Cooperation as the highest principle of morality is grounded in society and social activity itself; it can be rationally explained within society and need not refer to a highest transcendental absolute principle, such as God, that can't be justified within society. Cooperative ethics is a critique of lines of thought and arguments that want to advance exclusion and heteronomy in society. It is inherently critical; it subjects commonly accepted ideas, conventions, traditions, prejudices, and myths to critical questioning. It questions mainstream opinions and voices alternatives to them in order to avoid one-dimensional thinking and strengthen complex, dialectical, multidimensional thinking. The method of critique goes back to Socrates; in the twentieth century it has been advanced by approaches such as critical theory and discourse ethics.

James H. Moor (1985/2000) defined computer ethics as "the analysis of the nature and social impact of computer technology and the corresponding formulation and justification of policies for the ethical use of such technology" (Moor 1985, 23). With the rise of the Internet, computer ethics has been transformed into network ethics.

Rafael Capurro (Capurro 2003a, 2003b) offers an approach that is grounded in the social realm and explores and evaluates the development of moral values and new power structures in the information field, information myths, contradictions and intentionalities in information theories and practices, and the development of ethical conflicts in the information field. The main task of network ethics would be to pose the question of freedom in a digitally networked world.

The approach of cooperative cyberethics stresses that cooperation is a principle that could strengthen participation in the information society and that it should practically be applied to questions of the information society, a society that is increasingly shaped by technology (cyberspace), network logic, and information. *Cooperative information society* ethics is a more precise term, but, because of its clumsiness, the term *cooperative cyberethics* is preferred.

The task of cooperative cyberethics is to analyze the antagonisms of the information society, to question and deconstruct the uncritical appraisal and demonization of ICTs and the information society, and to stress the importance of the principle of cooperation for realizing a participatory development path of the information society. Cooperative cyberethics is oriented on social problems; it points out actual risks of the information society and tries to provide and discuss arguments that help people to practically strengthen real cooperation in the information society.

The goal of cooperative cyberethics is a cooperative society, or what Gunilla Bradley (2006) has termed a *good ICT society*, a society that is integrative, humane, bottom-up, and advances the common good and equality. There is no panacea for achieving a cooperative information society and for avoiding the further colonization of society by the instrumental reason of competition. If opportunities can be advanced and risks minimized, it is decided by political action and in social struggles. Hence, there is no panacea or recipe of how to achieve a cooperative society. However, at the policy level I want to give some personal suggestions for potential reforms that could strengthen cooperation, inclusion, and participation in society. I am not confident that a cooperative society can be achieved, but the task of cooperative cyberethics is also to give an idea of potential reforms that could in principle be taken. The measures suggested concern both the techno-social and the societal level because Internet and society is an integrative relational domain that needs to be considered as a whole. The list is fragmentary and tries to give only some potential examples.

- The support of the development of resource- and energy-saving ICTs.
- The legalization of file sharing on the Internet.

- The advancement of free software in society and the economy.
- The support of the growth of the free software and the open-content movement.
- The support of the diffusion of technologies of cooperation and cooperative online platforms (such as Wikipedia).
- The economic redistribution from high-profit corporations, upper classes, and the rich, towards low-income classes by increasing taxation of capital and high incomes.
- The support of the growth and diffusion of the Internet gift economy.
- The global redistribution of wealth.
- The full cancellation of all debts of developing countries.
- The multiplication of development aid.
- The introduction of a basic income guarantee for all absolutely poor individuals in the world (which could be financed, e.g., by the introduction of the Tobin tax).
- The support of local hardware production that aims at free or cheap local products and the large-scale adoption and production of free software technologies (that are adapted to local needs) by developing countries.
- The rigid enforcement of antitrust laws.
- The introduction of rigidly regulated employment contracts (definition of minimum wage and participation rights, extending and enforcing labor legislation, limit and control of working hours, maximum workload, abolition of precarious jobs, securing of training and education opportunities, etc., minimization of psychological and physical risks at work, etc).
- The support of self-managed corporations and cooperatives.
- The reduction of working hours without loss of income for employees.
- The launching of unions for the unemployed, precarious workers, migrant workers, reproductive workers, and the poor.
- The taxation of large ICT corporations (and large corporations in general) in order to support public goals.
- The introduction of an unconditional guaranteed basic income that secures basic needs for all, attenuates poverty and precarious living and working conditions that have been coproduced by technological rationality and rationalization, gives people more freedom from economic compulsion, and could potentially give them more time for rational and critical political discourse (given the conditions that an infrastructure that secures opportunities for political education and participation for all is given). A redistributive basic income could be one among several mechanisms that advance the reclaiming of the commons by its cooperative producers, given the condition that it is implemented as a basic right for everyone and considered as a share of the value that is produced cooperatively by all in society but that is now exploited by capital for free.

- The implementation of free public ICT access points for all.
- The universal availability of ICT infrastructure and network connectivity for free or at very low prices for all.
- The financial support for civil-society protest organizations.
- The support of open-media initiatives.
- The funding of civil-society new media projects.
- The large-scale implementation of open social software tools (mailing lists, discussion boards, wikis, blogs, political chats, etc.) that support political citizen-citizen communication on government and civil society Web sites.
- The support of cyberprotest that questions oppressive political, economic, and cultural regimes.
- The financial support for projects that implement open political communication on the Internet.
- The introduction of compulsory participatory and critical political-education courses in secondary education.
- Campaigns that stress the importance of social movements, protest, and critical capacities as democratic forces in society.
- The creation of public discussion forums in public spaces and on public television.
- The financial support of political open TV channels and programs.
- The support of social movements that struggle for participatory democracy and for reclaiming the commons.
- The stronger enforcement of data protection and privacy mechanisms for Internet users. Introduction of global-privacy and data-protection laws.
- The establishment of funds for universal free telecommunications services financed by a tax on the profits of large telecommunications and Internet corporations.
- The support of publicly provided free access to computers and Internet for all in developing countries.
- The definition of more mechanisms that help advance international understanding, inter- and transcultural dialogue.
- The provision of free universal basic services in areas such as health, primary, secondary and higher education, and pension.
- Full disarmament.
- The strengthening of mechanisms of international right such as the International Court of Justice, international treaties, and the UNO (United Nations Organization), and the minimization of the influence of transnational institutions that advance particularized interests.
- The advancement of participation in education, schools, universities, administrations, government, parliament, and so on.
- The support of digital literacy and digital involvement for excluded groups such as the elderly, the disabled, migrants, rural areas, developing countries, low-income groups, and so on.

- ICT diffusion in public institutions such as hospitals, libraries, schools, universities, public spaces, and so on, so that free public access is enabled.
- The provision of free public-health and educational programs in developing and developed countries.
- The public provision of free digital-literacy programs in developing and developed countries.
- The funding of alternative online-media projects.
- The advancement of comprehensive schools in countries that favor differentiated school systems.

The global networking of society by new media gives us an impression of the overall wealth and innovative capacities of contemporary society. However, due to the colonization of society by the instrumental reason of competition, new achievements remain limited to certain classes and don't benefit all. The overall impression is that the material conditions for a cooperative society (in which all live in wealth, hard labor can be abolished, and all participate) exist today, but human reason lags behind these material potentials. It seems that a cooperative society has never been more realistic in an objective sense but has never been more unrealistic in a subjective sense. The networking of the world advances the idea of bottom-up, grassroots self-organization and of a participatory society. However, this principle contradicts the dominance of competition and the logic of profitability; an antagonism of cooperation and competition shapes contemporary society. Under the given conditions, humans are confronted with a colonization of ever more spheres of society to an ever-larger extent by economic reason and the competitive logic of accumulation. A foundation of a cooperative society is the decolonization of society and an overall paradigm shift towards cooperation and participation. It is feasible that a cooperative society and a cooperative social system can best be constructed in bottom-up, grassroots self-organization processes, in which civil society plays an important role. Such a society can't be rigidly planned by state institutions; however, it probably is necessary that infrastructures are organized that enable and empower self-organization processes and provide them with resources.

What remains is the active hope for self-organizing processes that transform the competitive information society into a cooperative information society. The transformation of the established competitive direction, towards which the information society is heading, into a cooperative direction would mean elementary social change, but such a change presupposes that humans feel a vital need and desire for self-organization and cooperation. If such needs and resulting political practices will be able to develop in a significant degree is uncertain.

Notes

NOTES TO CHAPTER TWO

1. All references to and quotations from the works of Marx and Engels in this monograph give page numbers according to the German version of the Marx-Engels-Works (MEW). The translations of quotations are taken from marxists.org. The page numbers of such quotations refer to the original German sources.
2. The German term used by Bloch is *ausgebären*, which corresponds on the one hand to "bearing" but not only points at an active production; it also refers to a developing process.

NOTE TO CHAPTER THREE

1. Giddens summarizes his criticism of evolutionism in four points: unilinear compression, homological compression, normative illusion, and temporal distortion (Giddens 1984, 239sqq.).

NOTE TO CHAPTER FIVE

1. The idea of Web 3.0 as cooperative Internet was coined by Wolfgang Hofkirchner in cooperation with Robert Bichler, Celina Raffl, Matthias Schafranek and myself on December 21st, 2006.

NOTES TO CHAPTER SEVEN

1. The more famous formulation is: "At a certain stage of development, the material productive forces of society come into conflict with the existing relations of production or—this merely expresses the same thing in legal terms—with the property relations within the framework of which they have operated hitherto. From forms of development of the productive forces these relations turn into their fetters" (Marx 1858/59, 9).
2. Excluded were e.g. mobile phone producers such as Motorola and Nokia because although the mobile phone is arguably also a computer, it lacks the storage and calculation capacities and hence the multidimensionality of digital applications of home computers and laptops. The mobile phone industry should best be treated as a separate subindustry within the knowledge industries.

3. English translation from http://www.marxists.org.

NOTES TO CHAPTER 8

1. Moore's law says that the number of transistors on integrated circuits and hence processing power doubles every 18 months while the costs don't increase.
2. http://www.geni.org/globalenergy/library/donor-letters/2000/Donor2000-07. shtml, accessed on October 31, 2006.
3. For a discussion of cyberprotest and ATTAC, see Grignou/Patou (2004).
4. An example for the usage of FloodNet: In 1999, the toy-selling company etoys. com sued the art collective etoy.com because they worried that its customers would get confused by similar URLs. The answer of the collective was a two-week-long online campaign that blocked etoys.com with FloodNet, parodied the toy sellers on faked Web sites, and mass e-mailed the toy seller's staff, informing them about the lawsuit. The share value of etoys.com started dropping and finally it dropped the suit.
5. E.g.: "Although I commend you for your prompt customer service, I disagree with the claim that my personal iD was inappropriate slang. After consulting Webster's Dictionary, I discovered that "sweatshop" is in fact part of standard English, and not slang. The word means: "a shop or factory in which workers are employed for long hours at low wages and under unhealthy conditions" and its origin dates from 1892. So my personal iD does meet the criteria detailed in your first email. Your web site advertises that the NIKE iD program is "about freedom to choose and freedom to express who you are." I share Nike's love of freedom and personal expression. The site also says that "If you want it done right . . . build it yourself." I was thrilled to be able to build my own shoes, and my personal iD was offered as a small token of appreciation for the sweatshop workers poised to help me realize my vision. I hope that you will value my freedom of expression and reconsider your decision to reject my order".

References

Adorno, Theodor W. 1970. *Ästhetische Theorie*. Frankfurt/Main: Suhrkamp.
Aglietta, Michel. 1979. A theory of capitalist regulation. The US experience. London: NLB.
Alakeson, Vidhya, Tim Aldrich, James Goodman, and Britt James. 2003. *Making the net work: Sustainable development in a digital society*. Teddington: Forum for the Future.
Alexy, Eileen M., Ann W. Burgess, Timothy Baker, and Shirley A. Smoyak. 2005. Perceptions of cyberstalking among college students. *Brief Treatment and Crisis Intervention* 5 (3): 279–289.
Althusser, Louis. 1971. Ideology and ideological state apparatuses. In *Lenin and philosophy and other essays*, 121–173. London: New Left Books.
Anders, Günther. 1980. *Der Antiquierte Mensch*. 2 vols. München: Beck.
Argyris, Chris, and Donald A. Schön. 1996. *Organizational learning II*. Reading, MA: Addison-Wesley.
Arnett, Eric H. 1992. Welcome to hyperwar. *The Bulletin of the Atomic Scientists* 48 (7): 14–21.
Arquilla, John, and David Ronfeldt. 1996. *The Advent of netwar*. Santa Monica, CA: RAND.
———. 1997. Cyberwar is coming! In *In Athena's camp*, ed. John Arquilla and David Ronfeldt, 23–60. Santa Monica, CA: RAND.
———. 1999. *The emergence of noopolitik*. Santa Monica, CA: RAND.
———. 2000. *Swarming and the future of conflict*. Santa Monica, CA: RAND.
———. 2001. What next for networks and netwars? In *Networks and netwars*, ed. John Arquilla and David Ronfeldt, 311–361. Santa Monica, CA: RAND.
Arshinov, Vladimir, and Christian Fuchs, eds. 2003. *Causality, emergence, self-organisation*. Moscow: NIA-Priroda.
Arterton, Christopher. 1987. *Teledemocracy: Can technology protect democracy?* Newbury Park, CA: Sage.
Atton, Chris. 2004. *An alternative Internet*. Edinburgh: Edinburgh University Press.
Bak, Per. 1996. *How nature works*. New York: Copernicus/Springer.
Bakardijeva, Maria. 2003. Virtual togetherness. *Media, Culture & Society* 25 (3): 201–313.
———. 2005. *Internet society: The Internet in everyday life*. London: Sage.
Ball, Kirstie S., and Frank Webster, eds. 2003. *The intensification of surveillance: Crime, terrorism and warfare in the information age*. London: Pluto Press.
Banathy, Bela H. 1996. *Designing social systems in a changing world*. New York: Plenum.
Barabási, Albert-László. 2003. *Linked*. New York: Plume.

Barber, Benjamin. 1997. The new telecommunications technology: Endless frontier or the end of democracy? *Constellations* 4 (2): 208–228.

———. 1998. *Which technology and which democracy?* Transcript of a talk at the Democracy and Digital Media conference, MIT, May 8–9, http://web.mit.edu/m-i-t/articles/barber.html.

———. 2002. *The ambiguous effects of digital technology on democracy in a globalizing world.* Berlin. Heinrich-Böll-Stiftung, http://www.wissensgesellschaft.org/themen/demokratie/democratic.pdf.

Barbrook, Richard. 1998. The hi-tech gift economy. *First Monday* 3 (12).

Barney, Darin. 2004. *The network society.* Cambridge: Polity.

Barthes, Roland. 1972. *Mythologies.* London: Cape.

Batinic, Bernard, Ulf-Dietrich Reips, and Michael Bosnjak, eds. 2002. *Online social sciences.* Seattle: Hogrefe & Huber.

Bauman, Zygmunt. 1998. *Globalization.* Cambridge: Polity.

Bayer, Martin. 2006. Virtual violence and real war. In *Cyberwar, netwar and the revolution in military affairs,* ed. Edward Halpin et al., 12–31. Basingstoke, UK: Palgrave Macmillan.

Baym, Nancy K. 1998. The emergence of on-line community. In *Cybersociety 2.0: Revisiting computer-mediated communication and community,* ed. Steven G. Jones, 35–68. London: Sage.

———. 2006 Interpersonal life online. In *Handbook of new media,* ed. Leah Lievrouw and Sonia Livingstone, 35–54. London: Sage.

Beck, Ulrich. 1983. Jenseits von Stand und Klasse? In *Soziale Welt. Sonderband 2: Soziale Ungleichheiten,* ed. Reinhard Kreckel, 35–74. Göttingen: Otto Schwarz.

———. 1992. Modern society as a risk society. In *The culture and power of knowledge,* ed. Nico Stehr and Richard V. Ericson, 199–214. Berlin: De Gruyter.

Becker, Theodore, and Christa Daryl Slaton. 1997. *Transforming modern representative democracy via advanced telecommunications.* FUTU-Publication 7/97. Turku: Finland Futures Research Centre.

Bell, Daniel. 1976. *The coming of post-industrial society.* New York: Basic Books.

Ben-Ze'ev, Aaron. 2004. *Love online: Emotions on the Internet.* Cambridge, MA: Cambridge University Press.

Benjamin, Walter. 1934. Der Autor als Produzent. In *Medienästhetische Schriften,* 231–247. Frankfurt/Main: Suhrkamp.

Benkler, Yochai. 2002. Coase's penguin, or, Linux and The Nature of the Firm. *The Yale Law Journal* 112 (3): 369–446.

Bennett, Tony. 1986/1998. Popular Culture and the 'Turn to Gramsci.' In *Cultural theory and popular culture,* ed. John Storey, 217–224. Harlow, UK: Pearson.

Bennett, W. Lance. 2003. Communicating global activism. *Information, Communication & Society* 6 (2): 143–167.

Bennholdt-Thomsen, Veronika, Maria Mies, and Claudia von Werlhof. 1992. *Frauen, die letzte Kolonie: Zur Hausfrauisierung der Arbeit,* 3rd ed. Zürich: Rotpunktverlag.

Berardi, Franco. 2003. What is the meaning of autonomy? http://www.republicart.net/disc/realpublicspaces/berardi01_en.pdf.

Best, Steven, and Douglas Kellner. 2001. *The postmodern adventure: Science, technology and cultural studies at the third millennium.* New York: Guilford Press.

Bey, Hakim. 1991. T.A.Z.: The temporary autonomous zone. New York: Autonomedia.

———. 1995. The information war. *CTheory,* http://www.ctheory.net/articles.aspx?id=64.

Beyerle, Matthias. 1994. Staatstheorie und Autopoiesis: Über die Auflösung der modernen Staatsidee im nachmodernen Denken durch die Theorie autopoietischer

Systeme und der Entwurf eines nachmodernen Staatskonzepts, Frankfurt/Main: Peter Lang.

Bloch, Ernst. 1963. *Tübinger Einleitung in die Philosophie.* Frankfurt/Main: Suhrkamp.

———. 1975. *Experimentum Mundi.* Frankfurt/Main: Suhrkamp.

———. 1986. *The principle of hope.* Cambridge, MA: MIT Press.

Böcher, Wolfgang. 1996. *Selbstorganisation. Verantwortung. Gesellschaft: Von suba-tomaren Strukturen zu politischen Zukunftsvisionen.* Opladen, Germany: West-deutscher Verlag.

Bocij, Paul. 2003. Victims of cyberstalking: An exploratory study of harassment per-petrated via the Internet. First Monday 8 (10).

———. 2004. *Cyberstalking.* Westport, CT: Praeger.

Bogard, William. 2006. Surveillance assemblages and lines of flight. In *Theorizing surveillance,* ed. David Lyon, 97–122. Cullompton, UK: Willan.

Boltanski, Luc, and Ève Chiapello. 2006. *The new spirit of capitalism.* London: Verso.

Bookchin, Murray. 1987. The rise of urbanization and the decline of citizenship. San Francisco: Sierra Club Books.

———. 1994. What is communalism? Green Perspectives 31:1–6.

Bourdieu, Pierre. 1977. *Outline of a theory of practice.* Cambridge: Cambridge Uni-versity Press.

———. 1986a. *Distinction: A social critique of the judgement of taste.* New York: Routledge.

———. 1986b. The (three) forms of capital. In *Handbook of theory and research in the sociology of education,* ed. John G. Richardson, 241–258. New York: Green-wood Press.

———. 1990a. *In other words: Essays towards a reflexive sociology.* Cambridge: Polity Press.

———. 1990b. *The logic of practice.* Stanford: Stanford University Press.

———. 1993. *Sociology in question.* London: Sage.

boyd, danah. 2006a. Friends, friendsters, and top 8: Writing community into being on social networking sites. *First Monday* 11 (12).

———. 2006b. *Identity production in a networked culture: Why youth heart MySpace.* Talk at AAAS 2006 (part of panel: "It's 10PM: Do You Know Where Your Children Are . . . Online!"). St. Louis, MO: February 19, 2006, http://www.danah.org/papers/AAAS2006.html.

Boyer, Robert. 1990. *The regulation school: A critical introduction.* New York: Columbia University Press.

Bradley, Gunilla. 2006. *Social and community informatics. Humans on the Net.* New York: Routledge.

Brecht, Bert. 1932. *Radiotheorie.* Gesammelte Werke, vol. 8. Frankfurt/Main: Suhrkamp.

Brush, Heidi Marie. 2003. Cyberwarfare. In *Encyclopedia of new media,* ed. Steve Jones, 114–116. London: Sage.

Bryant, Susan, Andrea Forte, and Amy Bruckman. 2005. *Becoming Wikipedian: Transformation of participation in a collaborative online encyclopedia.* Paper presented at the GROUP International Conference on Supporting Group Work 2005, http://www.cc.gatech.edu/~aforte/134-Bryant.pdf.

Bühl, Walter L. 1991. Politische Grenzen der Autopoiese sozialer Systeme. In *Auto-poiesis,* ed. Hans Rudi Fischer, 201–226. Heidelberg: Carl-Auer-Systeme.

Butler, Judith. 1990. *Gender trouble: Feminism and the subversion of identity.* New York: Routledge.

Byrne, John A., Richard Brandt, and Otis Port. 1993. The virtual corporation. *Busi-ness Week* 8 (2): 36–41.

Calcutt, Andrew. 1999. *Whitenoise. An A-Z of the contradictions in cyberculture.* New York: St. Martin's Press.

Capurro, Rafael. 2003a. Ansätze zur Begründung einer Netzethik. In *Medientheorie und Medientheologie,* ed. Klaas Huizing and Horst F. Rupp, 122–137. Münster: Lit.

———. 2003b. *Ethik im Netz.* Stuttgart: Steiner.

Castells, Manuel. 1989. *The informational city: Information technology, economic restructuring and the urban regional process.* Malden, MA: Blackwell.

———. 2000a. *The rise of the network society. The information age: Economy, society and culture,* 2nd ed., vol. 1. Malden, MA: Blackwell.

———. 2000b. *End of millennium. The information age: Economy, society and culture,* 2nd ed., vol. 3. Malden, MA: Blackwell.

———. 2001. *The Internet galaxy.* Oxford: Oxford University Press.

———. 2004. *The power of identity. The information age: Economy, society and culture,* 2nd ed., vol. 2. Malden, MA: Blackwell.

———. 2006. The network society: From knowledge to policy. In: *The network society: From knowledge to policy,* ed. Manuel Castells and Gustavo Cardoso, 3–21. Washington, DC: Center for Transatlantic Relations.

Castells, Manuel, Mireia Fernández-Ardèvol, Jack Linchuan Qiu, and Araba Sey. 2007. *Mobile communication and society.* Cambridge, MA: MIT Press.

Castoriadis, Cornelius. 2005. *Figures of the thinkable,* http://www.costis.org/x/castoriadis/Castoriadis-Figures_of_the_thinkable.pdf.

Catinat, Michel, and Thierry Vedel. 2000. Public policies for digital democracy. In *Digital democracy. Issues of theory and practice,* ed. Kenneth L. Hacker and Jan Van Dijk, 184–208. London: Sage.

Cedergren, Magnus. 2003. Open content and value creation. *First Monday* 8 (8).

Cerny, Philip G. 1997. Paradoxes of the competition state: The dynamic of political globalization. *Government and Opposition* 32 (2): 251–274.

Cheal, David. 1988. *The gift economy.* New York: Routledge.

Checkland, Peter. 1981. *Systems thinking: Systems practice.* Chichester, UK: Wiley.

Chomsky, Noam. 2001. *9-11.* New York: Seven Stories Press.

Ciffolilli, Andrea. 2003. Phantom authority, self-selective recruitment and retention of members in virtual communities: The case of Wikipedia. *First Monday* 8 (12).

Clausewitz, Carl Von. 1997. *On war.* Hertfordshire, UK: Wortsworth.

Cleaver, Harry. 1993. *Theses on secular crisis in capitalism: The insurpassability of class antagonism,* http://www.eco.utexas.edu/facstaff/Cleaver/secularcrisis.html.

———. 1994. The Chiapas uprising and the future of class struggle in the new world order. *Common Sense* 15 (1994): 5–17.

———. 1995. *The Zapatistas and the electronic fabric of struggle,* http://www.eco.utexas.edu/faculty/Cleaver/zaps.html.

———. 1999. *Computer-linked social movements and the global threat to capitalism,* http://www.eco.utexas.edu/facstaff/Cleaver/polnet.html.

Clynes, Manfred, and Nathan Kline. 1960/1995. *Drugs, space and cybernetics.* In *The cyborg-handbook,* ed. Chris Hables Gray, Heidi J. Figueroa-Sarriera, and Steven Mentor, 1–14. New York: Routledge.

Coe, Neil M., Martin Hess, Henry Wai-chung Yeung, Peter Dicken, and Jeffrey Henderson. 2004. 'Globalizing' regional development: A global production networks perspective. *Transactions Institute of British Geographers* 29 (4): 468–484.

Coe, Neil M., and Timothy G. Bunnell. 2003. 'Spatializing' knowledge communities. Towards a conceptualization of transnational innovation networks. *Global Networks* 3 (4): 437–456.

Coleman, Stephen. 2005. Blogs and the new politics of listening. *The Political Quarterly* 76 (2): 273–280.

Collier, John. 2003. Fundamental properties of self-organization. In *Causality, emergence, self-organisation*, ed. Vladimir Arshinov and Christian Fuchs, 287–302. Moscow: NIA-Priroda.

———. 2004. Self-organisation, individuation and identity. *Revue Internationale de Philosophie* 59: 151–172.

Compaine, Benjamin M. 2001. Information gaps: Myth or reality? In *The digital divide: Facing a crisis or creating a myth?*, ed. Benjamin Compaine, 105–117. Cambridge, MA: MIT Press.

Corning, Peter A. 1998. The synergism hypothesis. *Journal of Social and Evolutionary Systems* 21 (2): 133–172.

Coté, Mark and Jennifer Pybus. 2007. Learning to Immaterial Labour 2.0: MySpace and Social Networks. *Ephemera* 7 (1): 88–106.

Coyle, Diane. 1997. *The weightless world: Strategies for managing the digital economy*. London: Capstone.

Critical Arts Ensemble. 1996. *Electronic civil disobedience*. New York: Autonomedia.

Crossley, Nick. 2002a. Global anti-corporate struggle: A preliminary analysis. *British Journal of Sociology* 53 (4): 667–691.

———. 2002b. *Making sense of social movements*. Buckingham/Philadelphia: Open University Press.

———. 2003. Even newer social movements? *Organization* 10 (2): 287–305.

Cult of the Dead Cow. Undated. *Hacktivismo FAQ*, http://www.cultdeadcow.com/cDc_files/HacktivismoFAQ.html.

Cunningham, Ward, and Bo Leuf. 2001. *The wiki way. Quick collaboration on the Web*. Reading, MA: Addison-Wesley.

Curry, James. 1997. The dialectic of knowledge-in-production: Value creation in late capitalism and the rise of knowledge-centered production. *Electronic Journal of Sociology* 2 (3).

Davidow, William H., and Michael S. Malone. 1992. *The virtual corporation*. New York: HarperCollins.

Davison, Robert, Doug Vogel, Roger Harris, and Noel Jones. 2000. Technology leapfrogging in developing countries—an inevitable luxury? *Electronic Journal of Information Systems in Developing Countries* 1 (5): 1–10.

Dawson, Michael, and John Bellamy Foster. 1998. Virtual capitalism. In *Capitalism and the information age*, ed. Robert W. McChesney, Ellen Meiksins Wood, and John Bellamy Foster, 51–67. New York: Monthly Review Press.

Deleuze, Gilles. 1995. Postscript on the societies of control. In *Negotiations*, 177–182. New York: Columbia University Press.

Deleuze, Gilles, and Félix Guattari. 1976. *Rhizome*. Paris: Les Éditions de Minuit.

Demirovic, Alex. 1997. *Demokratie und Herrschaft: Aspekte kritischer Gesellschaftstheorie*. Münster: Westfälisches Dampfboot.

Dery, Mark. 1993. Culture jamming: Hacking, slashing and sniping in the empire of signs, http://www.levity.com/markdery/culturjam.html.

Deutsch, Karl. 1983. Soziale und politische Aspekte der Informationsgesellschaft. In *Die Zukunft der Informationsgesellschaft*, ed. Philipp Sonntag, 68–88. Frankfurt/Main: Haag & Herchen.

Dicken, Peter, Philip F Kelly, Kris Olds, and Henry Wai-Chung Yeung. 2001. Chains and networks, territories and scales: Towards a relational framework for analysing the global economy. *Global Networks* 1 (2): 89–112.

Dominguez, Ricardo. Undated. *Digital Zapatismo*, http://www.thing.net/~rdom/ecd/DigZap.html.

Donath, Judith, and danah boyd. 2004. Public displays of connection. *BT Technology Journal* 22 (4): 71–82.

Döring, Nicola. 2002. Studying online-love and cyber-romance. In *Online social sciences*, ed. Bernard Batinic, Ulf-Dietrich Reips, and Michael Bosnja, 333–356. Göttingen: Hogrefe.

———. 2003. *Sozialpsychologie des Internet*. Göttingen: Hogrefe.

Drahos, Peter, and John Braithwaite. 2002. *Information feudalism: Who owns the knowledge economy?* London: Earthscan.

Drucker, Peter. 1969. *The age of discontinuity*. London: Heinemann.

Duff, Alistair S. 2000. *Information society studies*. New York: Routledge.

Dunning, John H. 1997. *Alliance capitalism and global business*. New York: Routledge.

Dunsire, Andrew. 1996. Tipping the balance: Autopoiesis and governance. *Administration and Society* 28 (3): 299–334.

Durkheim. Emile. 1982. *Rules of Sociological Method*. New York: Free Press.

Dutton, William H. 1999. *Society on the line: Information politics in the digital age*. Oxford: Oxford University Press.

Dwyer, Cathy. 2007. *Digital relationships in the 'MySpace' generation: Results from a qualitative study*. Paper presented at Hawaiian International Conference on System Sciences 2007, http://csis.pace.edu/~dwyer/research/DwyerHICSS2007. pdf.

Dyer-Witheford, Nick. 1997. Cycles and circuits of struggle in high-technology capitalism. In *Cutting edge: Technology, information, capitalism and social revolution*, ed. Jim Davis, Thomas Hirschl, and Michael Stack, 195–242. London: Verso.

———. 1999. *Cyber-Marx. Cycles and circuits of struggle in high-technology capitalism*. Urbana: University of Illinois Press.

———. 2006. Species-being and the new commonism. Notes on an interrupted cycle of struggles. *The Commoner* 11: 15–32.

Dyson, Esther, George Gilder, George Keyworth, and Alvin Toffler. 1994. Cyberspace and the American dream: A Magna Carta for the knowledge age. *Future Insight* 1 (2).

Ebeling, Werner, and Rainer Feistel. 1994. *Chaos und Kosmos—Prinzipien der Evolution*. Heidelberg/Berlin/Oxford: Spektrum.

Edmonds, Bruce. 1999. What is complexity?—the philosophy of complexity per se with application to some examples in evolution. In *The evolution of complexity*, ed. Francis Heylighen, Johan Bollen, and Alexander Riegler, 1–16. Dordrecht, Netherlands: Kluwer.

Ehrenreich, Barbara. 1997/1976. What is socialist feminism? In *Materialist feminism: A reader in class, difference, and women's lives*, ed. Rosemary Hennessy and Chrys Ingraham, 65–70. New York: Routledge.

Eigen, Manfed, and Peter Schuster. 1979. *The hypercycle*. Heidelberg: Springer.

Electrohippies Collective. 2003. Who does the Internet serve? http://www.fraw.org. uk/ehippies/papers/op3.pdf.

Elias, Norbert. 1971. Sociology of knowledge: New perspectives. *Sociology* 5(2+3): 149–168, 355–370.

Ellison, Nicole, Charles Steinfield, and Cliff Lampe. 2006. *Spatially bounded online social networks and social capital: The role of Facebook*. Paper presented at the annual meeting of the International Communication Association, Dresden, June 19–23, http://msu.edu/~nellison/Facebook_ICA_2006.pdf.

Emigh, William, and Susan C. Herring. 2005. Collaborative authoring on the Web: A genre analysis of online encyclopedias. In *Proceedings of the 38th Hawai'i International Conference on Systems Sciences (HICSS-38)*. Los Alamitos, CA: IEEE Press.

Engels, Friedrich. 1845. *Zwei Reden in Elberfeld*. MEW, vol. 2, 536–557. Berlin: Dietz.

————. 1850. *Die englische Zehstundenbill*. MEW, vol. 7, 233–243. Berlin: Dietz.

————. 1878. *Herrn Eugen Dühring's Umwälzung der Wissenschaft*. MEW, vol. 20, 1–303. Berlin: Dietz.

————. 1886a. *Dialektik der Natur*. MEW, vol. 20, 305–570. Berlin: Dietz.

————. 1886b. Ludwig Feuerbach und der Ausgang der klassischen deutschen Philosophie. In Karl Marx and Friedrich Engels, 1974, *Ausgewählte Schriften in zwei Bänden*, vol. 2, 328–369. Berlin: Dietz.

Enzensberger, Hans Magnus. 1970. Baukasten zu einer Theorie der Medien. In *Baukasten zu einer Theorie der Medien*, 97–132. Munich: Fischer.

Erikson, Erik. 1959. *Identity and the life cycle*. New York: Norton.

Escobar, Arturo. 1994. Welcome to Cyberia. Notes on the anthropology of cyberculture. *Current Anthropology* 35 (3): 211–231.

————. 2003. *Other worlds are (already) possible: Cyber-internationalism and post-capitalist cultures*. Contribution to the forum "Life after Capitalism," World Social Forum, January 23–28, Porto Alegre. In Z magazine, http://www.zmag.org/escobarcyner.htm.

Espejo, Raul. 2000. Self-construction of desirable social systems. *Kybernetes* 29 (7/8): 949–963.

Etzioni, Amitai. 1971. *The active society*. New York: Free Press.

European Information Technology Observatory (EITO). 2002. *Jahrbuch 2002*. Frankfurt/Main: EITO.

Fernback, Jan. 1999. There is a there there. Notes towards definition of cybercommunity. In *Doing Internet Research*, ed. Steven G. Jones, 203–220. London: Sage.

Fiske, John. 1996. *Media matters: Everyday culture and political change*. Minneapolis: University of Minnesota Press.

Fitzpatrick, Tony. 2002. Critical theory, information society and surveillance technologies. *Information, Communication and Society* 5 (3): 357–378.

Fleissner, Peter. 2005. Commodification, information, value and profit. *Poiesis & Praxis: International Journal of Technology Assessment and Ethics of Science* 3.

Flood, Robert L., and Ewart R. Carson. 1993. Dealing with complexity: An introduction to the theory and application of systems science. New York: Plenum Press.

Florida, Richard. 2002. *The rise of the creative class*. New York: Basic Books.

Flusser, Vilém. 1996a. *Ins Universum der technischen Bilder*. Göttingen: European Photography.

————. 1996b, *Kommunikologie*. Frankfurt/Main: Fischer.

Foster, John Bellamy. 2002. *Ecology against capitalism*. New York: Monthly Review Press.

Foucault, Michel. 1979. *Discipline and punish*. New York: Vintage.

François, Charles. 1997. International encyclopedia of systems and cybernetics. Munich: Saur.

Fraser, Nancy. 1982. Rethinking the public sphere. A contribution to the critique of the actually existing democracy. In *Habermas and the Public Sphere*, ed. Craig Calhoun, 109–142. Cambridge: MIT Press.

Fraunhofer Institut für Systemtechnik und Innovationsforschung (ISI)/Centre for Energy Policy and Economics (CEPE). 2005. Der Einfluss moderner Gerätegenerationen der Informations- und Kommunikationstechnik auf den Energieverbrauch in Deutschland bis zum Jahr 2010. Möglichkeiten zur Erhöhung der Energieeffizienz und zur Energieeinsparung in diesen Bereichen. Abschlussbericht an das BM für Wirtschaft und Arbeit. Karlsruhe/Zürich: ISI/CEPE.

Free Software Foundation. 1996. *The free software definition*, http://www.gnu.org/philosophy/free-sw.html.

French, Hilary. 2000. *Vanishing Borders: Protecting the planet in the age of globalization*. New York. Norton.

Friedewald, Michael, Elena Vildjiounaite, Yves Punie, and David Wright. 2007. Privacy, identity and security in ambient intelligence: A scenario analysis. *Telematics and Informatics* 24 (1): 15–29.

Fuchs, Christian. 2002. *Krise und Kritik in der Informationsgesellschaft*. Norderstedt, Germany: Libri.

———. 2003a. Co-operation and self-organisation. *tripleC* (http://triplec.uti.at) 1 (1): 1–52.

———. 2003b. Globalization and self-organization in the knowledge-based society. *tripleC* (http://triplec.uti.at) 1 (2): 105–169.

———. 2003c. Some implications of Pierre Bourdieu's works for a theory of social self-organization. *European Journal of Social Theory* 6 (4): 387–408.

———. 2003d. Structuration theory and self-organization. *Systemic Practice and Action Research* 16 (2): 133–167.

———. 2003e. The self-organization of matter. *Nature, Society, and Thought* 16 (3): 281–313.

———. 2004. The antagonistic self-organization of modern society. *Studies in Political Economy* 73:183–209.

———. 2005a. *Emanzipation! Technik und Politik bei Herbert Marcuse*. Aachen: Shaker.

———. 2005b. The mass media, politics, and warfare. In *Bring 'em on: Media and politics in the Iraq war*, ed. Lee Artz and Yahya B. Kamalipour, 189–207. Lanham, MD: Rowman & Littlefield.

———. 2005c. *Herbert Marcuse interkulturell gelesen*. Interkulturelle bibliothek, vol. 15. Nordhausen, Germany: Bautz.

———. 2007a. Anti-globalization. In *Encyclopedia of governance*, ed. Mark Bevir. London: Sage.

———. 2007b. Transnational space and the "network society." *21st Century Society* 2 (1): 49–78.

Fuchs, Christian, and Wolfgang Hofkirchner. 2002. Ein einheitlicher Informationsbegriff für eine einheitliche Informationswissenschaft. In *Stufen zur Informationsgesellschaft: Festschrift zum 65. Geburtstag von Klaus Fuchs-Kittowski*, ed. Christiane Floyd, Christian Fuchs, and Wolfgang Hofkirchner, 241–281. Frankfurt/Main: Peter Lang.

———. 2003. *Studienbuch Informatik und Gesellschaft*. Norderstedt, Germany: Libri.

———. 2005. Self-organization, knowledge, and responsibility. *Kybernetes* 34 (1–2): 241–260.

———. 2006. Informatik und Gesellschaft: Ein notwendiger Zusammenhang. In *Technik und Wissenschaftssoziologie in Österreich: Stand und Perspektiven*, ed. Eva Buchinger and Ulrike Felt, 205–224. Wiesbaden: Verlag für Sozialwissenschaften.

Fuchs, Christian, and Eva Horak. 2007a. Africa and the digital divide. *Telematics and Informatics* 24 (4).

———. 2007b. Informational capitalism and the digital divide in Africa. In *Proceedings of the Conference Cyberspace 2006*, ed. Radim Polčák and Martin Škop. Brno: Faculty of Law, Masaryk University.

Fuchs, Christian, and Rainer E. Zimmermann. 2008. *Criteria for practical civil virtues: Towards the utopian identity of civitas and multitudo*. Münchener schriften zur design science: Gestaltung in Systemtheorie, Modellbildung & Wissensmanagement, vol. 10. Aachen: Shaker.

Fuchs-Kittowski, Klaus. 2002. Wissens-Ko-Produktion: Verarbeitung, Verteilung und Entstehung von Informationen in kreativ-lernenden Organisationen. In *Stufen zur Informationsgeselllschaft. Festschrift zum 65. Geburtstag von*

Klaus Fuchs-Kittowski, ed. Christiane Floyd, Christian Fuchs, and Wolfgang Hofkirchner, 59–125. Frankfurt/Main: Peter Lang.

Funken, Christiane, and Martina Löw, eds. 2003. *Raumsimulation und Zeitraffer. Raum- und zeittheoretische Überlegungen zum Internet*. Opladen, Germany: Leske&Budrich.

Fussey, Pete. 2004. New labour and new surveillance: Theoretical and political ramifications of CCTV implementation in the UK. *Surveillance & Society* 2 (2/3): 251–269.

Galtung, Johan. 1975. *Essays in peace research*, vol. 1. Copenhagen: Ejlers.

Garcia, David, and Geert Lovink. 1997. The ABC of tactical media, http://www.ljudmila.org/nettime/zkp4/74.htm.

Garnham, Nicholas. 1990. *Capitalism and communication*. London: Sage.

———. 1990/1997. Contribution to a political economy of mass communication. In *The political economy of the media*, ed. Peter Golding and Graham Murdock, 51–86. Cheltenham, UK: Edward Elgar.

———. 2004. Information society theory as ideology. In *The information society reader*, ed. Frank Webster. New York: Routledge.

Gergen, Kenneth J. 2003. Self and community in the new floating worlds. In *Mobile democracy*, ed. Kristóf Nyiri, 103–114. Vienna: Passagen.

Gibson, William. 1984. *Neuromancer*. London: Gollancz.

Giddens, Anthony. 1977. *Studies in social and political theory*. London: Hutchinson.

———. 1979. *Central problems in social theory: Action structure and contradiction in social analysis*. London: Macmillan.

———. 1980. *The class structure of the advanced societies*, 2nd ed. London: Hutchinson.

———. 1981. *A contemporary critique of historical materialism. Vol. 1: Power, property and the state*. London: Macmillan.

———. 1984. *The constitution of society. Outline of the theory of structuration*. Cambridge: Polity Press.

———. 1985. *A contemporary critique of historical materialism. Vol. 2: The nation-state and violence*. Cambridge: Polity Press.

———. 1990. *The consequences of modernity*. Stanford, CA: Stanford University Press.

———. 1991. *Modernity and self-identity. Self and society in the late modern age*. Stanford, CA: Stanford University Press.

Giles, Jim. 2005. Internet encyclopaedias go head to head. *Nature* (online), December 14.

Gillmor, Dan. 2006. *We the media: Grassroots journalism by the people, for the people*. Beijing: O'Reilly.

Glotz, Peter. 1999. *Die beschleunigte Gesellschaft: Kulturkämpfe im digitalen Kapitalismus*. München: Kindler.

Goguen, Joseph A., and Francisco A. Varela. 1979. Systems and distinctions. Duality and complementarity. *International Journal of General Systems* 5 (1): 31–43.

Goldstein, Jeffrey. 1999. Emergence as a construct: History and issues. *Emergence* 1 (1): 49–72.

Goldthorpe, John H. 2000. *On sociology*. Oxford: Oxford University Press.

Gomery, Douglas. 1989/1997. Media economics. Terms of analysis. In *The political economy of the media*, ed. Peter Golding and Graham Murdock, 33–50. Cheltenham, UK: Edward Elgar.

Görg, Christoph. 2001. Risikogesellschaft: Naturverhältnisse in der Theorie Luhmanns. In *Komplexität und Emanzipation. Kritische Gesellschaftstheorie und die Herausforderung der Systemtheorie Niklas Luhmanns*, ed. Alex Demirovic, 255–288. Münster: Westfälisches Dampfboot.

Gorz, André. 1980. *Farewell to the working class*. London: Pluto.
———. 2000. Auswege aus der Misere. In *Existenzgeld*, ed. Hans-Peter Krebs and Harald Rein, 170–187. Münster: Westfälisches Dampfboot.
———. 2004. *Wissen, Wert und Kapital*. Zürich: Rotpunkt.
Gramsci, Antonio. 1971. *Selections from the prison notebooks*. New York: International Publishers.
———. 1980. *Zu Politik, Geschichte und Kultur*. Leipzig: Reclam.
Gras, Marianne L. 2004. The legal regulation of CCTV in Europe. *Surveillance and Society* 2 (2/3): 216–229.
Grassmuck, Volker. 2004. *Freie Software. Zwischen Privat- und Gemeineigentum*. Bonn: Bundeszentrale für politische Bildung.
Gray, Chris Hables. 2002. *Cyborg citizen*. New York: Routledge.
Gray, Mitchell. 2003. Urban surveillance and panopticism: Will we recognize the facial recognition society? *Surveillance & Society* 1 (3): 314–330.
Grignon, Brigitte Le, and Charles Pulver. 2004. ATTAC(k)ing Expertise: does the Internet really democratize knowledge? In *Cyberprotest*, ed. Wim van de Donk, Brian Loeder, Paul Nixon, and Dieter Rucht, 166–178. New York, Routledge.
Grote, Andreas. 1994. Grüne Rechnung. das Produkt Computer in der Ökobilanz. *CT* 1994 (12).
Guevara, Ernesto Che. 2005. Instructions to urban cadres. In *The Bolivian diary*, 257–264. Melbourne: Ocean Press.
Gurak, Laura J., and John Logie. 2003. Internet protest, from text to Web. In *Cyberactivism*, ed. Martha McCaughey and Michael D. Ayers, 25–46. New York: Routledge.
Habermas, Jürgen. 1968. *Strukturwandel der Öffentlichkeit*. Neuwied: Luchterhand.
———. 1981. *Theorie des kommunikativen Handelns*. 2 vols. Frankfurt/Main: Suhrkamp.
———. 1987. *The theory of communicative action. Vol. II: System and lifeworld*. Cambridge: Polity.
———. 2006a. Does democracy still enjoy an epistemic dimension? *Communication Theory* 16 (4): 411–426.
———. 2006b. *Ein avantgardistischer Spürsinn für Relevanzen*. Talk at the Renner Institute, Vienna, March 9, 2006, http://www.renner-institut.at/download/texte/habermas2006-03-09.pdf.
Habermas, Jürgen, and Niklas Luhmann. 1971. *Theorie der Gesellschaft oder Sozialtechnologie*. Frankfurt/Main: Suhrkamp.
Hacker, Kenneth L. 1996. The role of the Clinton White House in facilitating electronic democratization and political interactivity. Paper presented to the Political Communication Division of the Speech Communication Association, November 1996. http://web.nmsu.edu/~comstudy/pch.htm
Hacker, Kenneth L., and Jan Van Dijk, eds. 2000. *Digital democracy: Issues of theory and practice*. London: Sage.
Hagen, Martin. 1997. *A typology of electronic democracy*, http://www.uni-giessen.de/fb03/vinci/labore/netz/hag_en.htm.
Haggerty, Kevin D. 2006. Tear down the walls: On Demolishing the panopticon. In *Theorizing surveillance*, ed. David Lyon, 23–45. Cullompton, UK: Willan.
Haggerty, Kevin D., and Richard V. Ericson. 2000. The surveillant assemblage. *British Journal of Sociology* 51 (4): 605–622.
Haken, Hermann. 1978. *Synergetics*. Heidelberg: Springer.
———. 1983. *Advanced synergetics*. Heidelberg: Springer.
Hall, Stuart. 1999. Encoding/decoding. In *The cultural studies reader*, 2nd ed., ed. Simon During, 507–517. New York: Routledge.
Hampton, Keith N., and Barry Wellman. 2002. The not so global village of Netville. In *The Internet in everyday life*, ed. Barry Wellman and Caroline Haythornthwaite, 345–371. Malden. MA: Blackwell.

Haraway, Donna. 1985/2004. A manifesto for cyborgs. In *The Haraway reader*, 7–45. New York: Routledge.

Hardin, Garrett. 1968. The tragedy of the commons. *Science* 162 (1968): 1243–1248.

Hardt, Michael, and Antonio Negri. 2000. *Empire*. Cambridge, MA: Harvard University Press.

———. 2005. *Multitude*. London: Hamish Hamilton.

Harvey, David. 1989. The condition of postmodernity. London: Blackwell.

———. 2003. The New Imperialism. Oxford,UK: Oxford University Press.

———. 2005. A Brief History of Neoliberalism. Oxford, UK: Oxford University Press.

Haug, Wolfgang Fritz. 2003. *High-Tech-Kapitalismus*. Hamburg: Argument.

Hayek, Friedrich August. 1949. *Individualism and economic order*. London: Routledge & Kegan.

———. 1988. *The fatal conceit: The errors of socialism: Collected works*, vol. 1. London: Routledge.

Hegel, Georg Wilhelm Friedrich. 1812. *The science of logic*. Trans. A. Miller. London: Allen & Unwin.

———. 1874. *The logic of Hegel*. Trans. from the *Encyclopaedia of the philosophical sciences* by William Wallace. 2nd ed. London: Oxford University Press.

Heim, Michael. 1998. *Virtual realism*. Oxford: Oxford University Press.

Held, David. 1996. *Models of democracy*. Cambridge: Polity Press.

Held, David, Anthony McGrew, David Goldblatt, and Jonatan Perraton. 1999. *Global transformations*. Cambridge: Polity.

Herdin, Thomas, Wolfgang Hofkirchner, and Ursula Maier-Rabler. 2007. Culture and technology: A mutual shaping approach. In *Information technology ethics: Cultural perspectives*, ed. Soraj Hongladarom and Charles Ess, 54–67. Hershey: Idea Group Reference.

Heylighen, Francis. 1996. *What is complexity?* http://pespmc1.vub.ac.be/COMPLEXI.html.

———. 1999. The growth of structural and functional complexity during evolution. In *The evolution of complexity*, ed. Francis Heylighen, Johan Bollen, and Alexander Riegler, 17–44. Dordrecht, Netherlands: Kluwer.

Hirsch, Joachim. 1995. *Der nationale Wettbewerbsstaat*. Berlin: ID Verlag.

———. 2002. *Herrschaft, Hegemonie und politische Alternativen*. Hamburg: VSA.

Hodgson, Geoffrey. 2000. The concept of emergence in social science: Its history and importance. *Emergence* 2 (4): 65–77.

Hofkirchner, Wolfgang. 1993. Zwischen Chaos und Versklavung: Die Entgrenzung der Naturwissenschaften und die Mauern im Kopf. *Forum Wissenschaft* 37:7–18.

———. 1998. Emergence and the logic of explanation. *Acta Polytechnica Scandinavica, Mathematics, Computing and Management in Engineering Series* 91:23–30.

———. 2002. *Projekt Eine Welt. Oder Kognition Kommunikation Kooperation. Versuch über die Selbstorganisation der Informationsgesellschaft*. Münster: LIT.

———. 2004. Unity through diversity: Dialectics—systems thinking—semiotics. Trans 15 (1/2), http://www.inst.at/trans/15Nr/01_2/hofkirchner15.htm.

Hofkirchner, Wolfgang, and Christian Fuchs. 2000. The Architecture of the Information Society. In *Proceedings of the 47th annual conference of the international society for the systems sciences (ISSS): Agoras of the global village*, Iraklion, Crete, July 7–11, ed. Jennifer Wilby and Janet K. Allen.

Holloway, John. 2002. *Change the world without taking power: The meaning of revolution today*. London: Pluto Press.

Holzkamp, Klaus. 1985. *Grundlegung der Psychologie*. Frankfurt/Main: Campus.

Horkheimer, Max. 1937. *Traditionelle und Kritische Theorie*. Frankfurt/Main: Fischer.

Hörz, Herbert. 1976. *Marxistische Philosophie und Naturwissenschaften*. Berlin: Akademie.

———. 1993. *Selbstorganisation sozialer Systeme: Ein Verhaltensmodell zum Freiheitsgewinn*. Münster: LIT.

Howard, Michael W. 2002. *Liberal and Marxist justifications for basic income*. Paper presented at the 1st Congress of the US Basic Income Guarantee Network, New York, March 8–9, 2002.

Howard, Philip N. 2004. Embedded media: Who we know, what we know, and society online. In *Society online*, ed. Philip N. Howard and Steven G. Jones, 1–27. London: Sage.

Howard, Philip N., Lee Rainie, and Steven Jones. 2002. Days and nights on the Internet. In *The Internet in everyday life*, ed. Barry Wellman and Caroline Haythornthwaite, 45–73. Malden, MA: Blackwell.

Hunsinger, Jeremy. 2005. Toward a transdisciplinary Internet research. *The Information Society* 21 (4): 277–279.

Huws, Ursula. 2003. *The making of a cybertariat*. New York: Monthly Review Press.

Hyde, Lewis. 1983. *The gift: Imagination and the erotic life of property*. New York: Vintage.

Iglhaut, Stefan, Armin Medosch, and Florian Rötzer, eds. 1996. *Stadt am Netz*. Mannheim: Bollmann.

Introna, Lucas D. 2000. Privacy and the computer: Why we need privacy in the information society. In *Cyberethics*, ed. Robert M. Baird, Reagan Ramsower, and Stuart E. Rosenbaum, 188–199. New York: Prometheus Books.

James, Jeffrey. 2003. *Bridging the global digital divide*. Cheltenham, UK: Edward Elgar.

Jankowski, Nicholas, and Martine van Selm. 2000. The promise and practice of public debate in cyberspace. In *Digital democracy: Issues of theory and practice*, ed. Kenneth L. Hacker and Jan Van Dijk, 149–165. London: Sage.

Jantsch, Erich. 1975. *Design for evolution*. George Braziller: New York.

———. 1979. *Die Selbstorganisation des Universums*. Hanser: Munich.

Jessop, Bob. 2002. *The future of the capitalist state*. Cambridge: Polity.

Johns, Mark D., Shing-Ling Sarina Chen, and G. Jon Hall, eds. 2004. *Online social research*. New York: Peter Lang.

Jones, Steven G. 1995. Understanding community in the information age. In *Cybersociety: Computer-mediated communication and community*, ed. Steven G. Jones, 10–35. London: Sage.

Jordan, Tim, and Paul A. Taylor. 2004. *Hacktivism and cyberwars: Rebels with a cause?* New York: Routledge.

Kahn, Richard, and Douglas Kellner. 2004. New media and Internet activism. From the 'Battle of Seattle' to blogging. In *New Media & Society* 6 (1): 87–95.

Kalz, Marco. 2005. Strukturierungstheorie: Ein Rahmenwerk für die Wiki-Forschung? In *Proceedings of the wikimania 2005*. Frankfurt, http://meta.wikimedia.org/wiki/Transwiki:Wikimania05/Paper-MK3.

Katovsky, Bill, and Timothy Carlson, eds. 2003. *Embedded: The media at war in Iraq*. Guilford, CT: Lyons Press.

Katz, James E., and Ronald E. Rice. 2002. Syntopia: Access, civic involvement, and social interaction on the Net. In *The Internet in everyday life*, ed. Barry Wellman and Caroline Haythornthwaite, 114–138. Malden, MA: Blackwell.

Katz, Jon. 1997. The birth of a digital nation. *Wired* 5 (4) (April 1997).

Kauffman, Stuart. 1993. *The origins of order*. Oxford: Oxford University Press.

Keane, John. 2000. Structural transformation of the public sphere. In *Digital democracy: Issues of theory and practice*, ed. Kenneth L. Hacker and Jan Van Dijk, 71–89. London: Sage.

Kelly, Kevin. 1995. *Out of control: The new biology of machines*. London: Fourth Estate.

———. 1999. *New rules for the new economy*. New York: Viking.

Kenney, Martin. 1997. Value creation in the late twentieth century: The rise of the knowledge worker. In *Cutting edge*, ed. Jim Davis, Thomas Hirschl, and Michael Stack, 87–102. London: Verso.

Kenney, Martin, and James Curry. 1999. Knowledge creation and temporality in the information economy. In *Cognition, knowledge, and organizations*, ed. Raghu Garud and Joe Porac. Greenwich, CT: JAI Press.

Keohane, Robert O., and Joseph S. Nye Jr. 2000. Globalization: What's new = what's not? (and so what?). In *the global transformations reader*, ed. David Held and Anthony McGew, 75–83. Cambridge: Polity.

Khandwalla, Pradip N. 1977. *The design of organizations*. New York: Harcourt Brace Jovanovich.

Kidd, Dorothy. 2003. Indymedia.org: A new communication commons. In *Cyberactivism*, ed. Martha McCaughey and Michael D. Ayers, 47–70. New York: Routledge.

Klein, Naomi. 2004. Reclaiming the commons. In *A movement of movements: Is another world really possible?*, ed. Tom Mertes, 219–229. London: Verso.

Kline, David, and Dan Burstein. 2005. *Blog! How the newest media revolution is changing politics, business and culture*. New York: CDS Books.

Kling, Rob, Howard Rosenbaum, and Steve Sawyer. 2005. *Understanding and communicating social informatics*. Medford, NJ: Information Today.

Knoche, Manfred. 1999. Das Kapital als Strukturwandler der Medienindustrie—und der Staat als sein Agent? Lehrstücke der Medienökonomie im Zeitalter digitaler Kommunikation. In *Strukturwandel der Medienwirtschaft im Zeitalter digitaler Kommunikation*, ed. Manfred Knoche and Gabriele Siegert, 149–193. München: Fischer.

———. 2001. Kapitalisierung der Medienindustrie aus politökonomischer Perspektive. *Medien & Kommunikationswissenschaft* 49 (2): 177–194.

Kolbitsch, Josef, and Hermann Maurer. 2005. Community building around encyclopaedic knowledge, http://www.iicm.edu/iicm_papers/community_building_around_encyclopaedic_knowledge.pdf.

———. 2006. The Transformation of the Web: How Emerging Communities Shape the Information We Consume. *Journal of Universal Computer Science* 12 (2): 187–213.

Kollock, Peter, and Marc Smith. 1999. Communities in cyberspace. In *Communities in cyberspace*, ed. Peter Kollock and Marc Smith, 3–25. New York: Routledge.

Koskela, Hille. 2004. Webcams, TV shows and mobile phones: Empowering exhibitionism. *Surveillance & Society* 2 (2/3): 199–215.

———. 2006. 'The other side of surveillance': Webcams, power and agency. In *Theorizing surveillance*, ed. David Lyon, 163–181. Cullompton, UK: Willan.

Kraut, Robert, Michael Patterson, Vicki Lundmark, Sara Kiesler, Tridas Mukopadhyay, and William Scherlis. 1998. Internet paradox. A social technology that reduces social involvement and psychological well-being? *American Psychologist* 53 (9): 1017–1031.

Kraut, Robert, Sara Kiesler, Bonka Boneva, Jonathon Cummings, Vicki Helgeson, and Anne Crawford. 2002. Internet paradox revisited. *Journal of Social Issues* 58 (1): 49–74.

Krippendorff, Klaus. 1993. Major metaphors of communication and some constructivist reflections on their use. *Cybernetics & Human Knowing* 2 (1): 3–25.

———. 2004. Information and cyberspace: Re-embodying information theory, in *Proceedings des workshops "EU-media/ethik-media 03/04,"* ed. Gesellschaft für Pädagogik und Information e.V. and Deutsche Gesellschaft für Kybernetik, http://www.gpi-online.de/upload/PDFs/EU-Media/.

————. 2006. *The semantic turn*. Boca Raton, FL: Taylor & Francis.

Kroker, Arthur, and Michael Weinstein. 1994. *Data Trash. The Theory of the Virtual Class*. New York: St Martin's Press.

Kropotkin, Peter. 1902. *Mutual aid*. London: Heinemann.

————. 1906. *The conquest of bread*. London: Chapman and Hall.

Kuhndt, Michael. 2002. Project theme report: Virtual dematerialisation: eBusiness and factor X. Wuppertal, Germany: Wuppertal Institute.

Kuhns, Peter, and Adrienne Crew. 2006. *Blogosphere: Best of blogs*. Indianapolis: Que.

Küppers, Günter. 1999. Self-organisation—the emergence of order: From local interactions to global structures. SEIN-Project Paper No. 2. Bielefeld, Germany: University of Bielefeld.

Lamb, Roberta, and Steve Sawyer. 2005. On extending social informatics from a rich legacy of networks and conceptual resources. *Information Technology & People* 18 (1): 9–20.

Langrock, Thomas, Hermann E. Ott, and Tsuneo Takeuchi, eds. 2001. *Japan & Germany: International climate policy & the IT-sector*. Wuppertal, Germany: Wuppertal Institute.

Larkin, Bruce D. 2006. Nuclear weapons and the vision of command and control. In *Cyberwar, netwar and the revolution in military affairs*, ed. Edward Halpin et al., 113–138. Basingstoke, UK: Palgrave Macmillan.

Lash, Scott. 2002. *Critique of information*. London: Sage

————. 2006. Dialectic of information? *Information, Communication, and Society* 9 (5): 572–581.

Laszlo, Ervin. 1987. *Evolution: The grand synthesis*. Boston: Shambhala.

Leadbeater, Charles. 2000. *The weightless society*. New York: Texere Publishing.

Lessig, Lawrence. 2002. *The future of ideas*. New York: Vintage Books.

Lévy, Pierre. 1997. *Collective intelligence*. New York: Plenum.

————. 1998. *Becoming virtual. Reality in the digital age*. New York: Plenum.

————. 2001. *Cyberculture*. Minneapolis: University of Minnesota Press.

Levy, Steven. 1984. *Hackers*. Garden City, NY: Anchor Press.

Libicki, Martin C. 2000. Seven types of information age. In *Information age anthology volume II: National security implications of the information age*, ed. David S. Alberts and Daniel S. Papp, 77–113. Washington, DC: CCRP.

Lievrouw, Leah A., and Sonia Livingstone. 2006. Introduction to the updated student edition + introduction to the first edition. In *The handbook of new media*, ed. Leah A. Lievrouw and Sonia Livingstone, 1–32. London: Sage.

Lih, Andrew. 2004. *Wikipedia as participatory journalism: Reliable sources?* Paper presented at the 5th International Symposium on Online Journalism, April 16–17, Austin, TX, http://staff.washington.edu/clifford/teaching/readingfiles/utaustin-2004-wikipedia-rc2.pdf.

Lipietz, Alain. 1986. Behind the crisis. The exhaustion of a regime of accumulation. *Review of Radical and Critical Economics* 18 (1/2): 13–32.

————. 1987. *Mirages and miracles: The crises of global Fordism*. London: Verso.

Lipnack, Jessica, and Jeffrey Stamps. 2000. *Virtual teams*. New York: Wiley.

Lovink, Geert. 2005. *The principle of notworking. Concpets in critical Internet culture*. Amsterdam: Hogeschool van Amsterdam.

Löw, Martina. 2001. *Raumsoziologie*. Frankfurt/Main: Suhrkamp.

Lubbers, Eveline. 1997. Das müßt ihr uns erstmal nachmachen! Netzaktivitäten in Amsterdam. In *Netzkritik*, ed. nettime, 167–176. Berlin: Edition ID-Archiv.

Luhmann, Niklas. 1984. *Soziale Systeme*. Frankfurt/Main: Suhrkamp.

————. 1988. The autopoiesis of social systems. In: *Sociocybernetic paradoxes*, ed. Felix Geyer and Johannes van der Zouwen, 172–192. London: Sage.

————. 1994. *Die Wirtschaft der Gesellschaft*. Frankfurt/Main: Suhrkamp.

————. 1995. *Social systems.* Stanford, CA: Stanford University Press.

————. 1996a. *Die Realität der Massenmedien.* Opladen, Germany: Westdeutscher Verlag.

————. 1996b. *Protest: Systemtheorie und soziale Bewegungen.* Frankfurt/Main: Suhrkamp.

————. 2000. *Die Politik der Gesellschaft.* Frankfurt/Main: Suhrkamp.

————. 2004. *Ökologische Kommunikation.* Opladen, Germany: Westdeutscher Verlag.

Lukes, Steven. 1985. *Marxism and morality.* Oxford: Oxford University Press.

Luxemburg, Rosa. 1913/1979. *Die Akkumulation des Kapitals.* Berlin: Buchhandlung Vorwärts Paul Singer.

Lyon, David. 1994. *The electronic eye. The rise of surveillance society.* Cambridge: Polity Press.

————. 2001. *Surveillance society. Monitoring everyday life.* Buckingham, UK: Open University Press.

————. 2002. Surveillance studies. Understanding visibility, mobility and the phenetic fix. *Surveillance and Society* 1 (1).

————. 2003. *Surveillance after September 11.* Cambridge: Polity Press.

Lyotard, Jean-Fançois. 1984. *The postmodern condition.* Manchester: Manchester University Press.

Ma, Cathy. 2005. What makes Wikipedia so special? The social, cultural, economical implications of the Wikipedia, http://cathyma.net/wikipedia/cathyma_wikipedia.pdf.

Machlup, Fritz. 1962. *The production and distribution of knowledge in the United States.* Princeton, NJ: Princeton University Press.

Macintosh, Ann. 2004. Characterizing e-participation in policy-making. In *Proceedings of the Thirty-Seventh Annual Hawaii International Conference on System Sciences (HICSS-37)*, Big Island, Hawaii, January 5–8.

Mackay, Hughie. 1995. Theorising the IT/society relationship. In *Information technology and society*, ed. Nick Heap, Ray Thomas, Geoff Einon, Robin Mason, and Hughie Mackay, 41–53. London: Sage.

Macpherson, Crawford Brough. 1973. *Democratic theory: Essays in retrieval.* Oxford: Oxford University Press.

Mannheim, Karl. 1952. *Essays on the sociology of knowledge.* New York: Routledge.

Mansell, Robin. 2001. *New media and the power of networks.* Inaugural professorial lecture, http://www.lse.ac.uk/collections/media@lse/pdf/rmlecture.pdf.

————. 2004. Political economy, power and new media. *New Media & Society* 6 (1): 96–105.

Marcuse, Herbert. 1937a. Philosophie und Kritische Theorie. In *Schriften*, vol. 3, 227–249. Frankfurt/Main: Suhrkamp.

————. 1937b. Zum Begriff des Wesens. In *Schriften*, vol. 3, 45–84. Frankfurt/Main: Suhrkamp.

————. 1958. *Soviet Marxism.* New York: Columbia University Press.

————. 1964a. Ethik und Revolution. In *Schriften*, vol. 8, 100–114. Frankfurt/Main: Suhrkamp.

————. 1964b. *One-dimensional man.* Boston: Beacon Press.

————. 1966. The individual in the great society. In *Collected papers of Herbert Marcuse volume 2: Towards a critical theory of society*, 59–80. New York: Routledge.

————. 1969a. *An essay on liberation.* Boston: Beacon Press.

————. 1969b. Repressive tolerance. In *A critique of pure tolerance*, ed. Robert Paul Wolff, Barrington Moore Jr., and Herbert Marcuse, 95–137. Boston: Beacon Press.

————. 1972. *Counter-revolution and revolt.* Boston: Beacon Press.

————. 1999. *Reason and revolution: Hegel and the rise of social theory.* New York: Humanity Books.

————. 2004. Die Unterschiede zwischen alter und neuer Linker. In *Nachgelassene schriften,* vol. 4. Springe: Zu Klampen.

Marighella, Carlos. 1975. Minimanual of the urban guerrilla. In *Revolutionary guerrilla warfare,* ed. Sam Sarkesian, 507–532. New Brunswick, NJ: Transaction Publishers.

Marletta, Piercarlo, Alberto Pasquini, Glyn Stacey, and Lorenzo Vicario. 2004. *The environmental impact of ISTs.* E-Living Project report, http://www.eurescom. de/e-living/deliverables/e-liv-D14-Ch3-Environment.pdf.

Martens, Will. 1997. Organisation und gesellschaftliche Teilsysteme. In *Theorien der Organisation,* ed. Günther Ortmann, Jörg Sydow, and Klaus Türk, 263–311. Opladen, Germany: Westdeutscher Verlag.

Marx, Gary T. 2002. What's new about the "new surveillance"? *Surveillance & Society* 1 (1): 9–29.

————. 2004. Surveillance and society. In *Encyclopedia of social theory,* ed. George Ritzer, 275–280. London: Sage.

Marx, Karl. 1844a. *Einführung in die Kritik der Hegelschen Rechtsphilosophie.* MEW, vol. 1, 378–391. Berlin: Dietz.

————. 1844b. *Ökonomisch-philosophische Manuskripte von 1844.* MEW, Ergänzugsband 1, 465–588. Berlin: Dietz.

————. 1845. Thesen über Feuerbach. In *Gesammelte Schriften in zwei Bänden,* vol. 2, 370–372. Berlin: Dietz.

————. 1846/47. *Das Elend der Philosophie,* MEW, vol. 4, 63–182. Berlin: Dietz.

————. 1852. *Der 18: Brumaire des Louis Bonaparte.* MEW, vol. 8, 111–207. Berlin: Dietz.

————. 1857. *Einleitung zur Kritik der Politischen Ökonomie.* MEW, vol. 13, 615–641. Berlin: Dietz.

————. 1857/58. *Grundrisse der Kritik der Politischen Ökonomie.* MEW, vol. 42. Berlin: Dietz.

————. 1858/59. *Zur Kritik der Politischen Ökonomie.* MEW, vol. 13, 3–160. Berlin: Dietz.

————. 1861–63. *Theorien über den Mehrwert: Band 1.* MEW, vol. 26.1. Berlin: Dietz.

————. 1867. *Das Kapital: Band 1.* MEW, vol. 23. Berlin: Dietz.

————. 1869. *Über die Nationalisierung des Grund und Bodens.* MEW, vol. 18, 59–62. Berlin: Dietz.

————. 1875. *Kritik des Gothaer Programms.* MEW, vol. 19, 13–32. Berlin: Dietz.

————. 1885. *Das Kapital: Band 2.* MEW, vol. 24. Berlin: Dietz.

————. 1894. *Das Kapital: Band 3.* MEW, vol. 25. Berlin: Dietz.

Marx, Karl, and Friedrich Engels. 1844. Die Heilige Familie. MEW, vol. 2, 3–223. Berlin: Dietz.

————. 1846. Die Deutsche Ideologie. MEW, vol. 3. Berlin: Dietz.

————. 1848. *Manifest der Kommunistischen Partei.* MEW, vol. 4, 459–493. Berlin: Dietz.

————. 1985. *Briefe Jänner 1881–März 1883.* MEW, vol. 35. Berlin: Dietz.

Maturana, Humberto, and Francisco Varela. 1992. *The tree of knowledge: The biological roots of human understanding.* Boston: Shambhala.

Mauss, Marcel. 1954. *The Gift: Forms and functions of exchange in archaic societies.* Glencoe: Free Press.

May, Christopher. 2000. Knowledge workers, teleworkers and plumbers: Labour in the global information economy. In *Online-proceedings of the 41st annual convention of the International Studies Association,* http://www.ciaonet.org/isa/mac01/.

McAdam, Doug. 1982. *Political process and the development of black insurgency.* Chicago: University of Chicago Press.

McCarthy, John D., and Mayer N. Zald, 1977. Resource mobilization and social movements. *American Journal of Sociology* 82 (6): 1212–1241.

McChesney, Robert W. 1998. The political economy of global communication. In *Capitalism and the information age,* ed. Robert W. McChesney, Ellen Meiksins Wood, and John Bellamy Foster, 1–26. New York: Monthly Review Press.

———. 2003. The new global media. In *The global transformation reader,* edited by David Held and Anthony McGrew, 260–268. Cambridge: Polity.

McElroy, Mark W. 2000. Integrating complexity theory, knowledge management and organizational learning. *Journal of Knowledge Management* 4 (3): 195–203.

McKiernan, Gerry. 2005. Wikimediaworlds part I: Wikipedia. *Library Hi Tech News.* 22 (8).

McLaughlin, Margaret L., Kerry K. Osborne, and Christine B. Smith. 1996. Standards of conduct on usenet. In *Cybersociety. Computer mediated communication and community,* ed. Steven G. Jones, 90–111. London: Sage.

McLuhan, Marshall. 1962. *The Gutenberg galaxy.* London: Routledge & Kegan.

Mead, George H. 1934. *Mind, Self, and Society.* Chicago: University of Chicago Press.

Meikle, Graham. 2002. *Future Active. Media activism and the Internet.* New York: Routledge.

Melody, William H. 1993. On the political economy of communication in the information society. In *Illuminating the blindspots: Essays honoring Dallas W. Smythe,* ed. Janet Wasko, Vincent Mosco, and Manjuneth Pendaku, 63–81. Norwood, NJ: Ablex.

Mettler, Peter H. 1997. *Sustainable technology—sustainability of what?* FUTU publication 3/97. Turku: Finland Futures Research Centre.

Mies, Maria. 1996. *Patriarchat und Kapital: Frauen in der internationalen Arbeitsteilung,* 5th ed. Zürich: Rotpunkt.

Mingers, John. 1995. *Self-producing systems. Implications and applications of autopoiesis.* New York: Plenum.

———. 1996. A comparison of Maturana's autopoietic social theory and Giddens' theory of structuration. *Systems Research* 13 (4): 469–482.

———. 1999. Information, meaning, and communication: An autopoietic approach to linking the social and the individual. *Cybernetics & Human Knowing* 6 (4): 25–41.

Moor, James H. 1985/2000. What is computer ethics? In *Cyberethics,* ed. Robert M. Baird, Reagan Ramsower, and Stuart E. Rosenbaum, 23–33. New York: Prometheus Books.

———. 2000. Toward a theory of privacy in the information age. In *Cyberethics,* ed. Robert M. Baird, Reagan Ramsower, and Stuart E. Rosenbaum, 200–212. New York: Prometheus Books.

Moore, Mike. 2006. A bridge too far. In *Cyberwar, netwar and the revolution in military affairs,* ed. Edward Halpin et al., 199–218. Basingstoke, UK: Palgrave Macmillan.

Moore, Richard K. 1999. Democracy and cyberspace. In *Digital democracy: Discourse and decision making in the information age,* ed. Barry N. Hague and Brian D. Loader, 39–59. New York: Routledge.

Morahan-Martin, Janet, and Phyllis Schumacher. 2000. Incidence and correlates of pathological Internet use among college students. *Computers in Human Behavior* 16 (1): 13–29.

Morris-Suzuki, Tessa. 1997. Capitalism in the information age. In *Cutting edge,* ed. Jim Davis, Thomas Hirschl, and Michael Stack, 57–71. London: Verso.

Mosco, Vincent. 1996. *The political economy of communication.* London: Sage.

Mowshowitz, Abbe. 2002. *Virtual organization*. Westport, CT: Quorum.

Murdock, Graham, and Peter Golding. 1974/1997. For a political economy of mass communication. In *The political economy of the media*, ed. Peter Golding and Graham Murdock, 3–32. Cheltenham, UK: Edward Elgar.

Murelli, Elena. 2002. *Breaking the digital divide: Implications for developing countries*. London: Commonwealth Secretariat.

National Research Council. 1999. *Realizing the potential of C4I*. Washington, DC: National Academies Press.

———. 2004. *Army science and technology for homeland security. Report 2: C4ISR*. Washington, DC: National Academies Press.

Negri, Antonio. 2002. Approximations: Towards an ontological definition of the multitude. *Multitudes* 9:36–48.

———. 2004. *Subversive Spinoza*. Manchester: Manchester University Press.

Negroponte, Nicholas. 1996. *Being digital*. New York: Vintage Books.

Nicolis, Gregoire, and Ilya Prigogine. 1989. *Exploring complexity*. New York: Freeman.

Nie, Norman H., D. Sunshine Hillygus, and Lutz Erbring. 2002. Internet use, interpersonal relations, and sociability. In *The Internet in everyday life*, ed. Barry Wellman and Caroline Haythornthwaite, 215–243. Malden, MA: Blackwell.

Nonaka, Ikujiro. 1994. A dynamic theory of organizational knowledge creation. *Organization Science* 5 (1): 14–37.

Nonaka, Ikujiro, and Hirotaka Takeuchi. 1995. *The knowledge-creating company*. Oxford. Oxford University Press.

Norris, Pippa. 2001. *Digital divide: Civic engagement, information poverty, and the Internet worldwide*. New York: Cambridge University Press.

O'Connor, James. 1998. *Natural causes: Essays in ecological Marxism*. New York: Guilford Press.

O'Reilly, Tim (2005) What is Web 2.0? http://www.oreillynet.com/pub/a/oreilly/tim/news/2005/09/30/what-is-web-20.html?page=1.

Organisation for Economic Co-operation and Development (OECD). 1981. *Information activities, electronics and telecommunications technologies: Impact on employment, growth and trade*. Paris: OECD.

———. 1986. *Trends in the information economy*. Paris: OECD.

Ogura, Toshimaru. 2006. Electronic government and surveillance-oriented society. In *Theorizing surveillance*, ed. David Lyon, 270–295. Cullompton, UK: Willan.

Orwell, George. 1990. *Nineteen eighty-four*. London: Penguin.

Otto, Peter, and Philipp Sonntag. 1985. *Wege in die Informationsgesellschaft*. München: DTV.

Parks, Malcom R., and Kory Floyd. 1996. Making friends in cyberspace. *Journal of Computer-Mediated Communication* 1 (4).

Peery, Nelson. 1997. The birth of a modern proletariat. In *Cutting edge*, ed. Jim Davis, Thomas Hirschl, and Michael Stack, 297–302. London: Verso.

Perelman, Michael. 1998. *Class warfare in the information age*. New York: St. Martin's Press.

Peretti, Jonah. 2001. My Nike media adventure. *The Nation*, April 9, 2001, http://www.thenation.com/doc/20010409/peretti.

Piore, Michael J., and Charles Sabel. 1984. *The second industrial divide, possibilities for prosperity*. New York: Basic Books.

Porat, Marc. 1977. *The information economy*. Washington, DC: US Department of Commerce.

Poster, Mark. 1995a. Postmodern virtualities. In *Cyberspace, cyberbodies, cyberpunk*, ed. Mike Featherstone and Roger Burrows, 79–95. London: Sage.

———. 1995b. *The second media age*. Malden, MA: Blackwell.

————. 2001. *What's the matter with the Internet?* Minneapolis: University of Minnesota Press.

Poulantzas, Nicos. 1973/1982. On social classes. In *Classes, power, and conflict,* ed. Anthony Giddens and David Anthony, 101–111. Berkeley: University of California Press.

Prigogine, Ilya. 1980. *From being to becoming.* New York: Freeman.

Prigogine, Ilya, and Isabelle Stengers. 1984. *Order out of chaos.* New York: Bantam.

Quah, Danny T. 1999. The weightless economy in growth. *The Business Economist* 30 (1): 40–53.

Quan-Haase, Anabel, and Barry Wellman. 2002. Capitalizing on the Net. Social contact, civic engagement and sense of community. In *The Internet in everyday life,* ed. Barry Wellman and Caroline Haythornthwaite, 291–324. Malden, MA: Blackwell.

Raymond, Eric S. 1998a. Homesteading the noosphere. *First Monday* 3 (10).

————. 1998b. The cathedral and the bazaar. *First Monday* 3 (3).

®™ark. 1997. A system for change, http://www.rtmark.com/docsystem.html.

Resnick, Stephen A., and Richard D. Wolff. 1987. *Knowledge and class: A Marxian critique of political economy.* Chicago: University of Chicago Press.

Rheingold, Howard. 2000. *The virtual community.* Cambridge, MA: MIT Press.

————. 2002. *Smart mobs.* New York: Basic Books.

Rice, Ronald E. 2005. New media/Internet research topics of the Association of Internet Researchers. *The Information Society* 21 (4): 285–299.

Richard, Elisabeth. 1999. Tools of governance. In *Digital democracy: Discourse and decision making in the information age,* ed. Barry N. Hague and Brian D. Loader, 73–86. New York: Routledge.

Richta, Radovan. 1977. The scientific and technological revolution and the prospects of social development. In *Scientific-technological revolution: Social aspects,* ed. Ralf Dahrendorf, 25–72. London: Sage.

Robertson, Roland. 1992. *Globalization: Global theory and global culture.* London: Sage.

Robins, Kevin. 1995. Cyberspace and the world we live. In *Cyberspace, cyberbodies, cyberpunk,* ed. Mike Featherstone and Roger Burrows, 135–155. London: Sage.

Robins, Kevin, and Frank Webster. 1999. *Times of the technoculture.* New York: Routledge.

Robinson, John P., Meyer Kestnbaum, Alan Neustadtl, and Anthony S. Alvarez. 2002. The Internet and other uses of time. In *The Internet in everyday life,* ed. Barry Wellman and Caroline Haythornthwaite, 244–262. Malden, MA: Blackwell.

Rosenkrands, Jacob. 2004. Politicizing Homo economicus. Analysis of anti-corporate websites. In *Cyberprotest: New media, citizens and social movements,* ed. Wim van de Donk, Brian Loader, Paul Nixon, and Dieter Rucht, 57–76. New York: Routledge.

Salter, Lee. 2003. Democracy, new social movements, and the Internet: A Habermasian analysis. In *Cyberactivism,* ed. Martha McCaughey and Michael D. Ayers, 117–144. New York: Routledge.

Sanders, David, Harold D. Clarke, and Marianne C. Stewart. 2005. *Report on the dynamic of attitudes towards democracy and participation in contemporary Britain.* UK Data Archive, http://www.data-archive.ac.uk.

Saveri, Andrea, Howard Rheingold, and Kathi Vian. 2005. *Technologies of cooperation.* Palo Alto, CA: Institute for the Future.

Sawyer, Steve, and Michael Tyworth. 2006. Social informatics: Principles, theory, and practice. In *Social informatics: An information society for all?,* ed. Jacques Berleur, Markku I. Nurminen, and John Impagliazzo, 49–62. New York: Springer.

Schallaböck, Karl Otto, Iris Utzmann, Vidhya Alakeson, and Britt Jorgensen. 2003. *Telework and sustainable development*. Wuppertal, Germany: Wuppertal Institute.

Schiller, Dan. 2000. *Digital capitalism*. Cambridge, MA: MIT Press.

Schlemm, Annette. 1999. *Dass nichts bleibt, wie es ist . . . Philosophie der selbstorganisierten Entwicklung. Band II: Möglichkeiten menschlicher Zukünfte*. Münster: LIT.

Schmid, Alex P. 1993. The response problem as a definition problem. In *Western responses to terrorism*, ed. Alex P. Schmid and Ronald D. Crelinsten, 7–13. London: Frank Cass.

Schmiede, Rudi. 2006a. Knowledge, work and subject in informational capitalism. In *Social informatics: An information society for all?*, ed. Jacques Berleur, Markku I. Nurminen, and John Impagliazzo, 333–354. New York: Springer.

———. 2006b. Wissen und Arbeit im "informational capitalism". In *Informatisierung der arbeit—gesellschaft im umbruch*, ed. Andrea Baukrowitz, 455–488. Berlin: Edition Sigma.

Schmitt, Carl. 1932. *Legalität und Legitimität*. Berlin: Duncker + Humblot.

Schofield Clark, Lynn. 1998. Dating on the Net: Teens and the rise of the 'pure' relationships. In *Cybersociety 2.0*, ed. Steven G. Jones, 159–183. London: Sage.

Scholte, Jan Aart. 1999. Globalisation: Prospects for a paradigm shift. In *Politics and globalisation*, ed. Martin Shaw, 9–22. New York: Routledge.

Schuler, Douglas. 1996. *New community networks: Wired for change*. Reading, MA: Addison-Wesley.

Senge, Peter. 1990. *The fifth discipline: The art and practice of the learning organization*. London: Random House.

Sennett, Richard. 1998. *The corrosion of character. Personal consequences of work in the new capitalism*. New York: Norton.

Shaviro, Steven. 2003. *Connected: Or what it means to live in the network society?* Minneapolis: University of Minnesota Press.

Shrum, Wesley. 2005. Internet indiscipline: Two approaches to making a field. *The Information Society* 21 (4): 273–275.

Smith, Adam. 1976. *An inquiry into the nature and causes of the wealth of nations*. Chicago: University of Chicago Press.

Smythe, Dallas W. 1977/1997. Communications: Blindspot of Western Marxism. In *The political economy of the media*, ed. Peter Golding and Graham Murdock, 438–464. Cheltenham, UK: Edward Elgar.

Stadler, Felix, and Jesse Hirsh. 2002. Open source intelligence. *First Monday* 7 (6).

Stallman, Richard. 2005. Copyright and globalization in the age of computer networks. In *CODE: Collaborative ownership and the digital economy*, ed. Rishab Aiyer Ghosh, 317–335. Cambridge, MA: MIT Press.

Stehr, Nico. 1994. *Arbeit, Eigentum und Wissen*. Frankfurt/Main: Suhrkamp.

———. 2002a. *A world made of knowledge*. Lecture at the conference New Knowledge and New Consciousness in the Era of the Knowledge Society, Budapest, January 31, http://www.crsi.mq.edu.au/pdfworddocs/worldknowledge.pdf.

———. 2002b. *Knowledge and economic conduct*. Toronto: University of Toronto Press.

Steigerwald, Robert. 2000. Materialism and the Contemporary Natural Sciences. *Nature, Society, and Thought* 13 (3): 279–323.

Sternberg, Robert J. 1997. Construct validation of a triangular love scale. *European Journal of Social Psychology* 27 (3): 313–335.

Stone, Allucquère Rosanne. 1991. Will the real body please stand up? In *Cyberspace: First steps*, ed. Michael Benedikt, 81–118. Cambridge: MIT Press.

Sveiby, Karl. 1997. *The new organizational wealth: Managing and measuring knowledge-based assets*. San Francisco: Berrett-Koehler.

Tapscott, Don. 1996. *The digital economy*. New York: McGraw-Hill.

————. 1999. Introduction. In *Creating value in the network economy*, ed. Don Tapscott, vii–xxvi. Boston: Harvard Business Review.

Tapscott, Don and Anthony D. Williams. 2006. *Wikinomics: How Mass Collaboration Changes Everything*. London: Penguin.

Taylor, Paul A. 2006. Putting the critique back into a critique of information. *Information, Communication & Society* 9 (5): 553–571.

Terranova, Tiziana. 2000. Free labor: Producing culture for the digital economy. *Social Text* 18 (2): 33–57.

Titmuss, Richard Morris. 1970. *The gift relationship*. London: Allen & Unwin.

Toffler, Alvin. 1980. *The third wave*. London: Collins.

Tönnies, Ferdinand von. 1988. *Community & society*. New Brunswick, NJ: Transaction Books.

Touraine, Alain. 1988. *Return of the actor*. Minneapolis: University of Minnesota Press.

Tsagarousianou, Roza. 1999. Electronic democracy: Rhetoric and reality. *Communications. The European Journal of Communication Research* 24 (2): 189–208.

Türk, Volker. 2003. *The Social and environmental impacts of digital music: A case study with EMI*. Wuppertal, Germany: Wuppertal Institute.

Turkle, Sherry. 1997. *Life on screen: Identity in the age of the Internet*. New York: Touchstone.

Van Aelst, Peter, and Stefaan Walgrave. 2004. New media, new movements? The role of the Internet in shaping the 'anti-globalization' movement. In *Cyberprotest: New media, citizens and social movements*, ed. Wim van de Donk, Brian Loader, Paul Nixon, and Dieter Rucht, 97–122. New York: Routledge.

Van Dijk, Jan. 1999. The one-dimensional network society of Manuel Castells. *New Media & Society* 1 (1): 127–138.

————. 2000. Models of democracy and concepts of communication. In *Digital democracy: Issues of theory and practice*, ed. Kenneth L. Hacker and Jan Van Dijk, 30–53. London: Sage.

————. 2005. *The deepening divide: Inequality in the information society*. London: Sage.

————. 2006. *The network society*, 2nd ed. London: Sage.

Van Dijk, Jan, and Hacker, Kenneth. 2003. The digital divide as a complex and dynamic phenomenon. *The Information Society* 19 (4): 315–326.

Van Parijs, Philippe. 1989. A revolution in class theory. In *Approaches to class analysis*, ed. Erik Olin Wright, 213–241. Cambridge: Cambridge University Press.

————. 1995. *Real freedom for all*. Oxford: Oxford University Press.

Veale, Kylie J. 2003. Internet gift economies: Voluntary payment schemes as tangible reciprocity. *First Monday* 8 (12).

Vegh, Sandor. 2003. Classifying forms of online activism. In *Cyberactivism*, ed. Martha McCaughey and Michael D. Ayers, 71–95. New York: Routledge.

Vehovar, Vasja, 2006. Social informatics: An emerging discipline? In *Social informatics: An information society for all?*, ed. Jacques Berleur, Markku I. Nurminen, John Impagliazzo, 73–85. New York: Springer.

Vercellone, Carlo. 2007. From Formal Subsumption to General Intellect: Elements from a Marxist Reading of the Thesis of Cognitive Capitalism. *Historical Materialism* 15 (1): 13–36.

Von Foerster, Heinz. 1993. Lethologie: Eine Theorie des Lernens und Wissens angesichts von Unbestimmbarkeiten, Unentscheidbarkeiten, Unwißbarkeiten. In *KybernEthik*, 126–160. Berlin: Merve.

————. 1995. *Cybernetics of cybernetics*. Minneapolis: Future Systems.

————. 1999. *Wahrheit ist die Erfindung eines Lügners*. Heidelberg: Carl Auer Systeme.

————. 2002. *Teil der Welt*. Heidelberg: Carl Auer Systeme.

Voss, Jakob. 2005. *Measuring Wikipedia*. Paper presented at the International Conference of the International Society for Scientometrics and Informetrics 2005 (ISSI 2005). Online preprint: http://eprints.rclis.org/archive/00003610/01/Measuring Wikipedia2005.pdf.

Vowe, Gerhard, and Martin Emmer. 2001. Elektronische Agora? Digitale Spaltung? Der Einfluss des Internetzugangs auf politische Aktivitäten der Bürger. Ergebnisse einer empirischen Untersuchung. In *Fakten und Fiktionen: Über den Umgang mit Medienwirklichkeiten*, ed. Achim Baum and Siegfried J. Schmidt, 419–432. Konstanz, Germany: UVK.

Wallerstein, Immanuel. 1990. Culture as the ideological battleground of the modern world system. In *Global culture*, ed. Mike Featherstone, 31–55. London: Sage.

Wang, Georgette. 1997. Beyond media globalization: A look at cultural integrity from a policy perspective. *Telematics and Informatics* 14 (4): 309–321.

Wark, McKenzie. 2004. *A hacker manifesto: Version 4.0*, http://subsol.c3.hu/ subsol_2/contributors0/warktext.html.

Wayne, Mike. 2003. *Marxism and media studies*. London: Pluto Press.

Webb, David. 2006. Missile defence—the first steps towards war in space? In *Cyberwar, netwar and the revolution in military affairs*, ed. Edward Halpin et al., 82–97. Basingstoke, UK: Palgrave Macmillan.

Webb, Maureen. 2007. *Illusions of security: Global surveillance and democracy in the post-9/11 world*. San Francisco: City Lights.

Weber, Max. 1947. *The theory of social and economic organisation*. London: Hodge.

————. 1978. *Economy and society*. Berkeley: University of California Press.

Webster, Frank. 2002a. The information society revisited. In *Handbook of new media*, ed. Leah A. Lievrouw and Sonia Livingstone, 255–266. London: Sage.

————. 2002b. Theories of the information society. New York: Routledge.

Webster, William R. 2004. The diffusion, regulation and governance of CCTV in the UK. *Surveillance & Society* 2 (2/3): 230–250.

Weiser, Mark. 1991. The computer for the twenty-first century. *Scientific American* 265 (3): 94–104.

————. 1993. Hot topic: Ubiquitous computing. *IEEE Computer* October 1993:71–72.

Werlhof, Claudia von. 1991. Was haben die Hühner mit dem Dollar zu tun? München: Frauenoffensive.

Wiener, Norbert. 1948. *Cybernetics or control and communication in the animal and the machine*. Cambridge: MIT Press.

Wilhelm, Anthony G. 1999. Virtual sounding boards: How deliberative is online political discussion? In *Digital democracy: Discourse and decision making in the information age*, ed. Barry N. Hague and Brian D. Loader, 154–178. New York: Routledge.

————. 2004. *Digital nation: Towards an inclusive information society*. Cambridge, MA: MIT Press.

Williams, Raymond. 1961. *The long revolution*. London: Chatto & Windus.

————. 1977. *Marxism and literature*. Oxford: Oxford University Press.

————. 1983. *Keywords*. New York: Oxford University Press.

————. 2001. *The Raymond Williams reader*, ed. John Higgins. Oxford/Malden: Blackwell.

Willke, Helmut. 2001. *Systemisches wissensmanagement*. Stuttgart: Lucius & Lucius.

————. 2002. *Dystopia*. Frankfurt/Main: Suhrkamp.

Wilson, Ernest J. 2006. *The information revolution and developing countries*. Cambridge, MA: MIT Press.

Winkler, Roman. 2002. Deliberation on the Internet. Talkboard discussions on the UK parliamentarian elections 2001. *Medienjournal* 4 (2002): 1–20.

Winkler, Stefan. 2003. *Selbstorganisation der Kommunikation Wissenschaft—Öffentlichkeit im virtuellen Raum.* Koblenz, Germany: Forschungsstelle Wissenstransfer. Schriften zur Kommunikation Wissenschaft-Öffentlichkeit 1.

Winner, Langdon. 1997. Cyberlibertarian myths and the prospects for community. *Computers and Society*, September 1997:14–19.

Witt, Ulrich. 1997. Self-organization and economics—what is new? *Structural Change and Economic Dynamics* 8 (4): 489–507.

Woods, Alan, and Ted Grant (2002) *Reason in revolt: Dialectical philosophy and modern science*, vol. 1. New York: Algora.

World Commission on Environment and Development (WCED). 1987. *Our common future.* Oxford: Oxford University Press.

World Resource Institute (WRI). 2000. *The weight of nations: Material outflows from industrial economies. Developing environmental indicators.* Washington, DC: WRI.

World Summit on the Information Society (WSIS). 2003. *Plan of action*, http://www.itu.int/wsis/docs/geneva/official/poa.html.

Wright, Erik Olin. 1989. *The debate on classes.* London: Verso.

———. 1997. *Class counts: Comparative studies in class analysis.* Cambridge: Cambridge University Press.

———. 2005. Foundations of a neo-Marxist class analysis. In *Approaches to class analysis*, ed. Erik Olin Wright, 4–30. Cambridge: Cambridge University Press.

Wright, Steve. 2005. The ECHELON trail: An illegal vision. *Surveillance & Society* 3 (2/3): 198–215.

Young, Kimberley S. 1998. Internet addiction: The emergence of a new clinical disorder. *CyberPsychology and Behavior* 1 (3): 237–244.

Young, Kimberley S., and Robert C. Rodgers. 1998. The relationship between depression and Internet addiction. *CyberPsychology and Behavior* 1 (1): 25–28.

Zanini, Michele, and Sean J. A. Edwards. 2001. The networking of terror in the information age. In *Networks and netwars*, ed. John Arquilla and David Ronfeldt, 29–60. Santa Monica, CA: RAND.

Zeleny, Milan, and Kevin D. Hufford. 1992. The application of autopoiesis in systems analysis: Are autopoietic systems also social systems? *International Journal for General Systems* 21 (2): 145–160.

Zerdick, Axel. 1999. *Die Internet-Ökonomie.* Heidelberg: Springer.

Zeyer, Albert. 1997. *Die Kühnheit, trotzdem ja zu sagen.* Bern: Scherz.

Zhao, Shanyang. 2006. Do Internet users have more social ties? A call for differentiated analyses of Internet use. *Journal of Computer-Mediated Communication* 11 (3).

Žižek, Slavoj. 2001. *Repeating Lenin.* Zagreb: Bastard Books, http://www.marxists.org/reference/subject/philosophy/works/ot/zizek1.htm.

Index

Accumulation regime 30, 72, 74, 101, 103, 106–107, 110, 147, 273, 306–308, 340; *see also* Capital, capital accumulation

Actions 3, 6–8, 16–17, 21–25, 27, 29, 31, 34, 36–37, 40–41, 49–58, 62–70, 75, 77, 82, 88, 93, 96, 102, 104, 111, 115, 121, 123, 225, 289, 299, 317, 319, 336, 338, 340, 341; *see also* structures

Action theory 49

Activism 135–136, 234, 294; *see also* Antiglobalization movement; Antiwar movement; Cyber-activism; Green movement; Movement for democratic globalization; Social movements; Protest movements

Adorno, Theodor W. 6, 49, 175, 346

Aglietta, Michael 72

Alakeson, Vidhya 140

Alexy, Eileen M. 330

Alienation 1, 7, 31, 43, 46, 71, 75, 97, 109, 111, 127–228, 153, 227, 229, 230, 235, 290, 294, 297, 299–300, 308, 321, 327–328, 330, 331, 333–334, 337, 345–348

Althusser, Louis 73, 92, 275–276, 346

Ambient intelligence 270, 276–277

Anders, Günther 255

Anonymity 312, 314–315, 322–323, 332

Antagonism 22, 92, 94–95, 104, 111, 120, 127, 150, 218, 190, 230, 246, 337, 346, 350; *see also* Marx, Karl, antagonism between productive forces and relations of production

antagonism between cooperation and competition 7, 9–10, 30, 71, 97, 120, 127, 139, 148, 159–160, 311, 337, 340–341, 343, 346, 353
  cultural 90, 120, 139, 299–300, 302–303, 327, 331, 333–345
  ecological 139, 144, 146, 147
  economic 120, 139, 140, 161, 164, 174, 209–211
  political 120, 139, 213, 294–299
  societal 86, 97, 88, 89, 90, 103

Antiglobalization movement 83, 85, 243, 277, 283, 290–294, 297, 380; *see also* Globalization; Social movements; Protest movements

Antiwar movement 107, 259; *see also* Social movements; Protest movements

Argyris, Chris 115

Arnett, Eric H. 257

ARPANET 2, 121

Arshinov, Vladimir 11

Art 10, 46, 48, 73, 175, 294, 202, 208, 292, 302–303, 356
  Cyberart 302, 334, 345
  digital art 10
  web art 10

Arterton, Christopher 236

ATTAC 157, 280, 290, 356

Atton, Chris 133, 135

Arquilla, John 254–256, 261, 263, 264

Aufhebung (sublation) 14–15, 19, 34, 38, 55, 63–64, 153, 160, 163, 183, 290, 335, 347–348

Autopoiesis 21, 24–25, 35–37, 46, 50, 51, 65, 74–75, 78, 80–82, 225, 336

Bak, Per 20
Ball, Kirstie S. 268, 273
Bakardjieva, Maria 130, 309
Banathy, Bela H. 48, 61, 228
Barber, Benjamin 229–231, 237–238,
    242, 244
Barbrook, Richard 186
Barlow, John Perry 301
Barney, Darin 100–101
Barthes, Roland 92
Basic income 201, 207, 211, 223, 231,
    246, 251
Batinic, Bernard 4
Baudrillard, Jean 173
Bauer, Bruno 44
Bauman, Zygmunt 113, 156
Bayer, Martin 262
Baym, Nancy K. 308, 321
Beck, Ulrich 189, 305
Becker, Theodore 136
Bell, Daniel 99
Benjamin, Walter 241
Benkler, Yochai 316
Bennet, Lance W. 282
Bennholdt-Thomsen, Veronika 205
Ben-Ze`ev, Aaron 331–332
Berardi, Franco 193
Berners-Lee, Tim 121
Best, Steven 159, 261
Bey, Hakim 258–259, 288
Beyerle, Matthias 36
Bichler, Robert 355
Bloch, Ernst 18, 53, 348, 355
Blogs 1, 16, 129–136, 187–188, 237,
    240, 259, 267, 269–270, 278,
    323–324, 352
Bocij, Paul 330
Bogard, William 267
Boltanski, Luc 150
Bookchin, Murray 229, 231, 242
Bosnjak, Michael 4
Bourdieu, Pierre 49, 105, 200, 201,
    215, 294, 318, 322; *see also*
    Capital, cultural capital; Capi-
    tal, economic capital, Capital,
    political capital; Capital,
    symbolic capital
  capital 62, 72, 90, 311
  theory of habitus 3, 55, 56, 57, 58,
    336
Boyd, Danah 326
Boyer, Robert 73
Böcher, Wolfgang 31
Bradley, Gunilla 350

Brand, Stewart 301
Brecht, Bert 241
Bruckman, Amy 316, 319
Brush, Heidi Marie 262
Bryant, Susan 316, 319
Bunnel, Timothy G. 155
Burstein, Dan 134
Bush, George W. 134, 174, 285, 287
Bühl, Walter 31

C4I (Command, Control, Communica-
    tions, Computers, and Intel-
    ligence) 261–262
C4ISR (Command, Control, Com-
    munications, Computer,
    Intelligence, Surveillance and
    Reconnaissance) 262
Calcutt, Andrew 308
Capital 43, 57, 67, 72, 74, 76, 94–95,
    104, 106–107, 110–111, 113,
    115–116, 118, 141, 148,
    156, 168, 172, 174–177, 180,
    186, 191–192, 200, 202–203,
    205–207, 209–211, 253, 271,
    290, 301–302, 304, 306, 322,
    343, 351
  capital accumulation 30–31, 72–
    97, 101, 104, 111–112, 133,
    140, 143, 146, 148, 151–
    153, 155, 159, 164–165,
    171–172, 177, 180, 187,
    201, 205–206, 208–210,
    221–222, 253, 279, 300–301,
    306, 333, 337, 340–341, 343,
    346
  cultural capital 90–93, 97, 101, 110,
    119, 193, 201, 216, 217, 253,
    279, 295, 299, 311, 312, 322,
    333, 337, 339, 340, 344, 337,
    339, 340; *see also* Bourdieu,
    capital
  ecological capital 338
  economic capital 74–76, 90, 91, 97,
    101, 110, 119, 168, 193, 201,
    216, 217, 253, 279, 295, 318,
    322, 337, 338, 340, 344; *see
    also* Bourdieu, capital
  political capital 76–90, 91, 97, 101,
    110, 119, 193, 201, 216, 217,
    253, 279, 295, 318, 337, 339.
    340, 343, 344; *see also* Bour-
    dieu, capital
  social capital 201, 243, 318, 322; *see
    also* Bourdieu, capital

symbolic capital 90–91, 135, 201, 311, 312, 318, 333; *see also* Bourdieu, capital
taxation of capital 351
technological capital 338
Capitalism 7, 9, 17, 21–24, 26–31, 34, 41–42, 60, 66, 71–74, 83, 85, 90–91, 93, 96–97, 99–104, 109–110, 118–120, 131, 140, 143–145, 150, 155–156, 170–172, 190, 201, 206, 223, 240, 244, 270, 275, 290, 306–307, 337, 341, 346–348
   cognitive capitalism 104
   digtal capitalism 102, 186
   fordist capitalism 106, 110, 148, 150, 273, 306–307, 311, 340; *see also* Capitalism, global informational/network capitalism, *see* Capitalism, transnational post-fordist capitalism
   high-tech capitalism 102
   industrial capitalism 272
   informatic capitalism 102
   informational capitalism 102, 105–119, 148–211, 218, 295–297, 341, 343; *see also* Society, information society
   information/network capitalism
   knowledge capitalism 104, 118, 175, 209, 306; *see also* Society, knowledge society
   networked capitalism 104, 155, 159–160; *see also* Society, networked society
   post-Fordist capitalism 30, 107, 108–110, 150, 154–155, 205, 273, 279, 306, 311, 324, 340; *see also* Capitalism, fordist capitalism
   transnational information/network capitalism 7–8, 10, 98, 101, 105–120, 156, 161, 306, 340–341
   virtual capitalism 102
Capurro, Rafael 350
Carlson, Timothy 259, 260
Castells, Manuel 100–102, 113, 137, 148, 156, 160, 164, 193, 213–214, 237, 279, 305, 322, 326
Castoriadis, Cornelius 230, 231
Cedergren, Magnus 316–317

Censorship 170, 244–245, 250, 260, 284, 330
Centre for Energy Policy and Economics 145
Cerny, Phillip G. 109
Centralization 31, 150, 155, 170; *see also* Decentralization
Chase, Brian 317
Chat 1, 124, 126, 128–129, 136–137, 184, 187, 234, 237, 243, 271, 283, 292, 309, 323–324, 327–328, 332, 352
Checkland, Peter 13
Chen, Shing-Ling Sarina 4
Chiapello, Eve 150
Cheal, David 162
Chomsky, Noam 265
Ciffolillo, Andrea 316, 317
Civil Society 82–84, 86–87, 89, 109, 133–134, 228–229, 232, 236–237, 239, 245, 264, 276, 281, 283, 294, 296–297, 345, 352–353
Clark, Harold D. 89
Class 30–31, 56, 71–72, 75, 90–93, 97, 105–106, 109, 148, 150, 155, 189–209, 216, 218, 240, 270, 281, 294, 297, 300–301, 304, 307, 322, 337, 341, 343, 344, 351, 353
   class fractions 72, 90–91, 194, 201, 203, 205, 211, 216
   class model 192, 205, 206
   class struggle 59–61, 91–92, 97, 159–160, 192, 201, 210, 275
   economic class 193, 195, 200–201
   labor class 20, 190–191, 193, 200, 211, 306
   Marx on class, *see* Marx, class
   new class 155, 193
   nonclass 193
   revolutionary class 60, 193
   social class 55, 56, 91, 92, 105, 192, 245
Clausewitz, Carl von 247, 253, 257, 264, 266
Cleaver, Harry 279–280, 288
Clynes, Manfred 261
Coe, Neio M 155
Cognition 4, 16, 103–104, 115, 117–119, 122–123, 125, 128–129, 131–132, 183–184, 231–232, 237, 247, 257–258, 277, 280, 296, 219, 322, 331, 341, 344

Coleman, Stephen 133
Collective intelligence 127, 135, 227, 294
Collier, John 14
Compaine, Benjamin M. 219
Commodification 40, 109, 133, 143, 165, 180, 186, 238, 313, 321, 346
Commodities 25, 72, 74–76, 80, 90, 93–94, 96, 99, 105, 111, 113, 118, 133, 143, 148, 154–155, 157–158, 161–164, 166, 170–177, 180, 183, 185, 191–192, 197, 202–205, 208–211, 215, 238, 251, 254, 267, 272, 279, 300–301, 303, 306–307, 311, 313, 318, 338, 342, 343; *see also* Economy, commodity economy; Economy, internet economy, gift commodity economy
Commons 69, 109, 120, 163, 171, 203–211, 224, 286, 287, 343, 351–352
Communication 4, 7, 16–17, 33, 35–39, 50–51, 64, 78–79, 86–89, 103–104, 112, 115, 117–119, 121–123, 126, 128–129, 131–134, 140, 149, 153, 155, 180, 183–184, 216, 222, 227–229, 231–232, 236–240, 243, 245, 247, 257–258, 263, 268, 270, 272, 277–278, 280, 284, 289, 296, 299, 309, 311, 313–315, 319, 320, 322, 326–328, 330, 332–333, 336, 338, 340–341, 343–344, 349
    communication technologies, *see* Technologies, communication technologies
    computer-mediated communication 112, 115, 124, 233, 238, 243, 248, 251, 289, 309, 310, 315, 328, 330, 331, 333,
    face-to-face communication 314, 329, 331
    free communication 284
    many-to-many communication 112, 118, 130–133, 139–241, 248–249, 277
    mass communication 238
    online communication 125, 127–128, 130, 141, 184, 215, 233, 248–249, 251–252, 275, 309–311, 313–315, 318, 322–323, 329, 331, 333, 345
    political communication 248–252
Communism 17, 21, 41, 59, 160, 186, 209
Community 16, 180, 240, 243, 250, 304–308, 333
    community building 242, 309
    online community 127, 130, 184, 214, 238, 285, 304, 328
    self-organized community 249
    virtual community 5, 10, 16, 127, 137, 161, 218, 234, 238, 242–243, 252, 278, 299, 302–304, 308–316, 317, 319–321, 323–324, 327, 333, 345
    commodified virtual communities 333, 334
    cooperative virtual community 333, 345
    economic virtual communites 311
    levels of virtual communities 310–312
    mobile virtual community 304, 324
    political virtual communities 311
    self-organizing virtual community 315; *see also* Self-organization
Competition 7, 9–10, 23–26, 29–31, 33–34, 71, 74, 76–77, 79, 89, 91–93 , 97, 108, 120, 132, 144, 146, 148, 151, 154, 156, 158, 161–162, 164–165, 189, 209, 211, 213, 221–222, 224, 247, 253, 270, 294–298, 301, 304, 307–308, 311, 313, 334–335, 337, 341, 343, 349, 350, 353; *see also* Cooperation; Antagonism, antagonism between cooperation and competition
Complexity 11–34, 36, 61, 111, 115, 117, 136, 279, 287, 299, 335; *see also* Self-organization
Complex systems, *see* Complexity
Computer 2, 4, 30, 99, 102–103, 109–110, 112–113, 118, 121, 128, 136, 138, 144–145, 147, 158, 194, 213, 216, 220–221, 223, 240, 256–258, 262, 269, 271, 274, 275, 283, 295, 302, 350; *see also* ICTs; Technologies, computer technolgy

computer access 182, 214, 223, 301, 352

computer industry 166, 169

Computer-mediated communication, *see* Communication, computer-mediated communication

Contemporary society, *see* Society, contemporary society

Content industry 177, 220

Convergence 100, 118, 138, 324

Cooperation 4, 7, 9–11, 16, 23–25, 27, 29, 30–34, 44, 71, 89, 97, 103–104, 109, 114, 117–124, 126–129, 131–134, 148–149, 151–154, 156, 159–162, 164, 171, 183–185, 195, 209–211, 213, 225, 227–229, 231–232, 237, 243, 247, 257, 277–278, 280, 284, 290, 292, 294–298, 304, 310, 311, 313, 317, 319, 322, 326, 333–335, 337, 341, 343–345, 348–349, 353; *see also* Competition; Antagonism, antagonism between cooperation and competition

global cooperation 292

networked cooperation 240

online cooperation 112, 125, 184–185, 215, 216, 232, 234, 236

political cooperation 248–252

technologies of cooperation, *see* Technologies, technologies of cooperation

Corning, Peter A. 14

Corporations 70, 104–105, 107–109, 111, 134–135, 145, 148, 150–153, 160, 167–169, 177, 180, 183, 202, 207–210, 220, 222, 250, 267, 272, 301, 343, 351

transnational corporations 107, 110, 119, 154–156, 166, 186–187, 209

Coté, Mark 185, 186

Coyle, Diane 142, 143

Critical Arts Ensemble 285, 288

Critical theory 5–9, 34, 40, 151, 190, 241, 275, 335–337, 348; *see also* Critique; Frankfurt school

Critique 5, 8, 9, 34, 38, 86, 297, 298, 345, 348

critique of ideology 346; *see also* ideology

dialectical critique 6, 8; *see also* dialectics

immanent critique 7–8

transcendental critique 7–8

Crossley, Nick 85, 279, 291,

Cultural studies 3, 93

Culture 7, 10, 44, 47–48, 62–64, 66, 68–71, 73, 81, 90–93, 99–100, 113, 119, 135, 165, 207, 215, 227, 299–334, 337, 339, 340, 348

cultural actions 300

cultural capital, *see* Capital, cultural capital

cultural industry 40, 165, 166

cultural products 48, 68, 103, 115, 165

cultural structures 64, 68, 69, 300, 318

cyberculture 5, 9, 10, 298–334

alienated cyberculture 328, 330

cyberculture as dialectical system 62, 63, 300, 335, 341

cooperative cyberculture 300, 303, 333, 345

competitive cyberculture 300, 303, 33, 345

socialized cyberculture 327

gift culture 301

modern culture 90, 92, 299, 302

Cunningham, Ward 316

Curry, James 172, 173

Crews, Adrienne 135

Cyberactivism 279

Cyberattacks 283, 285, 286; *see also* Protest; Activism

Cyberculture, *see* Culture, cyberculture

Cyberlove 5, 243, 303, 331–332, 334, 345; *see also* Online dating system

Cyberhate 251, 303, 334, 345–346

Cybernetics 136, 261–262

Cyberprotest, *see* Protest, cyberprotest

Cybersex 332

Cyberspace 4, 16, 110, 119, 121, 124, 136–137, 161, 184, 218, 239, 242–244, 246–247, 251, 262, 269, 277–279, 281–284, 286–287, 297–298, 303, 209, 313–314, 320, 322–323, 328, 330–333, 340, 345, 350; *see also* Internet; Social software; WWW

Cyberstalking 330

Dahl, Robert A. 230
Davidow, William H. 153
Dawson, Michael 102
Dean, Howard 134
Decentralization 30–31, 107, 110,
    113–114, 150, 155, 232, 277,
    301; *see also* Centralization
Deleuze, Gilles 113, 149–150, 260, 267,
    277, 288
Deliberation 228, 231, 233, 234, 236,
    238
Dematerialization 10, 142–143, 173,
    342,
Democracy 32, 86, 133, 216, 225,
    230–231, 233–236, 238, 242,
    264, 283, 293, 294, 348
    digital democracy 5, 10, 134, 213,
        225, 233–247, 289, 292, 297,
        301
    grassroots digital democracy, *see*
        eParticipation
    plebiscitary digital democracy, *see*
        Plebiscitarianism, plebiscitary
        digital democracy
    representative digital democracy
        225, 233–235, 239, 296, 298,
        344
    direct democracy 78, 225–226,
        233–234, 238, 240
    electronic democracy 234–237, 247
    grassroots democracy, *see* Participa-
        tion, participatory democracy
    participatory democracy, *see*
        Participation, participatory
        democracy
    representative democracy 76, 77, 78,
        133, 225–226, 233–236, 253
    teledemocracy 234, 236
    democracy theory 225
Demirovic, Alex 84
Deregulation 28, 79, 101, 104, 135,
    218, 245, 307,
Dery, Mark 286
Determinism 22–23, 46, 58, 60–61, 70,
    92, 336; *see also* Marx, Karl,
    determinism
Deutsch, Karl 99
Dialectics 3–5, 9, 11, 17–18, 20, 22, 34,
    41, 49, 58, 102, 219, 222–223,
    247, 322, 336, 345; *see also*
    Antagonism; Aufhebung;
    Materialism, dialectical; Nega-
    tion of the negation
    dialectical development 18–20, 55

dialectical principles 18–20
dialectics of nature 22–23
dialectic of continuity and disconti-
    nuity 101, 102
dialectic of immanence and transcen-
    dence 7
dialectic of necessity and chance 12,
    14, 20, 61, 70
dialectic of structures and actions
    53, 54, 55, 57, 58, 65, 96, 104,
    337
dialectical system 62–63, 300, 335,
    341
social dialectics 22–23
Dicken, Peter 155
Digital divide 10, 213–224, 244–245,
    251, 281, 289, 295, 298, 343,
    346
Digital democracy, *see* democracy
Discussion boards 1, 16, 129–130, 233,
    235, 237, 239–240, 244, 271,
    280, 283, 285, 318, 352
Discussion list, *see* Mailing list
Domination 7, 22, 31, 34, 43, 47, 67,
    77, 90, 97, 101, 103, 107,
    113, 114, 119–120, 135, 149,
    213, 230, 284, 290, 293, 294,
    295, 340, 345, 347; *see also*
    eDomination
Donath, Judith 326
Döring, Nicola 314–315, 323,
    331–332
Drucker, Peter 98
Duff, Alistair 4
Dunning, John H. 155
Dunsire, Andrew 23
Durkheim, Emile 49, 54, 126, 128
Dutton, William H. 235
Dwyer, Catherine 312
Dyer-Witheford, Nick 193, 278, 279
Dyson, Esther 100, 245, 301

E-business 180
E-commerce 108, 154, 181, 222, 249,
    301
eDomination 213, 247, 266, 277, 294,
    296, 298, 341, 343–344; *see
    also* Domination
eGovernance 5
eGovernment 5, 296
E-mail 1, 16, 128–129, 136, 181–182,
    188, 233–234, 257, 262, 270–
    271, 273–275, 280, 283–285,
    287, 324, 327, 256

eParticipation 5, 134, 151, 224, 225, 230, 233, 236–252, 277, 295–298, 344–345

E-voting 233, 234, 236–238, 250, 280, 296

Ebeling, Werner 11

Ecology 140–147
  ecological problems 38–40, 83, 84, 88, 94–96,
  ecological system, ecosphere 10, 62, 64–66, 93, 95, 337, 338
  information ecology 9, 10, 140, 146, 341

Economy 10, 24, 28–29, 37, 39, 44, 62–67, 69–76, 78–79, 94, 96–97, 99–102, 108, 113, 119, 141–143, 146, 149, 151, 156, 166, 172, 186, 202, 210, 215, 222, 227, 245, 264, 272, 300, 303, 337–338, 340, 343, 348, 351; *see also* Antagonism, antagonism between productive forces and relations of production; Capital; Capitalism; Class; Exchange value; Labor; Use value
  commodity economy 148, 162, 171, 209, 211, 342, 343
  economic logic 28, 105, 145, 180, 205, 222, 297, 313, 333
  economic resources 30, 67, 82, 116, 209, 228, 230, 253, 275, 279, 342
  economic sectors 194, 195–200, 201
  economic strategies 178, 179
  information economy 89, 99, 148, 151, 161, 189
  internet economy 5, 9, 10, 148, 158, 160–189, 209–211, 301, 341, 343
    informational gift economy 148, 156, 158, 161, 185, 209, 211, 351, 341, 351
    informational commodity economy 148, 156, 158, 161, 209, 211, 341
    gift commodity internet economy 171
  gift economy 10, 133, 157, 158, 162, 163, 172, 178, 179, 186, 210, 244, 301, 342, 343;

Edmonds, Bruce 11, 12

Edwards, Sean J. A. 257

Eigen, Manfred 11, 278

Electrohippies 285, 288

Elias, Norbert 117

Ellison, Nicole 126, 127

Emancipation 5–6, 40, 150, 347

Emergence 8, 11–14, 16, 18–21, 24, 31, 33–34, 42, 45–47, 52, 54, 62, 67–69, 77, 83–85, 87–89, 114, 123, 335; *see also* Complexity; Self-organization
  aspects, qualities of emergence 14–15

Emigh, William 316

Emmer, Martin 238

Empire 103, 109, 156, 166, 257, 287, 292 *see also* Hardt, Michael; Negri, Antonio

Energy intensity 10, 142, 147, 342

Energy intensity of ICTs 10, 350

Engels, Friedrich 17–21, 45–46, 59, 60, 126–127, 160, 163, 190–191, 336, 346, 347, 349, 355

Enzensberger, Hans Magnus 241

Erbring, Lutz 329

Ericson, Richard V. 267

Erikson, Erik 322

Escobar, Arturo 278, 299

Espejo, Raul 31

Essence of society 6–8, 33–34, 42–43, 71, 97, 127, 140, 335–337, 347–349

Ethics 33–34, 39, 301, 303, 346–350
  cooperative cyberethics 350

Etzioni, Amitai 115

European Information Technology Observatory (EITO) 144

European Union 111, 146, 254, 275, 280

Evolution 20, 53, 58, 61, 88
  cultural evolution 25, 26, 27
  evolutionary theories 59

Exchange value 7 , 77, 162, 165, 177, 181

Exclusion 34, 71, 87, 80–81, 91–92, 101, 103, 119, 195, 213, 224, 235–236, 245, 272, 297, 337, 340, 349

EZLN (Ejército Zapatista de la Liberación Nacional) 263, 279, 284, 285, 290, 292

Facebook 125, 184, 188–189, 202, 267, 325–327

Feistel, Rainer 11

Fernback, Jan 309

Fishman, Steven 125

Fiske, John 165
Fitzpatrick, Tony 102
Fleissner, Peter 143, 180
Floyd, Kory 328
Flusser, Vilém 235, 240–242, 247
Foucault, Michel 139, 149, 267–270
Foerster, Heinz von 116, 136
Fordism, *see* Capitalism, fordist
    capitalism
Forte, Andrea 316, 319
Foster, John Bellamy 102, 143
Francois, Charles 61
Frankfurt School 8; *see also* Critical
    theory; Critique
Fraser, Nancy 229
Fraunhaufer Institut für Systemtechnik
    und Innovationsforschung
    145
Freedom 6, 13, 22–23, 40–43, 45,
    48–49, 56, 58, 61, 122, 162,
    163, 186, 209, 223, 230,
    245–246, 250–251, 260,
    264–265, 272, 284, 286, 291,
    301, 346–348, 350–351, 356
Free Software 157, 162, 170, 221, 223,
    280, 284, 301, 316, 351; *see
    also* Open source software;
    Open content
Friedman, Milton 301
Friendster 125, 184, 325–326
Fuchs, Christian 7, 11, 14, 18, 53, 102,
    106, 111–112, 114–115, 117,
    128, 183, 215–216, 218, 222,
    230–231, 257, 260, 290, 318,
    341, 348
Fuchs-Kittowski, Klaus 117
Functionalism 36, 40–41, 49, 53; *see
    also* Structuralism
Funken, Christiane 136
Fussey, Peter

Galtung, Johan 247
GATS (General Agreement on Trade
    and Service) 286, 292
Garcia, David 286
Garnham, Nicholas 102, 105, 245
Gergen, Kenneth 322
Gibson, William 136
Giddens, Anthony 27, 36, 49, 59, 61,
    80, 112–113, 115, 190, 192,
    270, 308, 318, 320, 336, 355
    institutions 62
    structuration theory 3, 50–51,
        53–56, 58, 318

Gift economy, *see* Economy, gift
    economy
Gilder, George 100, 245, 301
Gillmor, Dan 134
Globalization 4, 7, 28, 89, 102,
    110–113, 118, 120, 154–156,
    165, 171, 254, 271, 275, 277,
    283, 290–293, 320, 331, 340;
    see also Capitalism, transna-
    tional informational/network
    capitalism; Antiglobalization
    movement
    cultural globalization 165, 166
Glotz, Peter 102
GNU Free Documentation License 316
Goebbels, Jaoseph 238
Goldblatt, David 112, 154
Golding, Peter 105
Goldstein, Jeffrey 15
Gomery, Douglas 105
Google 126, 168–171, 177, 179,
    181–183, 185–187, 210, 267,
    286–287, 324
Gorz, André 193, 207
Görg, Christoph 39
GPL (General Public License) 157, 301
Gramsci, Antonio 73, 82, 93, 228, 275,
    346
Grant, Ted 18
Gras, Marianne 273
Grassmuck, Volker 221
Gray, Chris Hables 261
Gray, Mitchell 273
Green movement 39
Guattari, Félix 113, 267, 288
Guevara, Ernesto Che 265

Habermas, Jürgen 6, 8–9, 40, 49, 62,
    86, 105, 133–134, 229, 239,
    244, 281, 291, 313–314
Hacker, Kenneth 214, 233, 235
Hacktivism 285–286, 288; *see also*
    Activism; Protest
Haggerty, Kevin D. 267, 268
Haken, Hermann 11, 152
Hall, G. Jon 4
Hall, Stuart 92, 165
Hampton, Keith N. 328
Haraway, Donna 261
Hardin, Garret 163
Hardt, Michael 23, 103, 109, 113, 186,
    193, 202, 205, 208–209, 283,
    287, 289, 290, 292
Hardware industry 145, 177

Harvey, David 101, 103, 107, 112, 113
Haug, Wolfgang Fritz 102
Hayek, Friedrich August 23–31, 41, 301, 336
HCI (Human-Computer Interaction) 138
Hegel, Georg Wilhelm Friedrich 6, 8, 34, 38, 43, 55, 71, 172, 207, 337
essence 43, 71, 335, 337, 347–348
dialectics 17–22, 41, 117, 335
Heidegger, Martin 22
Hegemony 71, 73, 90, 91, 92, 93, 97, 104, 107, 118, 294, 337
Hillygus, D. Sunshine 329
Hirsch, Joachim 109
Held, David 112, 154, 229, 231, 254
Herdin, Thomas 4
Herring, Susan C. 316
Heteronomy 31, 32, 34, 71, 153, 228, 268, 290, 348, 268, 290, 349
Hirsch, Jesse 316
Hobbes, Thomas 43
Hofkirchner, Wolfgang ix–x, 2, 4, 18, 31, 52, 114–115, 117, 128, 131, 183, 219, 231, 257, 290, 300, 341, 355
Holloway, John 114
Holzkamp, Klaus 45
Horak, Eva 216, 219, 222
Horkheimer, Max 6, 346
Hörz, Herbert 20, 31
Howard, Michael W. 207, 243
Howard, Philip N. 327
HTML (Hypertext Markup Language) 124, 139
Hufford, Kevin D. 51
Hunsinger, Jeremy 4
Huws, Ursula 143, 193
Hypertext 124, 130, 132, 139

ICTs (information and communication technologies) 2, 101, 110–111, 140–147, 155, 169, 215, 226, 233, 235–236, 239, 242, 244, 248–252, 267, 294, 296, 344–345, 351–352; *see also* Technologies; Technologies, communication technologies; Technologies, information technologies
design of ICTs 1, 4, 5, 302
ICT access 214, 216, 245, 248, 252

ICTs and society 215; *see also* ICT&S
ICT industry 168
ICT sector 142–143, 222, 242, social shaping 2, 4
use of ICTs 1–5, 216, 233, 238, 239, 248, 297, 345
ICT&S (information and communication technologies & society); *see also* ICTs and society
Center 2
research 2–5
methodology 4
Idealism 70, 103
Identity 55, 68–69, 80–81, 85–88, 112, 117, 137, 150, 219, 260, 273, 275, 278, 280, 290, 291–293, 304–307, 309, 311–314, 316, 319–323, 333
online identity 312, 321–323
offline identity 323
social identity 321–322
virtual identity 322, 323
Ideology 5–6, 8, 22–23, 28, 37, 48, 59, 73, 85, 91–93, 100–101, 108, 113, 133, 134 148–149, 151–152, 190, 210, 245, 260, 272–273, 275–276, 290, 307, 322, 338, 339, 340, 343, 346–348
Iglhaut, Stefan 136
Inclusion 33, 71, 81, 119, 149, 213, 224–225, 277, 297, 337, 340, 349–350
Individualism 17–18, 27, 40–42, 49, 243, 245, 301, 305
Individualization 30, 80, 84, 108, 165, 190, 238, 242, 248–249, 179, 299–300, 303, 305–306, 308, 331, 333, 345
Informatics and society 1; *see also* Social Informatics
Information 7, 12–13, 16–17, 19, 25, 26–27, 34 47, 73, 80, 92, 98–101, 103–104, 111–115, 117–118, 128, 131, 133, 137–138, 153, 155, 159, 164, 172–173, 175, 209–210, 222, 234, 237, 250, 256, 268, 270–272, 280, 302, 326, 341
censorship of information 244
digital information 16, 139, 162–163, 179, 183–184, 263

Information (*continued*)
   information commodities 143, 154,
      171–173, 176, 185, 209–210,
      251, 343
   information ecology, *see* Ecology,
      information ecology
   information economy, *see* Economy,
      information economy; Econ-
      omy, internet economy
   information freedom 286
   information gifts 171, 185, 210
   informational monopolies 10, 164,
      170–171, 210, 238
   information politics 258
   information science 114
   information society, *see* Society,
      information
   information technologies, *see*
      Technologies, information
      technologies
   information warfare, *see* Warfare,
      information warfare
   political information 151
Informatization 7–8, 102, 110, 120,
   340
Instant messaging 1, 126, 271, 312
Instrumental reason 8, 28, 40, 84, 105,
   130, 181, 189, 255, 270, 294,
   296, 270, 294, 296, 297, 337,
   346, 350, 353
Intellectual property rights 104, 108,
   116, 157, 161, 170–171, 175,
   210, 245, 251, 286,192, 301,
   342
Interactivity 112, 118, 137–139, 235,
   240
Interdisciplinarity 1, 4
Internet 1, 2, 5, 9, 16–17, 97, 101,
   106, 110–112, 118, 120–124,
   130, 135–136, 138–140, 142,
   145, 148, 155, 161–164,
   166, 170–171, 175, 180–181,
   183, 185, 211, 213, 216,
   221, 234–235, 237, 239, 240,
   242–244, 248, 260, 268, 271,
   275, 277, 279–283, 287, 289,
   294, 298–299, 318, 320, 322,
   327–328, 330, 334, 340–341,
   343–346, 350, 352; *see also*
   Cyberspace; Social software;
   WWW
   Internet access 181–182, 214,
      181–182, 215, 218–219, 223,
      289, 352

Internet applications 121, 137
Internet as techno-social system 2, 9,
   121, 122, 146, 218, 278, 310,
   309, 341, 346
Internet censorship 250
Internet economy, *see* Economy,
   Internet economy
Internet phone 1–2, 4, 323
Internet research 1–2
Internet technologies, *see* Technolo-
   gies, Internet technologies
Internet usage 283, 290, 294,
   327–330
   self-organization of the Internet 123,
      125, 178
   wireless internet 182, 324
Immanence 7, 8, 32, 37
Introna, Lucas 272
Isolation, *see* Individualization

James, Jeffrey 216, 220, 221
Jankowski, Nicholas 239
Jantsch, Erich 36, 53
Jessop, Bob 109
Jones, Steven G. 308–309, 327, 330
Johns, Mark D. 4

Kahn, Richard 135
Kalz, Marco 318
Kant, Immanuel 349
Kauffmann, Stuart 11
Katovsky, Bill 259, 260
Katz, James E. 243 327
Katz, Jon 245
Keane, Jon 142
Kellner, Douglas 135, 259, 261
Kelly, Kevin 24, 142, 301
Kenney, Martin 172–173
Keohane, Robert O. 112
Keyworth, George 100, 245, 301
Khandwalla, Prodip N. 151
Klein, Naomi 286
Kline, David 134
Kline, Nathan 261
Kling, Rob 1, 5
Knoche, Manfred 166, 177, 180
Knowledge 5, 25–27, 31, 98–100,
   103–104, 112, 114–118,
   126, 133, 135, 138, 146,
   151–152, 156–158, 161,
   163, 165, 171–173, 175,
   194, 201–202, 205–209,
   220, 227–228, 231, 242,

270–271, 278–280, 295, 297,
307, 319, 341, 343
common knowledge 157, 202, 294
digital knowedge 158, 161–163,
283, 286
distribution of knowledge 163
knowledge industry 98, 142,
166–168, 355
knowledge management 29,
151–152, 210, 249,
knowledge products 143, 194,
202–203
knowledge production 116, 130–
131, 157, 172, 176, 227, 246,
277, 293, 316
knowledge society, *see* Society,
knowledge
knowledge work 140, 119, 151, 172,
195, 306, 318; *see also* Labor,
knowledge
objective knowledge 115, 118,
122–123, 138
open knowledge 161
subjective knowledge 104, 115, 118,
123, 138
technological knowledge 100, 116,
207, 208, 210
Kolbitsch, Joseph 127, 316–317
Kollock, Peter 128
Koskela, Hille 267, 270
Kraut, Robert 328, 329
Krippendorff, Klaus 47, 117
Kropotkin, Peter 162
Kuhndt, Michael 142
Kuhns, Peter 135
Küppers, Günter 50

Labor 28, 30, 42, 44–47, 51, 60, 64–67,
71–72, 74–75, 78–81, 84–85,
93–95, 101, 103–104, 107,
109, 118–119, 127, 141, 143,
148, 150–151, 155, 171, 174,
186, 189, 192, 195–200, 208,
303–304, 318, 338, 348
industrial labor 202, 208, 306–307
knowledge labor 133, 148, 174, 191,
193–195, 200–203
labor time 28, 104, 149, 175,
207–209, 239, 246, 307
labor force 66, 80–81, 141, 200, 306
precarious labor 114, 193, 200,
202–203, 205–206, 211, 343,
351; *see also* precarious working conditions

protest labor 293–294
reproductive labor 191, 202–206,
211, 297, 343, 351
self-employed labor 191, 102, 200,
202–203, 206
unpaid labor 200, 202, 204–205,
208–209
wage labor 67, 74, 78–79, 106, 163,
171, 190–192, 195, 200–203,
205, 211, 343, 347
Lamb, Roberta 4
Lampe, Cliff 126, 127
Langrock, Thomas 145
Lash, Scott 7, 8
Laszlo, Erwin 20, 61, 61
Larkin, Bruce D. 262
Leadbeater, Charles 142
Lenin, Wladimir Iljitsch Uljanow
160–161
Lessig, Lawrence 163, 170
Leuf, Bo 316
Lévy, Pierre 123–124, 135, 138
Levy, Stefen 301
Libicki, Martin 256
Lievrouw, Leah A. 4
Lih, Andrew 316–317
Lipietz, Alain 72–73
Lipnack, Jessica 153
Livingstone, Sonia 4
Locke, Johan 226
Lovink, Geert 114, 286
Löw, Martina 136
Lubbers, Eveline 125
Lukes, Steven 346
Luhmann, Niklas 8–9, 24, 28–29,
35–40, 49–50, 336
Luxemburg, Rosa 105
Lyon, David 268, 269, 271–273, 275
Lyotard, Jean-Francois 99

Ma, Cathy 316–317
Macpherson, Crawford Brough 7,
229–230, 246
Machlup, Fritz 98
Macintosh, Ann 237
Mackay, Hughie 3
Malone, Michael S. 153
Mannheim, Karl 115, 117
Mansell, Robin 105, 246
Maier-Rabler, Ursula 2, 4
Mailing lists 1, 124, 129–132, 137, 233,
237, 240, 256, 280, 283, 292,
318–319, 324, 352
Mao 21

Marcuse, Herbert 8, 55, 85, 89, 114,
    190, 246, 282, 347, 348
  cooperation 7, 32
  critical theory 6, 337
  dialectics 22–23
  technological rationality 88
  repressive tolerance 134
Marighella, Carlos 265
Marletta, Piercarlo 141
Marx, Gary T. 271, 272
Marx, Karl 8, 21, 41–46, 65, 70–71, 74,
    93–94, 96, 128, 161–162, 191,
    209, 313, 337, 346, 348, 355
  antagonism between the productive
    forces and the relations of pro-
    duction 30–31, 44, 95, 159–
    161, 186, 210, 342, 346–347,
    355; *see also* Antagonism
  capital accumulation 74–75,
    172, 174; *see also* Capital,
    accumulation
  class 190, 191, 192, 211, *see also*
    Class
  cooperation 7, 32–33, 126–127; *see
    also* Cooperation
  determinism 59, 60, 61, 336, 347;
    see also Determinism
  dialectics 17–18, 20, 22, 58–59; *see
    also* Dialectics
  dialectical philosophy of practice 55
  freedom 347; *see also* Freedom
  knowledge 106, 164, 175–176 *see
    also* Knowledge
  law of value 175, 208
  philosophy of practice 336, 347
  species being 47, 127
Marxism 18, 23, 73, 95, 103–104,
    190–191, 290, 347
  neo-Marxism 101–104, 195, 230,
    275
  contemporary Marxism 23
  Marxist feminism 204–205
  orthodox Marxism 21, 70–72
Materialism 18, 103
  cultural 69
  dialectical 20–21
  historical 59, 61
  mechanical 70
Maturana, Humberto 21, 35, 39, 46
Maurer, Hermann 127, 316–317
Mauss, Marcel 162
McAdam, Doug 85
McCarthy, John D. 84
McChesney, Robert 105

McElroy, Mark W. 151–152
McGrew, Anthony 112, 154
McKiernan, Gerry 216
McLaughlin, Margaret L. 315
McLuhan, Marshall 135, 246
Mead, George Herbert 46, 49
Media 37, 98, 105, 114, 117–118, 123,
    130, 175, 232, 238, 240, 259,
    263, 268, 281, 327
  alternative media 233, 248, 261,
    282
    alternative online media 135,
      239, 250, 280, 282, 283, 292,
      279, 345, 353
  media corporation 135, 165, 171,
    180, 187
  media coverage 77, 165, 259–261
  media industry 180
  mass media 139, 165, 166, 180,
    249, 250, 256–258, 260, 278,
    282, 286–287, 296, 302–303,
    307–308, 316–317, 344
  new media 177, 180, 240, 247, 308,
    353
  participatory online media 302, *see
    also* eParticipation
Medosch, Armin 137
Melody, William H. 105
Merton, Robert 49
Mettler, Peter H. 144
Microsoft 105, 175, 160, 167–170,
    178–179, 182, 184–185, 221,
    287
Mies, Maria 205
Mill, John Stuart 226
Mingers, John 36, 50
Mises, Ludwig van 41
Mobile phone 144–145, 270–271, 275,
    322, 324, 326, 355
Modern Society, *see* Society, modern
    society
Montesquieu 226
Moor, James H. 272, 350
Moore, Mike 257
Moore, Richard 236
Morahan-Martin, Janet 329–330
Morris-Suzuki, Tessa 102
Movement for democratic globaliza-
    tion, *see* Antiglobalization
    movement
Mowshowitz, Abbe 153
MUDs (Multi User Dungeons) 121,
    128–129, 167, 185, 330–331
Multimedia 112, 128, 139, 165, 251

Multitude 5, 103, 192, 201–203, 205–206, 208, 211–212, 283, 292, 297, 343, *see also* Hardt, Michael; Negri, Antonio
Murdock, Graham 105
Murdoch, Rupert 17, 260
Murelli, Elena 222
Mutal shaping of society and ICTs 4
MySpace 16–17, 125, 127, 129, 170, 179, 181, 184–188, 202, 323–327

Nature 8, 17–20, 22–23, 27, 38–39, 45–48, 53, 62–67, 70, 73, 93, 94, 95, 112, 146, 207, 297, 338, 343
Negation of the negation 19, 20, 34, 54, 290, 335, *see also* Dialectics, Aufhebung (sublation)
Negri, Antonio 21, 23, 103, 109, 113, 186, 193, 202, 205, 208–209, 283, 287, 289–290, 292
Negroponte, Nicholas 247, 301
Neoliberalism 11, 23–31, 34, 108–109, 180, 190, 200, 271, 275–276, 290, 297, 301, 307
Netwar, *see* War, netwar
Networks 4, 9, 26, 30, 37, 84, 89, 100–103 , 106, 109–114, 119–120, 135, 150, 155–156, 159, 160, 182, 209–210, 239, 258, 261, 263, 265, 271, 277–278, 293–294, 340, 344; *see also* Society, network society
    computer networks 2, 103, 109–110, 121–122, 137–139, 148–149, 153, 173, 234, 242, 333, 340–341
    communication network 11, 113, 119, 121, 173, 238, 240, 261
    digital networks 164, 177
    global networks 101, 290, 306
    grassroots networks 101, 290, 306,
    informational networks 159, 164, 210
    social movement networks 84, 88, 290, 292–293, 297
    social networks 111, 130, 258, 305, 307, 324–325, 328
    technological networks 2, 121–123, 266, 278, 341

transnational networks 106, 120, 341
Network enterprise 148–153, 305
New media, *see* Media, new media
Newsgroups 124, 130–132, 137, 140, 183, 328
New social movements, *see* social movenents
NGO (Nongovernmental organization) 84, 228, 253, 264, 284
Nicolis, Gregoire 11
Nie, Norman H. 243, 329
Nonaka, Ikujio 152
Norris, Pippa 214–216, 219–220, 234, 235
Nye, Joseph S. 112

O'Connor, James 95
O'Reilly, Tim 127–128
Online communication platform 184; *see also* Online dating system; Social networking platform
Online dating system 311; *see also* Cyberlove; Social networking platform; Online communication platform
Online journalism 5, 10, 162, 303, 334, 345,
Online love, *see* Cyberlove
Online politics 9, 10, 135, 248–252, 298
Online relations 153, 331–332
Open content 131, 133–134, 164, 313, 315–316, 151
Open source software10, 83, 131, 139, 157, 160–162, 164, 182–184, 221–224, 245, 251, 283–284, 286, 292, 300–302, 313, 317, 319 *see also* Free software, Open content
    open source community 161, 300, open source values 301, 302
Orwell, George 267–269, 277
Osborne, Kerry K. 315
Ott, Hermann E. 145
Otto, Peter 99

Participation 31–33, 40, 71, 97, 119–120, 133, 135, 146, 149–150, 213, 216, 222, 226–227, 229, 235, 240, 245, 277, 282, 284, 294, 297, 302, 306, 308, 313, 315, 324, 337, 343, 346, 350, 352–353

Participation (*continued*)
  participatory democracy 7, 31, 32,
    133, 136, 150, 210, 213,
    225–228, 230–231, 233,
    participatory/grassroots
    digital democracy, *see*
    eParticipation
  participatory management 30, 104,
    110, 148–151, 260, 273
  participatory society 151, 224, 228,
    231, 237, 251, 290, 294, 297,
    353
  participatory system 227–229, 237,
    240, 294, 296, 337, 334, 235,
    238–240, 242, 244, 246, 248,
    290, 292–293, 352
Parks, Malcolm 328
Parks, Rosa 89
Parsons, Talcott 49
Peer-to-peer networks 129, 137, 158,
    164
Peery, Nelson 193
Perelman, Michael 189–190
Peretti, Jonah 287
Perraton, Jonatan 112, 154
Piore, Michael J. 107
Plebiscitarianism 250
  plebiscitary system 226, 250
  plebiscitary digital democracy 134,
    225, 233, 235, 237, 296, 298,
    344
Political economy 105–106
Political economy of the media 105
Political system 10, 28–29, 37, 46,
    62–64, 66, 67–68, 70–73,
    76–90, 101, 113, 119, 131,
    215, 228, 253, 271, 294, 300,
    303, 337, 339, 340, 343, 348
Polity, *see* Political system
Porat, Marc 98
Poster, Mark 137, 321,
Postindustrial society, *see* Society,
    postindustrial society
Postman, Neil 247
Postmodern society *see* Society, post-
    modern society
Postmodern theory 173
Practice, *see* Action; Class, class
    struggle
Precarious working conditions 211,
    246, 307–308, 351; *see also*
    Labor, precarious labor
Privacy 24, 171, 188–189, 271–272,
    277, 326, 330, 352

Profit 25, 27, 28, 74–76, 94–95, 101–
    102, 104, 107, 109–110, 133,
    143–146, 149–151, 153–154,
    156, 161, 170, 172–173, 175–
    180, 183, 185–186, 191–192,
    203, 206, 209–210, 211, 218,
    221, 301, 306, 343
Progress 26, 30, 59–61, 113, 208; *see*
    also Technological progress
Prosumer 131, 157, 164, 202, 240, 248,
    282
Protest 38, 84–89, 124, 133, 239,
    277–294, 297, 344, 352
  cyberprotest 10, 133, 213, 239,
    248–249, 277–294, 297, 345,
    352, 356
    cognitive cyberprotest 280, 297
    communicative cyberprotest 280,
      283, 297
    cooperative cyberprotest 280,
      284, 297
    self-organization of cyberprotest
      278–279
  networked protest 114, 277–278,
    287, 290
  online protest 273, 278, 280–281,
    283–284, 292, 297
  protest movements 37–39, 70, 97,
    82–89, 92, 107, 114, 213, 228,
    232–233, 237, 243, 248, 251,
    264, 277–281, 283, 288–294,
    297, 345, 352; *see also*
    Antiglobalization movement;
    Antiwar movement; Green
    movement
  protest networks 278, 279, 293
  transnational protest 278, 289,
    292–293
  virtual protest 280, 284–285
Prigogine, Ilya 11, 18, 62
Public sphere 40, 86–87, 133–135, 229,
    238–239, 243–245, 250, 258,
    281, 283, 290, 296, 344,
Pybus, Jennifer 185, 186

Quah, Danny T. 142
Quan-Haase, Anabel 328

Raffl, Celina 355
Rainie, Lee 327
Raymond, Eric S. 162, 300–301
Regulation Theory 72
Reips, Ulf-Dietrich 4
Resource intensity 140, 147

Resource intensity of ICTs 10
RFID (radio frequency identification)
    273
Rheingold, Howard 17, 128, 130,
    137, 218, 237–238, 244,
    263, 277, 284, 309, 313,
    325–326
Rhizome 288–289
RIAA (Recording Industry Association
    of America) 158, 163
Rice, Ronald E. 5, 327
Richard, Elisabeth 134
Richta, Radovan 99
Robertson, Roland 112
Robins, Kevin 167, 321
Robinson, John P. 328
Rodgers, Robert C. 329
Ronfeldt, David 254, 256, 261,
    263–264
Rosenbaum, Howard 1, 5
Rosenkrands, Jacob 283
Rosseau, Jean-Jacques 226
Rötzer, Florian 137

Sabel, Charles, 107
Salter, Lee 281
Sanders, David 89
Sanger, Larry 315
Saveri, Andrea 128, 130
Sawyer, Steve 1, 4, 5
Schafranek, Matthias 355
Schallaböck, Karl Otto 141
Schiller, Herbert 102
Schlemm, Annette 31
Schmied, Alex 266
Schmiede, Rudi 102, 150
Schmitt, Carl 226
Schofield Clark, Lynn 323
Scholte, Jan Aart 112
Schön, Donald A. 114
Schumpeter, Joseph 41
Schuler, Douglas 315
Schumacher, Phyllis 329, 330
Schuster, Peter 11, 278
Schrum, Weley 4
Self-determination 6, 21, 31–32, 40, 48,
    71, 111, 163, 212, 229, 242,
    272, 276, 346–347, 349
Self-organization 7–8, 11–21, 23–24,
    26–27, 29, 31, 34, 61–62 65,
    75–76, 78–80, 82, 84, 87, 89,
    90, 97, 114, 117, 121, 134,
    136, 152–153, 160, 227, 229,
    279, 287, 292, 297, 299, 300,

    317, 318, 320, 333, 335–336,
    347, 353; *see also* Complexity
natural self-organization 65, 95
principles of self-organization,
    11–15
self-organization and dialectics
    17–23, 49
social self-organization 8, 35, 49–51,
    53–55, 65, 81
Self-organizing systems, *see* Self-
    organization
Selm, Martine van 239
Sennet, Richard 305
Shaviro, Steven 101
Slaton, Christa 236
Smith, Adam 24
Smith, Christine B. 315
Smith, Marc 128
Smythe, Dallas W. 105
Social constructivsm 3
Social informatics 1, 5
Social movements, *see* Protest, protest
    movements
Social networking platform 16, 127,
    129, 186–188, 210, 267, 271,
    312, 326, 330; *see also* Online
    communication platform
Social relationships 8, 9, 24–25, 27, 29,
    30–31, 40, 46, 51, 75, 92, 94,
    112–113, 115, 117, 118, 126,
    136, 140–141, 146, 155, 177,
    190, 194, 201, 225, 258, 295,
    297, 303–304, 308, 318, 320,
    326, 331, 343, 345, 348
Social software 5, 121, 126–128,
    130–131, 134–135, 185, 210,
    239, 240, 316, 323, 352; *see
    also* Cyberspace; Internet;
    WWW, Web 2.0
Socialism 21–23, 26–27, 29, 31,161,
    347
Socialization 74, 104, 152, 207, 299,
    300, 303, 305, 327, 331,
    333–334, 341, 345, 348
Society
    alienated society 71, 97, 297, 337
    agricultural society 93, 166, 171
    capitalist society, *see* capitalism
    class society 272
    contemporary society 7–9, 23, 37,
        59, 71, 97–98, 100–104, 114,
        119, 138, 146, 174, 189,
        201, 232, 246, 297, 320, 337,
        340–341, 345, 353

Society (*continued*)
  cooperative society 33–34, 71, 127, 212, 290, 294, 297, 335–336, 348, 350, 353; *see also* Cooperation
  cybersociety 300
  fordist society, *see* Capitalism, fordist
  industrial society 93, 118, 142
  information society 1, 7, 98–104, 108, 142–143, 145–146, 161, 175, 190, 193, 215–216, 218, 220, 222, 239, 245–246, 267, 269–270, 295, 299–301, 337, 350, 353
    cooperative information society 350, 353
    information society research 1
    information society theory 1, 100, 102
    participatory information society 239; *see also* Participation; eParticipation
    sustainable information society 7, 146
  Internet society 9, 97, 337
  knowledge society 100–101, 118, 144, 145, 208, 306, 337
    participatory knowledge society 2; *see also* Knowledge
  market society 42
  modern society 7, 9, 29, 20, 35, 37, 39, 42–43, 71–97, 99, 111, 113, 118, 120, 140, 166, 174, 213, 216, 223, 230, 253, 268, 272, 275, 294–295, 337–338, 340, 344, 346, 349
    late-modern society 305, 308, 311, 313, 331
  nature and society 63–66; *see* also Nature
  network society 98, 100–101, 113, 239; *see also* Networks
  participatory society, *see* Participation, participatory society
  postindustrial society 89–99, 101, 337
  post-fordist society, *see* Capitalism, post-fordist capitalism
  postmodern society 89–99, 101, 104
  self-organized society 97, 294, 336, 353
  society as dynamic system 62–71
  subsystems of society 24, 27, 29, 37, 39, 62–97, 105, 111, 120, 215, 300, 337, 340
  surveillance society 271–272
  transformation, development of society 1, 3, 5, 21–22, 30, 29, 57, 61, 65, 69, 73, 85, 87–8 8, 99, 114
Socrates 349
Software; *see also* Open source software; Social software
  Software industry 155, 177, 194, 220
  Software patents 157, 170, 280, 281, 286
Sonntag, Peter 99
Space 7, 16, 89, 113, 119, 120, 136, 137, 281, 313, 324, 326, 330
  space and time 62, 81, 111–113, 115, 118–119, 156, 254, 314
  electronic space 286
  global space 7, 113, 280
  global networked space 164
  transnational networked space 340
  social space 112–113, 119, 136–137, 164, 295, 311, 313, 343, 346
  virtual space 282–284, 286, 325
Spielberg, Steven 172
Spinoza 230
Superstructure 69–70, 93
Stadler, Felix 316
Stallman, Richard 161, 162
Stalin, Joseph 21–22
Stamps, Jeffrey 153
Stehr, Nico 100
Steigerwald, Robert 18
Steinfield, Charles 326–327
Stengers, Isabelle 18
Sternberg, Robert 332
Stewart, Marianne C. 89
Stirner, Max 16, 41, 44
Stone, Allucquère, Rosanne 309, 321
Structures 3, 6–7, 13, 15–17, 21, 23, 27, 31, 34, 36, 40–41, 49–58, 62–71, 75, 77, 82, 88, 93, 96, 102, 104, 111, 114–115, 121, 225, 289–299, 317, 319, 336, 338–341, 348 *see also* Open source software; Social software
Structuralism 22, 37, 40, 49, 92; *see also* Functionalism
Struggle, *see* Class, struggle

Sublation, *see* Aufhebung
Surplus value 75–76, 93–94, 96, 133,
    153, 159, 172–176, 181, 186,
    191, 202, 204, 318, 338
Surveillance 80, 149, 170, 250, 261,
    267–277, 284, 326, 330;
    see also Society, surveillance
    society
  economic surveillance 267, 268, 271,
    273
  electronic surveillance 10, 210, 213,
    266, 267–277, 295, 296, 298,
    343, 344, 346
  political surveillance 267, 268, 271
  private surveillance 268
  surveillance studies 267
Sustainability 6, 29, 94–96, 140,
    143–144, 146, 222, 341
  ecological sustainability 140,
    142–143, 145–146
Sveiby, Karl 115
Systems theory 8–9, 23
  critical systems theory 9

Takeuchi, Hirotaka 152
Takeuchi, Tsuneo 145
Tapscott, Don 127, 180
Taylor, Paul A. 8
Taylorism 106, 107
TCP/IP protocol 2, 121
Teamwork 107, 110, 148–152, 155,
    260, 273
Technological determinism 2–3, 5, 94,
    102–103, 121, 134, 140, 145,
    238, 245, 329, 340
Technological progress 94, 99, 113,
    144, 145, 203, 207–208,
    220–222, 306, 343
Technologies 47, 65, 93, 94, 103–104,
    113–115, 136, 138, 144, 155,
    162, 174, 208, 215, 218,
    220–221, 224, 227, 234–235,
    246, 253, 255, 279, 286, 294,
    297, 311–312, 330, 338, 340,
    343–345
  communication technologies 2, 7,
    110, 113, 115, 119, 136, 138,
    194, 201, 215, 235, 236, 243,
    257, 284, 321, 331; *see also*
    ICTs
  computer technology *see* Computer
  effects of technology 134
  information technologies 7, 98–100,
    102–104, 114, 136, 194, 201,

    215–216, 235, 256–258, 263,
    270, 271–172, 279, 284–295;
    see also ICTs
  infrastructure technology 122–123,
    242, 310, 318
  Internet technology 5, 16–17, 97,
    118, 129, 267, 296
  knowledge based technologies 2,
    103, 112, 118
  networked technologies 2, 4, 100,
    127–128, 165, 278, 279, 295,
    300, 302, 310, 337, 343
  technologies of cooperation 2, 128,
    138, 184, 224, 349
Technosphere, technological system 56,
    62, 70, 93, 96, 337–338
Telecommunication 142, 166, 180, 194,
    216, 244, 283, 352
Telework 141
Terranova, Tiziana 193, 202
Terrorism 86, 133, 265–266, 274–276
Titmuss, Richard Morris 162
Toffler, Alvin 100, 236, 245, 301
Touraine, Alain 99, 143
Tönnies, Ferdinand von 127–128,
    304–305, 309, 311–312
Transdisciplinarity 4, 8, 114
Transcendence 7–8
Transport 140–143, 147
TRIPS (Trade-Related Aspects of Inel-
    lectual Property Rights) 157,
    282, 292; *see also* Intellectual
    property rights
Tsagarousianou, Roza 233
Turkle, Sherry 314, 321, 331
Türk, Volker 143
Tyworth, Michael 4–5

Ubiquitous computing 276–277
USA 98, 107, 121, 134–135, 141, 157,
    166, 168, 188, 195–196,
    200, 225, 259–260, 262–263,
    265–266, 273–275, 315
Use value 7, 47, 65–67, 165, 172, 177,
    181, 215

Van Aelst; Peter 283
Van Dijk, Jan 100, 102, 113, 150, 156,
    213–214, 219, 233, 305–306
Van Parijs, Philippe 201, 205, 207
Varela, Francisco 21, 35, 39
Veale, Kylie J. 162
Vegh, Sandor 256, 280, 285
Vehovar, Vasja 4

Vercellone, Carlo 104
Vian, Kathi 128, 130
Video conferencing 1
Violence 268–271, 294–295
Virtual community, *see* Community
Virtual products 140, 142–143, 147
Virtual reality 112, 121, 136–139, 259,
        263, 322,
Virtualization 10
Voss, Jakob 316–317
Vowe, Gerhard 238

Wales, Jim 315, 319
Walgrave, Stefaan 283
Wallerstein, Immanuel 92
Wang, Georgette 165
War 33, 79, 104, 247, 253–256, 260, 263
    computer-related warfare 262
    cyberwar 256, 257, 261–262, 285,
    guerilla warfare 265
    information war 10, 213, 247,
        256–259, 261–263, 295–296,
        298, 343–344, 346,
        cognitive information war
            258–259
        communicative information war
            258, 261–262
        cooperative information war 258,
            263
    netwar 254, 257–258, 263–266,
        269, 244
    propaganda warfare 259,
    psychological warfare 256–257, 259
Wark, McKenzie 193
Web research 1
Wiener, Norbert 136, 261
Webb, David 262
Webb, Maureen 273
Weber, Max 40, 44, 49, 126–128, 190,
        192–193, 226, 315
Webster Frank 101, 267, 268, 273,
Weiser, Mark 276–277
Welhof, Claudia 205
Wellman, Barry 328
Wikipedia 125–126, 129, 130–133,
        135, 157, 162, 179, 181, 185,
        304, 311, 313, 315–320, 333,
        345, 351

Wikis 1, 126, 128–133, 139, 235, 237,
        240, 244, 283, 318, 352
Wilhelm, Anthony G. 239, 245
Willke, Helmut 115, 116
Williams, Anthony D. 127, 180
Williams, Raymond 68–70, 191, 309
Wilson III, Wenest J. 214–215
Winkler, Roman 239
Winkler, Stefan 316
Winner, Langdon 245, 301
Witt, Ulrich 24
Woods, Alan 18
World Resource Institute 142
Wright, Eric Olin 195, 200–201, 205,
        275
Wuppertal Institute 142–143, 145
WWW (World Wide Web) 121, 123–25,
        128, 130, 137–138, 161, 177,
        185, 244, 257, 282, 287, 302,
        323; *see also* Cyberspace;
        Internet; Social software
    self organzation of the WWW 123,
        124, 130
    web 1.0 17, 121, 123–129, 130,
        136
    web 2.0 5, 17, 121, 125–129,
        130–131, 133–134, 136, 138,
        185, 186, 343; *see also* Social
        software
    web 3.0 125–129, 130–131, 136,
        355
    web page 123–126, 131, 139, 158,
        168, 177, 182, 284
    WWW as techno-social system
        123–124

Young, Kimberly S. 329
YouTube 125, 170, 181, 186–188, 202,
        267

Zald, Mayer N. 84
Zanini, Michele 257
Zeleny, Milan 51
Zerdick, Axel 181
Zeyer, Albert 31
Zhao, Shanynag 328
Zimmermann, Rainer E. 7, 230
Zizek, Slavoj 160–161

Printed in the USA/Agawam, MA
January 15, 2015

606476.018